Con

All rights reserved under International and Pan American copyright conventions. Copyright © 2002 Publications International, Ltd. This book may not be reproduced or quoted in whole or in part by any means whatsoever without written permission from Louis Weber, CEO of Publications International, Ltd., 7373 North Cicero Avenue, Lincolnwood, Illinois 60712. Permission is never granted for commercial purposes. Printed in U.S.A.

Publications International, Ltd.

CONTENTS

Introduction 5	Chevrolet Prizm 102
2003 Acura CL 10	Chevrolet Tahoe and Suburban..................104
Acura MDX.....................12	Chevrolet Tracker........108
Acura NSX 14	Chevrolet TrailBlazer ...111
Acura RL.......................16	Chevrolet Venture 115
Acura RSX 18	Chrysler 300M.............118
Acura TL 20	Chrysler Concorde 121
Audi A4..........................22	Chrysler PT Cruiser 124
Audi A6/allroad quattro 25	Chrysler Sebring 126
Audi TT 29	Chrysler Town & Country and Voyager 131
BMW 3-Series................32	Daewoo Lanos 137
BMW 5-Series................37	Daewoo Leganza 139
BMW 7-Series................41	Daewoo Nubira 141
BMW X5.........................43	Dodge Caravan............143
BMW Z3 Series..............46	Dodge Durango...........149
Buick Century................49	Dodge Intrepid 152
Buick LeSabre...............51	Dodge Neon................155
Buick Park Avenue........54	Dodge Stratus.............159
Buick Regal...................57	Ford Crown Victoria......................162
Buick Rendezvous 60	Ford Escape................165
2003 Cadillac CTS........64	Ford Excursion............168
Cadillac DeVille.............66	Ford Expedition...........171
Cadillac Eldorado..........70	Ford Explorer 175
Cadillac Escalade and Escalade EXT............72	Ford Explorer Sport Trac and Sport.........178
Cadillac Seville...............74	Ford Focus..................181
Chevrolet Astro 77	Ford Mustang..............185
Chevrolet Blazer 80	Ford Taurus.................188
Chevrolet Camaro.........84	Ford Thunderbird 191
Chevrolet Cavalier 88	Ford Windstar 194
Chevrolet Corvette 90	Ford ZX2 197
Chevrolet Impala...........93	GMC Envoy..................199
Chevrolet Malibu 97	GMC Yukon/Denali 202
Chevrolet Monte Carlo..........................99	Honda Accord 207

Honda Civic	210
Honda CR-V	213
Honda Insight	215
Honda Odyssey	217
Honda Passport	219
Honda S2000	221
Hyundai Accent	223
Hyundai Elantra	225
Hyundai Santa Fe	228
Hyundai Sonata	230
Hyundai XG350	232
Infiniti G20	235
Infiniti I35	237
Infiniti Q45	239
Infiniti QX4	242
Isuzu Rodeo	244
Isuzu Rodeo Sport	247
Isuzu Trooper	250
Jaguar S-Type	252
Jaguar X-Type	255
Jaguar XJ Sedan	258
Jaguar XK8	260
Jeep Grand Cherokee	263
Jeep Liberty	268
Jeep Wrangler	272
Kia Optima	275
Kia Rio	278
Kia Sedona	280
Kia Spectra	282
Kia Sportage	285
Land Rover Discovery	288
Land Rover Freelander	290
Land Rover Range Rover	292
Lexus ES 300	295
Lexus GS 300/430	297
Lexus IS 300	300
Lexus LS 430	303
Lexus LX 470	306
Lexus RX 300	309
Lexus SC 430	311
Lincoln Continental	313
Lincoln LS	316
Lincoln Navigator	320
Lincoln Town Car	322
Mazda 626	325
Mazda Miata	328
Mazda Millenia	330
Mazda Protege	333
Mazda Tribute	335
Mercedes-Benz C-Class	338
Mercedes-Benz CLK	342
Mercedes-Benz E-Class	345
Mercedes-Benz M-Class	348
Mercedes-Benz S-Class/CL-Class	352
Mercedes-Benz SL-Class	356
Mercedes-Benz SLK-Class	357
Mercury Cougar	360
Mercury Grand Marquis	363
Mercury Mountaineer	365
Mercury Sable	368
Mercury Villager	371
Mini Cooper	374
Mitsubishi Diamante	375
Mitsubishi Eclipse	377
Mitsubishi Galant	380

Mitsubishi Lancer 382	Suzuki XL-7 475
Mitsubishi Mirage 384	Toyota 4Runner 477
Mitsubishi Montero 386	Toyota Avalon 481
Mitsubishi Montero Sport 389	Toyota Camry 484
Nissan Altima 391	Toyota Celica 487
Nissan Maxima 394	2003 Toyota Corolla 490
Nissan Pathfinder 397	Toyota Echo 491
Nissan Quest 400	Toyota Highlander 494
Nissan Sentra 403	Toyota Land Cruiser 497
Nissan Xterra 405	2003 Toyota Matrix 500
Oldsmobile Alero 409	Toyota MR2 Spyder 501
Oldsmobile Aurora 411	Toyota Prius 503
Oldsmobile Bravada 414	Toyota RAV4 505
Oldsmobile Intrigue 417	Toyota Sequoia 509
Oldsmobile Silhouette 419	Toyota Sienna 512
Pontiac Aztek 423	Toyota Solara 515
Pontiac Bonneville 426	Volkswagen Cabrio 519
Pontiac Firebird 428	Volkswagen EuroVan 521
Pontiac Grand Am 432	Volkswagen Jetta/Golf 523
Pontiac Grand Prix 435	Volkswagen New Beetle 528
Pontiac Montana 438	Volkswagen Passat 531
Pontiac Sunfire 442	Volvo 40 Series 534
Saab 9-3 445	Volvo S60 536
Saab 9-5 448	Volvo S80 540
Saturn L-Series 451	Volvo V70 543
Saturn S-Series 454	
Saturn VUE 457	Specifications 547
Subaru Forester 460	
Subaru Impreza 463	
Subaru Outback/Legacy 465	
Suzuki Esteem 470	
Suzuki Vitara 472	

INTRODUCTION

2002 Cars reports on more than 180 passenger cars, minivans, and sport-utility vehicles that are on sale or will be in the next few months. Key features, major changes for this year, and the latest available prices are included for each model. To help readers compare direct competitors, we divide vehicles into 12 model groups based on their size, price, and market position. Each report lists the model group that vehicle belongs to and suggests alternative choices from within the model group. Specifications for each vehicle are arranged by model group in charts that begin on **page 547**.

Best Buy and Recommended Choices

The Auto Editors of Consumer Guide® have selected Best Buys as the best overall values in their respective model categories. This is our highest rating. Other models labeled Recommended also merit serious consideration. This is our second-highest rating.

Ratings

Each vehicle is rated in ten categories on a 1-10 scale against the universe of vehicles, not just vehicles in its class. We use quantitative ratings for acceleration, fuel economy, and cargo space. The other category ratings are based on the subjective evaluations of our test drivers. **Note**: The cargo rating is based on the vehicle's maximum cargo volume, meaning with all rear seats folded or removed, when possible.

Specifications

Engine specifications supplied by the manufacturers are included with the vehicle report. Here's an explanation of our abbreviations:

All available engines, standard **(S)** or optional **(O)**. **Size, liters/cu. in.:** engine displacement in liters and cubic inches. **ohv:** overhead valve. **ohc:** overhead camshaft. **dohc:** dual overhead camshafts. **I:** inline arrangement of cylinders. **V:** cylinders in a V configuration. **H:** horizontally opposed cylinders. **I4/electric:** "hybrid" with both a gas engine and an electric motor. **rpm:** revolutions per minute. **CVT:** continuously variable (automatic) transmission. **SMT** = sequential manual transmission. **NA** = not available.

Other specifications, such as wheelbase and interior dimensions, are listed in the charts that begin on page 547. All dimensions and capacities are supplied by the manufacturers and represent the base model in the line. Optional equipment usually increases curb weight, and such items as larger tires or a roof rack may increase overall height.

INTRODUCTION
Price Information
• Retail price: the manufacturer's suggested retail price as set by the factory. "Suggested" is the key word here. The actual selling price is dictated by supply, demand, and competition.

• Invoice price: what the dealer pays to buy the car from the factory—the wholesale price.

• Destination charge: the cost of shipping the car to the dealership from the factory or port of entry.

• Note that the optional equipment section of some price lists includes a *Manufacturer's discount price*. This is the price of the option after the manufacturer's discount is calculated.

When a manufacturer offers such a discount, the vehicle's window sticker typically will show the full retail price of the option. The discounted amount will typically be displayed within a separate section on the window sticker. Regardless of how the discounted amount is represented on the window sticker, the *Manufacturer's discount price* is the actual price being charged for the option.

Car companies are free to change prices at any time, and may have done so after this book was published. If a dealer claims our prices are incorrect, or our information doesn't match what you see in showrooms, contact us and we'll do our best to help.

Consumer Guide®
7373 N. Cicero Ave.
Lincolnwood, IL 60712

SHOPPER'S GUIDE
Before you venture out to test drive and compare the new models, here are some suggestions to get you started on the right road:

• Determine how much you are willing, or can afford, to pay. If you plan to buy (instead of lease) shop for a loan at a bank or other lending institution before you shop for a car. It's better to figure out how much you can afford at a bank than in a dealer's showroom, where they can juggle numbers faster than you can count.

• Decide which vehicle or type of vehicle best suits your needs and pocketbook. Narrow the field to three or four choices.

Showroom Strategies
If you intend to buy a new vehicle instead of lease, remember:

• There are no formulas for calculating a "good deal." You can't just "knock 10 percent off the sticker." It depends on supply and demand for a particular model in your area and on competition among dealers.

• Don't tell a car salesperson how much you're willing to pay. Your price might be higher than what others are paying, and you may be

SHOPPER'S GUIDE

forfeiting your chance to get a lower price. Remember, it's the dealer's job to price the products they sell. It's your privilege to reject their price.

• Once you've settled on which vehicle you want to buy, shop at least three dealers to compare prices on the same model with the same equipment. Let each dealer know you're comparison shopping and that you'll buy from the dealer with the lowest price and best service.

• Get written price quotes that are good next week, not just today. A dealer won't give you a price in writing? Shop elsewhere. A salesperson who offers you a verbal quote "good for today only" is not being honest.

• Take your time and think about the deal at home. Don't be pressured into making a snap decision in the showroom.

• Don't put a deposit on a car just to get a price quote or a test drive. Dealers want a deposit because then you've made a commitment to them, and you're less likely to keep shopping.

• Don't shop for a monthly payment. Dealers will try to convince you to buy a car you can't afford by stretching the payments from 48 to 60 months. That lowers your monthly payment, but it means you'll pay more interest and be in debt longer. For example, if you borrow $15,000 for 48 months at 8 percent interest, you'll pay $366 per month, or $17,568 in total. If you borrow $15,000 for 60 months you'll likely pay a higher interest rate, say, 8.5 percent. Your monthly payment drops to $308.25, but you'll pay $18,495 over the 5-year life of the loan. That's $927 more in interest than you'll pay on a 4-year loan.

• Keep your trade-in out of the new-car price. If you're thinking about trading in your old vehicle, get a written trade-in value after you've settled on a price for the new car. When the dealer asks if you have a trade-in, say you haven't decided yet. The dealer may tempt you with the offer of a high trade-in allowance, then inflate the price of the new vehicle. Arrive at a price for the new car before you talk trade-in value.

Window Stickers

All cars sold in the U.S. must have posted on a side window what is called a "Monroney sticker" (named for the congressman who introduced the legislation). This law does not apply to light trucks, including passenger vans and most sport-utility vehicles, but most car companies and dealers voluntarily put the price sticker on trucks.

The Monroney sticker must show:
• The manufacturer's suggested retail price (MSRP) for the vehicle and all factory-installed options.
• A destination charge for shipping from final assembly point or port of importation to the dealer.
• EPA fuel economy estimates.

SHOPPER'S GUIDE

Dealer Price Stickers

Many dealers add a second window sticker that lists accessories installed at the dealership, and/or other charges. Everything on this added sticker should be considered "optional"—and probably overpriced. If you don't want a particular item—say, pinstriping or rustproofing—don't pay for it, even if it's already on the car.

Such add-on stickers typically include:

- Rustproofing: Most manufacturers advise against extra-cost rustproofing.
- Protection packages: These usually consist of dealer-applied paint sealers and fabric protectors, often in addition to rustproofing. They are of little or no value or duplicate the substances applied at the factory or those you can apply yourself for far less cost.
- M.V.A., A.D.P., or another abbreviation or code: These are smoke screens for dealer-invented profit-generators. M.V.A. stands for "Market Value Adjustment," and A.D.P. is "Additional Dealer Profit." Both sound official but are created by dealers to squeeze more money out of you. Some dealers dream up dandy new names for old add-on charges, such as "Currency Valuation Fee" and "Import Tariff." Those that do are best avoided.

Rather than arguing over individual charges like dealer prep, take the "bottom line" approach. Simply ask for a final price—the total amount you'll have to pay—and compare it to the price offered by competing dealers.

Lease Instead of Buy?

Leasing has become a popular alternative to buying, accounting for an estimated 30 percent of new-car sales and more than 50 percent of transaction on vehicles costing $30,000 or more.

Here are some guidelines to help you decide whether to lease or buy:

• When you buy a car, banks typically want a down payment of at least 20 percent. That requires $4000 in cash or trade-in value on a $20,000 vehicle. If you don't have that much, leasing might be a good deal because a large down payment isn't needed to lease. However, most leases require a substantial initial payment (usually called a "capital cost reduction"). Another plus is that monthly lease payments are generally lower than the monthly loan payment for an equivalent car.

• The major disadvantage to leasing is that unless you eventually buy a car, you'll always be making a monthly payment. At the end of a lease you have the option of returning the vehicle to the leasing company or buying it. Either way, you're going to have to dig into your pocket again to have a car. Think ahead two or three years. Will your financial situation allow you to lease another new car or to take out a loan to buy one?

SHOPPER'S GUIDE

• While the monthly payments may be lower on a lease, in the long run it is usually cheaper to buy if you keep cars five years or longer. For example, if you pay off a car loan in four years and keep the car another three years, your only expenses once the car is paid for will be for maintenance, repairs, and insurance.

• On the other hand, would you rather drive a 7-year-old car or a much newer one? A 2- or 3-year lease gives you the option of having a new car more often. The car you lease will probably always be under warranty and you don't have the hassle of selling or trading in an old car. After two or three years, you simply turn it in to the leasing agent.

• Leasing is generally less expensive than buying for those who claim their car as a business expense. You can write off more of the expense of a leased vehicle than one that is purchased and tie up less capital.

How do you find out if leasing is for you? Talk to your accountant or financial adviser. Everyone has a different situation, so leasing can be a great deal for your next-door neighbor but of no real benefit to you.

Read the Fine Print on Leases

Here's where leasing gets tricky. If you're enticed by leasing ads that tout "No money down, $299 a month" for a $25,000 car, read the fine print. It should explain some of the following:

• Most leases allow you to put 10,000 to 12,000 miles per year on the vehicle. Exceed the mileage limit and you'll pay a penalty of 10 to 15 cents per mile. A higher mileage limit can usually be negotiated.

• On most leases, you have to pay the first month's payment and a refundable security deposit up front.

• Some states require that the lessee—that's you—pay sales tax on the full suggested retail price of the car. If the sales tax is 8 percent in your area and you're leasing a $30,000 car, that's $2400 you have to pay. You usually have the option of rolling the sales tax into your monthly payment. In addition, if you purchase the car at the end of the lease, you may have to pay sales tax on that amount. Check your local tax laws.

• You'll also probably have to pay an "acquisition fee" when you sign the lease and may be hit with a "disposition fee" when you return it at the end. The amount is usually $250 to $500.

• Early termination and purchase options: Before signing, learn whether you can terminate the lease early and how much of a penalty you must pay. It might cost hundreds of dollars to terminate early.

• End-of-lease costs: You'll be liable for "excessive wear" or may be charged for having the car prepped for resale. It pays to take good care of a leased car so it passes inspection when you turn it in.

Good luck shopping for your next new vehicle!

ACURA

2003 ACURA CL

Acura CL

Front-wheel-drive near-luxury car
2002 base price range: $28,030-$30,380. Built in USA.
Also consider: BMW 3-Series, Toyota Solara, Mercedes-Benz CLK

FOR • Acceleration • Steering/handling • Build quality
AGAINST • Navigation system controls • Rear-seat entry/exit • Rear-seat head room

The coupe cousin of Acura's TL sedan jumps into the 2003 model early, gaining a 6-speed manual transmission, styling updates, and available General Motors' OnStar service. Two V6 models continue. The base 225-hp 3.2 CL uses a 5-speed automatic transmission with manual-shift feature. The 260-hp Type-S offers the automatic teamed with an antiskid system or the new manual with a limited-slip differential. Both CLs include antilock 4-wheel disc brakes, front side airbags, and sunroof. A satellite navigation system remains the sole factory option and now includes OnStar's emergency assistance and concierge services. The Type-S upgrades the base model with a firmer suspension and 17-inch wheels instead of 16s. Appearance changes for '03 involve new-design wheels, revised headlamps and taillights, body-color instead of bright grille surround and outside door handles, and interior trim revisions.

RATINGS	3.2 CL	Type-S w/nav. sys.
ACCELERATION	6	7
FUEL ECONOMY	6	5
RIDE QUALITY	7	5
STEERING/HANDLING	7	8
QUIETNESS	7	6
INSTRUMENTS/CONTROLS	8	6
ROOM/COMFORT (FRONT)	7	7

Specifications begin on page 551.

CONSUMER GUIDE®

ACURA

	3.2 CL	Type-S w/nav. sys.
ROOM/COMFORT (REAR)	3	3
CARGO ROOM	3	3
VALUE	5	4

The CL lacks the outright agility of a BMW 3-Series coupe, but appeals for brisk acceleration, an adept ride/handling balance, and now the extra sportiness of an available manual transmission. And like the TL sedan on which it's based, the CL is quite well equipped for the money.

TOTAL	59	54

Average total for near-luxury cars: 54.5

ENGINES

	ohc V6	ohc V6
Size, liters/cu. in.	3.2/196	3.2/196
Horsepower @ rpm	225 @ 5600	260 @ 6100
Torque (lb-ft) @ rpm	216 @ 4700	232 @ 3500
Availability	S[1]	S[2]
EPA city/highway mpg		
6-speed manual		19/28
5-speed automatic	19/29	19/29

1. 3.2CL. 2. Type-S.

2003 prices unavailable at time of publication.

PRICES

2002 Acura CL

	Retail Price	Dealer Invoice
3.2CL 2-door coupe	$28030	$25839
Type-S 2-door coupe	30380	28003
Destination charge	480	480

STANDARD EQUIPMENT

3.2CL: 3.2-liter V6 225-horsepower engine, 5-speed automatic transmission w/manual-shift capability, traction control, dual front airbags, front side airbags, antilock 4-wheel disc brakes, emergency inside trunk release, air conditioning w/automatic climate control, interior air filter, power steering, leather-wrapped tilt steering wheel, cruise control, leather upholstery, heated front bucket seats, 8-way power driver seat w/lumbar adjustment, 4-way power passenger seat, center console, cupholders, rear bucket seats w/trunk pass-through, memory driver seat and mirrors, heated power mirrors w/passenger-side tilt-down back-up aid, power windows, power door locks, remote keyless entry, Bose AM/FM/cassette w/in-dash 6-disc CD changer, steering wheel radio controls, automatic day/night rearview mirror, rear defogger, power sunroof, variable intermittent wipers, illuminated visor mirrors, universal garage door opener, map

Prices are accurate at time of publication; subject to manufacturer's change.

ACURA

lights, automatic-off headlights, floormats, theft-deterrent system, Xenon headlights, fog lights, 205/60VR16 tires, alloy wheels.

Type-S adds: 3.2-liter V6 260-horsepower engine, antiskid system, sport suspension, 215/50VR17 tires.

OPTIONAL EQUIPMENT

	Retail Price	Dealer Invoice
Navigation system	$2000	$1841

ACURA MDX

Acura MDX

All-wheel-drive midsize sport-utility vehicle

Base price range: $34,700-$39,300. Built in Canada.

Also consider: Ford Explorer, GMC Envoy, Lexus RX 300, Toyota Highlander

FOR • Passenger and cargo room **AGAINST** • Climate controls • Fuel economy • Navigation system controls

Noise-reduction measures highlight the 2002 Acura MDX, which is derived from parent-company Honda's Odyssey minivan. MDX seats seven and is longer overall than the rival 5-seat BMW X5 and Lexus RX 300. Its 2nd- and 3rd-row bench seats fold flat with the load floor. Standard are front side airbags, antilock 4-wheel disc brakes, rear air conditioning, leather upholstery, heated front seats, 17-inch alloy wheels, and now a rear wiper/washer. A V6 teams with a 5-speed automatic transmission and an all-wheel-drive system without low-range gearing. A navigation system is optional. The Touring model adds a power passenger seat, in-dash CD changer, and other features. Both models get thicker windshield glass, added sound dampening material in the roof and other areas, reshaped door mirrors and a repositioned roof rack, all said to reduce noise levels. Child-seat anchors also are added.

Specifications begin on page 551.

ACURA

RATINGS

	Base	Touring w/nav. sys.
ACCELERATION	5	5
FUEL ECONOMY	4	4
RIDE QUALITY	5	5
STEERING/HANDLING	5	5
QUIETNESS	3	3
INSTRUMENTS/CONTROLS	6	4
ROOM/COMFORT (FRONT)	8	8
ROOM/COMFORT (REAR)	7	7
CARGO ROOM	8	8
VALUE	6	5

A highly desirable blend of competence and convenience. Its ride can be truck-lumpy at times, but overall refinement, generous standard equipment, and attractive relative pricing make MDX a Best Buy.

TOTAL	57	54

Average total for midsize sport-utility vehicles: 49.6

ENGINES

	ohc V6
Size, liters/cu. in.	3.5/212
Horsepower @ rpm	240 @ 5300
Torque (lb-ft) @ rpm	245 @ 3000
Availability	S

EPA city/highway mpg
5-speed automatic 17/23

PRICES

Acura MDX

	Retail Price	Dealer Invoice
Base 4-door wagon	$34700	$31262
Base w/navigation system 4-door wagon	36700	33062
Touring 4-door wagon	37300	33602
Touring w/navigation system 4-door wagon	39300	35402
Destination charge	480	480

STANDARD EQUIPMENT

Base: 3.5-liter V6 engine, 5-speed automatic transmission, all-wheel drive, dual front airbags, front side airbags, antilock 4-wheel disc brakes, air conditioning w/front and rear automatic climate controls, power steering, tilt leather-wrapped steering w/radio controls, cruise control, leather upholstery, 7-passenger seating, heated front bucket seats, 8-way power driver seat, center console, cupholders, second and third row split-folding bench seats, heated power mirrors, power windows, power door locks, remote keyless entry,

Prices are accurate at time of publication; subject to manufacturer's change.

ACURA

AM/FM/cassette/CD player, digital clock, power sunroof, illuminated visor mirrors, universal garage door opener, automatic day/night rearview mirror, trip computer, map lights, rear defogger, intermittent rear wiper/washer, automatic-off headlights, floormats, theft-deterrent system, rear privacy glass, fog lights, 235/65R17 tires, alloy wheels.

Touring adds: 8-way power passenger seat, memory system for driver seat and mirrors, tilt-down passenger-side mirror back-up aid, Bose AM/FM/cassette w/in-dash 6-disc CD changer, roof rack.

Options are available as dealer-installed accessories.

Acura NSX

Rear-wheel-drive sports car
2001 base price range: $84,100-$88,100. Built in Japan.
Also consider: BMW Z8, Chevrolet Corvette, Porsche 911

FOR	• Acceleration • Steering/handling • Build quality
AGAINST	• Price

The midengine sports car from Honda's premium division gets the first noticeable appearance changes in its 12-year history. Acura says reshaped nose and lower-body areas are designed to make the 2002 NSX look more "substantial." Flip-up headlamps give way to fixed, glass-covered Xenon units. Also new are gold-colored brake calipers, larger exhaust ports, slightly wider rear tires and axle, 17-inch wheels all-around instead of 16s in front, suspension revisions, and reinforced roof pillars. The sole NSX-T model comes with a lift-off "targa" roof panel, 290-hp 3.2-liter V6, 6-speed manual transmission, antilock 4-wheel disc brakes, traction control, and a leather-upholstered cockpit that can be newly keyed to exterior color. The previous fixed-roof model is dropped. A 4-speed automatic transmission with manual-shift feature is available by special order and teams with a 252-hp 3.0-liter V6. Side airbags are still not available.

Specifications begin on page 551.

ACURA

RATINGS

	NSX-T, man.
ACCELERATION	9
FUEL ECONOMY	6
RIDE QUALITY	2
STEERING/HANDLING	10
QUIETNESS	4
INSTRUMENTS/CONTROLS	7
ROOM/COMFORT (FRONT)	5
ROOM/COMFORT (REAR)	0
CARGO ROOM	1
VALUE	2

The 2002 changes aren't the major improvements some had hoped for, and the NSX still trails most rivals for sheer horsepower. It also costs a mint, and aluminum-intensive construction means even minor accident repairs can be very expensive. But this sophisticated, well-built, high-performance sports car offers its own special thrills, yet is fairly practical day-to-day. It's also exclusive, with just 200 a year earmarked for the U.S.

TOTAL	46

Average total for sports cars: 41.3

ENGINES

	dohc V6	dohc V6
Size, liters/cu. in.	3.0/181	3.2/194
Horsepower @ rpm	252 @ 6600	290 @ 7100
Torque (lb-ft) @ rpm	210 @ 5300	224 @ 5500
Availability	O	S
EPA city/highway mpg		
6-speed manual		17/24
4-speed automatic	17/24	

2002 prices unavailable at time of publication.

PRICES

2001 Acura NSX	Retail Price	Dealer Invoice
Base 2-door coupe	$84100	$74013
T 2-door coupe	88100	77532
Destination charge	745	745

STANDARD EQUIPMENT

Base: 3.2-liter dohc V6 engine w/6-speed manual transmission or 3.0-liter dohc V6 engine w/4-speed automatic transmission w/manual-shift capability, traction control, limited-slip differential (6-speed manual), dual front airbags, antilock 4-wheel disc brakes, air conditioning w/automatic climate control, variable-assist power steering,

Prices are accurate at time of publication; subject to manufacturer's change.

ACURA

tilt/telescopic leather-wrapped steering wheel, cruise control, leather upholstery, 4-way power bucket seats, center console, cupholders, power mirrors, power windows, power door locks, Bose AM/FM/cassette, power antenna, digital clock, tachometer, variable intermittent wipers, rear defogger, illuminated visor mirrors, remote fuel door and decklid releases, floormats, rear spoiler, theft-deterrent system, 215/45ZR16 front tires, 245/40ZR17 rear tires, alloy wheels.

T adds to Base: removable roof panel.

Options are available as dealer-installed accessories.

Acura RL

Front-wheel-drive luxury car
Base price range: $43,150-$45,150.   Built in Japan.
Also consider: BMW 5-Series, Lexus GS 300/430, Mercedes-Benz E-Class

FOR • Acceleration • Steering/handling • Ride • Build quality
AGAINST • Navigation system controls

Driver-oriented changes highlight the latest version of Honda's luxury-brand flagship sedan. The 2002 RL went on sale in spring 2001, retaining its V6 engine and 4-speed automatic transmission, but gaining 15 hp. Tires are wider, the chassis firmer, and the standard antilock 4-wheel disc brake system is modified in an effort to improve pedal feel. There's more sound deadening, subtle styling revisions, and a standard General Motors OnStar assistance system. Continuing standard are a traction control/antiskid system, front side airbags, leather/wood interior trim, power tilt/telescopic steering wheel, heated front seats with memory, and a trunk-mounted CD changer. A touch-screen navigation system is the sole option and is priced as a separate model.

RATINGS	**Base**	**Base w/nav. sys.**
ACCELERATION	6	6

ACURA

	Base	Base w/nav. sys.
FUEL ECONOMY	4	4
RIDE QUALITY	9	9
STEERING/HANDLING	7	7
QUIETNESS	9	9
INSTRUMENTS/CONTROLS	8	7
ROOM/COMFORT (FRONT)	8	8
ROOM/COMFORT (REAR)	7	7
CARGO ROOM	3	3
VALUE	7	7

A 5-speed automatic transmission would be more up to date, but RL's road manners are luxury-class competitive and acceleration—admittedly not as strong as that of V8 rivals—is fine. Bottom line: A Best Buy becomes more entertaining for '02 while keeping its terrific refinement, quality, and value, plus strong reliability record.

TOTAL	68	67

Average total for luxury cars: 59.4

ENGINES

	dohc V6
Size, liters/cu. in.	3.5/212
Horsepower @ rpm	225 @ 5200
Torque (lb-ft) @ rpm	213 @ 2800
Availability	S

EPA city/highway mpg
4-speed automatic 18/24

PRICES

Acura RL	Retail Price	Dealer Invoice
Base 4-door sedan	$43150	$38421
Base w/navigation system	45150	40200
Destination charge	480	480

STANDARD EQUIPMENT

Base: 3.5-liter V6 engine, 4-speed automatic transmission, traction control, dual front airbags, front side airbags, antilock 4-wheel disc brakes, antiskid system, emergency inside trunk release, air conditioning w/front and rear automatic climate controls, interior air filter, power steering, power tilt/telescoping leather-wrapped steering wheel w/memory, cruise control, OnStar System w/one year service (roadside assistance, emergency services; other services available), leather upholstery, heated front bucket seats, 8-way power driver seat w/memory and lumbar adjustment, 4-way power passenger seat, center console, cupholders, rear seat trunk pass-through, wood interior trim, heated power mirrors, power windows, power

Prices are accurate at time of publication; subject to manufacturer's change.

ACURA

door locks, remote keyless entry, Bose AM/FM/cassette w/6-disc CD changer, steering wheel radio controls, digital clock, tachometer, power sunroof, rear defogger, automatic day/night rearview mirror, remote fuel door and decklid releases, variable intermittent wipers, illuminated visor mirrors, map lights, universal garage door opener, automatic headlights, floormats, theft-deterrent system, Xenon headlights, fog lights, 225/55VR16 tires, alloy wheels.

Base w/navigation system adds: touch screen navigation system.

Options are available as dealer-installed accessories.

Acura RSX Type-S

Front-wheel-drive sporty coupe
Base price range: $19,950-$23,170. Built in Japan.
Also consider: Toyota Celica, Volkswagen New Beetle

FOR	• Acceleration • Steering/handling • Instruments/controls
AGAINST	• Noise • Rear-seat room • Rear-seat entry/exit

RSX replaces Acura's entry-level Integra for 2002. It has similar dimensions, but new styling and more power. RSX comes only as a 2-dr hatchback; Integra offered 2- and 4-dr body styles. Base and performance-oriented Type-S models are offered, both with a 2.0-liter 4-cyl engine. In the base model, it has 160 hp and comes with 5-speed manual or 5-speed automatic transmission; in the Type-S, it makes 200 hp and teams only with 6-speed manual. Type-S has a stiffer suspension but the same 16-inch wheels and tires as the base model. Antilock 4-wheel disc brakes and front side airbags are standard, as are automatic climate control and sunroof. Leather upholstery is standard on the Type-S and optional on the base model. Type-S also comes with a 6-disc in-dash CD changer.

RATINGS	Base, man.	Base, auto.	Type-S
ACCELERATION	6	5	7

Specifications begin on page 551.

ACURA

	Base, man.	Base, auto.	Type-S
FUEL ECONOMY	7	6	6
RIDE QUALITY	4	4	3
STEERING/HANDLING	8	8	8
QUIETNESS	3	3	3
INSTRUMENTS/CONTROLS	8	8	8
ROOM/COMFORT (FRONT)	4	4	4
ROOM/COMFORT (REAR)	2	2	2
CARGO ROOM	3	3	3
VALUE	4	4	3

The fun-to-drive RSX is priced competitively, and the base version delivers most of the Type-S's thrills at slightly less money. This Acura is better executed than main rivals Toyota Celica and Mitsubishi Eclipse, though its high-strung 4 cyl may not appeal to those seeking relaxed day-to-day transportation.

TOTAL	49	47	47

Average total for sporty coupes: 43.4

ENGINES

	dohc I4	dohc I4
Size, liters/cu. in.	2.0/122	2.0/122
Horsepower @ rpm	160 @ 6500	200 @ 7400
Torque (lb-ft) @ rpm	141 @ 4000	142 @ 6000
Availability	S[1]	S[2]

EPA city/highway mpg
5-speed manual	27/33	
6-speed manual		24/31
5-speed automatic	24/33	

1. Base. 2. Type-S.

PRICES

Acura RSX

	Retail Price	Dealer Invoice
Base 2-door hatchback, manual	$19950	$18193
Base 2-door hatchback, automatic	20850	19012
Base w/leather 2-door hatchback, manual	20950	19103
Base w/leather 2-door hatchback, automatic	21850	19922
Type-S 2-door hatchback	23170	21124
Destination charge	480	480

STANDARD EQUIPMENT

Base: 2.0-liter dohc 4-cylinder 160-horsepower engine, 5-speed manual or 5-speed automatic transmission w/manual-shift capability, dual front airbags, front side airbags, antilock 4-wheel disc brakes, air conditioning w/automatic climate control, interior air filter, power steering, leather-wrapped steering wheel, cruise control, front

Prices are accurate at time of publication; subject to manufacturer's change.

ACURA

bucket seats w/driver seat lumbar adjustment, center console, cupholders, split folding rear seat, power mirrors, power windows, power door locks, remote keyless entry, AM/FM/CD player, digital clock, tachometer, power sunroof, rear defogger, rear wiper/washer, remote fuel door release, intermittent wipers, map lights, visor mirrors, floormats, theft-deterrent system, 205/55R16 tires, alloy wheels.

Base w/leather adds: leather upholstery.

Type-S adds: 2.0-liter dohc 4-cylinder 200-horsepower engine, 6-speed manual transmission, Bose AM/FM/cassette w/in-dash 6-disc CD changer, sport suspension.

Options are available as dealer installed accessories.

Acura TL Type-S

Front-wheel-drive near-luxury car
Base price range: $28,880-$33,230. Built in USA.
Also consider: BMW 3-Series, Infiniti I35, Lexus ES 300

FOR • Acceleration • Steering/handling • Refinement • Build quality **AGAINST** • Road noise (Type-S) • Climate controls with navigation system

Released in March 2001 as an early '02 model, the best-seller at Honda's upscale division gains revised front styling and a sporty Type-S version. Both models have a 5-speed automatic transmission with manual shift gate, but the Type-S gets a 260-hp edition of the base TL's 225-hp V6. Antilock, 4-wheel disc brakes, traction control, and front side airbags are standard on both. Type-S adds standard antiskid system, firmer suspension with 17-inch wheels instead of 16s, sport bucket front seats, and metal-look gauges. A navigation system with dashboard screen is the only option for either model. Both models now have a 6-disc in-dash CD changer, 2-position seat/mirrors memory linked to the remote keyfob, and revised cupholders.

Specifications begin on page 551.

ACURA

RATINGS	Base	Type-S w/nav. sys.
ACCELERATION	6	7
FUEL ECONOMY	6	5
RIDE QUALITY	8	7
STEERING/HANDLING	7	8
QUIETNESS	8	7
INSTRUMENTS/CONTROLS	8	6
ROOM/COMFORT (FRONT)	7	7
ROOM/COMFORT (REAR)	5	5
CARGO ROOM	3	3
VALUE	8	8

Solidly built, impeccably finished, and equal or superior to any class rival for refinement, quality, and features per dollar. Type-S gives the already sporty TL even better go and extra nimbleness without compromising comfort.

TOTAL	66	63

Average total for near-luxury cars: 54.5

ENGINES

	dohc V6	dohc V6
Size, liters/cu. in.	3.2/196	3.2/196
Horsepower @ rpm	225 @ 5600	260 @ 6100
Torque (lb-ft) @ rpm	216 @ 4700	232 @ 3500
Availability	S[1]	S[2]
EPA city/highway mpg		
5-speed automatic	19/29	19/29

1. Base model. 2. Type S.

PRICES

Acura TL	Retail Price	Dealer Invoice
Base 4-door sedan	$28880	$26322
Base w/navigation system 4-door sedan	30880	28143
Type-S 4-door sedan	31230	28462
Type-S w/navigation system 4-door sedan	33230	30283
Destination charge	480	480

STANDARD EQUIPMENT

Base: 3.2-liter V6 225-horsepower engine, 5-speed automatic transmission w/manual-shift capability, traction control, dual front airbags, front side airbags, antilock 4-wheel disc brakes, emergency inside trunk release, air conditioning w/automatic climate control, interior air filter, power steering, tilt leather-wrapped steering wheel, cruise control, leather upholstery, heated front bucket seats, 8-way power driver seat w/memory and lumbar adjustment, 4-way power passenger seat, center console, cupholders, trunk pass-through, heated

Prices are accurate at time of publication; subject to manufacturer's change.

ACURA • AUDI

power mirrors w/memory, power windows, power door locks, remote keyless entry, Bose AM/FM/cassette w/in-dash 6-disc CD changer, digital clock, steering wheel radio controls, power sunroof, rear defogger, automatic day/night rearview mirror, outside temperature indicator, universal garage door opener, variable intermittent wipers, illuminated visor mirrors, map lights, automatic-off headlights, remote fuel door/decklid release, floormats, theft-deterrent system, Xenon headlights, 205/60VR16 tires, alloy wheels.

Base w/navigation system adds: touch screen navigation system.

Type-S adds to Base: 3.2-liter V6 260-horsepower engine, antiskid system, upgraded variable-assist power steering, sport suspension, 215/50VR17 tires.

Type-S w/navigation system adds: touch screen navigation system.

Options are available as dealer-installed accessories.

AUDI A4

Audi A4 1.8T

Front- or all-wheel-drive near-luxury car
Base price range: $24,900-$40,500. Built in Germany.
Also consider: BMW 3-Series, Lexus IS 300, Mercedes-Benz C-Class

FOR • Acceleration (V6) • Automatic transmission performance (CVT) • Steering/handling • Ride • Interior materials • Available AWD **AGAINST** • Rear-seat room (S4)

Audiís least-expensive car is redesigned for 2002. The new A4 is slightly larger inside and out and introduces an optional continuously variable automatic transmission (CVT). Carried over for '02 are the 250-hp S4 sedan and S4 Avant wagon. The redesigned 1.8T sedan has a turbocharged 170-hp 4-cyl engine. The 3.0 model has a V6 with 220 hp, a gain of 30 hp. Audi's quattro all-wheel drive is standard on S4 models and available on other models in place of

Specifications begin on page 551.

AUDI

front-wheel drive. Quattro A4s use manual transmission or a conventional 5-speed automatic. The CVT is available with front-wheel drive. Audi's CVT furnishes variable drive ratios instead of conventional gears, and also has six "manual-shift" ratios accessed via a separate shift gate. ABS, an antiskid system and curtain and front side airbags are standard; rear side airbags are optional. Options include a navigation system, rear obstacle warning, and a Sport package with 17-inch wheels.

RATINGS	1.8T sdn w/Sport, man.	1.8T sdn, CVT	1.8T Sdn w/ quattro, auto.	3.0 sdn w/quattro, man.
ACCELERATION	6	6	5	7
FUEL ECONOMY	7	6	5	5
RIDE QUALITY	6	7	7	7
STEERING/HANDLING	7	7	7	7
QUIETNESS	6	6	6	7
INSTRUMENTS/CONTROLS	8	8	8	8
ROOM/COMFORT (FRONT)	7	7	7	7
ROOM/COMFORT (REAR)	3	3	3	3
CARGO ROOM	3	3	3	3
VALUE	5	6	5	4

The redesigned A4 matches or beats most any near-luxury rival in ride comfort, drivetrain smoothness, and features. BMW and Jaguar offer all-wheel drive, but no rival has the impressive new CVT.

TOTAL	58	59	56	58

Average total for near-luxury cars: 54.5

ENGINES	Turbocharged dohc I4	dohc V6	Turbocharged dohc V6
Size, liters/cu. in.	1.8/109	3.0/182	2.7/163
Horsepower @ rpm	170 @ 5900	220 @ 6300	250 @ 5800
Torque (lb-ft) @ rpm	166 @ 1950	221 @ 3200	258 @ 1850
Availability	S[1]	S[2]	S[3]

EPA city/highway mpg

5-speed manual	22/31[4]		
6-speed manual		18/25	17/23
5-speed automatic	19/28	17/25	17/24
CVT automatic	20/29	19/27	

1. 1.9T. 2. 3.0. 3. S4, S4 Avant. 4. 21/29 w/quattro.

PRICES

Audi A4

	Retail Price	Dealer Invoice
A4 1.8T 4-door sedan, manual	$24900	$22506
A4 1.8T 4-door sedan, CVT	26050	23628
A4 1.8T quattro 4-door sedan, manual	26650	24256
A4 1.8T quattro 4-door sedan, automatic	27800	25378

Prices are accurate at time of publication; subject to manufacturer's change.

CONSUMER GUIDE®

AUDI

	Retail Price	Dealer Invoice
A4 1.8T Avant quattro 4-wagon sedan, manual ...	$27650	$25146
A4 1.8T Avant quattro 4-wagon sedan, automatic...	28800	26268
A4 3.0 4-door sedan, CVT	31390	28370
A4 3.0 quattro 4-door sedan, manual	32090	29098
A4 3.0 quattro 4-door sedan, automatic	33140	30120
A4 3.0 Avant quattro 4-door wagon, manual	33090	29988
A4 3.0 Avant quattro 4-door wagon, automatic	34140	31010
S4 quattro 4-door sedan, manual	38900	35252
S4 quattro 4-door sedan, automatic	38900	35252
S4 Avant quattro 4-door wagon, manual	40500	36676
S4 Avant quattro 4-door wagon, automatic	40500	36676
Destination charge	575	575

STANDARD EQUIPMENT

A4 1.8T: 1.8-liter dohc turbocharged 4-cylinder engine, 5-speed manual or continuously-variable automatic transmission (CVT) w/manual-shift capability, traction control, front limited-slip differential, dual front airbags, front side airbags, curtain side airbags, antilock 4-wheel disc brakes, brake-assist, antiskid system, air conditioning w/dual-zone automatic climate control, interior air filter, power steering, tilt/telescoping leather-wrapped steering wheel, cruise control, cloth upholstery, front bucket seats w/height-adjustment and power lumbar adjustment, center console, cupholders, split folding rear seat, heated power mirrors, power windows, power door locks, remote keyless entry, AM/FM/cassette w/6-disc CD changer, digital clock, tachometer, trip computer, outside temperature indicator, rear window defogger, illuminated visor mirrors, map lights, variable intermittent wipers, remote fuel door and decklid release, floormats, theft-deterrent system, headlight washers, front and rear fog lights, full-size spare tire, 205/65HR15 tires, alloy wheels.

A4 1.8T quattro adds: all-wheel drive, 5-speed manual or 5-speed automatic transmission w/manual-shift capability, front and rear limited-slip differentials, cargo cover (wagon), rear wiper/washer (wagon), roof rails (wagon).

A4 3.0 adds to A4 1.8T: 3.0-liter dohc V6 engine, continuously variable automatic transmission (CVT) w/manual-shift capability, 12-way power driver seat, wood interior trim, 215/55HR16 tires.

A4 3.0 quattro adds: all-wheel drive, 6-speed manual or 5-speed automatic transmission w/manual-shift capability, front and rear limited-slip differentials, cargo cover (wagon), rear wiper/washer (wagon), roof rails (wagon).

S4 quattro adds: 2.7-liter dohc turbocharged V6 engine, single-zone automatic climate control, leather upholstery, 10-way power front seats, AM/FM/cassette/CD player, ski sack (wagon), Xenon headlights, sport

Specifications begin on page 551.

AUDI

suspension, 225/45R17 tires. *Deletes:* traction control, brake-assist, 6-disc CD changer, full-size spare tire (wagon).

OPTIONAL EQUIPMENT

	Retail Price	Dealer Invoice
Major Packages		
Sport Pkg., 1.8T, 1.8T quattro	$1000	$890
3.0, 3.0 quattro	750	668
Sport suspension, 235/45YR17 tires.		
Sport Trim Pkg., S4	400	356
Leather/alcantara upholstery, aluminum exterior trim.		
Premium Pkg., 1.8T, 1.8T quattro	350	312
3.0, 3.0 quattro	550	490
Automatic day/night rearview and outside mirrors, compass, driver seat and mirror memory (3.0, 3.0 quattro), universal garage door opener.		
Premium Pkg., S4	1200	1068
Power sunroof, automatic day/night rearview and outside mirrors, universal garage door opener.		
Preferred Pkg., 3.0, 3.0 quattro	1800	1674
Leather upholstery, power sunroof.		
Cold Weather Pkg., S4 sedan	600	534
Heated front seats, ski sack.		
Safety		
Rear side airbags, A4	350	312
Parktronic rear obstacle detection system, 3.0, 3.0 quattro	350	312
Comfort & Convenience Features		
Navigation system, 3.0, 3.0 quattro, S4	1350	1219
Power sunroof, A4	1000	890
Leather upholstery, 3.0, 3.0 quattro	1320	1175
Heated front and rear seats, A4	525	467
Heated front seats, S4 wagon	450	401
Bose sound system	650	579
6-disc CD changer, S4	550	490
Power rear and manual side sunshades, 3.0/3.0 quattro sedan	375	334
Manual side sun shades, 3.0 quattro wagon	150	134
Appearance and Miscellaneous		
Xenon headlights, A4	500	445
215/55HR16 tires, 1.8T, 1.8T quattro	450	401

AUDI A6/ALLROAD QUATTRO

Front- or all-wheel-drive luxury car
Base price range: $35,400-$58,700. Built in Germany.

Prices are accurate at time of publication; subject to manufacturer's change.

AUDI

Audi A6

Also consider: Acura RL, BMW 5-Series, Lexus GS 300/430

FOR • Acceleration (2.7T, 4.2, A6) • Available AWD • Passenger and cargo room • Steering/handling • Build quality **AGAINST** • Climate controls

The less-expensive of Audi's two luxury lines gets revised styling, a larger V6 engine, and a continuously variable automatic transmission for 2002. A6 comes as a sedan, wagon, or the high-riding allroad wagon. The 3.0 sedan and Avant wagon replace last year's 2.8 models and have a 220-hp 3.0-liter V6 instead of a 200-hp 2.8 V6. The turbo V6 2.7T and V8 4.2 sedans return, as does the allroad quattro—an SUV-inspired AWD wagon with the 2.7T engine and height-adjustable suspension. New for '02 is the S6 Avant with a 340-hp 4.2 V8, sport suspension and tires, and aluminum exterior trim. The 3.0 sedan comes with front-wheel drive or quattro AWD; all other models come with quattro. Front side airbags, curtain side airbags, antilock 4-wheel disc brakes, and antiskid system are standard. Rear side airbags are optional. A 6-speed manual transmission is available on the 2.7T. A 5-speed automatic with manual shift gate is optional on the 2.7T and standard on other A6s except the front-drive 3.0. That model uses a continuously variable automatic transmission. Like other CVTs, it furnishes variable drive ratios instead of conventional gears, but it also offers six manual-shift ratios accessed via a separate shift gate. Leather upholstery is standard on V8 models, optional elsewhere. All '02 A6s get an in-dash 6-disc CD changer, new front and rear appearance touches, and revised dashboards.

RATINGS	3.0 quattro sdn, auto.	2.7T w/ Sport Pkg., man.	allroad quattro, man.	S6
ACCELERATION	6	7	6	8
FUEL ECONOMY	5	6	4	3
RIDE QUALITY	8	7	6	5
STEERING/HANDLING	7	7	6	8
QUIETNESS	7	6	7	5

Specifications begin on page 551.

AUDI

	3.0 quattro sdn, auto.	2.7T w/ Sport Pkg., man.	allroad quattro, man.	S6
INSTRUMENTS/CONTROLS	8	8	8	8
ROOM/COMFORT (FRONT)	8	8	8	8
ROOM/COMFORT (REAR)	7	7	7	7
CARGO ROOM	6	6	7	7
VALUE	7	5	3	2

A6's distinctive blend of spaciousness, performance, design sophistication, and powertrain choice is unique among luxury cars. Prices generally run below those of directly competing models.

TOTAL	69	67	62	61

Average total for luxury cars: 59.4

ENGINES

	dohc V6	Turbocharged dohc V6	dohc V8	dohc V8
Size, liters/cu. in.	3.0/182	2.7/163	4.2/255	4.2/255
Horsepower @ rpm	220 @ 6300	250 @ 5800	300 @ 6200	340 @ 7000
Torque (lb-ft) @ rpm	221 @ 3200	258 @ 1850	295 @ 3000	310 @ 3400
Availability	S[1]	S[2]	S[3]	S[4]
EPA city/highway mpg				
6-speed manual		16/21		
5-speed automatic	17/25	15/21	17/25	14/21
CVT automatic	19/25			

1. 3.0. 2. 2.7T, allroad quattro. 3. 4.2. 4. S6.

PRICES

Audi A6/allroad quattro	Retail Price	Dealer Invoice
3.0 4-door sedan	$35400	$31950
3.0 quattro 4-door sedan	37150	33700
3.0 Avant quattro 4-door wagon	38350	34768
2.7T 4-door sedan, manual	39750	36014
2.7T 4-door sedan, automatic	39750	36014
allroad quattro 4-door wagon, manual	39900	36049
allroad quattro 4-door wagon, automatic	40950	37071
4.2 4-door sedan	49650	44825
S6 4-door wagon	58700	52879
Destination charge	575	575

STANDARD EQUIPMENT

3.0: 3.0-liter dohc V6 engine, continuously variable automatic transmission, traction control, dual front airbags, front side airbags, curtain side airbags, antilock 4-wheel disc brakes, antiskid system,

Prices are accurate at time of publication; subject to manufacturer's change.
CONSUMER GUIDE®

AUDI

emergency inside trunk release, air conditioning w/dual-zone automatic climate controls, interior air filter, power steering, tilt/telescoping steering wheel, leather-wrapped steering wheel, cruise control, cloth upholstery, 12-way power front bucket seats w/power lumbar adjustment, center console, cupholders, split folding rear seat, wood interior trim, heated power mirrors, power windows, power door locks, remote keyless entry, AM/FM/cassette w/in-dash 6-disc CD changer, digital clock, tachometer, trip computer, outside-temperature indicator, map lights, illuminated visor mirrors, rear defogger, variable intermittent wipers, remote fuel-door and decklid release, floormats, theft-deterrent system, headlight washers, front and rear fog lights, 205/55R16 tires, alloy wheels.

3.0 quattro/Avant quattro adds: all-wheel drive, 5-speed automatic transmission w/manual-shift capability, electronic limited-slip front and rear differentials, rear wiper/washer (wagon), ski sack (wagon), manual rear window sunshade (wagon), cargo cover (wagon), roof rails (wagon), 215/55HR16 tires. *Deletes:* traction control.

2.7T adds: 2.7-liter dohc turbocharged V6 engine, 6-speed manual or 5-speed automatic transmission w/manual-shift capablity, full-size spare tire.

allroad quattro adds: leather upholstery, height-adjustable suspension, 225/55WR17 tires. *Deletes:* ski sack, full-size spare tire.

4.2 adds: 4.2-liter dohc V8 engine, 5-speed automatic transmission w/manual-shift capability, power sunroof, power tilt/telescoping steering wheel w/manual-shift and radio controls, driver seat and mirror memory, Bose sound system, automatic day/night outside and rearview mirrors, compass, universal garage door opener, ski sack, 235/50HR16 tires. *Deletes:* height-adjustable suspension.

S6 adds: heated front seats, Xenon headlights, sport suspension, full size spare tire, 255/40ZR17 tires.

OPTIONAL EQUIPMENT
Major Packages

	Retail Price	Dealer Invoice
Convenience Pkg., 3.0, 3.0 quattro, 3.0 Avant, 2.7T, allroad	$730	$650

Front seat memory, automatic day/night rearview and outside mirrors, compass, universal garage door opener.

	Retail Price	Dealer Invoice
Preferred Luxury Pkg., 3.0, 3.0 quattro, }3.0 Avant, 2.7T, allroad	1800	1602

Leather upholstery, power sunroof.

	Retail Price	Dealer Invoice
Premium Pkg., 3.0, 3.0 quattro, 3.0 Avant	1200	1068
allroad	1225	1090
2.7T	1275	1135

Steering wheel radio and manual-shift controls, heated steering wheel (allroad), rear obstacle detection system, Xenon headlights. allroad requires heated front and rear seats.

Specifications begin on page 551.

AUDI

	Retail Price	Dealer Invoice
Premium Pkg., 4.2	$850	$757

Heated front and rear seats, heated steering wheel, rear obstacle detection system, Xenon headlights.

Sport Pkg., 2.7T	1425	1268
4.2	1750	1558

Front sport seats, sport suspension, 235/45HR17 tires (2.7T), 255/40R17 tires (4.2), special alloy wheels.

Warm Weather Pkg., 4.2	1000	890
S6	750	668

Solar sunroof, power rear sunshade (4.2), manual side sunshades.

Safety

Rear obstacle detection system, S6	350	312
Tire pressure monitor, allroad	390	347
Rear side airbags	350	312

Comfort & Convenience Features

Power sunroof, 3.0, 3.0 quattro, 3.0 Avant, 2.7T, allroad	1000	890
Leather upholstery, 3.0, 3.0 quattro, 2.8 Avant, 2.7T, allroad	1550	1380
Alcantara seat trrim, S6	250	223
Heated front and rear seats, 3.0, 3.0 quattro, 3.0 Avant, 2.7T, allroad	550	490
Heated rear seats, S6	250	223
Rear-facing seat, wagon	750	668
Bose sound system	750	668

Std. 4.2, S6.

Power rear and manual side sunshades, 3.0, 2.7T	450	401

Appearance and Miscellaneous

Cross spoke alloy wheels, 2.7T	675	601

Includes 235/45HR17 tires.

Cast alloy wheels, 4.2	750	668

Includes 255/40HR17 tires.

Forged alloy wheels, 4.2	1000	890

Include 255/40ZR17 tires.

Dual spoke alloy wheels, allroad	950	846

AUDI TT

Front- or all-wheel-drive sports car
Base price range: $31,200-$38,900. Built in Hungary.
Also consider: Chevrolet Corvette, Mazda Miata, Mercedes-Benz SLK-Class

Prices are accurate at time of publication; subject to manufacturer's change.

AUDI

Audi TT 2-door convertible

FOR • Build quality • Handling/roadholding • Interior materials • Acceleration • Available AWD **AGAINST** • Noise • Visibility • Rear-seat room • Rear-seat entry/exit • Ride

Audi's retro-look TT comes as a 4-seat hatchback coupe and a 2-seat convertible. Both have a turbo 4-cyl engine and a choice of 180 hp and a 5-speed manual transmission or 225 hp and a 6-speed manual. Automatic transmission is unavailable. The base 180-hp models come with front-wheel drive and traction control. Quattro all-wheel drive is available for the 180-hp coupe and is standard on 225-hp models. An antiskid system and rear spoiler are standard on all. A power top is standard on 225-hp convertibles and optional for 180-hp versions; both have a heated glass rear window. Changes for 2002 include a new radio with in-dash CD and an optional universal garage door opener.

RATINGS	Base conv 2WD	225-hp cpe
ACCELERATION	6	7
FUEL ECONOMY	7	6
RIDE QUALITY	3	3
STEERING/HANDLING	8	10
QUIETNESS	2	2
INSTRUMENTS/CONTROLS	6	6
ROOM/COMFORT (FRONT)	3	3
ROOM/COMFORT (REAR)	0	1
CARGO ROOM	1	6
VALUE	2	2

We recommend the TT based on its solidity, style, features, and road manners. Most rival sports cars with swifter acceleration cost thousands more, and none in this price range has the all-weather advantage of the TT's available quattro AWD.

TOTAL	38	46

Average total for sports cars: 41.3

AUDI

ENGINES	Turbocharged dohc I4	Turbocharged dohc I4
Size, liters/cu. in.	1.8/107	1.8/107
Horsepower @ rpm	180 @ 5500	225 @ 5900
Torque (lb-ft) @ rpm	173 @ 1950	207 @ 2200
Availability	S	S[1]
EPA city/highway mpg		
5-speed manual	23/31[2]	
6-speed manual		20/28

1. 225-hp models. 2. 20/29 w/Quattro.

PRICES

Audi TT	Retail Price	Dealer Invoice
Base 2-door hatchback	$31200	$28113
Base 2-door convertible	33200	29893
quattro 2-door hatchback	32950	29863
225-hp 2-door hatchback	36100	32667
225-hp 2-door convertible	38900	35159
Destination charge	575	575

STANDARD EQUIPMENT

Base: 1.8-liter dohc turbocharged 4-cylinder 180-horsepower engine, 5-speed manual transmission, traction control, limited-slip differential, dual front airbags, front side airbags, antilock 4-wheel disc brakes, antiskid system, emergency inside trunk release, air conditioning w/automatic climate control, interior air filter, power steering, tilt/telescoping leather-wrapped steering wheel, cruise control, leather upholstery, height-adjustable front bucket seats, center console, cupholders, split folding rear seat, heated power mirrors, power windows, power door locks, remote keyless entry, AM/FM/CD player, digital clock, tachometer, trip computer, outside temperature indicator, rear defogger, remote fuel door/decklid release, illuminated visor mirrors, map lights, variable-intermittent wipers, power retractable windbreak (convertible), floormats, theft-deterrent system, rear spoiler, fog lights, headlight washers, 205/55WR16 tires, alloy wheels.

quattro adds: all-wheel drive, center differential. *Deletes:* traction control.

225hp adds: 1.8-liter dohc turbocharged 4-cylinder 225-horsepower engine, 6-speed manual transmission, power convertible top (convertible), 225/45YR17 tires.

OPTIONAL EQUIPMENT
Major Packages

Premium Pkg., Base, quattro	1600	1424

Prices are accurate at time of publication; subject to manufacturer's change.

AUDI • BMW

	Retail Price	Dealer Invoice
225-hp	$1100	$979

Xenon headlights, heated front seats, universal garage door opener, 225/45YR17 tires (Base, quattro), 6-spoke alloy wheels.

Comfort & Convenience Features

Navigation system	1350	1219
Audio Pkg.	1200	1068

Bose premium sound system, 6-disc CD changer.

Power convertible top, Base convertible	800	712
Baseball optic leather upholstery	1000	890
Alcantara steering wheel	275	245

BMW 3-SERIES

BMW 325i 4-door wagon

Rear- or all-wheel-drive near-luxury car
Base price range: $27,100-$53,900. Built in Germany.
Also consider: Audi A4, Mercedes-Benz C-Class and CLK

FOR • Acceleration • Steering/handling • Build quality • Exterior finish **AGAINST** • Cargo room (convertible) • Rear-seat entry/exit (coupe)

More standard features, subtle styling changes, and a new type of transmission highlight 2002 additions to BMW's most popular lineup. All 3-Series models have inline 6-cyl engines. The 325i sedan and wagon and the 325Ci coupe and convertible have a 2.5 liter. The 330i/Ci versions have a 3.0 liter. The 325xi sedan and wagon and 330xi sedan have all-wheel drive vs. the other models' rear-wheel drive. The top-line M3 coupe and convertible use a high-power 3.2-liter six and either 6-speed manual transmission or, new for 2002, a sequential manual transmission (SMT). The computer-controlled 6-speed SMT doesn't have a clutch pedal, shifts via steering-wheel

BMW

"paddles," and can be set to shift like an automatic. Other models offer a conventional 5-speed manual or optional 5-speed automatic. Traction control, an antiskid system, and front torso side airbags are standard; rear side airbags are now available for 2-dr as well as 4-dr models. Front head-protecting tubular airbags are standard except in convertibles. Other across-the-board changes include recalibrated steering, reshaped headrests, standard in-dash CD player, titanium-color interior trim, and revised automatic climate controls. Newly optional are high/low-beam Xenon headlights. Sedans and wagons get a minor facelift, and the optional navigation system has a wider dashboard screen.

RATINGS	325i, auto.	330i, auto	330i w/Sport Pkg., man.	330xi w/nav. sys., man.
ACCELERATION	6	7	7	7
FUEL ECONOMY	6	5	6	5
RIDE QUALITY	7	7	5	7
STEERING/HANDLING	8	8	9	8
QUIETNESS	7	6	7	6
INSTRUMENTS/CONTROLS	7	7	7	5
ROOM/COMFORT (FRONT)	6	6	6	6
ROOM/COMFORT (REAR)	3	3	3	3
CARGO ROOM	2	2	2	2
VALUE	5	4	4	4

Still the class choice for driving enthusiasts. Some competitors deliver more room, standard features, and even more power for less money. But no rival line is more refined or dynamically capable overall. Resale values are strong, too.

TOTAL	57	55	54	53

Average total for near-luxury cars: 54.5

ENGINES

	dohc I6	dohc I6	dohc I6
Size, liters/cu. in.	2.5/152	3.0/182	3.2/192
Horsepower @ rpm	184 @ 5550	225 @ 5900	333 @ 7900
Torque (lb-ft) @ rpm	175 @ 3500	214 @ 3500	262 @ 4900
Availability	S[1]	S[2]	S[3]
EPA city/highway mpg			
5-speed manual	20/29	21/30	
6-speed manual			16/24
SMT manual			NA
5-speed automatic	19/27	19/27	

1. 325i, 325Ci. 2. 330i, 330Ci. 3. M3.

PRICES

BMW 3-Series	Retail Price	Dealer Invoice
325i 4-door sedan	$27100	$24550

Prices are accurate at time of publication; subject to manufacturer's change.

BMW

	Retail Price	Dealer Invoice
325xi AWD 4-door sedan	$28850	$26125
325i 4-door wagon	29500	26710
325xi AWD 4-door wagon	31250	28285
325Ci 2-door coupe	29100	26350
325Ci 2-door convertible	36100	32650
330i 4-door sedan	33990	30750
330xi AWD 4-door sedan	35740	32325
330Ci 2-door coupe	34990	31650
330Ci 2-door convertible	42400	38320
M3 2-door coupe	45900	41470
M3 2-door convertible	53900	48670
Destination charge	645	645

AWD denotes all-wheel drive. M3 adds $1000 Gas Guzzler Tax.

STANDARD EQUIPMENT

325i/325xi: 2.5-liter dohc 6-cylinder engine, 5-speed manual transmission, traction control, dual front airbags, front side airbags, front side head-protection airbags, antiskid system, antilock 4-wheel disc brakes, brake assist, daytime running lights, air conditioning w/automatic climate control, interior air filter, power steering, tilt/telescoping leather-wrapped steering wheel w/radio controls, cruise control, vinyl upholstery, front bucket seats, cupholders, split folding rear seat (wagon), heated power mirrors, power windows, power door locks, remote keyless entry, AM/FM/CD player, digital clock, tachometer, remote fuel door and decklid release, variable intermittent wipers, rear defogger, rear wiper/washer (wagon), theft-deterrent system, fog lights, roof rails (wagon), full-size spare tire (sedan), 205/55HR16 tires, alloy wheels. **AWD** adds: all-wheel drive, hill descent control, illuminated visor mirrors, map lights.

325Ci coupe adds: split folding rear seat, trip computer, illuminated visor mirrors, sport suspension, full-size spare tire.

325Ci convertible adds: rollover protection system, 8-way power front seats, passenger-side mirror tilt-down back-up aid, memory system for driver seat and power mirrors. *Deletes:* front side head-protection airbags, split folding rear seat, full-size spare tire, sport suspension.

330i sedan/330Ci coupe adds to 325i: 3.0-liter dohc 6-cylinder engine, 6-way power front seats, driver seat and mirror memory, center console, split folding rear seat (330Ci coupe), passenger-side mirror tilt-down back-up aid, Harman/Kardon sound system, trip computer, illuminated visor mirrors, map lights, sport suspension, full-size spare tire, 205/50HR17 tires. **AWD** adds: all-wheel drive, hill descent control.

330Ci convertible adds: rollover protection system, leather upholstery,

Specifications begin on page 551.

BMW

power convertible top. *Deletes:* front side head-protection airbags, split folding rear seat, sport suspension, full-size spare tire.

M3 coupe adds to 330i/330Ci coupe: 3.2-liter dohc 6-cylinder engine, 6-speed manual transmission, limited-slip differential, tire-pressure monitor, leather/cloth upholstery, automatic day/night rearview mirror, outside temperature display, heated door locks, M sport suspension, 225/45ZR18 front tires, 255/40ZR18 rear tires, chrome alloy wheels. *Deletes:* 6-way power front seats, driver seat and mirror memory, Harman/Kardon sound system, full-size spare tire.

M3 convertible adds: rollover protection system, leather upholstery, 8-way power front seats w/memory and thigh support adjustment, mirror memory, power convertible top. *Deletes:* front side head-protection airbags.

OPTIONAL EQUIPMENT
Major Packages

	Retail Price	Dealer Invoice
Premium Pkg., 325i, 325xi	$2700	$2295

6-way power front seats, driver seat and mirror memory, passenger-side mirror tilt-down back-up aid, center armrest, power sunroof, automatic day/night rearview mirror, trip computer, illuminated visor mirrors (325i), map lights (325i), wood interior trim.

Premium Pkg., 325Ci coupe	2300	1955

6-way power front seats, driver seat and mirror memory, passenger-side mirror tilt-down back-up aid, automatic climate control, power sunroof, automatic day/night rearview mirror, wood interior trim.

Premium Pkg., 325Ci convertible	1600	1360

Power convertible top, wood interior trim, automatic day/night rearview mirror, universal garage door opener.

Premium Pkg., 330i, 330Ci coupe	2900	2465

Leather upholstery, front seat power lumbar support, wood interior trim, power sunroof, automatic day/night rearview mirror, rain-sensing wipers, automatic headlights.

Premium Pkg., 330Ci convertible	800	680

Wood interior trim, front seat power lumbar support, automatic day/night rearview mirror, universal garage door opener, rain-sensing wipers, automatic headlights.

Premium Pkg., M3 coupe	3200	2720

Power sunroof, leather upholstery, 8-way power front seats w/memory, mirror memory, passenger-side mirror, tilt-down back-up aid, rain-sensing wipers, automatic headlights.

Sport Pkg., 325i	1400	1190

Sport steering wheel, 10-way power sport bucket seats w/adjustable thigh support, driver seat and mirror memory, passenger-side mirror tilt-down back-up aid, sport suspension, 225/45WR17 tires, special alloy wheels.

Prices are accurate at time of publication; subject to manufacturer's change.

BMW

	Retail Price	Dealer Invoice
Sport Pkg., 325xi	$1100	$935

Sport steering wheel, 10-way power front sport seats, driver seat and mirror memory, passenger-side mirror tilt-down back-up aid, 205/50HR17 tires, special alloy wheels.

Sport Pkg., 325Ci coupe	1000	850

8-way adjustable front sport seats w/adjustable thigh support, driver seat and mirror memory, passenger-side mirror tilt-down back-up aid, white turn signal indicators, 225/45WR17 tires, special alloy wheels.

Sport Pkg., 325Ci convertible	1200	1020

10-way power sport bucket seats w/adjustable thigh support, white turn signal indicators, sport suspension, 225/45WR17 tires, special alloy wheels. Requires leather upholstery.

Sport Pkg., 330i	1200	1020

Sport steering wheel, 10-way power front sport seats, driver seat and mirror memory, aerodynamic pkg., 225/45ZR17 front tires, 245/40ZR17 rear tires.

Sport Pkg., 330xi	900	765

Sport steering wheel, 10-way power front sport bucket seats w/adjustable thigh support, aerodynamic pkg., 205/50R17 tires, special alloy wheels.

Sport Pkg., 330Ci coupe	600	510
330Ci convertible	800	680

10-way power front sport seats w/adjustable thigh support, aerodynamic pkg., white turn signal indicators, sport suspension (330Ci convertible), 225/45ZR17 front tires, 245/40ZR17 rear tires.

Power Seat Pkg., M3 coupe	1200	1020

Power front seats w/memory, front seat lumbar adjustment and seat width adjustment, mirror memory, passenger-side mirror tilt-down back-up aid.

Cold Weather Pkg.,		
325i/325xi sedan, 330i	1000	850
325i/325xi wagon, 325Ci, 330Ci, M3	700	595

Heated front seats, split folding rear seat w/armrest (325i sedan, 330i), ski sack, headlight washers.

Powertrain

5-speed automatic trans. w/manual-shift capability	1275	1210
NA M3.		
6-speed sequential manual gearbox, M3	2400	2040

Safety

Rear side airbags	385	325
Rear obstacle detection system,		
325i/325xi wagon, M3	350	300

Specifications begin on page 551.

BMW

Comfort & Convenience Features

	Retail Price	Dealer Invoice
Navigation system..	$1800	$1530

325i/325xi require Premium Pkg. or trip computer. Replaces CD player w/cassette player.

Leather upholstery, 325, 330..	1450	1235
M3 coupe..	1100	935

Std. 330Ci convertible, M3 convertible.

6-way power front seats, 325i, 325xi, 325Ci............	945	805

Includes driver seat and mirror memory, passenger-side mirror tilt-down back-up aid.

Adjustable seats, M3 coupe...................................	500	425

Front seat lumbar adjustment and adjustable seat width. Requires Premium Pkg.

Heated front seats...	500	425
Split folding rear seat w/ski sack, 325i/325xi sedan, 330i..	475	405
Harman/Kardon sound system, 325, M3................	675	575
Trip computer, 325i, 325xi......................................	300	255
Power sunroof..	1050	895

NA convertible.

Rain-sensing wipers, M3 convertible.....................	100	85

Appearance and Miscellaneous

Removable hardtop, 325Ci/330Ci/M3 convertibles.	2295	1950
Xenon headlights..	700	595
Double spoke alloy wheels, 330	300	255

Includes tire-inflation monitor, 205/50R17 run-flat tires. NA w/Sport Pkg.

V-spoke alloy wheels, 330i, 330Ci	900	765

Includes 225/40R18 front tires, 255/35R18 rear tires. Requires Sport Pkg.

BMW 5-SERIES

Rear-wheel-drive luxury car

2001 base price range: $35,400-$69,400. Built in Germany.

Also consider: Acura RL, Lexus GS 300/430, Mercedes-Benz E-Class

FOR • Acceleration (540i, M5) • Steering/handling • Ride • Cargo room (wagon) • Quietness • Build quality **AGAINST** • Fuel economy (540i, M5)

BMW's midsize line makes few changes pending release of redesigned models for 2003. The 525i sedan and wagon use a

Prices are accurate at time of publication; subject to manufacturer's change.

BMW

BMW 530i 4-door sedan

2.5-liter inline 6-cyl engine, the 530i sedan a 3.0 version. The 540i sedan and wagon have a 4.4-liter V8 with 290 hp, up 8 hp from last year. The high-performance M5 sedan comes only with a 4.9-liter V8 and manual transmission. Other models offer manual or an optional automatic with manual shift gate. All 5s include an antiskid system, front side airbags, and front head-protecting tubular airbags. Rear torso and head-protecting side airbags are optional except for the M5, where they're a no-charge option. All 2002 models get a standard in-dash CD player; 6-cyl models add a standard power passenger seat but drop their Convenience and Sport Premium package options; and 525s replace manual climate control with automatic.

RATINGS	525iT wgn, auto.	530i, man.	540i sdn, man.	M5
ACCELERATION	5	7	8	9
FUEL ECONOMY	4	5	4	2
RIDE QUALITY	9	10	9	7
STEERING/HANDLING	8	8	9	10
QUIETNESS	7	7	7	6
INSTRUMENTS/CONTROLS	6	5	5	5
ROOM/COMFORT (FRONT)	8	8	8	8
ROOM/COMFORT (REAR)	6	6	6	6
CARGO ROOM	7	3	3	3
VALUE	7	7	6	2

For premium engineering and superior road manners, we recommend any 5-Series model you can afford. BMW's strong resale values help offset stiff sticker prices.

TOTAL	67	66	65	58

Average total for luxury cars: 59.4

ENGINES	dohc I6	dohc I6	dohc V8	dohc V8
Size, liters/cu. in.	2.5/152	3.0/182	4.4/268	4.9/303
Horsepower @ rpm	184 @ 6000	225 @ 5900	290 @ 5400	394 @ 6600

Specifications begin on page 551.

BMW

	dohc I6	dohc I6	dohc V8	dohc V8
Torque (lb-ft) @ rpm	175 @ 3500	214 @ 3500	324 @ 3600	368 @ 3800
Availability	S[1]	S[2]	S[3]	S[4]
EPA city/highway mpg				
5-speed manual	20/29	21/30		
6-speed manual			15/23	13/21
5-speed automatic	19/27	18/26	18/24	

1. 525i, 525iT. 2. 530i. 3. 540i, 540iT. 4. M5.

2002 prices unavailable at time of publication.

PRICES

2001 BMW 5-Series

	Retail Price	Dealer Invoice
525i 4-door sedan, manual	$35400	$32020
525iT 4-door wagon, manual	37200	33640
530i 4-door sedan, manual	39400	35620
540i 4-door sedan, automatic	51100	46150
540i 4-door sedan, manual	53900	48670
540iT 4-door wagon, automatic	53480	48290
M5 4-door sedan, manual	69400	62620
Destination charge	645	645

540i w/6-speed manual transmission and 540i with automatic transmission and Sport Pkg. add $1300 Gas Guzzler Tax. M5 add $2100 Gas Guzzler Tax.

STANDARD EQUIPMENT

525: 2.5-liter dohc 6-cylinder engine, 5-speed manual transmission, traction control, dual front airbags, front side airbags, front side head-protection airbags, antilock 4-wheel disc brakes, antiskid system, daytime running lights, variable-assist power steering, power tilt/telescopic steering wheel, leather-wrapped steering w/radio controls, cruise control, air conditioning, vinyl upholstery, 10-way power driver seat, power front head restraints, cupholders, memory system (driver seat, steering wheel, power mirrors), heated power mirrors w/passenger-side tilt-down parking aid, power windows, power door locks, remote keyless entry, AM/FM/cassette, tachometer, outside temperature display, trip computer, map lights, variable intermittent wipers, remote decklid release, rear defogger, illuminated visor mirrors, cargo cover (wagon), theft-deterrent system, fog lights, tool kit, roof rails (wagon), full-size spare tire, 225/55HR16 tires, alloy wheels.

530i adds: 3.0-liter dohc 6-cylinder engine, dual-zone automatic climate controls.

540i automatic add: 4.4-liter dohc V8 engine, 5-speed automatic

Prices are accurate at time of publication; subject to manufacturer's change.

BMW

transmission (sedan), 5-speed automatic transmission w/manual-shift capability (wagon), 10-way power passenger seat, leather upholstery, wood interior trim, power sunroof, automatic day/night rearview mirror, universal garage door opener, rain-sensing wipers, split folding rear seat (wagon), rain-sensing intermittent wipers, Xenon headlights, self-leveling suspension (wagon).

540i manual adds: 6-speed manual transmission, 12-way power front sport seats, sport suspension, 235/45WR17 front tires, 255/40WR17 rear tires. *Deletes:* power headrests.

M5 adds: 5.0-liter dohc V8 engine, limited-slip differential, rear side-airbags, rear side head-protection airbags, navigation system, automatic climate control, interior air filter, heated 16-way power front sport seats, alcantara headliner, automatic day/night driver-side mirror, AM/FM/cassette/CD player w/6-disc CD changer, heated door locks, heated headlight washers, rear spoiler, tire pressure monitor, M calibration suspension, front 245/40ZR18 tires, rear 275/35ZR18 tires. *Deletes:* wood interior trim.

OPTIONAL EQUIPMENT
Major Packages

	Retail Price	Dealer Invoice
Premium Pkg., 525	$2950	$2510
530i	3100	2635

Leather upholstery, wood interior trim, power sunroof, automatic day/night rearview mirror (530), rain-sensing wipers (530).

Sport Pkg., 525 sedan	1500	1275
525 wagon	1975	1680
530i	1970	1675

Sport steering wheel (530), sport suspension, self-leveling suspension (wagon), cross-spoke alloy wheels, 235/45WR17 tires.

Sport Premium Pkg., 525 sedan	3900	3315
525 wagon	4550	3870
530i	4300	3655

Includes Premium Pkg. and Sport Pkg.

Convenience Pkg., 525, 530i	1300	1105

Automatic climate control, power passenger seat, universal garage door opener. Requires Premium Pkg. or Sport Premium Pkg.

540i Sport Pkg., 540i sedan automatic, 540i wagon	2800	2380

Automatic transmission w/manual-shift capability (sedan), performance axle ratio, 12-way power front sport seats, Sport steering wheel, sport suspension, 235/45WR17 front tires (sedan), 255/40WR17 rear tires (sedan), 235/45WR17 tires (wagon).

Luxury/All Leather Trim Pkg., M5	NC	NC

Includes wood interior trim.

Cold Weather Pkg.	600	510

Heated front seats, heated headlight washers. Std. M5.

Specifications begin on page 551.

BMW

	Retail Price	Dealer Invoice
Powertrain		
5-speed automatic trans. w/manual-shift capability, 525, 530i	$1275	$1210
Safety		
Rear side airbags	550	470
Includes rear side head-protection airbags. Std. M5.		
Front and rear obstacle detection system	700	595
Comfort & Convenience Features		
Power sunroof, 525, 530i	1050	895
Navigation system, 525, 530i	1990	1690
540i	1800	1530
NA w/AM/FM/CD player.		
Leather upholstery, 525, 530i	1450	1235
Comfort 16-way power front seats, 530i	1800	1530
540i	1200	1020
Includes power lumbar support. 530i includes Convenience Pkg. 530i requires Sport Pkg. and leather upholstery or Premium Pkg.		
Power lumbar support, 530i, 540i automatic	400	340
NA with 540i Sport Pkg. or 12-way power sport seats.		
12-way power sport seats, 530i	475	405
Requires Sport Pkg. and leather upholstery or Premium Pkg.		
Split folding rear seat, sedans	475	405
Includes ski sack. 530i requires Premium Pkg.		
AM/FM/CD player	200	170
Premium sound system	1200	1020
NA M5.		
M Audio System, M5	900	765
Power rear and manual rear-door sunshades, sedans	575	490
Manual rear-door sunshades, wagons	180	155
Appearance and Miscellaneous		
Xenon headlights, 525, 530i	500	425
Self-leveling suspension, 525 wagon	760	645
Mixed parallel spoke alloy wheels, 540i	300	255
540i automatic requires Sport Pkg.		

BMW 7-SERIES

Rear-wheel-drive luxury car
Base price range: $62,900-$92,100. Built in Germany.
Also consider: Audi A8, Lexus LS 430, Mercedes-Benz S-Class

BMW redesigns its flagship sedans for 2002, with fresh styling, an

Prices are accurate at time of publication; subject to manufacturer's change.

BMW

BMW 7-Series

innovative control layout, and the industry's first 6-speed automatic transmission. Against the old 7-Series, the '02s are about 2 inches longer in wheelbase, overall length, and height. They're 1.6 inches wider and 120 lb heavier.

A 4.4-liter V8 continues in renamed 745i and long-wheelbase 745Li models, but it's a new design with 43 hp more than last year's 740i/740iL. The 6-speed automatic operates from a stalklike steering column control instead of a console-mounted lever. Joining standard antilock 4-wheel disc brakes and the traction control/antiskid system is BMW's new Active Roll Stabilization which adjusts front and rear antiroll bars to minimize body lean in turns. An Adaptive Ride Package with electronically adjusted shock absorbers and rear self-leveling via new air springs is an Li option. Both models have standard 18-inch wheels and offer 19s at extra cost.

Inside, front knee airbags join torso and head-protecting side airbags as standard; rear torso side airbags are available and come with tubular head-protecting airbags running the full interior length on each side. Sensors deploy any airbag only if an occupant is detected. Antiwhiplash front head restraints are standard. The new 7s also introduce BMW's iDrive control that uses a console "joystick" to select and change various audio, climate, navigation, and available phone functions. The settings display on a dashboard screen. Conventional switches are provided for a few frequently used functions. Among options are tire-pressure monitor, front/rear obstacle detection, in-dash CD changer, break-resistant window glass, power rear sunshades, and 20-way power front seats with internal fan ventilation and power "massage" feature. Prices were unavailable for this report. A V12 replacement for the 750iL is due for 2003. We have not yet tested the 2002 7-Series.

ENGINES

	dohc V8
Size, liters/cu. in.	4.4/268
Horsepower @ rpm	325 @ 6000
Torque (lb-ft) @ rpm	330 @ 3600
Availability	S

EPA city/highway mpg

6-speed automatic	NA

2002 prices unavailable at time of publication.

Specifications begin on page 551.

BMW

BMW X5

BMW X5

All-wheel-drive midsize sport-utility vehicle
Base price range: $38,900-$66,200. Built in USA.
Also consider: Acura MDX, Lexus RX 300, Mercedes-Benz M-Class

FOR • Acceleration • Build quality • Cargo room • Exterior finish • Interior materials **AGAINST** • Navigation system controls • Fuel economy

A new high-performance model and revised option-package content highlight BMW's American-built SUVs for 2002. Joining the V8 4.4i and 6-cyl 3.0i is the 4.6is, which aims at Mercedes' ML500/ML55 AMG with a 340-hp V8, 20-inch wheels, aero body add-ons, and special sports interior. All X5s have all-wheel drive without low-range gearing, plus antilock 4-wheel disc brakes, front torso side airbags and head-protection side airbags. The 3.0i offers manual transmission or 5-speed automatic with manual shift gate; V8 models get the automatic only. Options include rear torso side airbags, navigation system, and a Sport Package with firmer suspension. The Premium Package now includes rain-sensing windshield wipers, automatic climate control for the 3.0i, and sunroof for the 3.0i and 4.4i. The 4.4i also offers a new Rear Climate Package with privacy glass and rear window shades.

RATINGS	3.0i, auto.	3.0i w/ Sport Pkg., man.	4.4i w/Sport Pkg., nav. sys.
ACCELERATION	6	6	7
FUEL ECONOMY	4	3	3
RIDE QUALITY	6	5	3

Prices are accurate at time of publication; subject to manufacturer's change.
CONSUMER GUIDE®

BMW

	3.0i, auto.	3.0i w/ Sport Pkg., man.	4.4i w/Sport Pkg., nav. sys.
STEERING/HANDLING	5	6	6
QUIETNESS	6	6	4
INSTRUMENTS/CONTROLS	7	7	4
ROOM/COMFORT (FRONT)	8	8	8
ROOM/COMFORT (REAR)	5	5	5
CARGO ROOM	7	7	7
VALUE	3	3	2

The SUV of choice for sporty on-road driving. But BMW's strong resale values don't fully offset stiff prices. The RX 300 lacks X5's breeding, but is a better value in a carlike SUV. Ditto Acura's MDX with its three-row seating and extra cargo space.

TOTAL	57	56	49

Average total for midsize sport-utility vehicles: 49.6

ENGINES

	dohc I6	dohc V8	dohc V8
Size, liters/cu. in.	3.0/181	4.4/268	4.6/281
Horsepower @ rpm	225 @ 5900	282 @ 5400	340 @ 5700
Torque (lb-ft) @ rpm	214 @ 3500	324 @ 3600	350 @ 3700
Availability	S[1]	S[2]	S[3]
EPA city/highway mpg			
5-speed manual	15/21		
5-speed automatic	15/21	13/17	12/17

1. 3.0i. 2. 4.4i. 3. 4.6is.

PRICES

BMW X5	Retail Price	Dealer Invoice
3.0i 4-door wagon	$38900	$35170
4.4i 4-door wagon	49400	44620
4.6is 4-door wagon	66200	59740
Destination charge	645	645

STANDARD EQUIPMENT

3.0i: 3.0-liter dohc 6-cylinder engine, 5-speed manual transmission, all-wheel drive, traction control, dual front airbags, front side airbags, front side head-protection airbags, antilock 4-wheel disc brakes, anti-skid system, hill descent control, air conditioning, interior air filter, power steering, power tilt/telescoping leather-wrapped steering wheel w/radio controls, cruise control, vinyl upholstery, front bucket seats, 8-way power driver seat, memory system (driver seat, mirrors, steering wheel), center console, cupholders, split folding rear seat, heated power mirrors w/passenger-side tilt-down parking aid, power windows, power door locks, remote keyless entry, AM/FM/CD player, map lights, variable intermittent wipers, trip computer, outside temperature indicator, illuminated visor mir-

Specifications begin on page 551.

BMW

rors, universal garage door opener, rear defogger, intermittent rear wiper/washer, power tailgate release, cargo cover, theft-deterrent system, fog lights, roof rails, full-size spare, 235/65HR17 tires, alloy wheels.

4.4i adds: 4.4-liter dohc V8 engine, 5-speed automatic transmission w/manual-shift capability, dual-zone automatic climate control, rear climate controls, leather upholstery, 6-way-power passenger seat, wood interior trim, rear automatic-leveling suspension, 255/55HR18 tires. *Deletes:* full-size spare tire.

4.6is adds: 4.6-liter dohc V8 engine, front and rear obstacle detection system, heated steering wheel, front seat 4-way power lumbar adjustment, heated front and rear seats, power sunroof, premium AM/FM/cassette w/6-disc CD changer, automatic day/night outside and rearview mirrors, rain-sensing wipers, ski sack, rear side-window shades, rear privacy glass, Xenon headlights, sport suspension, 275/40WR20 front tires, 315/35WR20 rear tires.

OPTIONAL EQUIPMENT

	Retail Price	Dealer Invoice

Major Packages

Premium Pkg., 3.0i $3900 $3315
Leather upholstery, 6-way power passenger seat, adjustable rear seatbacks, wood interior trim, power sunroof, automatic climate control, upgraded trip computer, rain-sensing wipers, body-colored exterior trim.

Premium Pkg., 4.4i 2100 1785
Power sunroof, front lumbar adjustment, adjustable rear seatbacks, automatic day/night outside and rearview mirrors, upgraded trip computer, rain-sensing wipers, body-colored exterior trim.

Sport Pkg., 3.0i 2100 1785
4.4i 1600 1360
Sport seats (4.4i), sport steering wheel, black headliner, light-colored wood interior trim (4.4i), titanium-colored grille insert, Shadowline trim, white turn signal lenses, black chrome exhaust pipes, speed limiter delete (4.4i), sport suspension, 255/55HR18 tires (3.0i), unique alloy wheels. NA w/heated steering wheel, adjustable ride height suspension.

Cold Weather Pkg., 3.0i, 4.4i 750 640
Heated front seats, ski sack, headlight washers.

Rear Climate Pkg., 3.0i 850 725
4.4i 600 340
Rear climate controls (3.30i), rear side-window shades, rear privacy glass.

Powertrain

5-speed automatic transmission
   "w/manual-shift capability, 3.0i 1275 1210

Safety

Rear side airbags 550 470

Prices are accurate at time of publication; subject to manufacturer's change.

BMW

	Retail Price	Dealer Invoice
Front and rear obstacle detection system, 3.0i, 4.4i	$700	$595

Comfort & Convenience Features

Navigation system	1800	1530

3.0i and 4.4i replace CD player w/cassette player. 3.0i and 4.4i require Premium Pkg.

Power sunroof, 3.0i, 4.4i	1050	895
Premium sound system, 3.0i, 4.4i...........................	1200	1020
Heated steering wheel, 3.0i, 4.4i.............................	150	130

Requires Cold Weather Pkg.

Comfort seats, 4.4i	1200	1020
Heated rear seats, 4.4i..	350	300

Requires Cold Weather Pkg.

Front lumbar adjustment, 3.0i	400	340
Automatic day/night outside and rearview mirrors, 3.0i	300	255
Retractable load floor	380	325

Appearance and Miscellaneous

Xenon headlights, 3.0i, 4.4i.....................................	500	425

Special Purpose, Wheels and Tires

Rear automatic-leveling suspension, 3.0i	700	595
Adjustable ride height suspension, 4.4i	500	425
Y spoke alloy wheels, 4.4i.......................................	950	810

255/50R19 front tires, 285/45R19 rear tires. Requires Sport Pkg.

BMW Z3 SERIES

BMW Z3 M 2-door convertible

Rear-wheel-drive sports car

Specifications begin on page 551.

BMW

2001 base price range: $31,300-$45,990. Built in USA.
Also consider: Honda S2000, Mazda Miata, Mercedes-Benz SLK-Class, Porsche Boxster

FOR • Steering/handling • Acceleration • Exterior finish
AGAINST • Noise • Cargo space • Rear visibility (convertible)

BMW's American-built 2-seat sports cars are being redesigned for 2003, and so are little changed for '02. All use inline 6-cyl engines: a 2.5-liter for the Z3 2.5i convertible, a 3.0-liter for the Z3 3.0i convertible and hatchback coupe, and a high-performance 3.2 for the M Roadster and M Coupe. A 5-speed automatic transmission is optional except for M models. Linewide standards include antilock 4-wheel disc brakes, antiskid system, and BMW's Dynamic Brake Control that helps maintain braking stability in turns. M models include a low tire-pressure warning system. An in-dash CD player is now standard across the board.

RATINGS	2.5i, man.	3.0i hatch, man.	M-Series conv
ACCELERATION	7	7	10
FUEL ECONOMY	5	5	5
RIDE QUALITY	4	4	3
STEERING/HANDLING	8	9	9
QUIETNESS	2	3	2
INSTRUMENTS/CONTROLS	6	6	6
ROOM/COMFORT (FRONT)	3	4	3
ROOM/COMFORT (REAR)	0	0	0
CARGO ROOM	1	2	1
VALUE	2	2	2

These are aged but still-entertaining sports cars, with highish prices partly offset by BMW's strong resale values. M models are fastest but hardest to live with. We judge the 2.5i the best dollar value, though 3.0i models are slightly quicker, more relaxed performers, especially with automatic transmission.

TOTAL	38	42	41

Average total for sports cars: 41.3

ENGINES	dohc I6	dohc I6	dohc I6
Size, liters/cu. in.	2.5/152	3.0/182	3.2/192
Horsepower @ rpm	184 @ 5500	225 @ 5900	315 @ 7400
Torque (lb-ft) @ rpm	175 @ 3500	214 @ 3500	251 @ 4900
Availability	S[1]	S[2]	S[3]
EPA city/highway mpg			
5-speed manual	20/27	21/29	17/25
5-speed automatic	19/26	19/27	

1. Z3 2.5i. 2. Z3 3.0i. 3. M-Series.

Prices are accurate at time of publication; subject to manufacturer's change.
CONSUMER GUIDE®

BMW

2002 prices unavailable at time of publication.

PRICES

2001 BMW Z3 Series

	Retail Price	Dealer Invoice
2.5i 2-door convertible	$31300	$28330
3.0i 2-door convertible	37700	34090
3.0i 2-door hatchback	37900	34270
M-Series 2-door convertible	45990	41550
M-Series 2-door hatchback	44990	40650
Destination charge	645	645

STANDARD EQUIPMENT

2.5i: 2.5-liter dohc 6-cylinder engine, 5-speed manual transmission, limited-slip differential, traction control, dual front airbags, side airbags, antilock 4-wheel disc brakes, antiskid system, roll bars (convertible), air conditioning, cruise control, vinyl upholstery, 4-way power bucket seats, center console, cupholders, AM/FM/cassette, analog clock, power mirrors, power door locks, power windows, tachometer, visor mirrors, intermittent wipers, fog lights, 225/50VR16 tires, alloy wheels.

3.0i adds: 3.0-liter dohc 6-cylinder engine, leather upholstery, sport seats (hatchback), wood interior trim (hatchback), Harman/Kardon sound system, 225/45ZR17 front tires, 245/40ZR17 rear tires.

M-Series adds: 3.2-liter dohc 6-cylinder engine, power convertible top (convertible), upgraded leather upholstery, heated sport seats, heated mirrors and washer jets, heated driver door lock, automatic day/night rearview mirror, outside temperature indicator, tire pressure monitor, sport suspension. *Deletes:* wood interior trim.

OPTIONAL EQUIPMENT
Major Packages

Premium Pkg., 2.5i	1600	1360
3.0i	950	810

Power convertible top, leather upholstery (2.5i), wood interior trim.

Sport Pkg., convertible	600	510

Sport seats, cross-spoke composite wheels. NA M-Series.

Powertrain

5-speed automatic transmission w/manual-shift capability, 2.5i, 3.0i
  1275..................1210

Comfort & Convenience Features

Leather upholstery, 2.5i	1150	980
Extended leather upholstery, 3.0i	1200	1020

Includes color-keyed leather steering wheel, instrument cluster hood, console sides, door upper ledges and pulls.

Specifications begin on page 551.

BMW • BUICK

	Retail Price	Dealer Invoice
Heated seats	$500	$425
Includes heated mirrors. Std. M-Series.		
AM/FM/CD player..	200	170
Harman/Kardon sound system, 2.5i.....................	675	575
Trip computer, 2.5i, 3.0i.....................................	300	255
Power convertible top, 2.5i/3.0i convertible	750	640
Power tilt-up roof panel, hatchback.....................	300	255

Appearance and Miscellaneous

Hardtop, convertible	1900	1615
Cross-spoke composite wheels, hatchback..........	300	255

BUICK CENTURY

Buick Century Limited

Front-wheel-drive midsize car
Base price range: $20,285-$23,285. Built in Canada.
Also consider: Honda Accord, Mercury Sable, Toyota Camry

FOR • Ride **AGAINST** • Steering feel • Handling

Bucket seats are newly available for 2002 on Buick's lowest-priced car. Century shares its basic platform with the Regal, which targets a younger audience. A 3.1-liter V6 is Century's sole engine. Automatic transmission, traction control, a tire-pressure monitor, and ABS are standard. Custom and up-trim Limited models are offered, both with a standard front bench seat for 6-passenger capacity. Bucket seats are part of the 5-Passenger Appearance Package. Exclusive to Limited are standard leather upholstery and a side airbag for the driver. General Motors' OnStar assistance system is standard on Limited, optional on Custom.

RATINGS   Custom/Limited
ACCELERATION   4

Prices are accurate at time of publication; subject to manufacturer's change.

BUICK

	Custom/Limited
FUEL ECONOMY	5
RIDE QUALITY	7
STEERING/HANDLING	5
QUIETNESS	6
INSTRUMENTS/CONTROLS	5
ROOM/COMFORT (FRONT)	5
ROOM/COMFORT (REAR)	4
CARGO ROOM	5
VALUE	6

A well-thought-out sedan with a no-surprises formula that's proved appealing to conservative buyers. As such, it's worth a look.

TOTAL	**52**

Average total for midsize cars: 57.0

ENGINES

	ohv V6
Size, liters/cu. in.	3.1/191
Horsepower @ rpm	175 @ 5200
Torque (lb-ft) @ rpm	195 @ 4000
Availability	S

EPA city/highway mpg
4-speed automatic 20/29

PRICES

Buick Century	Retail Price	Dealer Invoice
Custom 4-door sedan	$20285	$18561
Limited 4-door sedan	23285	21306
Destination charge	610	610

STANDARD EQUIPMENT

Custom: 3.1-liter V6 engine, 4-speed automatic transmission, traction control, dual front airbags, antilock brakes, daytime running lights, emergency inside trunk release, tire-pressure monitor, air conditioning w/dual-zone manual climate control, interior air filter, power steering, tilt steering wheel, cloth upholstery, front split bench seat, front storage armrest, cupholders, power mirrors, power windows, power door locks, remote keyless entry, AM/FM radio, digital clock, rear defogger, variable intermittent wipers, visor mirrors, map lights, remote decklid release, automatic headlights, theft-deterrent system, cornering lights, 205/70R15 tires, wheel covers.

Limited adds: driver-side side airbag, leather-wrapped steering wheel w/radio controls, cruise control, OnStar System w/one year service (roadside assistance, emergency services; other services available), leather upholstery, 6-way power driver seat, AM/FM/cassette, heated

Specifications begin on page 551.

BUICK

power mirrors, illuminated visor mirrors, floormats.

	Retail Price	Dealer Invoice

OPTIONAL EQUIPMENT
Major Packages

Premium Pkg. PCH, Custom $605 $520
Cruise control, heated power mirrors, AM/FM/cassette, integrated rear window antenna, cargo net, floormats.

Special Edition Pkg. 1SB, Custom 1672 1438
Manufacturer's Discount Price 1172 1008
Premium Pkg. PCH plus 6-way power driver seat, AM/FM/cassette w/steering wheel radio controls, illuminated visor mirrors, chrome/black grille, bodyside moldings, chrome wheel covers.

Luxury Pkg. PCI, Limited 745 641
Dual-zone automatic climate control, 6-way power passenger seat, automatic day/night rearview and outside mirrors.

Special Edition Pkg. 1SD, Limited 2550 2193
Manufacturer's Discount Price 2050 1763
Luxury Pkg. PCI plus AM/FM/cassette/CD player, upgraded sound system, split folding rear seat w/storage armrest and cupholders, chrome/black grille, bodyside moldings, cast alloy wheels.

5-Passenger Appearance Pkg. PCJ, Custom 625 538
Limited 500 430
Front bucket seats, center console, alloy wheels (Custom). Custom requires Pkg. 1SB. Limited requires Pkg. 1SD.

Comfort & Convenience Features

Split folding rear seat 275 237
Includes armrest, cupholders.

Power sunroof 795 684
Custom requires Pkg. 1SB. Limited requires Pkg. 1SD.

AM/FM/cassette, Custom 195 168
AM/FM/cassette/CD player 280 241
Custom includes steering-wheel radio controls. Custom requires Pkg. PCH.

Steering-wheel radio controls, Custom 130 112

Appearance and Miscellaneous

Alloy wheels 375 323
Custom requires Pkg. 1SB. Limited requires Pkg. 1SD.

Cast alloy wheels, Custom 425 366
Requires Pkg. 1SB.

BUICK LE SABRE

Front-wheel-drive full-size car
Base price range: $24,290-$29,990. Built in USA.

Prices are accurate at time of publication; subject to manufacturer's change.

BUICK

RECOMMENDED

Buick LeSabre Custom

Also consider: Chrysler Concorde, Dodge Intrepid, Toyota Avalon

FOR • Acceleration • Automatic transmission performance • Instruments/controls • Ride **AGAINST** • Fuel economy • Rear-seat comfort

The top-line model of America's best-selling full-size car gets standard instead of optional leather seats for 2002. LeSabre is offered in Custom and Limited versions. Both use a 3.8-liter V6 and automatic transmission. Antilock 4-wheel-disc brakes and front side airbags are standard. Traction control and General Motors' OnStar assistance system are standard on Limited, optional on Custom. GM's Stabilitrak antiskid system is available on Limited. The optional Gran Touring Package includes firmer suspension and 16-inch wheels vs. 15s. The standard front bench seat allows 6-passenger seating; bucket seats are optional. Leather upholstery is standard on Limited, optional on Custom. Power memory front seats are also newly standard on Limited. LeSabre shares its structure with Cadillac Seville, Pontiac Bonneville, and Oldsmobile Aurora.

RATINGS	Custom	Limited w/Gran Touring Pkg.
ACCELERATION	6	6
FUEL ECONOMY	4	4
RIDE QUALITY	7	6
STEERING/HANDLING	4	5
QUIETNESS	7	7
INSTRUMENTS/CONTROLS	4	4
ROOM/COMFORT (FRONT)	7	7
ROOM/COMFORT (REAR)	4	4
CARGO ROOM	6	6
VALUE	7	6

LeSabre imparts a feeling of size and substance, and its standard-equipment list is well thought out. Subpar rear-seat accommodations and indifferent interior furnishings are letdowns. Base prices are competitive but options add up quickly.

TOTAL	**56**	**55**

Average total for full-size cars: 58.7

Specifications begin on page 551.

BUICK

ENGINES

	ohv V6
Size, liters/cu. in.	3.8/231
Horsepower @ rpm	205 @ 5200
Torque (lb-ft) @ rpm	230 @ 4000
Availability	S

EPA city/highway mpg
4-speed automatic	20/29

PRICES

Buick Le Sabre	Retail Price	Dealer Invoice
Custom 4-door sedan	$24290	$22225
Limited 4-door sedan	29990	27441
Destination charge	685	685

STANDARD EQUIPMENT

Custom: 3.8-liter V6 engine, 4-speed automatic transmission, dual front airbags, front side airbags, antilock 4-wheel disc brakes, emergency inside trunk release, daytime running lights, air conditioning, power steering, tilt steering wheel, cruise control, cloth upholstery, front split bench seat, 8-way power driver seat, cupholders, power mirrors, power windows, power door locks, remote keyless entry, overhead console, map lights, AM/FM/cassette, digital clock, variable intermittent wipers, rear defogger, visor mirrors, power decklid release, automatic headlights, floormats, theft-deterrent system, automatic level control, 215/70R15 tires, wheel covers.

Limited adds: traction control, tire-pressure monitor, OnStar System w/one year service (roadside assistance, emergency services; other services available), front dual-zone automatic climate control and rear climate control, interior air filter, leather upholstery, heated 10-way power front seats w/power recliners, trunk pass-through, memory package (seats, mirrors, climate control, radio presets), AM/FM/cassette/CD player, steering wheel radio controls, tachometer, heated power mirrors, automatic day/night driver-side and rearview mirrors, passenger-side mirror tilt-down parking aid, compass, universal garage door opener, illuminated visor mirrors, rain-sensing variable intermittent wipers, cornering lights, alloy wheels.

OPTIONAL EQUIPMENT
Major Packages

Luxury Pkg. 1SD, Custom	1404	1207

AM/FM/CD player w/upgraded sound system, steering wheel radio controls, tachometer, automatic day/night rearview mirror, driver information center (including tire-pressure monitor and dual trip odometers), interior air filter, cargo net, bodyside stripes, alloy wheels.

Prices are accurate at time of publication; subject to manufacturer's change.

BUICK

	Retail Price	Dealer Invoice
Prestige Pkg. 1SE, Custom	$2684	$2308

Luxury Pkg. 1SD plus OnStar System w/one year service (roadside assistance, emergency services; other services available), AM/FM/cassette/CD player, 8-way power passenger seat, rain-sensing wipers, illuminated visor mirrors, universal garage door opener, compass, theft-deterrent system w/alarm.

Seating/Convenience Console Pkg.	70	60

Front bucket seats, center console w/storage, leather armrest, additional cupholders and power outlets, rear climate controls, provisions for cellular telephone and fax. Custom requires leather upholstery and Pkg. 1SD or Pkg. 1SE.

Gran Touring Pkg.	235	202

Leather-wrapped steering wheel, sport suspension, rear stabilizer bar, 225/60R16 tires. Custom requires Pkg. 1SD or Pkg. 1SE.

Driver Confidence Pkg., Limited w/cross lace alloy wheels	880	757
Limited w/Gran Touring Pkg.	730	628

Antiskid system, head-up instrument display, self-sealing tires.

Powertrain

Traction control, Custom	175	151

Includes 225/60R16 tires. Requires Pkg. 1SD or Pkg. 1SE.

Comfort & Convenience Features

Power sunroof, Limited	900	774
Leather upholstery, Custom	780	671

Requires Pkg. 1SD or Pkg. 1SE.

Heated front seats, Custom	295	254

Custom requires Pkg. 1SD or Pkg. 1SE, leather upholstery, power passenger seat.

8-way power passenger seat, Custom	330	284

Requires Pkg. 1SD.

AM/FM/cassette/CD player, Custom	100	86

Includes automatic tone control and steering-wheel radio controls. Requires Pkg. 1SD.

Appearance and Miscellaneous

Cross lace alloy wheels	200	172

Includes 225/60R16 tires. Custom requires Pkg. 1SD or Pkg. 1SE. NA w/Gran Touring Pkg.

BUICK PARK AVENUE

Front-wheel-drive near-luxury car
Base price range: $33,420-$37,930. Built in USA.
Also consider: Acura TL, BMW 3-Series, Lexus ES 300

Specifications begin on page 551.

BUICK

Buick Park Avenue Ultra

FOR • Acceleration • Passenger and cargo room • Steering/handling (Ultra) **AGAINST** • Fuel economy (supercharged V6) • Steering/handling (base suspension) • Rear visibility

Buick's flagship comes in base and Ultra models, both with a V6 and automatic transmission. Ultras have a supercharger for more power. ABS, self-leveling rear suspension, leather upholstery, and power front seats are standard. Standard front bench allows 6-passenger seating; bucket seats are optional on Ultra. The Gran Touring option includes firmer suspension and more aggressive tires. General Motors' OnStar assistance and StabiliTrak antiskid systems are standard on Ultra, optional on base, as are traction control and a tire-pressure monitor. A rear obstacle warning system is optional on both. Among the few changes for 2002: Steering wheel radio and climate controls are now standard on the base model as well as the Ultra.

RATINGS	Base	Ultra w/Gran Touring Pkg.
ACCELERATION	5	6
FUEL ECONOMY	5	4
RIDE QUALITY	7	8
STEERING/HANDLING	5	6
QUIETNESS	7	7
INSTRUMENTS/CONTROLS	7	7
ROOM/COMFORT (FRONT)	7	7
ROOM/COMFORT (REAR)	6	6
CARGO ROOM	6	6
VALUE	6	6

In a class dominated by imports, Park Avenue gives up some prestige in exchange for traditional American room, power, and amenities at a competitive price.

TOTAL	61	63

Average total for near-luxury cars: 54.5

ENGINES	ohv V6	Supercharged ohv V6
Size, liters/cu. in.	3.8/231	3.8/231

Prices are accurate at time of publication; subject to manufacturer's change.

CONSUMER GUIDE®

BUICK

	ohv V6	Supercharged ohv V6
Horsepower @ rpm	205 @ 5200	240 @ 5200
Torque (lb-ft) @ rpm	230 @ 4000	280 @ 3600
Availability	S[1]	S[2]
EPA city/highway mpg		
4-speed automatic	20/29	18/27

1. Base. 2. Ultra.

PRICES

Buick Park Avenue

	Retail Price	Dealer Invoice
Base 4-door sedan	$33420	$30245
Ultra 4-door sedan	37930	34327
Destination charge	745	745

STANDARD EQUIPMENT

Base: 3.8-liter V6 engine, 4-speed automatic transmission, dual front airbags, front side airbags, antilock 4-wheel disc brakes, daytime running lights, air conditioning w/dual-zone automatic climate control, interior air filter, power steering, tilt leather-wrapped steering wheel w/radio and climate controls, cruise control, leather upholstery, front split bench seat, 10-way power front seats, center console, cupholders, rear seat trunk pass-through, power mirrors, power windows, power door locks, remote keyless entry, overhead console, rear defogger, AM/FM/cassette, digital clock, tachometer, power remote decklid and fuel-door releases, map lights, illuminated visor mirrors, variable intermittent wipers, automatic headlights, floormats, automatic level-control suspension, theft-deterrent system, cornering lights, 225/60R16 tires, alloy wheels.

Ultra adds: supercharged 3.8-liter V6 engine, traction control, antiskid system, tire-pressure monitor, OnStar System w/one year service (roadside assistance, emergency services; other services available), variable-assist power steering, heated front seats w/power lumbar adjustment, memory system (seats, mirrors, climate controls, radio), passenger-side mirror tilt-down back-up aid, automatic day/night rearview and driver-side mirrors, compass, rain-sensing windshield wipers, AM/FM/cassette/CD player w/upgraded sound system, rear illuminated vanity mirrors, universal garage door opener.

OPTIONAL EQUIPMENT
Major Packages

Gran Touring Pkg., Base	285	245
Ultra	200	172

Includes Gran Touring suspension, variable-assist power steering (Base), 225/60R16 touring tires, unique alloy wheels. Base requires Prestige Pkg. 1SE

Specifications begin on page 551.

BUICK

	Retail Price	Dealer Invoice
Prestige Pkg. 1SE, Base..........................	$1867	$1606

Traction control, OnStar System w/one year service (roadside assistance, emergency services; other services available), AM/FM/cassette/CD player, power front lumbar adjustment, driver seat memory, automatic day/night rearview and driver-side mirrors, compass, universal garage door opener, driver information center (tire-pressure monitor, oil-life/level monitor, dual trip odometers, additional warning lights, trip computer), heated power mirrors w/memory and passenger-side back-up aid, rain-sensing wipers, 3-note horn. Std. Ultra.

Safety

StabiliTrak antiskid system, Base w/Pkg. 1SE........	495	426
Rear obstacle detection system	295	254

Requires head-up display. Base requires Prestige Pkg. 1SE.

Comfort & Convenience Features

AM/FM/cassette/CD player, Base	215	185
12-disc CD changer	595	512

Base requires Prestige Pkg. 1SE, Concert Sound III speakers.

Concert Sound III speakers, Base w/Pkg. 1SE	295	254
Power sunroof	1095	942

Base requires Prestige Pkg. 1SE.

Heated front seats, Base..	295	254
Convenience Console/Five Person Seating Pkg., Ultra	185	159

Bucket seats, console with writing surface, rear climate controls, cupholders, auxiliary power outlets.

Head-up display	300	258

Requires rear obstacle detection system. Base requires Prestige Pkg. 1SE

Appearance and Miscellaneous

Chrome alloy wheels	760	654

BUICK REGAL

Front-wheel-drive midsize car

Base price range: $23,230-$27,285. Built in Canada.

Also consider: Honda Accord, Nissan Altima, Toyota Camry

FOR • Acceleration   **AGAINST** • Fuel economy (supercharged V6)

Regal shares a basic design with Buick's conservative Century

Prices are accurate at time of publication; subject to manufacturer's change.

BUICK

Buick Regal GS

sedan, but is more similar in market positioning and performance to its other platform-mates, the Oldsmobile Intrigue and Pontiac Grand Prix. Regal comes in LS and uplevel GS sedans. Both have automatic transmission and a V6 engine; the GS adds a supercharger for more power. Antilock 4-wheel disc brakes, a tire-pressure monitor, and traction control are standard. Leather upholstery, side airbag for the driver, and firmer Gran Touring suspension are standard on GS, optional on LS. A package named for fashion designer Joseph Abboud adds power sunroof, and special paint and trim. On LS, the Abboud option brings much of the GS's standard equipment, including Gran Touring suspension and 16-inch wheels. Among the few 2002 changes: Steering wheel radio controls are newly standard on the GS.

RATINGS

	LS	GS
ACCELERATION	6	7
FUEL ECONOMY	5	5
RIDE QUALITY	7	7
STEERING/HANDLING	6	7
QUIETNESS	6	6
INSTRUMENTS/CONTROLS	5	5
ROOM/COMFORT (FRONT)	5	5
ROOM/COMFORT (REAR)	4	4
CARGO ROOM	5	5
VALUE	5	5

Regal is less refined than Honda Accord or Toyota Camry, though it is competitively priced and well-equipped.

TOTAL	54	56

Average total for midsize cars: 57.0

ENGINES

	ohv V6	Supercharged ohv V6
Size, liters/cu. in.	3.8/231	3.8/231
Horsepower @ rpm	200 @ 5200	240 @ 5200
Torque (lb-ft) @ rpm	225 @ 4000	280 @ 3600
Availability	S[1]	S[2]

Specifications begin on page 551.

BUICK

EPA city/highway mpg	ohv V6	Supercharged ohv V6
4-speed automatic	19/29	18/27

1. LS. 2. GS.

PRICES

Buick Regal	Retail Price	Dealer Invoice
LS 4-door sedan	$23230	$21255
GS 4-door sedan	27285	24966
Destination charge	610	610

STANDARD EQUIPMENT

LS: 3.8-liter V6 engine, 4-speed automatic transmission, traction control, dual front airbags, antilock 4-wheel disc brakes, daytime running lights, emergency inside trunk release, tire-pressure monitor, power steering, leather-wrapped tilt steering wheel, cruise control, air conditioning w/dual-zone manual climate control, interior air filter, cloth upholstery, front bucket seats, center console, cupholders, 6-way power driver seat, split folding rear seat, power mirrors w/heated driver-side, power windows, power door locks, remote keyless entry, tachometer, variable intermittent wipers, rear defogger, map lights, visor mirrors, AM/FM/cassette, digital clock, remote decklid release, automatic headlights, theft-deterrent system, cornering lights, fog lights, 215/70R15 tires, wheel covers.

GS adds: supercharged 3.8-liter V6 engine, full traction control, driver-side side airbag, OnStar System w/one year service (roadside assistance, emergency services; other services available), leather upholstery, dual-zone automatic climate control, Monsoon AM/FM/cassette/CD player, steering wheel radio controls, illuminated visor mirrors, automatic day/night rearview and outside mirrors, driver information center (supercharger boost gauge, oil-change monitor, additional warning lights, trip computer), floormats, Gran Touring Suspension, 225/60R16 tires, alloy wheels.

OPTIONAL EQUIPMENT

Major Packages

Luxury Pkg. PCI, LS	767	660

Dual-zone automatic climate control, AM/FM/cassette/CD player, illuminated visor mirrors, cargo net, floormats.

Gran Touring Pkg. Y56, LS	600	516

Gran Touring suspension, 225/60R16 tires, alloy wheels. Requires Luxury Pkg. PCI.

Touring Pkg. 1SB, LS	2502	2152

Includes Gran Touring Pkg. Y56, Premium Pkg. PCH, Luxury Pkg. PCI, steering wheel radio controls, automatic day/night rearview and outside mirrors, driver information center, floormats.

Prices are accurate at time of publication; subject to manufacturer's change.

BUICK

	Retail Price	Dealer Invoice
Premium Pkg. PCH, LS..	$1160	$998

Leather upholstery, driver-side side airbag, alloy wheels.

Prestige Pkg. PCK, LS..	2190	1883

Power sunroof, 6-way power passenger seat, Monsoon sound system, chrome alloy wheels. Requires Touring Pkg. 1SB.

Joseph Abboud Special Appearance Pkg. B2E, LS	3647	3136
Manufacturer's Discount Price............................	3147	2706

Touring Pkg. 1SB plus power sunroof, Monsoon sound system, 6-way power passenger seat, Light Sandrift lower accent paint.

Joseph Abboud Special Appearance Pkg. B2E, GS	1495	1286
Manufacturer's Discount Price............................	995	856

Power sunroof, 6-way power passenger seat, Light Sandrift lower accent paint.

Comfort & Convenience Features

Power sunroof...	795	684

LS requires Touring Pkg. 1SB.

Heated front seats..	295	254

LS requires Touring Pkg. 1SB.

6-way power passenger seat, LS............................	350	301

Requires Touring Pkg. 1SB.

Monsoon sound system, LS....................................	395	340

Requires Touring Pkg. 1SB.

Appearance and Miscellaneous

Alloy wheels, LS...	350	301

Requires Luxury Pkg. PCI.

Chrome alloy wheels...	650	559

LS requires Touring Pkg. 1SB. NA w/Joseph Abboud Special Appearance Pkg. B2E.

BUICK RENDEZVOUS

Front- or all-wheel-drive midsize sport-utility vehicle
Base price range: $25,024-$27,552. Built in Mexico.
Also consider: Acura MDX, Lexus RX 300, Mercury Mountaineer, Toyota Highlander

FOR • Interior storage space • Passenger and cargo room
AGAINST • Acceleration • Fuel economy • Steering/handling

This new crossover SUV is related to the Pontiac Aztek, but has a 4-inch longer wheelbase and body to allow 3rd-row seating. Like Aztek, Rendezvous is based on General Motors' front-wheel-drive minivans and uses a 3.4-liter V6 and automatic transmission.

Specifications begin on page 551.

BUICK

Buick Rendezvous

Rendezvous offers front-wheel drive with optional traction control, or GM's Versatrak all-wheel drive without low-range gearing. Trim levels are base CX and better-equipped CXL, both with antilock 4-wheel disc brakes and front side airbags. The optional 2-passenger 3rd-row seat folds flush with the floor. Second-row seating is a 3-person split bench or optional twin buckets; both types have reclining backrests and move fore/aft. Other options include GM's OnStar assistance system, rear obstacle detection, head-up instrument display, rear self-leveling suspension, and a 3500-lb trailering package.

RATINGS

	CX 2WD	CXL
ACCELERATION	4	4
FUEL ECONOMY	4	4
RIDE QUALITY	4	4
STEERING/HANDLING	3	3
QUIETNESS	5	5
INSTRUMENTS/CONTROLS	6	6
ROOM/COMFORT (FRONT)	7	7
ROOM/COMFORT (REAR)	5	5
CARGO ROOM	9	9
VALUE	4	4

Buick's first SUV takes aim at the likes of the RX 300 and Acura MDX, which cost more similarly equipped. Still, at nearly $34,000, a loaded 7-seat AWD Rendezvous is not bargain-priced, and clearly lags the Lexus and Acura in performance, refinement, and quality of assembly and materials.

TOTAL	51	51

Average total for midsize sport-utility vehicles: 49.6

ENGINES

	ohv V6
Size, liters/cu. in.	3.4/204
Horsepower @ rpm	185 @ 5200

Prices are accurate at time of publication; subject to manufacturer's change.

BUICK

	ohv V6
Torque (lb-ft) @ rpm	210 @ 4000
Availability	S

EPA city/highway mpg

4-speed automatic	18/24[1]

1. 19/26 w/2WD.

PRICES

Buick Rendezvous

	Retail Price	Dealer Invoice
FWD CX 4-door wagon	$25024	$22647
AWD CX 4-door wagon	27552	24935
AWD CXL 4-door wagon	27552	24935
Destination charge	575	575

CXL requires option pkg. AWD denotes all-wheel drive. FWD denotes front-wheel drive.

STANDARD EQUIPMENT

CX: 3.4-liter V6 engine, 4-speed automatic transmission, dual front airbags, front side airbags, antilock 4-wheel disc brakes, daytime running lights, air conditioning, power steering, tilt leather-wrapped steering wheel, cruise control, cloth upholstery, front bucket seats w/lumbar adjustment, center console, cupholders, second row split folding seat, power mirrors, power windows, power door locks, remote keyless entry, AM/FM/CD player, digital clock, rear defogger, rear wiper/washer, illuminated visor mirrors, map lights, variable intermittent wipers, remote hatch release, cargo cover, automatic headlights, floormats, theft-deterrent system, fog lights, rear privacy glass, roof rails, 215/70R16 tires, wheel covers. **AWD** adds: all-wheel drive.

CXL adds: all-wheel drive, dual-zone automatic climate control, interior air filter, leather upholstery, heated power mirrors, AM/FM/cassette/CD player, automatic day/night rearview mirror, alloy wheels.

OPTIONAL EQUIPMENT
Major Packages

Security Pkg. 1SB, FWD CX	1471	1265

Traction control, OnStar System w/one year service (roadside assistance, emergency services; other services available), rear obstacle detection system, universal garage door opener, driver information center, overhead console, rear storage system, theft-deterrent system w/alarm, special wheel covers.

Versatility Pkg. 1SC, FWD CX	1960	1686

Traction control, leather/cloth upholstery, 6-way power driver seat, third row seat, universal garage door opener, driver information center, overhead console, rear storage system, alloy wheels.

Specifications begin on page 551.

BUICK

	Retail Price	Dealer Invoice
Luxury Pkg. 1SD, FWD CX	$3261	$2804

Versatility Pkg. 1SC plus OnStar System w/one year service (roadside assistance, emergency services; other services available), memory driver seat and mirrors, 6-way power passenger seat, rear radio controls, theft-deterrent system w/alarm, rear obstacle detection system, 215/70SR16 touring tires.

Security Pkg. 1SB, AWD CX	1296	1115

OnStar System w/one year service (roadside assistance, emergency services; other services available), universal garage door opener, driver information center, overhead console, rear storage system, cargo mat, rear obstacle detection system, theft-deterrent system w/alarm.

Security Pkg. 1SC, CXL	3475	2989

OnStar System w/one year service (roadside assistance, emergency services; other services available), 6-way power front seats, universal garage door opener, driver information center, overhead console, cargo mat, rear storage system, rear obstacle detection system, body-colored outside mirrors, theft-deterrent system w/alarm.

Versatility Pkg. 1SD, CXL	4030	3466

Security Pkg. 1SC plus third row seat, rear radio controls, 215/70SR16 touring tires, alloy wheels.

Luxury Pkg. 1SE, CXL	5015	4313

Versatility Pkg. 1SD plus heated front seats, head-up instrument display, memory driver seat and mirrors, chrome alloy wheels.

Trailer Tow Pkg., FWD CX, CXL	325	280

Heavy-duty engine cooling and alternator, air compressor, load-leveling rear suspension, wiring harness. CX requires Pkg. 1SC or 1SD. CXL requires Pkg. 1SD or 1SE.

Comfort & Convenience Features

Power sunroof, FWD CX, CXL	695	598

CX requires Pkg. 1SC or 1SD. CXL requires Pkg. 1SD or 1SE.

AM/FM/cassette/CD player, CX	350	301
AM/FM/cassette w/6-disc CD changer	395	340

FWD CX requires Pkg. 1SD. NA AWD CX.

Head-up instrument display, FWD CX	275	237

Requires Pkg. 1SD.

Memory Pkg., CXL	225	194

Driver seat and mirror memory.

Heated front seats, CXL	225	194

Requires Memory Pkg.

Third row split folding seat, FWD CX	750	645

Requires Pkg. 1SD.

Prices are accurate at time of publication; subject to manufacturer's change.

BUICK • CADILLAC

	Retail Price	Dealer Invoice
Second row captain chairs , FWD CX, CXL	$250	$215

CX requires Pkg. 1SD, third row split folding seat. CXL requires Pkg. 1SE.

Leather upholstery, FWD CX 655 563
Requires Pkg. 1SD.

Special Purpose, Wheels and Tires

Chrome alloy wheels, CXL....................................... 650 559
Requires Pkg. 1SD.

2003 CADILLAC CTS

Cadillac CTS

Rear-wheel-drive near-luxury car
Base price: $29,350. Built in USA.
Also consider: Acura TL, BMW 3-Series, Mercedes-Benz C-Class

FOR • Brake-pedal feel • Build quality • Steering/handling
AGAINST • Navigation system controls

This new American-built sedan replaces the German-sourced Catera as the entry-level Cadillac for 2003. The CTS competes with near-luxury mainstays such as the BMW 3-Series and Mercedes-Benz C-Class, but is among the largest, heaviest cars in that class. It has rear-wheel drive and a V6 engine. It offers a 5-speed manual transmission or a 5-speed automatic, both firsts for Cadillac. The automatic is the same one GM supplies for BMW's 3- and 5-Series cars. It has Sport and Winter modes, but no manual shift gate, as in the BMWs. Standard on CTS are antilock 4-wheel disc brakes, traction control, front side and curtain side airbags, leather upholstery, and GM's OnStar assistance system. An antiskid system is part of a Luxury Sport Package option, which also contains 17-inch wheels vs. 16s, and sport-oriented suspension, steering, and brake calibrations. Other options include a navigation system with dashboard

Specifications begin on page 551.

CADILLAC

screen and related voice activation for navigation and audio functions. A sunroof, in-dash CD changer, and Xenon headlamps are among other extra-cost items.

RATINGS	Base w/Lux. Pkg., auto.	Base w/Luxury Sport Pkg., man.	Base w/Luxury Sport Pkg. and nav. sys., auto.
ACCELERATION	6	6	6
FUEL ECONOMY	5	5	5
RIDE QUALITY	7	6	6
STEERING/HANDLING	6	7	7
QUIETNESS	7	6	6
INSTRUMENTS/CONTROLS	7	7	5
ROOM/COMFORT (FRONT)	7	7	7
ROOM/COMFORT (REAR)	5	5	5
CARGO ROOM	3	3	3
VALUE	5	5	4

Its bold styling may polarize, but there's no doubt the CTS is an upper-echelon driving machine. Solid and sporty, it delivers much of the feel of the BMW 5-Series, its acknowledged inspiration, but at 3-Series prices. There's more here than meets the eye.

TOTAL	58	57	54

Average total for near-luxury cars: 54.5

ENGINES

	dohc V6
Size, liters/cu. in.	3.2/194
Horsepower @ rpm	220 @ 6000
Torque (lb-ft) @ rpm	218 @ 3400
Availability	S
EPA city/highway mpg	
5-speed manual	18/25
5-speed automatic	18/25

PRICES

Cadillac CTS	Retail Price	Dealer Invoice
Base 4-door sedan	$29350	$27149
Destination charge	640	640

STANDARD EQUIPMENT

Base: 3.2-liter dohc V6 engine, 5-speed manual transmission, traction control, dual front airbags, front side airbags, curtain side airbags, antilock 4-wheel disc brakes, wiper-activated headlights, daytime running lights, emergency inside trunk release, air conditioning w/dual-zone automatic climate controls, OnStar System w/one year service (roadside assistance, emergency services; other services available), power steering, tilt leather-wrapped steering

Prices are accurate at time of publication; subject to manufacturer's change.

CADILLAC

wheel w/climate controls, cruise control, leather upholstery, front bucket seats, 8-way power driver seat, center console, cupholders, heated power mirrors, power windows, power door locks, remote keyless entry, AM/FM/cassette/CD player, analog clock, automatic day/night rearview mirror, illuminated visor mirrors, rear defogger, variable intermittent wipers, remote fuel door and decklid release, automatic headlights, floormats, fog lights, cornering lights, 225/55HR16 tires, alloy wheels.

OPTIONAL EQUIPMENT

	Retail Price	Dealer Invoice
Major Packages		
Luxury Pkg. 1SB	$2000	$1700

8-way power passenger seat, memory driver seat and mirrors, wood interior trim, compass, universal garage door opener, digital memo recorder.

Luxury Sport Pkg. 1SC	3500	2975

Luxury Pkg. plus Stabilitrak antiskid system, variable-assist power steering, upgraded brake pads, sport suspension, load-leveling rear suspension, 225/50VR17 tires, polished alloy wheels.

Powertrain

5-speed automatic transmission	1200	1020

Comfort & Convenience Features

Navigation system	2700	2295

CD Rom navigation system. Includes Bose AM/FM/cassette w/in-dash 6-disc CD changer. Requires Luxury Pkg. or Sport Luxury Pkg.

Bose AM/FM/cassette w/in-dash 6-disc CD changer	1275	1084
Power sunroof	1100	935

Requires Luxury Pkg. or Sport Luxury Pkg.

Heated front seats	400	340

Requires Luxury Pkg. or Sport Luxury Pkg.

Split folding rear seat	300	255

Requires Luxury Pkg. or Sport Luxury Pkg.

Appearance and Miscellaneous

Xenon headlights	500	425

Includes headlight washers. Requires Luxury Pkg. or Sport Luxury Pkg.

Polished alloy wheels	795	509

Requires Luxury Pkg.

CADILLAC DE VILLE

Front-wheel-drive luxury car
Base price range: $42,325-$47,255. Built in USA.
Also consider: Lexus LS 430, Mercedes-Benz E-Class

Specifications begin on page 551.

CADILLAC

Cadillac DeVille DHS

FOR • Acceleration • Build quality • Entry/exit • Interior materials • Quietness • Passenger and cargo room **AGAINST** • Navigation system controls • Fuel economy • Rear visibility

A new navigation system that plays DVD movies is the marquee addition to Cadillac's largest car for 2002. Base and DHS DeVilles have a bench front seat, the sportier DTS model has buckets. The V8 makes 300 hp in the DTS, 275 in the others. All have a 4-speed automatic transmission, traction control, antilock 4-wheel disc brakes, front head-and-torso side airbags, load-leveling suspension, and General Motors' OnStar assistance system. Rear side airbags and a rear obstacle warning system are optional. An antiskid system is standard on DTS, optional elsewhere. Infrared Night Vision is optional on DHS and DTS. The optional navigation system now incorporates voice recognition and DVD mapping; it can play entertainment DVDs over the 6.5-inch dashboard screen with the transmission in Park. Also for '02: Leather upholstery is standard instead of optional on the base model, and a tire pressure monitor is standard on DHS and DTS. Due later in the model year is an optional satellite radio that plays commercial-free programs for a $9.98 monthly fee.

RATINGS	Base	DHS	DTS
ACCELERATION	7	7	7
FUEL ECONOMY	3	3	3
RIDE QUALITY	9	9	8
STEERING/HANDLING	6	6	7
QUIETNESS	8	8	8
INSTRUMENTS/CONTROLS	6	6	6
ROOM/COMFORT (FRONT)	8	9	9
ROOM/COMFORT (REAR)	9	9	9
CARGO ROOM	6	6	6
VALUE	5	6	6

Spacious and powerful, brims with space-age gizmos, and priced below most V8 luxury rivals. Affluent younger buyers still favor imports, but DeVille's virtues make it worth considering.

| **TOTAL** | 67 | 69 | 69 |

Average total for luxury cars: 59.4

Prices are accurate at time of publication; subject to manufacturer's change.

CADILLAC

ENGINES

	dohc V8	dohc V8
Size, liters/cu. in.	4.6/279	4.6/279
Horsepower @ rpm	275 @ 5600	300 @ 6000
Torque (lb-ft) @ rpm	300 @ 4000	295 @ 4400
Availability	S[1]	S[2] |//
EPA city/highway mpg		
4-speed automatic	18/27	18/27

1. Base, DHS. 2. DTS.

PRICES

Cadillac De Ville

	Retail Price	Dealer Invoice
Base 4-door sedan	$42325	$38727
DHS 4-door sedan	47255	43238
DTS 4-door sedan	47255	43238
Destination charge	745	745

STANDARD EQUIPMENT

Base: 4.6-liter dohc V8 275-horsepower engine, 4-speed automatic transmission, traction control, dual front airbags, front side airbags, antilock 4-wheel disc brakes, wiper-activated headlights, daytime running lights, OnStar System w/one year service (roadside assistance, emergency services; other services available), air conditioning w/tri-zone automatic climate control, power steering, tilt leather-wrapped steering wheel, cruise control, leather upholstery, split front bench seat, 8-way power front seats, front storage armrest, cupholders, rear seat trunk pass-through, heated power mirrors w/driver-side automatic day/night, power windows, power door locks, remote keyless entry, AM/FM/cassette/CD player, digital clock, steering wheel radio and climate controls, trip computer, outside temperature indicator, illuminated front visor mirrors, variable intermittent wipers, power decklid release and power pull-down, remote fuel door release, rear defogger, automatic day/night rearview mirror, compass, map lights, automatic headlights, automatic parking brake release, floormats, theft-deterrent system, cornering lights, load-leveling suspension, 225/60SR16 tires, alloy wheels.

DHS adds: tire-pressure monitor, heated front and rear seats, front and rear power lumbar adjustment, front seat lumbar massage, memory system (driver seat, mirrors, steering wheel), power tilt/telescoping wood and leather-wrapped steering wheel, wood shift knob, Bose sound system, analog instruments, tachometer, wood interior trim, rear illuminated visor mirrors, rain-sensing automatic wipers, power rear window sunshade, manual rear side sunshades, chrome alloy wheels.

DTS adds: 4.6-liter dohc V8 300-horsepower engine, StabiliTrak

Specifications begin on page 551.

CADILLAC

antiskid system, front bucket seats, center console, tilt leather-wrapped steering wheel, fog lights, Continuously Variable Road Sensing Suspension, 235/55HR17 tires, alloy wheels. *Deletes:* memory system, power tilt/telescoping wood and leather-wrapped steering wheel, wood shift knob, rear seat lumbar adjustment, rear illuminated visor mirrors, power rear window sunshade, manual rear side sunshades, chrome alloy wheels.

OPTIONAL EQUIPMENT

	Retail Price	Dealer Invoice

Major Packages

Comfort and Convenience Pkg., Base $1095 $931
Heated front and rear seats, front seat lumbar adjustment, memory system (driver seat, mirrors), trunk mat.

Premium Luxury Pkg., DTS 1985 1687
Rear side airbags, power tilt/telescoping wood/leather-wrapped steering wheel, memory system (seats, steering wheel, mirrors), rear obstacle detection system, universal garage door opener, trunk mat.

Safety and Security Pkg., Base 1045 888
DHS 895 761
StabiliTrak antiskid system, rear obstacle detection system, tire-pressure monitor (Base), universal garage door opener. Base requires Comfort and Convenience Pkg.

Safety

Rear side airbags 295 251
Night Vision, DHS, DTS 2250 1913
DHS requires Safety and Security Pkg. DTS requires Premium Equipment Pkg.

Comfort & Convenience Features

Navigation system, DHS, DTS 1995 1696
Navigation system with Global Positioning System, DVD player, LCD screen, voice recognition, 6-disc CD changer. NA w/satellite radio.

Power sunroof 1550 1318
DHS deletes rear illuminated visor mirrors.

Adaptive front seats, DHS, DTS 995 846
DTS requires Premium Luxury Pkg.

6-disc CD changer 595 506
Satellite radio, DHS, DTS....................................... 295 251
Requires monthly fee. DHS requires Safety and Security Pkg. DTS requires Premium Luxury Pkg. NA w/Navigation system, 6-disc CD changer.

Hands-free cellular telephone 325 276

Appearance and Miscellaneous

Chrome alloy wheels, Base, DTS 795 509

Prices are accurate at time of publication; subject to manufacturer's change.

CADILLAC

CADILLAC ELDORADO

Cadillac Eldorado

Front-wheel-drive luxury car
Base price range: $41,865-$45,000. Built in USA.
Also consider: Jaguar XK8, Mercedes-Benz CLK

FOR • Acceleration • Steering/handling • Interior materials
AGAINST • Fuel economy • Rear visibility • Climate controls (base model) • Rear-seat entry/exit

Cadillac's slow-selling V8 luxury coupe is offered in base Sport Coupe (ESC) and uplevel Touring Coupe (ETC). The ESC has 275 hp, the ETC 300; both use regular-grade fuel. All Eldos come with a 4-speed automatic transmission, traction control, antilock 4-wheel disc brakes, and General Motors' OnStar assistance system. Eldorado is the only Cadillac without front side airbags. An antiskid system is standard on ETC, optional on ESC.

RATINGS

	ESC	ETC
ACCELERATION	7	7
FUEL ECONOMY	4	4
RIDE QUALITY	7	7
STEERING/HANDLING	6	7
QUIETNESS	7	7
INSTRUMENTS/CONTROLS	5	5
ROOM/COMFORT (FRONT)	6	6
ROOM/COMFORT (REAR)	3	3
CARGO ROOM	4	4
VALUE	2	2

Slow sales spell big discounts. We'd choose the less-expensive, softer-riding ESC over the sport-oriented ETC.

TOTAL	51	52

Average total for luxury cars: 59.4

ENGINES

	dohc V8	dohc V8
Size, liters/cu. in.	4.6/279	4.6/279

Specifications begin on page 551.

CADILLAC

	dohc V8	dohc V8
Horsepower @ rpm	275 @ 5600	300 @ 6000
Torque (lb-ft) @ rpm	300 @ 4000	295 @ 4400
Availability	S[1]	S[2]
EPA city/highway mpg		
4-speed automatic	18/27	18/27

1. ESC. 2. ETC.

PRICES

Cadillac Eldorado

	Retail Price	Dealer Invoice
ESC 2-door coupe	$41865	$38306
ETC 2-door coupe	45000	41175
Destination charge	745	745

STANDARD EQUIPMENT

ESC: 4.6-liter dohc V8 275-horsepower engine, 4-speed automatic transmission, traction control, dual front airbags, antilock 4-wheel disc brakes, wiper-activated headlights, emergency inside trunk release, daytime running lamps, air conditioning w/dual-zone automatic climate control, OnStar System w/one year service (roadside assistance, emergency services; other services available), power steering, leather-wrapped steering wheel with controls for radio and climate, tilt steering wheel, cruise control, leather upholstery, heated power front bucket seats w/4-way power lumbar support, center console, cupholders, rear seat trunk pass-through, overhead console, Memory Pkg. (memory seats, mirrors, climate control, and radio presets), heated power mirrors w/driver-side automatic day/night, power windows, power door locks, remote keyless entry, rear defogger, automatic day/night rearview mirror, compass, outside temperature indicator, AM/FM/cassette, power antenna, digital clock, tachometer, remote fuel-door release, remote decklid release w/power pull-down, trip computer, wood interior trim, variable intermittent wipers, automatic parking-brake release, automatic headlights, map lights, illuminated visor mirrors, floormats, automatic level control suspension, theft-deterrent system, fog lights, cornering lights, 225/60SR16 tires, alloy wheels.

ETC adds: 4.6-liter dohc V8 300-horsepower engine, StabiliTrak antiskid system, wood/leather-wrapped steering wheel, Bose AM/FM/weatherband/cassette/CD player, passenger-side mirror tilt-down parking aid, rain-sensing windshield wipers, Continuously Variable Road Sensing Suspension, 235/60HR16 tires.

OPTIONAL EQUIPMENT
Major Packages

Luxury Pkg. 1SB, ESC	2900	2465

StabiliTrak antiskid system, Bose AM/FM/cassette/CD player, wood/leather-wrapped steering wheel, chrome alloy wheels.

Prices are accurate at time of publication; subject to manufacturer's change.

CADILLAC

	Retail Price	Dealer Invoice
Luxury Pkg. 1SC, ETC	$1390	$1182

12-disc CD changer, chrome alloy wheels.

Comfort & Convenience Features

Power sunroof	1550	1318
Universal garage door opener	107	91

CADILLAC ESCALADE AND ESCALADE EXT

Cadillac Escalade

Rear- or all-wheel-drive full-size sport-utility vehicle
Base price range: $47,790-$51,235. Built in USA, Mexico.
Also consider: Lexus LX 470, Lincoln Navigator

FOR • Acceleration • Quietness • Passenger and cargo room • Trailer towing capability **AGAINST** • Steering feel (Escalade) • Fuel economy • Entry/exit (Escalade)

Escalade comes as a luxury SUV and a crossover SUV/pickup-truck called the EXT. The SUV shares a platform with the GMC Yukon/Denali and Chevrolet Tahoe but has more power and unique appointments. The EXT is a similarly embellished version of the Chevrolet Avalanche. Standard on both are front side airbags, antilock 4-wheel disc brakes, traction control, Cadillac's automatic-adjusting road-sensing suspension, 17-inch alloy wheels, and rear obstacle warning and OnStar assistance systems.

The SUV seats seven and offers rear-wheel drive or all-wheel drive without low-range gearing. AWD Escalades have a 6.0-liter V8 and tow up to 8500 lb, 2WD models have a 5.3 V8 and tow 7700 lb.

EXT is a 4-dr crew cab with a "midgate" separating cab from cargo bed. The rear window removes and the midgate folds along with the rear seat to extend the bed from 5.3 ft to 8.1. EXT seats five with the

Specifications begin on page 551.

CADILLAC

midgate upright and two with it folded. It comes only with AWD and the 6.0 V8; towing capacity is 8000 lb. AWD versions of both vehicles have antiskid control.

RATINGS

	Escalade AWD
ACCELERATION	5
FUEL ECONOMY	2
RIDE QUALITY	5
STEERING/HANDLING	3
QUIETNESS	6
INSTRUMENTS/CONTROLS	6
ROOM/COMFORT (FRONT)	9
ROOM/COMFORT (REAR)	8
CARGO ROOM	9
VALUE	2

Interior detail execution and ride quality aren't up to the $50,000 price, but Escalade fights back with plenty of power, no-fuss AWD, and styling that exudes attitude.

TOTAL	55

Average total for full-size sport-utility vehicles: 50.9

ENGINES

	ohv V8	ohv V8
Size, liters/cu. in.	5.3/327	6.0/366
Horsepower @ rpm	285 @ 5200	345 @ 5200
Torque (lb-ft) @ rpm	325 @ 4000	380 @ 4000
Availability	S[1]	S[2]
EPA city/highway mpg		
4-speed automatic	14/18	12/15

1. 2WD Escalade. 2. AWD Escalade and EXT.

PRICES

Cadillac Escalade and Escalade EXT	Retail Price	Dealer Invoice
2WD Base 4-door wagon	$47790	$43682
AWD Base 4-door wagon	51235	46880
AWD EXT 4-door crew cab	49245	45059
Destination charge	745	745

STANDARD EQUIPMENT

2WD Base: 5.3-liter V8 engine, 4-speed automatic transmission, traction control, dual front airbags, front side airbags, antilock 4-wheel disc brakes, rear obstacle detection system, daytime running lights, OnStar System w/one year service (roadside assistance, emergency services; other services available), air conditioning w/dual-zone automatic climate control, rear climate controls, power

Prices are accurate at time of publication; subject to manufacturer's change.

CADILLAC

steering, tilt leather-wrapped/wood steering wheel, cruise control, leather upholstery, 10-way power front bucket seats w/driver seat memory, heated front and second-row seats, cupholders, stowable split folding second-row seat, split folding third-row seat, wood interior trim, overhead console (universal garage door opener, rear radio controls, rear headphone jacks), heated power mirrors w/automatic day/night and tilt-down back-up aid, power windows, power door locks, remote keyless entry, Bose AM/FM radio w/in-dash 6-disc CD changer, digital clock, steering wheel radio controls, tachometer, automatic day/night rearview mirror, compass, outside temperature display, trip computer, map lights, rain-sensing intermittent wipers, rear defogger, intermittent rear wiper/washer, illuminated visor mirrors, automatic headlights, floormats, theft-deterrent system, fog lights, running boards, roof rack, front tow hooks, 7-lead trailer wiring harness, trailer hitch, automatic shock absorber control, load leveling rear suspension, full-size spare tire, 265/70R17 tires, alloy wheels.

AWD Base adds: 6.0-liter V8 engine, all-wheel drive, antiskid system.

AWD EXT adds: split folding rear seat, removable rear window, folding midgate, stowable cargo cover. *Deletes:* rear climate controls, second row seat heating, split folding third row seat, rear wiper/washer.

OPTIONAL EQUIPMENT

	Retail Price	Dealer Invoice
Power sunroof	$1550	$1318

Deletes rear climate controls.

CADILLAC SEVILLE

Cadillac Seville STS

Front-wheel-drive luxury car
Base price range: $43,524-$49,080. Built in USA.
Also consider: BMW 5-Series, Lexus LS 430, Mercedes-Benz E-Class

FOR • Acceleration • Automatic transmission performance • Handling/roadholding • Interior storage space • Interior materials
AGAINST • Fuel economy • Rear visibility

Specifications begin on page 551.

CADILLAC

A new navigation system that plays DVD movies tops 2002 additions to Cadillac's midsize sedan. Seville offers 275-hp SLS and sportier 300-hp STS models. Both have a V8 engine and 4-speed automatic transmission, plus front side airbags, antilock 4-wheel disc brakes, traction and antiskid control, and GM's OnStar assistance system. Heated front and rear seats and a rear obstacle warning system are new standard features for 2002. The optional navigation system now incorporates voice recognition and DVD mapping; it can play entertainment DVDs over the 6.5-inch dashboard screen with the transmission in Park. Due later in the model year is an optional satellite radio that plays commercial-free programs for a $9.98 monthly fee. And the STS's automatically adjusting road-sensing suspension is due for new technology designed to improve ride and handling.

RATINGS

	SLS	STS
ACCELERATION	7	7
FUEL ECONOMY	4	4
RIDE QUALITY	8	7
STEERING/HANDLING	6	7
QUIETNESS	7	7
INSTRUMENTS/CONTROLS	6	6
ROOM/COMFORT (FRONT)	7	7
ROOM/COMFORT (REAR)	5	5
CARGO ROOM	4	4
VALUE	3	3

SLS models furnish the better balance of comfort and performance, but no Seville matches the overall refinement and precision feel of like-priced imports.

TOTAL	57	57

Average total for luxury cars: 59.4

ENGINES

	dohc V8	dohc V8
Size, liters/cu. in.	4.6/279	4.6/279
Horsepower @ rpm	275 @ 5600	300 @ 6000
Torque (lb-ft) @ rpm	300 @ 4000	295 @ 4400
Availability	S[1]	S[2]
EPA city/highway mpg		
4-speed automatic	18/27	18/27

1. SLS. 2. STS.

PRICES

Cadillac Seville

	Retail Price	Dealer Invoice
SLS 4-door sedan	$43524	$39824
STS 4-door sedan	49080	44908
Destination charge	745	745

Prices are accurate at time of publication; subject to manufacturer's change.

CADILLAC
STANDARD EQUIPMENT

SLS: 4.6-liter dohc V8 275-horsepower engine, 4-speed automatic transmission, traction control, dual front airbags w/automatic child recognition system, front side airbags, antilock 4-wheel disc brakes, StabiliTrak antiskid system, wiper-activated headlights, emergency inside trunk release, daytime running lights, rear obstacle detection system, OnStar System w/one year service (roadside assistance, emergency services; other services available), air conditioning w/dual zone automatic climate control, outside temperature display, interior air filter, power steering, leather-wrapped tilt steering wheel w/radio and climate controls, cruise control, leather upholstery, power front seats w/power lumbar adjustment, heated front and rear seats, center console, cupholders, overhead console, trunk pass-through, wood interior trim, heated power mirrors w/driver-side automatic day/night, power windows, power door locks, remote keyless entry, AM/FM/cassette/CD player, digital clock, tachometer, automatic day/night rearview mirror, compass, map lights, illuminated visor mirrors, automatic parking brake release, remote fuel door and decklid releases, rain-sensing variable intermittent wipers, automatic headlights, rear defogger, floormats, theft-deterrent system, cornering lights, automatic level control suspension, 235/60SR16 tires, alloy wheels.

STS adds: 4.6-liter dohc V8 300-horsepower engine, memory system (seat, mirrors, steering wheel, climate control and radio presets), power tilt/telescoping steering wheel, Bose AM/FM/weatherband/cassette/CD player w/radio data system, parking-assist passenger-side mirror, fog lights, road-sensing suspension, 235/60HR16 tires.

OPTIONAL EQUIPMENT
Major Packages

	Retail Price	Dealer Invoice
Luxury Pkg. 1SB, SLS............	$675	$574

Power tilt/telescoping steering wheel, memory system (driver seat, mirrors, steering wheel, climate control and radio presets).

Premium Luxury Pkg. 1SC, SLS............	3015	2563

Luxury Pkg. plus Bose AM/FM/weatherband/cassette/CD player w/radio data system, wood/leather-wrapped steering wheel, wood shift knob, chrome alloy wheels.

Luxury Pkg. 1SD, STS............	1985	1687

6-disc CD changer in console, wood trimmed steering wheel and shift knob, chrome alloy wheels.

Premium Luxury Pkg. 1SE, STS............	2635	2240

Luxury Pkg. plus tire pressure monitor, high intensity discharge headlights, 235/55HR17 tires, chrome alloy wheels.

Premium Performance Pkg. 1SF, STS............	5305	4509

Premium Luxury Pkg. plus navigation system, hands-free cellular telphone.

CADILLAC • CHEVROLET

Comfort & Convenience Features	Retail Price	Dealer Invoice
Navigation system, SLS	$2945	$2503
STS	1995	1696

Navigation system w/Global Positioning System, DVD player, LCD screen, voice recognition, 6-disc CD changer in console. SLS requires Luxury Pkg. STS requires option pkg.

UM5 Bose sound system, SLS	950	808

Includes AM/FM/weatherband/cassette/CD w/radio data system, automatic volume control. Requires Luxury Pkg.

Satellite radio	295	251

Requires monthly fee. SLS requires UM5 Bose sound system.

6-disc CD player, SLS	595	506

Requires option pkg.

Hands-free cellular telephone	325	276
Power sunroof	1550	1318

Requires option group.

Wood Trim Pkg.	595	506

Wood/leather-wrapped steering wheel, wood shift knob. SLS requires Luxury Pkg.

Appearance and Miscellaneous

Chrome alloy wheels, SLS	795	509

Requires Luxury Pkg.

235/60ZR16 tires, STS	250	213

CHEVROLET ASTRO

Chevrolet Astro LS

Rear- or all-wheel-drive minivan
Base price range: $21,113-$25,576. Built in USA.
Also consider: Dodge Caravan, Ford Windstar, Honda

Prices are accurate at time of publication; subject to manufacturer's change.

CHEVROLET

Odyssey

FOR • Passenger and cargo room • Trailer towing capability
AGAINST • Fuel economy • Entry/exit • Ride

Also sold as the GMC Safari, Astro comes in one body length with a passenger-side sliding door. It's offered in LS and LT trim, both with 8-passenger seating: two front buckets, two 3-place rear benches; 2nd-row buckets are optional. Astro offers a choice of side-by-side rear cargo doors or Dutch doors with separate-opening glass. There is also a 2-seat Cargo Van. The only powertrain is a V6 and automatic transmission featuring a Tow/Haul mode, with rear-wheel drive or all-wheel drive. Antilock brakes are standard; traction control and side airbags are unavailable. Cargo models offer remote keyless entry and a rear heater for 2002.

RATINGS

	2WD LS	AWD LS
ACCELERATION	4	4
FUEL ECONOMY	3	3
RIDE QUALITY	3	3
STEERING/HANDLING	3	3
QUIETNESS	3	3
INSTRUMENTS/CONTROLS	6	6
ROOM/COMFORT (FRONT)	3	3
ROOM/COMFORT (REAR)	6	6
CARGO ROOM	10	10
VALUE	4	4

Consider Astro or Safari if you're looking for a minivan to haul cargo and handle light-duty towing. For primarily passenger use, go with one of the many front-drive alternatives.

TOTAL	45	45

Average total for minivans: 56.0

ENGINES

	ohv V6
Size, liters/cu. in.	4.3/262
Horsepower @ rpm	190 @ 4400
Torque (lb-ft) @ rpm	250 @ 2800
Availability	S
EPA city/highway mpg	
4-speed automatic	15/20[1]

1. 15/18 w/AWD.

PRICES

Chevrolet Astro	Retail Price	Dealer Invoice
2WD 3-door Cargo van	$21113	$19107
AWD 3-door Cargo van	23513	21279

Specifications begin on page 551.

CHEVROLET

	Retail Price	Dealer Invoice
2WD LS 3-door van	$23761	$21504
AWD LS 3-door van	25576	23146
Destination charge	655	655

STANDARD EQUIPMENT

Cargo: 4.3-liter V6 engine, 4-speed automatic transmission, dual front airbags, antilock brakes, daytime running lamps, front air conditioning, power steering, vinyl upholstery, front bucket seats, cupholders, black rubber floor covering, variable intermittent wipers, AM/FM radio, digital clock, automatic headlights, theft-deterrent system, dual manual outside mirrors, 215/75R15 tires. **AWD** models add: all-wheel drive.

LS adds: tilt steering wheel, cruise control, cloth upholstery, 8-passenger seating with front bucket seats and two 3-passenger rear bench seats, carpeting, power mirrors, power windows, power door locks, remote keyless entry, AM/FM/CD player, overhead console, trip computer, compass, outside temperature indicator, illuminated visor mirrors, map lights, floormats, rear privacy glass, swing-out rear side windows, roof rack, chrome steel wheels. **AWD** models add: all-wheel drive.

OPTIONAL EQUIPMENT
Major Packages

LS Preferred Equipment Group 1SD, LS	1527	1313
Front and rear air conditioning, rear heater, 6-way power driver seat, AM/FM/cassette/CD player, rear defogger, rear Dutch doors.		
LT Preferred Equipment Group 1SE, LS	3178	2733
LS Preferred Equipment Group plus leather-wrapped steering wheel, rear radio controls, headphone jacks, universal garage door opener, 215/75R15 white-letter tires, alloy wheels.		
ZQ3 Convenience Pkg., Cargo	383	329
Tilt steering wheel, cruise control.		
ZQ2 Convenience Group, Cargo	474	408
Power windows and door locks.		
Trailering Special Equipment	309	266
Platform trailer hitch, 8-lead wiring harness.		

Powertrain

Limited-slip rear differential	252	217

Comfort & Convenience Features

Front and rear air conditioning, LS	523	450
Rear heater, LS	205	176
Cargo	NA	NA

Prices are accurate at time of publication; subject to manufacturer's change.

CHEVROLET

	Retail Price	Dealer Invoice
Dutch doors, LS	$459	$395
Includes rear defogger.		
7-passenger seating, LS	NC	NC
Front- and second-row bucket seats, third-row bench seat. Requires LT Group.		
Leather upholstery, LS	950	817
Requires LT Group.		
Remote keyless entry, Cargo	170	146
Requires ZQ2 Convenience Group.		
AM/FM/CD player, Cargo	407	350
Rear radio controls, LS	125	108
Includes headphone jacks. Requires LS Group 1SD.		

Appearance and Miscellaneous

Running boards, LS	400	344
Requires Preferred Equipment Group, alloy wheels.		
Alloy wheels, LS	25	22
Requires LS Group 1SD.		
Chrome styled steel wheels, LS	25	22

CHEVROLET BLAZER

Chevrolet Blazer LS 4-door wagon

Rear- or 4-wheel-drive midsize sport-utility vehicle
Base price range: $19,295-$25,530. Built in USA.
Also consider: Dodge Durango, Ford Explorer, Toyota 4Runner

FOR • Acceleration • Cargo room **AGAINST** • Rear-seat comfort • Fuel economy • Rear-seat entry/exit (2-door)

With the debut of the 2002 TrailBlazer, the 1995-vintage Blazer is

Specifications begin on page 551.

CHEVROLET

repositioned as a lower-priced companion to Chevrolet's larger, more-powerful new SUV. Blazer will be sold at least through 2003. Blazer offers 2- and 4-dr models with rear-wheel drive, 4WD that must be disengaged on dry pavement, or General Motors' Autotrac 4WD that can be left engaged on dry pavement; 4x4s include low-range gearing. A 4.3-liter V6 is the only engine and comes with automatic or manual transmission on 2-dr models, automatic only on 4 drs. ABS is standard. The Xtreme is a 2WD 2-dr with low-riding sport suspension, unique 5-spoke 16-inch alloy wheels, and special trim and cladding.

RATINGS

	LS 2-dr 2WD, auto.	LS 4-dr 4WD, auto.
ACCELERATION	5	5
FUEL ECONOMY	4	4
RIDE QUALITY	3	4
STEERING/HANDLING	2	3
QUIETNESS	3	3
INSTRUMENTS/CONTROLS	6	6
ROOM/COMFORT (FRONT)	5	5
ROOM/COMFORT (REAR)	2	3
CARGO ROOM	7	7
VALUE	2	3

It's overshadowed by roomier successors and newer-design rivals, but comfortable ride, capable engine, and regularly available discounts are Blazer assets.

TOTAL	39	43

Average total for midsize sport-utility vehicles: 49.6

ENGINES

	ohv V6
Size, liters/cu. in.	4.3/262
Horsepower @ rpm	190 @ 4400
Torque (lb-ft) @ rpm	250 @ 2800
Availability	S
EPA city/highway mpg	
5-speed manual	14/17[1]
4-speed automatic	15/20[2]

1. 16/22 w/2WD. 2. 17/22 w/2WD.

PRICES

Chevrolet Blazer	Retail Price	Dealer Invoice
LS 2-door wagon, 2WD	$19295	$17462
LS 2-door wagon, 4WD	22295	20177
Xtreme 2-door wagon, 2WD	21360	19331
LS 4-door wagon, 2WD	23530	21295
LS 4-door wagon, 4WD	25530	23105

Prices are accurate at time of publication; subject to manufacturer's change.

CHEVROLET

	Retail Price	Dealer Invoice
Destination charge	$600	$600

STANDARD EQUIPMENT

LS: 4.3-liter V6 engine, 5-speed manual transmission (2-door), 4-speed automatic transmission w/column shift (4-door), dual front airbags, antilock 4-wheel disc brakes, daytime running lights, power steering, air conditioning, cloth upholstery, front bucket seats w/driver seat manual lumbar adjustment (2-door), front console (2-door), split front bench seat with storage armrest (4-door), cupholders, split folding rear seat, AM/FM/cassette, digital clock, tachometer, passenger-side visor mirror, automatic headlights, variable intermittent wipers, floormats, theft-deterrent system, roof rack, tailgate, 6-lead trailer wiring harness, full-size spare tire, 235/70R15 tires, alloy wheels. **4WD** adds: 4-wheel drive, 2-speed transfer case, front tow hooks.

Xtreme adds to LS 2-door: leather-wrapped steering wheel, rear defogger, color-keyed body cladding, fog lights, deep-tinted glass, heavy-duty trailer hitch, lowered sport suspension, 235/60R16 tires.

OPTIONAL EQUIPMENT
Major Packages

1SB Preferred Equipment Group, LS 2-door................ 1200 1032
Tilt steering wheel, cruise control, floor-mounted shifter (w/automatic transmission), heated power mirrors, power windows and door locks, AM/FM/cassette w/automatic tone control, rear defogger, rear wiper/washer, power tailgate window release, deep-tinted rear glass, bodyside moldings (4WD).

1SC Preferred Equipment Group, LS 2-door................ 2300 1978
1SB Preferred Equipment Group plus remote keyless entry, AM/FM/CD player, 6-way power driver seat, leather-wrapped steering wheel, overhead console, compass, outside temperature indicator, illuminated visor mirrors.

1SC Preferred Equipment Group, LS 4-door................ 1630 1402
Manufacturer's Discount Price.................................. 630 542
Tilt leather-wrapped steering wheel, cruise control, front bucket seats, center console, heated power mirrors, power windows and door locks, AM/FM/cassette w/automatic tone control, overhead console, compass, outside temperature indicator, illuminated visor mirrors, rear defogger, rear wiper/washer, power tailgate window release, cargo net, deep-tinted rear glass.

1SH Preferred Equipment Group, LS 4-door................ 3810 3277
Manufacturer's Discount Price.................................. 2810 2417
1SC Preferred Equipment Group plus Autotrac 4WD transfer case (4WD), leather upholstery, 8-way power driver seat, remote keyless entry, AM/FM/CD player, universal garage door opener, trip computer, automatic day/night rearview and driver-side mirrors, cargo cover.

Specifications begin on page 551.

CHEVROLET

	Retail Price	Dealer Invoice
1SX Preferred Equipment Group, Xtreme	$995	$856
Manufacturer's Discount Price	*495*	*426*

Tilt steering wheel, cruise control, floor-mounted shifter (w/automatic transmission), heated power mirrors, power windows, power door locks, remote keyless entry, AM/FM/cassette w/automatic tone control, power tailgate window, rear wiper/washer.

1SY Preferred Equipment Group, Xtreme	2040	1754
Manufacturer's Discount Price	*1540*	*1325*

1SX Preferred Equipment Group plus 6-way power driver seat, AM/FM/CD player, overhead console, compass, outside temperature indicator, illuminated visor mirrors.

Power sunroof/Bose sound system discount (credit)	(500)	(430)

Requires power sunroof and Bose sound system. LS, Xtreme require Preferred Equipment Group.

ZR2 Wide Stance Performance Pkg., 4WD LS 2-door	2000	1720

Heavy-duty wide stance chassis, heavy-duty suspension, raised ride height, Bilstein shock absorbers, Shield Pkg., heavy-duty differential gears and axles, fender flares.

Trailering Special Equipment	210	181

Includes platform hitch, heavy-duty flasher. 2WD models require automatic transmission. Std. Xtreme.

Powertrain

4-speed automatic transmission, LS 2-door, Xtreme	1000	860
Limited-slip rear differential	270	232
Autotrac 4WD transfer case, 4WD LS	225	194

Comfort & Convenience Features

Heated front seats, LS 4-door	250	215

Requires 1SH Preferred Equipment Group.

Driver seat memory, LS 4-door	NA	NA

Requires 1SH Preferred Equipment Group.

Power sunroof	800	688

Requires Preferred Equipment Group.

Deluxe overhead console, LS 2-door, Xtreme	332	286

Includes universal garage door opener, trip computer, automatic day/night rearview and driver-side mirrors. LS requires 1SC Preferred Equipment Group. Xtreme requires 1SY Preferred Equipment Group.

AM/FM/CD player	100	86

Requires Preferred Equipment Group.

AM/FM/cassette/CD player, LS 2-door w/1SB Group, LS 4-door w/1SC, Xtreme w/1SX	200	172
LS 2-door w/1SC Group, LS 4-door w/1SH, Xtreme w/1SY	100	86

Requires automatic transmission.

Prices are accurate at time of publication; subject to manufacturer's change.

CHEVROLET

	Retail Price	Dealer Invoice
6-disc CD changer	$395	$340

Requires Preferred Equipment Group, automatic transmission.

Bose sound system	495	426

NA with AM/FM/cassette/CD player. Requires automatic transmission Preferred Equipment Group.

Steering-wheel radio controls	125	108

Requires automatic transmission, Preferred Equipment Group.

Cargo cover, LS 4-door	69	59

Requires 1SC Preferred Equipment Group.

Appearance and Miscellaneous

Fog lights, LS	115	99

Requires Preferred Equipment Group.

Special Purpose, Wheels and Tires

Shield Pkg., 4WD	126	108

Includes transfer case and front differential skid plates, fuel tank and steering linkage shields.

ZM6 Off-Road Suspension Pkg., 4WD LS 2-door	NA	NA

Heavy-duty suspension and shock absorbers, jounce bumpers. Requires exterior spare tire carrier, 235/75R15 on/off-road white-letter tires.

235/75R15 on/off-road white-letter tires, 4WD LS	168	144

2-door requires exterior spare tire carrier.

CHEVROLET CAMARO

Chevrolet Camaro Convertible Z28 SS w/35th Anniversary Pkg.

Rear-wheel-drive sporty coupe
Base price range: $18,080-$29,590. Built in Canada.
Also consider: Chevrolet Corvette, Ford Mustang

FOR • Acceleration (Z28) • Handling **AGAINST** • Fuel economy (Z28) • Ride (Z28) • Rear-seat room • Wet-weather traction (without traction control) • Rear visibility • Entry/exit

Specifications begin on page 551.

CHEVROLET

For what is Camaro's final year in its present form, Chevrolet's rear-wheel-drive sports coupe offers a 35th Anniversary Package for the SS version. Camaro comes as a hatchback coupe and a convertible in base V6 or Z28 V8 form. Manual transmission (5-speed on V6, 6-speed on V8) and automatic are available. The Z28 SS package adds a higher-power V8 with functional ram-air hood. All Camaros have antilock 4-wheel disc brakes. Traction control is optional. Convertibles have a power top with glass rear window; V6 versions now have standard automatic transmission. A T-top is optional for coupes. For '02, a CD player is standard. The anniversary package includes red paint, dual silver stripes, and special wheels and trim. Pontiac's Firebird shares Camaro's design and also is due for retirement after the 2002 model year.

RATINGS	Base conv, man.	Z28 hatch, auto.	SS hatch, man.
ACCELERATION	5	8	8
FUEL ECONOMY	5	4	4
RIDE QUALITY	3	2	2
STEERING/HANDLING	7	9	9
QUIETNESS	2	3	3
INSTRUMENTS/CONTROLS	6	6	6
ROOM/COMFORT (FRONT)	4	4	4
ROOM/COMFORT (REAR)	2	2	2
CARGO ROOM	1	3	3
VALUE	3	4	3

V8 models are among the world's best high-performance values, but Camaro and Firebird are out of step with today's tastes and trends, hence their imminent demise.

TOTAL	38	45	44

Average total for sporty coupes: 43.4

ENGINES	ohv V6	ohv V8	ohv V8
Size, liters/cu. in.	3.8/231	5.7/346	5.7/346
Horsepower @ rpm	200 @ 5200	310 @ 5200	325 @ 5200
Torque (lb-ft) @ rpm	225 @ 4000	340 @ 4000	350 @ 4000
Availability	S[1]	S[2]	S[3]

EPA city/highway mpg
5-speed manual	19/31		
6-speed manual		19/28	19/28
4-speed automatic	19/30	18/25	18/25

1. Base. 2. Z28. 3. SS; 335-345 hp w/SLP accessories.

PRICES

Chevrolet Camaro	Retail Price	Dealer Invoice
Base 2-door hatchback	$18080	$16543
Base 2-door convertible	26075	23859

Prices are accurate at time of publication; subject to manufacturer's change.

CHEVROLET

	Retail Price	Dealer Invoice
Z28 2-door hatchback	$22495	$20583
Z28 2-door convertible	29590	27075
Destination charge	575	575

STANDARD EQUIPMENT

Base hatchback: 3.8-liter V6 engine, 5-speed manual transmission, dual front airbags, antilock 4-wheel disc brakes, daytime running lights, air conditioning, power steering, tilt steering wheel, cloth upholstery, front bucket seats, center console, cupholders, folding rear seat, AM/FM/CD player, digital clock, tachometer, intermittent wipers, map lights, visor mirrors, automatic headlights, floormats, 235/55R16 tires, theft-deterrent system, rear spoiler, alloy wheels.

Base convertible adds: 4-speed automatic transmission, power mirrors, power windows, power door locks, remote keyless entry, rear defogger, Monsoon sound system, leather-wrapped steering wheel w/radio controls, cruise control, power convertible top, fog lights.

Z28 hatchback adds to Base hatchback: 5.7-liter V8 310-horsepower engine, 4-speed automatic transmission, limited-slip differential, Monsoon sound system, performance ride and handling suspension, 245/50R16 tires.

Z28 convertible adds: power mirrors, power windows, power door locks, remote keyless entry, rear defogger, leather-wrapped steering wheel w/radio controls, cruise control, 6-way power driver seat, power convertible top, fog lights.

OPTIONAL EQUIPMENT

Major Packages

1SB Preferred Equipment Group 1, Base hatchback   1170   1041
Cruise control, power mirrors and windows, power door locks, remote keyless entry, remote hatch release, theft-deterrent system w/alarm, fog lights.

1SD Preferred Equipment Group 1, Z28 hatchback   1700   1513
1SB Pkg. plus 6-way power driver seat, leather-wrapped steering wheel w/radio controls, bodyside moldings.

SS Performance/Appearance Pkg., Z28 3625   3226
Includes 325-horsepower engine, composite hood w/functional air scoop, forced-air induction system, low-restriction dual exhaust, power steering fluid cooler, special rear spoiler, Special High Performance Ride and Handling Pkg., 275/40ZR17 tires, special alloy wheels. Requires Preferred Equipment Group 1.

Sport Appearance Pkg. 1345   1197
Front and rear body moldings, rocker panels.

Specifications begin on page 551.

CHEVROLET

	Retail Price	Dealer Invoice
Camaro SS 35th Anniversary Edition, Z28	NA	NA

325-horsepower engine, Bright Rally Red paint w/graphics pkg., hood scoop, removable roof panels (hatchback), Ebony/Pewter leather upholstery w/embroidered emblems, owner's portfolio, badging, anodized brake calipers, special black-painted alloy wheels. Hatchback requires Preferred Equipment Group 1.

Performance Handling Pkg., Base	$275	$245

Limited-slip differential, performance axle ratio (w/automatic transmission), dual exhaust, sport steering ratio. Hatchback requires Preferred Equipment Group 1.

RS Pkg., Base	849	NA

Body stripes, badging, Z28 exhaust system, silver painted exhaust outlets. NA w/Sport Appearance Pkg., RS Pkg.

Powertrain

4-speed automatic transmission, Base hatchback	815	725
6-speed manual transmission, Z28	NC	NC
Hurst shifter, Z28	325	289

Requires 6-speed manual transmission.

Traction control, Z28	450	401
Base	250	223

Requires Preferred Equipment Group. Base requires Performance Handling Pkg.

Performance axle ratio, Z28	300	267

Requires automatic transmission.

Comfort & Convenience Features

12-disc CD changer	595	530

Base hatchback requires Monsoon sound system.

Monsoon sound system, Base hatchback	350	311
Leather-wrapped steering wheel, hatchback	170	151

Includes radio controls. Base requires Monsoon sound system.

6-way power driver seat, Base hatchback	270	240
Leather upholstery	500	445
Rear defogger, hatchback	170	151

Appearance and Miscellaneous

Removable roof panels, hatchback	995	886

Includes locks, storage provsions, sun shades.

Chrome alloy wheels, Base	975	868
Base w/Sport Appearance Pkg, Z28	725	645

SLP performance accessories available through dealer.

Prices are accurate at time of publication; subject to manufacturer's change.

CHEVROLET

CHEVROLET CAVALIER

Chevrolet Cavalier 2-door coupe

Front-wheel-drive subcompact car
Base price range: $13,860-$16,380. Built in USA.
Also consider: Ford Focus, Honda Civic, Mazda Protege

FOR • Fuel economy **AGAINST** • Rear-seat room • Interior materials • Rear-seat entry/exit (coupe)

Cavalier offers 2-dr coupes and 4-dr sedans in three trim levels: base, LS, and LS Sport. The LS Sport replaced the Z24 model shortly after the start of the 2002 model year. All Cavaliers come with a 4-cyl engine: Base and LS have a 115-hp 2.2 liter. The LS Sport comes with a new 140-hp dual overhead-cam 2.2 that replaces the 150-hp dohc 2.4 used in the Z24. The new engine rates 1 mpg higher than the 2.4 in EPA fuel-economy estimates. All offer manual or automatic transmission; traction control is included with the automatic, but is not offered with manual. Standard on all models are ABS and air conditioning. New standard features for 2002 include tilt steering wheel, CD player, tachometer, and power trunk release. New chrome 16-inch wheels are standard on the LS Sport. Cavalier shares its design with Pontiac's Sunfire.

RATINGS	Base cpe, man.	LS sdn, auto	LS Sport cpe, man.
ACCELERATION	3	3	5
FUEL ECONOMY	6	6	5
RIDE QUALITY	4	4	3
STEERING/HANDLING	4	5	6
QUIETNESS	3	3	3
INSTRUMENTS/CONTROLS	4	4	4
ROOM/COMFORT (FRONT)	3	3	3
ROOM/COMFORT (REAR)	2	3	2
CARGO ROOM	3	3	3

Specifications begin on page 551.

CHEVROLET

	Base cpe, man.	LS sdn, auto	LS Sport cpe, man.
VALUE	3	4	3

They fall far short of the refinement of Japanese subcompacts, but Cavalier and Sunfire include plenty of useful standard features and should be available with discounts. Cavalier edges out Sunfire as the better overall value.

TOTAL	35	38	37

Average total for subcompact cars: 43.7

ENGINES

	ohv I4	dohc I4
Size, liters/cu. in.	2.2/134	2.2/134
Horsepower @ rpm	115 @ 5000	140 @ 5600
Torque (lb-ft) @ rpm	135 @ 3600	150 @ 4000
Availability	S[1]	S[2]
EPA city/highway mpg		
5-speed manual	25/33	24/33
4-speed automatic	24/32	24/32

1. Base and LS. 2. LS Sport.

PRICES

Chevrolet Cavalier	Retail Price	Dealer Invoice
Base 2-door coupe	$13860	$12960
Base 4-door sedan	13960	13053
LS 2-door coupe	14910	13941
LS 4-door sedan	15010	14034
LS Sport 2-door coupe	16280	15222
LS Sport 4-door sedan	16380	15315
Destination charge	540	540

STANDARD EQUIPMENT

Base: 2.2-liter 4-cylinder engine, 5-speed manual transmission, dual front airbags, antilock brakes, daytime running lights, air conditioning, power steering, tilt steering wheel, cloth and vinyl reclining front bucket seats, center console, cupholders, folding rear seat, AM/FM/CD player, digital clock, tachometer, intermittent wipers, rear defogger, visor mirrors, power remote decklid release, floormats, theft-deterrent system, 195/70R14 tires, wheel covers.

LS adds: cruise control, cloth upholstery, power mirrors, power windows, power door locks, map lights, remote keyless entry, variable intermittent wipers, 195/65R15 tires.

LS Sport adds: 2.2-liter dohc 4-cylinder engine, AM/FM/cassette/CD player, premium speakers, rear spoiler, fog lights, sport suspension, 205/55R16 tires, chrome alloy wheels.

Prices are accurate at time of publication; subject to manufacturer's change.

CHEVROLET

OPTIONAL EQUIPMENT

	Retail Price	Dealer Invoice
Major Packages		
1SB Preferred Equipment Group 1, Base	$850	$765

Rocker panel moldings, rear spoiler, chrome exhaust tips, 205/55R16 tires, alloy wheels.

Powertrain

4-speed automatic transmission	780	702

Includes traction control.

Comfort & Convenience Features

Power sunroof, coupe	595	536
Cruise control, Base	235	212
Remote keyless entry, Base coupe	370	333
Base sedan	410	369

Includes power door locks, theft-deterrent system w/alarm.

AM/FM/cassette/CD player, Base, LS	230	207

Includes premium speakers.

Premium speakers, Base, LS	100	90

Appearance and Miscellaneous

Rear spoiler, Base coupe, LS	150	135
Alloy wheels, Base coupe, LS	295	266

Base coupe includes 195/65R15 tires.

CHEVROLET CORVETTE

CG BEST BUY AUTO

Chevrolet Corvette Z06

Rear-wheel-drive sports car
Base price range: $41,005-$49,705. Built in USA.
Also consider: Chevrolet Camaro, Dodge Viper, Mercedes-Benz SLK-Class

FOR • Acceleration • Steering/handling • Instruments/controls
AGAINST • Fuel economy • Ride • Rear visibility

CHEVROLET

More power for the Z06 model highlights the 2002 Corvette. Three body styles return: convertible with manual fabric top and glass rear window, hatchback coupe with removable roof panel, and fixed-roof Z06 hardtop. All have a 5.7-liter V8. Convertibles and hatchbacks stay at 350 hp; the Z06 has 405, up 20 hp from '01. The Z06 comes only with the 6-speed manual transmission, the others also offer a 4-speed automatic. Antilock 4-wheel disc brakes and an antiskid/traction system are standard. Z06 now comes with the head-up instrument display that's optional on other 'Vettes, plus revisions to its unique chassis tuning. Other models offer two suspension options, but are no longer available with magnesium wheels. A CD player replaces a cassette as standard equipment.

RATINGS	Base hatch, man.	Base hatch w/Z51, auto.	Base conv, auto.	Z06
ACCELERATION	9	9	9	10
FUEL ECONOMY	5	5	4	5
RIDE QUALITY	3	2	3	1
STEERING/HANDLING	10	10	10	10
QUIETNESS	3	2	2	1
INSTRUMENTS/CONTROLS	6	6	6	6
ROOM/COMFORT (FRONT)	5	5	5	5
ROOM/COMFORT (REAR)	0	0	0	0
CARGO ROOM	6	6	3	3
VALUE	4	4	4	1

Not inexpensive, but if you like your sports cars big, bold, and brawny, there's no better high-performance value. The Z06, though, is best left to the racetrack.

TOTAL	51	49	46	42

Average total for sports cars: 41.3

ENGINES

	ohv V8	ohv V8
Size, liters/cu. in.	5.7/346	5.7/346
Horsepower @ rpm	350 @ 5600	405 @ 6000
Torque (lb-ft) @ rpm	375 @ 4400	400 @ 4800
Availability	S[1]	S[2]
EPA city/highway mpg		
6-speed manual	19/28	19/28
4-speed automatic	18/25	

1. Base models; torque is 360 @ 4000 w/automatic transmission. 2. Z06.

PRICES

Chevrolet Corvette — Retail Price / Dealer Invoice

	Retail Price	Dealer Invoice
Base 2-door hatchback	$41005	$35879
Base 2-door convertible	47530	41589

Prices are accurate at time of publication; subject to manufacturer's change.

CHEVROLET

	Retail Price	Dealer Invoice
Z06 2-door coupe	$49705	$43492
Destination charge	645	645

STANDARD EQUIPMENT

Base: 5.7-liter V8 350-horsepower engine, 4-speed automatic transmission, limited-slip differential, traction control, dual front airbags, antilock 4-wheel disc brakes, antiskid system, tire-pressure monitor, daytime running lights, air conditioning, power steering, tilt leather-wrapped steering wheel, cruise control, leather upholstery, bucket seats, 6-way power driver seat, center console, cupholders, heated power mirrors, power windows, power door locks, remote keyless entry, Bose AM/FM/CD player, digital clock, power antenna (convertible), tachometer, intermittent wipers, rear defogger, map lights, illuminated visor mirrors, remote decklid/hatchback release, floormats, theft-deterrent system, body-colored removable roof panel (hatchback), manually folding convertible top (convertible), extended-mobility tires, (245/45ZR17 front, 275/40ZR18 rear), alloy wheels.

Z06 adds: 5.7-liter V8 405-horsepower engine, 6-speed manual transmission, dual-zone automatic climate controls, head-up instrument display, Z06 suspension, 265/40ZR17 front tires, 295/35ZR18 rear tires. *Deletes:* tire-pressure monitor, removable roof panel, extended mobility tires.

OPTIONAL EQUIPMENT
Major Packages

1SB Preferred Equipment Group 1, hatchback	$1700	$1462
convertible	1800	1548

Dual-zone automatic climate control, sport bucket seats, 6-way power passenger seat, Memory System (driver seat, mirrors, climate control, radio), cargo cover and net (hatchback), automatic headlights (convertible), automatic day/night rearview and driver-side mirrors (convertible), fog lights.

1SC Preferred Equipment Group 2, hatchback	2700	2322
convertible	2600	2236

Preferred Equipment Group 1 plus power tilt/telescoping steering wheel w/memory, head-up instrument display, automatic headlights (hatchback), automatic day/night rearview and driver-side mirrors, (hatchback).

Memory Pkg., Z06	150	129

Memory System (driver seat, mirrors, climate control, radio). Requires automatic day/night rearview and driver-side mirrors.

Selective Real Time Dampening Suspenion, Base.	1695	1458

Adjustable ride control.

Specifications begin on page 551.

CHEVROLET

	Retail Price	Dealer Invoice
Z51 Performance Handling Pkg., Base....................	$350	$301

Stiffer springs and stabilizer bars. Automatic transmission requires performance axle ratio. NA w/Selective Real Time Dampening Suspension.

Powertrain
6-speed manual transmission, Base.......................	815	701

Includes performance axle ratio.

Performance axle ratio, Base.................................	300	258

Comfort & Convenience Features
AM/FM/cassette, Base (credit)...............................	(100)	(86)

Requires 12-disc CD changer.

12-disc CD changer, Base	600	516
Automatic day/night rearview and driver-side mirrors, Z06	120	103

Appearance and Miscellaneous
Corvette Museum Delivery.......................................	490	421

Includes tour of Corvette factory and museum, delivery of car in museum w/broadcast on Internet, plaque, door badges, one year Corvette Museum membership. In addition to normal delivery charge.

Transparent roof panel, hatchback..........................	750	645
Dual roof panels, hatchback....................................	1200	1032

Standard removable roof panel and transparent roof panel.

Polished alloy wheels, Base....................................	1200	1032

CHEVROLET IMPALA

Chevrolet Impala

Front-wheel-drive midsize car
Base price range: $19,960-$23,660. Built in Canada.
Also consider: Ford Taurus, Honda Accord, Toyota Camry

Prices are accurate at time of publication; subject to manufacturer's change.

CHEVROLET

FOR • Passenger and cargo room • Handling/roadholding • Instruments/controls **AGAINST** • Rear-seat comfort • Road noise

Impala plays the role of Chevrolet's "large" midsize sedan, while the smaller, lower-priced Malibu sells in greater volume. Impala offers base and LS versions with V6s of 3.4 or 3.8 liters, plus automatic transmission and 4-wheel disc brakes. The base Impala has a front bench seat and can be ordered with the LS's buckets. Also optional on the base and standard on LS are ABS, traction control, a side airbag for the driver, a tire-inflation monitor, and General Motors' OnStar assistance system. For 2002, the base model adds dual-zone climate controls and a cassette player as standard equipment. Impala shares its basic design with the Buick Century and Regal, the Oldsmobile Intrigue, and the Pontiac Grand Prix.

RATINGS

	Base, 3.4 V6	LS
ACCELERATION	5	6
FUEL ECONOMY	5	5
RIDE QUALITY	6	6
STEERING/HANDLING	6	6
QUIETNESS	6	6
INSTRUMENTS/CONTROLS	6	6
ROOM/COMFORT (FRONT)	6	6
ROOM/COMFORT (REAR)	5	5
CARGO ROOM	6	6
VALUE	7	6

An alternative to Ford Taurus, featuring comfort-oriented American style to Taurus's sportier influences. Impala leads in powertrain response, Taurus in safety features and rear-seat comfort. Discounts on this Chevy are available, but compromised refinement and low resale value are part of the deal.

TOTAL	58	58

Average total for midsize cars: 57.0

ENGINES

	ohv V6	ohv V6
Size, liters/cu. in.	3.4/205	3.8/231
Horsepower @ rpm	180 @ 5200	200 @ 5200
Torque (lb-ft) @ rpm	205 @ 4000	225 @ 4000
Availability	S[1]	S[2]

EPA city/highway mpg
4-speed automatic	21/32	19/29

1. Base. 2. LS; optional, Base.

PRICES

Chevrolet Impala

	Retail Price	Dealer Invoice
Base 4-door sedan	$19960	$18263

Specifications begin on page 551.

CHEVROLET

	Retail Price	Dealer Invoice
LS 4-door sedan	$23660	$21649
Destination charge	610	610

STANDARD EQUIPMENT
Base: 3.4-liter V6 engine, 4-speed automatic transmission, dual front airbags, 4-wheel disc brakes, daytime running lights, emergency inside trunk release, air conditioning w/manual dual-zone climate controls, power steering, tilt steering wheel, cloth upholstery, front split bench seat, cupholders, overhead console, power mirrors, power windows, power door locks, AM/FM/cassette, digital clock, rear defogger, variable intermittent wipers, map lights, visor mirrors, power remote decklid release, automatic headlights, floormats, theft-deterrent system, 225/60R16 tires, wheel covers.

LS adds: 3.8-liter V6 engine, traction control, driver-side side airbag, antilock brakes, tire-pressure monitor, OnStar System w/one year service (roadside assistance, emergency services; other services available), interior air filter, cruise control, leather-wrapped steering wheel, front bucket seats, 6-way power driver seat, center console, split folding rear seat, overhead console w/storage, heated power mirrors, remote keyless entry, tachometer, automatic day/night rearview mirror, illuminated visor mirrors, rear spoiler, fog lights, Sport Touring Suspension, tire inflation monitor, 225/60R16 touring tires, alloy wheels.

OPTIONAL EQUIPMENT
Major Packages

1SB Preferred Equipment Group 1, Base	980	872

Cruise control, remote keyless entry, AM/FM/CD player, overhead console w/storage, illuminated visor mirrors, cargo net.

1SC Preferred Equipment Group 2, Base	1989	1770

Preferred Equipment Group 1 plus OnStar System w/one year service (roadside assistance, emergency services; other services available), leather-wrapped steering-wheel w/radio controls, automatic day/night rearview mirror, alloy wheels.

1SB Preferred Equipment Group 1, LS	580	516

Steering-wheel radio controls, AM/FM/CD player, Driver Information/Convenience Center (trip computer, compass, outside temperature indicator, universal garage door opener, theft-deterrent system w/alarm).

Custom Cloth Trim, Base	785	699

Driver-side side airbag, 6-way power driver seat, split folding rear seat. Requires Preferred Equipment Group.

Custom Cloth Seat Trim w/bucket seats, Base	835	743

Custom Cloth Seat Trim plus front bucket seats, center console. Requires Preferred Equipment Group.

Prices are accurate at time of publication; subject to manufacturer's change.

CHEVROLET

	Retail Price	Dealer Invoice
Leather Seat Trim, Base	$1390	$1237

Custom Cloth Seat Trim w/bucket seats plus leather upholstery. Requires Preferred Equipment Group, steering-wheel radio controls.

Comfort Seating Pkg.	445	396

Heated front seats, 6-way power passenger seat. Requires Leather Seat Trim. Base requires Preferred Equipment Group.

Powertrain

3.8-liter V6 engine, Base	995	886

Includes traction control, antilock brakes, tire-pressure monitor, Sport Touring Suspension. Requires Preferred Equipment Group, 225/60R16 touring tires, alloy wheels.

Safety

Antilock brakes, Base	600	534

Includes tire inflation monitor.

Comfort & Convenience Features

Power sunroof	795	708

Base requires Preferred Equipment Group.

Driver Information/Convenience Center, Base	295	262

Trip computer, compass, outside temperature indicator, universal garage door opener, theft-deterrent system w/alarm. Requires Preferred Equipment Group, antilock brakes.

6-way power driver seat, Base	325	289
6-way power passenger seat	325	289

Base requires Custom Cloth Trim. Base NA w/bucket seats.

Leather Seat Trim, LS	835	743
LS w/split bench seat	625	556
AM/FM/CD player	345	307

Includes premium speakers.

AM/FM/cassette/CD player, LS	445	396
Base, LS w/Preferred Equipment Group	100	89

Includes premium speakers. Base requires Preferred Equipment Group.

Steering-wheel radio controls, Base	195	173

Includes leather-wrapped steering wheel. Requires Preferred Equipment Group 1.

Appearance and Miscellaneous

Alloy wheels, Base	350	312

Requires Preferred Equipment Group 1.

225/60R16 touring tires, Base	45	40

Requires 3.8-liter engine.

Specifications begin on page 551.

CHEVROLET

CHEVROLET MALIBU

Chevrolet Malibu

Front-wheel-drive midsize car
Base price range: $17,535-$19,740. Built in USA.
Also consider: Honda Accord, Nissan Altima, Toyota Camry

FOR • Ride • Build quality **AGAINST** • Steering feel

The smaller of Chevrolet's two midsize sedans slots below Impala in size, price, and market position. Malibu offers base and LS models, both with a V6, automatic transmission, and ABS. Impala can seat six; Malibu has front bucket seats for 5-passenger capacity. For 2002, a CD player and floormats are standard on the base model.

RATINGS

	Base/LS
ACCELERATION	5
FUEL ECONOMY	5
RIDE QUALITY	6
STEERING/HANDLING	6
QUIETNESS	6
INSTRUMENTS/CONTROLS	7
ROOM/COMFORT (FRONT)	5
ROOM/COMFORT (REAR)	4
CARGO ROOM	6
VALUE	8

It's no cut-rate Camry, but Malibu delivers a fine blend of utility, driving ease, and features at an attractive price.

TOTAL	**58**

Average total for midsize cars: 57.0

ENGINES

	ohv V6
Size, liters/cu. in.	3.1/191
Horsepower @ rpm	170 @ 5200

Prices are accurate at time of publication; subject to manufacturer's change.

CHEVROLET

	ohv V6
Torque (lb-ft) @ rpm	190 @ 4000
Availability	S

EPA city/highway mpg
4-speed automatic	20/29

PRICES

Chevrolet Malibu	Retail Price	Dealer Invoice
Base 4-door sedan	$17535	$16045
LS 4-door sedan	19740	18062
Destination charge	585	585

STANDARD EQUIPMENT

Base: 3.1-liter V6 engine, 4-speed automatic transmission, dual front airbags, antilock brakes, daytime running lights, air conditioning, power steering, tilt steering wheel, cloth upholstery, front bucket seats, center console, cupholders, power door locks, AM/FM/CD player, digital clock, tachometer, variable intermittent wipers, rear defogger, visor mirrors, remote decklid release, automatic headlights, floormats, theft-deterrent system, 215/60R15 tires, wheel covers.

LS adds: cruise control, 6-way power driver seat, split folding rear seat, power mirrors, power windows, remote keyless entry, upgraded sound system, passenger-side illuminated visor mirror, map lights, fog lights, alloy wheels.

OPTIONAL EQUIPMENT

Major Packages

1SB Preferred Equipment Group 1, Base	995	896
Power windows, power mirrors, remote keyless entry, cruise control, map lights.		
1SB Preferred Equipment Group 1, LS	1365	1229
Leather upholstery, power sunroof, rear spoiler.		

Comfort & Convenience Features

Cruise control, Base	240	216
Power sunroof, LS	695	626
Split folding rear seat, Base	195	176
Includes cargo net. Requires Preferred Equipment Group 1.		
Leather upholstery, LS	595	536
Includes leather-wrapped steering wheel.		
AM/FM/cassette/CD player	150	135
Base requires Preferred Equipment Group 1.		

Appearance and Miscellaneous

Rear spoiler, LS	175	158

Specifications begin on page 551.

CHEVROLET

	Retail Price	Dealer Invoice
Alloy wheels, Base	$375	$338

Requires Preferred Equipment Group 1.

CHEVROLET MONTE CARLO

Chevrolet Monte Carlo

Front-wheel-drive midsize car

Base price range: $20,060-$22,860. Built in USA.

Also consider: Dodge Stratus coupe, Honda Accord coupe, Toyota Solara

FOR • Acceleration (SS) • Steering/handling (SS) • Instruments/controls **AGAINST** • Engine noise • Road noise • Rear-seat entry/exit

A coupe based on Chevrolet's Impala sedan, Monte Carlo has front bucket seats for 5-passenger capacity. The LS model uses a 3.4-liter V6, the sporty SS a 3.8-liter V6; both come with automatic transmission only. SS has firmer suspension settings, a standard side airbag for the driver, and General Motors' OnStar assistance system; the last is optional on LS. Antilock 4-wheel disc brakes, traction control, and tire-inflation monitor are standard on both. Dual-zone climate controls and a rear-seat center shoulder belt are newly standard for 2002.

RATINGS	LS	SS
ACCELERATION	5	6
FUEL ECONOMY	5	5
RIDE QUALITY	6	6
STEERING/HANDLING	6	7
QUIETNESS	6	6
INSTRUMENTS/CONTROLS	6	6
ROOM/COMFORT (FRONT)	6	6
ROOM/COMFORT (REAR)	3	3

Prices are accurate at time of publication; subject to manufacturer's change.

CHEVROLET

	LS	SS
CARGO ROOM	4	4
VALUE	4	4

Monte Carlo beats most like-priced coupes on a features-per-dollar basis. It's not as polished as Japanese-brand rivals and won't hold its value as well, but this Chevy has its own American-car character.

TOTAL	51	53

Average total for midsize cars: 57.0

ENGINES

	ohv V6	ohv V6
Size, liters/cu. in.	3.4/205	3.8/231
Horsepower @ rpm	180 @ 5200	200 @ 5200
Torque (lb-ft) @ rpm	205 @ 4000	225 @ 4000
Availability	S[1]	S[2]
EPA city/highway mpg		
4-speed automatic	21/32	19/29

1. LS. 2. SS.

PRICES

Chevrolet Monte Carlo	Retail Price	Dealer Invoice
LS 2-door coupe	$20060	$18355
SS 2-door coupe	22860	20917
Destination charge	610	610

STANDARD EQUIPMENT

LS: 3.4-liter V6 engine, 4-speed automatic transmission, traction control, dual front airbags, antilock 4-wheel disc brakes, daytime running lights, emergency inside trunk release, air conditioning w/dual-zone manual climate controls, power steering, tilt steering wheel, cloth upholstery, front bucket seats, center console, cupholders, split folding rear seat, overhead console, AM/FM/cassette, digital clock, tachometer, tire inflation monitor, power mirrors, power windows, power door locks, rear defogger, variable intermittent wipers, power decklid release, map lights, automatic headlights, visor mirrors, floormats, theft-deterrent system, 225/60R16 tires, wheel covers.

SS adds: 3.8-liter engine, driver-side side airbag, OnStar System w/one year service (roadside assistance, emergency services; other services available), driver seat lumbar adjustment, interior air filter, cruise control, leather-wrapped steering wheel w/radio controls, remote keyless entry, automatic day/night rearview mirror, illuminated visor mirrors, fog lights, rear spoiler, sport suspension, 225/60SR16 performance tires, alloy wheels.

Specifications begin on page 551.

CHEVROLET

OPTIONAL EQUIPMENT

	Retail Price	Dealer Invoice

Major Packages

1SB Preferred Equipment Group 1, LS.................. $815 $725
Cruise control, remote keyless entry, cargo net, alloy wheels.

1SC Preferred Equipment Group 2, LS 1275 1135
Preferred Equipment Group 1 plus 6-way power driver seat, heated power mirrors, illuminated visor mirrors.

Sport Appearance Pkg., LS.. 615 547
Rear spoiler, special alloy wheels. Requires Preferred Equipment Group.

1SB Preferred Equipment 1, SS..................................... 660 587
Heated power mirrors, 6-way power driver seat, Driver Information/Convenience Center (includes trip computer, compass, outside temperature indicator, universal garage door opener, theft-deterrent system w/alarm).

High Sport Appearance Pkg., SS 2100 1869
Ground effects body cladding, special rear spoiler, stainless steel exhaust tips, badging, special alloy wheels.

Comfort & Convenience Features

Driver Information/Convenience Center, LS 295 263
Trip computer, compass, outside temperature indicator, universal garage door opener, theft-deterrent system w/alarm. Requires Preferred Equipment Group.

AM/FM/CD player 345 307
Includes 6-speaker sound system, Radio Display System.

AM/FM/cassette/CD player 445 396
Includes Radio Display System and 6-speaker sound system.

Steering wheel radio controls, LS 195 174
Includes leather-wrapped steering wheel. Requires Preferred Equipment Group.

Leather upholstery, LS... 770 686
SS 625 556
LS includes driver-side side airbag. Requires power driver seat.

Heated front seats.. 120 107
Requires leather upholstery, power driver and passenger seats.

6-way power driver seat 325 289
6-way power passenger seat 325 289
Requires leather upholstery, 6-way power driver seat, heated front seats.

Power sunroof 795 708
LS requires Preferred Equipment Group.

Appearance and Miscellaneous

Alloy wheels, LS 350 312

Prices are accurate at time of publication; subject to manufacturer's change.

CHEVROLET

CHEVROLET PRIZM

Chevrolet Prizm

Front-wheel-drive subcompact car
Base price range: $14,330-$16,395. Built in USA.
Also consider: Ford Focus, Honda Civic, Mazda Protege

FOR • Fuel economy   **AGAINST** • Rear-seat room
• Automatic transmission performance

Prizm is unchanged for 2002, its final model year. This sedan is a slightly retrimmed version of the 1998-2002 Toyota Corolla, but will not carry over to the redesigned 2003 Corolla model. It uses a Toyota-designed 4-cyl engine. Manual transmission is standard, 3- and 4-speed automatics are optional. Air conditioning is standard. ABS and front side airbags are optional. An integrated rear child safety seat is optional on the uplevel LSi model.

RATINGS

	Base, man.	LSi, auto.
ACCELERATION	4	4
FUEL ECONOMY	8	7
RIDE QUALITY	4	4
STEERING/HANDLING	4	5
QUIETNESS	4	4
INSTRUMENTS/CONTROLS	7	7
ROOM/COMFORT (FRONT)	4	4
ROOM/COMFORT (REAR)	2	2
CARGO ROOM	2	2
VALUE	4	4

Performance is conservative and rear-seat space is tight, even for a subcompact. But fuel economy is good, and overall, the solid and reliable Prizm makes fine use of its Toyota genes. Corolla always outsold Prizm, and now more than ever, Chevy dealers are likely to be discounting their lame-duck small sedan.

Specifications begin on page 551.

CHEVROLET

	Base, man.	LSi, auto.
TOTAL	43	43

Average total for subcompact cars: 43.7

ENGINES

	dohc I4
Size, liters/cu. in.	1.8/110
Horsepower @ rpm	125 @ 5800
Torque (lb-ft) @ rpm	125 @ 4000
Availability	S

EPA city/highway mpg

5-speed manual	32/41
3-speed automatic	29/33

PRICES

Chevrolet Prizm	Retail Price	Dealer Invoice
Base 4-door sedan	$14330	$13642
LSi 4-door sedan	16395	15116
Destination charge	485	485

STANDARD EQUIPMENT

Base: 1.8-liter dohc 4-cylinder engine, 5-speed manual transmission, dual front airbags, daytime running lights, emergency inside trunk release, air conditioning, power steering, cloth upholstery, front bucket seats, center console, cupholders, AM/FM radio, digital clock, variable intermittent wipers, visor mirrors, remote fuel door/decklid release, automatic headlights, floormats, 175/65R14 tires, wheel covers.

LSi adds: cruise control, tilt steering wheel, split folding rear seat w/trunk pass-through, power mirrors, power windows, power door locks, remote keyless entry, AM/FM/cassette, tachometer, outside temperature indicator, rear window defogger, map lights, 185/65R14 tires.

OPTIONAL EQUIPMENT
Major Packages

Preferred Equipment Group 2, Base	570	490

Cruise control, power door locks, AM/FM/cassette.

Powertrain

3-speed automatic transmission	495	426
4-speed automatic transmission	800	688

Safety

Antilock brakes	645	555

Prices are accurate at time of publication; subject to manufacturer's change.

CHEVROLET

	Retail Price	Dealer Invoice
Front side airbags	$295	$254
Integrated child safety seat, LSi	125	108

Comfort & Convenience Features
Power sunroof, Base	675	581
LSi	655	563
Tilt steering wheel, Base	80	69
Power windows, Base	300	258
Rear defogger, Base	180	158
AM/FM/CD player, Base	215	185
Base w/Preferred Group 2, LSi	50	43

Appearance and Miscellaneous
Alloy wheels	283	243

CHEVROLET TAHOE AND SUBURBAN

CG BEST BUY AUTO

Chevrolet Tahoe LS 4WD

Rear- or 4-wheel-drive full-size sport-utility vehicle

Base price range: $32,489-$39,686. Built in Canada.

Also consider: Ford Expedition and Excursion, Toyota Land Cruiser and Sequoia

FOR • Passenger and cargo room • Towing ability **AGAINST** • Rear-seat entry/exit (Tahoe) • Fuel economy

Tahoe and Suburban come standard with a host of previously optional equipment for 2002, triggering base-price increases up to $9177. Most features of last year's LS package are now standard, including air conditioning, power windows, power front seats, heated power mirrors, rear climate controls, CD player, and alloy wheels.

Specifications begin on page 551.

CHEVROLET

Leather upholstery is again optional as part of the LS package. Base-price increases range from $7423 for the 2WD Tahoe to $9177 for the 2WD Suburban 1500.

Tahoe shares its design with the GMC Denali and Yukon and the Cadillac Escalade. The longer Suburban is kin to XL versions of Denali and Yukon. Tahoe comes in the half-ton 1500 series, Suburban in 1500 and three-quarter-ton 2500 models. Both offer swing-open rear cargo doors or a liftgate with separate-opening glass. All have V8s, ranging from a 275-hp 4.8 liter to the 340-hp 8.1 optional on 2500 Suburbans. Standard are automatic transmission with Tow/Haul mode, antilock 4-wheel disc brakes, and front side airbags. Available are rear load leveling and General Motors' OnStar assistance system. Tahoe and Suburban offer rear-wheel drive or GM's Autotrac 4WD that can be left engaged on dry pavement and includes low-range gearing. Traction control is optional for 2WD models. Third-row bench seats (standard on Suburban, optional on Tahoe) create 9-passenger seating. The 4WD Z71 package adds special wheel flares, body trim, and shock absorbers, plus 17-inch wheels in place of 16s.

RATINGS	Tahoe LS 2WD, 4.8 V8	Tahoe LT 4WD, 5.3 V8	Suburban LT 4WD, 5.3 V8
ACCELERATION	4	5	4
FUEL ECONOMY	3	2	2
RIDE QUALITY	6	6	6
STEERING/HANDLING	3	3	3
QUIETNESS	6	6	6
INSTRUMENTS/CONTROLS	7	7	7
ROOM/COMFORT (FRONT)	9	9	9
ROOM/COMFORT (REAR)	8	8	8
CARGO ROOM	9	9	9
VALUE	4	6	4

Capable, comfortable, competitively priced, GM's full-size SUVs fit nicely into size gaps between Expedition and Excursion, and beat Toyota Sequoia in payload and towing capacity. The GMC models already came with most of the items now standard on their Chevy counterparts. And while only the Chevys get the big base-price hikes, most Tahoe and Suburban buyers opted for the LS package anyway, tempering the increases somewhat. Overall, the Tahoe and Suburban are the top values in this GM family and are Best Buys.

TOTAL	59	61	58

Average total for full-size sport-utility vehicles: 50.9

ENGINES	ohv V8	ohv V8	ohv V8	ohv V8
Size, liters/cu. in.	4.8/294	5.3/327	6.0/364	8.1/496
Horsepower @ rpm	275 @	285 @	320 @	340 @

Prices are accurate at time of publication; subject to manufacturer's change.

CHEVROLET

	ohv V8	ohv V8	ohv V8	ohv V8
	5200	5200	5000	4200
Torque (lb-ft) @ rpm	290 @ 4000	325 @ 4000	360 @ 4000	455 @ 3200
Availability	S[1]	S[2]	S[3]	O[3]
EPA city/highway mpg				
4-speed automatic	14/17[4]	13/17[5]	NA	NA

1. Tahoe LS. 2. Tahoe LT, Suburban 1500; optional Tahoe LS. 3. Suburban 2500. 4. 15/19 w/2WD. 5. 14/18 w/2WD.

PRICES

Chevrolet Tahoe and Suburban

	Retail Price	Dealer Invoice
Tahoe 4-door wagon, 2WD	$32489	$28428
Tahoe 4-door wagon, 4WD	35255	30848
Suburban 1500 4-door wagon, 2WD	35223	30820
Suburban 2500 4-door wagon, 2WD	36836	32232
Suburban 1500 4-door wagon, 4WD	37989	33240
Suburban 2500 4-door wagon, 4WD	39686	34725
Destination charge: Tahoe	730	730
Destination charge: Suburban	765	765

STANDARD EQUIPMENT

Tahoe: 4.8-liter V8 engine, 4-speed automatic transmission, dual front airbags, front side airbags, antilock 4-wheel disc brakes, power steering, air conditioning, front and rear manual climate controls, tilt leather-wrapped steering wheel, cruise control, cloth upholstery, front split bench seat w/lumbar adjustment, 6-way power front seats, second-row split folding bench seat, cupholders, heated power mirrors w/driver-side automatic day/night, power windows, power door locks, remote keyless entry, AM/FM/CD player, digital clock, tachometer, engine hour meter, overhead console, intermittent wipers, automatic day/night rearview mirror, compass, outside temperature indicator, universal garage door opener, illuminated visor mirrors, rear defogger, cargo cover, carpeting, floormats, theft-deterrent system, rear cargo doors, rear privacy glass, roof rack, fog lights, 7-lead trailer harness, full-size spare tire, P265/70R16 tires, alloy wheels. **4WD** models add: 4-wheel drive, 2-speed transfer case, variable-assist power steering, front tow hooks.

Suburban adds: 5.3-liter V8 engine (1500), 6.0-liter V8 engine (2500), third-row bench seat, LT245/75R16E tires (2500). **4WD** models add: 4-wheel drive, 2-speed transfer case, limited-slip rear differential, variable-assist power steering (1500), wheel flares (2500), front tow hooks.

Specifications begin on page 551.

CHEVROLET

OPTIONAL EQUIPMENT
Major Packages

	Retail Price	Dealer Invoice
LS Preferred Equipment Group 1SK, Tahoe	$2320	$1995
Suburban	1620	1393

5.3-liter V8 engine (Tahoe), leather upholstery, front bucket seats, center console, AM/FM/cassette/CD player, rear radio controls.

LT Preferred Equipment Group 1SM, Tahoe	3421	2942
Suburban	2996	2577

Preferred Equipment Group 1SK plus OnStar System w/one year service (roadside assistance, emergency services; other services available), heated 8-way power front seats, driver seat memory, automatic climate control.

LT Preferred Equipment Group 1SN, 2WD Tahoe	5806	4993
4WD Tahoe	5321	4576

Preferred Equipment Group 1SM plus traction control (2WD), limited-slip rear differential (2WD), third row split folding seat, rear heater, liftgate/liftglass rear door, rear wiper/washer, variable rate shock absorbers, load-leveling rear suspension, front tow hooks (2WD).

LT Preferred Equipment Group 1SN,		
2WD Suburban 1500	5361	4610
4WD Suburban 1500	4896	4193

Preferred Equipment Group 1SM plus traction control (2WD), limited-slip rear differential (2WD), center row bucket seats, liftgate/liftglass rear door, rear wiper/washer, variable rate shock absorbers, load-levelling rear suspension, front tow hooks (2WD).

Z71 Off-Road Equipment Group 1SL, 4WD Tahoe	3126	2688
4WD Suburban 1500	2631	2263

Preferred Equipment Group 1SK plus OnStar System w/one year service (roadside assistance, emergency services; other services available), limited-slip rear differential (Tahoe), tubular side steps, lower bodyside moldings, wheel flares, color-keyed grille, bumpers, door handles and mirrors, skid plates, Trailer Pkg., special shock absorbers, P265/70R17 on-off road tires. NA w/Third Seat Pkg.

Third Row Seat Pkg., Tahoe	360	310
Tahoe w/Preferred Equipment Group	760	654

Split folding third row seat, rear heater, liftgate/liftglass rear door, rear wiper/washer, Premium Ride Suspension.

Traction Pkg., 2WD	485	417

Traction control, limited-slip rear differential, cruise control, front tow hooks. NA w/8.1-liter V8 engine.

Snow Plow Prep Pkg., 4WD Suburban 2500	253	218

Instrument panel switch, roof beacon and forward light wiring, heavy-duty front springs. NA w/8.1-liter V8 engine, Autoride Suspension, power sunroof.

Prices are accurate at time of publication; subject to manufacturer's change.

CONSUMER GUIDE®

CHEVROLET

	Retail Price	Dealer Invoice
Trailer Pkg., Tahoe, Suburban 1500	$260	$224
Suburban 2500	164	141

Trailer hitch platform, transmission oil cooler, trailer brake wiring harness. Requires special axle ratio w/4.8-liter V8 engine.

Powertrain
8.1-liter V8 engine, Suburban 2500	700	602

Comfort & Convenience Features
OnStar System, Tahoe, Suburban 1500	695	598

OnStar System w/one year service (roadside assistance, emergency services; other services available)

Power sunroof, w/1SK or 1SL	988	850
w/1SM or 1SN	938	807

Deletes rear climate controls.

Second row bucket seats, Suburban	490	421

Requires Preferred Equipment Group.

Rear liftgate/liftglass	250	215

Includes rear wiper/washer. Requires LS or LT Group.

Appearance and Miscellaneous
Wheel-flares	180	155

Std. 4WD Suburban 2500.

Special Purpose, Wheels and Tires
Autoride Suspension, Tahoe, Suburban 1500	875	753
Suburban 2500	925	796

Includes variable rate shock absorbers, load-leveling rear suspension. Tahoe, Suburban 1500 require Preferred Equipment Group 1SM.

Skid Plate Pkg., 4WD	95	82
P265/70R16 white-letter tires, Tahoe, Suburban 1500	125	108

NA w/Preferred Equipment Group 1SL.

CHEVROLET TRACKER

Rear- or 4-wheel-drive compact sport-utility vehicle

Base price range: $15,865-$21,700. Built in Canada.

Also consider: Honda CR-V, Subaru Forester, Toyota RAV4

FOR • Maneuverability • Cargo room **AGAINST** • Ride • Steering/handling • Rear-seat room • Rear visibility • Acceleration • Rear-seat entry/exit (2-dr)

Tracker offers a 2-dr convertible and a longer 4-dr wagon. Both

Specifications begin on page 551.

CHEVROLET

Chevrolet Tracker 4-door wagon

have body-on-frame construction and are designed by Suzuki, which markets its own versions as the Vitara. Tracker is available with rear-wheel drive or with 4WD that must be disengaged on dry pavement but includes low-range gearing. A 4-cyl engine is offered in both bodies. A V6 is standard in ZR2- and top-line LT-model wagons. Automatic transmission is standard with the V6, optional with the 4-cyl in place of a 5-speed manual. For 2002, a CD player is standard, wagons get a standard roof rack, and ZR2s join the LT in offering optional leather upholstery.

RATINGS	Base conv 2WD, man.	LT 4WD
ACCELERATION	2	3
FUEL ECONOMY	5	4
RIDE QUALITY	1	2
STEERING/HANDLING	2	2
QUIETNESS	1	2
INSTRUMENTS/CONTROLS	3	3
ROOM/COMFORT (FRONT)	3	3
ROOM/COMFORT (REAR)	2	3
CARGO ROOM	6	6
VALUE	2	2

They have some off-road prowess going for them, but Tracker and Vitara are also-rans among compact SUVs in the kind of driving most people do. Rivals from Ford, Mazda, Honda, Subaru, and Toyota are more pleasant, roomier, and have higher resale values.

TOTAL	27	30

Average total for compact sport-utility vehicles: 44.4

ENGINES	dohc I4	dohc V6
Size, liters/cu. in.	2.0/121	2.5/152
Horsepower @ rpm	127 @ 6000	155 @ 6500
Torque (lb-ft) @ rpm	134 @ 3000	160 @ 4000
Availability	S[1]	S[2]

Prices are accurate at time of publication; subject to manufacturer's change.

CHEVROLET

EPA city/highway mpg

	dohc I4	dohc V6
5-speed manual	23/25[3]	
4-speed automatic	22/25[3]	18/20[4]

1. Base, ZR2 conv. 2. ZR2 wagon, LT. 3. 23/26 w/2WD. 4. 19/21 w/2WD.

PRICES

Chevrolet Tracker

	Retail Price	Dealer Invoice
Base 2-door convertible, 2WD	$15865	$14945
Base 4-door wagon, 2WD	16555	15595
LT 4-door wagon, 2WD	20600	19405
Base 2-door convertible, 4WD	16965	15981
Base 4-door wagon, 4WD	17655	16631
ZR2 2-door convertible, 4WD	18835	17743
ZR2 4-door wagon, 4WD	21270	20036
LT 4-door wagon, 4WD	21700	20441
Destination charge	450	450

STANDARD EQUIPMENT

Base: 2.0-liter dohc 4-cylinder engine, 5-speed manual transmission, dual front airbags, daytime running lights, air conditioning, power steering, cloth/vinyl upholstery, front bucket seats, center console, cupholders, split folding rear seat (wagon), folding rear seat (convertible), AM/FM/CD player, digital clock, tachometer, variable intermittent wipers, passenger-side visor mirror, map lights, rear defogger (wagon), rear wiper/washer (wagon), automatic headlights, cargo cover (wagon), floormats, roof rack (wagon), skid plate, front and rear tow hooks, outside-mounted full-size spare tire, 195/75R15 tires. **4WD adds:** 4-wheel drive, 2-speed transfer case, 205/75R15 tires.

ZR2 convertible adds: 4-wheel drive, 2-speed transfer case, tilt steering wheel, cruise control, cloth upholstery, power mirrors, power windows, power door locks, remote keyless entry, wheel flares, 215/75R15 white-letter tires, alloy wheels.

ZR2 wagon adds: 2.5-liter dohc V6 engine, 4-speed automatic transmission.

LT adds to Base: 2.5-liter dohc V6 engine, 4-speed automatic transmission, tilt steering wheel, cruise control, cloth upholstery, power mirrors, power windows, power door locks, remote keyless entry, 215/70R15 tires, alloy wheels. **4WD adds:** 4-wheel drive, 2-speed transfer case.

OPTIONAL EQUIPMENT
Major Packages

Preferred Equipment Group 2, Base convertible	$1470	$1308

Specifications begin on page 551.

CHEVROLET

	Retail Price	Dealer Invoice
Base wagon	$1415	$1259

Power mirrors, power windows and door locks, remote keyless entry, cruise control, tilt steering wheel, cargo storage compartment (convertible), alloy wheels.

Powertrain
4-speed automatic transmission, Base, ZR2 convertible	1000	890

Safety
Antilock brakes	595	530

Comfort & Convenience Features
Leather upholstery, ZR2, LT	595	530
Lockable storage compartment, Base convertible	125	111

Special Purpose, Wheels and Tires
Alloy wheels, Base	365	325

CHEVROLET TRAILBLAZER

Chevrolet TrailBlazer LT

Rear- or 4-wheel-drive midsize sport-utility vehicle
Base price range: $25,305-$33,965. Built in USA.
Also consider: Dodge Durango, Ford Explorer, Toyota 4Runner

FOR • Passenger and cargo room • Towing ability	**AGAINST** • Steering/handling • Fuel economy

Chevrolet's all-new midsize SUV shares its design, powertrain, and new body-on-frame platform with the '02 Oldsmobile Bravada and GMC Envoy. Each is a 4-dr wagon with its own styling details

Prices are accurate at time of publication; subject to manufacturer's change.

CHEVROLET

inside and out, and is larger than the model it replaces. TrailBlazer's wheelbase is 6 inches longer than the 1995-vintage Blazer's, and its body is longer by 10 inches, wider and taller by 5. It's bigger inside, too, though seating is limited to five. To match rivals with 3rd-row seating, a longer-wheelbase 7-passenger TrailBlazer is planned for sometime in calendar '02 as a 2003 model. These redesigned General Motors SUVs share a new 270-hp inline 6-cyl engine linked to a 4-speed automatic transmission. Offered is rear-wheel drive with available traction control or GM's Autotrac 4WD that can be left engaged on dry pavement and includes low-range gearing. Standard are antilock 4-wheel disc brakes and front side airbags (the driver's bag covers head and torso). LTZ models have 17-inch wheels, other TrailBlazers get 16s. Note that the 1995-vintage Blazer continues, repositioned as budget SUV.

RATINGS

	LT/LTZ 4WD
ACCELERATION	6
FUEL ECONOMY	4
RIDE QUALITY	5
STEERING/HANDLING	3
QUIETNESS	4
INSTRUMENTS/CONTROLS	7
ROOM/COMFORT (FRONT)	7
ROOM/COMFORT (REAR)	6
CARGO ROOM	8
VALUE	4

Lack of 3rd-row seating and curtain side airbags are shortfalls in today's midsize SUV environment—though the elongated TrailBlazer and Envoy due within the year will seat seven. GM's newest match any rival in terms of powertrain and roominess, but we judge Envoy as a better value than its Chevy and Olds siblings. It has the best interior design details, but more important, offers the rear air suspension, which firms up road manners and avoids the sloppy ride and handling you're stuck with on the TrailBlazer. The demise of the Olds brand makes the costly-to-begin-with Bravada the least-sound investment.

TOTAL	54

Average total for midsize sport-utility vehicles: 49.6

ENGINES

	dohc I6
Size, liters/cu. in.	4.2/256
Horsepower @ rpm	270 @ 6000
Torque (lb-ft) @ rpm	275 @ 3600
Availability	S
EPA city/highway mpg	
4-speed automatic	15/21[1]

1. 16/22 w/2WD.

Specifications begin on page 551.

CHEVROLET

PRICES

Chevrolet TrailBlazer	Retail Price	Dealer Invoice
LS 4-door wagon, 2WD	$25305	$22901
LS 4-door wagon, 4WD	27530	24915
LT 4-door wagon, 2WD	28665	25942
LT 4-door wagon, 4WD	30890	27955
LTZ 4-door wagon, 2WD	31740	28725
LTZ 4-door wagon, 4WD	33965	30738
Destination charge	600	600

STANDARD EQUIPMENT

LS: 4.2-liter dohc 6-cylinder engine, 4-speed automatic transmission, dual front airbags, front side airbags, antilock 4-wheel disc brakes, daytime running lights, air conditioning w/dual-zone manual controls, power steering, tilt steering wheel, cloth upholstery, front bucket seats w/lumbar adjustment, center console, cupholders, split folding rear seat, power windows, power door locks, AM/FM/CD player, digital clock, tachometer, variable intermittent wipers, power rear window release, rear intermittent wiper/washer, visor mirrors, map lights, automatic headlights, theft-deterrent system, rear liftgate, roof rack, platform hitch, 7-wire trailer harness, full-size spare tire, 245/70R16 tires, alloy wheels. **4WD** adds: 4-wheel drive, 2-speed transfer case, front tow hooks.

LT adds: OnStar System w/one year service (roadside assistance, emergency services; other services available), leather-wrapped steering wheel, cruise control, 8-way power driver seat, heated power mirrors, remote keyless entry, rear defogger, automatic day/night rearview mirror, compass, outside temperature indicator, overhead console, universal garage door opener, digital memo recorder, illuminated visor mirrors, cargo cover, floormats, rear privacy glass, fog lights. **4WD** adds: 4-wheel drive, 2-speed transfer case, front tow hooks.

LTZ adds: leather upholstery, 8-way power passenger seat, driver seat and mirror memory, dual-zone automatic climate control, steering wheel radio and climate controls, rear climate controls, AM/FM/cassette/CD player, rear radio controls, outside-mirror mounted turn signal lights, outside-mirror reverse tilt-down and driver-side automatic day/night, 245/65R17 on-off road tires. **4WD** adds: 4-wheel drive, 2-speed transfer case, front tow hooks.

OPTIONAL EQUIPMENT
Major Packages

Preferred Equipment Group 1SB, LS	880	757

Cruise control, heated power mirrors, rear defogger, floormats, rear privacy glass, bodyside moldings.

Prices are accurate at time of publication; subject to manufacturer's change.
CONSUMER GUIDE®

CHEVROLET

	Retail Price	Dealer Invoice
Preferred Equipment Group 1SC, LS	$1180	$1015

Preferred Equipment Group 1SB plus leather-wrapped steering wheel, remote keyless entry, cargo cover, theft-deterrent system w/alarm.

Preferred Equipment Group 1SE, LT	1860	1600

Leather upholstery, 8-way power passenger seat, dual-zone automatic climate controls, rear climate controls, steering wheel radio and climate controls, rear radio controls, driver message center.

Driver Convenience Pkg., LT	585	503

Dual-zone automatic climate controls, rear climate controls, steering wheel radio and climate controls, rear radio controls, driver message center.

Powertrain

Traction control, 2WD LT, 2WD LTZ	195	168

Requires locking rear differential.

Locking rear differential	270	232

Comfort & Convenience Features

OnStar System, LS	965	830

Includes one year service (roadside assistance, emergency services; other services available), overhead console, universal garage door opener, digital memo recorder, automatic day/night rearview mirror, compass, outside temperature indicator, illuminated visor mirrors.

Rear Seat Entertainment System, LT, LTZ	995	856

DVD player, screen, headphones. NA w/power sunroof.

Power sunroof	800	688

LS requires OnStar System.

AM/FM/cassette/CD player, LS	100	86
AM/FM radio w/in-dash 6-disc CD changer, LT	395	340
LTZ	295	254
Bose sound system, LT, LTZ	495	426

Requires AM/FM/cassette/CD player or AM/FM radio w/in-dash 6-disc CD changer.

Rear defogger, LS	197	169
Heated front seats, LTZ	250	215

Appearance and Miscellaneous

Running boards, LT, LTZ	325	280

Special Purpose, Wheels and Tires

Skid plates, 4WD	130	112
245/70R16 white-letter tires, LS, LT	140	120
245/65R17 white-letter tires, LTZ	140	120

Specifications begin on page 551.

CHEVROLET

CHEVROLET VENTURE

CG RECOMMENDED AUTO

Chevrolet Venture LT

Front-wheel-drive minivan
Base price range: $21,380-$33,120. Built in USA.
Also consider: Dodge Caravan, Ford Windstar, Honda Odyssey

FOR • Ride • Passenger and cargo room • Available all-wheel-drive   **AGAINST** • Fuel economy • Rear-seat comfort

Optional all-wheel drive and a DVD rear-entertainment system are the top additions to the 2002 Venture. This minivan is offered in regular- and extended-length models, both with dual sliding side doors. Power operation is available for the right-side door on most models, while LT and top-trim Warner Bros Edition models offer power for both side doors. All seat seven; LS and LT extendeds optionally seat eight. Venture is available with front-wheel drive or GM's Versatrak AWD that includes independent rear suspension and 4-wheel disc brakes. ABS and front side airbags are standard, as are a V6 engine and automatic transmission. Optional are traction control and a rear obstacle warning system. A stowable 3rd-row seat and a rear floor-mounted covered storage tray are available. The Warner Bros Edition includes a rear-seat entertainment system with the new DVD player, which replaces the former standard VCR. Integrated child safety seats are standard with the 2nd-row bench seat. Venture's design is shared by the Oldsmobile Silhouette and Pontiac Montana.

RATINGS	LS reg. length	LT ext. length
ACCELERATION	4	4
FUEL ECONOMY	4	4
RIDE QUALITY	6	7
STEERING/HANDLING	5	5
QUIETNESS	6	6
INSTRUMENTS/CONTROLS	6	6

Prices are accurate at time of publication; subject to manufacturer's change.
CONSUMER GUIDE®

CHEVROLET

	LS reg. length	LT ext. length
ROOM/COMFORT (FRONT)	6	6
ROOM/COMFORT (REAR)	5	7
CARGO ROOM	9	9
VALUE	7	8

These minivans merit strong consideration. Venture is the best value of the three, but base prices on all are reasonable and include a fine array of standard features. And only Dodge and Chrysler offer AWD among direct competitors. Note, however, that the phaseout of Oldsmobile has damaged Silhoutte's near-term resale value and lease residual value.

TOTAL	58	62

Average total for minivans: 56.0

ENGINES

	ohv V6
Size, liters/cu. in.	3.4/207
Horsepower @ rpm	185 @ 5200
Torque (lb-ft) @ rpm	210 @ 4000
Availability	S

EPA city/highway mpg

4-speed automatic	19/26[1]

1. 18/24 w/AWD.

PRICES

Chevrolet Venture

	Retail Price	Dealer Invoice
Value regular length 4-door van, FWD	$21380	$19777
Plus regular length 4-door van, FWD	24600	22263
Plus extended 4-door van, FWD	25600	23168
LS regular length 4-door van, FWD	25450	23032
LS extended 4-door van, FWD	26450	23937
LT extended 4-door van, FWD	29720	26897
LT extended 4-door van, AWD	32150	29096
Warner Bros Edition extended 4-door van, FWD	30500	27603
Warner Bros Edition extended 4-door van, AWD	33120	29974
Destination charge	655	655

FWD denotes front-wheel drive. AWD denotes all-wheel drive.

STANDARD EQUIPMENT

Value: 3.4-liter V6 engine, 4-speed automatic transmission, dual front airbags, front side impact airbags, antilock brakes, daytime running lights, front air conditioning, power steering, tilt steering wheel, cloth upholstery, 7-passenger seating (front bucket seats, center 2-passenger split bench seat, rear 3-passenger split bench seat, integrated child seat, center console, cupholders, power door locks, dual sliding rear doors,

Specifications begin on page 551.

CHEVROLET

AM/FM radio, digital clock, variable intermittent wipers, visor mirrors, automatic headlights, theft-deterrent system, 215/70R15 tires, wheel covers.

Plus adds: cruise control, heated power mirrors, power front windows, remote keyless entry, center row split folding bench seat, overhead console, AM/FM/CD player, rear defogger, rear wiper/washer, floormats, deep-tinted rear glass.

LS adds: power rear quarter windows, illuminated visor mirrors, roof rack, alloy wheels.

LT adds: traction control, rear obstacle detection system, OnStar System w/one year service (roadside assistance, emergency services; other services available), front and rear air conditioning, 6-way power driver seat, two center row captain chairs, rear stowable bench seat, rear convenience tray, power sliding rear doors, AM/FM/cassette/CD player, rear radio controls, rear headphone jacks, universal garage door opener, theft-deterrent system w/alarm, air inflation kit, Touring Suspension w/automatic load-leveling. **AWD** adds: all-wheel drive, 4-wheel disc brakes, 215/60R16 tires. *Deletes:* traction control.

Warner Bros Edition adds: cloth/leather upholstery, three center-row bucket seats, LCD screen, DVD player w/remote control, wireless headphones. *Deletes:* traction control, power driver-side sliding door, air inflation kit, Touring Suspension w/automatic load-leveling. **AWD** adds: all-wheel drive, 4-wheel disc brakes, air inflation kit, Touring Suspension w/automatic load levelling, 215/60R16 tires.

OPTIONAL EQUIPMENT

	Retail Price	Dealer Invoice
Major Packages		
Safety and Security Pkg., Plus	$450	$387
LS	510	439

OnStar System w/one year service (roadside assistance, emergency services; other services available), extended overhead console, universal garage door opener (LS), theft-deterrent system w/alarm.

Touring Suspension, LS, Warner	555	477
LS/Warner w/self-sealing tires	405	348

Traction control, air inflation kit, Touring Suspension w/automatic load-leveling, 215/70R15 self-sealing tires.

Trailering Pkg., LS, LT, Warner	165	142

Includes heavy-duty engine and transmission oil cooling. LS, FWD Warner require Touring Suspension.

Powertrain
Traction control, LS, FWD Warner	195	168

Safety
Rear obstacle detection system, LS extended	195	168

Prices are accurate at time of publication; subject to manufacturer's change.

CHEVROLET • CHRYSLER

Comfort & Convenience Features

	Retail Price	Dealer Invoice
Front and rear air conditioning, Plus extended, LS extended..................	$475	$409
Power passenger-side sliding door, Plus...............	770	662
LS	720	620
Includes 6-way power driver seat, power rear quarter windows.		
Power driver-side sliding door, LS extended, Warner	350	301
LS requires Safety and Security Pkg., front and rear air conditioning, power passenger-side sliding door, rear obstacle detection system.		
6-way power driver seat, Plus, LS	270	232
ABC 7-passenger seating, LS extended.....................	525	452
Two center row bucket seats, rear stowable bench seat, rear convenience tray.		
ABD 7-passenger seating, LS regular........................	290	249
Two center row captain chairs, third row split folding bench seat. Deletes integrated child seat.		
ABE 8-passenger seating, LS regular.........................	290	249
Three center row bucket seats, split folding rear seat, integrated child seat.		
ABF 8-passenger seating, LS extended	525	452
LT	NC	NC
Three center-row bucket seats, rear stowable 3-passenger bench seat, integrated child seat, rear convenience tray. NA w/leather upholstery.		
Leather upholstery, LT	625	538
AM/FM/cassette/CD player, Plus, LS........................	100	86
AM/FM/cassette w/in-dash 6-disc CD changer, LS......	395	340
LT, Warner	295	254
Rear-seat audio controls, LS......................................	155	133
Includes headphone jacks. Requires optional radio.		
Rear defogger, Value	180	155
Rear wiper/washer, Value..	125	108
Requires rear defogger.		

Appearance and Miscellaneous

Roof rack, Plus..	225	194
Self-sealing 215/70R15 tires, LS, FWD Warner, LT AWD	300	258
FWD LT	150	129
Alloy wheels, Plus	295	254

CHRYSLER 300M

Front-wheel-drive near-luxury car
Base price: $28,340. Built in Canada.
Also consider: Acura TL, BMW 3-Series, Lexus GS 300

Specifications begin on page 551.

CHRYSLER

Chrysler 300M Special

FOR • Acceleration • Passenger and cargo room • Ride/handling
AGAINST • Rear visibility • Trunk liftover

Chrysler's sporty near-luxury sedan gains an even sportier edition for 2002. Called the 300M Special, the new version is due at midyear with unique trim, stiffer suspension, 18-inch wheels vs. 17s, and brighter Xenon headlights. Both the 300M and 300M Special use the same front-wheel-drive chassis as the Chrysler Concorde and Dodge Intrepid, but have distinct styling and shorter bodies. Standard is a 250-hp V6 (255 hp on Special) and 4-speed automatic transmission with Chrysler's AutoStick, which has a separate gate for manual shifting. Antilock 4-wheel disc brakes and traction control are standard. Front side airbags are optional. Newly available is a tire inflation monitor.

RATINGS	300M	300M Special
ACCELERATION	6	6
FUEL ECONOMY	5	5
RIDE QUALITY	6	5
STEERING/HANDLING	6	7
QUIETNESS	5	5
INSTRUMENTS/CONTROLS	6	6
ROOM/COMFORT (FRONT)	8	8
ROOM/COMFORT (REAR)	7	7
CARGO ROOM	5	5
VALUE	4	4

300Ms give up a measure of refinement to the top competition, and their cabin decor isn't as sophisticated. But few similarly priced rivals match this blend of interior space and overall performance.

TOTAL	58	58

Average total for near-luxury cars: 54.5

ENGINES

	ohc V6
Size, liters/cu. in.	3.5/215

Prices are accurate at time of publication; subject to manufacturer's change.

CHRYSLER

	ohc V6
Horsepower @ rpm	250 @ 6400
Torque (lb-ft) @ rpm	255 @ 3950
Availability	S[1]
EPA city/highway mpg	
4-speed automatic	18/26

1. Special has 255 hp and 258 lb-ft.

PRICES

Chrysler 300M	Retail Price	Dealer Invoice
Base 4-door sedan	$28340	$26356
Special 4-door sedan	NA	NA
Destination charge	655	655

STANDARD EQUIPMENT

Base: 3.5-liter V6 250-horsepower engine, 4-speed automatic transmission w/manual-shift capability, traction control, dual front airbags, antilock 4-wheel disc brakes, emergency inside trunk release, power steering, tilt leather-wrapped steering wheel w/radio controls, cruise control, air conditioning w/automatic climate control, leather upholstery, heated 8-way power front bucket seats w/driver-side lumbar adjustment, center console, cupholders, split folding rear seat, memory system (driver seat, mirrors, radio), heated power mirrors, power windows, power door locks, remote keyless entry, Infinity AM/FM/CD player, analog clock, tachometer, trip computer, universal garage door opener, automatic day/night rearview mirror, rear defogger, power decklid release, variable intermittent wipers, illuminated visor mirrors, automatic headlights, map lights, overhead console, floormats, theft-deterrent system, fog lights, 225/55R17 tires, alloy wheels.

Special adds: 3.5-liter V6 255-horsepower engine, AM/FM/cassette w/in-dash 4-disc CD changer, tilt-down back-up aid mirrors w/driver-side automatic day/night, Xenon headlights, sport suspension, 245/45ZR18 tires.

OPTIONAL EQUIPMENT
Major Packages

Luxury Group, Base	920	846

Wood/leather-wrapped steering wheel, tilt-down back-up aid mirrors w/driver-side automatic day/night, wood interior trim, tire pressure monitor, vehicle information center.

Luxury Group w/chrome alloy wheels, Base	1055	971
Performance Handling Group, Base	560	515

Performance antilock 4-wheel disc brakes, performance power steering and suspension, 225/55VR17 tires.

Specifications begin on page 551.

CHRYSLER

	Retail Price	Dealer Invoice
Safety		
Front side airbags	$390	$359
Comfort & Convenience Features		
Power sunroof	895	823
Infinity AM/FM/cassette/CD player, Base	100	92
Infinity AM/FM/cassette w/4-disc CD changer, Base	390	359
Smoker's Group	30	28
Ashtrays, lighter.		
Appearance and Miscellaneous		
Chrome alloy wheels, Base	750	690

CHRYSLER CONCORDE

Chrysler Concorde Limited

Front-wheel-drive full-size car
Base price range: $22,370-$27,870. Built in Canada.
Also consider: Buick LeSabre, Pontiac Bonneville, Toyota Avalon

FOR • Acceleration (3.5 V6) • Passenger and cargo room • Ride • Steering/handling **AGAINST** • Rear visibility • Trunk liftover

Chrysler's mainstream full-size sedan adopts the body of its discontinued LHS near-luxury sedan counterpart and adds a new top-line trim level for 2002. The LHS continues in spirit as the new top-of-the-line Concorde Limited. Concorde shares its underskin design with the Dodge Intrepid. It's also the foundation for Chrysler's sporty 300M near-luxury sedan. Concorde has standard seating for five and an optional front bench for six. The base LX has a 200-hp 2.7-liter V6, the LXi a newly available 234-hp 3.5-liter V6, the Limited a 250-hp 3.5. All team with automatic transmission. Four-wheel disc brakes are standard. ABS and traction control are standard on Limited, optional on LXi. ABS is optional on LX. Front side airbags are optional on all. Concorde's performance and accommodations

Prices are accurate at time of publication; subject to manufacturer's change.

CHRYSLER

mirror those of like-equipped Dodge Intrepids.

RATINGS

	LX	LXi	Limited
ACCELERATION	4	6	6
FUEL ECONOMY	6	5	5
RIDE QUALITY	7	7	7
STEERING/HANDLING	6	6	6
QUIETNESS	5	5	5
INSTRUMENTS/CONTROLS	6	6	7
ROOM/COMFORT (FRONT)	7	7	7
ROOM/COMFORT (REAR)	7	7	7
CARGO ROOM	6	6	6
VALUE	8	8	7

Distinctive styling, roomy interior, and fine handling make this an impressive value. And Concordes with the 3.5 V6 are quite quick.

TOTAL	62	63	63

Average total for full-size cars: 58.7

EXTENDED-USE TEST UPDATE

The 2002 Concorde LXi is functionally equivalent to the now-retired LHS. We put an LHS through an extended-use test, during which it averaged 21.6 mpg over 14,480 mi. That test car tended to drift left at freeway speeds, but dealer service technicians found no alignment problems. Nor did they determine any malfunction of the transmission when we complained that it would shift in and out of overdrive with a modest jolt in 40-mph cruising. The LHS was otherwise mechanically trouble-free during its 12-month test period.

ENGINES

	dohc V6	ohc V6	ohc V6
Size, liters/cu. in.	2.7/167	3.5/215	3.5/215
Horsepower @ rpm	200 @ 5800	234 @ 6000	250 @ 6400
Torque (lb-ft) @ rpm	190 @ 4850	241 @ 4400	250 @ 3900
Availability	S[1]	S[2]	S[3]

EPA city/highway mpg
4-speed automatic	20/28	18/26	18/26

1. LX. 2. LXi. 3. Limited.

PRICES

Chrysler Concorde	Retail Price	Dealer Invoice
LX 4-door sedan	$22370	$20803
LXi 4-door sedan	24975	23148
Limited 4-door sedan	27870	25753
Destination charge	625	625

Specifications begin on page 551.

CHRYSLER

STANDARD EQUIPMENT

LX: 2.7-liter dohc V6 engine, 4-speed automatic transmission, dual front airbags, 4-wheel disc brakes, emergency inside trunk release, air conditioning, power steering, tilt steering wheel, cruise control, cloth upholstery, front bucket seats, 8-way power driver seat w/manual lumbar adjustment, center console, cupholders, trunk pass-through, power mirrors, power windows, power door locks, remote keyless entry, AM/FM/cassette, digital clock, tachometer, visor mirrors, rear defogger, variable intermittent wipers, power decklid release, map lights, floormats, fog lights, 225/60R16 tires, wheel covers.

LXi adds: 3.5-liter V6 engine, leather-wrapped steering wheel w/radio controls, leather upholstery, AM/FM/CD player, automatic climate control, trip computer, illuminated visor mirrors, automatic day/night rearview mirror, universal garage door opener, overhead console, automatic climate control, theft-deterrent system, alloy wheels.

Limited adds: traction control, antilock brakes, heated front seats, memory driver seat and mirrors, 8-way power passenger seat, heated power mirrors, Infinity sound system, analog clock, 225/55R17 tires, chrome alloy wheels.

OPTIONAL EQUIPMENT

	Retail Price	Dealer Invoice
Major Packages		
Quick Order Pkg. 22D, LX	$1400	$1288
Manufacturer's Discount Price	915	842

   AM/FM/CD player w/Premium sound system, illuminated visor mirrors, automatic day/night mirror, universal garage door opener, trip computer, cargo net, alloy wheels.

Luxury Touring Group, LXi	1690	1555

   Traction control, antilock brakes, variable-assist power steering, 225/55R17 tires, chrome alloy wheels.

Luxury Group, Limited	420	478

   Automatic day/night driver-side mirror, tilt-down back-up aid mirrors, wood/leather-wrapped steering wheel, wood interior trim, vehicle information center.

Safety

Antilock brakes, LX, LXi	600	552
Front side impact airbags	390	359

Comfort & Convenience Features

Power sunroof	895	823
LX requires Quick Order Pkg. 22D.		
Front split bench seat, LX, LXi	150	138
AM/FM/CD player, LX	525	483
Includes premium sound system.		

Prices are accurate at time of publication; subject to manufacturer's change.

CHRYSLER

	Retail Price	Dealer Invoice
AM/FM/cassette/CD player, LX	$625	$575
LX w/Pkg. 22D, LXi, Limited	100	92
LX, LXi include premium sound system.		
AM/FM/cassette w/in-dash 4-disc CD changer, LX.	1210	1113
LX w/Pkg. 22D	510	469
LXi	375	345
Limited	390	359

Includes Infinity sound system, leather-wrapped steering wheel w/radio controls. Limited includes upgraded Infinity sound system.

CHRYSLER PT CRUISER

Chrysler PT Cruiser

Front-wheel-drive compact car
Base price range: $16,200-$20,265. Built in Mexico.
Also consider: Ford Focus wagon, Toyota Matrix, Volkswagen Jetta wagon

FOR • Handling/roadholding • Entry/exit • Passenger and cargo room   **AGAINST** • Acceleration w/automatic transmission

Chrysler's hot-selling PT Cruiser gets even hotter for 2002 with the addition of optional flame accent decals for the hood and front fenders. This retro-styled 4-dr compact hatchback seats five; its rear seat and front passenger seat fold and the rear seat removes. Sole engine is a 2.4-liter 4 cyl with manual or optional automatic transmission. PT Cruiser is offered in Base, Touring, and Limited versions. For '02, Base models add some previously optional features as standard, such as CD player and underseat storage bin, while Limited gets adjustable driver's lumbar support. Front side airbags are standard on Limited, optional on others; antilock 4-wheel disc brakes with traction control are optional on all models.

Specifications begin on page 551.

CHRYSLER

RATINGS

	Limited, man.	Limited, auto.
ACCELERATION	5	4
FUEL ECONOMY	5	5
RIDE QUALITY	6	6
STEERING/HANDLING	6	6
QUIETNESS	4	4
INSTRUMENTS/CONTROLS	6	6
ROOM/COMFORT (FRONT)	7	7
ROOM/COMFORT (REAR)	6	6
CARGO ROOM	7	7
VALUE	8	8

The Cruiser is roomy, comfortable, adaptable, and fun, with mediocre acceleration the only real flaw. It's affordable too, but strong demand keeps prices high and delivery times long.

TOTAL	60	59

Average total for compact cars: 51.6

ENGINES

	dohc I4
Size, liters/cu. in.	2.4/148
Horsepower @ rpm	150 @ 5500
Torque (lb-ft) @ rpm	162 @ 4000
Availability	S

EPA city/highway mpg

5-speed manual	21/29
4-speed automatic	19/25

PRICES

Chrysler PT Cruiser	Retail Price	Dealer Invoice
Base 4-door wagon	$16200	$15242
Touring Edition 4-door wagon	17915	16803
Limited Edition 4-door wagon	20265	18941
Destination charge	565	565

STANDARD EQUIPMENT

Base: 2.4-liter dohc 4-cylinder engine, 5-speed manual transmission, dual front airbags, air conditioning, power steering, tilt steering wheel, cloth upholstery, front bucket seats, under-seat storage bin, center console, cupholders, split folding rear seat, power windows, AM/FM/CD player, digital clock, tachometer, rear defogger, intermittent rear wiper/washer, visor mirrors, variable intermittent wipers, floormats, 195/65TR15 tires, wheel covers.

Touring Edition adds: heated power mirrors, power door locks, remote keyless entry, fold-flat passenger seat, illuminated visor mir-

Prices are accurate at time of publication; subject to manufacturer's change.

CHRYSLER

rors, overhead console, map lights, theft-deterrent system, deep-tinted rear glass, fog lights, Touring Suspension, 205/55TR16 tires, alloy wheels.

Limited Edition adds: front side airbags, leather/suede upholstery, driver-seat power height adjuster and lumbar adjustment, leather-wrapped steering wheel, cruise control, power sunroof, chrome alloy wheels.

OPTIONAL EQUIPMENT

	Retail Price	Dealer Invoice
Major Packages		
Power Conveninece Group, Base	$570	$524
Heated power mirrors, power door locks, remote keyless entry.		
Light Group, Base	300	276
Manufacturer's Discount Price	*250*	*230*
Illuminated visor mirrors, map and console lights, additional auxiliary power outlets.		
Powertrain		
4-speed automatic transmission	825	759
Safety		
Front side airbags, Base, Touring Edition	350	322
Antilock Braking System	790	727
Manufacturer's Discount Price	*595*	*548*
Antilock 4-wheel disc brakes, traction control.		
Comfort & Convenience Features		
Power sunroof, Base	895	823
Manufacturer's Discount Price	*845*	*777*
Touring	595	547
Base includes Light Group.		
Cruise control, Base, Touring	235	216
AM/FM/cassette/CD player	100	92
Driver-seat power height adjuster, Touring	100	92
Heated front seats, Limited	250	230
Appearance and Miscellaneous		
Flame accent decals	495	NA
Deep tinted glass, Base	275	253
Roof rack	175	161
Chrome alloy wheels, Touring	600	552

CHRYSLER SEBRING

Front-wheel-drive midsize car
Base price range: $17,705-$28,795. Built in USA.

Specifications begin on page 551.

CHRYSLER

Chrysler Sebring LXi sedan

Also consider: Ford Taurus, Honda Accord, Toyota Camry

FOR • Steering/handling **AGAINST** • Acceleration (4-cylinder)
• Rear-seat entry/exit (coupe, convertible) • Rear-seat comfort (coupe)

Chrysler's midsize line consists of sedans, convertibles, and coupes. Curtain side airbags are optional on sedans; no Sebring offers torso side airbags. All models except the base coupe have 4-wheel disc brakes and offer ABS.

The sedan and convertible share a Chrysler platform and use Chrysler powertrains with a base 4-cyl engine or available V6. All have automatic transmission, though the new GTC convertible due later in the model year will offer a V6/manual combination. Chrysler's AutoStick automatic with manual shift gate is available on the top-line Limited convertible.

The coupe takes its platform and powertrains from Mitsubishi's Galant and Eclipse. It has a standard 4-cyl engine or optional V6. The 4 cyl comes only with automatic transmission, the V6 with manual or automatic. AutoStick is available with the V6. The convertible is exclusive to the Sebring line, but sedans and coupes have Dodge Stratus counterparts.

RATINGS	LX sdn, V6	LXi cpe, V6 auto.	Limited conv
ACCELERATION	5	6	5
FUEL ECONOMY	5	6	5
RIDE QUALITY	6	5	6
STEERING/HANDLING	6	7	6
QUIETNESS	5	5	4
INSTRUMENTS/CONTROLS	6	4	6
ROOM/COMFORT (FRONT)	5	4	5
ROOM/COMFORT (REAR)	4	2	3
CARGO ROOM	5	5	2

Prices are accurate at time of publication; subject to manufacturer's change.
CONSUMER GUIDE®

CHRYSLER

	LX sdn, V6	LXi cpe, V6 auto.	Limited conv
VALUE	6	4	6

Though Sebrings lack the polish of some import-brand rivals, prices are competitive, sedans qualify as relatively sporty family cars, and along with the convertible, have a comfortable interior. All in all, though, the real gem here is that roomy, stylish ragtop.

TOTAL	53	48	48

Average total for midsize cars: 57.0

ENGINES

	ohc I4	dohc I4	dohc V6	ohc V6
Size, liters/cu. in.	2.4/143	2.4/148	2.7/167	3.0/181
Horsepower @ rpm	142 @ 5500	150 @ 5200	200 @ 5800	200 @ 5500
Torque (lb-ft) @ rpm	158 @ 4000	167 @ 4000	190 @ 4850	205 @ 4500
Availability	S[1]	S[2]	S[3]	S[4]
EPA city/highway mpg				
5-speed manual				20/29
4-speed automatic	21/28	21/30	20/27	20/28

1. LX coupe. 2. LX sedan and convertible. 3. LXi sedan, LXi and Limited convertible; optional LX sedan. 4. LXi coupe; optional LX coupe.

PRICES

Chrysler Sebring

	Retail Price	Dealer Invoice
LX 4-door sedan	$17705	$16500
LXi 4-door sedan	20280	18817
LX 2-door coupe	20020	18623
LXi 2-door coupe	21710	20144
LX 2-door convertible	23075	21463
LXi 2-door convertible	26160	24239
Limited 2-door convertible	28795	26611
Destination charge	595	595

STANDARD EQUIPMENT

LX sedan: 2.4-liter dohc 4-cylinder engine, 4-speed automatic transmission, dual front airbags, 4-wheel disc brakes, emergency inside trunk release, air conditioning, power steering, tilt steering wheel, cloth upholstery, front bucket seats w/height-adjustable driver seat, center console, cupholders, split folding rear seat, power mirrors, power windows, power door locks, AM/FM/cassette, tachometer, rear defogger, variable-intermittent wipers, remote decklid release, floormats, 205/65R15 tires, wheel covers.

LXi sedan adds: 2.7-liter dohc V6 engine, leather-wrapped steering wheel, cruise control, 8-way power driver seat, remote keyless entry,

Specifications begin on page 551.

CHRYSLER

AM/FM/CD player, trip computer, compass, outside temperature indicator, illuminated visor mirrors, map lights, automatic-off headlights, fog lights, touring suspension, 205/60TR16 tires, alloy wheels.

LX coupe adds to LX sedan: 2.4-liter 4-cylinder engine, cruise control, remote keyless entry, illuminated visor mirrors, automatic day/night rearview mirror, map lights, theft-deterrent system, fog lights, 205/60HR16 tires. *Deletes:* 4-wheel disc brakes, split folding rear seat, emergency inside trunk release.

LXi coupe adds: 3.0-liter V6 engine, 5-speed manual transmission, 4-wheel disc brakes, leather-wrapped steering wheel, Infinity AM/FM radio w/in-dash 4-disc CD changer, outside temperature indicator, compass, 215/50HR17 tires, alloy wheels.

LX convertible adds to LX sedan: heated power mirrors, remote keyless entry, illuminated visor mirrors, power convertible top, automatic-off headlights.

LXi convertible adds: 2.7-liter dohc V6 engine, leather-wrapped steering wheel, cruise control, leather upholstery, 6-way power driver seat, trip computer, Infinity AM/FM/CD player, theft-deterrent system, fog lights, touring suspension, 205/60R16 tires, alloy wheels.

Limited convertible adds: manual-shift capability, antilock 4-wheel disc brakes, front seat lumbar adjustment, Infinity sound system, universal garage door opener, automatic day/night rearview mirror, chrome alloy wheels.

OPTIONAL EQUIPMENT

	Retail Price	Dealer Invoice
Major Packages		
Quick Order Group 24/28J, LX sedan	$850	$782

Cruise control, AM/FM/CD player, remote keyless entry, illuminated visor mirrors, trip computer, automatic-off headlights, rear passenger assist handles.

Remote/Illuminated Entry Group, LX sedan	170	156

Remote keyless entry, illuminated entry, automatic-off headlights.

Enthusiast Group, LXi sedan	400	368
LXi sedan w/Luxury Group	250	230

Manual-shift capability for automatic transmission, firm-feel power steering, sport suspension, electroluminescent instrument cluster.

Luxury Group, LXi sedan	1465	1348
Manufacturer's Discount Price	*1265*	*1164*

Leather upholstery, universal garage door opener, premium sound system, electroluminescent instrument cluster, automatic door locks, cargo net, theft-deterrent system w/alarm.

Touring Group, LX coupe	485	446

AM/FM radio w/in-dash 4-disc CD changer, 6-way power driver seat, outside temperature gauge, compass.

Prices are accurate at time of publication; subject to manufacturer's change.

CHRYSLER

	Retail Price	Dealer Invoice
Leather Interior Group, LXi coupe	$1045	$961

Leather upholstery, 6-way power driver seat, universal garage door opener.

Electronics Convenience Group, LXi conv.	325	299

Automatic day/night rearview mirror, universal garage door opener, automatic door locks, theft-deterrent system w/alarm.

Security Information Group, LX sedan	355	327
LX conv.	175	161

Theft-deterrent system w/alarm, automatic door locks, trip computer. LX sedan requires Quick Order Group.

Security Group, LXi sedan, LX conv.	195	179

Theft-deterrent system w/alarm, automatic door locking.

Powertrain

3.0-liter V6 engine, LX coupe	885	814
2.7-liter dohc V6 engine, LX sedan	1085	998
LX sedan w/Quick Order Group, LX conv.	850	782

LX sedan includes cruise control.

4-speed automatic transmission, LXi coupe	825	759
Autostick manual-shift capability, LXi coupe	165	152

Require 4-speed automatic transmission.

Safety

Curtain side airbags, sedans	390	359
Antilock brakes, LXi coupe w/manual trans., sedans, LX/LXi conv.	565	520
LXi coupe w/automatic transmission	740	681

LXi coupe w/automatic transmission includes traction control.

Comfort & Convenience Features

Power sunroof, sedans, coupes	695	639

LX sedan requires Quick Order Group.

Cruise control, LX sedan/conv.	235	216
AM/FM/CD player, LX sedan	125	115
AM/FM/cassette/CD player, LX sedan	100	92
LXi coupe	NC	NC

LX sedan requires Quick Order Group.

AM/FM/cassette w/in-dash 4-disc CD changer, LXi convertible, Limited	250	230
AM/FM radio w/in-dash 4-disc CD changer, LX conv.	375	345
Premium sound system, sedans	350	322

LX requires Quick Order Group.

Infinity sound system, LX/LXi conv.	475	437
8-way power driver seat, LX sedan	380	350
6-way power driver seat, LX conv.	350	322

Specifications begin on page 551.

CHRYSLER

	Retail Price	Dealer Invoice
Leather upholstery, LXi sedan.................................	$650	$598
Appearance and Miscellaneous		
Alloy wheels, LX coupe..	365	336
Alloy wheels w/205/60R16 tires, LX sedan/conv. ...	325	299
Chrome alloy wheels, LXi coupe.............................	750	690
LXi sedan...	600	552

LXi coupe requires Leather Interior Group.

CHRYSLER TOWN & COUNTRY AND VOYAGER

Chrysler Town & Country Limited

Front- or all-wheel-drive minivan
Base price range: $16,355-$37,660. Built in USA.
Also consider: Chevrolet Venture, Honda Odyssey, Toyota Sienna

FOR • Available all-wheel drive • Entry/exit • Interior storage space • Passenger and cargo room **AGAINST** • Fuel economy • Acceleration (4-cylinder)

Power-adjustable brake and accelerator pedals, a DVD rear-seat entertainment system, and a tire inflation monitor are newly available on the 2002 Town & Country and Voyager. The luxury Town & Country is nearly a foot longer than Voyager, an entry-level model. The Dodge Caravan shares this design and most mechanical features.

All Chrysler minivans seat seven and have two sliding side doors. Power operation for one or both side doors is available and includes a manual override that allows them to be closed or opened by hand

Prices are accurate at time of publication; subject to manufacturer's change.

CHRYSLER

during the powered phase. A power liftgate is available on Town & Country. Also offered is a 50-50 split 3rd-row bench seat; its 55-lb portions remove individually, recline, or fold flat. Available on Town & Country is a rear parcel shelf that locates at floor or midlevel positions and includes popup storage dividers.

Voyager comes with a 4-cyl engine or a 3.3-liter V6. Town & Country offers V6s of 3.3 and 3.8 liters. All engines team with automatic transmissions. Town & Country is available with all-wheel drive. ABS is unavailable on Voyager eC models, optional on other Voyagers, and standard on Town & Country, where it teams with 4-wheel disc brakes. Front side airbags are available on all models. The DVD system is a dealer-installed option with a suggested retail of $1650 plus about $150 installation. A VCR-based system is similarly available for around $1400. Chrysler positions its Voyager eC as a high-value entry-level minivan, with Town & Country eL and eX models equipped to compete directly with corresponding Honda Odyssey models, but to sell for less.

RATINGS	Voyager LX, 4 cyl	Town & Country LXi, 3.3 V6	Town & Country Limited AWD
ACCELERATION	2	4	5
FUEL ECONOMY	4	4	4
RIDE QUALITY	5	7	7
STEERING/HANDLING	4	5	6
QUIETNESS	4	6	7
INSTRUMENTS/CONTROLS	7	7	7
ROOM/COMFORT (FRONT)	7	7	7
ROOM/COMFORT (REAR)	6	8	8
CARGO ROOM	9	10	10
VALUE	6	8	6

DaimlerChrysler's lineup is strong at the "shoulders" of the minivan market, with 62 percent of sales under $20,000, 37 percent over $30,000. That's testimony to the appeal of the entry-level Voyager and luxury Town & Country, which are fine values.

TOTAL	54	66	67

Average total for minivans: 56.0

ENGINES	dohc I4	ohv V6	ohv V6
Size, liters/cu. in.	2.4/153	3.3/202	3.8/231
Horsepower @ rpm	150 @ 5200	180 @ 5000	215 @ 5000
Torque (lb-ft) @ rpm	167 @ 4000	210 @ 4000	245 @ 4000
Availability	S[1]	S[2]	S[3]
EPA city/highway mpg			
4-speed automatic	NA	18/24	18/24[4]

1. Base and eC Voyager. 2. Voyager LX, Town & Country eL, LX and LXi; optional base Voyager. 3. Town & Country eX, Limited, and AWD; optional Town & Country LXi. 4. 17/22 w/AWD.

CHRYSLER

PRICES

Chrysler Town & Country and Voyager

	Retail Price	Dealer Invoice
Voyager eC regular length 4-door van, FWD	$16355	$15498
Voyager Base regular length 4-door van, FWD	19155	18046
Voyager LX regular length 4-door van, FWD	23420	21459
Town & Country LX extended 4-door van, FWD	24880	22973
Town & Country LX extended 4-door van, AWD	30980	28402
Town & Country eL extended 4-door van, FWD	23675	22374
Town & Country eX extended 4-door van, FWD	26175	24649
Town & Country LXi extended 4-door van, FWD	29175	26796
Town & Country LXi extended 4-door van, AWD	33045	30240
Town & Country Limited extended 4-door van, FWD	35335	32456
Town & Country Limited extended 4-door van, AWD	37660	34347
Destination charge: Voyager eC, Voyager Base, Voyager/Town & Country LX FWD	640	640
Destination charge: Voyager/Town & Country LX FWD, Town & Country LX AWD, Town & Country eL, Town & Country eX, Town & Country LXi FWD, Town & Country LXi AWD, Town & Country Limited	655	655

AWD denotes all-wheel drive. FWD denotes front-wheel drive.

STANDARD EQUIPMENT

Voyager eC: 2.4-liter dohc 4-cylinder engine, 4-speed automatic transmission, dual front airbags, front air conditioning, power steering, cloth upholstery, 5-passenger seating, front bucket seats, center console, cupholders, second row 3-passenger bench seat, AM/FM/cassette, digital clock, variable intermittent wipers, visor mirrors, intermittent rear wiper/washer, 215/70R15 tires, wheel covers.

Voyager Base adds: 7-passenger seating, second row 2-passenger bench seat, third row 3-passenger bench seat.

Voyager/Town & Country LX FWD adds: 3.3-liter V6 engine, antilock 4-wheel disc brakes (Town & Country), tilt steering wheel, cruise control, heated power mirrors, power windows, power door locks, tachometer, rear defogger, floormats, rear privacy glass.

Town & Country LX AWD adds: 3.8-liter V6 engine, all-wheel drive, tri-zone manual climate control, rear air conditioning and heater, interior air filter, 8-way power driver seat, second row bucket seats, third row split-folding bench seat, power sliding passenger-side rear door, remote keyless entry, AM/FM/cassette/CD player, illuminated visor mirrors, windshield wiper de-icer, automatic-off headlights, load-leveling height-control suspension, 215/65R16 tires.

Town & Country eL adds to Town & Country LX FWD: tri-zone manual climate control (including rear controls), rear air conditioning and heater, interior air filter, second row bucket seats, third row-split

Prices are accurate at time of publication; subject to manufacturer's change.

CHRYSLER

bench seat, remote keyless entry, overhead console, trip computer, illuminated visor mirrors, universal garage door opener, windshield wiper de-icer, automatic-off headlights.

Town & Country eX adds: 3.8-liter V6 engine, traction control, 8-way power driver seat, removable center console, power sliding passenger-side rear door, power rear liftgate, AM/FM/cassette/CD player, roof rack, 215/65R16 tires, alloy wheels.

Town & Country LXi FWD adds: 3.3-liter V6 engine, tri-zone automatic climate controls, driver seat lumbar adjustment, power sliding driver-side rear door, Infinity AM/FM/cassette, map lights, fog lights. *Deletes:* traction control, power rear liftgate, removable center console, alloy wheels.

Town & Country LXi AWD adds: 3.8-liter V6 engine, all-wheel drive, leather-wrapped steering wheel w/radio controls, removable center console, load-leveling height-control suspension, alloy wheels.

Town & Country Limited adds: traction control, front side airbags, tire pressure monitor, leather upholstery, 8-way power passenger seat, memory system (driver seat, mirrors, radio), power adjustable pedals, third row bench seat w/armrests, power rear liftgate, Infinity AM/FM/cassette/CD player, vehicle information center, automatic day/night rearview mirror, theft-deterrent system w/alarm, full-size spare tire, chrome alloy wheels. **AWD** adds: all-wheel drive. *Deletes:* traction control.

OPTIONAL EQUIPMENT

	Retail Price	Dealer Invoice
Quick Order Pkg. 25H, Voyager LX	$1375	$1166
Manufacturer's Discount Price	*575*	*506*

Major Packages

Antilock brakes, dual-zone manual climate controls, interior air filter, windshield wiper de-icer, remote keyless entry, overhead console, trip computer, illuminated visor mirrors, glove box light, map lights, automatic-off headlights.

Quick Order Pkg. 25H, Town & Country LX FWD........ 1300 1144
Tri-zone manual climate control (including rear controls), rear air conditioning and heater, interior air filter, remote keyless entry, overhead console, trip computer, universal garage door opener, automatic-off headlights, windshield wiper de-icer.

Quick Order Pkg. 25K, Town & Country LX FWD........ 3240 2851
Manufacturer's Discount Price *3040* *2675*
Quick Order Group 25H plus power sliding passenger-side rear door, 8-way power driver seat, second row bucket seats, third row split-folding bench seat, AM/FM/cassette/CD player, illuminated visor mirrors, glove box light.

Quick Order Pkg. 29U, LXi FWD 2220 1954
Leather upholstery, 8-way power passenger seat, removable center console, leather-wrapped steering wheel w/radio controls, theft-deterrent system w/alarm, alloy wheels.

Specifications begin on page 551.

CHRYSLER

	Retail Price	Dealer Invoice
Power Convenience Group, Base	$755	$664
Power mirrors (heated when ordered w/rear defogger), power windows and door locks.		
Deluxe Convenience Group, Base	375	330
Tilt steering wheel, cruise control.		
Climate Group II, Base	645	568
Base w/Power Convenience Group	680	598
Heated power mirrors, rear defogger, windshield wiper de-icer, rear privacy glass.		
Climate Group III, Town & Country LX FWD	660	581
Town & Country LX FWD w/Trailer Tow Prep	595	524
Tri-zone manual climate control (including rear controls), rear air conditioning and heater, interior air filter, windshield wiper de-icer.		
Electronics Convenience Group, LXi	305	268
Tire pressure monitor, vehicle information center, rear reading lights. Requires Touring Suspension or alloy wheels.		
Trailer Tow Prep Group, Town & Country LX/LXi FWD	645	568
LX/LXi AWD	355	312
Limited	195	172
Heavy-duty engine cooling, heavy-duty alternator and battery, trailer wiring harness, load-leveling height-control suspension (LX/LXi FWD), full-size spare tire (LX, LXi). LX FWD requires Quick Order Pkg.		

Powertrain

3.3-liter V6 engine, Base	970	854
3.8-liter V6 engine, LXi FWD	335	295
Traction control, LXi FWD	175	154

Safety

Antilock brakes, Base, Voyager LX	565	497
Base requires 3.3-liter V6 engine. LX requires Quick Order Pkg.		
Front side airbags	390	343
Std. Limited.		

Comfort & Convenience Features

AM/FM/CD player, Base	225	198
Requires 3.3-liter V6 engine.		
AM/FM/cassette/CD player, LX FWD, LXi	225	198
Voyager LX requires Quick Order Pkg. 25H.		
AM/FM/cassette/CD player w/rear controls,		
Town & Country LX FWD, LXi	450	396
LX AWD, Limited	225	198
Includes wireless headphones.		
In-dash 4-disc CD changer, LX w/Pkg. 25H,		
LXi, LX AWD/Limited w/rear radio controls	375	330

Prices are accurate at time of publication; subject to manufacturer's change.

CHRYSLER

	Retail Price	Dealer Invoice
LX FWD w/Pkg. 25K, LX AWD	$150	$132
Includes Infinity speakers.		
Infinity speakers, LX	495	436
FWD models require Quick Order Pkg., optional radio.		
Steering wheel radio controls, LXi	135	119
Power door locks, eC, Base	315	277
Remote keyless entry, LX FWD	150	132
Rear defogger, eC, Base	195	172
Base w/Power Convenience Group	230	202
Third row bench seat, eC	450	396
CYG 7-passenger seating, LX FWD	945	832
Quad bucket seats, third row split folding bench seat. LX requires Quick Order Pkg. 25H.		
CYK/CYR 7-passenger seating, Base, LX FWD	225	198
Front bucket seats, second row bench seat w/dual integrated child seats, third row bench seat.		
CYL 7-passenger seating, LX FWD w/Pkg. 25H	1070	942
LX FWD w/25K, LX AWD, LXi, Limited	125	110
Quad bucket seats, second row integrated child seat, third row split folding bench seat. NA LXi w/leather upholstery.		
CYS 7-passenger seating, LX FWD	745	656
Quad bucket seats, third row bench seat. Requires Quick Order Pkg. 25H.		
CYT 7-passenger seating, LX FWD	870	766
Quad bucket seats w/second row integrated child seat, third row bench seat. Requires Quick Order Pkg. 25H.		
Power adjustable pedals	185	163
Std. Limited.		
Leather upholstery, LXi	890	783
Heated front seats, LXi, Limited	250	220
LXi requires Quick Order Pkg. or leather upholstery.		
Removable center console, Town & Country LX, LXi	195	172
Requires quad bucket seats. LX requires Quick Order Pkg.		
Power sliding passenger-side rear door, LX FWD, eL	400	352
LX requires Quick Order Pkg.		
Power sliding driver-side rear door, eX	400	352
Power rear liftgate, Town & Country LX, LXi	400	352
LX FWD requires Quick Order Pkg., power sliding passenger-side rear door.		
Rear cargo organizer, Town & Country LX, LXi, Limited	250	220

Appearance and Miscellaneous

Theft-deterrent system w/alarm, Town & Country LX, LXi	195	172
LX requires Quick Order Pkg.		

Specifications begin on page 551.

CHRYSLER • DAEWOO

	Retail Price	Dealer Invoice
Roof rack, Base, LX, LXi	$250	$220
Touring Suspension Pkg., LXi FWD	540	475
LXi FWD w/Pkg. 29U	95	84
Suspension upgraded for handling, alloy wheels.		
Alloy wheels, Town & Country LX	535	471
LXi FWD	445	392
Requires Quick Order Pkg.		

DAEWOO LANOS

Daewoo Lanos 4-door sedan

Front-wheel-drive subcompact car
Base price range: $9,199-$12,999. Built in South Korea.
Also consider: Ford Focus, Honda Civic, Toyota Echo

FOR • Fuel economy **AGAINST** • Acceleration • Automatic transmission performance • Rear-seat room • Rear-seat entry/exit (hatchback)

Lanos is the smallest model offered in the U.S. by this South Korean automaker. It comes as a 2-dr hatchback in S and Sport trim and as the S 4-dr sedan. All have a 4-cyl engine and manual or optional automatic transmission. The Sport comes with air conditioning and leather upholstery, but Lanos and Daewoo's slightly larger Nubira (see separate report) are among the few cars that do not offer ABS. For 2002, power steering is optional rather than standard on Lanos S models, and alloy wheels are no longer available on the Sport. Daewoo's warranty covers normal maintenance and roadside assistance for the first year.

RATINGS

	S sdn, auto.	Sport hatch, man.
ACCELERATION	2	2
FUEL ECONOMY	6	7
RIDE QUALITY	3	3

Prices are accurate at time of publication; subject to manufacturer's change.

DAEWOO

	S sdn, auto.	Sport hatch, man.
STEERING/HANDLING	3	3
QUIETNESS	3	3
INSTRUMENTS/CONTROLS	6	6
ROOM/COMFORT (FRONT)	4	4
ROOM/COMFORT (REAR)	3	2
CARGO ROOM	2	6
VALUE	1	1

Lanos isn't that cheap for what it is and does, and Daewoo's future is very uncertain despite talks of a General Motors buyout. In all, a poor entry-level choice, especially now that Korean rivals Hyundai and Kia offer longer, more comprehensive warranties.

TOTAL	33	37

Average total for subcompact cars: 43.7

ENGINES

	dohc I4
Size, liters/cu. in.	1.6/98
Horsepower @ rpm	105 @ 5800
Torque (lb-ft) @ rpm	106 @ 3400
Availability	S

EPA city/highway mpg
5-speed manual	25/35
4-speed automatic	22/32

PRICES

Daewoo Lanos	Retail Price	Dealer Invoice
S 2-door hatchback	$9199	$8555
S 4-door sedan	10099	9392
Sport 2-door hatchback	12999	12089
Destination charge	495	495

STANDARD EQUIPMENT

S: 1.6-liter dohc 4-cylinder engine, 5-speed manual transmission, dual front airbags, cloth upholstery, front bucket seats w/height-adjustable driver seat, height-adjustable driver seat, center console, cupholders, split folding rear seat, rear defogger, AM/FM/cassette, rear wiper/washer (hatchback), passenger-side visor mirror, remote fuel door/decklid release, cargo cover (hatchback), 185/60R14 tires, wheel covers.

Sport adds: air conditioning, power steering, leather-wrapped steering wheel, leather upholstery, power passenger-side mirror, power windows, power door locks, AM/FM/cassette/CD player, rear spoiler.

Specifications begin on page 551.

DAEWOO

OPTIONAL EQUIPMENT	Retail Price	Dealer Invoice
Major Packages		
Comfort Pkg., S	$950	$855
Air conditioning, power steering.		
Convenience Pkg., S	400	360
Power passenger-side mirror, power windows and door locks. Requires Comfort Pkg.		
Powertrain		
4-speed automatic transmission	800	720
Comfort & Convenience Features		
AM/FM/cassette/CD player, S	500	450

DAEWOO LEGANZA

Daewoo Leganza

Front-wheel-drive compact car
Base price range: $14,599-$18,599. Built in South Korea.
Also consider: Chrysler PT Cruiser, Mazda 626, Subaru Outback/Legacy, Volkswagen Passat

FOR • Ride **AGAINST** • Acceleration (w/automatic transmission) • Automatic transmission performance

Daewoo trims some standard equipment from its largest sedan for 2002. Pitched as an "affordable luxury" compact, Leganza comes with a 4-cyl engine, air conditioning, power windows/locks, and 4-wheel disc brakes. Automatic transmission is standard on the uplevel CDX model and optional on the base SE in place of manual. For '02, the CDX gets a $600 price reduction but traction control, ABS, leather upholstery, and a sunroof are now optional instead of standard. Automatic climate control is no longer available. This South

Prices are accurate at time of publication; subject to manufacturer's change.
CONSUMER GUIDE®

DAEWOO

Korean automaker's warranty includes free scheduled maintenance and roadside assistance for the first year of ownership.

RATINGS

	SX, CDX
ACCELERATION	3
FUEL ECONOMY	6
RIDE QUALITY	6
STEERING/HANDLING	4
QUIETNESS	5
INSTRUMENTS/CONTROLS	4
ROOM/COMFORT (FRONT)	4
ROOM/COMFORT (REAR)	3
CARGO ROOM	3
VALUE	2

In performance, comfort, and features, Legaza is generally class-competitive. But most rivals sell for the same or less money and carry stronger warranties. Worse, Daewoo's uncertain future means big-time depreciation today and poor trade-in value tomorrow.

TOTAL	**40**

Average total for compact cars: 51.6

ENGINES

	dohc I4
Size, liters/cu. in.	2.2/134
Horsepower @ rpm	131 @ 5200
Torque (lb-ft) @ rpm	148 @ 2800
Availability	S

EPA city/highway mpg

5-speed manual	20/28
4-speed automatic	20/28

PRICES

Daewoo Leganza	Retail Price	Dealer Invoice
SE 4-door sedan	$14599	$13139
CDX 4-door sedan	18599	16739
Destination charge	495	495

STANDARD EQUIPMENT

SE: 2.2-liter dohc 4-cylinder engine, 5-speed manual transmission, dual front airbags, 4-wheel disc brakes, air conditioning, power steering, tilt steering wheel, cloth upholstery, front bucket seats w/height-adjustable driver seat, center console, cupholders, split folding rear seat, heated power mirrors, power windows, power door locks, AM/FM/cassette, digital clock, tachometer, rear defogger, variable intermittent wipers, illuminated visor mirrors, remote fuel

Specifications begin on page 551.

DAEWOO

door/decklid release, map lights, full-size spare tire, 205/60R15 tires, wheel covers.

CDX adds: 4-speed automatic transmission, variable-assist power steering, cruise control, 6-way power driver seat, remote keyless entry, AM/FM/cassette/CD player, power antenna, theft-deterrent system, fog lights, alloy wheels.

OPTIONAL EQUIPMENT

	Retail Price	Dealer Invoice
Major Packages		
Premium Pkg., SE	$1400	$1218
Cruise control, AM/FM/cassette/CD player, remote keyless entry, woodgrain interior trim, theft-deterrent system w/alarm.		
Luxury Pkg., CDX	1550	1349
Leather upholstery, leather-wrapped steering wheel, power sunroof.		
Powertrain		
4-speed automatic transmission, SE	1000	850
Safety		
Antilock brakes, CDX	800	696
Includes traction control.		

DAEWOO NUBIRA

Daewoo Nubira 4-door sedan

Front-wheel-drive subcompact car
Base price range: $11,699-$13,999. Built in South Korea.
Also consider: Ford Focus, Honda Civic, Mazda Protege

FOR • Fuel economy **AGAINST** • Engine noise • Automatic

DAEWOO

transmission performance • Rear-seat entry/exit

ABS is no longer available on the larger of Daewoo's two subcompact cars. Nubira comes as the SE sedan and CDX wagon. Both have a 4-cyl engine and manual or optional automatic transmission. The CDX's base price is cut $1200 for 2002 with the removal of such standard features as ABS, cruise control, CD player, remote keyless entry, fog lights, theft-deterrent system, and alloy wheels. All but ABS return in the new $800 Premium Package option. Daewoo's warranty includes free scheduled maintenance and roadside assistance for the first year of ownership.

RATINGS

	SE sdn, man.	CDX wgn, auto.
ACCELERATION	3	3
FUEL ECONOMY	7	7
RIDE QUALITY	4	4
STEERING/HANDLING	4	4
QUIETNESS	3	3
INSTRUMENTS/CONTROLS	6	6
ROOM/COMFORT (FRONT)	4	4
ROOM/COMFORT (REAR)	3	3
CARGO ROOM	3	7
VALUE	1	1

Nubira may be attractive on a features-for-money basis, but it's really an average car from a troubled South Korean company with a doubtful future. Consider it with caution—and not before checking out rivals, most of which have much longer warranties and return more at trade-in time.

TOTAL	38	42

Average total for subcompact cars: 43.7

ENGINES

	dohc I4
Size, liters/cu. in.	2.0/122
Horsepower @ rpm	129 @ 5400
Torque (lb-ft) @ rpm	136 @ 4400
Availability	S
EPA city/highway mpg	
5-speed manual	22/31
4-speed automatic	22/31

PRICES

Daewoo Nubira	Retail Price	Dealer Invoice
SE 4-door sedan	$11699	$10046
CDX 4-door wagon	13999	12739
Destination charge	495	495

Specifications begin on page 551.

DAEWOO • DODGE

STANDARD EQUIPMENT

SE: 2.0-liter dohc 4-cylinder, 5-speed manual transmission, dual front airbags, 4-wheel disc brakes, power steering, cloth upholstery, front bucket seats w/height-adjustable driver seat, center console, cupholders, split folding rear seat, power front windows, AM/FM/cassette, digital clock, tachometer, rear defogger, variable intermittent wipers, remote fuel door/decklid or hatch release, visor mirrors, 185/65R14 tires, wheel covers.

CDX adds: air conditioning, tilt steering wheel, heated power mirrors, power rear windows, power door locks, rear wiper/washer, roof rack.

OPTIONAL EQUIPMENT

	Retail Price	Dealer Invoice
Major Packages		
Convenience Pkg., SE	$1500	$1320
Air conditioning, tilt steering wheel, heated power mirrors, power rear windows and door locks, upgraded sound system.		
Premium Pkg.	800	704
Cruise control, remote keyless entry, theft-deterrent system w/alarm, AM/FM/cassette/CD player. SE requires Convenience Pkg.		
Powertrain		
4-speed automatic transmission	800	720
Comfort & Convenience Features		
Air conditioning, SE	850	748

DODGE CARAVAN

Dodge Grand Caravan ES

Front- or all-wheel-drive minivan
Base price range: $16,355-$33,320. Built in USA.
Also consider: Chevrolet Venture, Honda Odyssey, Toyota Sienna

Prices are accurate at time of publication; subject to manufacturer's change.
CONSUMER GUIDE®

DODGE

FOR • Available all-wheel drive • Entry/exit • Interior storage space • Passenger and cargo room **AGAINST** • Fuel economy • Acceleration (4-cylinder)

Newly available for 2002 on America's best-selling minivan are power-adjustable brake and accelerator pedals, a DVD rear-seat entertainment system, and a tire-pressure monitor. Caravan offers regular-length models and extended-length Grand versions. All seat seven and have two sliding side doors. Caravan shares its design with the Chrysler Town & Country and Voyager.

Front-wheel drive is standard. All-wheel drive is available on Grand Caravans. Regular-length models use a 4-cyl engine or a 180-hp 3.3-liter V6. Grands get the 3.3 V6 or a 215-hp 3.8 V6. All use automatic transmission. On the front-drive Grand ES model, the automatic is available with Chrysler's AutoStick feature, which facilitates manual shifting. ABS is standard on all but the base regular-length Caravan. Front side airbags are optional.

Grands offer power operation for both side doors, regular-length models for the right door only. A minivan exclusive shared with Voyager and Town & Country allows the side doors to be closed or opened by hand during the powered phase. The Grand's optional power liftgate is also a minivan exclusive and is shared with Town & Country. The center console with internal power outlet can be placed between front or 2nd-row seats. And a rear parcel shelf has floor- and midheight mounting positions and popup storage dividers. The 3rd-row seats don't fold into the floor, but there's a 50-50 split 3rd-row bench available. Each portion weighs 55 lbs and can be removed, reclined, or folded flat. The DVD system is a dealer-installed option with a suggested retail of $1650 plus about $150 installation. A VCR-based system is similarly available for around $1400. Dodge positions its Caravan eC as a high-value entry-level minivan, with Grand Caravan eL and eX models equipped to compete directly with corresponding Honda Odyssey models, but to sell for less.

RATINGS	SE, 4 cyl	Grand Sport, 3.3 V6	Grand eX	ES AWD, 3.8 auto
ACCELERATION	2	4	5	5
FUEL ECONOMY	4	4	5	4
RIDE QUALITY	5	6	7	7
STEERING/HANDLING	4	5	6	6
QUIETNESS	4	6	6	6
INSTRUMENTS/CONTROLS	7	7	7	7
ROOM/COMFORT (FRONT)	7	7	7	7
ROOM/COMFORT (REAR)	6	8	8	8
CARGO ROOM	9	10	10	10
VALUE	7	9	10	8

Caravan is hard to beat for refinement, utility, and carlike road manners. Our extended-use test is intended to address reliability woes that have nagged previous Dodge and Chrysler minivans. But don't buy a minivan without checking out Dodge's latest.

Specifications begin on page 551.

DODGE

	SE, 4 cyl	Grand Sport, 3.3 V6	Grand eX	ES AWD, 3.8 auto
TOTAL	55	66	71	68

Average total for minivans: 56.0

EXTENDED-USE TEST UPDATE

Eleven months and 19,472 mi. into its extended-use test, our Grand Caravan ES AWD has required no unscheduled service. The optional towing package gives it a 3500-lb trailer rating (2000 lb is standard), and we had a Dodge dealer service department install a trailer hitch and wiring harness. Pulling a loaded 5x8-ft enclosed trailer, the ES was predictably slower to accelerate from a stop and required slightly longer stopping distances, but otherwise performed flawlessly. And the standard rear-leveling suspension did its job, offsetting the tongue weight of the trailer to keep the Grand Caravan's ride height even.

ENGINES

	dohc I4	ohv V6	ohv V6
Size, liters/cu. in.	2.4/153	3.3/202	3.8/231
Horsepower @ rpm	150 @ 5200	180 @ 5000	215 @ 5000
Torque (lb-ft) @ rpm	167 @ 4000	210 @ 4000	245 @ 4000
Availability	S[1]	S[2]	S[3]

EPA city/highway mpg
3-speed automatic	19/24		
4-speed automatic	NA	18/24	17/23[4]

1. eC, SE. 2. Sport FWD, eL, Grand SE; optional SE reg. 3. Sport AWD, eX, ES. 4. 17/23 w/AWD.

PRICES

Dodge Caravan

	Retail Price	Dealer Invoice
eC regular length 4-door van, FWD	$16355	NA
SE regular length 4-door van, FWD	19155	18046
Sport regular length 4-door van, FWD	23420	21459
Grand SE 4-door van, FWD	21785	20494
Grand Sport 4-door van, FWD	24275	22275
Grand Sport 4-door van, AWD	29825	27214
Grand eL 4-door van, FWD	23520	NA
Grand eX 4-door van, FWD	26070	24394
Grand ES 4-door van, FWD	29480	26907
Grand ES 4-door van, AWD	33320	30325
Destination charge: eC, SE, Sport FWD	640	640
Destination charge: Grand SE, Sport FWD, Sport AWD, eL, eX, ES FWD	655	655

Prices are accurate at time of publication; subject to manufacturer's change.

CONSUMER GUIDE®

DODGE

AWD denotes all-wheel drive. FWD denotes front-wheel drive.

STANDARD EQUIPMENT

eC: 2.4-liter dohc 4-cylinder engine, 4-speed automatic transmission, dual front airbags, front air conditioning, power steering, cloth upholstery, 5-passenger seating, front bucket seats, center console, cupholders, second row 3-passenger bench seat, AM/FM/cassette, digital clock, variable intermittent wipers, visor mirrors, intermittent rear wiper/washer, 215/70R15 tires, wheel covers.

SE adds: 7-passenger seating, second row 2-passenger bench seat, third row 3-passenger bench seat.

Grand SE adds: 3.3-liter V6 engine, antilock brakes.

Sport FWD adds: tilt steering wheel, cruise control, heated power mirrors, power windows, power door locks, tachometer, rear defogger, floormats, rear privacy glass (regular cab).

Sport AWD adds: 3.8-liter V6 engine, all-wheel drive, antilock 4-wheel disc brakes, tri-zone manual climate control (including rear controls), rear air conditioning and heater, interior air filter, leather-wrapped steering wheel, remote keyless entry, overhead console, trip computer, universal garage door opener, windshield wiper de-icer, automatic-off headlights, fog lights, rear privacy glass, 215/65R16 tires, alloy wheels.

eL adds to Sport FWD: tri-zone manual climate control (including rear controls), rear air conditioning and heater, interior air filter, second row bucket seats, third row split bench seat, remote keyless entry, overhead console, trip computer, illuminated visor mirrors, universal garage door opener, windshield wiper de-icer, automatic-off headlights, rear privacy glass.

eX adds: 3.8-liter V6 engine, traction control, antilock 4-wheel disc brakes, 8-way power driver seat, removable center console, AM/FM/cassette/CD player, power passenger-side rear door, power rear liftgate, roof rack, 215/65R16 tires, alloy wheels.

ES FWD adds: leather-wrapped steering wheel, driver seat lumbar adjustment, Infinity AM/FM/cassette, power sliding driver-side rear door, map lights, fog lights. *Deletes:* traction control, power liftgate, removable center console.

ES AWD adds: all-wheel drive, Infinity AM/FM/cassette/CD player, steering wheel radio controls, automatic day/night rearview mirror, load-leveling height-control suspension, full-size spare tire.

OPTIONAL EQUIPMENT
Major Packages

	Retail Price	Dealer Invoice
Quick Order Pkg. 25H, Sport FWD regular length..	$1325	$1166
Manufacturer's Discount Price............................	*575*	*506*

Antilock brakes, dual-zone manual climate controls, rear air conditioning, remote keyless entry, overhead console, trip computer, illuminated visor mirrors, additional interior lights, windshield wiper de-icer, automatic-off headlights.

Specifications begin on page 551.

DODGE

	Retail Price	Dealer Invoice
Quick Order Pkg. 25H, Grand Sport FWD	$1750	$1540

Tri-zone manual climate controls, rear air conditioning and heater, interior air filter, remote keyless entry, overhead console, trip computer, windshield wiper de-icer, automatic-off headlights, rear privacy glass

Quick Order Pkg. 25K, Grand Sport FWD	3690	3247
Manufacturer's Discount Price	3490	3071

Quick Order Pkg. 25H plus AM/FM/cassette/CD player, power sliding passenger-side rear door, quad bucket seats, third row split folding bench seat, 8-way power driver seat, illuminated visor mirrors, additional interior lights.

Quick Order Pkg. 29S, ES FWD	2000	1760

AutoStick automatic transmission w/manual-shift capability, traction control, removable center console, AM/FM/cassette/CD player, steering wheel radio controls, automatic day/night rearview mirror, touring suspension, full-size spare tire, 215/60R17 tires, chrome alloy wheels.

Power Convenience Group, SE	755	664

Power mirrors (heated when ordered w/rear defogger), power windows and door locks, overwrhead console, map lights.

Deluxe Convenience Group, SE	375	330

Tilt steering wheel, cruise control.

Climate Group II, SE	645	568
SE w/Power Convenience Group	680	598

Heated power mirrors, rear defogger, rear privacy glass.

Climate Group II, Grand Sport FWD	450	396

Rear privacy glass.

Climate Group III, Grand Sport FWD	1110	977
Grand Sport FWD w/Trailer Tow Prep Group	1045	920

Rear air conditioning, rear privacy glass.

Touring Group, Sport FWD regular length	870	766
Grand Sport FWD	820	722
Grand Sport FWD w/Trailer Tow Prep Group	770	678

Leather-wrapped steering wheel, 4-wheel disc brakes, fog lights, touring suspension, 215/65R16 tires, alloy wheels. Requires Quick Order Pkg.

Courtesy Light Group, Grand Sport	100	88

Illuminated visor mirrors, additional interior lights. Sport FWD requires Quick Order Pkg. 25H.

Electronics Convenience Group, ES	305	268

Tire pressure monitor, vehicle information system, rear reading lights.

Trailer Tow Prep Group, Grand Sport FWD	695	612
Grand Sport AWD	355	312

Prices are accurate at time of publication; subject to manufacturer's change.

CONSUMER GUIDE®

DODGE

	Retail Price	Dealer Invoice
ES FWD	$645	$568
ES FWD w/Pkg. 29S	485	427
ES AWD	195	172

Heavy-duty engine cooling, heavy-duty alternator and battery, load-leveling height-control suspension (FWD), 4-wheel disc brakes, trailer wiring harness, full-size spare tire. Sport FWD requires Quick Order Pkg.

Powertrain

3.3-liter V6 engine, SE reg. length	970	854
Traction control, ES FWD	175	154

Safety

Antilock brakes, SE/Sport reg. length	565	497

SE requires 3.3-liter V6 engine.

Front side airbags	390	343

Comfort & Convenience Features

Power adjustable pedals	185	163
AM/FM/CD player, SE	225	198

Includes CD changer controls. Requires 3.3-liter V6 engine.

AM/FM/cassette/CD player, Sport, ES FWD	225	198
AM/FM/cassette/CD player w/rear controls, Sport, ES FWD	450	396
Sport w/Pkg. 25K, ES FWD w/Pkg. 29S, ES AWD	225	198

Includes wireless headphones. Sport FWD requires Quick Order Pkg. 25H.

In-dash 4-disc CD changer, Sport, ES FWD, Sport/ES w/rear radio controls	375	330
Sport FWD w/Pkg. 25K, ES FWD w/Pkg. 29S, ES AWD	150	132

Sport requires Pkg. 25H.

Infinity speakers, Sport	495	436

Requires optional radio. Sport FWD requires Quick Order Pkg.

Steering wheel radio controls, ES FWD	75	66
Third row bench seat, eC	450	NA
CYG 7-passenger seating, Sport	945	832

Quad bucket seats, third row split folding bench seat. Sport FWD requires Quick Order Pkg. 25H.

CYK/CYR 7-passenger seating, SE, Sport	225	198

Front bucket seats, second row 2-passenger bench seat w/dual integrated child seats, third row 3-passenger bench seat. Sport FWD NA w/Quick Order Pkg. 25H/K.

CYS 7-passenger seating, Sport	745	656

Quad bucket seats, third row 3-passenger folding bench seat. Sport FWD requires Pkg. 25H.

Specifications begin on page 551.

DODGE

	Retail Price	Dealer Invoice
CYT 7-passenger seating, Sport.............................	$870	$766
Quad bucket seats w/integrated child seat, third row 3-passenger bench seat. Sport FWD requires Pkg. 25H.		
CYL 7-passenger seating, Sport FWD w/Pkg. 25H	1070	942
Sport FWD w/Pkg. 25K, Sport AWD, ES.............	125	110
Quad bucket seats w/integrated child seat, third row 3-passenger split-folding bench seat. NA w/leather upholstery.		
Leather upholstery, ES FWD....................................	890	783
ES w/Pkg. 29S, ES AWD......................................	1250	1100
Heated front seats, ES..	250	220
Requires leather upholstery. ES FWD requires Quick Order Pkg.		
Removable console, Grand Sport, ES FWD............	195	172
Sport FWD requires Quick Order Pkg., 7-passenger seating CYG, CYL, CYS, or CYT. Sport AWD requires CYS or CYT seating.		
Rear cargo organizer, Grand Sport, ES..................	250	220
Sport FWD requires Quick Order Pkg. or Climate Group III.		
Rear defogger, eC, SE..	195	172
SE w/Power Convenience Group.......................	230	202
Power sliding passenger-side rear door, eL, Sport.	400	352
Sport FWD requires Quick Order Pkg. 25H.		
Power sliding driver-side rear door, eX...................	400	352
Power liftgate, Grand Sport, eL, ES........................	400	352
Sport FWD requires Quick Order Pkg., power sliding passenger-side rear door.		

Appearance and Miscellaneous

Theft-deterrent system w/alarm, Sport, ES.............	195	172
Sport FWD requires Quick Order Pkg.		
Roof rack, SE, Sport, eL, ES	250	220
Touring Suspension, ES FWD.................................	95	84
Chrome alloy wheels, ES FWD................................	680	598
Includes 215/60R17 tires.		

DODGE DURANGO

Rear- or 4-wheel-drive midsize sport-utility vehicle
Base price range: $24,875-$36,470. Built in USA.
Also consider: Chevrolet Blazer, Ford Explorer Sport Trac and Sport, Jeep Grand Cherokee

FOR • Passenger and cargo room • Acceleration (5.9-liter V8)
AGAINST • Rear-seat comfort • Fuel economy

Dodge's SUV gains optional curtain side airbags and a DVD entertainment system for 2002. Durango is sized between midsize and

Prices are accurate at time of publication; subject to manufacturer's change.
CONSUMER GUIDE®

DODGE

Dodge Durango

full-size SUVs and offers three rows of seats. A 235-hp 4.7-liter V8 is standard on the base Sport model. A 245-hp 5.9 V8 is optional on the SLT models and standard on the R/T model. Both engines come with a 4-speed automatic transmission, though the 4.7 is due to get a 5-speed automatic midyear. Durango is available with rear-wheel drive, 4WD that must be disengaged on dry pavement, or 4WD that can be left engaged on dry pavement; 4x4s include low-range gearing. Rear ABS is standard; 4-wheel ABS is optional. Front bucket seats and a 3-passenger 2nd-row bench seat are standard. A front bench is available, as is a 2-place 3rd-row seat for a maximum 8-passenger capacity. The new curtain side airbags cover the front and 2nd-row seats. The DVD rear-seat entertainment system is a dealer-installed option and is expected to cost about $1800, including installation.

RATINGS	Sport 4WD, 4.7 V8	SLT Plus 4WD, 5.9 V8
ACCELERATION	5	5
FUEL ECONOMY	2	2
RIDE QUALITY	5	5
STEERING/HANDLING	3	3
QUIETNESS	4	4
INSTRUMENTS/CONTROLS	7	8
ROOM/COMFORT (FRONT)	8	8
ROOM/COMFORT (REAR)	6	6
CARGO ROOM	8	8
VALUE	6	5

Durango approaches full-size SUVs for roominess and power but sells at midsize-SUV prices. That merits our Recommended rating.

TOTAL	54	54

Average total for midsize sport-utility vehicles: 49.6

ENGINES	ohc V8	ohv V8
Size, liters/cu. in.	4.7/287	5.9/360

Specifications begin on page 551.

DODGE

	ohc V8	ohv V8
Horsepower @ rpm	235 @ 4800	245 @ 4000
Torque (lb-ft) @ rpm	295 @ 3200	335 @ 3200
Availability	S[1]	S[2]
EPA city/highway mpg		
4-speed automatic	13/18[3]	12/16[5]
5-speed automatic	13/17[4]	

1. Sport, SLT Plus. 2. R/T; optional SLT, SLT Plus. 3. 15/20 w/2WD. 4. 14/19 w/2WD. 5. 12/17 w/2WD.

PRICES

Dodge Durango	Retail Price	Dealer Invoice
Sport 4-door wagon, 2WD	$24875	$22819
Sport 4-door wagon, 4WD	26995	24741
SLT 4-door wagon, 2WD	29095	26575
SLT 4-door wagon, 4WD	31215	28496
SLT Plus 4-door wagon, 2WD	31705	28897
SLT Plus 4-door wagon, 4WD	33825	30819
R/T 4-door wagon, 4WD	36470	33170
Destination charge	600	600

STANDARD EQUIPMENT

Sport: 4.7-liter V8 engine, 4-speed automatic transmission, dual front airbags, rear antilock brakes, front air conditioning w/manual dual-zone controls, power steering, tilt steering wheel, cruise control, cloth upholstery, front bucket seats, center console, cupholders, second row split folding seat, power mirrors, power windows, power door locks, remote keyless entry, AM/FM/cassette, digital clock, tachometer, visor mirrors, map lights, variable intermittent wipers, rear defogger, variable-intermittent rear wiper/washer, rear privacy glass, full-size spare tire, 235/75R15XL tires, alloy wheels. **4WD** adds: 4-wheel drive, 2-speed transfer case.

SLT adds: rear air conditioning/heater, 6-way power driver seat, third row folding seat, AM/FM/CD player, floormats, roof rack, fog lights, 255/65R16 white-letter tires.

SLT Plus adds: leather upholstery, leather-wrapped steering wheel w/radio controls, heated power mirrors w/driver-side automatic day/night, Infinity sound system, automatic day/night rearview mirror, universal garage door opener, illuminated visor mirrors, running boards. **4WD** adds: 4-wheel drive, 2-speed transfer case, 265/70R16 all-terrain white-letter tires.

R/T adds: 5.9-liter V8 engine, 4-wheel drive, 2-speed transfer case, limited-slip differential, 6-way power passenger seat, steering wheel radio controls, theft-deterrent system, performance suspension, 275/60R17 tires.

Prices are accurate at time of publication; subject to manufacturer's change.

DODGE

OPTIONAL EQUIPMENT

	Retail Price	Dealer Invoice
Major Packages		
SXT Quick Order Pkg. 24F, Sport	$1000	$880

AM/FM/CD player, floormats, roof rack, wheel flares, graphite-colored front and rear fascias, 265/70R16 white-letter tires (2WD), 265/70R16 all-terrain white-letter tires (4WD).

Overhead Convenience Group, SLT	415	365

Overhead console, illuminated visor mirrors, trip computer, universal garage door opener.

Trailer Tow Group, SLT	590	519
SLT Plus, R/T	465	409

Includes 7-wire harness, 4-pin wire adaptor, Class IV platform hitch, heavy-duty alternator and battery, heavy-duty engine and power steering fluid cooling, transmission oil cooler, heated power mirrors.

Powertrain

5.9-liter V8 engine, SLT, SLT Plus	595	524
Full-time transfer case, 4WD SLT/SLT Plus	395	348
Std. R/T.		
Limited-slip differential, Sport, SLT, SLT Plus	285	251

Safety

Front and second row curtain side airbags	495	436
Front and rear antilock brakes	495	436

Comfort & Convenience Features

Leather upholstery, SLT	795	700
Heated front seats, SLT Plus, R/T	250	220
Manufacturer's Discount Price	*140*	*123*
Front split bench seat, Sport	150	132
AM/FM/cassette/CD player, Sport	225	198
Sport w/Pkg. 24F, SLT, SLT Plus, R/T	100	88
Infinity sound system, SLT	535	471

Appearance and Miscellaneous

Fog lights, Sport	120	106
Requires Quick Order Pkg. 24F.		
Running boards, Sport, SLT	395	348
Sport requires Quick Order Pkg 24F.		

DODGE INTREPID

Front-wheel-drive full-size car
Base price range: $20,370-$26,615. Built in Canada.
Also consider: Buick LeSabre, Toyota Avalon

Specifications begin on page 551.

DODGE

BEST BUY

Dodge Intrepid R/T

FOR • Passenger and cargo room • Ride • Steering/handling
AGAINST • Trunk liftover • Rear visibility

Dodge's full-size sedan shares a basic design with the Chrysler Concorde and 300M but has different styling. Intrepid comes in base SE, uplevel ES, and performance-oriented R/T models. SE comes with a 200-hp 2.7-liter V6, ES with a 234-hp 3.5 V6. R/T has a 244-hp 3.5 V6, along with firmer suspension, unique trim, and 17-inch wheels that will be available in chrome midyear. All use a 4-speed automatic transmission; on R/T it's Chrysler's AutoStick with separate gate for manual shifting. All Intrepids have 4-wheel disc brakes; ABS is optional on SE and ES, standard on R/T. Traction is optional on ES, standard on R/T. Front side airbags are optional on all. Front bucket seats are standard, but an optional bench for the SE gives 6-passenger seating.

RATINGS	Base	ES	R/T
ACCELERATION	4	5	6
FUEL ECONOMY	6	5	5
RIDE QUALITY	7	7	6
STEERING/HANDLING	6	6	7
QUIETNESS	5	5	4
INSTRUMENTS/CONTROLS	6	6	6
ROOM/COMFORT (FRONT)	7	7	7
ROOM/COMFORT (REAR)	7	7	7
CARGO ROOM	6	6	6
VALUE	8	8	8

Intrepid targets the sportier buyer, while Concorde's message is one of stylish comfort. Both do their jobs well, being roomy, athletic, and competitively priced. Their reputation for reliability trails that of such rivals as the Toyota Avalon and Buick LeSabre, but overall, Concorde and Intrepid are impressive values.

TOTAL	62	62	62

Average total for full-size cars: 58.7

Prices are accurate at time of publication; subject to manufacturer's change.
CONSUMER GUIDE®

DODGE

ENGINES

	dohc V6	ohc V6	ohc V6
Size, liters/cu. in.	2.7/167	3.5/215	3.5/215
Horsepower @ rpm	200 @ 5800	234 @ 6000	244 @ 6400
Torque (lb-ft) @ rpm	190 @ 4850	241 @ 4400	250 @ 3950
Availability	S[1]	O[2]	S[3]
EPA city/highway mpg			
4-speed automatic	20/28	18/26	18/26

1. SE. 2. ES. 3. R/T.

PRICES

Dodge Intrepid	Retail Price	Dealer Invoice
SE 4-door sedan	$20370	$18938
ES 4-door sedan	22530	20882
R/T 4-door sedan	26615	24559
Destination charge	625	625

STANDARD EQUIPMENT

SE: 2.7-liter dohc V6 engine, 4-speed automatic transmission, dual front airbags, 4-wheel disc brakes, emergency inside trunk release, air conditioning, power steering, tilt steering wheel, cloth upholstery, front bucket seats, center console, cupholders, power mirrors, power windows, power door locks, rear defogger, variable intermittent wipers, AM/FM/cassette, digital clock, tachometer, visor mirrors, map lights, power remote decklid release, automatic-off headlights, floormats, 225/60R16 tires, wheel covers.

ES adds: 3.5-liter V6 234-horsepower engine, cruise control, 8-way power driver seat w/lumbar adjustment, split folding rear seat, remote keyless entry, AM/FM/CD player, fog lights, alloy wheels.

R/T adds: 3.5-liter V6 244-horsepower engine, traction control, 4-speed automatic transmission w/manual-shift capability, antilock brakes, leather-wrapped steering wheel, automatic climate control, upgraded sound system, overhead console, automatic day/night rearview mirror, universal garage door opener, trip computer, illuminated visor mirrors, rear spoiler, performance suspension, 225/55VR17 tires, chrome alloy wheels.

OPTIONAL EQUIPMENT
Major Packages

Quick Order Pkg. 22D, SE	1670	1536
Manufacturer's Discount Price	*1160*	*1067*

Cruise control, 8-way power driver seat, split folding rear seat w/rear armrest and additional cupholder, AM/FM/CD player, remote keyless entry, cargo net, bodyside moldings, alloy wheels.

Specifications begin on page 551.

DODGE

	Retail Price	Dealer Invoice
Quick Order Pkg. 27M, ES	$1870	$1720

Leather upholstery, leather-wrapped steering wheel, automatic climate control, upgraded sound system, overhead console, automatic day/night rearview mirror, trip computer, illuminated visor mirrors, universal garage door opener, theft-deterrent system w/alarm.

Safety
Antilock brakes, SE, ES	600	552
ES w/Pkg. 27M	775	713
ES with Quick Order Pkg. 27M includes traction control.		
Front side airbags	390	359

Comfort & Convenience Features
Power sunroof	895	823
SE require Quick Order Pkg. 22D.		
Cruise control, SE	235	216
AM/FM/cassette/CD player, SE	625	575
ES	450	414
ES w/Pkg. 27M, R/T	100	92
Includes upgraded sound system.		
AM/FM/cassette w/in-dash 4-disc CD changer, SE, ES	725	667
ES w/Pkg. 27M, R/T	375	345
Includes Infinity sound system. SE requires Quick Order Pkg. 22D.		
Leather upholstery, R/T	640	589
Front split bench seat, SE	150	138

Appearance and Miscellaneous
Chrome aloy wheels, ES	600	552

DODGE NEON

Dodge Neon SE

Front-wheel-drive subcompact car

Prices are accurate at time of publication; subject to manufacturer's change.

DODGE

Base price range: $12,240-$16,190. Built in USA.
Also consider: Ford Focus, Honda Civic, Toyota Corolla

FOR • Fuel economy • Steering/handling	AGAINST • Noise

Plymouth's retirement gives Dodge sole possession of the Neon. A new automatic transmission, available chrome wheels, and a compass/outside temperature display are its 2002 highlights. Front side airbags, ABS, and traction control are optional. Base models have a 132-hp 4-cyl engine and are available with manual transmission or a 4-speed automatic, which replaces a 3-speed for 2002. A no-charge option for the R/T and race-track oriented ACR models is a 150-hp 4 cyl that's available only with manual transmission. Both those models have 4-wheel disc brakes. The R/T also has 16-inch wheels vs. the other models' 14s and 15s. Chrome 15-inch alloys are a new SE-model option.

RATINGS

	ES, auto.	R/T, 150 hp
ACCELERATION	4	5
FUEL ECONOMY	6	7
RIDE QUALITY	4	4
STEERING/HANDLING	6	7
QUIETNESS	4	4
INSTRUMENTS/CONTROLS	6	6
ROOM/COMFORT (FRONT)	4	4
ROOM/COMFORT (REAR)	4	4
CARGO ROOM	3	3
VALUE	6	6

Pressured by newer, more polished rivals such as the Ford Focus and Honda Civic, Neon's sales are slow and getting slower, so don't buy one without taking advantage of factory incentives and/or dealer discounts. On the upside, prices are attractive to start with, and Neon is capable enough to stand comparison with most subcompact competitors.

TOTAL	47	50

Average total for subcompact cars: 43.7

ENGINES

	ohc I4	ohc I4
Size, liters/cu. in.	2.0/122	2.0/122
Horsepower @ rpm	132 @ 5600	150 @ 6600
Torque (lb-ft) @ rpm	130 @ 4600	135 @ 4800
Availability	S	O[1]
EPA city/highway mpg		
5-speed manual	28/34	28/34
4-speed automatic	24/31	

1. R/T, ACR.

Specifications begin on page 551.

DODGE

PRICES

Dodge Neon

	Retail Price	Dealer Invoice
Base 4-door sedan	$12240	$11498
ACR 4-door sedan	14305	13378
SE 4-door sedan	14015	13114
ES 4-door sedan	14545	13596
R/T 4-door sedan	16190	15093
Destination charge	490	490

STANDARD EQUIPMENT

Base: 2.0-liter 4-cylinder 132-horsepower engine, 5-speed manual transmission, dual front airbags, emergency inside trunk release, power steering, tilt steering wheel, cloth upholstery, front bucket seats, center console, cupholders, split folding rear seat, AM/FM/cassette, variable intermittent wipers, rear defogger, visor mirrors, floormats, 185/65R14 tires, wheel covers.

ACR adds: traction control, antilock 4-wheel disc brakes, leather-wrapped steering wheel, tachometer, competition suspension, 185/60HR15 tires, alloy wheels.

SE adds to Base: air conditioning, power mirrors, power windows, power door locks, remote keyless entry, AM/FM/CD player, power decklid release, theft-deterrent system, 185/60R15 tires.

ES adds: tachometer, rear spoiler, fog lights, alloy wheels.

R/T adds: traction control, antilock 4-wheel disc brakes, leather-wrapped steering wheel, cruise control, map lights, sport suspension, 195/50VR16 tires.

OPTIONAL EQUIPMENT
Major Packages

Buyer Security Group, Base	1770	1628
Manufacturer's Discount Price	*895*	*823*
SE	1270	1168
Manufacturer's Discount Price	*695*	*639*
ES	1170	1076
Manufacturer's Discount Price	*695*	*639*
R/T	1120	1030
Manufacturer's Discount Price	*695*	*639*

Front side airbags, power door locks (Base), remote keyless entry (Base), tachometer (Base, SE), power decklid release (Base), map and additional interior lights (Base, SE, ES), theft-deterrent system w/alarm, 5-year/60,000 mile powertrain warranty, service contract. Base requires AM/FM/cassette w/CD changer controls.

Antilock Brake Group, Base, SE	840	773

Prices are accurate at time of publication; subject to manufacturer's change.

DODGE

	Retail Price	Dealer Invoice
Manufacturer's Discount Price.............................	*$595*	*$548*
SE w/Buyer Security Group, ES........................	740	681
Manufacturer's Discount Price.............................	*595*	*548*
Antilock 4-wheel disc brakes, traction control, tachometer.		
Sun/Sound Group, SE, ES................................	985	906
Manufacturer's Discount Price.............................	*795*	*731*
SE/ES w/Buyer Security Group	935	860
Manufacturer's Discount Price.............................	*795*	*731*
Power sunroof, AM/FM/cassette w/in-dash 4-disc CD changer, map lights, additional interior lights, passenger assist handles.		
Driver Convenience Group, ACR.......................	2100	1932
Manufacturer's Discount Price.............................	*1695*	*1559*
Air conditioning, power door locks, remote keyless entry, AM/FM/cassette w/CD changer controls, map lights, additional interior lights, power decklid release, floormats, theft-deterrent system w/alarm.		
Leather Interior Group, ES...............................	820	754
Manufacturer's Discount Price.............................	*695*	*639*
ES w/Buyer Security Group..............................	790	727
Manufacturer's Discount Price.............................	*680*	*626*
R/T	715	658
Manufacturer's Discount Price.............................	*620*	*571*
Leather upholstery, leather-wrapped steering wheel and shifter, compass, outside temperature indicator, map lights, additional interior lights.		
Convenience Group, SE, ES.............................	285	262
SE/ES w/Buyer Security Group	235	216
Cruise control, map lights, additional interior lights.		

Powertrain
2.0-liter 4-cylinder 150-horsepower engine, ACR, R/T	NC	NC
4-speed automatic transmission, Base, SE, ES	825	759

Safety
Front side airbags	350	322

Comfort & Convenience Features
Air conditioning, Base	1000	920
AM/FM/cassette w/CD changer controls, Base	50	46
Requires Buyer Security Group.		
AM/FM/CD player, Base...	175	161

Appearance and Miscellaneous
Alloy wheels, SE	355	327
Chrome alloy wheels, SE	955	879

Specifications begin on page 551.

DODGE

DODGE STRATUS

Dodge Stratus ES sedan

Front-wheel-drive midsize car
Base price range: $17,400-$20,940. Built in USA.
Also consider: Chevrolet Malibu, Honda Accord, Toyota Camry

FOR • Steering/handling **AGAINST** • Acceleration (4-cylinder) • Rear-seat entry/exit (coupe) • Rear-seat comfort (coupe)

Stratus sedans share a design with the Chrysler Sebring sedan and convertible. Stratus coupes share a design with the Chrysler Sebring coupe; both coupes use powertrains and platforms from Mitsubishi's Eclipse and Galant.

Base SE and uplevel SE Plus sedans come with a 4-cyl engine and offer an optional Chrysler-made 2.7-liter V6. The V6 is standard on the top-line ES sedan. Both engines come only with automatic transmission. All sedans have 4-wheel disc brakes, with ABS optional. Curtain side airbags are optional on sedans; no torso side airbags are offered. Due later in the model year is an R/T sedan with the 2.7 V6, 5-speed manual transmission, and antilock 4-wheel disc brakes. The R/T will offer Chrysler's AutoStick automatic transmission with manual shift gate.

Coupes offer SE and R/T models. The SE comes with a 4-cyl engine or optional 3.0-liter V6. The V6 is standard on the R/T. Both coupes use manual transmission or optional automatic. R/T automatics come with traction control, and can be ordered with AutoStick. Four-wheel disc brakes are included with the V6. ABS is optional only on the R/T.

RATINGS	SE cpe, 4-cyl auto.	R/T cpe, man.	SE sdn, 4-cyl auto.	ES sdn
ACCELERATION	4	7	4	5
FUEL ECONOMY	5	5	5	5
RIDE QUALITY	5	4	6	6

Prices are accurate at time of publication; subject to manufacturer's change.

DODGE

	SE cpe, 4-cyl auto.	R/T cpe, man.	SE sdn, 4-cyl auto.	ES sdn
STEERING/HANDLING	6	7	6	7
QUIETNESS	5	4	5	5
INSTRUMENTS/CONTROLS	4	4	6	6
ROOM/COMFORT (FRONT)	4	4	5	5
ROOM/COMFORT (REAR)	2	2	4	4
CARGO ROOM	5	5	5	5
VALUE	3	4	6	6

Stratus and Sebring lack the polish of some import-brand rivals, but all three body styles fulfill their mission and are competitively priced. Stratus R/T appeals for its performance image and the sedans are sporty-feeling family cars, but the real gem here is the roomy, stylish Sebring convertible.

TOTAL	43	46	52	54

Average total for midsize cars: 57.0

ENGINES

	ohc I4	dohc I4	dohc V6	ohc V6
Size, liters/cu. in.	2.4/143	2.4/148	2.7/167	3.0/181
Horsepower @ rpm	147 @ 5500	150 @ 5200	200 @ 5900	200 @ 5000
Torque (lb-ft) @ rpm	158 @ 4000	167 @ 4000	192 @ 4300	205 @ 4500
Availability	S[1]	S[2]	S[3]	S[4]

EPA city/highway mpg

5-speed manual	22/29			20/29
4-speed automatic	21/28	21/30	20/28	20/28

1. SE coupe. 2. SE sedan. 3. ES; optional SE sedan. 4. R/T; optional SE coupe.

PRICES

Dodge Stratus

	Retail Price	Dealer Invoice
SE 2-door coupe	$17920	$16648
R/T 2-door coupe	20940	19366
SE 4-door sedan	17400	16195
SE Plus 4-door sedan	18845	17496
ES 4-door sedan	20660	19129
Destination charge	595	595

STANDARD EQUIPMENT

SE coupe: 2.4-liter 4-cylinder engine, 5-speed manual transmission, dual front airbags, air conditioning, power steering, tilt steering wheel, cruise control, cloth upholstery, front bucket seats, height-adjustable driver seat, center console, cupholders, power mirrors, power windows, power door locks, AM/FM/cassette, digital clock, tachometer, variable

Specifications begin on page 551.

DODGE

intermittent wipers, rear defogger, visor mirrors, map lights, remote decklid release, floormats, theft-deterrent system, 205/60HR16 tires, wheel covers.

R/T adds: 3.0-liter V6 engine, 4-wheel disc brakes, leather-wrapped steering wheel, remote keyless entry, Infinity AM/FM/cassette/CD player, automatic day/night rearview mirror, compass, fog lights, sport suspension, 215/50HR17 tires, alloy wheels.

SE sedan adds to SE coupe: 2.4-liter dohc 4-cylinder engine, 4-speed automatic transmission, 4-wheel disc brakes, emergency inside trunk release, split folding rear seat, 205/65TR15 tires. *Deletes:* power mirrors.

SE Plus adds: 8-way power driver seat, power mirrors, remote keyless entry, AM/FM/CD player, automatic-off headlights, 205/60TR16 tires, alloy wheels.

ES adds: 2.7-liter dohc V6 engine, leather-wrapped steering wheel, driver seat lumbar adjustment, Premium sound system, illuminated visor mirrors, trip computer, sport suspension, fog lights.

OPTIONAL EQUIPMENT

	Retail Price	Dealer Invoice
Major Packages		
Touring Group, SE coupe	$545	$501
Remote keyless entry, AM/FM radio w/in-dash 4-disc CD changer, theft-deterrent system w/alarm.		
Leather Interior Group, R/T	1045	961
Leather upholstery, 6-way power driver seat, universal garage door opener. Requires polished alloy wheels.		
Security Information Group, SE Plus	355	327
Trip computer, central locking system, theft-deterrent system w/alarm.		
Convenience Group, ES	285	262
Universal garage door opener, central locking system, theft-deterrent system w/alarm.		
Powertrain		
3.0-liter V6 engine, SE coupe	885	814
Includes 4-wheel disc brakes. Requires 4-speed automatic transmission.		
2.7-liter dohc V6 engine, SE sedan	1210	1113
SE Plus	850	782
SE includes cruise control, AM/FM/CD player.		
4-speed automatic transmission, SE coupe, R/T	825	759
AutoStick manual-shift capability, R/T	165	152
Requires 4-speed automatic transmission.		
Safety		
Curtain side airbags, sedans	390	359
Antilock brakes, R/T manual, sedans	565	520

Prices are accurate at time of publication; subject to manufacturer's change.

DODGE • FORD

	Retail Price	Dealer Invoice
R/T automatic	$740	$680

R/T automatic includes traction control.

Comfort & Convenience Features

Leather upholstery, ES..	600	552
Power mirrors, SE sedan	60	55
Power sunroof, SE Plus	805	741
coupes, ES	695	638

SE Plus includes illuminated visor mirrors, map lights.

Cruise control, SE sedan	235	216
Remote keyless entry, SE sedan	170	156
AM/FM/CD player, SE sedan	125	115
AM/FM/cassette/CD player, SE Plus.......................	100	92
AM/FM/cassette w/in-dash 4-disc CD changer, ES	250	230
Premium sound system, SE Plus............................	350	322

Appearance and Miscellaneous

Alloy wheels, SE coupe..	365	336
Chrome alloy wheels, ES	600	552
Polished alloy wheels, R/T	375	345

FORD CROWN VICTORIA

Ford Crown Victoria

Rear-wheel-drive full-size car
Base price range: $22,855-$28,060. Built in Canada.
Also consider: Buick LeSabre, Dodge Intrepid, Toyota Avalon

FOR • Passenger and cargo room   **AGAINST** • Fuel economy

Added standard equipment marks the 2002 version of Ford's rear-

Specifications begin on page 551.

FORD

wheel-drive full-size sedan. Crown Victoria is similar to Mercury's Grand Marquis, and the platform is shared by the luxury Lincoln Town Car. Crown Vic is offered in base, LX, and LX Sport trim. LX Sport comes with bucket seats, center console, sport suspension with rear leveling, leather interior, and 17-inch wheels vs. 16s. Automatic transmission is standard on all models. The sole engine is a 4.6-liter V8 that makes 220 hp in base form and 235 in the LX Sport and with the optional Handling and Performance Package. ABS is standard on LX and LX Sport, optional on the base model. Traction control is optional for LX and LX Sport. Side airbags are unavailable. New standard features for 2002 include a standard power driver's seat and heated mirrors on base models, and automatic climate control and power-adjustable brake and accelerator pedals for the LX.

RATINGS

	LX
ACCELERATION	6
FUEL ECONOMY	4
RIDE QUALITY	7
STEERING/HANDLING	5
QUIETNESS	6
INSTRUMENTS/CONTROLS	4
ROOM/COMFORT (FRONT)	7
ROOM/COMFORT (REAR)	6
CARGO ROOM	6
VALUE	5

We favor the more modern approach of front-wheel-drive rivals like the Dodge Intrepid and Buick LeSabre, but rear-drive V8 traditionalists won't be disappointed with the reasonably priced Crown Victoria and Grand Marquis.

TOTAL	56

Average total for full-size cars: 58.7

ENGINES

	ohc V8	ohc V8
Size, liters/cu. in.	4.6/281	4.6/281
Horsepower @ rpm	220 @ 4750	235 @ 4750
Torque (lb-ft) @ rpm	265 @ 4000	275 @ 4000
Availability	S[1]	S[2]
EPA city/highway mpg		
4-speed automatic	17/25	17/25

1. Base, LX. 2. LX Sport; optional base, LX.

PRICES

Ford Crown Victoria	Retail Price	Dealer Invoice
Base 4-door sedan	$22855	$21487

Prices are accurate at time of publication; subject to manufacturer's change.

FORD

	Retail Price	Dealer Invoice
LX 4-door sedan	$26445	$24789
LX Sport 4-door sedan	28060	26275
Destination charge	680	680

STANDARD EQUIPMENT

Base: 4.6-liter V8 220-horsepower engine, 4-speed automatic transmission, dual front airbags, 4-wheel disc brakes, emergency inside trunk release, air conditioning, power steering, tilt steering wheel, cruise control, column shift, cloth upholstery, front split bench seat, 6-way power driver seat, cupholders, AM/FM/cassette, digital clock, heated power mirrors, power windows, power door locks, power decklid release, rear defogger, intermittent wipers, wiper-activated automatic headlights, floormats, theft-deterrent system, 225/60SR16 tires, wheel covers.

LX adds: antilock brakes, automatic climate control, driver seat power lumbar adjustment, power passenger seat, power adjustable pedals, leather-wrapped steering wheel w/radio controls, illuminated visor mirrors, map lights, remote keyless entry, automatic day/night rearview mirror, compass, 225/60R16 tires, alloy wheels.

LX Sport adds: 4.6-liter V8 235-horsepower engine, leather upholstery, front bucket seats, center console w/floor shifter, Premium Audio System, Handling and Performance Suspension, rear air suspension, 225/60TR16 touring tires.

OPTIONAL EQUIPMENT
Major Packages

Safety and Convenience Group, Base	670	597

Antilock brakes, power adjustable pedals, remote keyless entry.

Handling and Performance Pkg., LX	615	547

Includes 235-horsepower engine, dual exhaust, performance springs, shocks and stabilizer bars, rear air suspension, 3.27 axle ratio, 225/60TR16 touring tires, unique alloy wheels. Std. LX Sport.

Powertrain

Traction control, LX, LX Sport	175	156

Safety

Antilock brakes, Base	600	534

Comfort & Convenience Features

Power adjustable pedals, Base	120	107
Remote keyless entry, Base	240	213
Leather upholstery, LX	795	708
Manufacturer's Discount Price	NC	NC

Includes power passenger seat.

Specifications begin on page 551.

FORD

	Retail Price	Dealer Invoice
AM/FM/CD player, Base..	$140	$124
6-disc CD changer, LX, LX Sport.............................	350	312
LX requires Premium Audio System.		
Premium Audio System, LX	360	321
Upgraded amplifier and six speakers.		
Electronic instruments, LX	235	209
Digital instruments, trip computer.		
Trunk storage unit, LX, LX Sport.............................	190	169

Appearance and Miscellaneous
225/60SR16 whitewall tires, Base, LX	80	71
NA with Handling and Performance Pkg.		

FORD ESCAPE

Ford Escape XLT

Front- or all-wheel-drive compact sport-utility vehicle

Base price range: $18,415-$24,630. Built in USA.

Also consider: Honda CR-V, Subaru Forester, Toyota RAV4

FOR • Cargo room • Maneuverability • Visibility **AGAINST** • Noise

Introduced for 2001 and now America's best-selling compact SUV, Escape for 2002 gets new model names and plans for a modified shift lever. This 4-dr wagon has a rear liftgate with separate-opening glass. For '02, base XLS and uplevel XLT versions get new sub-series models called Value, Sport, Choice, and Premium. Each has escalating levels of equipment. Escape is offered with two powertrain combinations: a 4-cyl engine with manual transmission, or a V6 with automatic. Both combinations are available with front-wheel drive or all-wheel drive without low-range gearing; a dashboard

Prices are accurate at time of publication; subject to manufacturer's change.

FORD

switch on AWD models locks in a 50/50 front/rear torque split. ABS is standard on XLT versions, optional on XLS models. Front side airbags are optional on both. Standard equipment includes air conditioning, power windows/locks/mirrors, front bucket seats with console, and folding rear seatback (split/folding on XLTs). XLS models have 15-inch wheels, XLTs get 16s. For 2002, XLSs have a CD/cassette, XLTs a 6-disc CD changer. Due later in the model year is a shortened automatic-transmission shift lever designed to provide easier access to some dashboard controls. Also due later as an option is Ford's No Boundaries roof rack that slides back and down to ease loading.

RATINGS

	XLT Sport
ACCELERATION	5
FUEL ECONOMY	5
RIDE QUALITY	4
STEERING/HANDLING	5
QUIETNESS	4
INSTRUMENTS/CONTROLS	5
ROOM/COMFORT (FRONT)	6
ROOM/COMFORT (REAR)	5
CARGO ROOM	7
VALUE	7

Substantial feeling, roomy, comfortable, even fun to drive, Escape and Tribute are compact SUV all-stars. Priced in the mid-$20,000 range fully equipped, they're also imminently sensible alternatives to any number of midsize SUVs, especially truck-based wagons less efficient in their use of space and fuel.

TOTAL	53

Average total for compact sport-utility vehicles: 44.4

ENGINES

	dohc I4	dohc V6
Size, liters/cu. in.	2.0/121	3.0/182
Horsepower @ rpm	127 @ 5400	201 @ 5900
Torque (lb-ft) @ rpm	135 @ 4500	196 @ 4700
Availability	S[1]	S[2]
EPA city/highway mpg		
5-speed manual	22/25[3]	
4-speed automatic		18/23[4]

1. XLS Value, XLS Sport. 2. XLS Choice, all XLT models. 3. 23/27 w/2WD. 4. 19/24 w/2WD.

PRICES

Ford Escape	Retail Price	Dealer Invoice
XLS Value 4-door wagon, 2WD	$18415	$17171
XLS Value 4-door wagon, AWD	20040	18651

Specifications begin on page 551.

FORD

	Retail Price	Dealer Invoice
XLS Sport 4-door wagon, 2WD	$19210	$17895
XLS Sport 4-door wagon, AWD	20835	19375
XLS Choice 4-door wagon, 2WD	19925	18546
XLS Choice 4-door wagon, AWD	21550	20026
XLT Choice 4-door wagon, 2WD	21950	20390
XLT Choice 4-door wagon, AWD	23575	21867
XLT Choice 2 4-door wagon, 2WD	22125	20549
XLT Sport 4-door wagon, AWD	24525	22732
XLT Premium 4-door wagon, 2WD	23180	21508
XLT Premium 4-door wagon, AWD	24630	22828
Destination charge	540	540

STANDARD EQUIPMENT

XLS Value: 2.0-liter dohc 4-cylinder engine, 5-speed manual transmission, dual front airbags, air conditioning, power steering, tilt steering wheel, cloth/vinyl upholstery, front bucket seats, console, cupholders, folding rear seat, power mirrors, power windows, power door locks, remote keyless entry, AM/FM/cassette/CD player, digital clock, tachometer, variable intermittent wipers, rear wiper/washer, automatic-off headlights, theft-deterrent system, roof rack, 225/70R15 tires. **AWD** adds: all-wheel drive.

XLS Sport adds: floormats, side step bars, rear privacy glass, 225/70R15 white-letter tires, alloy wheels.

XLS Choice adds to XLS Value: 3.0-liter dohc V6 engine, 4-speed automatic transmission. **AWD** adds: all-wheel drive.

XLT Choice adds: antilock brakes, cruise control, cloth upholstery, 6-way power driver seat w/adjustable lumbar support, split folding rear seat, AM/FM radio w/in-dash 6-disc CD changer, map lights, visor mirrors, cargo cover, floormats, theft-deterrent system w/perimeter alarm, rear privacy glass, fog lights, 225/70R15 white-letter tires, alloy wheels. **AWD** adds: all-wheel drive, trailer hitch, 4-pin wiring harness, wheel lip moldings, 235/70R16 white-letter tires.

XLT Choice 2 adds: wheel lip moldings, 235/70R16 white-letter tires.

XLT Sport adds: all-wheel drive, side step bars, unique roof rack, trailer hitch, 4-pin wiring harness. *Deletes:* wheel lip moldings.

XLT Premium adds to XLT Choice 2: leather upholstery, leather-wrapped steering wheel, power sunroof. **AWD** adds: all-wheel drive, trailer hitch, 4-pin wiring harness..

OPTIONAL EQUIPMENT
Major Packages

Convenience Group, XLS Value/Sport/Choice	325	293

Cruise control, cargo cover, floormats, perimeter alarm system.

Prices are accurate at time of publication; subject to manufacturer's change.

FORD

	Retail Price	Dealer Invoice
Leather Comfort Group, 4WD XLT Choice, XLT Choice 2, XLT Sport	$575	$517

Leather upholstery, leather-wrapped steering wheel, front passenger under-seat storage compartment, overhead console w/storage, front door map pockets.

Class II Trailer Towing Pkg., XLS Choice, 2WD XLT Choice/Choice 2/Sport /Premium	350	316

Trailer hitch, 7-wire harness, wiring kit, oil cooler.

Safety

Front side airbags	345	310
Antilock brakes, XLS Value/Sport/Choice	575	517

Comfort & Convenience Features

Power sunroof, XLT Choice/Choice 2	585	527
Mach sound system, XLT Choice/Choice 2/Sport/Premium	505	454

Appearance and Miscellaneous

Side step bars	275	248

Std. XLS Sport, XLT Sport.

Special Purpose, Wheels and Tires

Alloy wheels, XLS Value/Choice	375	337

Includes 225/70R15 white-letter tires.

235/70R16 white-letter tires, 2WD XLT Choice	175	157

Includes wheel lip moldings.

FORD EXCURSION

Ford Excursion

Rear- or 4-wheel-drive full-size sport-utility vehicle
Base price range: $35,110-$47,035. Built in USA.

Specifications begin on page 551.

FORD

Also consider: Chevrolet Tahoe and Suburban, GMC Yukon/Denali

FOR • Passenger and cargo room • Trailer towing capability • Seat comfort **AGAINST** • Fuel economy • Maneuverability • Rear visibility

Power adjustable brake and throttle pedals highlight changes to the 2002 version of the largest SUV sold in America. Excursion is 7.4 inches longer than Chevrolet Suburban, 6 inches taller, and 2000 lb heavier. It seats up to nine and offers rear-wheel drive or 4WD that must be disengaged on dry pavement but includes low-range gearing. A V8 is the base engine. A V10 and a turbodiesel V8 are also available. Antilock 4-wheel disc brakes are standard. Side airbags aren't offered. An available rear obstacle warning system sounds an alert of objects when backing up. The optional rear video entertainment system has wireless headphones and a VCR; a DVD player is expected to be offered later in the '02 model year. A 6-disc in-dash CD player is also optional. The power adjustable pedals move fore and aft a few inches via a dashboard control. They're optional on XLT and XLT Premium models, standard on Limited and Limited Ultimate models; on Ultimate, they come with a seat-and-pedal memory feature. Excursion can tow up to 11,000 lb.

RATINGS

	XLT 2WD, V10	Limited 4WD, V10
ACCELERATION	3	3
FUEL ECONOMY	1	1
RIDE QUALITY	3	3
STEERING/HANDLING	2	2
QUIETNESS	3	3
INSTRUMENTS/CONTROLS	6	6
ROOM/COMFORT (FRONT)	9	9
ROOM/COMFORT (REAR)	9	9
CARGO ROOM	9	9
VALUE	2	2

Too cumbersome for a "suburban utility vehicle." But if you tow extremely heavy loads, need 4WD, and can accept abysmal fuel economy, the Excursion is actually a good SUV value.

TOTAL	47	47

Average total for full-size sport-utility vehicles: 50.9

ENGINES

	ohc V8	ohc V10	Turbodiesel ohc V8
Size, liters/cu. in.	5.4/330	6.8/415	7.3/444
Horsepower @ rpm	255 @ 4250	310 @ 4250	250 @ 2600
Torque (lb-ft) @ rpm	350 @ 2500	425 @ 3250	505 @ 1600
Availability	S[1]	S[2]	O
EPA city/highway mpg			
4-speed automatic	NA	NA	NA

1. 2WD. 2. 4WD; optional 2WD.

Prices are accurate at time of publication; subject to manufacturer's change.

FORD

PRICES

Ford Excursion

	Retail Price	Dealer Invoice
XLT V8 4-door wagon, 2WD	$35110	$30959
XLT V10 4-door wagon, 2WD	35695	31463
XLT turbodiesel 4-door wagon, 2WD	39715	34920
XLT V8 4-door wagon, 4WD	38365	33759
XLT V10 4-door wagon, 4WD	38365	33759
XLT turbodiesel 4-door wagon, 4WD	42380	37211
XLT Premium V8 4-door wagon, 2WD	36460	32121
XLT Premium V10 4-door wagon, 2WD	37045	32623
XLT Premium turbodiesel 4-door wagon, 2WD	41065	36081
XLT Premium V8 4-door wagon, 4WD	39715	34920
XLT Premium V10 4-door wagon, 4WD	39715	34920
XLT Premium turbodiesel 4-door wagon, 4WD	43730	38373
Limited V8 4-door wagon, 2WD	38925	34241
Limited V10 4-door wagon, 2WD	39510	34743
Limited turbodiesel 4-door wagon, 2WD	43530	38201
Limited V10 4-door wagon, 4WD	42025	36907
Limited turbodiesel 4-door wagon, 4WD	46040	40359
Limited Ultimate V8 4-door wagon, 2WD	39920	35097
Limited Ultimate V10 4-door wagon, 2WD	40505	35599
Limited Ultimate turbodiesel 4-door wagon, 2WD	44525	39057
Limited Ultimate V10 4-door wagon, 4WD	43020	37763
Limited Ultimate turbodiesel 4-door wagon, 4WD	47035	41215
Destination charge	750	750

STANDARD EQUIPMENT

XLT: 5.4-liter V8 engine, 6.8-liter V10 engine, or 7.3-liter turbo-diesel V8 engine, 4-speed automatic transmission, dual front airbags, antilock 4-wheel disc brakes, front and rear air conditioning, power steering, tilt leather-wrapped steering wheel, cruise control, cloth upholstery, front split bench seat w/driver-side lumbar adjustment, second-row split-folding bench seat, third-row folding bench seat, cupholders, overhead console, heated power mirrors, power front windows, power door locks, remote keyless entry, AM/FM/cassette/CD player, digital clock, tachometer, automatic day/night rearview mirror, map lights, illuminated visor mirrors, intermittent wipers, rear defogger, intermittent rear wiper/washer, floormats, theft-deterrent system, rear liftgate w/lower Dutch doors, roof rack, privacy glass, running boards, engine block heater (7.3-liter), front tow hooks, 7-lead trailer harness, Class IV trailer hitch, full-size spare tire, LT265/75R16 white-letter tires, chrome steel wheels. **4WD** adds: 4-wheel drive, 2-speed transfer case, limited-slip differential (5.4), LT265/75R16 all-terrain white-letter tires.

XLT Premium adds: 6-way power front captain chairs, center console, rear radio controls, trip computer, power rear quarter windows, automat-

Specifications begin on page 551.

FORD

ic headlights, illuminated running boards, alloy wheels. **4WD** adds: 4-wheel drive, 2-speed transfer case, limited-slip differential (5.4-liter), LT265/75R16 all-terrain white-letter tires.

Limited adds: front and rear automatic climate controls, leather upholstery, power adjustable pedals, outside-mirror mounted turn signal lights, variable intermittent wipers, fog lights. **4WD** adds: 4-wheel drive, 2-speed transfer case, 6.8-liter V10 engine or 7.3-liter turbo-diesel V8 engine, LT265/75R16 all-terrain white-letter tires.

Limited Ultimate adds: rear obstacle detection system, heated front seats, driver seat and pedal memory, steering wheel climate controls, universal garage door opener. **4WD** adds: 4-wheel drive, 2-speed transfer case, 6.8-liter V10 engine or 7.3-liter turbo-diesel V8 engine, LT265/75R16 all-terrain white-letter tires.

OPTIONAL EQUIPMENT	Retail Price	Dealer Invoice
Major Packages		
No Boundaries Group, Limited, Limited Ultimate....	$95	$81
Monochromatic black exterior, chrome accents, black illuminated running boards.		
Powertrain		
Limited-slip differential..	250	213
Std. 4WD w/5.4-liter V8 engine.		
Safety		
Rear obstacle detection system, XLT Premium	245	208
Comfort & Convenience Features		
Rear Seat Entertainment System, XLT Premium, Limited, Limited Ultimate..	1525	1297
Videocassette player, fold-down color monitor, 2 wireless headphones.		
Telescoping heated power trailer tow mirrors	95	81
Leather upholstery, XLT Premium	1360	1156
Heated front seats, Limited	290	247
Second-row captain chairs, Limited Ultimate..........	795	676
Power adjustable pedals, XLT, XLT Premium	120	102
In-dash 6-disc CD changer	255	217

FORD EXPEDITION

Rear- or 4-wheel-drive full-size sport-utility vehicle
Base price range: $30,430-$40,960. Built in USA.
Also consider: Chevrolet Tahoe and Suburban, GMC Yukon/Denali

Prices are accurate at time of publication; subject to manufacturer's change.

FORD

Ford Expedition

FOR • Acceleration (5.4-liter) • Passenger and cargo room • Visibility • Towing ability • Build quality **AGAINST** • Fuel economy • Entry/exit (4WD models)

The smaller of Ford's two full-size SUVs sees only detail changes for 2002. Expedition shares its design with the Lincoln Navigator, which offers more luxury features and a more powerful engine. Expedition is available in XLT and Eddie Bauer trim levels, with front bench or bucket seats. Three-passenger 2nd- and 3rd-row benches are standard, 2nd-row buckets are optional. Power adjustable gas and brake pedals are standard. Available engines are V8s of 4.6 or 5.4 liters, teamed only with automatic transmission. Expedition is offered with rear-wheel drive or Ford's Control Trac 4WD that can be left engaged on dry pavement and includes low-range gearing. Antilock 4-wheel disc brakes are standard. Front side airbags are optional. A rear entertainment system is also optional, and for '02 is available on the XLT as well as the Eddie Bauer.

RATINGS	XLT 2WD, 4.6 V8	Eddie Bauer 4WD, 5.4 V8
ACCELERATION	3	4
FUEL ECONOMY	3	2
RIDE QUALITY	6	4
STEERING/HANDLING	3	3
QUIETNESS	6	6
INSTRUMENTS/CONTROLS	7	7
ROOM/COMFORT (FRONT)	9	9
ROOM/COMFORT (REAR)	9	9
CARGO ROOM	9	9

Specifications begin on page 551.

FORD

	XLT 2WD, 4.6 V8	Eddie Bauer 4WD, 5.4 V8
VALUE	5	5

Chevrolet's Tahoe and Suburban rate as Best Buys, but the modern, refined Expedition is also a good choice in a full-size SUV and earns our Recommended nod. The costlier Navigator isn't as strong a value, though it offers some luxury options unavailable on Expedition.

TOTAL	60	58

Average total for full-size sport-utility vehicles: 50.9

ENGINES

	ohc V8	ohc V8
Size, liters/cu. in.	4.6/281	5.4/330
Horsepower @ rpm	232 @ 4750	260 @ 4500
Torque (lb-ft) @ rpm	291 @ 3450	350 @ 2500
Availability	S[1]	S[2]
EPA city/highway mpg		
4-speed automatic	14/17[3]	12/16[4]

1. XLT and Eddie Bauer 2WD. 2. Eddie Bauer 4WD, optional others. 3. 15/20 w/2WD. 4. 13/18 w/2WD.

PRICES

Ford Expedition	Retail Price	Dealer Invoice
XLT 4-door wagon, 2WD	$30430	$26840
XLT 4-door wagon, 4WD	33300	29308
Eddie Bauer 4-door wagon, 2WD	36815	32331
Eddie Bauer 4-door wagon, 4WD	40960	35896
Destination charge	715	715

STANDARD EQUIPMENT

XLT: 4.6-liter V8 engine, 4-speed automatic transmission, dual front airbags, antilock 4-wheel disc brakes, front air conditioning, power steering, tilt steering wheel, cruise control, cloth upholstery, front split bench seat, 6-way power driver seat w/lumbar adjustment, second-row split-folding bench seat, third-row folding bench seat, cupholders, power adjustable pedals, power mirrors, power front windows, power door locks, remote keyless entry, AM/FM/cassette, digital clock, tachometer, map lights, passenger-side visor mirror, variable intermittent wipers, rear defogger, intermittent rear wiper/washer, floormats, theft-deterrent system, rear privacy glass, rear liftgate with flip-up glass, roof rack, full-size spare tire, 255/70R16 tires. **4WD** adds: 4-wheel drive, 2-speed transfer case, front tow hooks.

Eddie Bauer adds: automatic climate control, rear air conditioning and heater w/rear controls, leather upholstery, front captain chairs, driver seat and power adjustable pedal memory, leather-wrapped steering wheel, front storage console, rear radio controls and headphone jacks, over-

Prices are accurate at time of publication; subject to manufacturer's change.
CONSUMER GUIDE®

FORD

head storage console (trip computer, compass, storage), heated power mirrors w/memory, automatic day/night rearview mirror, universal garage door opener, Mach sound system system, 6-disc CD changer, illuminated visor mirrors, power rear-quarter windows, automatic headlights, illuminated running boards, outside-mirror mounted turn signal lights, fog lights, 275/60R17 white-letter tires, chrome styled steel wheels. **4WD** adds: 4-wheel drive, 2-speed transfer case, 5.4-liter V8 engine, 7-lead trailer harness, frame-mounted hitch, 265/70R17 all-terrain white-letter tires.

OPTIONAL EQUIPMENT
Major Packages

	Retail Price	Dealer Invoice
Comfort/Convenience Pkg., XLT	$1935	$1645

Captain's chairs, floor console, rear air conditioning and heater w/rear controls, automatic day/night rearview mirror, overhead console, compass, outside temperature indicator, illuminated visor mirrors, rear radio controls, heated power mirrors, illuminated running boards (when ordered w/Premium Sport Appearance Group), 255/70R16 all-terrain tires; alloy wheels.

Premium Sport Appearance Group, XLT 2WD	860	731
XLT 4WD	960	816

Captain chairs, color-keyed bumpers and grille, side step bars, wheel lip moldings, fog lights, skid plates (4WD), 275/60R17 white-letter tires (2WD), 265/70R17 all-terrain white-letter tires (4WD), alloy wheels. Requires Comfort/Convenience Group.

No Boundaries Group, 2WD XLT	860	731
4WD XLT	960	816

Captain's chairs, illuminated running boards, fog lights, chrome mirrors and grille surround, color-keyed bodyside and wheel lip moldings, 275/60R17 white-letter tires (2WD), 265/70R17 white-letter tires (4WD), alloy wheels. Requires Comfort/Convenience Pkg.

Premier Group, Eddie Bauer	1595	1356
Manufacturer's Discount Price	795	676

Monochromatic Arizona Beige exterior color, second row captain chairs, unique leather trim, power sunroof, special alloy wheels. NA w/front side airbags, rear obstacle detection system.

Class III Trailer Tow Group, 2WD	880	748
4WD XLT	390	332

7-lead trailer wiring harness, frame-mounted hitch, auxiliary transmission-oil cooler, 30-gallon fuel tank (2WD), rear load-leveling suspension (2WD). Std. 4WD Eddie Bauer.

Powertrain

5.4-liter V8 engine, XLT, Eddie Bauer 2WD	695	591
Limited-slip differential	255	217

Specifications begin on page 551.

FORD

	Retail Price	Dealer Invoice

Safety
Front side airbags $395 $336
 Requires rear obstacle detection system. XLT requires Comfort/Convenience Pkg.
Rear obstacle detection system............................. 200 170
 Requires front side airbags.

Comfort & Convenience Features
Rear Entertainment System 1345 1143
 Videocassette player, LCD screen. XLT requires Comfort/Convenience Pkg., 6-disc CD changer.
Power sunroof 800 680
 XLT requires Premium Sport Appearance Group or No Boundaries Group.
Heated front seats, Eddie Bauer............................ 295 251
Leather upholstery, XLT 1360 1156
 Requires Comfort/Convenience Pkg.
Second row captain chairs, Eddie Bauer 795 676
6-disc CD changer, XLT 495 421
 Requires Comfort/Convenience Group.

Special Purpose, Wheels and Tires
Load-leveling suspension, 4WD.............................. 815 692
 XLT requires Class III Trailer Tow Group.

FORD EXPLORER

Ford Explorer

Rear- or 4-wheel-drive midsize sport-utility vehicle
Base price range: $24,335-$34,085. Built in USA.
Also consider: Acura MDX, Dodge Durango, GMC Envoy, Toyota Highlander

FOR • Passenger and cargo room   **AGAINST** • Fuel economy

Prices are accurate at time of publication; subject to manufacturer's change.

FORD

America's top-selling SUV was redesigned as an early 2002 model and went on sale in Spring 2001. Explorer retains body-on-frame construction, but gets new styling, a wider stance, longer wheelbase, independent rear suspension, and an available 3rd-row seat for 7-passenger capacity. Mercury's upscale Mountaineer is similarly revamped, but with more differentiated styling. Explorer offers V6 and V8 engines; the V6 teams with manual or automatic transmission, the V8 with automatic only. With either, the automatic is a 5 speed. Available is rear-wheel drive or Ford's Control Trac 4WD that can be left engaged on dry pavement and includes low-range gearing. Antilock 4-wheel disc brakes are standard. Torso side airbags are unavailable, but curtain side airbags are optional; due later in the model year are sensors that deploy them in a rollover accident. Also due later is an antiskid system. A rear obstacle warning system is optional. Standard on top Eddie Bauer and Limited models are driver seat memory, tilt/telescopic steering wheel, and power adjustable pedals. Still sold alongside this redesigned 4-dr wagon are the Explorer Sport Trac crew cab and Explorer Sport 2-dr wagon (see separate entry), both using Explorer's 1995-vintage design.

RATINGS

	XLT 4WD, V6	Limited 4WD, V8
ACCELERATION	4	5
FUEL ECONOMY	4	3
RIDE QUALITY	4	4
STEERING/HANDLING	4	4
QUIETNESS	4	5
INSTRUMENTS/CONTROLS	7	7
ROOM/COMFORT (FRONT)	7	8
ROOM/COMFORT (REAR)	7	7
CARGO ROOM	8	8
VALUE	6	5

Explorer and Mountaineer are competent overall performers with an unmatched array of useful features: available V8 power, 7-passenger seating, adjustable pedals, curtain airbags, and reverse sensing system. The coming antiskid system is also a plus. Mountaineer's higher sticker price brings more expressive styling and slightly sharper handling feel, but in all, Explorer is the better value and earns our Recommended label.

TOTAL	55	56

Average total for midsize sport-utility vehicles: 49.6

ENGINES

	ohc V6	ohc V8
Size, liters/cu. in.	4.0/245	4.6/281
Horsepower @ rpm	210 @ 5250	240 @ 4750
Torque (lb-ft) @ rpm	250 @ 4000	280 @ 4000
Availability	S	O[1]

Specifications begin on page 551.

FORD

EPA city/highway mpg	ohc V6	ohc V8
5-speed manual	16/20[2]	
5-speed automatic	15/20[3]	14/19

1. XLT, Eddie Bauer, Limited. 2. 17/21 w/2WD. 3. 16/21 w/2WD.

PRICES

Ford Explorer

	Retail Price	Dealer Invoice
XLS 4-door wagon, 2WD	$24335	$22228
XLS 4-door wagon, 4WD	26215	23901
XLT 4-door wagon, 2WD	28095	25575
XLT 4-door wagon, 4WD	30060	27324
Eddie Bauer 4-door wagon, 2WD	32120	29157
Eddie Bauer 4-door wagon, 4WD	34085	30906
Limited 4-door wagon, 2WD	32120	29157
Limited 4-door wagon, 4WD	34085	30906
Destination charge	600	600

STANDARD EQUIPMENT

XLS: 4.0-liter V6 engine, 5-speed manual transmission, limited-slip differential, dual front airbags, antilock 4-wheel disc brakes, air conditioning, power steering, tilt steering wheel, cruise control, cloth upholstery, front captain chairs, center console, cupholders, split folding rear seat, power mirrors, power windows, power door locks, remote keyless entry, AM/FM/cassette, digital clock, tachometer, variable intermittent wipers, rear defogger, intermittent rear wiper/washer, visor mirrors, map lights, cargo management system, theft-deterrent system, rear liftgate, rear privacy glass, roof rails, Class II trailer hitch receiver, 4-pin connector, full-size spare tire, 235/70R16 white-letter tires. **4WD** adds: 4-wheel drive, 2-speed transfer case.

XLT adds: 5-speed automatic transmission, front bucket seats w/lumbar adjustment, 6-way power driver seat, AM/FM/CD player, overhead console, outside temperature indicator, compass, illuminated visor mirrors, rear climate controls, cargo cover, automatic headlights, floormats, roof rack, alloy wheels. **4WD** adds: 4-wheel drive, 2-speed transfer case.

Eddie Bauer/Limited adds: leather upholstery, heated front seats, 6-way power passenger seat, driver seat memory, tilt/telescoping leather-wrapped steering wheel w/radio and climate controls, power adjustable pedals w/memory, dual-zone automatic climate control, heated power mirrors, AM/FM radio w/in-dash 6-disc CD changer, automatic day/night rearview mirror, universal garage door opener, fog lights, two-tone paint (Eddie Bauer), monotone paint (Limited), 245/70R16 all-terrain white-letter tires. **4WD** adds: 4-wheel drive, 2-speed transfer case.

Prices are accurate at time of publication; subject to manufacturer's change.

FORD

OPTIONAL EQUIPMENT

	Retail Price	Dealer Invoice
Major Packages

Sport Group, XLS.. $1150 $978
AM/FM/CD player, high series center console w/rear climate controls, floormats, side step bars, wheel lip moldings, alloy wheels.
Class III/IV Trailer Towing Prep Pkg., XLT,
 Eddie Bauer, Limited 395 336
Engine oil cooler, special axle ratio, 7-wire harness, hitch, heavy-duty flasher.

Powertrain

4.6-liter V8, XLT, Eddie Bauer, Limited 800 680
5-speed automatic transmission, XLS..................... 1095 931

Safety

Front and second row curtain side airbags............. 495 421
Rear obstacle detection system, XLT,
 Eddie Bauer, Limited 255 217

Comfort & Convenience Features

Rear air conditioning and heater, XLT,
 Eddie Bauer, Limited 610 518
Requires folding third row seat.
Power sunroof, XLT, Eddie Bauer, Limited............. 800 680
NA w/rear air conditioning and heater.
Power adjustable pedals, XLT................................ 120 102
AM/FM/cassette/CD player, XLT 130 111
AM/FM radio w/in-dash 6-disc CD changer, XLT.... 395 336
Leather upholstery, XLT 655 557
Includes 6-way power passenger seat.
Folding third row seat, XLT, Eddie Bauer, Limited.. 670 569
Includes 40/20/40 split folding second row seat. Deletes cargo cover.

Appearance and Miscellaneous

Running boards, XLT, Eddie Bauer, Limited 395 336

Special Purpose, Wheels and Tires

Chrome steel wheels, Eddie Bauer, Limited 245 208

FORD EXPLORER SPORT TRAC AND SPORT

Rear- or 4-wheel-drive midsize sport-utility vehicle
Base price range: $21,220-$28,210. Built in USA.

Specifications begin on page 551.

FORD

Ford Explorer Sport Trac

Also consider: Chevrolet Blazer, Dodge Dakota Quad Cab, Isuzu Rodeo Sport, Toyota Tacoma Double Cab

FOR • Cargo room • Build quality **AGAINST** • Ride • Fuel economy

Sport and Sport Trac carry on for 2002 with their 1995-vintage Explorer design, their 4-dr wagon companion having been replaced by the all-new 2002 Explorer (see separate entry). Sport is a 2-dr wagon. Sport Trac has a 4-dr SUV cabin, but gets a 4-ft-long pickup-truck bed in lieu of an enclosed cargo area. Both use a V6 engine with manual or 5-speed automatic transmission. They offer rear-wheel drive or Ford's Control Trac 4WD that can be left engaged on dry pavement and includes low-range gearing. ABS is standard. Sport has 4-wheel disc brakes, Sport Trac has rear drums. Front side airbags are optional on Sport but unavailable on Sport Trac. For 2002, major option packages are designated as separate models called Value, Choice, and Premium. Also, Sport Trac's fuel tank increases to 23 gal, from 20.5.

RATINGS	Sport Choice 2WD	Sport Trac Premium 4WD
ACCELERATION	5	5
FUEL ECONOMY	4	4
RIDE QUALITY	2	4
STEERING/HANDLING	2	3
QUIETNESS	3	3
INSTRUMENTS/CONTROLS	7	7
ROOM/COMFORT (FRONT)	6	6
ROOM/COMFORT (REAR)	2	6
CARGO ROOM	7	6
VALUE	2	6

The uncomfortable 2-dr Sport is of limited appeal, while the Sport Trac has a deserved following based on its unique blend of passenger space and open-bed versatility.

Prices are accurate at time of publication; subject to manufacturer's change.

CONSUMER GUIDE®

FORD

	Sport Choice 2WD	Sport Trac Premium 4WD
TOTAL	**40**	**50**

Average total for midsize sport-utility vehicles: 49.6

ENGINES

	ohc V6
Size, liters/cu. in.	4.0/245
Horsepower @ rpm	210 @ 5200
Torque (lb-ft) @ rpm	240 @ 3000
Availability	S[1]

EPA city/highway mpg

5-speed manual	16/19[2]
5-speed automatic	15/20[3]

1. Sport, 203 hp, 237 lb-ft torque. 2. 17/22 w/2WD. 3. 17/21 w/2WD.

PRICES

Ford Explorer Sport Trac and Sport	Retail Price	Dealer Invoice
Sport Value 2-door wagon, 2WD	$21220	$19376
Sport Choice 2-door wagon, 2WD	23055	21009
Sport Premium 2-door wagon, 2WD	24470	22268
Sport Value 2-door wagon, 4WD	24240	22063
Sport Choice 2-door wagon, 4WD	26075	23697
Sport Premium 2-door wagon, 4WD	27635	25085
Sport Trac Value 4-door crew cab, 2WD	22120	20177
Sport Trac Choice 4-door crew cab, 2WD	23880	21743
Sport Trac Premium 4-door crew cab, 2WD	25440	23131
Sport Trac Value 4-door crew cab, 4WD	24890	22642
Sport Trac Choice 4-door crew cab, 4WD	26650	24209
Sport Trac Premium 4-door crew cab, 4WD	28210	25597
Destination charge	600	600

STANDARD EQUIPMENT

Value: 4.0-liter V6 engine, 5-speed manual transmission, dual front airbags, antilock brakes, 4-wheel disc brakes (Sport), air conditioning, power steering, cloth upholstery, front captain chairs, center console, cupholders, split folding rear seat, power mirrors, power windows, power rear window (Sport Trac), power door locks, front-hinged rear doors (Sport Trac), variable intermittent wipers, AM/FM/cassette/CD player, digital clock, tachometer, map light, rear defogger, intermittent rear wiper/washer (Sport), visor mirrors, floormats, theft-deterrent system, rear privacy glass, rear cargo box w/composite bed (Sport Trac), roof rack, 4-wire trailering harness, full-size spare tire, 235/70R16 white-letter tires, alloy wheels. **4WD** models add: 4-wheel drive, 2-speed transfercase, skid plate (Sport Trac).

Choice adds: 5-speed automatic transmission, tilt leather-wrapped

Specifications begin on page 551.

FORD

steering wheel, cruise control, remote keyless entry, key pad entry, cargo cover (Sport). **4WD** adds: 4-wheel drive, 2-speed transfer case, skid plate (SportTrac), front tow hooks.

Premium adds: leather upholstery, front bucket seats, 6-way power driver seat, rear climate controls, overhead console, outside temperature indicator, compass, side step bars, fog lights, front tow hooks, 255/70R16 all-terrain white-letter tires (Sport Trac), bright cast alloy wheels. **4WD** adds: 4-wheel drive, 2-speed transfer case, skid plate (SportTrac), 255/70R16 all-terrain white-letter tires.

OPTIONAL EQUIPMENT

	Retail Price	Dealer Invoice
Major Packages		
Convenience Group, Sport Value	$830	$706
Sport Trac Value	750	635
Cruise control, tilt leather-wrapped steering wheel, remote keyless entry, key pad entry, automatic door locks, cargo cover (Sport).		
Comfort Group, Choice	935	795
Front bucket seats, 6-way power driver seat, overhead console, outside temperature indicator, compass, rear radio and climate controls.		
Leather Comfort Group, Premium	655	557
Leather upholstery, front seat lumbar adjustment.		
Premium Sport Group, 2WD Sport Choice	550	468
4WD Sport Choice, Sport Trac Choice	700	595
Side step bars, fog lights, front tow hooks, 255/70R16 all-terrain white-letter tires (4WD Sport, Sport Trac), bright cast alloy wheels.		
Powertrain		
Limited-slip differential	355	302
Safety		
Front side airbags, Sport Premium/Choice	390	332
Requires Comfort Group. Choice requires Premium Sport Group.		
Comfort & Convenience Features		
Power sunroof, Premium	800	680
Pioneer AM/FM radio, Choice, Premium	510	433
Includes in-dash 6-disc CD changer.		
Appearance and Miscellaneous		
Cargo cage, Sport Trac	195	166
Locking tonneau cover, Sport Trac	590	502

FORD FOCUS

Front-wheel-drive subcompact car
Base price range: $12,445-$17,735. Built in USA.

Prices are accurate at time of publication; subject to manufacturer's change.

FORD

Ford Focus ZTS 4-door sedan

Also consider: Honda Civic, Mazda Protege, Volkswagen Jetta/Golf

FOR • Control layout • Handling/roadholding • Fuel economy • Cargo room (wagon) **AGAINST** • Acceleration (exc. SVT) • Engine noise • Rear-seat entry/exit (hatchback)

Ford's popular subcompact adds a new body style, a sport-trim wagon, and a sporty SVT variant for 2002. Focus comes as a 4-dr sedan, 4-dr wagon, and a 2- and 4-dr hatchback; the 4-dr hatchback is new for '02. All have a 4-cyl engine. It has 110 or 130 hp, depending on model, with the new SVT rated at 170 hp. The SVT comes only as a 2-dr hatchback and includes a sport suspension and 17-inch wheels. And a new ZTW wagon has standard leather upholstery, fog lights, and 16-inch wheels. The base sedan, base 2-dr hatchback, and SVT come only with manual transmission; other models are available with manual or automatic. ABS is standard on the SVT, optional on other Focus models. Head-and-torso front side airbags are optional on all but the SVT. Newly optional on higher-line models is an anti-skid system that includes ABS and traction control. A sunroof and 6-disc in-dash CD player are other new options.

RATINGS	LX sdn, auto.	SE wgn, auto.	ZTS, man.	ZX3, auto.
ACCELERATION	3	4	4	4
FUEL ECONOMY	7	6	7	7
RIDE QUALITY	5	5	4	3
STEERING/HANDLING	6	6	7	7
QUIETNESS	4	4	4	4
INSTRUMENTS/CONTROLS	7	7	7	7
ROOM/COMFORT (FRONT)	5	5	5	5
ROOM/COMFORT (REAR)	5	5	5	3
CARGO ROOM	3	6	3	6
VALUE	8	8	8	5

Though not as refined as a Honda Civic or Volkswagen Jetta, Focus offers generous subcompact passenger and cargo room. It's fun to drive, too, despite timid engines. And prices are very competitive.

| TOTAL | 53 | 56 | 54 | 51 |

Average total for subcompact cars: 43.7

Specifications begin on page 551.

FORD

EXTENDED-USE TEST UPDATE

Our Focus test cars have had a solid on-road feel. However, our extended-use ZTS was built without the model's standard tilt/telescopic steering wheel, which had to be retrofitted by a dealer service department. It also was the subject of emissions-systems and cruise-control recalls, and a creaking suspension led to the warranty replacement of an upper strut bearing. No other unscheduled service was required during the 12-month test.

ENGINES

	ohc I4	dohc I4	dohc I4
Size, liters/cu. in.	2.0/121	2.0/121	2.0/121
Horsepower @ rpm	110 @ 5000	130 @ 5300	170 @ 7000
Torque (lb-ft) @ rpm	125 @ 3750	135 @ 4500	145 @ 5500
Availability	S^1	S^2	S^3

EPA city/highway mpg

5-speed manual	28/36	28/36	25/34
4-speed automatic	26/32	26/32	

1. LX, SE sedan. 2. SE wagon, SE Comfort/Zetec sedan, ZX3, ZTS; optional SE sedan. 3. SVT.

PRICES

Ford Focus	Retail Price	Dealer Invoice
LX 4-door sedan	$12760	$12019
LX Premium 4-door sedan	13605	12796
SE 4-door sedan	14350	13483
SE 4-door wagon	16555	15511
SE Comfort 4-door sedan	14695	13800
SE Comfort 4-door wagon	16900	15828
SE Comfort/Zetec 4-door sedan	14945	14029
ZTS 4-door sedan	15270	14328
ZX5 4-door hatchback	15645	14673
ZTW 4-door wagon	17735	16596
ZX3 2-door hatchback	12445	11729
ZX3 Premium 2-door hatchback	13540	12737
ZX3 Power Premium 2-door hatchback	14480	13601
SVT 2-door hatchback	17505	NA
Destination charge	490	490

STANDARD EQUIPMENT

LX: 2.0-liter 4-cylinder engine, 5-speed manual transmission, dual front airbags, emergency inside trunk release, power steering, cloth upholstery, front bucket seats, height-adjustable driver seat, center

Prices are accurate at time of publication; subject to manufacturer's change.
CONSUMER GUIDE®

FORD

console, cupholders, split folding rear seat, AM/FM/cassette, digital clock, visor mirrors, rear defogger, intermittent wipers, remote fuel door and decklid release, floormats, theft-deterrent system, 185/65R14 tires, wheel covers.

LX Premium adds: air conditioning, front armrest.

SE sedan adds: power mirrors, power windows, power door locks, remote entry system, AM/FM/CD player, variable intermittent wipers, 195/60R15 tires, alloy wheels.

SE Comfort sedan adds: tilt/telescoping steering wheel, cruise control, map lights.

SE Comfort/Zetec sedan adds: 2.0-liter dohc 4-cylinder engine.

ZTS adds: leather-wrapped steering wheel, driver seat lumbar adjustment, tachometer, rear spoiler, fog lights, sport suspension, 205/50R16 tires.

ZX5 adds: AM/FM radio w/in-dash 6-disc CD changer, rear wiper/washer.

SE wagon adds to SE sedan: 2.0-liter dohc 4-cylinder engine, 4-speed automatic transmission, cargo cover, rear wiper/washer, roof rack.

SE Comfort wagon adds: tilt/telescoping steering wheel, cruise control, map lights.

ZTW adds: leather-wrapped steering wheel, leather upholstery, driver seat lumbar adjustment, AM/FM radio w/in-dash 6-disc CD changer, tachometer, fog lights, 205/50R16 tires.

ZX3 adds to LX: 2.0-liter dohc 130-horsepower engine, AM/FM/CD player, leather-wrapped steering wheel, tachometer, rear wiper/washer, fog lights, 195/60R15 tires, alloy wheels.

ZX3 Premium adds: air conditioning, tilt/telescoping steering wheel, cruise control, front armrest, map lights, 205/50R16 tires.

ZX3 Power Premium adds: power mirrors, power windows, power door locks, remote keyless entry, AM/FM radio w/in-dash 6-disc CD changer.

SVT adds: 2.0-liter dohc 170-horsepower 4-cylinder engine, 6-speed manual transmission, antilock 4-wheel disc brakes, leather/cloth upholstery, power driver seat, heated power mirrors, variable intermittent wipers, rear spoiler, SVT Suspension, 215/45ZR17 tires. *Deletes: Deletes:* drive-side visor mirror.

OPTIONAL EQUIPMENT

	Retail Price	Dealer Invoice
Major Packages		
Cold Weather Pkg., SVT	$395	NA
Traction control, heated front seats, engine block heater.		
Powertrain		
5-speed manual transmission, SE/SE Comfort wagon, ZTW (credit)	(815)	(725)

Specifications begin on page 551.

FORD

	Retail Price	Dealer Invoice
4-speed automatic transmission	$815	$725
NA LX, ZX3, SVT. Std. wagons.		

Safety
Antilock brakes	400	356
Std. SVT.		
Advance Trac, ZTS, ZX5, ZTW, ZX3 Power Premium	1625	1447
Antiskid system, antilock brakes, traction control.		
Front side airbags	350	312
NA SVT.		

Comfort & Convenience Features
Air conditioning, ZX3	795	708
Leather upholstery, ZTS, ZX5	695	619
AM/FM radio w/in-dash 6-disc CD changer, SE Comfort, SE Comfort/Zetec, ZTS, ZX3 Premium, ZX3 Power Premium	280	249
Audiophile Pkg., SVT	695	NA
AM/FM radio w/in-dash 6-disc CD changer, upgraded sound system.		
Power sunroof, SE Comfort, SE Comfort/Zetec, ZTS, ZX5, ZTW, ZX3 Power Premium, SVT	595	530

FORD MUSTANG

Ford Mustang GT 2-door convertible

Rear-wheel-drive sporty coupe
Base price range: $17,305-$28,390. Built in USA.
Also consider: Acura RSX, Toyota Celica, Volkswagen New Beetle

FOR • Acceleration (V8) • Steering/handling **AGAINST** • Rear visibility (convertible) • Fuel economy (V8) • Rear-seat

Prices are accurate at time of publication; subject to manufacturer's change.

FORD

room • Wet weather traction (without traction control) • Rear-seat entry/exit

New audio choices, larger standard wheels, and a revised Cobra update the original pony car for 2002. Mustang's Base and GT models are offered in coupe and convertible body styles. Convertibles have a power top and glass rear window. For '02, major option packages are redesignated as submodels called Standard, Deluxe, and Premium. All Base Mustangs have a 190-hp V6, GTs a 260-hp V8. A 5-speed manual transmission is standard, with automatic optional on Base and GT. All Mustangs have 4-wheel disc brakes; ABS coupled with traction control is standard or optional on all but the Base Standard model. Side airbags are unavailable. For '02, an MP3/CD radio is newly available, and Base Mustangs get 16-inch alloy wheels to replace 15s. Details on the 2002 Cobra were not announced in time for this report. It's to go on sale in early calendar '02. Cobra is the only Mustang with independent rear suspension. The 2001 model had a 320-hp V8.

RATINGS

	Base cpe, auto.	GT conv, auto.
ACCELERATION	5	7
FUEL ECONOMY	5	4
RIDE QUALITY	3	2
STEERING/HANDLING	6	8
QUIETNESS	3	2
INSTRUMENTS/CONTROLS	6	6
ROOM/COMFORT (FRONT)	5	5
ROOM/COMFORT (REAR)	2	2
CARGO ROOM	2	1
VALUE	4	3

Mustang has outlasted its soon-to-be discontinued GM competition because it has broader appeal. This is still an impractical car, but easily fulfills its core mission: Deliver sporty performance and looks for a reasonable price.

TOTAL	41	40

Average total for sporty coupes: 43.4

ENGINES

	ohv V6	ohc V8
Size, liters/cu. in.	3.8/232	4.6/281
Horsepower @ rpm	190 @ 5250	260 @ 5250
Torque (lb-ft) @ rpm	220 @ 2750	302 @ 4000
Availability	S[1]	S[2]
EPA city/highway mpg		
5-speed manual	20/29	18/26
4-speed automatic	19/27	17/24

1. Base models. 2. GT models.

Specifications begin on page 551.

FORD

PRICES

Ford Mustang

	Retail Price	Dealer Invoice
Base Standard 2-door coupe	$17305	$15989
Base Deluxe 2-door coupe	17910	16534
Base Deluxe 2-door convertible	22745	20885
Base Premium 2-door coupe	19025	17538
Base Premium 2-door convertible	25330	23212
GT Deluxe 2-door coupe	22965	21084
GT Deluxe 2-door convertible	27220	24913
GT Premium 2-door coupe	24135	22136
GT Premium 2-door convertible	28390	25966
Destination charge	600	600

Cobra prices and equipment not available at time of publication.

STANDARD EQUIPMENT

Base Standard: 3.8-liter V6 engine, 5-speed manual transmission, dual front airbags, 4-wheel disc brakes, emergency inside trunk release, air conditioning, power steering, tilt steering wheel, cloth upholstery, front bucket seats, center console, cupholders, split folding rear seat, power mirrors, power windows, power door locks, remote keyless entry, AM/FM/cassette/CD player, digital clock, tachometer, visor mirrors, rear defogger, remote decklid release, theft-deterrent system, 225/55R16 tires, alloy wheels.

Base Deluxe adds: cruise control, 6-way power driver seat, illuminated visor mirrors (convertible), power convertible top (convertible), floormats, rear spoiler (coupe), bright alloy wheels (convertible). *Deletes:* split folding rear seat (convertible).

Base Premium adds: 4-speed automatic transmission (convertible), traction control, antilock brakes, leather-wrapped steering wheel, leather upholstery (convertible), Mach 460 AM/FM radio w/in-dash 6-disc CD changer, rear spoiler, bright alloy wheels.

GT Deluxe adds: 4.6-liter V8 engine, limited-slip differential, AM/FM/cassette/CD player, fog lights, GT suspension, 245/45ZR17 tires. *Deletes:* 4-speed automatic transmission (convertible), leather upholstery.

GT Premium adds: leather upholstery, Mach 460 AM/FM radio w/in-dash 6-disc CD changer.

OPTIONAL EQUIPMENT
Major Packages

Sport Appearance Group, Base Deluxe coupe	125	112

Leather-wrapped steering wheel, bodyside stripes, bright alloy wheels.

Prices are accurate at time of publication; subject to manufacturer's change.

FORD

Powertrain

	Retail Price	Dealer Invoice
4-speed automatic transmission	$815	$725

Std. Base Deluxe convertible.

Safety

Antilock brakes, Base Deluxe	730	650

Includes traction control. Coupe requires 4-speed automatic transmission.

Comfort & Convenience Features

Leather upholstery, Base Deluxe convertible, Base Premium coupe, GT Deluxe	525	468
Mach 460 AM/FM radio w/in-dash 6-disc CD changer, Base Deluxe, GT Deluxe	550	490
Mach 1000 sound system, Base Premium, GT Premium	1295	1153
AM/FM/CD/MP3 player, Base Standard, Base Deluxe, GT Deluxe	NC	NC

FORD TAURUS

Ford Taurus 4-door sedan

Front-wheel-drive midsize car

Base price range: $18,750-$23,015. Built in USA.

Also consider: Honda Accord, Nissan Altima, Pontiac Grand Prix, Toyota Camry

FOR • Handling/roadholding • Rear-seat comfort • Cargo room **AGAINST** • Midrange acceleration

Ford's best-selling car makes some previously optional features standard for 2002, and former option packages become separate models. Base LX sedan models return, while SE, SES, and SEL sedans and wagons gain new submodels. Front bucket seats are

FORD

standard on SES Deluxe and SEL sedans and optional for the SEL Deluxe wagon. The standard front bench seat gives sedans 6-passenger capacity, while a 2-passenger rear-facing 3rd-row seat is now standard on wagons for 8-passenger seating. The base engine is an overhead-valve 155-hp V6. Available on higher-line models is a 200-hp dual overhead-cam V6. Both engines come only with automatic transmission. Antilock brakes are standard on all but the LX and SE sedan, where theyíre optional; wagons get rear discs in place of drums. Traction control and head and torso front side airbags are standard on the SEL Premium sedan, and optional on all but the LX sedan and SE Standard wagon. Power-adjustable brake and accelerator pedals are available on all but the LX sedan. Taurus shares its basic design with the Mercury Sable.

RATINGS	LX sdn, ohv V6	SE Prem. wgn, dohc V6	SEL Prem. sdn, dohc V6
ACCELERATION	4	5	5
FUEL ECONOMY	5	5	5
RIDE QUALITY	6	6	6
STEERING/HANDLING	6	6	6
QUIETNESS	5	5	5
INSTRUMENTS/CONTROLS	6	6	6
ROOM/COMFORT (FRONT)	6	6	6
ROOM/COMFORT (REAR)	6	6	6
CARGO ROOM	6	8	6
VALUE	7	7	6

Acceleration and ride comfort are only average, but the competitively priced Taurus and Sable merit your consideration for their good road manners, utility, and range of safety features.

TOTAL	57	60	57

Average total for midsize cars: 57.0

ENGINES

	ohv V6	dohc V6
Size, liters/cu. in.	3.0/182	3.0/181
Horsepower @ rpm	155 @ 4900	200 @ 5650
Torque (lb-ft) @ rpm	185 @ 3960	200 @ 4400
Availability	S	O[1]

EPA city/highway mpg

4-speed automatic	20/28	20/27

1. Optional SE wagon, SES; standard SEL.

PRICES

Ford Taurus	Retail Price	Dealer Invoice
LX 4-door sedan	$18750	$17438
SE 4-door sedan	19560	17979
SE Standard 4-door wagon	21495	19721

Prices are accurate at time of publication; subject to manufacturer's change.

FORD

	Retail Price	Dealer Invoice
SE Deluxe 4-door wagon	$22120	$20283
SE Premium 4-door wagon	22810	20904
SES Standard 4-door sedan	20575	18892
SES Deluxe 4-door sedan	21675	19882
SEL Deluxe 4-door sedan	22445	20575
SEL Deluxe 4-door Wagon	22695	20801
SEL Premium 4-door sedan	23015	21088
Destination charge	625	625

STANDARD EQUIPMENT

LX: 3.0-liter V6 engine, 4-speed automatic transmission, dual front airbags, emergency inside trunk release, air conditioning, power steering, tilt steering wheel, cloth upholstery, 6-passenger seating, front split bench seat w/flip fold center console, column shift, center console, cupholders, power mirrors, power windows, power door locks, AM/FM radio, digital clock, tachometer, variable intermittent wipers, visor mirrors, rear defogger, remote decklid release, floormats, theft-deterrent system, 215/60R16 tires, wheel covers.

SE sedan adds: remote keyless entry, cruise control, AM/FM/cassette, alloy wheels.

SE Standard wagon adds: antilock 4-wheel disc brakes, split folding rear seat, rear-facing third row seat, power antenna, cargo cover, rear wiper/washer, roof rack.

SE Deluxe wagon adds: 6-way power driver seat w/lumbar adjustment, AM/FM/CD player.

SE Premium wagon adds: 3.0-liter dohc V6 engine.

SEL Deluxe wagon adds: 3.0-liter V6 engine, automatic climate control, leather-wrapped steering wheel, power adjustable pedals, keypad entry, automatic headlights.

SES Standard sedan adds to SE sedan: antilock brakes, 6-way power driver seat w/lumbar adjustment, split folding rear seat, AM/FM/CD player, illuminated visor mirrors.

SES Deluxe sedan adds: 3.0-liter dohc V6 engine, leather-wrapped steering wheel, 5-passenger seating, front bucket seats, floor shift, rear spoiler.

SEL Deluxe sedan adds: automatic climate control, power adjustable pedals, AM/FM/cassette/CD player, keypad entry, automatic headlights.

SEL Premium sedan adds: traction control, front side airbags.

OPTIONAL EQUIPMENT
Major Packages

Value Pkg., SE sedan	535	476

Specifications begin on page 551.

FORD

	Retail Price	Dealer Invoice
Manufacturer's Discount Price................................	*NC*	*NC*
6-way power driver seat, AM/FM/CD player.		
Safety Pkg..	$565	$503
Traction control, front side airbags. SE sedan requires antilock brakes. NA LX, SE Standard wagon. Std. SEL Premium.		
Premium Audio Group, SES standard/Deluxe	530	472
AM/FM/cassette w/in-dash 6-disc CD changer, Mach Premium Sound.		
Luxury and Convenience Pkg., SES Standard/Deluxe, SEL Deluxe/Premium..	185	165
Heated power mirrors, automatic day/night rearview mirror, compass.		
Duratec Pkg., SEL Deluxe wagon............................	1120	997
3.0-liter dohc V6 engine, AM/FM radio w/in-dash 6-disc CD changer, Mach Premium Sound, 5-passenger seating, front bucket seats, floor shift.		

Safety
Antilock brakes, LX, SE sedan	600	534

Comfort & Convenience Features
Leather upholstery, SES Standard/Deluxe, SEL Deluxe/Premium...	895	797
6-passenger seating, SEL Deluxe sedan (credit)............	(105)	(93)
Front split bench seat w/flip-fold seating console, column shift. NA w/leather upholstery.		
6-way power passenger seat, SEL Premium	350	312
Power-adjustable pedals, SE sedan, SE Deluxe/Premium wagon, SES Standard/Deluxe	120	107
AM/FM/cassette, LX...	185	165
Mach Premium Sound, SEL Deluxe sedan, SEL Premium	320	285
Power sunroof, SES Standard/Deluxe sedan, SEL Deluxe/Premium sedan...	895	797

Appearance and Miscellaneous
Rear spoiler, SEL Deluxe/Premium sedan	230	205

FORD THUNDERBIRD

Rear-wheel-drive near-luxury car
Base price range: $34,965-$38,465. Built in USA.
Also consider: Audi TT, BMW 3-Series convertible, Mercedes-Benz SLK-Class

FOR • Acceleration • Steering/handling **AGAINST** • Climate controls • Cargo room • Rear visibility

Ford restores a famous name to its lineup with the 2002

FORD

Ford Thunderbird

Thunderbird, a 2-seat convertible with retro styling cues. It's built on a shortened version of the rear-wheel-drive platform developed for the Lincoln LS and Jaguar S-Type sedans. A removable hardtop with T-Bird's trademark porthole windows is available to supplement the standard power-folding soft top with heated glass rear window. The only engine is the LS's 252-hp 3.9-liter V8. Also shared is the Lincoln/Jaguar 5-speed automatic transmission. Standard features include antilock 4-wheel disc brakes, side airbags, 17-inch alloy wheels, and CD changer. A premium model adds chrome wheels and traction control. Interior upgrade packages match various trim pieces to the exterior color.

RATINGS

	Premium
ACCELERATION	6
FUEL ECONOMY	4
RIDE QUALITY	5
STEERING/HANDLING	6
QUIETNESS	4
INSTRUMENTS/CONTROLS	6
ROOM/COMFORT (FRONT)	6
ROOM/COMFORT (REAR)	0
CARGO ROOM	2
VALUE	4

Ford aims Thunderbird at "relaxed sportiness," and pretty much hits the mark. It is not as mechanically refined as it should be, and its interior feels cheap. But it is more practical than a genuine sports car, and as a near-luxury 2-passenger V8 convertible, is in a class by itself. Just don't expect discounts.

TOTAL	43

Average total for near-luxury cars: 54.5

ENGINES

	dohc V8
Size, liters/cu. in.	3.9/241

Specifications begin on page 551.

FORD

	dohc V8
Horsepower @ rpm	252 @ 6100
Torque (lb-ft) @ rpm	261 @ 4300
Availability	S

EPA city/highway mpg

5-speed automatic 17/23

PRICES

Ford Thunderbird	Retail Price	Dealer Invoice
Deluxe 2-door convertible	$34965	$32174
Deluxe 2-door convertible w/removable hardtop	37465	34424
Premium 2-door convertible	35965	33074
Premium 2-door convertible w/removable hardtop	35324	38465
Destination charge	530	530

STANDARD EQUIPMENT

Deluxe: 3.9-liter dohc V8 engine, 5-speed automatic transmission, dual front airbags, side airbags, antilock 4-wheel disc brakes, emergency inside trunk release, air conditioning w/dual-zone automatic climate control, power steering, tilt/telescoping leather-wrapped steering wheel, cruise control, leather upholstery, bucket seats, 6-way power driver seat w/lumbar adjustment, 2-way power passenger seat, center console, cupholders, power mirrors, power windows, power door locks, remote keyless entry, AM/FM radio w/in-dash 6-disc CD changer, digital clock, steering wheel radio controls, tachometer, power convertible top, variable intermittent wipers, rear defogger, remote power decklid release, visor mirrors, automatic headlights, floormats, theft-deterrent system, 235/50VR17 tires, alloy wheels.

Premium adds: traction control, chrome alloy wheels.

OPTIONAL EQUIPMENT

Major Packages

Partial Interior Color Accent Pkg., Premium	595	530

Exterior-color steering wheel, and shifter trim, exterior-color seat insert.

Full Interior Color Accent Pkg., Premium	800	712

Exterior-color dashboard, console, door, steering wheel, and shifter trim, exterior-color seat insert.

Black Accent Pkg.	295	263

Black steering wheel and shifter trim.

Powertrain

Traction control, Deluxe w/hardtop	230	205

Prices are accurate at time of publication; subject to manufacturer's change.

FORD

FORD WINDSTAR

Ford Windstar

Front-wheel-drive minivan

Base price range: $20,385-$33,840. Built in Canada.

Also consider: Chevrolet Venture, Dodge Caravan, Honda Odyssey, Toyota Sienna

FOR • Passenger and cargo room   **AGAINST** • Fuel economy

Former option packages become separate trim levels for 2002, while an antiskid system is due later in the model year. Windstar offers LX models with new Base, Standard, and Deluxe versions. SE, SEL, and Limited models return. A 3.8-liter V6 with automatic transmission is the only powertrain. Windstar comes in a single, 7-passenger body length, and dual sliding doors are now standard. ABS is also standard. Traction control is standard on Limited, optional on LX Deluxe, SE, and SEL models. The antiskid system due later is designed to automatically apply select brakes to counteract skids in turns. Head/torso front side airbags are standard on Limited, optional on other Windstars. Also offered are power adjustable brake and accelerator pedals, power sliding doors, rear obstacle warning system, and a rear entertainment system with ceiling mounted screen and removable VCR. Windstar is also available in a cargo model.

RATINGS	LX Standard	SEL
ACCELERATION	5	5
FUEL ECONOMY	3	3
RIDE QUALITY	5	5
STEERING/HANDLING	4	4
QUIETNESS	5	5
INSTRUMENTS/CONTROLS	6	6
ROOM/COMFORT (FRONT)	7	7
ROOM/COMFORT (REAR)	6	8

Specifications begin on page 551.

FORD

	LX Standard	SEL
CARGO ROOM	9	9
VALUE	6	6

Minivans from Dodge, Chrysler, and Honda are our Best Buys, but the roomy Windstar boasts some noteworthy safety and convenience features.

TOTAL	56	58

Average total for minivans: 56.0

ENGINES

	ohv V6
Size, liters/cu. in.	3.8/232
Horsepower @ rpm	200 @ 4900
Torque (lb-ft) @ rpm	240 @ 3600
Availability	S
EPA city/highway mpg	
4-speed automatic	17/23

PRICES

Ford Windstar	Retail Price	Dealer Invoice
Cargo 3-door van	$20385	$18658
LX Base 4-door van	22340	20844
LX Standard 4-door van	26175	23811
LX Deluxe 4-door van	27260	24777
SE 4-door van	28760	26112
SEL 4-door van	31430	28488
Limited 4-door van	33840	30632
Destination charge	655	655

STANDARD EQUIPMENT

Cargo: 3.8-liter V6 engine, 4-speed automatic transmission, dual front airbags, antilock brakes, air conditioning, power steering, 2-passenger seating (cloth front buckets), front passenger area carpeting and cloth headliner, cupholders, power mirrors, power windows, power door locks, AM/FM radio, digital clock, tachometer, intermittent wipers, rear defogger, rear wiper/washer, visor mirrors, theft-deterrent system, full-size spare tire, 215/70R15 tires, wheel covers.

LX Base adds: tire pressure monitor, driver-side rear door, 7-passenger seating (front bucket seats, 2-place second row bench seat and 3-place third row bench seat), rear passenger area carpeting and cloth headliner, map lights, floormats. *Deletes:* full-size spare tire.

LX Standard adds: front and rear automatic climate controls, tilt steering wheel, cruise control, driver-side sliding rear door, remote keyless entry, key pad entry, second and third row adjustable seat-tracks and rollers,

Prices are accurate at time of publication; subject to manufacturer's change.

FORD

AM/FM/cassette, conversation mirror, rear privacy glass, roof rack.

LX Deluxe adds: power adjustable pedals, center console, AM/FM/cassette/CD player, 225/60R16 tires, alloy wheels.

SE adds: quad bucket seats, 6-way power driver seat w/power lumbar adjustment, heated power mirrors w/turn signals, rear radio controls, illuminated visor mirrors, cornering lights, 215/65R16 tires. *Deletes:* center console.

SEL adds: power sliding rear doors, leather upholstery, 6-way power passenger seat w/power lumbar adjustment, center console, automatic day/night rearview mirror, universal garage door opener, compass, automatic headlights.

Limited adds: traction control, front side airbags, rear obstacle detection system, heated front seats, wood/leather-wrapped steering wheel, driver seat and mirror memory, AM/FM radio w/in-dash 6-disc CD changer, theft-deterrent system w/alarm, trailer wiring harness, full-size spare tire, self-sealing tires.

OPTIONAL EQUIPMENT

	Retail Price	Dealer Invoice
Major Packages		
Van Value Group, Cargo	$910	$773

Tilt steering wheel, cruise control, remote keyless entry, AM/FM/cassette, privacy glass.

Value Group, LX Base	585	498

AM/FM/cassette, rear privacy glass.

Electronics Group, SE	485	413

Automatic day/night rearview mirror, compass, universal garage door opener, additional warning messages, automatic headlights.

Family Security Group I, LX Deluxe	455	387

Traction control, perimeter alarm, self-sealing tires.

Family Security Group II, SE, SEL	600	510

Traction control, rear obstacle detection system, theft-deterrent system w/alarm, 215/65R16 self-sealing tires.

Class II Trailer Towing Pkg., SEL	445	378

Heavy-duty battery, trailer tow wiring, full-size spare tire. Std. Limited.

Powertrain

Traction control, Cargo	395	336

Safety

Front side airbags	390	332

NA Cargo. Std. Limited.

Comfort & Convenience Features

Rear Seat Entertainment System, SE, SEL, Limited	995	846

Videocassette player, LCD screen, two headphones, headphone jacks, remote control. Deletes center console.

Specifications begin on page 551.

FORD

	Retail Price	Dealer Invoice
Power driver- and passenger-side sliding rear doors, SE	$900	$765
Center console, LX Standard, SE	155	132
Quad bucket seats, LX Standard/Deluxe	745	633

FORD ZX2

Ford ZX2

Front-wheel-drive sporty coupe
Base price range: $12,500-$14,000. Built in Mexico.
Also consider: Ford Focus ZX3, Toyota Celica, Volkswagen New Beetle

FOR • Fuel economy **AGAINST** • Rear-seat room • Noise • Rear-seat entry/exit

Ford's 'budget' sporty coupe is based on the 1997-2000 Escort sedan. Base Standard models are joined for 2002 by Deluxe and Premium trim levels. All have a 4-cyl engine teamed with manual or optional automatic transmission. ABS is optional. Deluxe and Premium offer an optional sunroof. Available only on Premium are leather upholstery and a 6-disc, in-dash CD player.

RATINGS	Standard, man.	Standard, auto.
ACCELERATION	5	4
FUEL ECONOMY	7	7
RIDE QUALITY	4	4
STEERING/HANDLING	5	5
QUIETNESS	2	2
INSTRUMENTS/CONTROLS	4	4
ROOM/COMFORT (FRONT)	4	4
ROOM/COMFORT (REAR)	2	2
CARGO ROOM	2	2

Prices are accurate at time of publication; subject to manufacturer's change.

FORD

	Standard, man.	Standard, auto.
VALUE	3	3

ZX2 looks sportier than it performs. Honda's Civic coupe or the ZX3 rate far higher overall.

TOTAL	38	37

Average total for sporty coupes: 43.4

ENGINES

	dohc I4
Size, liters/cu. in.	2.0/121
Horsepower @ rpm	130 @ 5750
Torque (lb-ft) @ rpm	127 @ 4250
Availability	S

EPA city/highway mpg

5-speed manual	26/33
4-speed automatic	25/33

PRICES

Ford ZX2	Retail Price	Dealer Invoice
Standard 2-door coupe	$12500	$11765
Deluxe 2-door coupe	13545	12726
Premium 2-door coupe	14000	13145
Destination charge	490	490

STANDARD EQUIPMENT

Standard: 2.0-liter dohc 4-cylinder engine, 5-speed manual transmission, dual front airbags, emergency inside trunk release, power steering, cloth upholstery, bucket seats, center console, cupholders, split folding rear seat, power mirrors, AM/FM/cassette, digital clock, tachometer, rear defogger, variable intermittent wipers, visor mirrors, rear spoiler, 185/60R15 tires, alloy wheels.

Deluxe adds: air conditioning, tilt leather-wrapped steering wheel, cruise control, map lights, floormats.

Premium adds: power windows, power door locks, remote keyless entry, fog lights.

OPTIONAL EQUIPMENT

Powertrain

4-speed automatic transmission	815	725

Safety

Antilock brakes	400	356

Comfort & Convenience Features

Air conditioning, Standard	795	708

Specifications begin on page 551.

FORD • GMC

	Retail Price	Dealer Invoice
Leather upholstery, Premium	$395	$352
Premium AM/FM/cassette w/6-disc CD changer, Premium	295	263
Power sunroof, Deluxe, Premium	595	530

Appearance and Miscellaneous
Chrome alloy wheels, Premium	595	530

Includes 185/65R14 tires.

GMC ENVOY

GMC Envoy

Rear- or 4-wheel-drive midsize sport-utility vehicle
Base price range: $28,945-$33,985. Built in USA.
Also consider: Acura MDX, Dodge Durango, Ford Explorer, Mercury Mountaineer

FOR • Passenger and cargo room • Towing ability **AGAINST** • Steering/handling • Fuel economy

Envoy is a new 5-passenger 4-dr wagon that shares its design, powertrain, and new body-on-frame platform with the '02 Chevrolet TrailBlazer and Oldsmobile Bravada. Each has its own styling details inside and out. Compared to its retired Jimmy predecessor, Envoy has a 6-inch longer wheelbase, 10-inch longer body, and is 5 inches wider and taller. A new 270-hp inline 6 cyl and 4-speed automatic transmission are the sole powertrain. Envoy offers rear-wheel drive with available traction control or General Motors' Autotrac 4WD that can be left engaged on dry pavement and includes low-range gearing. Unlike Ford's '02 Explorer, GM's new SUVs do not adopt independent rear suspension. But in lieu of standard coil-spring rear suspension, Envoy offers an optional load-leveling air suspension. Standard are antilock 4-wheel disc brakes, front side airbags (driver's covers head and torso), and 17-inch alloy wheels. Options

Prices are accurate at time of publication; subject to manufacturer's change.

GMC

include a DVD rear-seat entertainment system. A longer Envoy with 3rd-row seating is planned for spring 2002. Envoy's performance and accommodations mirror those of comparably equipped TrailBlazers.

RATINGS	Envoy 4WD w/coil springs	Envoy 4WD w/air suspension
ACCELERATION	6	6
FUEL ECONOMY	4	4
RIDE QUALITY	5	6
STEERING/HANDLING	3	4
QUIETNESS	4	4
INSTRUMENTS/CONTROLS	7	7
ROOM/COMFORT (FRONT)	7	7
ROOM/COMFORT (REAR)	6	6
CARGO ROOM	8	8
VALUE	4	4

Lack of 3rd-row seating and curtain side airbags are shortfalls in today's SUV environment—though the elongated Envoy due within the year will seat seven. But if you're shopping GM for a midsize 4x4, we recommend the Envoy over the TrailBalzer and Bravada. The GMC version has the best interior design details, but more important, offers the rear air suspension, which firms up road manners and avoids the sloppy ride/handling feel you're stuck with on the TrailBlazer. The demise of the Olds brand does not make the costly-to-begin-with Bravada a sound investment.

TOTAL	54	56

Average total for midsize sport-utility vehicles: 49.6

ENGINES

	dohc I6
Size, liters/cu. in.	4.2/256
Horsepower @ rpm	270 @ 6000
Torque (lb-ft) @ rpm	275 @ 3600
Availability	S
EPA city/highway mpg	
4-speed automatic	15/21[1]

1. 16/22 w/2WD.

PRICES

GMC Envoy	Retail Price	Dealer Invoice
SLE 4-door wagon, 2WD	$28945	$26195
SLE 4-door wagon, 4WD	31170	28743
SLT 4-door wagon, 2WD	31760	28743
SLT 4-door wagon, 4WD	33985	30756
Destination charge	600	600

Specifications begin on page 551.

GMC

STANDARD EQUIPMENT

SLE: 4.2-liter dohc 6-cylinder engine, 4-speed automatic transmission, dual front airbags, front side airbags, antilock 4-wheel disc brakes, daytime running lights, air conditioning w/dual-zone manual controls, power steering, tilt leather-wrapped steering wheel, cruise control, OnStar System w/one year service (roadside assistance, emergency services; other services available), cloth upholstery, front bucket seats w/lumbar adjustment, 8-way power driver seat, center console, cupholders, split folding rear seat, heated power mirrors, power windows, power door locks, remote keyless entry, AM/FM/CD player, digital clock, tachometer, variable intermittent wipers, rear defogger, intermittent rear wiper/washer, automatic day/night rearview mirror, compass, outside temperature indicator, overhead console, universal garage door opener, illuminated visor mirrors, map lights, cargo cover, automatic headlights, floormats, theft-deterrent system, rear liftgate, rear privacy glass, roof rack, fog lights, platform hitch, 7-wire trailer harness, full-size spare tire, 245/65R17 tires, alloy wheels. **4WD** adds: 4-wheel drive, 2-speed transfer case.

SLT adds: leather upholstery, 8-way power passenger seat, driver seat and mirror memory, dual-zone automatic climate control, steering wheel radio and climate controls, rear climate controls, rear radio controls, rear headphone jacks, trip computer, driver-side automatic day/night mirror, outside-mirror mounted turn signal lights, headlight washers. **4WD** adds: 4-wheel drive, 2-speed transfer case.

OPTIONAL EQUIPMENT
Major Packages

Enhanced Preferred Equipment Group 1SB, SLE ..   400   344
AM/FM/cassette/CD player, 8-way power passenger seat, theft-deterrent system w/alarm

Off-Road Preferred Equipment Group w/Professional
Towing1SC, 4WD SLE..   700   602
Locking rear differential, special axle ratio, AM/FM/cassette/CD player, skid plates, 245/65R17 on-off road tires.

Premium Preferred Equipment Group w/Professional Towing1SD,
2WD SLE   1525   1312
4WD SLE   1350   1161
Enhanced Preferred Equipment Group 1SB plus traction control (2WD), locking rear differential, special axle ratio, rear load-leveling suspension, polished alloy wheels.

Enhanced Preferred Equipment Group 1SF, SLT ...   400   344
AM/FM/cassette/CD player, heated front seats, theft-deterrent system w/alarm.

Off-Road Preferred Equipment Group w/Professional
Towing 1SG, 4WD SLT   1500   1290
Locking rear differential, special axle ratio, Bose AM/FM radio w/in-dash 6-disc CD changer, heated front seats, theft-deterrent system w/alarm, skid plates, 245/65R17 on-off road tires.

Prices are accurate at time of publication; subject to manufacturer's change.

GMC

	Retail Price	Dealer Invoice
Premium Preferred Equipment Group w/ Professional Towing1SH, 2WD SLT	$2425	$2086
4WD SLT	2250	1935

Locking rear differential, special axle ratio, taction control (2WD), Bose AM/FM radio w/in-dash 6-disc CD changer, heated front seats, digital memo recorder, rain-sensing wipers, rear load-leveling suspension, polished alloy wheels.

Professional Technology Group 1SJ, SLE	NA	NA

Premium Preferred Equipment Group 1SD plus rear entertainment system w/DVD, AM/FM radio w/in-dash 6-disc CD changer, digital memo recorder, reversible cargo mat. NA w/power sunroof.

Professional Technology Group 1SK, SLT	NA	NA

Premium Preferred Equipment Group 1SH plus entertainment system w/DVD, reversible cargo mat. NA w/power sunroof.

Powertrain

Traction control, 2WD	175	151
Locking rear differential	270	232

Comfort & Convenience Features

Power sunroof	800	688
Requires Preferred Equipment Group.		
AM/FM/cassette/CD player	100	86
AM/FM radio w/in-dash 6-disc CD changer, SLT	395	340
SLE, SLT w/Preferred Equipment Group	295	254
SLE requires Preferred Equipment Group.		
Bose sound system, SLT	495	426
Requires Preferred Equipment Group 1SF.		

Appearance and Miscellaneous

Running boards	325	280

Special Purpose, Wheels and Tires

Rear load-leveling suspension	375	323
Requires Preferred Equipment Group.		

GMC YUKON/DENALI

Rear- or 4-wheel-drive full-size sport-utility vehicle

Base price range: $33,377-$48,125. Built in USA.

Also consider: Ford Expedition and Excursion, Toyota Land Cruiser and Sequoia

FOR • Acceleration (Denali) • Passenger and cargo room • Trailer towing capability **AGAINST** • Steering feel • Fuel economy

Specifications begin on page 551.

GMC

GMC Yukon

Yukon is GMC's version of the Chevrolet Tahoe, while the longer Yukon XL is a companion to the Chevy Suburban. GMC also has luxury versions called Denali and Denali XL. Cadillac's Escalade is basically a retrimmed Denali. Yukon XL comes in half-ton 1500- and three-quarter-ton 2500-series models; the others are 1500-series trucks. Yukons offer side-opening rear cargo doors as an alternative to the one-piece liftgate. Front bucket seats are standard on Denali and optional on Yukon in place of a front bench. XL models offer 2nd-row bucket seats. A 3rd-row bench seat is standard on XLs and Denalis, optional on regular Yukons. All have front side airbags and antilock 4-wheel disc brakes.

A 4.8-liter V8 is standard on Yukon. A 5.3 V8 is standard on Yukon XL and optional on Yukon. Both Denalis and the Yukon XL 2500 come with a 6.0-liter V8. An 8.1-liter V8 is optional for the Yukon XL 2500. All have an automatic transmission with GM's Tow/Haul mode; it gets revisions for 2002 designed to improve durability. Maximum towing capacity is 8100 lb on Yukon, 12,000 on Yukon XL 2500. Yukons have rear-wheel drive or General Motors' Autotrac 4WD that can be left engaged on dry pavement and includes low-range gearing. Denalis have all-wheel drive without low-range gearing. For 2002, front and rear automatic climate controls are newly standard on Yukons, and 2WD versions get standard limited-slip rear differential and traction control. GM's OnStar assistance system is also available. Denalis for '02 add heated 2nd-row seats to the already-standard heated front seats, plus load-leveling rear suspension. Performance and accommodations mirror those of like-equipped Tahoes and Suburbans.

RATINGS	Yukon 2WD, 5.3 V8	Yukon XL 4WD, 5.3 V8	Denali
ACCELERATION	4	4	5
FUEL ECONOMY	3	2	1
RIDE QUALITY	6	6	6

Prices are accurate at time of publication; subject to manufacturer's change.

GMC

	Yukon 2WD, 5.3 V8	Yukon XL 4WD, 5.3 V8	Denali
STEERING/HANDLING	3	3	4
QUIETNESS	6	6	6
INSTRUMENTS/CONTROLS	7	7	7
ROOM/COMFORT (FRONT)	9	9	9
ROOM/COMFORT (REAR)	8	8	8
CARGO ROOM	9	9	9
VALUE	4	4	2

Yukon and Yukon XL offer fine value in base form and most of the sensible luxury options anyone could want. They earn our Recommended label. Denalis mix those basic virtues with more standard power and extra amenities, but not enough of either to warrant their higher prices.

TOTAL	59	58	57

Average total for full-size sport-utility vehicles: 50.9

ENGINES

	ohv V8	ohv V8	ohv V8	ohv V8
Size, liters/cu. in.	4.8/294	5.3/327	6.0/364	8.1/496
Horsepower @ rpm	275 @ 5200	285 @ 5200	320 @ 5000	340 @ 4200
Torque (lb-ft) @ rpm	290 @ 4000	325 @ 4000	360 @ 4000	455 @ 3200
Availability	S[1]	S[2]	S[3]	O[4]

EPA city/highway mpg

4-speed automatic	14/17[5]	14/17[6]	12/15	NA

1. Yukon. 2. Yukon XL 1500; optional Yukon. 3. Denali, Yukon XL 2500. 4. Yukon XL 2500. 5. 15/19 w/2WD. 6. 14/18 w/2WD.

PRICES

GMC Yukon/Denali

	Retail Price	Dealer Invoice
Yukon 2WD 4-door wagon	$33377	$29205
Yukon 4WD 4-door wagon	35910	31421
Denali AWD 4-door wagon	46625	40797
Yukon XL 1500 2WD 4-door wagon	36282	31747
Yukon XL 1500 4WD 4-door wagon	38815	33963
Denali XL AWD 4-door wagon	48125	42109
Yukon XL 2500 2WD 4-door wagon	37654	32947
Yukon XL 2500 4WD 4-door wagon	40271	35237
Destination charge: Yukon, Denali/Denali XL	730	730
Destination charge: Denali/Denali XL, Yukon XL	765	765

STANDARD EQUIPMENT

Yukon: 4.8-liter V8 engine, 4-speed automatic transmission, traction

Specifications begin on page 551.

GMC

control, limited-slip rear differential, dual front airbags, front side airbags, antilock 4-wheel disc brakes, daytime running lights, front and rear air conditioning w/front and rear automatic climate controls, interior air filter, rear heater, power steering, tilt leather-wrapped steering wheel, cruise control, cloth upholstery, split front bench seat, 6-way power front seats w/lumbar adjustment, cupholders, second row split folding seat, heated power mirrors, power windows, power door locks, remote keyless entry, AM/FM/CD player, digital clock, tachometer, engine hour meter, overhead console, illuminated visor mirrors, intermittent wipers, map lights, rear defogger, rear wiper/washer, cargo cover, automatic day/night rearview mirror, compass, outside temperature indicator, automatic headlights, carpeting, floormats, theft-deterrent system, fog lights, roof rack, rear liftgate/liftglass, deep-tinted rear glass, 7-lead trailer wiring harness, front tow hooks, full-size spare tire, P265/70R16 tires, alloy wheels. **4WD** adds: 4-wheel drive, Autotrac 2-speed transfer case, variable-assist power steering. *Deletes:* traction control.

Denali/Denali XL add: 6.0-liter V8 engine, all-wheel drive, variable-assist power steering, OnStar System w/one year service (roadside assistance, emergency services; other services available), leather upholstery, 10-way power front bucket seats w/driver seat memory, heated front and second row seats, third row split folding seat, Bose AM/FM/cassette w/in-dash 6-disc CD changer, steering wheel radio controls, rear radio controls, rear headphone jacks, driver-side automatic day/night mirror, trip computer, universal garage door opener, running boards, Autoride suspension, load-leveling rear suspension, trailer hitch platform, brake wiring harness, P265/70R17 tires. *Deletes:* traction control.

Yukon XL adds to Yukon: 5.3-liter V8 engine (1500), 6.0-liter V8 engine (2500), third row bench seat, trailer hitch platform, brake wiring harness, LT245/75R16E tires (2500). **4WD** adds: 4-wheel drive, 2-speed transfer case, variable-assist power steering (1500). *Deletes:* traction control.

OPTIONAL EQUIPMENT
Major Packages

	Retail Price	Dealer Invoice
SLT Marketing Option Pkg. 1SC, Yukon	$1455	$1251
Yukon XL	2105	1810

Leather upholstery, front bucket seats, center console, AM/FM/cassette/CD player.

SLT Marketing Option Pkg. 1SD, Yukon	3723	3202
Yukon XL	3273	2815

SLT Pkg. 1SC plus 5.3-liter V8 engine (Yukon), OnStar System w/one year service (roadside assistance, emergency services; other services available), heated 10-way power front seats, driver seat memory, rear seat radio controls and headphone jacks, universal garage door opener, driver-side automatic day/night rearview mirror.

Prices are accurate at time of publication; subject to manufacturer's change.

GMC

	Retail Price	Dealer Invoice
Z71 Off-Road Suspension Pkg., 4WD Yukon	$619	$532

Gas shock absorbers, skid plates, high-capacity air cleaner, LT265/75R16C on/off-road tires, polished alloy wheels. Requires 5.3-liter V8 engine. NA with third row seat.

Heavy-Duty Trailering Equipment, Yukon 169   145

Trailer hitch platform, brake wiring harness. 2WD requires 5.3-liter V8 engine.

Powertrain

	Retail Price	Dealer Invoice
5.3-liter V8 engine, Yukon	700	602
8.1-liter V8 engine, 2WD Yukon XL 2500	1405	1208
4WD Yukon XL 2500	1600	1376

Includes Autoride Suspension. 2WD deletes traction control.

Special axle ratio, Yukon, Yukon XL	50	43

Comfort & Convenience Features

	Retail Price	Dealer Invoice
Power sunroof, Yukon, Yukon XL	1045	899
Yukon/Yukon XL ordered w/SLT Pkg. 1SD	938	807
Denali, Denali XL	1000	860

Yukon/Yukon XL include universal garage door opener. Downgrades rear automatic climate controls to manual climate controls.

Front bucket seats, Yukon, Yukon XL	375	323

Includes floor console.

Second-row bucket seats, Yukon XL, Denali XL	490	421

Yukon XL requires front bucket seats or SLT Pkg.

Third-row split folding rear seat, Yukon	360	310
Yukon w/SLT Pkg.	760	654

Includes floormat. Deletes cargo cover.

AM/FM/cassette/CD player, Yukon, Yukon XL	180	155

Requires bucket seats.

Rear seat radio controls, Yukon, Yukon XL	165	142

Includes headphone jacks. Requires front bucket seats.

Appearance and Miscellaneous

	Retail Price	Dealer Invoice
Rear panel doors, Yukon, Yukon XL (credit)	(250)	(215)

NA with Yukon third-row seat. Deletes rear wiper/washer.

Running boards, Yukon, Yukon XL	395	340

Special Purpose, Wheels and Tires

	Retail Price	Dealer Invoice
Skid Plates, 4WD	95	82
Autoride Suspension, Yukon, Yukon XL 1500	850	731
Yukon XL 2500	900	774
Polished alloy wheels, Yukon, Yukon XL	200	172
P265/70R16 white-letter tires, Yukon, Yukon XL 1500	125	108

NA w/Z71 Off-Road Suspension Pkg.

Specifications begin on page 551.

HONDA

HONDA ACCORD

Honda Accord 4-door sedan

Front-wheel-drive midsize car
Base price range: $15,500-$25,300. Built in USA.
Also consider: Ford Taurus, Nissan Altima, Toyota Camry

FOR • Acceleration (V6 models) • Quietness • Instruments/controls • Steering/handling • Build quality • Exterior finish • Interior materials **AGAINST** • Automatic transmission performance • Rear-seat entry/exit (2-door)

Addition of a popularly equipped SE model signals 2002 as the final model year for the current Accord design. The redesigned 2003 Accord will reportedly retain the current car's styling themes and basic exterior dimensions, but have more interior space and a larger available V6 engine. The 1998-2002 generation closes out with a price-leader DX sedan and DX-based VP sedan, both with a 4-cyl engine. The top-selling LX and upscale EX coupes and sedans offer 4-cyl and V6 power. Four cyl models come with manual or automatic transmission, V6s with automatic only. The new SEs are 4-cyl coupes and sedans that upgrade LX equipment with standard alloy wheels, sunroof, remote keyless entry, cassette/CD player, imitation-wood interior trim, and power driver's-seat height adjuster. ABS is standard on V6s and 4-cyl EXs, optional for the 4-cyl LX sedan with automatic transmission. All Accords offer optional front side airbags. The dashboard airbags have occupant-position sensors. V6 models have standard traction control. EX versions gain steering wheel audio controls for '02.

RATINGS	LX cpe, 4 cyl auto.	DX sdn, man.	LX sdn, 4 cyl auto.	EX sdn, V6
ACCELERATION	5	4	5	6
FUEL ECONOMY	6	6	6	6
RIDE QUALITY	7	7	7	7
STEERING/HANDLING	7	6	7	7

Prices are accurate at time of publication; subject to manufacturer's change.

HONDA

	LX cpe, 4 cyl auto.	DX sdn, man.	LX sdn, 4 cyl auto.	EX sdn, V6
QUIETNESS	6	6	6	6
INSTRUMENTS/CONTROLS	10	10	10	10
ROOM/COMFORT (FRONT)	6	6	6	6
ROOM/COMFORT (REAR)	3	5	5	5
CARGO ROOM	3	4	4	4
VALUE	8	10	10	8

Accord is a perennial Best Buy and a must-see midsize: roomy, well built from top-grade materials, and a cut above the family-car norm for road manners. Terrific reliability and strong resale values complete the picture. These cars are much in demand and so are rarely discounted, but dealers should become more willing to negotiate in the face of intensified competition from the Toyota Camry and Nissan Altima, both of which are all-new for 2002.

TOTAL	61	64	66	65

Average total for midsize cars: 57.0

EXTENDED-USE TEST UPDATE

Our extended-use EX coupe required no unscheduled maintenance over its 12-month test period, though a recent test sedan's power front-passenger window worked only intermittently.

ENGINES

	ohc I4	ohc I4	ohc V6
Size, liters/cu. in.	2.3/137	2.3/137	3.0/183
Horsepower @ rpm	135 @ 5400	150 @ 5700	200 @ 5500
Torque (lb-ft) @ rpm	145 @ 4700	152 @ 4900	195 @ 4700
Availability	S[1]	S[2]	S[3]

EPA city/highway mpg

5-speed manual	26/32	25/32	
4-speed automatic	23/30	23/30	20/28

1. DX, VP models. 2. LX, SE, EX models; 148 hp, 148 lb-ft with ULEV equipment. 3. V6 models.

PRICES

Honda Accord

	Retail Price	Dealer Invoice
DX 4-door sedan, manual	$15500	$13959
DX 4-door sedan, automatic	16300	14678
DX 4-door sedan w/side airbags, manual	15750	14183
DX 4-door sedan w/side airbags, automatic	16550	14902
VP 4-door sedan, automatic	17300	15576
VP 4-door sedan w/side airbags, automatic	17550	15801
LX 2-door coupe, manual	18890	17005

Specifications begin on page 551.

HONDA

	Retail Price	Dealer Invoice
LX 2-door coupe, automatic	$19690	$17724
LX 2-door coupe w/side airbags, manual	19140	17230
LX 2-door coupe w/side airbags, automatic	19940	17949
LX 4-door sedan, manual	18890	17005
LX 4-door sedan, automatic	19690	17724
LX 4-door sedan w/side airbags, manual	19140	17230
LX 4-door sedan w/side airbags, automatic	19940	17949
LX 4-door sedan w/ABS, automatic	20690	18623
LX 4-door sedan w/ABS and side airbags, automatic	20940	18847
LX V6 2-door coupe, automatic	22600	20339
LX V6 4-door sedan, automatic	22600	20339
SE 2-door coupe, automatic	20850	18767
SE 2-door coupe w/side airbags, automatic	21100	18991
SE 4-door sedan, automatic	20850	18767
SE 4-door sedan w/side airbags, automatic	21100	18991
EX 2-door coupe, manual	21500	19351
EX 2-door coupe, automatic	22300	20070
EX 2-door coupe w/leather, manual	22650	20384
EX 2-door coupe w/leather, automatic	23450	21103
EX 4-door sedan, manual	21500	19351
EX 4-door sedan, automatic	22300	20070
EX 4-door sedan w/leather, manual	22650	20384
EX 4-door sedan w/leather, automatic	23450	21103
EX V6 2-door coupe, automatic	25300	22765
EX V6 4-door sedan, automatic	25300	22768
Destination charge	440	440

STANDARD EQUIPMENT

DX: 2.3-liter 4-cylinder 135-horsepower engine, 5-speed manual or 4-speed automatic transmission, dual front airbags, emergency inside trunk release, power steering, tilt steering wheel, cloth upholstery, front bucket seats, driver seat manual height adjustment, center console, cupholders, folding rear seat, AM/FM/cassette, digital clock, tachometer, intermittent wipers, rear defogger, remote fuel-door and decklid releases, visor mirrors, theft-deterrent system, 195/70R14 tires, wheel covers.

VP adds: air conditioning, interior air filter, AM/FM/cassette/CD player, floormats.

LX adds to DX: 2.3-liter 4-cylinder VTEC 150-horsepower engine, cruise control, air conditioning, power mirrors, power windows, power door locks, AM/FM/CD player, illuminated visor mirrors, driver seat manual height adjustment, map lights, rear seat w/trunk

Prices are accurate at time of publication; subject to manufacturer's change.

HONDA

pass-through (sedan), split folding rear seat (coupe), variable intermittent wipers, 195/65HR15 tires.

LX V6 adds: 3.0-liter V6 engine, 4-speed automatic transmission, traction control, front side airbags, antilock 4-wheel disc brakes, 8-way power driver seat, floormats, 205/65VR15 tires.

SE adds to LX: power sunroof, remote keyless entry, driver seat power height adjustment, AM/FM/cassette/CD player, floormats, alloy wheels.

EX adds: front side airbags, antilock 4-wheel disc brakes, driver seat adjustable lumbar support, AM/FM/cassette w/in-dash 6-disc CD changer, steering wheel radio controls, automatic-off headlights, power decklid release.

EX w/leather adds: leather upholstery, leather-wrapped steering wheel w/radio controls, 8-way power driver seat.

EX V6 adds: 3.0-liter V6-cylinder engine, 4-speed automatic transmission, traction control, automatic climate control, 4-way power passenger seat, universal garage door opener, 205/65VR15 tires.

Options are available as dealer-installed accessories.

Honda Civic EX 4-door sedan

Front-wheel-drive subcompact car

Base price range: $12,810-$18,060. Built in USA, England.

Also consider: Ford Focus, Mazda Protege, Toyota Corolla, Volkswagen Jetta/Golf

FOR • Fuel economy • Visibility • Build quality • Acceleration (Si) • Handling (Si) **AGAINST** • Steering feel (exc. Si) • Rear-seat entry/exit (coupes, Si)

Specifications begin on page 551.

HONDA

A sporty new Si hatchback joins the Civic line for 2002, and coupes and sedans get suspension revisions designed to improve ride and handling, plus added sound insulation. Due during the model year is a gas/electric hybrid sedan. For now, Civic coupes and sedans come in DX, LX, and top-rung EX trim. There's also a fuel-economy-oriented HX coupe. All use a 1.7-liter 4-cyl engine and manual or optional automatic transmission. The HX's automatic is a continuously variable transmission (CVT) with, in effect, an infinite number of ratios. Front side airbags are optional. ABS is standard on EXs and unavailable otherwise. The new Si is a 2-dr hatchback 9 inches shorter than other Civics. Its anticipated base price of around $18,000 includes a 160-hp 2.0-liter 4 cyl, 5-speed manual transmission (no automatic offered), ABS, electric-assist power steering, sport suspension, and sunroof; front side airbags are optional. Price of the hybrid sedan wasn't available in time for this report, but the car will have a 4-cyl gas engine supplemented by an electric motor and manual or CVT transmission (Honda already offers a hybrid in the 3-cyl Insight 2-seat coupe.)

RATINGS	HX cpe, CVT	LX sdn, auto.	EX sdn, auto.	Si, man.
ACCELERATION	4	4	5	6
FUEL ECONOMY	7	7	7	6
RIDE QUALITY	6	6	6	5
STEERING/HANDLING	5	5	6	7
QUIETNESS	5	5	5	5
INSTRUMENTS/CONTROLS	7	7	7	7
ROOM/COMFORT (FRONT)	5	5	5	5
ROOM/COMFORT (REAR)	3	4	4	3
CARGO ROOM	3	3	3	4
VALUE	7	10	10	8

Minor test-car workmanship glitches and worrisome non-ABS braking dim its luster, but Civic is a clear Best Buy. The competition can't match its blend of comfort and refinement, fuel thrift, great resale value, and strong reliability record. Si offers good combinaton of sportiness and utility.

| TOTAL | 52 | 56 | 58 | 56 |

Average total for subcompact cars: 43.7

EXTENDED-USE TEST UPDATE

Initial automatic-transmission EX sedan required no unscheduled maintenance during its 5206 mi. as part of our extended-use test fleet. That car was damaged in a flood and was replaced by an identical Civic, which is has been trouble-free over its first 1045 mi.

Prices are accurate at time of publication; subject to manufacturer's change.

HONDA

ENGINES

	ohc I4	ohc I4	ohc I4	dohc I4
Size, liters/cu. in.	1.7/102	1.7/102	1.7/102	2.0/122
Horsepower @ rpm	115 @ 6100	117 @ 6100	127 @ 6300	160 @ 6500
Torque (lb-ft) @ rpm	110 @ 4500	111 @ 4500	114 @ 4800	132 @ 5000
Availability	S[1]	S[2]	S[3]	S[4]
EPA city/highway mpg				
5-speed manual	33/39	36/44	32/37	26/30
4-speed automatic	30/38		31/38	
CVT automatic		35/40		

1. DX, LX. 2. HX. 3. EX. 4. Si.

PRICES

Honda Civic

	Retail Price	Dealer Invoice
DX 2-door coupe, manual	$12810	$11715
DX 2-door coupe, automatic	13610	12445
DX 2-door coupe w/side airbags, manual	13060	11943
DX 2-door coupe w/side airbags, automatic	13860	12673
DX 4-door sedan, manual	13010	11898
DX 4-door sedan, automatic	13810	12627
DX 4-door sedan w/side airbags, manual	13260	12126
DX 4-door sedan w/side airbags, automatic	14060	12856
HX 2-door coupe, manual	13610	12445
HX 2-door coupe, CVT	14610	13357
HX 2-door coupe w/side airbags, manual	13860	12673
HX 2-door coupe w/side airbags, CVT	14860	13585
LX 2-door coupe, manual	14910	13631
LX 2-door coupe, automatic	15710	14361
LX 2-door coupe w/side airbags, manual	15160	13859
LX 2-door coupe w/side airbags, automatics	15960	14589
LX 4-door sedan, manual	15110	13813
LX 4-door sedan, automatic	15910	14543
LX 4-door sedan w/side airbags, manual	15360	14041
LX 4-door sedan w/side impact airbags, automatic	16160	14771
EX 2-door coupe, manual	16510	15090
EX 2-door coupe, automatic	17310	15820
EX 2-door coupe w/side airbags, manual	16760	15318
EX 2-door coupe w/side airbags, automatic	17560	16048
EX 4-door sedan, manual	17010	15547
EX 4-door sedan, automatic	17810	16276
EX 4-door sedan w/side impact airbags, manual	17260	15775

Specifications begin on page 551.

HONDA

	Retail Price	Dealer Invoice
EX 4-door sedan w/side impact airbags, automatic..........	$18060	$16504
Destination charge	440	440

STANDARD EQUIPMENT

DX: 1.7-liter 4-cylinder 115-horsepower engine, 5-speed manual or 4-speed automatic transmission, dual front airbags, emergency inside trunk release, power steering, tilt steering wheel, cloth upholstery, front bucket seats, cupholders, split folding rear seat, AM/FM radio, digital clock, rear defogger, remote fuel-door and decklid releases, intermittent wipers, visor mirrors, theft-deterrent system, 185/70R14 tires, wheel covers.

HX adds: 1.7-liter 4-cylinder VTEC 117-horsepower engine, 5-speed manual or continuously-variable automatic transmission (CVT), cruise control, power mirrors, power door locks, AM/FM/cassette, tachometer, alloy wheels.

LX adds to DX: air conditioning, interior air filter, cruise control, center console, power mirrors, power windows, power door locks, AM/FM/cassette, tachometer, map lights.

EX adds: 1.7-liter 4-cylinder VTEC 127-horsepower engine, antilock brakes, height-adjustable driver seat, power sunroof, remote keyless entry, AM/FM/CD player, variable intermittent wipers, 185/65R15 tires.

Options are available as dealer-installed accessories.

Honda CR-V

Front- or all-wheel-drive compact sport-utility vehicle

Prices are accurate at time of publication; subject to manufacturer's change.

HONDA

Base price range: $18,750-$22,800. Built in Japan.
Also consider: Ford Escape, Mazda Tribute, Subaru Forester

FOR • Passenger and cargo room • Maneuverability • Build quality • Exterior finish **AGAINST** • Brake-pedal feel • Road noise

More interior room, more power, new styling, and new features keynote the redesigned 2002 CR-V. Like the 1997-2001 original, the 2002 is a 4-dr, 5-passenger wagon with a side-hinged tailgate and 4-cyl engine. Wheelbase is unchanged and no exterior dimension grows more than 1.3 inches. But new interior panels expand cabin width 3.6 inches, rear leg room increases 2.7 inches, and cargo volume gains 5 cu ft. A new 160-hp 2.4-liter engine replaces a 146-hp 2.0. Manual and automatic transmissions are available. The LX model comes with front-wheel drive or all-wheel drive. The EX comes only with AWD. The AWD system does not have low-range gearing. Power windows and locks, cruise control, cassette/CD audio, tilt steering column, and height-adjustable driverís seat are standard. ABS is limited to the EX, where itís standard. Front side airbags—new to CR-V—are standard on EX and optional on LX, as are alloy wheels. Also new is a sunroof; itís exclusive to the EX as standard equipment. Leather upholstery is unavailable. A 60/40 split folding rear seat is standard, as is the innovative rear-cargo floor that doubles as a folding picnic table. Full prices were unavailable in time for this report, but Honda announced starting prices of $18,800 for a 2WD LX, $21,500 for the EX.

RATINGS

	LX 2WD, auto.	LX AWD, man.	EX, auto.
ACCELERATION	4	4	4
FUEL ECONOMY	6	6	6
RIDE QUALITY	5	5	5
STEERING/HANDLING	4	4	4
QUIETNESS	4	4	4
INSTRUMENTS/CONTROLS	8	8	8
ROOM/COMFORT (FRONT)	7	7	7
ROOM/COMFORT (REAR)	7	7	7
CARGO ROOM	7	7	7
VALUE	8	8	8

Terrifically efficient and satisfyingly well-built, CR-V also appeals for relative comfort, refinement, and spaciousness. V6 competitors have more outright power, but no small SUV beats this Honda for design intelligence, proven reliability, and resale value.

TOTAL	60	60	60

Average total for compact sport-utility vehicles: 44.4

HONDA

ENGINES

	dohc I4
Size, liters/cu. in.	2.4/146
Horsepower @ rpm	160 @ 6000
Torque (lb-ft) @ rpm	162 @ 3600
Availability	S

EPA city/highway mpg
5-speed manual	NA
4-speed automatic	NA

2002 prices unavailable at time of publication.

HONDA INSIGHT

Honda Insight

Front-wheel-drive subcompact car
Base price range: $19,080-$21,280. Built in Japan.
Also consider: Ford Focus ZX3, Toyota Prius

FOR • Fuel economy • Maneuverability • Automatic transmission performance   **AGAINST** • Acceleration • Rear visibility • Road noise • Ride • Interior storage space

Honda's first hybrid-power car is a 2-seat hatchback coupe that leads all other cars in EPA fuel-economy ratings. It has aerodynamic styling, lightweight aluminum-intensive construction, and an electric motor to assist its 3-cyl gasoline engine. When coasting or decelerating, the motor becomes a generator for recharging its own battery pack, so no plug-in charging is required. Manual transmission is standard and a continuously variable transmission (CVT) is optional. The CVT furnishes variable drive ratios instead of conventional gear changes but has steering-wheel "D" and "S" buttons to select normal and higher-performance ranges. Antilock brakes are standard, but air conditioning is optional. Honda limits U.S. sales to about 6500 a year. Due in early 2002 is a Civic Hybrid sedan, a direct challenger to Toyota's 5-passenger Prius hybrid.

Prices are accurate at time of publication; subject to manufacturer's change.

HONDA

RATINGS

	Base w/air conditioning	CVT
ACCELERATION	2	2
FUEL ECONOMY	10	10
RIDE QUALITY	2	3
STEERING/HANDLING	4	4
QUIETNESS	3	4
INSTRUMENTS/CONTROLS	5	5
ROOM/COMFORT (FRONT)	4	4
ROOM/COMFORT (REAR)	0	0
CARGO ROOM	2	2
VALUE	2	3

Despite modest acceleration and a stiff ride, Insight is a useful city/suburban commuter, especially in CVT form, with high-tech, environment-friendly appeal. But like the larger Toyota Prius, it's costly for an economy car, and the payback in fuel savings will take years to recoup. Insight has its charms, but we'd opt for the more practical, similarly priced Prius or a conventional subcompact.

TOTAL	34	37

Average total for subcompact cars: 43.7

ENGINES

	ohc I3/electric
Size, liters/cu. in.	1.0/61
Horsepower @ rpm	73 @ 5700
Torque (lb-ft) @ rpm	91 @ 2000
Availability	S[1]

EPA city/highway mpg

5-speed manual	61/68
CVT automatic	57/56

1. 71 hp, 90 lb-ft w/CVT.

PRICES

Honda Insight	Retail Price	Dealer Invoice
Base 2-door hatchback	$19080	$17824
Base w/air conditioning 2-door hatchback	20280	18943
CVT 2-door hatchback	21280	19876
Destination charge	440	440

STANDARD EQUIPMENT

Base: 1.0-liter 3-cylinder gasoline engine/electric motor, 5-speed manual transmission, dual front airbags, antilock brakes, interior air filter, power steering, front bucket seats, cupholders, power mirrors, power windows, power door locks, remote keyless entry, AM/FM/cassette, digital clock, tachometer, trip computer, intermit-

HONDA

tent wipers, rear defogger, rear wiper/washer, map lights, driver-side visor mirror, remote fuel door release, theft-deterrent system, 165/65R14 tires, alloy wheels.

Base w/air conditioning adds: air conditioning w/automatic climate control.

CVT adds: continuously-variable automatic transmission.

Options are available as dealer-installed accessories.

HONDA ODYSSEY

Honda Odyssey

Front-wheel-drive minivan
Base price range: $24,250-$30,250. Built in Canada.
Also consider: Chrysler Town & Country and Voyager, Dodge Caravan, Toyota Sienna

FOR • Entry/exit • Passenger and cargo room **AGAINST** • Navigation system controls

More horsepower, standard front side airbags, available leather upholstery, and a DVD rear-seat entertainment system lead Odyssey's 2002 updates. Odyssey's 3.5-liter V6 engine gains 30 hp and replaces its 4-speed automatic transmission with a 5-speed. Minor cosmetic changes, retuned suspension, and standard rear disc brakes vs. drums also are new. The front side airbags join standard ABS and traction control. LX, EX, and EX-L models are offered. All have dual sliding side doors, which are powered on all but the LX. Odyssey seats seven and includes a 3rd-row seat that folds into the floor. EX-Ls add leather upholstery and are available with a factory-installed video system that includes a 7-inch ceiling-mounted LCD screen, remote control, wireless headsets, and front-mount DVD

Prices are accurate at time of publication; subject to manufacturer's change.

HONDA

player. The EX-L is also available with a satellite/DVD navigation system, but not in combination with the rear video package.

RATINGS

	LX	EX-L w/nav. sys.
ACCELERATION	5	5
FUEL ECONOMY	4	4
RIDE QUALITY	6	6
STEERING/HANDLING	6	6
QUIETNESS	5	5
INSTRUMENTS/CONTROLS	7	6
ROOM/COMFORT (FRONT)	7	7
ROOM/COMFORT (REAR)	8	8
CARGO ROOM	10	10
VALUE	9	8

Not perfect, but a solid Best Buy: roomy, refined, well built, reasonably priced, plus an even bigger performance edge for '02 versus most rivals with no apparent loss in fuel economy. Demand continues strong, though, so you'll likely pay full sticker or more.

TOTAL	67	65

Average total for minivans: 56.0

ENGINES

	ohc V6
Size, liters/cu. in.	3.5/212
Horsepower @ rpm	240 @ 5500
Torque (lb-ft) @ rpm	242 @ 4500
Availability	S

EPA city/highway mpg
5-speed automatic	18/25

PRICES

Honda Odyssey	Retail Price	Dealer Invoice
LX 4-door van	$24250	$21822
EX 4-door van	26750	24068
EX-L 4-door van	28250	25416
EX-L w/DVD 4-door van	29750	26764
EX-L w/navigation system 4-door van	30250	27214
Destination charge	440	440

STANDARD EQUIPMENT

LX: 3.5-liter V6 engine, 5-speed automatic transmission, traction control, dual front airbags, front side airbags, antilock 4-wheel disc brakes, front and rear air conditioning, power steering, tilt steering wheel, cruise control, cloth upholstery, 7-passenger seating, front bucket seats, height-adjustable driver seat, center console, cuphold-

Specifications begin on page 551.

HONDA

ers, two second-row bucket seats, third row 3-passenger stowable bench seat, power mirrors, power windows, power door locks, AM/FM/cassette, digital clock, tachometer, variable intermittent wipers, rear defogger, intermittent rear wiper/washer, illuminated visor mirrors, map lights, remote fuel door release, floormats, theft-deterrent system, rear privacy glass, 225/65R16 tires, wheel covers.

EX adds: 8-way power driver seat w/lumbar adjustment, dual power-sliding rear doors, remote keyless entry, automatic climate control, AM/FM/CD player, steering wheel radio controls, universal garage door opener, automatic-off headlights, alloy wheels.

EX-L adds: leather upholstery, heated front seats.

EX-L w/DVD adds: DVD player, fold-down LCD screen, wireless headphones, remote control.

EX-L w/navigation system adds to EX-L: navigation system.

Options are available as dealer-installed accessories.

HONDA PASSPORT

Honda Passport EX

Rear- or 4-wheel-drive midsize sport-utility vehicle
Base price range: $23,300-$30,900. Built in USA.
Also consider: Dodge Durango, Ford Explorer, Toyota Highlander

FOR • Cargo room **AGAINST** • Road and wind noise • Fuel economy • Ride • Rear-seat entry/exit

The larger and older of Honda's two SUVs is a retrimmed Isuzu Rodeo and is built at the same Isuzu-run Indiana plant. Passport will reportedly be replaced for the 2003 model year by an SUV based on the MDX from Honda's upscale Acura division. Passport comes in LX, EX, and luxury EX-L trim. All use an Isuzu V6. LXs are available with manual or automatic transmission, the others with automatic

HONDA

only. Passport's 4WD must be disengaged on dry pavement but includes low-range gearing and a limited-slip rear differential. Antilock brakes are standard, and 4WD versions have 4-wheel disc brakes. Exclusive to the EX-L are standard leather upholstery, power driver's seat, and in-dash CD changer. Passport's performance and accommodations mirror those of similarly equipped Rodeos.

RATINGS	LX 2WD, auto.	EX-L 4WD
ACCELERATION	5	5
FUEL ECONOMY	3	3
RIDE QUALITY	2	2
STEERING/HANDLING	4	4
QUIETNESS	4	4
INSTRUMENTS/CONTROLS	6	6
ROOM/COMFORT (FRONT)	6	6
ROOM/COMFORT (REAR)	4	4
CARGO ROOM	8	8
VALUE	3	3

Like Rodeo, Passport emphasize the sport in sport-utility, but has no outstanding feature to distinguish it. Subpar refinement and comfort and an antiquated 4WD system are among its demerits.

TOTAL	45	45

Average total for midsize sport-utility vehicles: 49.6

ENGINES

	dohc V6
Size, liters/cu. in.	3.2/193
Horsepower @ rpm	205 @ 5400
Torque (lb-ft) @ rpm	214 @ 3000
Availability	S

EPA city/highway mpg

5-speed manual	17/20
4-speed automatic	16/20[1]

1. 17/21 w/2WD.

PRICES

Honda Passport	Retail Price	Dealer Invoice
LX 2WD 4-door wagon, 5-speed	$23300	$21047
LX 2WD 4-door wagon, automatic	24450	22084
LX 4WD 4-door wagon, 5-speed	26450	23888
LX 4WD 4-door wagon, automatic	27600	24925
EX 2WD 4-door wagon, automatic	27100	24474
EX 4WD 4-door wagon, automatic	29550	26684
EX-L 2WD 4-door wagon, automatic	28450	25692
EX-L 4WD 4-door wagon, automatic	30900	27902

Specifications begin on page 551.

HONDA

	Retail Price	Dealer Invoice
Destination charge	$440	$440

STANDARD EQUIPMENT

LX: 3.2-liter dohc V6 engine, 5-speed manual or 4-speed automatic transmission, dual front airbags, antilock brakes, air conditioning, power steering, tilt steering wheel, cruise control, cloth upholstery, front bucket seats, center console, cupholders, split folding rear seat, power mirrors, power windows, power door locks, AM/FM/cassette, digital clock, tachometer, map lights, illuminated visor mirrors, variable intermittent wipers, power tailgate release, cargo cover, rear defogger, intermittent rear wiper/washer, roof rack, skid plates, outside-mounted full-size spare tire, 225/75R16 tires. **4WD** models add: 4-wheel drive, 2-speed transfer case, limited-slip differential, 4-wheel disc brakes, 245/70R16 tires, alloy wheels.

EX adds: 4-speed automatic transmission, power sunroof, leather-wrapped steering wheel, heated power mirrors, remote keyless entry, theft-deterrent system, fog lights, rear privacy glass, underfloor full-size spare tire, 245/70R16 tires, alloy wheels. **4WD** models add: 4-wheel drive, 2-speed transfer case, limited-slip differential, 4-wheel disc brakes.

EX-L adds: leather upholstery, 4-way power driver seat, AM/FM/cassette w/in-dash 6-disc CD changer. **4WD** models add: 4-wheel drive, 2-speed transfer case, limited-slip differential, 4-wheel disc brakes.

Options are available as dealer-installed accessories.

HONDA S2000

Honda S2000

Rear-wheel-drive sports car

Prices are accurate at time of publication; subject to manufacturer's change.

HONDA

2001 base price: $32,300. Built in Japan.
Also consider: Audi TT, BMW Z3 Series, Mazda Miata

FOR • Acceleration • Steering/handling • Brake performance
AGAINST • Engine noise • Ride • Passenger and cargo room

S2000's power soft top exchanges a plastic rear window for a glass pane with electric defroster in one of several changes for 2002. Honda's high-performance 4-cyl 2-seat convertible has a mandatory 6-speed manual transmission. The gearbox is reworked for '02 in an effort to provide smoother, quieter shifting. The interior gets extra aluminum trim, a leather-wrapped shift knob in place of an alloy piece, and a restyled console. Revised taillights wear chrome rings. Suzuka Blue is a new exterior color choice. Continuing as standard: antilock 4-wheel disc brakes, 16-inch alloy wheels, high-intensity headlamps, leather upholstery, wind deflector, and AM/FM/CD stereo—the last upgraded and more powerful this year. A removable aluminum hard top is optional. Side airbags are unavailable.

RATINGS

	Base
ACCELERATION	8
FUEL ECONOMY	6
RIDE QUALITY	2
STEERING/HANDLING	10
QUIETNESS	1
INSTRUMENTS/CONTROLS	3
ROOM/COMFORT (FRONT)	3
ROOM/COMFORT (REAR)	0
CARGO ROOM	1
VALUE	2

The '02 changes begin to civilize the S2000, but this remains a noisy, hard-riding, high-strung thoroughbred sports car for performance purists. Strong demand and limited availability send transaction prices way above sticker. S2000 is terrific on a sports-car road, but a BMW Z3 2.5 or Mazda Miata offers similar fun and better day-to-day livability for the same or less money.

TOTAL	36

Average total for sports cars: 41.3

ENGINES

	dohc I4
Size, liters/cu. in.	2.0/122
Horsepower @ rpm	240 @ 8300
Torque (lb-ft) @ rpm	153 @ 7500
Availability	S

EPA city/highway mpg
6-speed manual	20/26

Specifications begin on page 551.

HONDA • HYUNDAI

2002 prices unavailable at time of publication.

PRICES

2001 Honda S2000

	Retail Price	Dealer Invoice
Base 2-door convertible	$32300	$28733
Destination charge	440	440

STANDARD EQUIPMENT

Base: 2.0-liter dohc 4-cylinder engine, 6-speed manual transmission, limited-slip differential, dual front airbags, antilock 4-wheel disc brakes, roll bars, emergency inside trunk release, air conditioning, interior air filter, power steering, leather-wrapped steering wheel, cruise control, leather upholstery, bucket seats, center console, cupholders, power mirrors, power windows, power door locks, remote keyless entry, AM/FM/CD player, digital clock, tachometer, intermittent wipers, wind deflector, power convertible top, remote decklid release, floormats, theft-deterrent system, high-intensity headlights, 205/55WR16 front tires, 225/50WR16 rear tires, alloy wheels.

Options are available as dealer-installed accessories.

HYUNDAI ACCENT

Hyundai Accent 4-door sedan

Front-wheel-drive subcompact car
Base price range: $8,999-$11,249. Built in South Korea.
Also consider: Ford Focus, Honda Civic, Toyota Echo

FOR • Fuel economy • Visibility **AGAINST** • Noise • Acceleration • Ride • Rear-seat entry/exit (2-door)

Air conditioning is standard for 2002 on higher-trim versions of Hyundai's smallest car. Accent comes in three models. The base L is a 2-dr hatchback with a 1.5-liter 4-cyl engine and comes only with

Prices are accurate at time of publication; subject to manufacturer's change.
CONSUMER GUIDE®

HYUNDAI

manual transmission. GS hatchbacks and GL 4-dr sedans have a 1.6-liter engine and either manual or automatic transmission. Air conditioning is now standard on GS and GL, optional on L. Accent is among the few cars that isn't available with ABS. This South Korean automaker offers one of the industry's longest warranties: 5-years/60,000-mi. bumper-to-bumper, 10-years/100,000 powertrain.

RATINGS

	L, man.
ACCELERATION	2
FUEL ECONOMY	8
RIDE QUALITY	3
STEERING/HANDLING	3
QUIETNESS	3
INSTRUMENTS/CONTROLS	5
ROOM/COMFORT (FRONT)	4
ROOM/COMFORT (REAR)	2
CARGO ROOM	5
VALUE	2

Accent makes some sense as a budget-priced commuter car that's reasonably well made and comes with a generous warranty. However, most rivals offer better performance and refinement than Accent for little more money. And Hyundai lags most every non-Korean brand in resale value.

TOTAL	37

Average total for subcompact cars: 43.7

ENGINES

	ohc I4	dohc I4
Size, liters/cu. in.	1.5/91	1.6/98
Horsepower @ rpm	92 @ 5500	105 @ 5800
Torque (lb-ft) @ rpm	97 @ 3000	106 @ 3000
Availability	S[1]	S[2]
EPA city/highway mpg		
5-speed manual	28/36	27/37
4-speed automatic	25/35	25/35

1. L. 2. GS, GL.

PRICES

Hyundai Accent	Retail Price	Dealer Invoice
L 2-door hatchback, manual	$8999	$8610
GS 2-door hatchback, manual	10249	9593
GS 2-door hatchback, automatic	10849	10155
GL 4-door sedan, manual	10649	9967
GL 4-door sedan, automatic	11249	10529
Destination charge	495	495

Specifications begin on page 551.

HYUNDAI

STANDARD EQUIPMENT

L: 1.5-liter 4-cylinder engine, 5-speed manual transmission, dual front airbags, power steering, cloth upholstery, front bucket seats, center console, cupholders, folding rear seat, AM/FM/cassette, rear defogger, remote fuel-door release, variable intermittent wipers, 175/70R13 tires, wheel covers.

GS and GL add: 1.6-liter dohc 4-cylinder engine, 5-speed manual or 4-speed automatic transmission, air conditioning, height-adjustable driver seat w/lumbar support, split folding rear seat, tachometer, digital clock, passenger-side visor mirror, cargo cover (GS), remote decklid release (GL), rear wiper/washer (GS).

OPTIONAL EQUIPMENT

	Retail Price	Dealer Invoice
Major Packages		
AB Option Pkg. 2, L	$750	$686
Air conditioning		
AC Option Pkg. 3, GS, GL	400	367
Power mirrors, power windows and door locks, AM/FM/CD player.		
Powertrain		
California and Northeast emissions	75	70
Required on cars purchased in Calif., N.H., N.Y., Mass.		
Appearance and Miscellaneous		
Rear spoiler	395	264

Postproduction options also available.

HYUNDAI ELANTRA

Hyundai Elantra GT 4-door hatchback

Front-wheel-drive subcompact car

Prices are accurate at time of publication; subject to manufacturer's change.

HYUNDAI

Base price range: $12,499-$14,799. Built in South Korea.
Also consider: Ford Focus, Honda Civic, Mazda Protege, Nissan Sentra

FOR • Fuel economy • Maneuverability **AGAINST** • Acceleration (auto. trans.)

The larger of Hyundai's two subcompact cars for 2002 comes as the GLS 4-dr sedan and GT 4-dr hatchback. Both have a 2.0-liter 4-cyl engine and manual or optional automatic transmission. Front side airbags are standard. ABS with traction control is optional; 4-wheel disc brakes are standard on the GT and included with ABS on the GLS. Standard equipment includes air conditioning and power windows/locks/mirrors. GTs add a sport suspension, alloy wheels, and leather upholstery. Hyundai's warranty is one of the industry's longest: 5-years/60,000-mi. basic, 10/100,000 powertrain.

RATINGS

	GLS, man.	GLS, auto.	GT, man.
ACCELERATION	5	4	5
FUEL ECONOMY	7	6	7
RIDE QUALITY	5	5	5
STEERING/HANDLING	5	5	5
QUIETNESS	4	4	4
INSTRUMENTS/CONTROLS	6	6	6
ROOM/COMFORT (FRONT)	4	4	4
ROOM/COMFORT (REAR)	4	4	4
CARGO ROOM	2	2	6
VALUE	4	4	4

In features, comfort, and even road manners, Elantra is a budget alternative to the class-leading but costlier Honda Civic and Ford Focus. However, cars from this South Korean automaker haven't earned a reputation for long-term reliability, and their resale values are low.

TOTAL	46	44	50

Average total for subcompact cars: 43.7

ENGINES

	dohc I4
Size, liters/cu. in.	2.0/121
Horsepower @ rpm	140 @ 6000
Torque (lb-ft) @ rpm	133 @ 4800
Availability	S

EPA city/highway mpg
5-speed manual	25/33
4-speed automatic	24/33

Specifications begin on page 551.

HYUNDAI

PRICES

Hyundai Elantra

	Retail Price	Dealer Invoice
GLS 4-door sedan, 5-speed	$12499	$11504
GLS 4-door sedan, automatic	13299	12236
GT 4-door hatchback, 5-speed	13999	12885
GT 4-door hatchback, automatic	14799	13617
Destination charge	495	495

STANDARD EQUIPMENT

GLS: 2.0-liter dohc 4-cylinder engine, 5-speed manual or 4-speed automatic transmission, dual front airbags, front side airbags, air conditioning, power steering, tilt steering wheel, cloth upholstery, front bucket seats w/driver seat lumbar adjustment, center console, cupholders, split folding rear seat, heated power mirrors, power windows, power door locks, AM/FM/cassette, digital clock, tachometer, visor mirrors, variable intermittent wipers, rear defogger, remote fuel-door and decklid release, map lights, 195/60HR15 tires, wheel covers.

GT adds: 4-wheel disc brakes, leather-wrapped steering wheel, cruise control, leather upholstery, remote keyless entry, AM/FM/CD player, rear wiper/washer, cargo cover, theft-deterrent system, fog lights, sport suspension, alloy wheels.

OPTIONAL EQUIPMENT

Major Packages

Option Pkg. 2, GLS	400	344

Cruise control, remote keyless entry, theft-deterrent system w/alarm.

Option Pkg. 3	750	633

Option Pkg. 2 plus AM/FM/CD player.

Option Pkg. 4, GLS	1400	1174

Option Pkg. 3 plus power sunroof.

Option Pkg. 5, GLS	1275	1125

Option Pkg. 3 plus traction control, antilock 4-wheel disc brakes.

Option Pkg. 10, GT	650	541

Power sunroof.

Option Pkg. 11, GT	1175	1033

Traction control, antilock brakes, power sunroof.

Powertrain

California and Northeast emissions	100	94

Required on cars purchased in Calif., N.H., N.Y., Mass.

Postproduction options also available.

Prices are accurate at time of publication; subject to manufacturer's change.

HYUNDAI

HYUNDAI SANTA FE

Hyundai Santa Fe

Front- or all-wheel-drive compact sport-utility vehicle

Base price range: $17,199-$23,299. Built in South Korea.
Also consider: Ford Escape, Honda CR-V, Mazda Tribute, Subaru Forester

FOR • Instruments/controls • Entry/exit • Cargo room • Ride/handling **AGAINST** • Acceleration • Interior materials

Hyundai's SUV is based on the Sonata car platform. The base 4-cyl Santa Fe GL has front-wheel drive. V6-powered GLS and top-line LX models offer front-wheel drive or all-wheel drive without low-range gearing. The 4 cyl comes with manual or automatic transmission, the V6 with automatic only; the automatic includes a manual shift feature. Traction control is optional on the GLS and standard on LX. ABS is standard on LX and optional on other models. The right-side dashboard airbag automatically shuts off if a sensor detects a child or no occupant, but side airbags aren't available. In the only change of note for 2002, the 4-cyl GL exchanges front-disc/rear-drum brakes for the 4-wheel discs of the V6 models.

RATINGS

	GLS 4WD
ACCELERATION	3
FUEL ECONOMY	6
RIDE QUALITY	4
STEERING/HANDLING	4
QUIETNESS	4
INSTRUMENTS/CONTROLS	5
ROOM/COMFORT (FRONT)	6
ROOM/COMFORT (REAR)	5

Specifications begin on page 551.

HYUNDAI

	GLS 4WD
CARGO ROOM	7
VALUE	4

It needs more V6 muscle and better interior detailing, but Santa Fe is a high features-per-dollar SUV with a generous 5-year/60,000-mi. basic warranty and 10/100,000 powertrain coverage.

TOTAL	48

Average total for compact sport-utility vehicles: 44.4

ENGINES

	dohc I4	dohc V6
Size, liters/cu. in.	2.4/143	2.7/165
Horsepower @ rpm	150 @ 5500	185 @ 6000
Torque (lb-ft) @ rpm	156 @ 3000	187 @ 4000
Availability	S[1]	S[2]
EPA city/highway mpg		
5-speed manual	21/28	
4-speed automatic	20/27	19/23[3]

1. GL. 2. GLS, LX. 3. 19/26 w/2WD.

PRICES

Hyundai Santa Fe	Retail Price	Dealer Invoice
2WD Base 4-door wagon, manual	$17199	$16098
2WD Base 4-door wagon, automatic	17999	16847
2WD GLS 4-door wagon, automatic	19599	18304
AWD GLS 4-door wagon, automatic	21099	19705
2WD LX 4-door wagon, automatic	21799	20336
AWD LX 4-door wagon, automatic	23299	21735
Destination charge	495	495

STANDARD EQUIPMENT

Base: 2.4-liter dohc 4-cylinder engine, 5-speed manual or 4-speed automatic transmission w/manual-shift capability, dual front airbags, 4-wheel disc brakes, air conditioning, power steering, tilt steering wheel, cruise control, cloth upholstery, front bucket seats, center console, cupholders, split folding rear seat, heated power mirrors, power windows, power door locks, AM/FM/CD player, digital clock, tachometer, variable intermittent wipers, illuminated passenger-side visor mirror, map lights, rear defogger, remote fuel door release, roof rails, rear privacy glass, full-size spare wheel, 225/70R16 tires, alloy wheels.

GLS adds: 2.7-liter dohc V6 engine, 4-speed automatic transmission w/manual-shift capability, leather-wrapped steering wheel, remote keyless entry, AM/FM/cassette/CD player, rear wiper/washer, cargo

Prices are accurate at time of publication; subject to manufacturer's change.

HYUNDAI

cover, theft-deterrent system, fog lights. **AWD** adds: all-wheel drive.

LX adds: limited-slip differential, traction control, antilock brakes, automatic climate control, leather upholstery, heated front seats, automatic day/night rearview mirror. **AWD** adds: all-wheel drive.

OPTIONAL EQUIPMENT
Major Packages

	Retail Price	Dealer Invoice
Option Pkg. 2, Base	$495	$463
Remote keyless entry, rear wiper/washer, cargo cover and net, theft-deterrent system, first aid kit.		
Option Pkg. 3, Base	990	926
Option Pkg. 2 plus antilock brakes.		
Option Pkg. 4, GLS	595	557
Traction control, antilock brakes.		

Comfort & Convenience Features
Cargo organizer	95	60

Appearance and Miscellaneous
Roof rack	180	105
Tow hitch	295	215

Postproduction options also available.

HYUNDAI SONATA

Hyundai Sonata

Front-wheel-drive compact car
Base price range: $15,499-$18,824. Built in South Korea.
Also consider: Chrysler PT Cruiser, Mazda 626, Volkswagen Passat

FOR • Ride • Instruments/controls **AGAINST** • Automatic transmission performance • Rear-seat comfort

Specifications begin on page 551.

HYUNDAI

Hyundai's compact sedan gets revised styling and a larger V6 engine for 2002. Sonata shares its mechanical components with the Kia Optima. Hyundai owns Kia. Sonata offers base, GLS, and LX models. Base models come with a 4-cyl engine. GLS and LX come with a 181-hp 2.7-liter V6, which for '02 replaces a 170-hp 2.5. Manual transmission is standard with both engines; an automatic with manual shift gate is optional. Front side airbags are again standard. GLS and LX have standard 4-wheel disc brakes; ABS is optional on all models. Optional traction control is exclusive to GLS and LX. This South Korean automaker's basic warranty is among the industry's longest: 5-years/60,000-mi. bumper-to-bumper, 10/100,000 powertrain.

RATINGS

	Base, man.	GLS, auto.
ACCELERATION	4	5
FUEL ECONOMY	6	5
RIDE QUALITY	7	7
STEERING/HANDLING	4	5
QUIETNESS	5	6
INSTRUMENTS/CONTROLS	6	7
ROOM/COMFORT (FRONT)	7	7
ROOM/COMFORT (REAR)	4	4
CARGO ROOM	5	5
VALUE	4	4

In terms of equipment and comfort, Sonata and Optima offer impressive value for the money. But both suffer from low resale values associated with South Korean cars, a burden the generous warranties don't offset.

TOTAL	52	55

Average total for compact cars: 51.6

ENGINES

	dohc I4	dohc V6
Size, liters/cu. in.	2.4/146	2.7/162
Horsepower @ rpm	149 @ 5500	181 @ 6000
Torque (lb-ft) @ rpm	156 @ 3000	177 @ 4000
Availability	S[1]	S[2]
EPA city/highway mpg		
5-speed manual	22/30	20/27
4-speed automatic	22/30	20/27

1. Base. 2. GLS, LX.

PRICES

Hyundai Sonata	Retail Price	Dealer Invoice
Base 4-door sedan, manual	$15499	$14104
Base 4-door sedan, automatic	15999	14603

Prices are accurate at time of publication; subject to manufacturer's change.

HYUNDAI

	Retail Price	Dealer Invoice
GLS 4-door sedan, manual	$16999	$15381
GLS 4-door sedan, automatic	17499	15880
LX 4-door sedan, manual	18324	16484
LX 4-door sedan, automatic	18824	16983
Destination charge	495	495

STANDARD EQUIPMENT

Base: 2.4-liter dohc 4-cylinder engine, 5-speed manual or 4-speed automatic transmission w/manual-shift capability, dual front airbags, front side airbags, air conditioning, variable-assist power steering, tilt steering wheel, cruise control, cloth upholstery, front bucket seats w/driver seat lumbar adjustment, center console, cupholders, split folding rear seat, power mirrors, power windows, power door locks, remote keyless entry, AM/FM/CD player, digital clock, tachometer, driver-side visor mirror, illuminated passenger-side visor mirror, remote fuel-door and decklid releases, rear defogger, variable intermittent wipers, fog lights, 205/60R15 tires, wheel covers.

GLS adds: 2.7-liter dohc V6 engine, 4-wheel disc brakes, leather-wrapped steering wheel (automatic), heated power mirrors, AM/FM/cassette/CD player, power antenna, map lights, alloy wheels.

LX adds: automatic climate control, leather upholstery, power driver seat, leather-wrapped steering wheel.

OPTIONAL EQUIPMENT
Major Packages

Option Pkg. 2, Base manual	550	526
Antilock brakes.		
Option Pkg. 3, Base automatic	550	458
Power sunroof.		
Option Pkg. 4, Base automatic	1100	984
Antilock brakes, power sunroof.		
Option Pkg. 5, GLS, LX	550	458
Power sunroof.		
Option Pkg. 6, GLS, LX	1250	1113
Traction control, antilock brakes, power sunroof.		

Postproduction options also available.

HYUNDAI XG350

Front-wheel-drive midsize car
Base price range: $23,999-$25,599. Built in South Korea.

Specifications begin on page 551.

HYUNDAI

Hyundai XG350

Also consider: Honda Accord, Nissan Altima, Toyota Camry

FOR • Ride • Front-seat room/comfort **AGAINST** • Road noise

Hyundai's flagship sedan gains a larger engine for 2002, a change reflected in its new model name. The XG350 has a 3.5-liter V6 vs. the 3.0 used in the XG300. The new engine gains only 2 hp, but has 38 more lb-ft of torque. A 5-speed automatic with manual shift gate is the only transmission. Standard equipment includes front side airbags, antilock 4-wheel disc brakes, traction control, and leather upholstery. The XG350L model includes a sunroof and seat/mirror memory. Hyundai is South Korea's biggest automaker and the XG350 is basically its compact Sonata stretched to midsize dimensions and given different styling. Hyundai's basic warranty is among the industry's longest: 5-years/60,000-mi. bumper-to-bumper, 10/100,000 powertrain.

RATINGS

	Base/L
ACCELERATION	5
FUEL ECONOMY	6
RIDE QUALITY	7
STEERING/HANDLING	6
QUIETNESS	6
INSTRUMENTS/CONTROLS	6
ROOM/COMFORT (FRONT)	6
ROOM/COMFORT (REAR)	5
CARGO ROOM	4

Prices are accurate at time of publication; subject to manufacturer's change.

HYUNDAI

	Base/L
VALUE	4

The XG350 isn't as solidly built as the leading midsize cars, specifically the Toyota Camry and Honda Accord. And it isn't as sporty as the Nissan Altima. It does deliver perfectly adequate performance; quiet, comfort-oriented road manners; and good interior room. It's real lure, of course, is a long warranty and lots of features for the money. But we're not convinced those assets fully offset Hyundai's unproven track record and the low resale values associated with <u>Korean cars.</u>

TOTAL	55

Average total for midsize cars: 57.0

ENGINES

	dohc V6
Size, liters/cu. in.	3.5/221
Horsepower @ rpm	194 @ 5500
Torque (lb-ft) @ rpm	216 @ 3500
Availability	S

EPA city/highway mpg

5-speed automatic	18/26

PRICES

Hyundai XG350	Retail Price	Dealer Invoice
Base 4-door sedan	$23999	$21465
L 4-door sedan	25599	22896
Destination charge	495	495

STANDARD EQUIPMENT

Base: 3.5-liter dohc V6 engine, 5-speed automatic transmission w/manual-shift capability, traction control, dual front airbags, front side airbags, antilock 4-wheel disc brakes, air conditioning w/automatic climate control, power steering, tilt leather-wrapped steering wheel, cruise control, leather upholstery, front bucket seats, 8-way power driver seat, 4-way power passenger seat, center console, cupholders, split folding rear seat, heated power mirrors, power windows, power door locks, remote keyless entry, AM/FM/cassette/CD player, digital clock, tachometer, trip computer, rear defogger, illuminated visor mirrors, map lights, variable intermittent wipers, remote fuel door/decklid release, automatic headlights, theft-deterrent system, fog lights, 205/60HR16 tires, alloy wheels.

L adds: power sunroof, heated front seats, driver seat and mirror memory, woodgrain/leather-wrapped steering wheel, automatic day/night rearview mirror.

Specifications begin on page 551.

HYUNDAI • INFINITI

OPTIONAL EQUIPMENT	Retail Price	Dealer Invoice
Option Pkg. 2/3	$500	$447

8-disc CD changer.

Postproduction options also available.

INFINITI G20

Infiniti G20

Front-wheel-drive near-luxury car
Base price range: $21,395-$22,195. Built in Japan.
Also consider: Acura TL, Audi A4, Lexus IS 300

FOR • Steering/handling • Instruments/controls • Visibility • Exterior finish **AGAINST** • Automatic transmission performance • Engine noise

Infiniti's entry-level sedan drops its sporty "Touring" model in favor of a new Sport option package for 2002. G20's only engine is a 4 cyl that comes with manual or optional automatic transmission. Standard are antilock 4-wheel disc brakes and front side airbags. Available are several option groups, including the new Sport package, which adds leather upholstery, power sunroof, and 16-inch alloy wheels instead of 15s.

RATINGS	Luxury w/Sport Pkg., auto.
ACCELERATION	3
FUEL ECONOMY	6
RIDE QUALITY	4
STEERING/HANDLING	6
QUIETNESS	4
INSTRUMENTS/CONTROLS	6
ROOM/COMFORT (FRONT)	5
ROOM/COMFORT (REAR)	3

Prices are accurate at time of publication; subject to manufacturer's change.

INFINITI

	Luxury w/Sport Pkg., auto.
CARGO ROOM	3
VALUE	3

G20 is really more of a dressy compact than a true near-luxury car. A similarly equipped Honda Accord or Toyota Camry offers better value despite Infiniti's superior warranty and customer service, but G20s should carry heavier-than-usual discounts.

TOTAL	43

Average total for near-luxury cars: 54.5

ENGINES

	dohc I4
Size, liters/cu. in.	2.0/122
Horsepower @ rpm	145 @ 6000
Torque (lb-ft) @ rpm	136 @ 4800
Availability	S
EPA city/highway mpg	
5-speed manual	24/31
4-speed automatic	23/30

PRICES

Infiniti G20	Retail Price	Dealer Invoice
Base 4-door sedan, manual	$21395	$19522
Base 4-door sedan, automatic	22195	20252
Destination charge	545	545

STANDARD EQUIPMENT

Base: 2.0-liter dohc 4-cylinder engine, 5-speed manual or 4-speed automatic transmission, dual front airbags, front side airbags, antilock 4-wheel disc brakes, emergency inside trunk release, air conditioning, power steering, tilt steering wheel, cruise control, cloth upholstery, front bucket seats, center console, cupholders, split folding rear seat, Bose AM/FM/cassette/CD player, digital clock, tachometer, power mirrors, power windows, power door locks, remote keyless entry, rear defogger, remote fuel door/decklid release, illuminated visor mirrors, variable intermittent wipers, automatic-off headlights, floormats, theft-deterrent system, 195/65R15 tires, alloy wheels.

OPTIONAL EQUIPMENT
Major Packages

Leather and Sunroof Pkg.	1600	1248

Leather upholstery, leather-wrapped steering wheel, 8-way power driver seat, power sunroof, automatic climate control, interior air filter, universal garage door opener, stainless steel door sills.

INFINITI

	Retail Price	Dealer Invoice
Sport Pkg.	$2700	$2217

Limited-slip differential, two-tone leather upholstery, leather-wrapped steering wheel, 8-way power driver seat, power sunroof, automatic climate control, interior air filter, universal garage door opener, stainless steel door sills, fog lights, rear spoiler, 205/50HR16 tires, unique alloy wheels.

Heated Seat Pkg.	420	362

Heated front seats, outside mirrors.

Comfort & Convenience Features

6-disc CD changer	99	93

INFINITI I35

Infiniti I35

Front-wheel-drive near-luxury car
Base price: $28,750. Built in Japan.
Also consider: Acura TL, BMW 3-Series, Lexus ES 300

FOR • Acceleration • Steering/handling   **AGAINST** • Navigation system controls

Revamped styling, more power, and new features highlight 2002 changes to Infiniti's near-luxury sedan. I35 is named for a new 3.5-liter V6, which has 28 hp more than the predecessor I30's 3.0 V6. A sunroof and rear sunshades are optional instead of standard for '02, but the I35 comes with several features that had cost extra, among them traction control, brake assist, 17-inch wheels, and Xenon headlamps. An antiskid system is newly available. Suspension revisions are intended to improve ride and handling. A 4-speed automatic remains the sole transmission. New front styling aims for visu-

INFINITI

al kinship with Infiniti's Q45 flagship. Rear styling and interior details also are retouched. I35 comes as a single Luxury model. Replacing the I30's Touring model is a similar Sport Package with high-performance tires, firmer suspension, and lower-body aero extensions, plus the antiskid system. Infiniti is the upscale division of Nissan, and the I35 is based on the Nissan Maxima, which is also revised for 2002 and includes the 255-hp V6.

RATINGS

	Luxury w/ Sport Pkg.
ACCELERATION	6
FUEL ECONOMY	5
RIDE QUALITY	5
STEERING/HANDLING	6
QUIETNESS	6
INSTRUMENTS/CONTROLS	8
ROOM/COMFORT (FRONT)	7
ROOM/COMFORT (REAR)	6
CARGO ROOM	4
VALUE	5

I35 is a capable near-luxury sedan and well equipped even without options. It's well worth considering as a bridge between the sportier-handling Acura TL, and the plusher but more-conservative Lexus ES 300.

TOTAL	**58**

Average total for near-luxury cars: 54.5

ENGINES

	dohc V6
Size, liters/cu. in.	3.5/214
Horsepower @ rpm	255 @ 6000
Torque (lb-ft) @ rpm	246 @ 3200
Availability	S

EPA city/highway mpg
4-speed automatic 20/26

PRICES

Infiniti I35	Retail Price	Dealer Invoice
Luxury 4-door sedan	$28750	$26044
Destination charge	545	545

STANDARD EQUIPMENT

Luxury sedan: 3.5-liter dohc V6 engine, 4-speed automatic transmission, traction control, dual front airbags, front side airbags, front seat active head restraints, antilock 4-wheel disc brakes, brake assist, emergency inside trunk release, air conditioning w/automatic

INFINITI

climate control, interior air filter, power steering, tilt woodtone/leather-wrapped steering wheel w/radio controls, cruise control, leather upholstery, front bucket seats, 8-way power driver seat w/memory and lumbar adjustment, 4-way power passenger seat, center console, cupholders, split folding rear seat, power mirrors, power windows, power door locks, remote keyless entry, Bose AM/FM/cassette w/in-dash 6-disc CD changer, analog clock, tachometer, trip computer, automatic day/night rearview mirror, outside temperature indicator, compass, illuminated visor mirrors, universal garage door opener, variable intermittent wipers, rear defogger, map lights, theft-deterrent system, Xenon headlights, fog lights, cornering lights, 215/55HR17 tires, alloy wheels.

OPTIONAL EQUIPMENT
Major Packages

	Retail Price	Dealer Invoice
Sport Pkg.	$1700	$1465

Antiskid system, leather-wrapped steering wheel, side sills, sport suspension, 225/50VR17 tires, unique alloy wheels. Requires Sunroof and Sun Shade Pkg.

Sunroof and Sun Shade Pkg.	1380	1217

Power sunroof, power rear sun shade.

Navigation Pkg.	2000	1805

Navigation system. Replaces in-dash CD changer w/trunk-mounted 6-disc CD changer. Requires Sunroof and Sun Shade Pkg.

Cold Weather Pkg.	700	604

Heated front and rear seats, heated steering wheel and mirrors. Requires Sunroof and Sun Shade Pkg.

Appearance and Miscellaneous

Rear spoiler	500	431

Requires Sport Pkg.

Chrome alloy wheels	1600	840

Requires Sport Pkg.

INFINITI Q45

Rear-wheel-drive luxury car
Base price: $50,500. Built in Japan.
Also consider: BMW 540i, Lexus GS 430, Mercedes-Benz E430

FOR • Acceleration • Quietness • Build quality • Exterior finish • Interior materials **AGAINST** • Fuel economy • Navigation system controls

The flagship sedan of Nissan's luxury brand is redesigned for 2002. It's wider and taller than the 1997-2001 version, on a longer

Prices are accurate at time of publication; subject to manufacturer's change.

INFINITI

Infiniti Q45

wheelbase for more interior room. New styling includes 7-lens headlamps claimed to be the world's brightest. Infiniti aims to revive Q45's performance roots with a new 4.5-liter V8 with 74 hp more than the prior 4.1. A 5-speed automatic transmission with manual shift feature supplants a 4-speed without. Also standard: antilock 4-wheel discs with brake assist, traction control/antiskid system, 17-inch wheels, front side airbags, curtain side airbags, and leather/wood interior trim. An in-dash information screen serves an available navigation system, and there's standard voice control for audio, climate, and navigation functions.

To the base Luxury model the Sport Package option adds 18-inch wheels and auto-adjusting shock absorbers with firmer sport setting. The Premium Package includes power-reclining rear seat, rear audio/climate controls, and a TV camera that displays a rear view on the dashboard screen when Reverse is selected. Due later in the year: optional radar cruise control designed to maintain a safe following distance automatically.

RATINGS	Luxury	Luxury w/Premium, Sport pkgs, nav. sys.
ACCELERATION	7	7
FUEL ECONOMY	4	4
RIDE QUALITY	8	7
STEERING/HANDLING	7	7
QUIETNESS	7	7
INSTRUMENTS/CONTROLS	7	4
ROOM/COMFORT (FRONT)	7	7
ROOM/COMFORT (REAR)	6	7
CARGO ROOM	3	3
VALUE	2	2

Premium sedans must deliver effortless performance in an atmosphere of spacious refinement. Materials and workmanship of the highest quality and at-your-service ergonomics are also essential when a car costs over $50,000. Q45 doesn't squarely hit any of these marks.

Specifications begin on page 551.

INFINITI

	Luxury	Luxury w/Premium, Sport pkgs, nav. sys.
TOTAL	58	55

Average total for luxury cars: 59.4

ENGINES

	dohc V8
Size, liters/cu. in.	4.5/274
Horsepower @ rpm	340 @ 6400
Torque (lb-ft) @ rpm	333 @ 4000
Availability	S

EPA city/highway mpg
5-speed automatic 17/25

PRICES

Infiniti Q45	Retail Price	Dealer Invoice
Luxury 4-door sedan	$50500	$45672
Destination charge	545	545

STANDARD EQUIPMENT

Luxury: 4.5-liter dohc V8 engine, 5-speed automatic transmission w/manual-shift capability, traction control, limited-slip differential, dual front airbags, front side airbags, curtain airbags, front seat active head restraints, antilock 4-wheel brakes, antiskid system, air conditioning w/dual-zone automatic climate control, interior air filter, power steering, power tilt/telescoping wood/leather-wrapped steering wheel w/memory, cruise control, leather upholstery, front bucket seats, 10-way power driver seat w/power lumbar adjustment and memory, 8-way power passenger seat, center console, cupholders, wood interior trim, power mirrors w/signal lights, power windows, power door locks, remote keyless entry, Bose AM/FM/cassette/CD player, 6-disc CD changer, steering wheel radio controls, analog clock, tachometer, outside temperature indicator, voice recognition system for radio and climate controls, power sunroof, rear defogger, automatic day/night rearview mirror, universal garage door opener, illuminated visor mirrors, map lights, variable intermittent wipers, remote fuel door/decklid release, automatic headlights, theft-deterrent system, Xenon headlights, tire pressure monitor, 225/55R17 tires, alloy wheels.

OPTIONAL EQUIPMENT
Major Packages

	Retail Price	Dealer Invoice
Premium Pkg.	$8000	$6893

Power reclining rear seat w/exit assist, rear radio controls, rear air conditioning controls w/additional rear vents, heated front and rear seats, navigation system, rear view monitor, power rear entry assistance,

INFINITI

heated mirrors w/automatic day/night and memory, passenger-side mirror tilt-down back-up aid, power rear sunshade, manual rear side sunshades, computer controlled and driver adjustable sport suspension, 245/45R18 tires, special alloy wheels.

Sport Pkg. 1500 1293
Graphite-tone wood interior trim, blue tone headlight trim, blue back-up light bulbs, computer controlled and driver adjustable sport suspension, 245/45R18 tires, special alloy wheels.

Sunshade Pkg. 500 431
Power rear sunshade, manual rear side sunshades.

Comfort & Convenience Features

Navigation system 2100 1896
Heated front seats 450 388

INFINITI QX4

Infiniti QX4

Rear- or 4-wheel-drive midsize sport-utility vehicle
2001 base price range: $34,150-$35,550. Built in Japan.
Also consider: Acura MDX, Ford Explorer, Lexus RX 300

FOR • Cargo room • Build quality • Acceleration **AGAINST** • Rear-seat comfort • Entry/exit

Cruise control designed to maintain a set distance from other traffic is the main QX4 addition for 2002. QX4 is essentially a dressed-up Nissan Pathfinder; Infiniti is Nissan's luxury division. QX4 shares Pathfinder's 240-hp V6 and automatic transmission. It offers rear-wheel drive or Nissan's All-Mode 4WD that can be left engaged on dry pavement and includes low-range gearing. Front side airbags are standard, as is ABS, though brakes are front disc/rear drum. QX4 shares Nissan's Intelligent Cruise Control with Infiniti's flagship Q45 sedan. Employing laser sensors, the system is designed to automatically speed or slow the QX4 to keep a constant distance from cars ahead. Also new for '02 is a revised audio system, plus

Specifications begin on page 551.

INFINITI

audio controls for the available leather and wood steering wheel. The optional rear-seat video entertainment system offers a choice of VCR or DVD player. QX4's performance and accommodations are similar to those of the Pathfinder.

RATINGS	Base 2WD	Base 4WD w/nav.sys.
ACCELERATION	6	6
FUEL ECONOMY	4	4
RIDE QUALITY	5	5
STEERING/HANDLING	4	4
QUIETNESS	5	5
INSTRUMENTS/CONTROLS	7	7
ROOM/COMFORT (FRONT)	5	5
ROOM/COMFORT (REAR)	3	3
CARGO ROOM	8	8
VALUE	3	3

It's too old a design and too cramped inside to qualify as a compelling value, but the QX4 packs lots of features into an upscale package, and owners benefit from Infiniti's red-carpet customer service.

TOTAL	50	50

Average total for midsize sport-utility vehicles: 49.6

ENGINES

	dohc V6
Size, liters/cu. in.	3.5/214
Horsepower @ rpm	240 @ 6000
Torque (lb-ft) @ rpm	265 @ 3200
Availability	S
EPA city/highway mpg	
4-speed automatic	15/18[1]

1. 15/19 w/2WD.

2002 prices unavailable at time of publication.

PRICES

2001 Infiniti QX4	Retail Price	Dealer Invoice
Base 2WD 4-door wagon	$34150	$30987
Base 4WD 4-door wagon	35550	32253
Destination charge	545	545

STANDARD EQUIPMENT

Base: 3.5-liter dohc V6 engine, 4-speed automatic transmission, dual front airbags, front side airbags, antilock brakes, air conditioning w/automatic climate control, interior air filter, variable-assist power steering, tilt leather-wrapped steering wheel, cruise control,

Prices are accurate at time of publication; subject to manufacturer's change.

INFINITI • ISUZU

leather upholstery, power front bucket seats, center console, cupholders, reclining split-folding rear seat, wood interior trim, heated power mirrors, power windows, power door locks, remote keyless entry, tachometer, Bose AM/FM/cassette/CD player, power antenna, analog clock, overhead console, outside temperature indicator, map lights, variable intermittent wipers, automatic-off headlights, universal garage door opener, illuminated visor mirrors, remote fuel door and hatch release, cargo cover, rear defogger, variable intermittent rear wiper/washer, floormats, theft-deterrent system, Xenon headlights, fog lights, step rails, roof rack, rear privacy glass, skid plates, full-size spare tire, 245/70SR16 tires, alloy wheels. **4WD** model adds: 4-wheel drive, 2-speed transfer case.

OPTIONAL EQUIPMENT
Major Packages

	Retail Price	Dealer Invoice
Premium Pkg.	$600	$450
Memory driver seat, leather/wood-grain steering wheel, 245/65SR17 tires.		
Sport Pkg., 4WD	900	813
Heated front and rear seats, limited-slip rear differential. Requires Premium Pkg.		
Towing Pkg.	400	307

Comfort & Convenience Features

Navigation system	2000	1805
Requires Premium Pkg., sunroof.		
Mobile Entertainment System Pkg.	1299	1120
Videocassette player, roof-mounted screen. Requires Premium Pkg.		
Power sunroof	950	858
Requires Premium Pkg.		
Heated front and rear seats, 2WD	600	541
Requires Premium Pkg.		

ISUZU RODEO

Rear- or 4-wheel-drive midsize sport-utility vehicle
Base price range: $18,380-$31,730. Built in USA.
Also consider: Dodge Durango, Ford Explorer, Nissan Xterra, Toyota Highlander

FOR • Cargo room **AGAINST** • Wind noise • Fuel economy • Ride • Rear-seat entry/exit

Isuzu builds only trucks, and its best seller is unchanged for 2002 except for options availability. Rodeo features a 4-cyl S model and V6 LS and LSE versions. All offer rear-wheel drive or 4WD that must

ISUZU

Isuzu Rodeo

be disengaged on dry pavement but includes low-range gearing. A side-hinged tailgate mounting the spare tire sits below a flip-up glass hatch. For 2002, the former Ironman option is effectively replaced by the 4WD LS Chrome Package, which includes 18-inch wheels and tires as well as Isuzu's Intelligent Suspension Control, which automatically varies shock-absorber firmness and is standard for Rodeo LSE. Honda's near-twin Passport is also built by Isuzu in Indiana, but doesn't offer the adjustable shocks.

RATINGS	S 2WD, auto.	LS 4WD, auto.	LSE 4WD
ACCELERATION	2	5	5
FUEL ECONOMY	4	3	3
RIDE QUALITY	2	2	2
STEERING/HANDLING	4	4	4
QUIETNESS	4	4	4
INSTRUMENTS/CONTROLS	6	6	6
ROOM/COMFORT (FRONT)	6	6	6
ROOM/COMFORT (REAR)	4	4	4
CARGO ROOM	8	8	8
VALUE	2	3	3

V6 Rodeos and Passports emphasize the sport in sport-utility, but an aging basic design leaves them way behind the competition in most respects, especially in ride and 4WD convenience. Prices aren't that attractive either.

TOTAL	42	45	45

Average total for midsize sport-utility vehicles: 49.6

ENGINES	dohc I4	dohc V6
Size, liters/cu. in.	2.2/134	3.2/193
Horsepower @ rpm	130 @ 5200	205 @ 5400
Torque (lb-ft) @ rpm	144 @ 4000	214 @ 3000
Availability	S[1]	S[2]

Prices are accurate at time of publication; subject to manufacturer's change.
CONSUMER GUIDE®

ISUZU

EPA city/highway mpg	dohc I4	dohc V6
5-speed manual	19/23	17/20[3]
4-speed automatic	17/22	16/20[4]

1. 2WD S. 2. S V6, LS, LSE. 3. 17/20 w/2WD. 4. 17/21 w/2WD.

PRICES

Isuzu Rodeo	Retail Price	Dealer Invoice
S 4-cylinder 2WD 4-door wagon, manual	$18380	$17885
S 4-cylinder 2WD 4-door wagon, automatic	19380	18830
S V6 2WD 4-door wagon, manual	21265	20020
S V6 2WD 4-door wagon, automatic	22265	20950
S V6 4WD 4-door wagon, manual	23695	22280
S V6 4WD 4-door wagon, automatic	24695	23210
LS 2WD 4-door wagon, automatic	25085	23350
LS 4WD 4-door wagon, automatic	27745	25800
LSE 2WD 4-door wagon, automatic	29295	27100
LSE 4WD 4-door wagon, automatic	31730	29340
Destination charge	610	610

STANDARD EQUIPMENT

S: 2.2-liter dohc 4-cylinder engine, 5-speed manual or 4-speed automatic transmission, dual front airbags, antilock brakes, power steering, cloth upholstery, front bucket seats, center console, cupholders, split folding rear seat, AM/FM/cassette, digital clock, tachometer, automatic day/night rearview mirror, intermittent wipers, illuminated visor mirrors, rear defogger, map lights, intermittent rear wiper/washer, trailer wiring harness, skid plates, tow hooks, full-size spare tire, 225/75R16 tires.

S V6 adds: 3.2-liter dohc V6 engine, tilt steering wheel, cruise control, 245/70R16 tires. **4WD** adds: 4-wheel drive, 2-speed transfer case, 4-wheel disc brakes, outside-mounted spare tire.

LS adds: 4-speed automatic transmission, air conditioning, heated power mirrors, power windows, power door locks, remote keyless entry, variable intermittent wipers, cargo cover, floormats, theft-deterrent system, rear privacy glass, roof rails. **4WD** adds: 4-wheel drive, 2-speed transfer case, limited-slip differential, 4-wheel disc brakes, outside-mounted spare tire.

LSE adds: leather upholstery, 4-way power front seats, leather-wrapped steering wheel, power sunroof, AM/FM/cassette w/in-dash 6-disc CD changer, fog lights, adjustable shock absorbers, alloy wheels. **4WD** adds: 4-wheel drive, 2-speed transfer case, limited-slip differential, 4-wheel disc brakes, outside-mounted spare tire.

Specifications begin on page 551.

ISUZU

OPTIONAL EQUIPMENT	Retail Price	Dealer Invoice
Major Packages		
Preferred Equipment Pkg. 1, S automatic, S V6	$2605	$2079
Manufacturer's Discount Price	*2080*	*1663*
Air conditioning, tilt steering wheel, power windows and door locks, upgraded sound system, cargo cover, variable intermittent wipers, courtesy lights, floormats, rear privacy glass, roof rack, overfenders.		
SE Pkg., S automatic, S V6	1075	863
Manufacturer's Discount Price	*859*	*689*
Bodyside moldings, fog lights, tubular side steps, alloy wheels. Requires Preferred Equipment Pkg. 1.		
Comfort Pkg., LS	805	677
Manufacturer's Discount Price	*645*	*546*
4-way power driver seat, AM/FM/cassette w/in-dash 6-disc CD changer, wood grain interior trim, bodyside moldings.		
Special Edition Pkg., LS	NA	NA
4-way power driver seat, upgraded sound system, side steps, overfenders, hood protector, bodyside moldings, rear spoiler, spare tire cover (4WD), painted alloy wheels.		
Chrome Pkg., LS 4WD	2275	1886
Manufacturer's Discount Price	*1815*	*1539*
Adjustable shock absorbers, tubular side steps, taillight trim, 245/60R18 tires, chrome alloy wheels.		
Comfort & Convenience Features		
Air conditioning, S manual	1000	890
Power sunroof, LS	700	623
AM/FM/cassette w/in-dash 6-disc CD changer, LS	NA	NA
Appearance and Miscellaneous		
Running boards	330	243
Special Purpose, Wheels and Tires		
Trailer hitch	240	175
Alloy wheels, LS	450	398

ISUZU RODEO SPORT

Rear- or 4-wheel-drive compact sport-utility vehicle
Base price range: $16,100-$22,045. Built in USA.
Also consider: Ford Escape, Honda CR-V, Mazda Tribute

FOR • Cargo room   **AGAINST** • Acceleration (4-cyl) • Ride • Noise • Entry/exit

Prices are accurate at time of publication; subject to manufacturer's change.

ISUZU

Isuzu Rodeo Sport

Once called Amigo, this 2-dr SUV is basically a shortened version of Isuzu's 4-dr Rodeo wagon. The Sport comes as a fixed-roof hardtop with a pop-up front sunroof, and as a semiconvertible that also has a folding soft top over the back seat. Base 4-cyl S models are rear-wheel drive only. V6 versions offer 4WD that must be disengaged on dry pavement but includes low-range gearing. For 2002, the Ironman and SE packages are dropped along with their adjustable shock absorbers. A Preferred Equipment Package with revised features content continues for V6 models.

RATINGS	S wgn	S V6 conv 4WD w/Ironman Pkg., man.	S V6 wgn 4WD, auto.
ACCELERATION	2	5	5
FUEL ECONOMY	4	4	3
RIDE QUALITY	3	3	3
STEERING/HANDLING	3	3	3
QUIETNESS	2	2	2
INSTRUMENTS/CONTROLS	4	4	4
ROOM/COMFORT (FRONT)	5	5	5
ROOM/COMFORT (REAR)	3	3	3
CARGO ROOM	7	7	7
VALUE	3	3	3

Two-door SUVs have limited appeal, but Rodeo Sport is more substantial than a Kia Sportage or Suzuki Vitara and more refined than a Jeep Wrangler. It's also worth considering against the 2-dr Chevrolet Blazer and Ford Explorer Sport.

TOTAL	36	39	38

Average total for compact sport-utility vehicles: 44.4

ENGINES	dohc I4	dohc V6
Size, liters/cu. in.	2.2/134	3.2/193
Horsepower @ rpm	130 @ 5200	205 @ 5400
Torque (lb-ft) @ rpm	144 @ 4000	214 @ 3000

Specifications begin on page 551.

ISUZU

	dohc I4	dohc V6
Availability	S	O
EPA city/highway mpg		
5-speed manual	19/23	17/20
4-speed automatic	17/22	16/20

PRICES

Isuzu Rodeo Sport	Retail Price	Dealer Invoice
2WD S 4-cylinder 2-door convertible, manual	$16375	$16030
2WD S 4-cylinder 2-door wagon, manual	16100	15740
2WD S 4-cylinder 2-door wagon, automatic	17100	16710
2WD S V6 2-door convertible, automatic	19570	18390
2WD S V6 2-door wagon, automatic	19295	18135
4WD S V6 2-door convertible, automatic	22045	20695
4WD S V6 2-door wagon, automatic	21770	20435
Destination charge	610	610

STANDARD EQUIPMENT

S 4-cylinder convertible: 2.2-liter dohc 4-cylinder engine, 5-speed manual or 4-speed automatic transmission, dual front airbags, antilock brakes, power steering, cloth upholstery, front bucket seats, center console, cupholders, folding rear seat, AM/FM/cassette, digital clock, tachometer, manual front sunroof, driver-side visor mirror, intermittent wipers, map lights, rear folding top, skid plates, 7-wire trailer harness, front and rear tow hooks, outside-mounted full-size spare tire, 245/70R16 tires.

S 4-cylinder wagon adds: manual rear sunroof, rear defogger, rear intermittent wiper. *Deletes:* rear folding top.

S V6 adds to S 4-cylinder convertible and S 4-cylinder wagon: 3.2-liter dohc V6 engine, tilt steering wheel, cruise control, variable intermittent wipers. **4WD** models add: 4-wheel drive, 2-speed transfer case, limited-slip differential, 4-wheel disc brakes.

OPTIONAL EQUIPMENT

Major Packages

Preferred Equipment Pkg., V6	2885	2240
Manufacturer's Discount Price	*2320*	*1795*

Air conditioning, heated power mirrors, power windows and door locks, remote keyless entry, AM/FM/cassette w/in-dash 6-disc CD changer, center armrest, courtesy lights, cargo tray, cargo net, floormats, dual note horns, theft-deterrent system.

Comfort & Convenience Features

Air conditioning, 4-cylinder, 2WD V6 wagon	1000	890

Prices are accurate at time of publication; subject to manufacturer's change.

INFINITI • ISUZU

Appearance and Miscellaneous	Retail Price	Dealer Invoice
Fog lights	$70	$56
Requires alloy wheels.		
Tubular side steps	320	240

Special Purpose, Wheels and Tires		
Alloy wheels	450	398

ISUZU TROOPER

Isuzu Trooper

Rear- or 4-wheel-drive full-size sport-utility vehicle

Base price range: $28,105-$36,660. Built in Japan.

Also consider: Chevrolet Tahoe/GMC Yukon, Ford Expedition, Toyota Land Cruiser

FOR • Passenger and cargo room **AGAINST** • Fuel economy • Ride

Isuzu's flagship SUV gets some new standard equipment for 2002. Trooper has 70/30 swing-out rear cargo doors, a 3.5-liter V6, and antilock 4-wheel disc brakes. The base S model offers manual or automatic transmission; LS and Limited models are automatic only. All offer rear-wheel drive or 4WD. Optional on the 4WD S and standard on the other 4x4s is Isuzu's Torque-On-Demand 4WD that can be left engaged on dry pavement. The S's standard 4WD must be disengaged on dry pavement. Both systems include low-range gearing. Maximum towing capacity is 5000 lb. For 2002, the S model adds standard privacy glass, the LS a sunroof that had been optional, the top-line Limited a premium Nakamichi audio system.

Specifications begin on page 551.

ISUZU

RATINGS

	LS/Limited 4WD
ACCELERATION	4
FUEL ECONOMY	2
RIDE QUALITY	4
STEERING/HANDLING	2
QUIETNESS	4
INSTRUMENTS/CONTROLS	5
ROOM/COMFORT (FRONT)	8
ROOM/COMFORT (REAR)	7
CARGO ROOM	8
VALUE	2

This Japanese-built SUV delivers fine workmanship, ample space, smooth powertrains and, with automatic transmission, convenient all-surface 4WD. But Trooper is priced against rivals that feature V8s, seat more than five, and have less trucky ride and handling. Subpar resale value is another competitive deficit.

TOTAL	46

Average total for full-size sport-utility vehicles: 50.9

ENGINES

	dohc V6
Size, liters/cu. in.	3.5/213
Horsepower @ rpm	215 @ 5400
Torque (lb-ft) @ rpm	230 @ 3000
Availability	S

EPA city/highway mpg

5-speed manual	16/19
4-speed automatic	15/19

PRICES

Isuzu Trooper	Retail Price	Dealer Invoice
S 4-door 2WD wagon, automatic	$28105	$25865
S 4-door 4WD wagon, manual	28555	26280
S 4-door 4WD wagon, automatic	29405	27055
LS 4-door 2WD wagon, automatic	30690	28230
LS 4-door 4WD wagon, automatic	32690	30065
Limited 4-door 2WD wagon, automatic	34460	31865
Limited 4-door 4WD wagon, automatic	36660	33695
Destination charge	610	610

STANDARD EQUIPMENT

S: 3.5-liter dohc V6 engine, 4-speed automatic transmission, dual front airbags, antilock 4-wheel disc brakes, air conditioning, power steering, tilt steering wheel, cruise control, cloth upholstery, front

Prices are accurate at time of publication; subject to manufacturer's change.
CONSUMER GUIDE®

ISUZU • JAGUAR

bucket seats, center console, cupholders, split folding rear seat, heated power mirrors, power windows, power door locks, remote keyless entry, AM/FM/cassette, digital clock, tachometer, rear defogger, remote fuel door release, intermittent wipers, illuminated visor mirrors, map lights, intermittent rear wiper/washer, cargo cover, floormats, theft-deterrent system, cornering lights, rear privacy glass, skid plates, front and rear tow hooks, outside-mounted full-size spare tire, 245/70R16 tires, alloy wheels. **4WD** adds: 4-wheel drive, 2-speed transfer case, 5-speed manual or 4-speed automatic transmission, limited-slip differential.

LS adds: limited-slip differential, automatic climate control, leather-wrapped steering wheel, heated front seats, 8-way power driver seat, 4-way power passenger seat, power sunroof, AM/FM/cassette w/in-dash 6-disc CD changer, variable intermittent wipers, fog lights. **4WD** adds: 4-wheel drive, 2-speed transfer case.

Limited adds: leather upholstery, Nakamichi sound system, compass, outside temperature indicator, barometer, altimeter. **4WD** adds: 4-wheel drive, 2-speed transfer case.

OPTIONAL EQUIPMENT	Retail Price	Dealer Invoice
Powertrain		
Torque-On-Demand, S 4WD	$700	$588
Full-time 4-wheel drive. Std. LS and Limited 4WD.		
Appearance and Miscellaneous		
Running boards, S, LS	320	243

JAGUAR S-TYPE

Jaguar S-Type

Rear-wheel-drive luxury car
2001 base price range: $43,655–$49,355. Built in England.
Also consider: BMW 5-Series, Lexus GS 300/430, Mercedes-Benz E-Class

Specifications begin on page 551.

JAGUAR

FOR • Acceleration (V8) • Handling/roadholding • Quietness • Ride **AGAINST** • Automatic transmission performance (V6) • Navigation system controls

Anchoring the middle of Jaguar's sedan line, the S-Type is built in Britain and shares its platform and basic engine design with the Lincoln LS. The S-Type offers V6 3.0 and V8 4.0 models, both with a 5-speed automatic transmission. Antilock 4-wheel disc brakes, traction control, front side airbags, and a rear obstacle warning system are standard. An antiskid system is optional. For 2002, the previous Sport option package is the basis for a new Sport edition. Available with either engine. the Sport edition has body-color exterior trim and sport front seats, plus the previous package's computer-controlled shock absorbers and 17-inch wheels with high-speed tires. The S-Type also gains rear cupholders. Options include the Deluxe Communications Package with emergency assistance and in-dash navigation systems, and voice-activated phone, audio, and climate functions.

RATINGS	3.0	4.0 w/Sport Pkg.
ACCELERATION	5	6
FUEL ECONOMY	5	5
RIDE QUALITY	8	6
STEERING/HANDLING	7	7
QUIETNESS	7	6
INSTRUMENTS/CONTROLS	4	4
ROOM/COMFORT (FRONT)	6	6
ROOM/COMFORT (REAR)	4	4
CARGO ROOM	3	3
VALUE	3	3

For performance and design sophistication, this is not a sports/luxury sedan in the BMW/Mercedes-Benz league, and it's not as refined as a Lexus, despite prices that mimic all those competitors. Overall, the S-Type is a nice premium midsize car, but more Lincoln-in-a-catsuit than bona fide Jaguar.

TOTAL	52	50

Average total for luxury cars: 59.4

ENGINES	dohc V6	dohc V8
Size, liters/cu. in.	3.0/181	4.0/244
Horsepower @ rpm	240 @ 6800	281 @ 6100
Torque (lb-ft) @ rpm	221 @ 4500	287 @ 4300
Availability	S[1]	S[2]
EPA city/highway mpg		
5-speed automatic	18/25	17/24

1. 3.0. 2. 4.0.

Prices are accurate at time of publication; subject to manufacturer's change.

CONSUMER GUIDE®

JAGUAR

2002 prices unavailable at time of publication.

PRICES

2001 Jaguar S-Type	Retail Price	Dealer Invoice
3.0 4-door sedan	$43655	$39289
4.0 4-door sedan	49355	44419
Destination charge	595	595

STANDARD EQUIPMENT

3.0: 3.0-liter dohc V6 engine, 5-speed automatic transmission, traction control, dual front airbags, front side airbags, antilock 4-wheel disc brakes, rear obstacle detection system, air conditioning w/dual-zone automatic climate control, interior air filter, variable-assist power steering, tilt/telescoping steering wheel, wood/leather-wrapped steering wheel, cruise control, leather upholstery, 8-way power front bucket seats, center console, cupholders, split folding rear seat, wood interior trim, heated power mirrors, power windows, power door locks, remote keyless entry, AM/FM/cassette w/CD changer controls, steering wheel radio controls, digital clock, tachometer, trip computer, illuminated visor mirrors, rear defogger, heated variable intermittent wipers, automatic headlights, floormats, theft-deterrent system, front and rear fog lights, full-sized spare tire, 225/55HR16 tires, alloy wheels.

4.0 adds: 4.0-liter dohc V8 engine, power sunroof, memory driver seat and mirrors, front seat power lumbar supports, power tilt/telescoping steering wheel w/memory, upgraded sound system, 6-disc CD changer, automatic day/night rearview mirror, universal garage door opener, compass.

OPTIONAL EQUIPMENT
Major Packages

Power/Memory Pkg., 3.0 .... 2000 1680
  Power sunroof, memory driver seat and mirrors, front seat lumbar supports, power tilt/telescoping steering wheel w/memory, automatic day/night rearview mirror, compass, universal garage door opener.

Deluxe Communications Pkg. 4300 3644
  Integrated navigation system, emergency services, voice activated controls (telephone, climate control, audio), portable cellular telephone. 3.0 requires Power/Memory Pkg.

Sport Pkg. 1100 924
  Computer-controlled shock absorbers, 235/50ZR17 tires, special alloy wheels. 3.0 requires Power/Memory Pkg.

Specifications begin on page 551.

JAGUAR

	Retail Price	Dealer Invoice
Weather Pkg.	$1200	$1008

Antiskid system, heated front seats, rain-sensing wipers. 3.0 requires Power/Memory Pkg.

Comfort & Convenience Features

Integrated navigation system	2000	1680

3.0 requires Power/Memory Pkg.

6-disc CD changer w/upgraded sound system, 3.0	1500	1260

Requires Power/Memory Pkg.

JAGUAR X-TYPE

Jaguar X-Type

All-wheel-drive near-luxury car
Base price range: $30,595-$38,595. Built in England.
Also consider: Acura TL, Audi A4, BMW 3-Series, Mercedes-Benz C-Class

FOR • All-wheel drive • Handling/roadholding • Quietness
AGAINST • Automatic transmission performance • Navigation system controls

Jaguar aims this new, compact-sized sedan at the Audi A4, BMW 3-Series, and Mercedes-Benz C-Class. The new entry-level Jaguar offers 194-hp 2.5-liter V6 models and 231-hp 3.0 V6 versions. Both are available with manual transmission or a 5-speed automatic. X-Type is manufactured in England and borrows its structure from the European Mondeo sedan built by Jaguar's U.S. owner, Ford. X-Type has a shorter wheelbase than Mondeo, different styling, and standard all-wheel drive vs. Mondeo's front-wheel drive. Competing Audis and BMWs have optional AWD. Standard on X-Type are antilock 4-wheel discs brakes, leather and wood interior trim, front

Prices are accurate at time of publication; subject to manufacturer's change.

JAGUAR

side airbags, and curtain side airbags. The AWD normally splits power 40 percent front/60 rear, reapportioning it automatically for best traction. Sport versions include 17-inch wheels vs. 16s, sport suspension, and unique trim. An antiskid system is standard on Sport models, optional on other X-Types. Xenon headlamps and a navigation system are optional. Voice activation for audio, climate, and navigation is a dealer-installed option.

RATINGS

	2.5 Sport, man.	3.0 w/nav. sys., auto.
ACCELERATION	6	6
FUEL ECONOMY	5	4
RIDE QUALITY	5	7
STEERING/HANDLING	8	7
QUIETNESS	5	7
INSTRUMENTS/CONTROLS	6	5
ROOM/COMFORT (FRONT)	6	6
ROOM/COMFORT (REAR)	5	5
CARGO ROOM	5	5
VALUE	3	3

Not a pure-pedigree sports sedan in the mold of the 3-Series and C-Class, but a pleasing blend of performance and Jaguar emotion. Prices escalate quickly: A base 2.5 is over $35,500 popularly optioned. A fully equipped 3.0 Sport tops $47,000. But X-Type makes Jaguar accessible to a new audience and will likely sell out its annual U.S. allotment of 35,000 units.

TOTAL	54	55

Average total for near-luxury cars: 54.5

ENGINES

	dohc V6	dohc V6
Size, liters/cu. in.	2.5/152	3.0/181
Horsepower @ rpm	194 @ 6800	231 @ 6800
Torque (lb-ft) @ rpm	180 @ 3000	209 @ 3000
Availability	S[1]	S[2]
EPA city/highway mpg		
5-speed manual	19/26	18/28
5-speed automatic	18/25	18/25

1. 2.5 models. 2. 3.0 models.

PRICES

Jaguar X-Type	Retail Price	Dealer Invoice
2.5 4-door sedan	$30595	$28900
2.5 Sport 4-door sedan	32595	30740
3.0 4-door sedan	36595	34300
3.0 Sport 4-door sedan	38595	36140

Specifications begin on page 551.

JAGUAR

	Retail Price	Dealer Invoice
Destination charge	$645	$645

STANDARD EQUIPMENT

2.5: 2.5-liter dohc V6 engine, 5-speed manual transmission, all-wheel drive, dual front airbags, front side airbags, curtain side airbags, antilock 4-wheel disc brakes, air conditioning w/automatic climate control, interior air filter, power steering, tilt/telescoping leather-wrapped steering wheel, cruise control, leather upholstery, front bucket seats, 8-way power driver seat, center console, cupholders, wood interior trim, heated power mirrors, power windows, power door locks, remote keyless entry, AM/FM/cassette, steering wheel radio controls, digital clock, rear defogger, heated variable-intermittent wipers, illuminated visor mirrors, theft-deterrent system, front and rear fog lights, 205/55HR16 tires, alloy wheels.

2.5 Sport adds: antiskid system, rear spoiler, sport suspension, 225/45ZR17 tires.

3.0 adds to 2.5: 3.0-liter dohc V6 engine, 5-speed automatic transmission.

3.0 Sport adds: antiskid system, rear spoiler, sport suspension, 225/45ZR17 tires.

OPTIONAL EQUIPMENT
Major Packages

X1 Premium Pkg.	2500	2100

Power sunroof, front seat power lumbar adjustment, 8-way power passenger seat, split folding rear seat, automatic day/night rearview mirror, universal garage door opener, rear parking assist, trip, computer, message center, rain-sensing wipers, automatic headlights.

X3 Weather Pkg., 2.5, 3.0	1200	1008
2.5 Sport, 3.0 Sport	600	504

Antiskid system (2.5, 3.0), heated front seats, heated headlight washers. Requires X1 Premium Pkg.

Powertrain

5-speed automatic transmission, 2.5, 2.5 Sport	1275	1071
5-speed manual transmission, 3.0, 3.0 Sport	NC	NC

Comfort & Convenience Features

Navigation system	2200	1848

Requires X1 Premium Pkg.

Emergency messaging system	1500	1260

Includes cellular telephone. Requires X1 Premium Pkg.

Prices are accurate at time of publication; subject to manufacturer's change.

JAGUAR

	Retail Price	Dealer Invoice
Alpine sound system	$1200	$1006

Includes 6-disc CD changer. Requires X1 Premium Pkg.

Appearance and Miscellaneous

Xenon headlights	675	567

Includes automatic headlight leveling. Requires X1 Premium Pkg.

JAGUAR XJ SEDAN

Jaguar XJ Sport

Rear-wheel-drive luxury car

2001 base price range: $56,355-$83,355. Built in England.

Also consider: BMW 7-Series, Lexus LS 430, Mercedes-Benz S-Class

FOR • Ride • Acceleration • Quietness • Build quality • Exterior finish • Interior materials **AGAINST** • Fuel economy • Cargo space

New sport and top-line models highlight 2002 for Jaguar's flagship. This sedan comes in two body lengths. For more rear leg room, Vanden Plas and Super V8 models are 5 inches longer than other versions. All have a 5-speed automatic transmission, traction control, antilock 4-wheel discs, front side airbags, and a 4.0-liter V8. XJ8, XJ Sport and premium-luxury Vanden Plas models have 290 hp. XJR, XJR 100, and Super V8 models use a supercharger for 370 hp. The XJ Sport is new for '02 and essentially combines the base powertrain with the XJR's 18-inch wheels, sport seats, and body-color exterior trim. Also new is the XJR 100, a limited-edition marking the 1902 birth of Jaguar founder William Lyons; it adds exclusive-design 19-inch wheels and special trim. The Super V8 replaces the Vanden Plas Supercharged model at the top of the line and includes a touring-tuned version of Jaguar's computer-controlled

Specifications begin on page 551.

JAGUAR

suspension. The XJR for '02 adds as standard a sport-tuned computer suspension and a navigation system.

RATINGS	XJ8	Vanden Plas	XJR
ACCELERATION	7	6	8
FUEL ECONOMY	4	4	3
RIDE QUALITY	10	10	8
STEERING/HANDLING	7	7	8
QUIETNESS	9	9	7
INSTRUMENTS/CONTROLS	3	3	3
ROOM/COMFORT (FRONT)	5	5	5
ROOM/COMFORT (REAR)	5	7	5
CARGO ROOM	2	2	2
VALUE	3	3	3

They're too cozy inside for their bulk outside, but the XJs shine for top-notch ride and refinement, potent, silky V8s, and evergreen British charm. Aging quickly, but under Ford's ownership, poor workmanship and reliability are no longer issues.

TOTAL	55	56	52

Average total for luxury cars: 59.4

ENGINES	dohc V8	Supercharged dohc V8
Size, liters/cu. in.	4.0/244	4.0/244
Horsepower @ rpm	290 @ 6100	370 @ 6150
Torque (lb-ft) @ rpm	290 @ 4250	387 @ 3600
Availability	S[1]	S[2]
EPA city/highway mpg		
5-speed automatic	17/24	16/22

1. XJ8, XJ Sport, Vanden Plas. 2. XJR, XJR 100, Super V8.

2002 prices unavailable at time of publication.

PRICES

2001 Jaguar XJ Sedan

	Retail Price	Dealer Invoice
XJ8 4-door sedan	$56355	$50719
XJ8L 4-door sedan	62355	56119
Vanden Plas 4-door sedan	67655	60889
XJR 4-door sedan	69355	62419
Vanden Plas Supercharged 4-door sedan	83355	75019
Destination charge	595	595

XJR and Vanden Plas Supercharged retail price includes $1000 Gas Guzzler tax.

STANDARD EQUIPMENT

Prices are accurate at time of publication; subject to manufacturer's change.

JAGUAR

XJ8: 4.0-liter dohc V8 engine, 5-speed automatic transmission, traction control, dual front airbags, front side airbags, antilock 4-wheel disc brakes, antiskid system, reverse sensing system, variable-assist power steering, power tilt/telescopic leather-wrapped steering wheel, cruise control, air conditioning w/automatic climate control, leather upholstery, 12-way power front bucket seats with power lumbar adjusters, center console, cupholders, wood interior trim, overhead console, driver memory system (driver seat, steering wheel, outside mirrors), heated power mirrors, power windows, power door locks, remote keyless entry, AM/FM/cassette w/6-disc CD changer, steering wheel radio controls, analog clock, tachometer, power sunroof, trip computer, outside-temperature indicator, automatic day/night rearview mirror, rear defogger, remote fuel-door and decklid releases, illuminated visor mirrors, universal garage-door opener, map lights, rain-sensing variable intermittent wipers, automatic headlights, floormats, theft-deterrent system, front and rear fog lights, full-size spare tire, 225/60ZR16 tires, alloy wheels.

XJ8L adds: 4.9-inch longer wheelbase.

Vanden Plas adds: wood and leather-wrapped steering wheel, wood shift knob, wood picnic trays on front seatbacks, upgraded leather upholstery and wood interior trim, heated front and rear seats, Alpine sound system, lamb's wool floormats.

Vanden Plas Supercharged adds: 4.0-liter dohc supercharged V8 engine, navigation system, computer-controlled shock absorbers, 235/50ZR17 tires.

XJR adds to XJ8: 4.0-liter dohc supercharged V8 engine, Alpine sound system, wood and leather-wrapped steering wheel, heated front and rear seats, sport suspension, 255/40ZR18 tires.

OPTIONAL EQUIPMENT
Comfort & Convenience Features

	Retail Price	Dealer Invoice
Navigation system	$1500	$1260
Std. Vanden Plas Supercharged.		
Heated front and rear seats, XJ8, XJ8L	500	420
Alpine sound system, XJ8, XJ8L	1000	840

JAGUAR XK8

Rear-wheel-drive luxury car

2001 base price range: $69,155-$96,905. Built in England.

Also consider: BMW Z8, Lexus SC 430, Mercedes-Benz SL-Class

FOR • Acceleration • Ride • Quietness • Build quality • Exterior finish • Interior materials **AGAINST** • Passenger

Specifications begin on page 551.

JAGUAR

Jaguar XKR 100 convertible

and cargo room • Entry/exit • Rear visibility

Jaguar's sporting coupe and convertible gain limited-edition models for 2002. All XKs have a 4.0-liter V8 and 5-speed automatic transmission. XK8s have 290 hp, the supercharged XKRs have 370. Both come as coupes or as convertibles with a power top and heated glass rear window. XKR versions have a louvered hood, rear spoiler, 18-inch wheels (vs. 17s), and computer-controlled shock absorbers. Commemorating the 1902 birth of Jaguar founder William Lyons, the new XKR 100 comes with 20-inch wheels, Brembro-brand brakes, Recaro-brand seats, and exclusive interior and exterior trim. Jaguar will import 270 XKR 100 convertibles and 30 coupes. Antilock 4-wheel disc brakes, traction control, front side airbags, and a rear obstacle warning system are standard on all models.

RATINGS

	XK8 conv	XKR cpe
ACCELERATION	7	8
FUEL ECONOMY	4	4
RIDE QUALITY	8	7
STEERING/HANDLING	7	8
QUIETNESS	5	5
INSTRUMENTS/CONTROLS	5	5
ROOM/COMFORT (FRONT)	4	4
ROOM/COMFORT (REAR)	1	1
CARGO ROOM	2	2
VALUE	2	2

XKs shine for silky performance in an elegant package with Jaguar's usual charm. Interior room is tight and prices are steep, though resale values compensate some.

| **TOTAL** | 45 | 46 |

Average total for luxury cars: 59.4

Prices are accurate at time of publication; subject to manufacturer's change.

JAGUAR

ENGINES

	dohc V8	Supercharged dohc V8
Size, liters/cu. in.	4.0/244	4.0/244
Horsepower @ rpm	290 @ 6100	370 @ 6150
Torque (lb-ft) @ rpm	290 @ 4250	387 @ 3600
Availability	S[1]	S[2]
EPA city/highway mpg		
5-speed automatic	17/24	16/22

1. XK8. 2. XKR, XKR 100.

2002 prices unavailable at time of publication.

PRICES

2001 Jaguar XK8

	Retail Price	Dealer Invoice
XK8 2-door coupe	$69155	$62239
XK8 2-door convertible	74155	66739
XKR 2-door coupe	80155	72139
XKR 2-door convertible	85155	76639
XKR Silverstone 2-door coupe	96905	86209
XKR Silverstone 2-door convertible	96905	86509
Destination charge	595	595

STANDARD EQUIPMENT

XK8: 4.0-liter dohc V8 engine, 5-speed automatic transmission, traction control, dual front airbags, front side airbags, antilock 4-wheel disc brakes, antiskid system, rear obstacle detection system, air conditioning w/automatic climate control, variable-assist power steering, power tilt/telescopic steering wheel, wood/leather-wrapped steering wheel, cruise control, power top (convertible), leather upholstery, heated 8-way power front bucket seats w/power lumbar support, memory system (driver seat, steering wheel, outside mirrors), center console, cupholders, wood interior trim and shifter, heated power mirrors, power windows, power door locks, remote keyless entry, Alpine AM/FM/cassette w/6-disc CD changer, steering wheel radio controls, analog clock, tachometer, trip computer, universal garage-door opener, illuminated visor mirrors, automatic day/night rearview mirror, outside-temperature indicator, rear defogger, remote fuel-door and decklid release, rain-sensing variable intermittent windshield wipers, map lights, automatic headlights, floormats, theft-deterrent system, front and rear fog lights, headlight washers, full-size spare tire, 245/50ZR17 tires, alloy wheels.

XKR adds: 4.0-liter dohc supercharged V8 engine, navigation system, computer-controlled shock absorbers, 245/45ZR18 front tires, 255/45ZR18 rear tires. *Deletes:* full-size spare tire.

XKR Silverstone adds: upgraded brakes, leather-wrapped steering

Specifications begin on page 551.

JAGUAR • JEEP

wheel, sport suspension (coupe), 255/35ZR20 front tires, 285/30ZR20 rear tires.

OPTIONAL EQUIPMENT	Retail Price	Dealer Invoice
Major Packages		
BBS Milan Wheels and Brake Pkg., XKR	$5700	$4788
18-inch BBS Milan wheels, Brembo brakes.		
BBS Paris/Detroit Wheels and Brake Pkg., XKR	8700	7308
18-inch BBS Paris or Detroit wheels, Brembo brakes.		
Comfort & Convenience Features		
Navigation system, XK8	2400	2016
Appearance and Miscellaneous		
18-inch alloy wheels, XK8	500	420
Includes 245/45ZR18 front tires, 255/45ZR18 rear tires, space-saver spare tire.		

JEEP GRAND CHEROKEE

Jeep Grand Cherokee Overland

Rear- or 4-wheel-drive midsize sport-utility vehicle
Base price range: $25,425-$36,830. Built in USA.
Also consider: Acura MDX, Ford Explorer, Toyota Highlander

FOR • Acceleration • Cargo room **AGAINST** • Fuel economy

Grand Cherokee adds a new top-line model for 2002 and makes available more power, side curtain airbags, and power-adjustable brake and accelerator pedals. Laredo, Limited, and new Overland models are offered. Overland has altered front and rear styling and special interior trim, including redwood accents. Inline-6 cyl and V8 engines are offered. The V8 has 235 hp in base form and 260 in the

JEEP

new high-output guise that's standard on Overland and optional for Limited. Both engines use automatic transmission: the 6 cyl a 4 speed, the V8s a 5 speed. Antilock 4-wheel disc brakes are standard. Grand Cherokee offers rear-wheel drive, Jeep's Selec-Trac 4WD that can be left engaged on dry pavement, or Jeep's Quadra-Drive or Quadra-Trac all-wheel drive; 4x4s include low-range gearing. The curtain side airbags provide head protection to outboard front and rear passengers in a side collision; they're standard on Overland, optional on Laredo and Limited. Torso side airbags are not offered. Rain-sensing windshield wipers are newly available.

RATINGS	Laredo 4WD w/Quadra-Drive, 6 cyl	Limited 4WD, V8
ACCELERATION	5	6
FUEL ECONOMY	4	3
RIDE QUALITY	4	4
STEERING/HANDLING	3	3
QUIETNESS	3	3
INSTRUMENTS/CONTROLS	7	7
ROOM/COMFORT (FRONT)	6	6
ROOM/COMFORT (REAR)	4	4
CARGO ROOM	7	7
VALUE	5	3

Performance and overall design are good, and prices competitive. But questions about long-term mechanical reliability keep Grand Cherokee from the Recommended category. Our extended-use test Laredo didn't entirely erase those concerns.

TOTAL	48	46

Average total for midsize sport-utility vehicles: 49.6

EXTENDED-USE TEST UPDATE

A pronounced brake shudder on our extended-use-test Grand Cherokee was eliminated at 15,400 mi. when a dealer service department replaced the front pads and rotors. A technician said the standard warranty covers these parts for 12 months/12,000 mi., but the dealer arranged to have the work performed under warranty. Also under warranty, a pressure transducer was replaced to fix a leaking transmission. No other unscheduled maintenance was required during this vehicle's 12-month test.

ENGINES

	ohv I6	ohc V8	ohc V8
Size, liters/cu. in.	4.0/242	4.7/287	4.7/287
Horsepower @ rpm	195 @ 4600	235 @ 4800	260 @ 5100
Torque (lb-ft) @ rpm	230 @ 3000	295 @ 3200	330 @ 3600

Specifications begin on page 551.

JEEP

	ohv I6	ohc V8	ohc V8
Availability	S[1]	O[1]	S[2]
EPA city/highway mpg			
4-speed automatic	15/20[3]		
5-speed automatic		14/19	14/19

1. Laredo, Limited. 2. Overland; optional Limited. 3. 15/21 w/2WD.

PRICES

Jeep Grand Cherokee	Retail Price	Dealer Invoice
Laredo 4-door wagon 2WD	$25425	$23408
Laredo 4-door wagon 4WD	27395	25197
Limited 4-door wagon 2WD	30270	27720
Limited 4-door wagon AWD	32700	29918
Overland 4-door wagon AWD	36830	33594
Destination charge	600	600

Laredo requires Convenience Group or Quick Order Pkg. 26/28F.

STANDARD EQUIPMENT

Laredo: 4.0-liter 6-cylinder engine, 4-speed automatic transmission, dual front airbags, antilock 4-wheel disc brakes, air conditioning, power steering, tilt steering wheel, cruise control, cloth upholstery, front bucket seats, 6-way power driver seat, center console, cupholders, split folding rear seat, power mirrors, power windows, power door locks, AM/FM/CD player, digital clock, tachometer, variable intermittent wipers, visor mirrors, rear defogger, cargo cover, intermittent rear wiper/washer, theft-deterrent system, rear privacy glass, roof rack, full-size spare tire, 225/75R16 tires, alloy wheels. **4WD** adds: 4-wheel drive, 2-speed transfer case.

Limited adds: dual-zone automatic climate control, leather upholstery, leather-wrapped steering wheel w/radio controls, 10-way power driver seat w/memory, 6-way power passenger seat, heated power mirrors w/driver-side memory and automatic day/night, remote keyless entry, Infinity sound system, automatic day/night rearview mirror, overhead console, trip computer, outside temperature indicator, universal garage door opener, illuminated visor mirrors, automatic headlights, fog lights, 235/65R17 tires. **AWD** adds: all-wheel drive, 2-speed transfer case.

Overland adds: 4.7-liter V8 260-horsepower engine, 5-speed automatic transmission, all-wheel drive, 2-speed transfer case, 2-speed transfer case, curtain side airbags, wood/leather-wrapped steering wheel, heated 10-way power front seats, power sunroof, Infinity AM/FM/cassette/CD player w/10-disc CD changer, rain-sensing wipers, floormats, skid plates, tow hooks, Up-Country Suspension, 235/65R17 all-terrain white-letter tires.

Prices are accurate at time of publication; subject to manufacturer's change.

JEEP

OPTIONAL EQUIPMENT
Major Packages

	Retail Price	Dealer Invoice
Quick Order Pkg. 26/28F, Laredo	$2195	$1932
Manufacturer's Discount Price	*1695*	*1492*

Remote keyless entry, 6-way power front passenger seat, automatic day/night rearview mirror, automatic headlights, leather-wrapped steering wheel, Infinity sound system, overhead console, trip computer, outside temperature indicator, universal garage door opener, illuminated visor mirrors, theft-deterrent system w/alarm, 225/75R16 white-letter tires.

Quick Order Pkg. 26/28G, Limited	NC	NC
Manufacturer's Discount Price (credit)	*(500)*	*(440)*

Standard equipment.

Quick Order Pkg. 26/28K, Limited 2WD	1595	1404
Manufacturer's Discount Price	*1095*	*964*
Limited AWD	2145	1888
Manufacturer's Discount Price	*1645*	*1448*

Heated front seats, 10-way power passenger seat, power sunroof, Infinity AM/FM/cassette/CD player, 10-disc CD changer, Quadra-Drive all-wheel drive (AWD).

Convenience Group, Laredo	640	563
Manufacturer's Discount Price	*140*	*123*

Remote keyless entry, overhead console, trip computer, outside temperature indicator, cargo cover and net, floormats, 225/75R16 white-letter tires.

Cold Weather Group,

Laredo	300	264
Limited	250	220

Heated power mirrors, heated front seats. Laredo requires Quick Order Pkg. 26/28F, leather upholstery.

Up-Country Suspension Group, Laredo 4WD	435	383
Limited AWD	290	255

Heavy-duty suspension, skid plates, tow hooks, 245/70R16 all-terrain white-letter tires (Laredo), 235/65R17 all-terrain white-letter tires (Limited). Laredo requires Quick Order Pkg. 26/28F. NA w/4.7-liter 260-horsepower engine.

Trailer Tow Prep Group	105	92

Trailer wiring harness, mechanical cooling fan.

Trailer Tow Group, Laredo, Limited	360	317

Frame mounted Class III receiver hitch, 7-wire connector, adapter plug. Requires 4.0-liter engine.

Trailer Tow Group IV	255	224

Frame mounted Class IV receiver hitch, 7-wire connector, adapter plug, power steering fluid cooler. NA w/4.0-liter engine.

Specifications begin on page 551.

JEEP

	Retail Price	Dealer Invoice
Powertrain		
4.7-liter V8 235-horsepower engine,		
Laredo 4WD	1165	1025
Laredo 2WD, Limited	1070	942
Manufacturer's Discount Price, Limited	*370*	*326*

Requires 5-speed automatic transmission. Laredo requires Quick Order Pkg. 26/28F. 4WD includes Quadra-Trac II AWD.

	Retail Price	Dealer Invoice
4.7-liter V8 260-horsepower engine,		
Limited 2WD	1935	1703
Manufacturer's Discount Price	*1235*	*1087*
Limited AWD	1590	1399
Manufacturer's Discount Price	*890*	*783*

Requires 5-speed automatic transmission. 2WD includes Vari-Lock progressive rear axle.

	Retail Price	Dealer Invoice
5-speed automatic transmission	75	66

Requires 4.7-liter V8 engine.

	Retail Price	Dealer Invoice
Quadra-Trac II AWD, Laredo 4WD	445	392
Quadra-Drive AWD, Limited	550	484

With 4.0-liter and 4.7 235-horsepower engines includes front and rear Vari-Lok progressive axles.

	Retail Price	Dealer Invoice
Vari-Lock progressive rear axle, Laredo, Limited	345	304

Requires Quick Order Pkg. 26/28F. NA w/Quadra-Trac II AWD. Std. Overland.

Safety

	Retail Price	Dealer Invoice
Curtain side air bags, Laredo, Limited	490	431
Tire pressure monitor, Limited, Overland	150	132

Comfort & Convenience Features

	Retail Price	Dealer Invoice
Power sunroof, Laredo, Limited	800	704
Leather upholstery, Laredo	655	576

Requires Quick Order Pkg. 26/28F.

	Retail Price	Dealer Invoice
Power adjustable pedals, Laredo	120	106
Limited, Overland	185	132

Laredo requires Quick Order Pkg. 26/28F. Limited, Overland include memory.

	Retail Price	Dealer Invoice
Infinity AM/FM/cassette/CD player, Laredo	495	436
Limited	100	88

Requires Quick Order Pkg. 26/28F.

	Retail Price	Dealer Invoice
Infinity AM/FM/cassette/CD player w/10-disc CD changer, Limited	495	436
Rain-sensing wipers, Limited	75	66

Appearance and Miscellaneous

	Retail Price	Dealer Invoice
Fog lights, Laredo	120	106

Requires Quick Order Pkg. 26/28F.

Prices are accurate at time of publication; subject to manufacturer's change.

JEEP

Special Purpose Wheels and Tires

	Retail Price	Dealer Invoice
Chrome alloy wheels, Limited	$870	$766

Require Quick Order Pkg. 26/28K.

JEEP LIBERTY

Jeep Liberty Limited Edition

Rear- or 4-wheel-drive compact sport-utility vehicle
Base price range: $16,450-$22,720. Built in USA.
Also consider: Ford Escape, Honda CR-V, Mazda Tribute

FOR • Build quality • Cargo room **AGAINST** • Rear-seat comfort • Ride

Replacing the 18-year old Cherokee is a roomier new SUV with a more-sophisticated suspension and available curtain side airbags. Liberty retains unibody construction, but is about three inches longer in wheelbase and seven inches longer overall than Cherokee. It's taller, wider, and about 400 lb heavier, too. The only body is a 4-dr wagon. Its tailgate opens to the left and carries the outside-mount spare tire. Liberty's coil-spring suspension is independent in front and replaces Cherokee's solid-axle, leaf-spring setup. Two models are offered. The Sport has contrasting-color body cladding. The Limited Edition has monochromatic exterior and brushed metallic interior trim. Sport comes with a 150-hp 4-cyl engine. Optional on Sport and standard on Limited is a new 210-hp 3.7-liter V6. The 4 cyl uses manual transmission, the V6 gets manual or automatic. Liberty offers rear-wheel drive, Jeep's Command-Trac 4WD that must be disengaged on dry pavement, or Jeep's Selec-Trac 4WD that can be left engaged on dry pavement; 4x4s include low-range gearing. Liberty's 5000-lb towing capacity is tops among compact SUVs. ABS and curtain side airbags are optional. Standard are 16-inch wheels

Specifications begin on page 551.

JEEP

and a 65/35 split/folding rear seat. Leather upholstery, heated front seats, and a sunroof are available.

RATINGS	Sport 4WD, V6 auto.	Limited Edition 4WD
ACCELERATION	3	3
FUEL ECONOMY	3	3
RIDE QUALITY	4	4
STEERING/HANDLING	4	4
QUIETNESS	4	4
INSTRUMENTS/CONTROLS	5	5
ROOM/COMFORT (FRONT)	5	5
ROOM/COMFORT (REAR)	4	4
CARGO ROOM	7	7
VALUE	5	4

Liberty is capable, solid, competitively priced, and the off-road leader among compact SUVs. But for better or worse, Jeep avoided making it as carlike as most of its rivals. That dictates some compromises in rear-seat comfort and handling.

TOTAL	44	43

Average total for compact sport-utility vehicles: 44.4

ENGINES

	ohc I4	ohc V6
Size, liters/cu. in.	2.4/148	3.7/226
Horsepower @ rpm	150 @ 5200	210 @ 5200
Torque (lb-ft) @ rpm	167 @ 4000	225 @ 4000
Availability	S[1]	S[2]
EPA city/highway mpg		
5-speed manual	19/23	16/21
4-speed automatic		16/20

1. Sport. 2. Limited Edition; optional on Sport.

PRICES

Jeep Liberty	Retail Price	Dealer Invoice
Sport 4-door wagon, 2WD	$16450	$15550
Sport 4-door wagon, 4WD	17960	16944
Limited 4-door wagon, 2WD	21210	19881
Limited 4-door wagon, 4WD	22720	21275
Destination charge	585	585

STANDARD EQUIPMENT

Sport: 2.4-liter dohc 4-cylinder engine, 5-speed manual transmission, dual front airbags, power steering, cloth upholstery, center console, cupholders, split folding rear seat, AM/FM/cassette, digital clock, tachometer, variable intermittent wipers, rear defogger, rear

Prices are accurate at time of publication; subject to manufacturer's change.

JEEP

wiper/washer, automatic-off headlights, outside-mounted spare tire, 215/75R16 tires. **4WD** adds: 4-wheel drive, 2-speed transfer case.

Limited adds: 3.7-liter V6 engine, 4-speed automatic transmission, air conditioning, tilt leather-wrapped steering wheel, cruise control, power mirrors, power windows, power door locks, remote keyless entry, AM/FM/CD player, illuminated visor mirrors, map lights, cargo cover, floormats, fog lights, roof rack, full-size spare tire, 235/70R16 tires, alloy wheels. **4WD** adds: 4-wheel drive, 2-speed transfer case.

OPTIONAL EQUIPMENT
Major Packages

	Retail Price	Dealer Invoice
23/26/27B Quick Order Pkg., Sport	$2445	$2201
Manufacturer's Discount Price	*1670*	*1503*

Air conditioning, tilt steering wheel, power mirrors, power windows, power door locks, remote keyless entry, illuminated visor mirrors, map lights, auxiliary power outlet, cargo net, floormats, roof rack, outside-mounted full-size spare wheel, styled steel wheels.

27G Quick Order Pkg., 2WD Limited	2550	2295
Manufacturer's Discount Price	*1925*	*1732*
4WD Limited	2945	2651
Manufacturer's Discount Price	*2320*	*2088*

Leather upholstery, 6-way power front seats, Infinity AM/FM/cassette/CD player, overhead console, universal garage door opener, trip computer, heated power mirrors, theft-deterrent system w/alarm, Selec-Trac 4-wheel drive (4WD).

AJP Power Convenience Group, Sport	485	437

Power mirrors and windows, power door locks, remote keyless entry.

AHM Convenience Group 1, Sport	185	167

Illuminated visor mirrors, map lights, auxiliary power outlet, cargo net.

Security Group, Sport	250	225
Limited	175	158

Cargo cover (Sport), theft-deterrent system w/alarm. Requires deep-tinted glass. Sport requires 23/26/27B Quick Order Pkg.

Off-Road Group, 4WD Sport	765	689
4WD Limited	520	468

Limited-slip rear differential, heavy-duty engine cooling, tow hooks, skid plates, 235/70R16 all-terrain white-letter tires. Sport requires 23/26/27B Quick Order Pkg., 3.7-liter engine.

Trailer Tow Group	325	293
ordered w/Off-Road Group	245	222

Heavy-duty engine cooling, 7-wire trailer harness, Class III hitch receiver. Sport requires, 3.7-liter engine, 4-speed automatic transmission, air conditioning.

Specifications begin on page 551.

JEEP

	Retail Price	Dealer Invoice
Powertrain		
3.7-liter V6 engine, Sport	$850	$765
4-speed automatic transmission, Sport	825	743
Requires 3.7-liter engine.		
Selec-Trac 4-wheel drive, 4WD	395	356
Sport requires 4-speed automatic transmission.		
Limited-slip rear differential	285	257
Requires 3.7-liter engine.		
Safety		
Curtain side airbags	390	351
Antilock brakes	600	540
Sport requires 3.7-liter engine.		
Comfort & Convenience Features		
Air conditioning, Sport	850	765
Power sunroof	700	630
Sport requires 23/26/27B Quick Order Pkg.		
AM/FM/CD player, Sport	125	113
AM/FM/cassette/CD player, Sport	225	203
Limited	100	90
Requires Infinity speakers. Sport requires 23/26/27B Quick Order Pkg.		
6-disc CD changer	415	374
Sport requires 23/26/27B Quick Order Pkg., optional radio.		
Infinity speakers	475	428
Includes steering wheel radio controls. Requires AM/FM/cassette/CD player. Sport requires 23/26/27B Quick Order Pkg., cruise control.		
Cruise control, Sport	300	270
Includes leather-wrapped steering wheel. Requires 23/26/27B Quick Order Pkg.		
6-way power driver seat, Limited	300	270
Heated front seats, Limited	250	225
Requires 27G Quick Order Pkg.		
Mini overhead console, Limited	300	270
Includes universal garage door opener, trip computer.		
Appearance and Miscellaneous		
Fog lights, Sport	120	108
Requires 23/26/27B Quick Order Pkg.		
Deep-tinted glass	270	243
Sport requires 23/26/27B Quick Order Pkg.		
Special Purpose, Wheels and Tires		
Alloy wheels, Sport	310	279
Requires 23/26/27B Quick Order Pkg.		

Prices are accurate at time of publication; subject to manufacturer's change.

JEEP

JEEP WRANGLER

Jeep Wrangler Sahara

4-wheel-drive compact sport-utility vehicle
Base price range: $15,230-$23,450. Built in USA.
Also consider: Honda CR-V, Subaru Forester, Toyota RAV4

FOR • Cargo room • Maneuverability **AGAINST** • Fuel economy • Acceleration (4-cylinder w/automatic) • Noise • Ride • Entry/exit

Jeep's tradition-bound compact SUV gains a new midlevel model that becomes the lowest-priced 6-cyl Wrangler. Wrangler is available with a soft top and plastic side windows or optional hardtop with glass windows. The base SE model has a 4-cyl engine; the new X model joins the Sport and Sahara in having a standard inline-6 cyl. Manual transmission is standard, a 3-speed automatic is optional. All Wranglers have Jeep's Command-Trac 4WD that must be disengaged on dry pavement but includes low-range gearing. ABS is available on all but the SE. A 30-inch tire package is optional on Sport and newly standard on Sahara, and the premium audio system gets front tweeters.

RATINGS	SE, man.	Sport/Sahara, auto.
ACCELERATION	2	4
FUEL ECONOMY	4	4
RIDE QUALITY	1	1
STEERING/HANDLING	2	3
QUIETNESS	1	1
INSTRUMENTS/CONTROLS	3	3
ROOM/COMFORT (FRONT)	4	4
ROOM/COMFORT (REAR)	2	2

Specifications begin on page 551.

JEEP

	SE, man.	Sport/Sahara, auto.
CARGO ROOM	6	6
VALUE	3	3

Wrangler isn't comfortable, but few vehicles have more personality or better off-road ability. All versions have strong resale value, but initial prices can be relatively steep—the Sport quickly tops $22,000, and Sahara starts above that. Positioned just above the 4-cyl SE, the new X delivers 6-cyl power for lower cost than a Sport model.

TOTAL	28	31

Average total for compact sport-utility vehicles: 44.4

ENGINES

	ohv I4	ohv I6
Size, liters/cu. in.	2.5/150	4.0/242
Horsepower @ rpm	120 @ 5400	190 @ 4600
Torque (lb-ft) @ rpm	140 @ 3500	235 @ 3200
Availability	S[1]	S[2]
EPA city/highway mpg		
5-speed manual	18/20	15/18
3-speed automatic	16/18	15/17

1. SE. 2. X, Sport, Sahara.

PRICES

Jeep Wrangler	Retail Price	Dealer Invoice
SE 2-door convertible	$15230	$14229
X 2-door convertible	18410	17248
Sport 2-door convertible	20080	18366
Sahara 2-door convertible	23450	21366
Destination charge	585	585

STANDARD EQUIPMENT

SE: 2.5-liter 4-cylinder engine, 5-speed manual transmission, 4-wheel drive, 2-speed transfer case, dual front airbags, roll bar, power steering, vinyl upholstery, front bucket seats, tachometer, front carpeting, mini floor console, cupholder, variable intermittent wipers, skid plates, 205/75R15 all-terrain tires.

X adds: 4.0-liter 6-cylinder engine, cloth upholstery, folding rear bench seat, rear carpeting, AM/FM/cassette w/rear sound bar and speakers, digital clock, 215/75R15 all-terrain tires.

Sport adds: full metal doors w/roll-up windows, fog lights, tow hooks, outside-mounted full-sized spare tire.

Sahara adds: air conditioning, tilt leather-wrapped steering wheel, full storage console, AM/FM/CD player w/upgraded sound system, front floormats, theft-deterrent system, deep-tinted rear glass, body-side steps, 30x9.5R15 all-terrain white-letter tires, alloy wheels.

Prices are accurate at time of publication; subject to manufacturer's change.

JEEP

OPTIONAL EQUIPMENT

	Retail Price	Dealer Invoice
Major Packages		

Pkg. 22/23N, SE $1310 $1153
  AM/FM/cassette, rear sound bar w/speakers, folding rear seat, rear carpeting.
Wheel Plus Group, X 1110 977
  Manufacturer's Discount Price *995* *876*
  AM/FM/CD player w/subwoofer and tweeter, 225/75R15 all-terrain tires, full-size spare tire, alloy wheels.
ADC Convenience Group, SE, X 165 145
  Full storage console, courtesy and underhood lights. SE requires Pkg. 22/23N.

Powertrain
3-speed automatic transmission, SE, X, Sport 625 550
  Sahara 315 277
Limited-slip rear differential, X, Sport, Sahara 285 251
Dana 44 rear axle, Sport, Sahara 310 273
  Includes limited-slip differential, special axle ratio. NA w/antilock brakes.

Safety
Antilock brakes, X, Sport, Sahara 600 528

Comfort & Convenience Features
Hard top, SE, X 920 810
  Sport, Sahara 795 700
  Includes full metal doors with roll-up windows, rear wiper/washer, deep-tinted glass (Sahara), rear defogger, cargo light.
Soft and hard tops, Sport 1435 1263
  Sahara 1675 1474
  Includes full metal doors.
Full metal doors w/roll-up windows,
  SE, X 125 110
  SE requires Pkg. 22/23N.
Air conditioning, SE, X, Sport 895 788
Folding rear seat, SE 595 524
Steering Group, SE, X 190 167
  Tilt leather-wrapped steering wheel. SE requires Pkg. 22/23N.
Cruise control, SE, X 300 264
  SE/X w/Steering Group, Sport, Sahara 250 220
  Includes leather-wrapped steering wheel. SE requires Pkg. 22/23N.
AM/FM/cassette, SE 715 629
  Includes rear sound bar with speakers.

Specifications begin on page 551.

JEEP • KIA

	Retail Price	Dealer Invoice
AM/FM/CD player, SE w/22/23N, X, Sport..............	$125	$110

Includes rear sound bar with speakers.

Upgraded sound system, Sport...............................	295	260

Includes 7 speakers, tweeter, subwoofer. Requires ADC Convenience Group. Std. Sahara.

Appearance and Miscellaneous

Add-A-Trunk lockable storage................................	125	110
SE requires Pkg. 22/23N.		
Deep-tinted rear glass, X/Sport w/hard top............	240	211
Sport w/soft and hard tops	365	321
Tinted soft top windows, X, Sport........................	125	110
Bodyside steps, Sport	75	66

Special Purpose, Wheels and Tires

Full Face Tire and Wheel Group, SE	700	616
X	425	374

Full-size spare tire, 225/75R15 all-terrain white-letter tires, full-face steel wheels.

Ecco Tire and Wheel Group, SE	965	849
Sport	575	506

Full-size spare tire (SE), 225/75R15 all-terrain white-letter tires, alloy wheels. SE requires Pkg. 22/23N.

Canyon Tire and Wheel Group, Sport w/automatic	670	590
Sport w/manual..	850	748

Five alloy wheels, heavy-duty shock absorbers and rear axle, Dana 44 rear axle (w/manual transmission), 30x9.5R15 all-terrain white-letter tires. Std. Sahara.

Full-size spare tire, SE, X	115	101

KIA OPTIMA

Front-wheel-drive compact car

2001 base price range: $15,299-$19,949. Built in South Korea.

Also consider: Chrysler PT Cruiser, Mazda 626, Volkswagen Passat

FOR • Instruments/controls • Ride **AGAINST** • Automatic transmission performance • Rear-seat room/comfort

A larger V6 engine tops a short list of 2002 changes to Kia's compact sedan. Optima is based on the Sonata produced by Kia's South Korean corporate parent, Hyundai. LX and uplevel SE Optimas use the Sonata's 4-cyl and V6 engines. The V6 grows from 2.5 liters to

Prices are accurate at time of publication; subject to manufacturer's change.

KIA

Kia Optima

2.7 this year for a gain of 8 hp. The 4 cyl teams with manual or automatic transmission, the V6 with automatic only. V6 Optimas have a separate gate for manual shifting. Front side airbags are standard. ABS and leather upholstery are optional with the V6, though Optima doesn't offer Sonata's available traction control. V6 Optimas also have rear disc brakes in place of drums. In other '02 changes, 15-inch wheels replace 14s as standard, and SEs gain standard automatic headlights and an available power front-passenger seat. Optima's performance and accommodations mirror those of like-equipped Sonatas.

RATINGS

	Optima SE V6
ACCELERATION	5
FUEL ECONOMY	5
RIDE QUALITY	7
STEERING/HANDLING	5
QUIETNESS	6
INSTRUMENTS/CONTROLS	7
ROOM/COMFORT (FRONT)	7
ROOM/COMFORT (REAR)	4
CARGO ROOM	5
VALUE	4

Optima isn't Honda Accord agile or Toyota Camry refined, and its resale values are much lower, though even the V6 Optima beats their 4-cyl models on price and has a longer warranty. Basically a decent car that needs more of a track record in the U.S.

TOTAL	55

Average total for compact cars: 51.6

ENGINES

	dohc I4	dohc V6
Size, liters/cu. in.	2.4/144	2.7/152
Horsepower @ rpm	149 @ 6000	178 @ 6000
Torque (lb-ft) @ rpm	159 @ 4500	181 @ 4000

Specifications begin on page 551.

KIA

	dohc I4	dohc V6
Availability	S[1]	S[2]
EPA city/highway mpg		
5-speed manual	21/28	
4-speed automatic	20/27	19/25

1. LX, SE. 2. LX V6, SE V6.

2002 prices unavailable at time of publication.

PRICES

2001 Kia Optima	Retail Price	Dealer Invoice
LX 4-cylinder 4-door sedan, manual	$15299	$13788
LX 4-cylinder 4-door sedan, automatic	16149	14542
LX V6 4-door sedan, automatic	18499	16120
SE 4-cylinder 4-door sedan, manual	17599	15601
SE 4-cylinder 4-door sedan, automatic	18449	16355
SE V6 4-door sedan, automatic	19949	17443
Destination charge	495	495

STANDARD EQUIPMENT

LX 4-cylinder: 2.4-liter dohc 4-cylinder engine, 5-speed manual or 4-speed automatic transmission, dual front airbags, front side airbags, air conditioning, power steering, cloth upholstery, front bucket seats, center console, cupholders, split folding rear seat, power mirrors, power windows, power door locks, AM/FM/cassette, digital clock, illuminated visor mirrors, variable intermittent wipers, map lights, 195/70HR14 tires, wheel covers.

LX V6 adds: 2.5-liter dohc V6 engine, 4-speed automatic transmission w/manual-shift capability, 4-wheel disc brakes, cruise control, 205/60HR15 tires, alloy wheels.

SE 4-cylinder adds to LX 4-cylinder: 8-way power driver seat, leather-wrapped steering wheel, cruise control, AM/FM/cassette/CD player, power antenna, remote keyless entry, sunroof, heated power mirrors, fog lights, 205/60HR15 tires, alloy wheels.

SE V6 adds: 2.5-liter dohc V6 engine, 4-speed automatic transmission w/manual-shift capability, 4-wheel disc brakes.

OPTIONAL EQUIPMENT

Safety
Antilock brakes, LX V6, SE V6	795	665

Comfort & Convenience Features
Leather upholstery, SE	995	865
Cruise control, LX 4-cylinder	250	210

Prices are accurate at time of publication; subject to manufacturer's change.

KIA

	Retail Price	Dealer Invoice
AM/FM/cassette/CD player, LX	$595	$525

KIA RIO

Kia Rio Cinco 4-door wagon

Front-wheel-drive subcompact car
Base price range: $9,095-$11,260. Built in South Korea.
Also consider: Ford Focus, Honda Civic, Toyota Echo

FOR • Fuel economy **AGAINST** • Acceleration • Rear-seat entry/exit • Rear-seat room (sedan)

Among the least-expensive cars on the market, Rio is sized and priced below Kia's Spectra subcompact. For 2002, Rio offers sedan and wagon body styles that share a 4-cyl engine and manual or optional automatic transmission. The wagon is called the Cinco. ABS and air conditioning are optional. Side airbags and power windows are unavailable. Included with the wagon and in the sedan's upgrade package are power steering and tilt steering wheel. Hyundai is Kia's corporate parent and that South Korean automaker's warranty applies here: 5 years/60,000 mi. basic, 10/100,000 powertrain, 5 years/unlimited roadside assistance.

RATINGS	Base sdn, man.	Base sdn, auto.	Cinco wgn, auto.
ACCELERATION	2	2	2
FUEL ECONOMY	6	7	6
RIDE QUALITY	4	4	3
STEERING/HANDLING	3	3	3
QUIETNESS	3	3	3
INSTRUMENTS/CONTROLS	5	5	5

Specifications begin on page 551.

KIA

	Base sdn, man.	Base sdn, auto.	Cinco wgn, auto.
ROOM/COMFORT (FRONT)	3	3	3
ROOM/COMFORT (REAR)	2	2	3
CARGO ROOM	2	2	6
VALUE	1	1	2

Rio offers "cheap wheels" economy and a generous warranty, but Kia's resale values are low, partly in recognition of its unproven record of reliability and low ratings on independent surveys of customer satisfaction. Our test Rios were optioned to $11,400 or more, which buys a larger, fancier used car in good condition—or a more-desirable Toyota Echo.

TOTAL	31	32	36

Average total for subcompact cars: 43.7

ENGINES

	dohc I4
Size, liters/cu. in.	1.5/91
Horsepower @ rpm	96 @ 5800
Torque (lb-ft) @ rpm	98 @ 4500
Availability	S

EPA city/highway mpg
5-speed manual	27/30
4-speed automatic	25/30

PRICES

Kia Rio

	Retail Price	Dealer Invoice
Base 4-door sedan, manual	$9095	$8450
Base 4-door sedan, automatic	9970	9250
Cinco 4-door wagon, manual	10385	NA
Cinco 4-door wagon, automatic	11260	NA
Destination charge	495	495

STANDARD EQUIPMENT

Base: 1.5-liter dohc 4-cylinder engine, 5-speed manual or 4-speed automatic transmission, dual front airbags, emergency inside trunk release, manual steering, cloth upholstery, front bucket seats w/height-adjustable driver seat, center console, cupholders, rear defogger, intermittent wipers, 175/65R14 tires, wheel covers.

Cinco adds: power steering, tilt steering wheel, split folding rear seat, AM/FM/cassette, tachometer, visor mirrors, cargo cover, rear wiper/washer.

Prices are accurate at time of publication; subject to manufacturer's change.

KIA

OPTIONAL EQUIPMENT	Retail Price	Dealer Invoice
Major Packages		
Upgrade Pkg., Base	$380	$315
Power steering, tilt steering wheel, visor mirrors, bodyside moldings.		
Safety		
Antilock brakes	400	350
Comfort & Convenience Features		
Air conditioning	750	650
AM/FM/cassette, Base	320	250
AM/FM/CD player, Base	425	350
Cinco	125	NA
Power door locks	95	75
Appearance and Miscellaneous		
Rear spoiler, Base	85	65
Alloy wheels	275	225

KIA SEDONA

Kia Sedona

Front-wheel-drive minivan

Base price range: $18,995-$20,995. Built in South Korea.

Also consider: Dodge Caravan, Honda Odyssey, Toyota Sienna

FOR • Passenger and cargo room • Instruments/controls • Interior storage space   **AGAINST** • Acceleration • Steering/handling • Brake-pedal feel

This South Korean automaker's first minivan has standard V6

KIA

power and 7-passenger seating. Sedona comes in a single body length and is about the size of a Toyota Sienna. Base LX and uplevel EX models are offered. Both use a 195-hp 3.5-liter V6 teamed with a 5-speed automatic transmission. Dual sliding rear side doors are standard, but power doors and side airbags are unavailable. ABS is optional. The LX's 2nd-row seat is a bench; the EX has buckets, plus standard heated outside mirrors, fog lights, keyless entry, and alloy wheels. EX-only options include a sunroof and leather upholstery. Kia is owned by Hyundai and duplicates Hyundai's warranty: 5-year/60,000-mi. bumper-to-bumper, 10/100,000 powertrain, and 5-year/unlimited roadside assistance.

RATINGS

	EX w/ABS
ACCELERATION	3
FUEL ECONOMY	3
RIDE QUALITY	6
STEERING/HANDLING	3
QUIETNESS	6
INSTRUMENTS/CONTROLS	8
ROOM/COMFORT (FRONT)	8
ROOM/COMFORT (REAR)	7
CARGO ROOM	9
VALUE	6

Korean automakers stake their fortunes on delivering more features-per-dollar than class competitors. On that basis, Sedona trumps all rivals. Additionally, Kia says its comprehensive warranty is the No. 1 reason buyers purchase its vehicles. Combine features and warranty coverage, and Sedona packs enough value to offset its performance shortfalls. However, Kia's customer satisfaction ratings and resale values are low.

TOTAL	59

Average total for minivans: 56.0

ENGINES

	dohc V6
Size, liters/cu. in.	3.5/213
Horsepower @ rpm	195 @ 5500
Torque (lb-ft) @ rpm	218 @ 3500
Availability	S

EPA city/highway mpg
5-speed automatic	15/20

PRICES

Kia Sedona	Retail Price	Dealer Invoice
LX 4-door van	$18995	NA
EX 4-door van	20995	NA

Prices are accurate at time of publication; subject to manufacturer's change.

KIA

	Retail Price	Dealer Invoice
Destination charge	$595	$595

STANDARD EQUIPMENT

LX: 3.5-liter dohc engine, 5-speed automatic transmission, dual front airbags, front and rear air conditioning, power steering, tilt steering wheel, cruise control, cloth upholstery, 7-passenger seating, front bucket seats w/driver seat lumbar adjustment, center console, cupholders, second and third row bench seats, dual sliding rear doors, power mirrors, power front windows, power door locks, AM/FM/cassette, digital clock, tachometer, variable intermittent wipers w/deicer, map lights, visor mirrors, rear defogger, intermittent rear wiper/washer, rear privacy glass, 215/70R15 tires, wheel covers.

EX adds: 8-way power driver seat w/power lumbar support, 4-way power passenger seat, second row bucket seats, leather-wrapped steering wheel, heated power mirrors, power rear quarter windows, remote keyless entry, AM/FM/cassette/CD player, illuminated visor mirrors, trip computer, automatic headlights, roof rack, fog lights, alloy wheels.

OPTIONAL EQUIPMENT
Safety
Antilock brakes	595	NA

Comfort & Convenience Features
Leather upholstery, EX	850	NA
Power sunroof, EX	575	NA
AM/FM/CD player, LX	195	NA
Universal garage door opener, EX	125	NA

Appearance and Miscellaneous
Roof rack, LX	175	NA
Rear spoiler	170	NA

KIA SPECTRA

Front-wheel-drive subcompact car

2001 base price range: $10,845-$14,170. Built in South Korea.

Also consider: Ford Focus, Mazda Protege, Toyota Echo

FOR • Fuel economy **AGAINST** • Acceleration (automatic) • Noise • Rear seat room • Cargo room

Spectra is the larger and costlier of Kia's two subcompact cars. It

Specifications begin on page 551.

KIA

Kia Spectra

comes as a 4-dr sedan and hatchback with a 4-cyl engine, manual or automatic transmission, and optional antilock 4-wheel disc brakes. The sedan was previously called the Sephia. Exterior and interior styling is slightly revised for 2002 and a driver's lumbar support and automatic on/off headlights are among new features. Kia also adds sound-deadening measures in an effort to reduce noise levels. Side airbags are unavailable. Kia is owned by Hyundai and uses that South Korean automaker's warranty coverage: 5 years/50,000 mi. basic, 10/100,000 powertrain, 5/unlimited roadside assistance.

RATINGS	Sedan, man.	Hatchback w/ABS, auto.
ACCELERATION	4	3
FUEL ECONOMY	6	6
RIDE QUALITY	3	3
STEERING/HANDLING	3	5
QUIETNESS	3	3
INSTRUMENTS/CONTROLS	6	6
ROOM/COMFORT (FRONT)	5	5
ROOM/COMFORT (REAR)	3	3
CARGO ROOM	2	3
VALUE	2	2

Spectra is a better value in every way than the Rio, at not that much more money. It's a generally competent car overall, too, though Kia's customer satisfaction ratings and resale values are quite low. Bottom line: Kia banks on its comprehensive warranty to attract buyers.

TOTAL	37	39

Average total for subcompact cars: 43.7

KIA

ENGINES

	dohc I4
Size, liters/cu. in.	1.8/109
Horsepower @ rpm	126 @ 6000
Torque (lb-ft) @ rpm	108 @ 4500
Availability	S

EPA city/highway mpg

5-speed manual	24/32
4-speed automatic	22/30

2002 prices unavailable at time of publication.

PRICES

2001 Kia Spectra

	Retail Price	Dealer Invoice
Sephia Base 4-door sedan, manual	$10845	$9846
Sephia Base 4-door sedan, automatic	11820	10706
Sephia LS 4-door sedan, manual	12445	11209
Sephia LS 4-door sedan, automatic	13420	12069
Spectra GS 4-door hatchback, manual	10955	9996
Spectra GS 4-door hatchback, automatic	11970	10856
Spectra GSX 4-door hatchback, manual	13195	11995
Spectra GSX 4-door hatchback, automatic	14170	12855
Destination charge	495	495

STANDARD EQUIPMENT

Sephia Base/Spectra GS: 1.8-liter dohc 4-cylinder engine, 5-speed manual or 4-speed automatic transmission, dual front airbags, emergency inside trunk release (Sephia), variable-assist power steering, cloth upholstery, front bucket seats, driver seat front cushion tilt, center console, cupholders, split folding rear seat, AM/FM/cassette, tachometer (Spectra GS), rear defogger, passenger-side visor mirror (Spectra GS), remote fuel-door/decklid release, intermittent wipers, dual remote outside mirrors, 185/65R14 tires, wheel covers.

Sephia LS adds to Sephia Base: air conditioning, tilt steering wheel, power windows, power door locks, tachometer, passenger-side visor mirror.

Spectra GSX adds to Spectra GS: air conditioning, tilt leather-wrapped steering wheel, power windows, power door locks, rear spoiler, bodyside cladding, alloy wheels.

OPTIONAL EQUIPMENT
Major Packages

Cruise Pkg., LS	400	350

Specifications begin on page 551.

KIA

	Retail Price	Dealer Invoice
GSX	$425	$350

Cruise control, power mirrors, variable intermittent wipers, upgraded sound system.

Sport Pkg., GS	499	375

Side skirts, front and rear air dams, rear spoiler. Std. GSX.

Safety

Antilock brakes, LS, GSX	800	745

Includes 4-wheel disc brakes.

Comfort & Convenience Features

Air conditioning, Base	900	745
GS	960	805
Cruise control, LS	250	200
GSX	275	225
AM/FM/CD player, LS, GSX	295	245
CD changer, LS, GSX	335	270

Requires AM/FM/CD player.

Remote keyless entry, LS, GSX	250	165

Appearance and Miscellaneous

Rear wiper/washer, Spectra	125	95
Rear spoiler, Base, LS	175	132
Alloy wheels, LS	340	274

KIA SPORTAGE

Kia Sportage 4-door wagon

Rear- or 4-wheel-drive compact sport-utility vehicle
Base price range: $14,645-$19,220. Built in South Korea.
Also consider: Ford Escape, Honda CR-V, Subaru

Prices are accurate at time of publication; subject to manufacturer's change.

KIA

Forester

FOR • Cargo room • Maneuverability • Visibility **AGAINST** • Acceleration (4-door) • Ride • Noise • Interior materials • Rear-seat entry/exit (2-door)

Sportage comes as a 4-dr wagon and a shorter 2-dr semi-convertible with a rear folding soft top. Both are among the few compact SUVs with body-on-frame instead of unibody construction. They share a 4-cyl engine. Wagons offer rear-wheel drive and 4WD, manual and automatic transmission. Convertibles come with 2WD and automatic transmission or with 4WD and manual. The 4WD system must be disengaged on dry pavement but includes low-range gearing. ABS is optional. Side airbags are unavailable, but the industry's only driver's knee airbag is standard. New for 2002 is an optional exterior trim package that includes two-tone body cladding and a hard-face spare tire cover. Kia is owned by Hyundai; both are based in South Korea and share warranty coverage of 5 years/50,000 mi. basic, 10/100,000 powertrain, 5/unlimited roadside assistance.

RATINGS

	Conv 4WD, man.	Wgn 4WD, auto.
ACCELERATION	2	1
FUEL ECONOMY	5	5
RIDE QUALITY	1	2
STEERING/HANDLING	2	2
QUIETNESS	1	2
INSTRUMENTS/CONTROLS	4	4
ROOM/COMFORT (FRONT)	4	4
ROOM/COMFORT (REAR)	1	2
CARGO ROOM	6	7
VALUE	1	2

Sportage trails other compact SUVs in performance and refinement. It depreciates faster too, and Kia ranks low in consumer satisfaction surveys.

TOTAL	27	31

Average total for compact sport-utility vehicles: 44.4

ENGINES

	dohc I4
Size, liters/cu. in.	2.0/122
Horsepower @ rpm	130 @ 5500
Torque (lb-ft) @ rpm	127 @ 4000
Availability	S
EPA city/highway mpg	
5-speed manual	19/22[1]
4-speed automatic	18/21

1. 19/23 w/2WD.

Specifications begin on page 551.

KIA

PRICES

Kia Sportage

	Retail Price	Dealer Invoice
2WD Base 2-door convertible, automatic	$14645	$13374
2WD Base 4-door wagon, manual	17095	15459
2WD Base 4-door wagon, automatic	18095	16369
4WD Base 2-door convertible, manual	15145	13708
4WD Base 4-door wagon, manual	18220	16379
4WD Base 4-door wagon, automatic	19220	17289
Destination charge	495	495

STANDARD EQUIPMENT

Base convertible: 2.0-liter dohc 4-cylinder engine, 5-speed manual or 4-speed automatic transmission, dual front airbags, driver-side knee airbag, power steering, tilt steering wheel, cloth upholstery, front bucket seats w/driver-side lumbar adjuster, center console, cupholders, folding rear seat, power mirrors, power windows, power door locks, tachometer, digital clock, remote fuel-door release, variable intermittent wipers, theft-deterrent system, rear folding soft top, rear-mounted full-size spare tire, 205/75SR15 tires. **4WD** models add: 4-wheel drive, 2-speed transfer case.

Base wagon adds: air conditioning, split folding rear seat, AM/FM/cassette, rear defogger, rear privacy glass. *Deletes:* rear folding soft top, alloy wheels. **4WD** adds: 4-wheel drive, 2-speed transfer case.

OPTIONAL EQUIPMENT

Major Packages

Two-Tone Pkg., wagon	325	270

Two-tone cladding, roof rack, spare tire cover.

Safety

Antilock brakes, wagon	490	410

Comfort & Convenience Features

Air conditioning, convertible	925	770
Cruise control	250	200
AM/FM/cassette, convertible	350	280
AM/FM/CD player, convertible	475	375
CD changer	335	270

Convertible requires AM/FM/CD player.

Remote keyless entry	225	140
Rear wiper/washer, wagon	145	120

Appearance and Miscellaneous

Rear spoiler, wagon	189	143

Prices are accurate at time of publication; subject to manufacturer's change.

KIA • LAND ROVER

	Retail Price	Dealer Invoice
Roof rack, wagon	$215	$170
Special Purpose, Wheels and Tires		
Alloy wheels, convertible	375	309

LAND ROVER DISCOVERY

Land Rover Discovery Series II HSE

All-wheel-drive midsize sport-utility vehicle
2001 base price range: $33,350-$36,350. Built in England.
Also consider: Acura MDX, Ford Explorer, Lexus RX 300

FOR • Ride • Exterior finish • Cargo room **AGAINST** • Instruments/controls • Fuel economy • Entry/exit

A new top-line HSE model with DVD entertainment and navigation systems is added to Land Rover's midsize SUV for 2002. The HSE joins base SD and midline SE versions of this British-built SUV. All have a 4.0-liter V8, automatic transmission, antilock 4-wheel disc brakes, and all-wheel drive with low-range gearing and traction control. An available Rear Seat Package increases passenger capacity from five to seven and changes badging to SD7, SE7 and HSE7. An optional Suspension Package for SE and HSE adds Land Rover's Active Cornering Enhancement (ACE) suspension that uses hydraulic rams to reduce body lean in turns. Also included in the package is the rear self-leveling suspension that's standard on 7-seat models. Standard on SE and HSE are leather upholstery and 18-inch wheels vs. the SD's 16s. Land Rover, which is owned by Ford, plans to offer a series of limited-production Discoverys during the model year, including the off-road-oriented Kalahari edition.

Specifications begin on page 551.

LAND ROVER

RATINGS	SD	SE w/Performance Pkg.
ACCELERATION	3	3
FUEL ECONOMY	2	2
RIDE QUALITY	3	4
STEERING/HANDLING	2	4
QUIETNESS	3	3
INSTRUMENTS/CONTROLS	2	2
ROOM/COMFORT (FRONT)	6	6
ROOM/COMFORT (REAR)	6	6
CARGO ROOM	7	7
VALUE	2	2

Discovery is an old soldier selling mainly on its off-road prowess and the toney Land Rover name, but most every similarly priced rival offers superior road manners, refinement, and materials quality.

TOTAL	36	39

Average total for midsize sport-utility vehicles: 49.6

ENGINES

	ohv V8
Size, liters/cu. in.	4.0/241
Horsepower @ rpm	188 @ 4750
Torque (lb-ft) @ rpm	250 @ 2600
Availability	S
EPA city/highway mpg	
4-speed automatic	13/17

2002 prices unavailable at time of publication.

PRICES

2001 Land Rover Discovery	Retail Price	Dealer Invoice
SD 4-door wagon	$33350	$29685
LE 4-door wagon	34350	30570
SE 4-door wagon	36350	32350
Destination charge	645	645

STANDARD EQUIPMENT

SD: 4.0-liter V8 engine, 4-speed automatic transmission, all-wheel drive, 2-speed transfer case, traction control, Hill Descent Control, dual front airbags, antilock 4-wheel disc brakes, air conditioning w/dual-zone control, outside temperature indicator, power steering, leather-wrapped tilt steering wheel, cruise control, vinyl upholstery, 8-way power front bucket seats, center console, cupholders, split folding rear seat, heated power mirrors, power windows, power door locks, remote keyless entry, AM/FM/cassette, digital clock, steering wheel radio controls, tachometer, rear defogger, rear wiper/washer,

Prices are accurate at time of publication; subject to manufacturer's change.

LAND ROVER

illuminated visor mirrors, automatic day/night rearview mirror, compass, map lights, variable intermittent wipers, remote fuel-door release, rear fog lights, theft-deterrent system, rear-mounted full-size spare tire, 255/65HR16 tires, alloy wheels.

LE adds: cloth/leather upholstery, wood interior trim, front fog lights, headlight washers.

SE adds: leather upholstery, front seat power lumbar adjustment, dual power sunroofs, Phillips/Lear sound system, in-dash 6-disc CD changer, universal garage door opener, cargo cover, Class III towing hitch receiver.

OPTIONAL EQUIPMENT

	Retail Price	Dealer Invoice
Major Packages		
Rear Seat Pkg.	$1750	$1558
Forward-facing third-row seats, hydraulic rear step, remote radio controls (SE), self-leveling rear suspension.		
Performance Pkg., SE	2900	2581
Active Cornering Enhancement, 255/55HR18 tires, special alloy wheels.		
Cold Climate Pkg.	500	445
Heated windshield, heated front seats.		
Comfort & Convenience Features		
Dual power sunroofs, SD, LE	1500	1335
Rear air conditioning, LE, SE	750	668
Special Purpose, Wheels and Tires		
Self-leveling rear suspension, LE, SE	750	668

LAND ROVER FREELANDER

Land Rover Freelander

Specifications begin on page 551.

LAND ROVER

All-wheel-drive compact sport-utility vehicle
Base price range: $24,975-$31,575. Built in England.
Also consider: Ford Escape, Honda CR-V, Mazda Tribute

FOR • Maneuverability • Visibility **AGAINST**
• Instruments/controls

Freelander is the first compact SUV from Britain's luxury 4x4 maker. This unibody 4-dr wagon uses a 175-hp V6 and 5-speed automatic transmission. All-wheel drive is standard; it doesn't have low-range gearing but includes traction control and hill descent control designed to limit speed when going down steep grades. ABS is standard, but side airbags are unavailable. Other standard features include power windows, air conditioning, heated power folding mirrors, and a class-exclusive power up/down rear window in a swing-out cargo door. Base S, SE, and top-line HSE models are offered. Standard on SE and HSE are leather upholstery and 17-inch wheels vs. 16s. The HSE includes a navigation system, plus a power sunroof that's optional on SE. Land Rover is owned by Ford. The British-built Freelander has slightly larger exterior dimensions than the Ford Escape/Mazda Tribute, but is an older, unrelated design.

RATINGS

	HSE
ACCELERATION	4
FUEL ECONOMY	4
RIDE QUALITY	5
STEERING/HANDLING	5
QUIETNESS	5
INSTRUMENTS/CONTROLS	4
ROOM/COMFORT (FRONT)	6
ROOM/COMFORT (REAR)	5
CARGO ROOM	5
VALUE	3

Fault Freelander for premium pricing, prosaic interior decor, and awkward details like the silly rear-seat-release design. It is solid, comfortable, and competent, but its key asset is whatever cachet the Land Rover image carries.

TOTAL	**46**

Average total for compact sport-utility vehicles: 44.4

ENGINES

	dohc V6
Size, liters/cu. in.	2.5/152
Horsepower @ rpm	175 @ 6250
Torque (lb-ft) @ rpm	177 @ 4000
Availability	S

Prices are accurate at time of publication; subject to manufacturer's change.

LAND ROVER

EPA city/highway mpg

dohc V6

5-speed automatic 16/19

PRICES

Land Rover Freelander	Retail Price	Dealer Invoice
S 4-door wagon	$24975	$23227
SE 4-door wagon	27775	25553
HSE 4-door wagon	31575	28773
Destination charge	625	625

STANDARD EQUIPMENT

S: 2.5-liter V6 dohc engine, 5-speed automatic transmission, all-wheel drive, traction control, hill descent control, dual front airbags, antilock brakes, hill descent control, air conditioning, power steering, tilt leather-wrapped steering wheel, cruise control, cloth upholstery, front bucket seats, center console, cupholders, split folding rear seat, heated power mirrors, power windows, power rear window, power door locks, remote keyless entry, AM/FM/CD player, digital clock, variable intermittent wipers, rear defogger, rear wiper/washer, 215/65R16 tires, alloy wheels.

SE adds: leather upholstery, steering wheel radio controls, illuminated visor mirrors, cargo cover, rear privacy glass, roof rails, 225/55R17 tires.

HSE adds: navigation system, power sunroof, Harman/Kardon sound system, 6-disc CD changer.

OPTIONAL EQUIPMENT
Comfort & Convenience Features

Power sunroof, SE	875	NA
Heated front seats	300	NA
Harman/Kardon sound system, S, SE	750	690

LAND ROVER RANGE ROVER

All-wheel-drive full-size sport-utility vehicle

2001 base price range: $62,000-$68,000. Built in England.

Also consider: BMW X5, Lexus LX 470, Mercedes-Benz M-Class

FOR • Passenger and cargo room **AGAINST** • Fuel economy • Entry/exit

Land Rover's flagship loses its base 4.6 SE model for 2002, leav-

Specifications begin on page 551.

LAND ROVER

Land Rover Range Rover HSE

ing only the top-line 4.6 HSE version. This British-built SUV has a 4.6-liter V8 and all-wheel drive that includes low-range gearing. Standard are automatic transmission, antilock 4-wheel disc brakes, traction control, front side airbags, and driver-adjustable self-leveling suspension. Also standard is a Navigation system that includes features designed for off-road use. The 4.6 SE had come with 16-inch wheels and lower-grade interior trim and had offered the navigation system as an option. Land Rover is owned by Ford.

RATINGS

	4.6 HSE
ACCELERATION	4
FUEL ECONOMY	2
RIDE QUALITY	4
STEERING/HANDLING	2
QUIETNESS	4
INSTRUMENTS/CONTROLS	2
ROOM/COMFORT (FRONT)	9
ROOM/COMFORT (REAR)	7
CARGO ROOM	7
VALUE	1

Range Rover attracts a small but enthusiastic following who appreciate its upper-crust image and impressive interior decor. However, it's an aged design with unexceptional performance and relatively limited cargo room. Less money buys similar luxury, better performance, and likely superior reliability in any number of premium SUVs.

TOTAL	42

Average total for full-size sport-utility vehicles: 50.9

ENGINES

	ohv V8
Size, liters/cu. in.	4.6/278
Horsepower @ rpm	222 @ 4750
Torque (lb-ft) @ rpm	300 @ 2600

Prices are accurate at time of publication; subject to manufacturer's change.

LAND ROVER

	ohv V8
Availability	S
EPA city/highway mpg	
4-speed automatic	12/15

2002 prices unavailable at time of publication.

PRICES

2001 Land Rover Range Rover	Retail Price	Dealer Invoice
4.6 SE 4-door wagon	$62000	$54870
4.6 HSE 4-door wagon	68000	60180
Destination charge	665	665

STANDARD EQUIPMENT

4.6 SE: 4.6-liter V8 engine, 4-speed automatic transmission, all-wheel drive, 2-speed transfer case, locking center differential, front and rear traction control, dual front airbags, front side airbags, antilock 4-wheel disc brakes, variable-assist power steering, tilt/telescopic leather-wrapped steering wheel, cruise control, air conditioning w/dual-zone automatic climate control, interior air filter, leather upholstery, heated 10-way power front bucket seats w/memory, center console, cupholders, split folding rear seat, wood interior trim, heated power mirrors w/memory and automatic day/night, outside mirror tilt-down back-up aid, power windows, power door locks, remote keyless entry, Harman/Kardon AM/FM/weatherband/cassette w/in-dash 6-disc CD changer, steering-wheel radio controls, tachometer, power sunroof, trip computer, automatic day/night rearview mirror, universal garage-door opener, remote fuel-door release, rear defogger, variable intermittent wipers, variable-intermittent rear wiper/washer, illuminated visor mirrors, map lights, cargo cover, theft-deterrent system, headlight wiper/washers, front and rear fog lights, trailer hitch and wiring harness, height-adjustable and automatic load-leveling suspension, full-size spare tire, 265/65HR16 tires, alloy wheels.

4.6 HSE adds: navigation system, upgraded Harman/Kardon sound system, upgraded leather and wood interior trim, 255/55HR18 tires.

OPTIONAL EQUIPMENT
Major Packages

Navigation/Audio Pkg., SE	3000	2650
Includes upgraded Harman/Kardon sound system.		

Comfort & Convenience Features

Wood/leather-wrapped steering wheel, HSE	400	354
Color-keyed carpets/seat piping, HSE	750	550

Specifications begin on page 551.

LEXUS

LEXUS ES 300

Lexus ES 300

Front-wheel-drive near-luxury car
Base price: $31,505. Built in Japan.
Also consider: Acura TL, Infiniti I35, Mercedes-Benz C-Class

FOR • Acceleration • Ride • Quietness • Build quality • Interior materials **AGAINST** • Rear visibility • Navigation system controls

Redesigned for 2002 with a greater luxury emphasis, ES 300 gains several features, including curtain side airbags, a 5-speed automatic transmission in place of a 4-speed, and an optional navigation system. This Lexus again shares its basic design with the redesigned 2002 Camry from parent Toyota. A 3.0-liter V6 returns with unchanged power. Styling is new, and exterior dimensions grow 2 inches in wheelbase, about 1 in length and width, and 2.4 in height. Leather upholstery is again optional, but new standard features include 16-inch wheels (replacing 15s), a trip computer, dual-zone automatic climate control, and auto up/down for all side windows. The available dashboard navigation screen has a 3-position tilt feature. Other options include premium Mark Levinson audio, power rear sunshade, high-intensity headlamps packaged with rain-sensing windshield wipers, and in-dash or console-mount CD changer. Standard ABS continues, but full-power brake assist is now included with optional antiskid or traction systems. Lexus' Adaptive Variable Suspension AVS option furnishes driver-selectable shock-absorber settings. Base price is unchanged from 2001.

RATINGS	Base	Base w/nav. sys. and AVS
ACCELERATION	6	6
FUEL ECONOMY	5	5
RIDE QUALITY	8	7

Prices are accurate at time of publication; subject to manufacturer's change.

LEXUS

	Base	Base w/nav. sys. and AVS
STEERING/HANDLING	6	6
QUIETNESS	9	9
INSTRUMENTS/CONTROLS	8	6
ROOM/COMFORT (FRONT)	8	8
ROOM/COMFORT (REAR)	6	6
CARGO ROOM	4	4
VALUE	7	5

With the IS 300 for sports-sedan lovers, Lexus remakes the ES into a baby LS 430, offering more comfort, refinement, and amenities, plus somewhat improved road manners. No excitement machine, just a very pleasant near-luxury sedan that's likely to have broad appeal.

TOTAL	67	62

Average total for near-luxury cars: 54.5

ENGINES

	dohc V6
Size, liters/cu. in.	3.0/183
Horsepower @ rpm	210 @ 5800
Torque (lb-ft) @ rpm	220 @ 4400
Availability	S
EPA city/highway mpg	
5-speed automatic	21/29

PRICES

Lexus ES 300	Retail Price	Dealer Invoice
Base 4-door sedan	$31505	$27935
Destination charge	575	575

STANDARD EQUIPMENT

Base: 3.0-liter dohc V6 engine, 5-speed automatic transmission, dual front airbags, front side airbags, curtain side airbags, antilock 4-wheel disc brakes, emergency inside trunk release, daytime running lights, air conditioning w/dual-zone automatic climate control, power steering, tilt leather-wrapped steering wheel, cruise control, cloth upholstery, front bucket seats, 10-way power driver seat w/power lumbar adjustment, 8-way power passenger seat, center console, cupholders, wood interior trim, heated power mirrors w/driver-side automatic day/night, power windows, power door locks, remote keyless entry, AM/FM/cassette/CD player, digital clock, tachometer, power sunroof, automatic day/night rearview mirror, universal garage door opener, overhead console, illuminated visor mirrors, rear defogger, trip computer, map lights, variable intermittent wipers,

Specifications begin on page 551.

LEXUS

remote fuel door and decklid release, automatic-off headlights, floormats, theft-deterrent system, fog lights, full-size spare tire, 215/60VR16 tires, alloy wheels.

OPTIONAL EQUIPMENT

	Retail Price	Dealer Invoice
Major Packages		
Leather Trim Pkg.	$1560	$1248
Leather upholstery, driver seat and mirror memory.		
Premium Pkg.	2110	1688
Leather upholstery, driver seat and mirror memory, in-dash 6-disc CD changer.		
Mark Levinson Audio Pkg.	3010	2363
Premium Pkg. plus Mark Levinson sound system.		
Navigation System Pkg.	3960	3261
Premium Pkg. plus navigation system. Moves in-dash CD changer to console.		
Navigation System/Mark Levinson Audio Pkg.	4860	3936
Navigation System Pkg. plus Mark Levinson sound system. Moves in-dash CD changer to console.		
Safety		
Antiskid system	650	520
Includes traction control, full-power brake assist. Requires leather upholstery.		
Comfort & Convenience Features		
Heated front seats	440	352
Requires leather upholstery.		
Wood/leather-wrapped steering wheel	330	264
Requires leather upholstery.		
Appearance and Miscellaneous		
High-intensity discharge headlights	640	512
Includes rain-sensing wipers. Requires leather upholstery.		
Adaptive variable suspension	620	496
Requires Navigation/Mark Levinson Audio Pkg., antiskid system, high-intensity discharge headlights.		

Postproduction options also available.

LEXUS GS 300/430

Rear-wheel-drive luxury car
Base price range: $38,605-$47,405. Built in Japan.
Also consider: BMW 5-Series, Jaguar S-Type, Mercedes-Benz E-Class

Prices are accurate at time of publication; subject to manufacturer's change.

LEXUS

Lexus GS 430

FOR • Acceleration • Steering/handling • Quietness • Build quality • Exterior finish • Interior materials **AGAINST** • Fuel economy • Navigation system controls

Navigation-system revisions aimed at greater convenience are the only change of note to these luxury sedans for 2002. The rear-wheel drive GS 300/430 and front-drive ES 300 share the middle range of the Lexus lineup, but the GS is designed to have a sportier personality. The GS 300 has a 3.0-liter inline 6-cyl engine, the GS 430 a 4.3 V8. Standard on both are 5-speed automatic transmission, front side airbags, antiskid system, traction control, and antilock 4-wheel disc brakes. The GS 430 adds standard leather upholstery and memory seats. Both are optional on the GS 300. Available on either model is a DVD navigation system. For '02 it gets new functions, including multiroute calculation, simplified graphics, and route preview. It also gains a faster computer intended speed up route processing and map scrolling.

RATINGS

	GS 300	GS 430 w/nav. sys.
ACCELERATION	6	8
FUEL ECONOMY	4	4
RIDE QUALITY	9	8
STEERING/HANDLING	7	8
QUIETNESS	8	8
INSTRUMENTS/CONTROLS	8	6
ROOM/COMFORT (FRONT)	8	8
ROOM/COMFORT (REAR)	4	4
CARGO ROOM	4	4

Specifications begin on page 551.

LEXUS

	GS 300	GS 430 w/nav. sys.
VALUE	6	4

Neither GS model is quite as athletic as the best German sports sedans, but these posh Lexuses compensate with their smooth-ride, plentiful features, and quality workmanship. Though not inexpensive, both GSs earn our Recommended nod for the value they provide against 6-cyl and V8 rivals.

TOTAL	64	62
Average total for luxury cars: 59.4		

ENGINES

	dohc I6	dohc V8
Size, liters/cu. in.	3.0/183	4.3/262
Horsepower @ rpm	220 @ 5800	300 @ 5600
Torque (lb-ft) @ rpm	220 @ 3800	325 @ 3400
Availability	S[1]	S[2]
EPA city/highway mpg		
5-speed automatic	18/25	18/23

1. GS 300. 2. GS 430.

PRICES

Lexus GS 300/430	Retail Price	Dealer Invoice
GS 300 4-door sedan	$38605	$33972
GS 430 4-door sedan	47405	41242
Destination charge	575	575

STANDARD EQUIPMENT

GS 300: 3.0-liter dohc 6-cylinder engine, 5-speed automatic transmission w/manual shift-capability, traction control, dual front airbags, front side airbags, front curtain side airbags, antilock 4-wheel disc brakes, antiskid system, daytime running lights, air conditioning w/automatic dual-zone climate control, interior air filter, power steering, power tilt/telescopic leather-wrapped steering wheel, cruise control, cloth upholstery, 10-way power front bucket seats w/power lumbar adjustment, center console, cupholders, wood interior trim, heated power mirrors w/automatic day/night, power windows, power door locks, remote keyless entry, AM/FM/cassette, digital clock, automatic day/night rearview mirror, compass, variable intermittent wipers, rear defogger, outside-temperature indicator, illuminated visor mirrors, universal garage door opener, remote fuel-door and trunk releases, map lights, automatic headlights, floormats, theft-deterrent system, fog lights, 215/60VR16 tires, alloy wheels.

GS 430 adds: 4.3-liter dohc V8 engine, leather upholstery, memory system (driver seat, steering wheel, outside mirrors), high-intensity headlights, 225/55VR16 tires.

Prices are accurate at time of publication; subject to manufacturer's change.

LEXUS

OPTIONAL EQUIPMENT
Major Packages

	Retail Price	Dealer Invoice
LA Leather Trim Pkg., GS 300	$1660	$1328

Leather upholstery, memory system (driver seat, steering wheel, outside mirrors).

PM Premium Pkg., GS 300	3740	2992

Leather Trim Pkg., power sunroof, in-dash 6-disc CD changer.

PM Premium Pkg., GS 430	2520	2016

Heated front seats, power sunroof, in-dash 6-disc CD changer.

ND Navigation System Pkg., GS 300	6695	5456
GS 430	4520	3716

Premium Pkg. plus navigation system, heated front seats, high-intensity headlights.

NL Navigation/Mark Levinson Radio

System Pkg., GS 300	7945	6394
GS 430	5770	4654

Navigation System Pkg. plus Premium Mark Levinson Radio System Pkg.

LI Premium Mark Levinson Radio System Pkg.,

GS 300	5945	4694
GS 430	3770	2954

Premium Pkg. plus Mark Levinson sound sytem, heated front seats, high-intensity headlights.

Comfort & Convenience Features

Heated front seats, GS 300	440	352

Requires Premium Pkg.

In-dash 6-disc CD changer	1080	864
Power sunroof	1000	800
Wood/leather-wrapped steering wheel, GS 430	300	240

Appearance and Miscellaneous

Rear spoiler, GS 430	440	352
235/45ZR17 tires, GS 430	215	172
Chrome alloy wheels	1700	850

Postproduction options also available.

LEXUS IS 300

Rear-wheel-drive near-luxury car
Base price range: $29,435-$32,305. Built in Japan.
Also consider: Acura TL, Audi A4, BMW 3-Series, Mercedes-Benz C-Class

Specifications begin on page 551.

LEXUS

Lexus IS 300 SportCross

FOR • Acceleration • Brake performance • Build quality • Steering/handling **AGAINST** • Rear-seat room

A wagon body style, a manual-transmission version, and standard curtain side airbags are 2002 additions to this compact sports sedan. IS 300's inline 6-cyl engine is unchanged. The sedan with the 5-speed manual has a firmer suspension than the 5-speed automatic-transmission model. Lexus labels the wagon the SportCross. It comes only with the automatic, plus a slightly different front-end look, a fold-down front passenger seat, a split-fold rear seat, and an upgraded stereo. All 2002 IS models get standard curtain side airbags, Lexus's full-power Brake Assist feature, and self-dimming inside mirror with integral compass. Options expand with addition of an antiskid system and a navigation system with dashboard display screen.

RATINGS	Base sdn, man.	Base sdn, auto.	SportCross w/nav. sys.
ACCELERATION	7	7	7
FUEL ECONOMY	4	4	4
RIDE QUALITY	6	6	6
STEERING/HANDLING	8	8	8
QUIETNESS	6	6	6
INSTRUMENTS/CONTROLS	6	6	4
ROOM/COMFORT (FRONT)	6	6	6
ROOM/COMFORT (REAR)	4	4	4
CARGO ROOM	2	2	6
VALUE	4	4	4

Rival BMW 3-Series and Audi A4 models feel more substantial, have "built for the autobahn" cachet, and perhaps more ultimate dynamic ability. But the IS 300 is sporty driving fun Lexus-style, and that's no bad thing.

TOTAL	53	53	55

Average total for near-luxury cars: 54.5

Prices are accurate at time of publication; subject to manufacturer's change.

CONSUMER GUIDE®

LEXUS

ENGINES

	dohc I6
Size, liters/cu. in.	3.0/183
Horsepower @ rpm	215 @ 5800
Torque (lb-ft) @ rpm	218 @ 3800
Availability	S

EPA city/highway mpg
5-speed manual	18/25
4-speed automatic	18/25

PRICES

Lexus IS 300	Retail Price	Dealer Invoice
Base 4-door sedan, manual	$29435	$25091
Base 4-door sedan, automatic	30805	27108
SportCross 4-door wagon, automatic	32305	28428
Destination charge	545	545

STANDARD EQUIPMENT

Base: 3.0-liter dohc 6-cylinder engine, 5-speed manual or 5-speed automatic transmission w/manual-shift capability, traction control, dual front airbags, front side airbags, front curtain side airbags, antilock 4-wheel disc brakes, daytime running lights, emergency inside trunk release, air conditioning w/automatic climate control, interior air filter, power steering, tilt leather-wrapped steering wheel, cruise control, cloth upholstery, front bucket seats, center console, cupholders, trunk pass-through, heated power mirrors, power windows, power door locks, remote keyless entry, AM/FM/cassette w/in-dash 6-disc CD changer, digital clock, tachometer, automatic day/night rearview mirror, compass, rear defogger, map lights, visor mirrors, floormats, theft-deterrent system, high-intensity discharge headlights, fog lights, 215/45ZR17 tires, alloy wheels.

SportCross adds: 5-speed automatic transmission w/manual-shift capability, fold-down front passenger seat, split folding rear seat, cargo cover, rear wiper/washer, rear spoiler, 215/45ZR17 front tires, 225/45ZR17 rear tires. *Deletes:* emergency inside trunk release, trunk pass-through.

OPTIONAL EQUIPMENT
Major Packages

LS Leather Pkg., Base	1805	1444
SportCross	1845	1476
Leather/ultra-suede upholstery, 8-way power front seats, universal garage door opener.		
LA Leather Pkg., Base	2105	1684

Specifications begin on page 551.

LEXUS

	Retail Price	Dealer Invoice
SportCross	$2145	$1716

Leather upholstery, 8-way power front seats, universal garage door opener.

Powertrain
Limited-slip differential	390	312

Safety
Antiskid system, Base w/automatic, SportCross	350	280

Includes limited-slip differential.

Comfort & Convenience Features
Navigation system	2000	1700
Power sunroof	500	400
Heated front seats	440	352

Requires Leather Pkg.

Appearance and Miscellaneous
Rear spoiler, Base	440	325
Polished alloy wheels	400	320

Post production options also available.

LEXUS LS 430

CG BEST BUY AUTO

Lexus LS 430

Rear-wheel-drive luxury car
Base price: $54,405. Built in Japan.
Also consider: Audi A8, BMW 7-Series, Mercedes-Benz S-Class/CL-Class

FOR • Acceleration • Ride • Quietness • Build quality
AGAINST • Automatic transmission performance

Prices are accurate at time of publication; subject to manufacturer's change.

LEXUS

• Instruments/controls

Lexus' flagship sedan gets a new lower-priced luxury package for '02. The LS 430's sole powerteam is a 4.3-liter V8 with 5-speed automatic transmission. Standard are a traction/antiskid system, antilock 4-wheel disc brakes, curtain side airbags, and a leather/wood interior. Firm Euro-Tuned suspension is a no-charge option but requires available 17-inch wheels. The new $6895 Custom Luxury Package includes a navigation system, heated/cooled front seats, heated rear seats, rear-seat audio controls, and cruise control that automatically maintains a safe following distance. This equipment had been in the $12,505 Ultra Luxury Package, which returns for 2002 at $12,485 and includes the Custom package, plus rear-seat climate controls, massaging rear seats, self-adjusting air suspension, and Lexus Link assistance service provided in conjunction with GM's OnStar system. Both packages require optional upgraded leather upholstery.

RATINGS	Base	Base w/Euro suspension	Base w/Ultra Lux. Pkg.
ACCELERATION	7	7	7
FUEL ECONOMY	5	5	5
RIDE QUALITY	10	9	10
STEERING/HANDLING	6	7	6
QUIETNESS	10	10	10
INSTRUMENTS/CONTROLS	5	5	5
ROOM/COMFORT (FRONT)	10	10	10
ROOM/COMFORT (REAR)	9	9	10
CARGO ROOM	6	6	6
VALUE	6	6	4

LS 430's starting price is competitive with that of V8 rivals, but can quickly climb. Ultra Luxury-equipped models approach the Mercedes-Benz S-Class in cost and techno overload. Even the new Custom Luxury Package has to be ordered with a minimum of $1460 in leather trim. Still, an LS in any form is unsurpassed for comfort, coddling, and refinement at the price.

TOTAL	74	74	73

Average total for luxury cars: 59.4

ENGINES

	dohc V8
Size, liters/cu. in.	4.3/262
Horsepower @ rpm	290 @ 5600
Torque (lb-ft) @ rpm	320 @ 3400
Availability	S
EPA city/highway mpg	
5-speed automatic	18/25

Specifications begin on page 551.

LEXUS

PRICES

Lexus LS 430	Retail Price	Dealer Invoice
Base 4-door sedan	$54405	$47332
Destination charge	575	575

STANDARD EQUIPMENT

Base: 4.3-liter dohc V8 engine, 5-speed automatic transmission, traction control, dual front airbags, front side airbags, curtain side airbags, antilock 4-wheel disc brakes, antiskid system, emergency inside trunk release, daytime running lights, power steering, power tilt/telescoping steering wheel, leather-wrapped/wood steering wheel, cruise control, air conditioning w/dual zone automatic climate control, leather upholstery, 14-way power driver seat, 10-way power passenger seat, front power headrests and lumbar adjustment, memory system (driver seat and headrest, steering wheel, mirrors), center console, cupholders, wood interior trim, heated power mirrors w/tilt-down back-up aid, automatic day/night rearview and outside mirrors, power windows, power door locks, remote keyless entry, AM/FM/cassette w/in-dash 6-disc CD changer, steering wheel radio controls, digital clock, tachometer, outside temperature indicator, trip computer, compass, rear defogger, illuminated visor mirrors, universal garage door opener, map lights, rain-sensing variable intermittent wipers, remote fuel-door and decklid release, automatic headlights, floormats, theft-deterrent sytem, high-intensity discharge headlights, fog lights, tool kit, full-size spare tire, 225/60HR16 tires, alloy wheels.

OPTIONAL EQUIPMENT
Major Packages

Custom Luxury Pkg. 6895 5554
Navigation system, climate controlled front seats, heated rear seats, power sunroof, Mark Levinson sound system, rear radio controls, dynamic laser cruise control (maintains distance from vehicle in front of car), power rear sunshade, power door closers, laminated side glass, front and rear obstacle detection system. Requires Nappa Leather or Nappa Leather/Semi Anilin Leather Interior Pkg.

Ultra Luxury
Pkg. 12485 10086
Custom Luxury Pkg. plus Lexus Link, rear air conditioning w/rear climate control and interior air filter, rear seat power adjusters and massage, rear seat cooler box in armrest, suede headliner, manual rear side-window sunshades, self-adjusting air suspension. Requires Nappa Leather or Nappa Leather/Semi Anilin Leather Interior Pkg.

Prices are accurate at time of publication; subject to manufacturer's change.

LEXUS

	Retail Price	Dealer Invoice
Navigation System Pkg.	$3980	$3284

Navigation system, power sunroof, heated front and rear seats.

| Mark Levinson Radio System Pkg. | 3220 | 2514 |

Mark Levinson sound system, power sunroof, heated front and rear seats.

| Navigation System/Radio System | 5220 | 4214 |

Navigation System Pkg. plus Mark Levinson sound system.

Comfort & Convenience Features

| Lexus Link | 1215 | 1015 |

Emergency and roadside assistance, travel advice and information. Includes one year service fee.

Power sunroof	1100	880
Heated front and rear seats	880	704
Nappa Leather Interior Pkg.	1460	1168

Upgraded leather upholstery. Requires Ultra Luxury Pkg. or Custom Luxury Pkg.

| Nappa Leather/Semi Anilin Leather Interior Pkg. | 2100 | 1680 |

Upgraded leather upholstery. Requires Ultra Luxury Pkg. or Custom Luxury Pkg.

Appearance and Miscellaneous

| Euro-Tuned Suspension | NC | NC |

Requires 225/55R17 tires.

| 225/55R17 tires | 100 | 80 |
| Chrome alloy wheels | 1800 | 900 |

Includes 225/55R17 tires.

Postproduction options also available.

LEXUS LX 470

All-wheel-drive full-size sport-utility vehicle

Base price: $61,855. Built in Japan.

Also consider: BMW X5, Cadillac Escalade and Escalade EXT, Lincoln Navigator

FOR • Acceleration • Passenger and cargo room • Ride • Build quality • Exterior finish • Interior materials **AGAINST** • Fuel economy • Rear entry/exit

A navigation system is standard instead of optional on Lexus's full-size SUV for '02. The LX 470 is basically an upscale Toyota Land Cruiser with Lexus styling cues. It has more standard equipment than Land Cruiser, but the same V8, automatic transmission, traction/antiskid control, antilock 4-wheel disc brakes, and all-wheel

Specifications begin on page 551.

LEXUS

Lexus LX 470

drive that includes low-range gearing. Exclusive to LX 470 is Adaptive Variable Suspension with driver-adjusted shock-absorber damping and selectable ride height. For '02, the navigation system gets revisions aimed at greater convenience. These include multi-route calculation, simplified graphics, and route preview, along with a faster computer designed to speed up route processing and map scrolling. The system can also play DVD movies on the system's dashboard screen, but only with the transmission in Park. LX 470 performance and accommodations are similar to those of Land Cruiser.

RATINGS	Base
ACCELERATION	5
FUEL ECONOMY	2
RIDE QUALITY	7
STEERING/HANDLING	4
QUIETNESS	8
INSTRUMENTS/CONTROLS	7
ROOM/COMFORT (FRONT)	9
ROOM/COMFORT (REAR)	8
CARGO ROOM	8
VALUE	2

LX 470 and Land Cruiser may be the nicest truck-style SUVs around. The Lexus boasts a longer warranty, the promise of better customer service, and extra functional and luxury features, though its elaborate suspension seems of minimal benefit.

TOTAL	60

Average total for full-size sport-utility vehicles: 50.9

ENGINES

	dohc V8
Size, liters/cu. in.	4.7/285

Prices are accurate at time of publication; subject to manufacturer's change.

LEXUS

	dohc V8
Horsepower @ rpm	230 @ 4800
Torque (lb-ft) @ rpm	320 @ 3400
Availability	S

EPA city/highway mpg
4-speed automatic 13/16

PRICES

Lexus LX 470	Retail Price	Dealer Invoice
Base 4-door wagon	$61855	$53813
Destination charge	575	575

STANDARD EQUIPMENT

Base: 4.7-liter dohc V8 engine, 4-speed automatic transmission, all-wheel drive, 2-speed transfer case, locking center differential and limited-slip rear differential, traction control, dual front airbags, antiskid system, antilock 4-wheel disc brakes, daytime running lights, front and rear air conditioning w/front and rear automatic climate controls, interior air filter, power steering, power tilt and telescoping steering wheel w/memory, wood/leather-wrapped steering wheel, cruise control, leather upholstery, heated power front bucket seats with driver-side lumbar support and memory, center console, cupholders, reclining and split folding middle seat, split folding third-row seat, wood interior trim, heated power mirrors w/driver-side automatic day/night and memory, passenger-side mirror w/tilt-down back-up aid, power windows, power door locks, remote keyless entry, navigation system, DVD player, AM/FM/cassette, 6-disc CD changer, overhead console, power antenna, digital clock, tachometer, power sunroof, universal garage door opener, rear defogger, intermittent rear wiper/washer, outside temperature display, automatic day/night rearview mirror, compass, illuminated visor mirrors, map lights, variable intermittent wipers, automatic headlights, remote fuel-door release, floormats, running boards, rear privacy glass, fog lights, theft-deterrent system, adaptive-variable and height-adjustable suspension, full-size spare tire, 275/70HR16 tires, alloy wheels.

OPTIONAL EQUIPMENT
Comfort & Convenience Features
Mark Levinson
    Radio System 1280 960

Appearance and Miscellaneous
Roof rack... 621 373

Specifications begin on page 551.

LEXUS

Special Purpose, Wheels and Tires   Retail Price   Dealer Invoice
Chrome alloy wheels $1300 $650

Postproduction options also available.

LEXUS RX 300

Lexus RX 300

Front- or all-wheel-drive midsize sport-utility vehicle
Base price range: $33,955-$35,705. Built in Japan.
Also consider: Acura MDX, Ford Explorer, Toyota Highlander

FOR • Ride • Passenger and cargo room • Build quality • Exterior finish • Interior materials   **AGAINST** • Audio and climate controls

Navigation-system revisions aimed at greater convenience are the only 2002 change of note to the smaller of Lexus's two SUVs. RX 300 is based on the Lexus ES 300/Toyota Camry sedan platform and is an underskin sibling to the newer Toyota Highlander SUV. Highlander has a 4-inch longer wheelbase but, like the Lexus, seats five. RX 300 offers front-wheel drive or all-wheel drive without low-range gearing. Standard on either version is 3.0-liter V6, automatic transmission, traction control, front side airbags, antilock 4-wheel disc brakes, antiskid system and emergency-stop brake assist feature. For '02 the optional DVD navigation system gets new functions, including multi-route calculation, simplified graphics, and route preview. It also gains a faster computer intended to speed up route processing and map scrolling.

RATINGS	Base 2WD	Base AWD
ACCELERATION	5	5
FUEL ECONOMY	5	4

Prices are accurate at time of publication; subject to manufacturer's change.

LEXUS

	Base 2WD	Base AWD
RIDE QUALITY	6	6
STEERING/HANDLING	4	5
QUIETNESS	6	6
INSTRUMENTS/CONTROLS	6	6
ROOM/COMFORT (FRONT)	8	8
ROOM/COMFORT (REAR)	7	7
CARGO ROOM	7	7
VALUE	7	7

Highlander is our Best Buy pick, but RX 300 justifies its higher sticker price by being posh, refined, roomy, and pleasant to drive. Solid Lexus resale values add further luster to this premium midsize SUV.

TOTAL	61	61

Average total for midsize sport-utility vehicles: 49.6

ENGINES

	dohc V6
Size, liters/cu. in.	3.0/183
Horsepower @ rpm	220 @ 5800
Torque (lb-ft) @ rpm	222 @ 4400
Availability	S

EPA city/highway mpg
4-speed automatic .... 18/22[1]

1. 19/23 w/2WD.

PRICES

Lexus RX 300	Retail Price	Dealer Invoice
Base 2WD 4-door wagon	$33955	$29879
Base AWD 4-door wagon	35705	31420
Destination charge	545	545

STANDARD EQUIPMENT

Base: 3.0-liter dohc V6 engine, 4-speed automatic transmission, traction control, dual front airbags, front side airbags, antilock 4-wheel disc brakes, antiskid system, daytime running lights, air conditioning w/automatic climate control, power steering, tilt leather-wrapped steering wheel, cruise control, cloth upholstery, front bucket seats, 10-way power driver seat w/power lumbar support, 4-way power passenger seat, center console, cupholders, split folding rear seat, overhead console, wood interior trim, AM/FM/cassette, power antenna, digital clock, tachometer, heated power mirrors, power windows, power door locks, remote keyless entry, variable intermittent wipers, trip computer, outside temperature indicator, illuminated visor mirrors, rear defogger, intermittent rear wiper, remote fuel door

LEXUS

release, automatic headlights, map lights, cargo cover, floormats, theft-deterrent system, rear privacy glass, fog lights, 225/70SR16 tires, full-size spare tire, alloy wheels. **AWD** model adds: all-wheel drive, towing pkg. (heavy-duty radiator, transmission oil cooler).

OPTIONAL EQUIPMENT

Major Packages

	Retail Price	Dealer Invoice
PM Premium Pkg.	$1965	$1572

Leather upholstery, driver seat memory, universal garage door opener, automatic day/night rearview and outside mirrors, interior air filter.

VP Premium Plus Pkg.	2545	2291

Premium Pkg. plus in-dash 6-disc CD changer, power sunroof.

VN Navigation System Pkg.	5390	4667

Navigation system, leather upholstery, memory driver seat, wood/leather-wrapped steering wheel, in-dash 6-disc CD changer, automatic day/night rearview and outside mirrors, universal garage door opener, interior air filter, high-intensity discharge headlights.

Towing Pkg., 2WD	160	128

Heavy-duty radiator, transmission oil cooler. Requires towing hitch receiver.

Comfort & Convenience Features

Navigation system	2000	1700
Power sunroof	1000	800
Leather Trim Pkg.	1300	1040
Heated front seats	440	352
Wood/leather-wrapped steering wheel	330	264
In-dash 6-disc CD changer	1080	864

Appearance and Miscellaneous

High-intensity discharge headlights	515	412

Special Purpose, Wheels and Tires

Chrome alloy wheels	1700	850

Postproduction options also available.

LEXUS SC 430

Rear-wheel-drive luxury car
Base price: $58,455. Built in Japan.
Also consider: BMW Z8, Jaguar XK8, Mercedes-Benz CLK

Prices are accurate at time of publication; subject to manufacturer's change.

LEXUS

Lexus SC 430

FOR • Acceleration • Quietness • Ride/handling • Build quality **AGAINST** • Cargo room • Rear-seat entry/exit • Rear-seat room

Lexus's first convertible is an all-new car with a power-retractable metal roof and a small rear seat intended for occasional use, mainly by kids. The SC 430 takes its V8 engine and 5-speed automatic transmission from the LS 430 sedan. Standard features include front side airbags, antilock 4-wheel disc brakes with emergency-stop power assist, traction/antiskid system, tire-pressure monitor, 18-inch wheels, leather/wood cabin trim, and premium Mark Levinson audio. Options are few: rear spoiler, navigation system, and run-flat tires that eliminate the spare tire for a little extra trunk space.

RATINGS

	Base
ACCELERATION	8
FUEL ECONOMY	4
RIDE QUALITY	6
STEERING/HANDLING	8
QUIETNESS	7
INSTRUMENTS/CONTROLS	6
ROOM/COMFORT (FRONT)	7
ROOM/COMFORT (REAR)	1
CARGO ROOM	2
VALUE	2

Priced a bit above the CLK430 convertible but far below the ragtop XK8, the SC 430 offers a pleasing mix of performance and panache, plus the extra security and convenience of a power metal roof. Demand exceeds supply, so don't expect discounts.

TOTAL	51

Average total for luxury cars: 59.4

LEXUS • LINCOLN

ENGINES

	dohc V8
Size, liters/cu. in.	4.3/262
Horsepower @ rpm	300 @ 5600
Torque (lb-ft) @ rpm	320 @ 3400
Availability	S

EPA city/highway mpg
5-speed automatic 18/23

PRICES

Lexus SC 430	Retail Price	Dealer Invoice
Base 2-door convertible	$58455	$50855
Destination charge	545	545

STANDARD EQUIPMENT

Base: 4.3-liter dohc V8 engine, 5-speed automatic transmission, traction control, dual front airbags, front side airbags, antilock 4-wheel disc brakes, antiskid system, daytime running lights, air conditioning w/dual-zone automatic climate control, interior air filter, power steering, power tilt/telescoping wood/leather-wrapped steering wheel, cruise control, leather upholstery, heated 10-way power front seats, memory system (front seats, steering wheel, mirrors), center console, cupholders, wood interior trim, heated power mirrors w/automatic day/night, power windows, power door locks, remote keyless entry, Mark Levinson AM/FM radio w/in-dash 6-disc CD changer, steering wheel radio controls, digital clock, tachometer, power retractable steel hard top, rear defogger, automatic day/night rearview mirror, outside temperature indicator, universal garage door opener, remote fuel door/decklid release, theft-deterrent system, high-intensity discharge headlights, fog lights, tire pressure monitor, 245/40ZR18 tires, alloy wheels.

OPTIONAL EQUIPMENT
Comfort & Convenience Features

Navigation system	2000	1700

Appearance and Miscellaneous

Rear spoiler	440	352
Run-flat tires	400	320

LINCOLN CONTINENTAL

Front-wheel-drive luxury car
Base price range: $38,010-$39,720. Built in USA.
Also consider: Acura RL, Audi A6, Mercedes-Benz E-Class

Prices are accurate at time of publication; subject to manufacturer's change.

LINCOLN

Lincoln Continental

FOR • Acceleration • Passenger and cargo room **AGAINST** • Rear-seat comfort

For what is likely its final model year, the 2002 Continental redesignates former options packages as separate models. Lincoln's only front-wheel-drive car now offers Base, Driver Select, Personal Security, and Luxury Appearance models. All have a V8 engine, 4-speed automatic transmission, traction control, antilock 4-wheel disc brakes, and front side airbags. Six-passenger seating with a split front bench is standard; front buckets are a no-cost option. Driver Select and Luxury Appearance models allow switching between three levels of steering and suspension firmness. All Continentals come with a rear load-leveling suspension. The Personal Security includes run-flat tires with pressure-monitoring system. Lincoln's new Vehicle Communications System option provides "one-button" emergency assistance, concierge services, and information via a satellite link. It also includes voice-activated hands-free phone; Sprint PCS cell service is required. The slow-selling Continental is not expected to return for 2003.

RATINGS

	Driver Select
ACCELERATION	6
FUEL ECONOMY	5
RIDE QUALITY	7
STEERING/HANDLING	6
QUIETNESS	6
INSTRUMENTS/CONTROLS	5
ROOM/COMFORT (FRONT)	6
ROOM/COMFORT (REAR)	5
CARGO ROOM	6

Specifications begin on page 551.

LINCOLN

	Driver Select
VALUE	3

Quiet and powerful, but Continental is a near-luxury also-ran for comfort, room, and image. This slow-seller is worth considering only if you can get a big discount, which should be easy given its imminent phaseout, though you'll take a big hit in first-year depreciation.

TOTAL	**55**

Average total for luxury cars: 59.4

EXTENDED-USE TEST UPDATE

Our extended-use Continental required no unscheduled service during its 12-month test, though a minor dashboard rattle appeared intermittently.

ENGINES

	dohc V8
Size, liters/cu. in.	4.6/281
Horsepower @ rpm	275 @ 5750
Torque (lb-ft) @ rpm	275 @ 4750
Availability	S
EPA city/highway mpg	
4-speed automatic	17/25

PRICES

Lincoln Continental	Retail Price	Dealer Invoice
Base 4-door sedan	$38010	$34940
Driver Select 4-door sedan	38615	35483
Personal Security 4-door sedan	39600	36370
Luxury Appearance 4-door sedan	39720	36478
Destination charge	745	745

STANDARD EQUIPMENT

Base: 4.6-liter dohc V8 engine, 4-speed automatic transmission, traction control, dual front airbags, front side airbags, antilock 4-wheel disc brakes, emergency inside trunk release, programmable variable-assist power steering, tilt leather-wrapped steering wheel, cruise control, air conditioning w/automatic climate control, interior air-filter, leather upholstery, front split bench seat w/power lumbar adjustment, 6-way power front seats, memory system for driver seat and outside mirrors, cupholders, column shifter, overhead console, wood interior trim, heated power mirrors w/tilt-down back-up aid, power windows, power door locks, remote keyless entry, key pad entry, rear defogger, automatic day/night rearview mirror, compass,

Prices are accurate at time of publication; subject to manufacturer's change.

LINCOLN

variable intermittent wipers, wiper-activated headlights, AM/FM/cassette, analog clock, tachometer, remote fuel-door and decklid releases, map lights, illuminated visor mirrors, universal garage door opener, automatic headlights, automatic parking brake release, floormats, load leveling suspension, theft-deterrent system, cornering lights, 225/60R16 tires, alloy wheels.

Driver Select adds: Alpine sound system, steering wheel climate and radio controls, driver-side automatic day/night mirror, memory for power steering assist and ride control suspension settings, semi-active suspension w/selectable ride control.

Personal Security adds: tire-pressure monitor, run-flat tires, polished alloy wheels.

Luxury Appearance adds to Driver Select: two-tone leather upholstery, heated front seats, wood/leather-wrapped steering wheel, chrome alloy wheels.

OPTIONAL EQUIPMENT
Major Packages

	Retail Price	Dealer Invoice
Select Pkg.	$2705	$2353
Manufacturer's Discount Price	NC	NC
Power sunroof, Alpine sound system, 6-disc CD changer.		
Limited Edition Pkg., Driver Select	590	514
Upgraded leather upholstery, wood/leather-wrapped steering wheel, unique floormats.		

Comfort & Convenience Features

Vehicle Communications System	1295	1127
Includes voice-activated cellular telephone, route guide, emergency services, information services. Requires Sprint PCS Airtime Plan.		
Front bucket seats	NC	NC
Includes center console, floor shifter. NA Base.		
Heated front seats, Base, Driver Select, Personal Security	400	348

Appearance and Miscellaneous

Chrome alloy wheels, Base, Driver Select	855	744
Polished alloy wheels, Base, Driver Select	360	313

LINCOLN LS

Rear-wheel-drive near-luxury car
Base price range: $33,045-$39,395. Built in USA.
Also consider: Acura TL, BMW 3-Series, Lexus ES 300

FOR • Acceleration (V8) • Ride/handling • Seat comfort

Specifications begin on page 551.

LINCOLN

Lincoln LS

AGAINST • Automatic transmission performance • Climate controls

More V6 power and a new communications option update Lincoln's near-luxury sedan for 2002. LS shares a platform with the British-built Jaguar S-Type, but differs in styling and features. It offers a Ford V6 with an extra 10 hp this year, and a Jaguar-designed V8. Base, Sport, and Premium are the model names; there's also a V6 Convenience model. The V6 Sport has manual or automatic transmission, other models are automatic only. The automatic in Sports and Premiums has a manual shift gate. Standard are front side airbags, antilock 4-wheel disc brakes, traction control, and, for '02, an in-dash CD changer. Sports add firmer suspension, performance tires, and 17-inch wheels vs. 16s. Lincoln's new Vehicle Communications System provides "one-button" emergency assistance, concierge services, and information; Sprint cell service is required. Due midyear is an LSE Appearance Package that adds to Sport models a rear spoiler, fog lights, special wheels, and "aero" lower-body cladding.

RATINGS	V6 Sport, man.	V8 Premium
ACCELERATION	6	6
FUEL ECONOMY	5	4
RIDE QUALITY	6	8
STEERING/HANDLING	7	6
QUIETNESS	6	7
INSTRUMENTS/CONTROLS	6	6
ROOM/COMFORT (FRONT)	6	7
ROOM/COMFORT (REAR)	6	6
CARGO ROOM	3	3

Prices are accurate at time of publication; subject to manufacturer's change.

CONSUMER GUIDE®

LINCOLN

	V6 Sport, man.	V8 Premium
VALUE	3	3

Interior furnishings disappoint, but the LS offers lots of features for the money, capable road manners, and one of the few V8s in the near-luxury class.

TOTAL	54	56

Average total for near-luxury cars: 54.5

ENGINES

	dohc V6	dohc V8
Size, liters/cu. in.	3.0/181	3.9/235
Horsepower @ rpm	220 @ 6400	252 @ 6100
Torque (lb-ft) @ rpm	215 @ 4300	261 @ 4300
Availability	S[1]	S[2]

EPA city/highway mpg

5-speed manual	18/25	
5-speed automatic	18/25	17/23

1. LS V6. 2. LS V8.

PRICES

Lincoln LS

	Retail Price	Dealer Invoice
V6 Base 4-door sedan, automatic	$33045	$30456
V6 Convenience 4-door sedan, automatic	34230	31522
V6 Sport 4-door sedan, automatic	35030	32242
V6 Sport 4-door sedan, manual	35055	32264
V6 Premium 4-door sedan, automatic	36335	33417
V8 Base 4-door sedan, automatic	37220	34213
V8 Sport 4-door sedan, automatic	38075	34983
V8 Premium 4-door sedan, automatic	39395	36171
Destination charge	610	610

STANDARD EQUIPMENT

V6 Base: 3.0-liter dohc V6 engine, 5-speed automatic transmission, traction control, dual front airbags, front side-airbags, antilock 4-wheel disc brakes, emergency inside trunk release, air conditioning w/dual-zone automatic climate control, interior air filter, power steering, power tilt/telescoping wood/leather-wrapped steering wheel, cruise control, leather upholstery, front bucket seats w/manual lumbar adjustment, 8-way power driver seat, 6-way power passenger seat, center console, cupholders, split folding rear seat, heated power mirrors, power windows, power door locks, remote keyless entry, AM/FM/radio w/in-dash 6-disc CD changer, steering-wheel radio controls, tachometer, map lights, illuminated visor mirrors, rear defogger, variable intermittent wipers, automatic headlights, remote fuel door/decklid release, floormats, theft-deterrent system, fog

Specifications begin on page 551.

LINCOLN

lights, 215/60HR16 tires, alloy wheels.

V6 Convenience adds: front seat power lumbar adjustments, memory pkg. (driver seat, steering wheel, mirrors), automatic day/night rearview mirror, compass, universal garage door opener, rain-sensing wipers.

V6 Sport adds: 5-speed manual or 5-speed automatic transmission w/manual-shift capability, leather-wrapped steering wheel, sport suspension, 235/50VR17 tires.

V6 Premium adds: power sunroof, Alpine sound system, unique interior trim, chrome alloy wheels.

V8 Base adds to V6 Convenience: 3.9-liter dohc V8 engine, trip computer, 215/60VR16 tires.

V8 Sport adds: manual-shift capability, leather-wrapped steering wheel, sport suspension, 235/50VR17 tires.

V8 Premium adds: power sunroof, Alpine sound system, unique interior trim, chrome alloy wheels.

OPTIONAL EQUIPMENT

	Retail Price	Dealer Invoice
Major Packages		
All Season Pkg.	$1135	$988
Manufacturer's Discount Price	*735*	*640*
Antiskid system, heated front seats.		
LSE Appearance Pkg., V6/V8 Sport	NA	NA
Unique body cladding, special fog lights, rear spoiler, stainless steel exhaust tips, special alloy wheels.		

Comfort & Convenience Features

	Retail Price	Dealer Invoice
Vehicle Communications System	1295	1127
Includes voice-activated cellular telephone, route guide, emergency services, information services. Requires Sprint PCS Airtime Plan.		
Power sunroof, V8 Base, Convenience, V6/V8 Sport	1005	874
Alpine sound system, V8 Base, Convenience, V6/V8 Sport	575	501
Manufacturer's Discount Price, V6/V8 Sport	*NC*	*NC*
Alpine AM/FM/cassette w/6-disc CD changer, V8 Base, Convenience	605	526
CD changer located in glove box.		

Appearance and Miscellaneous

	Retail Price	Dealer Invoice
Polished alloy wheels, V8 Base, Convenience	405	353
Chrome alloy wheels, V6/V8 Sport	845	735

Prices are accurate at time of publication; subject to manufacturer's change.

LINCOLN

LINCOLN NAVIGATOR

Lincoln Navigator

Rear- or 4-wheel-drive full-size sport-utility vehicle
Base price range: $44,415-$48,165. Built in USA.
Also consider: Cadillac Escalade, GMC Yukon Denali and Denali XL, Lexus LX 470

FOR • Passenger and cargo room • Instruments/controls • Build quality • Interior materials **AGAINST** • Fuel economy • Entry/exit • Maneuverability

This luxury spinoff of the Ford Expedition seats up to eight, offers a rear-seat video entertainment option, and uses a 300-hp version of the Ford's 260-hp 5.4-liter V8. Navigator is available with rear-wheel drive or Control Trac 4WD that can be left engaged on dry pavement and includes low-range gearing. Standard are automatic transmission, front side airbags, antilock 4-wheel disc brakes, and power adjustable pedals. Seating comprises front- and 2nd-row buckets and a 3-passenger 3rd-row bench; a 3-place 2nd-row bench is available at no charge. Added for 2002 is a monochrome-black exterior trim option that includes unique wheels and standard rear obstacle warning system. Navigator's performance and accommodations are similar to those of its Ford sibling.

RATINGS	2WD	4WD w/nav. sys.
ACCELERATION	5	5
FUEL ECONOMY	2	2
RIDE QUALITY	6	5
STEERING/HANDLING	3	3
QUIETNESS	6	6
INSTRUMENTS/CONTROLS	7	4
ROOM/COMFORT (FRONT)	9	9
ROOM/COMFORT (REAR)	9	9
CARGO ROOM	9	9

Specifications begin on page 551.

LINCOLN

	2WD	4WD w/nav. sys.
VALUE	3	3

Between the Lincoln and the Ford, Expedition is now our Recommended choice, dethroned by Chevrolet's newer Tahoe and Suburban as itself class Best Buys. Navigator offers some luxury options not available on Expedition, but we don't think it's worth the extra money.

TOTAL	59	55

Average total for full-size sport-utility vehicles: 50.9

ENGINES

	dohc V8
Size, liters/cu. in.	5.4/330
Horsepower @ rpm	300 @ 5000
Torque (lb-ft) @ rpm	355 @ 2750
Availability	S
EPA city/highway mpg	
4-speed automatic	12/16[1]

1. 12/17 w/2WD.

PRICES

Lincoln Navigator	Retail Price	Dealer Invoice
4-door wagon, 2WD	$44415	$39082
4-door wagon, 4WD	48165	42307
Destination charge	715	715

STANDARD EQUIPMENT

2WD: 5.4-liter dohc V8 engine, 4-speed automatic transmission, limited-slip differential, antilock 4-wheel disc brakes, dual front airbags, front side airbags, air conditioning w/front and rear automatic climate controls, power steering, wood/leather-wrapped steering wheel w/radio and climate controls, tilt steering column, cruise control, power-adjustable pedals w/memory, leather upholstery, 7-passenger seating w/quad bucket seats, 6-way power front seats w/power lumbar adjustment, driver seat memory, third-row folding bench seat, wood interior trim, front floor console (rear audio controls and headphone jack, rear air conditioning/heater outlet), second row floor console, overhead console, trip computer, compass, cupholders, heated power mirrors w/memory and turn signal lights, power windows, power door locks, remote keyless entry, key pad entry, automatic day/night rearview mirror, AM/FM/cassette, digital clock, tachometer, illuminated visor mirrors, universal garage door opener, automatic headlights, variable intermittent wipers, automatic parking brake release, rear defogger, intermittent rear wiper/washer, map lights, automatic headlights, floormats, theft-deterrent system, rear

Prices are accurate at time of publication; subject to manufacturer's change.

LINCOLN

privacy glass, fog lights, roof rack, illuminated running boards, rear self-leveling suspension, Class III Trailer Towing Group (7-wire harness, hitch, heavy-duty flasher, engine-oil cooler, auxiliary transmission-oil cooler), full-size spare tire, 275/60R17 white-letter tires, alloy wheels.

4WD adds: 4-wheel drive, 2-speed transfer case, front and rear self-leveling suspension, front tow hooks, 255/75R17 all-terrain white-letter tires.

OPTIONAL EQUIPMENT

	Retail Price	Dealer Invoice
Major Packages		
Limited Edition Pkg.	$685	$589
Rear obstacle detection system, unique polished alloy wheels.		
Safety		
Rear obstacle detection system	255	219
Comfort & Convenience Features		
Navigation system	1995	1716
Requires 6-disc CD changer.		
Rear Entertainment System	1280	1101
Fold-down LCD screen, videocassette player, two wireless headphones. NA with navigation system, climate control seats. Requires 6-disc CD changer.		
Power sunroof	1495	1286
Replaces overhead console with mini overhead console. NA with navigation system.		
Climate control front seats	595	521
8-passenger seating	NC	NC
Second row 3-passenger split bench seat.		
Alpine AM/FM/cassette	580	499
6-disc CD changer	595	512
ordered w/Alpine AM/FM/cassette	NC	NC
Special Purpose, Wheels and Tires		
Chrome alloy wheels	595	512

LINCOLN TOWN CAR

Rear-wheel-drive luxury car
Base price range: $39,995-$49,060. Built in USA.
Also consider: Cadillac De Ville, Lexus LS 430

FOR • Passenger and cargo room • Quietness **AGAINST** • Fuel economy • Rear visibility

Specifications begin on page 551.

LINCOLN

Lincoln Town Car

America's only rear-wheel drive full-size luxury sedan is set to end its 2002 season in early Spring with the release of a more-powerful, restyled 2003 Town Car. Meantime, the '02 treats option packages as separate models. Town Car's V8 has 225 hp in the base Executive and regular Signature models. It has 235 hp in Signature Touring, Premium, and Premium Touring models and in Cartier, Cartier Premium, and Cartier L versions. Cartier L aims at the limousine trade with a 6-inch longer wheelbase and an extra 6 inches of rear leg room. Touring models include a firmer suspension and wider tires. All have antilock 4-wheel disc brakes, traction control, leather upholstery, front bench seat, power-adjustable pedals, and a 4-speed automatic transmission. New for '02 is an in-dash CD changer, standard for Cartier Premium and optional for others except the Executive. Available for all is Lincoln's new Vehicle Communications System, providing "one-button" emergency assistance, concierge services and information via satellite link and voice-activated hands-free phone; Sprint cell service is required.

RATINGS	Executive	Cartier L
ACCELERATION	4	4
FUEL ECONOMY	4	4
RIDE QUALITY	7	8
STEERING/HANDLING	5	5
QUIETNESS	7	7
INSTRUMENTS/CONTROLS	7	7
ROOM/COMFORT (FRONT)	7	7
ROOM/COMFORT (REAR)	6	8
CARGO ROOM	6	6
VALUE	4	4

Cadillac's DeVille is far more modern and better executed, but Town Car delivers traditional American luxury, spaciousness and isolation, and its base prices are among the lowest in this class.

TOTAL	57	60

Average total for luxury cars: 59.4

Prices are accurate at time of publication; subject to manufacturer's change.

LINCOLN

ENGINES

	ohc V8	ohc V8
Size, liters/cu. in.	4.6/281	4.6/281
Horsepower @ rpm	225 @ 4750	235 @ 4750
Torque (lb-ft) @ rpm	275 @ 4000	285 @ 4000
Availability	S[1]	S[2]

EPA city/highway mpg

| 4-speed automatic | 17/24 | 17/24 |

1. Executive, Signature. 2. Cartier; optional Signature.

PRICES

Lincoln Town Car

	Retail Price	Dealer Invoice
Executive 4-door sedan	$39995	$36781
Signature 4-door sedan	42165	38733
Signature Touring 4-door sedan	42875	39373
Signature Premium 4-door sedan	44295	40651
Signature Premium Touring 4-door sedan	45005	41289
Cartier 4-door sedan	44550	40880
Cartier Premium 4-door sedan	46680	42797
Cartier L 4-door sedan	49060	44939
Destination charge	745	745

STANDARD EQUIPMENT

Executive: 4.6-liter V8 220-horsepower engine, 4-speed automatic transmission, traction control, dual front airbags, front side airbags, antilock 4-wheel disc brakes, emergency inside trunk release, power steering, tilt leather-wrapped steering wheel, cruise control, air conditioning w/automatic climate control, leather upholstery, dual 8-way power front split bench seat w/power recliners and lumbar support, power-adjustable pedals, cupholders, heated power mirrors w/driver-side automatic day/night, power windows, power door locks, remote keyless entry, key pad entry, rear defogger, AM/FM/cassette, digital clock, automatic day/night rearview, compass, remote fuel-door release, power decklid pulldown, headlight-activated variable-intermittent wipers, illuminated visor mirrors, map lights, automatic headlights, automatic parking brake release, floormats, theft-deterrent system, cornering lights, 225/60SR16 tires, alloy wheels.

Signature adds: memory system (driver seat, mirrors, pedals), wood steering wheel w/radio and climate controls, universal garage-door opener, upgraded sound system.

Signature Touring adds: 4.6-liter V8 235-horsepower engine, sport suspension, 235/60SR16 tires.

Signature Premium adds to Signature: power sunroof, Alpine sound system, 6-disc CD changer.

Specifications begin on page 551.

LINCOLN • MAZDA

Signature Premium Touring adds: 4.6-liter 235-horsepower engine, sport suspension, 235/60SR16 tires.

Cartier adds to Signature: 4.6-liter V8 235-horsepower engine, upgraded leather upholstery, heated front seats, Alpine sound system, analog clock, gold pkg., chrome alloy wheels.

Cartier Premium adds: power sunroof, 6-disc CD changer.

Cartier L adds to Cartier: 6-inch longer wheelbase, rear radio and climate controls, rear controls for front passenger seat, heated rear seats, rear illuminated visor mirrors, 225/70R16 tires.

OPTIONAL EQUIPMENT
Comfort & Convenience Features

	Retail Price	Dealer Invoice
Vehicle Communications System	$1295	$1127
Includes voice-activated cellular telephone, route guide, emergency services, information services. Requires Sprint PCS Airtime Plan.		
Heated front seats, Signature, Signature Touring/Premium/Premium Touring	400	348
6-disc CD changer, Signature, Signature Touring, Cartier, Cartier L	605	526
Includes Alpine sound system.		

MAZDA 626

Mazda 626 LX

Front-wheel-drive compact car
Base price range: $18,735-$21,635. Built in USA.
Also consider: Subaru Outback/Legacy, Volkswagen Passat

FOR • Acceleration (V6) • Steering/handling • Build quality
AGAINST • Automatic transmission performance • Road noise

Prices are accurate at time of publication; subject to manufacturer's change.

MAZDA

The top-line 626 model for '02 trades its previously standard sunroof and CD player for a corresponding drop in base price. This line of compact sedans comes in base LX trim with 4-cyl or V6 power, or as the uplevel ES model with V6. All are available with manual transmission or optional automatic. V6 models have standard 4-wheel disc brakes. ABS and front-side airbags are grouped into a single option. On the ES, that package includes traction control, which is unavailable on LXs. For '02, the ES's base price drops $1300, but its CD player and sunroof are available only as part of the $1300 Premium Package option.

RATINGS

	LX, 4 cyl auto.	ES, V6 auto.
ACCELERATION	3	5
FUEL ECONOMY	6	5
RIDE QUALITY	6	6
STEERING/HANDLING	5	6
QUIETNESS	5	5
INSTRUMENTS/CONTROLS	6	6
ROOM/COMFORT (FRONT)	5	5
ROOM/COMFORT (REAR)	5	5
CARGO ROOM	3	3
VALUE	6	6

Not the sportiest compact sedan, but all-around competence makes it worth considering. The solid 626 tends to be overlooked by buyers, so moderate demand and stiff competition should mean attractive discounts.

TOTAL	50	52

Average total for compact cars: 51.6

ENGINES

	dohc I4	dohc V6
Size, liters/cu. in.	2.0/122	2.5/152
Horsepower @ rpm	125 @ 5500	165 @ 6000
Torque (lb-ft) @ rpm	127 @ 3000	161 @ 5000
Availability	S[1]	S[2]

EPA city/highway mpg

5-speed manual	26/32	21/27
4-speed automatic	22/28	20/26

1. LX. 2. LX V6, ES V6.

PRICES

Mazda 626	Retail Price	Dealer Invoice
LX 4-door sedan	$18735	$17281
LX V6 4-door sedan	19935	18386
ES 4-door sedan	21635	19949

Specifications begin on page 551.

MAZDA

	Retail Price	Dealer Invoice
Destination charge	$480	$480

STANDARD EQUIPMENT

LX: 2.0-liter dohc 4-cylinder engine, 5-speed manual transmission, dual front airbags, emergency inside trunk release, air conditioning, power steering, tilt steering wheel, cruise control, cloth upholstery, front bucket seats w/driver seat height adjustment, center console, cupholders, split folding rear seat, power mirrors, power windows, power door locks, remote keyless entry, AM/FM/CD player, digital clock, tachometer, variable intermittent wipers, rear defogger, map lights, illuminated visor mirrors, automatic-off headlights, remote fuel-door and decklid releases, 205/60R15 tires, wheel covers.

LX V6 adds: 2.5-liter dohc V6 engine, 4-wheel disc brakes.

ES adds: leather upholstery, 6-way power driver seat, leather-wrapped steering wheel, heated power mirrors, floormats, 205/55HR16 tires, alloy wheels.

OPTIONAL EQUIPMENT
Major Packages

Luxury Pkg., LX	1800	1440
Power sunroof, 6-way power driver seat, floormats, theft-deterrent system w/alarm, alloy wheels.		
Premium Pkg., ES	1300	1040
Power sunroof, Bose AM/FM/cassette/CD player.		

Powertrain

4-speed automatic transmission	800	696

Safety

Antilock brakes w/front side airbags, LX, LX V6	800	640
Requires automatic transmission.		
Antilock brakes w/front side airbags, traction control, ES	950	760
Requires automatic transmission.		

Comfort & Convenience Features

AM/FM/cassette/CD player	150	120
In-dash 6-disc CD changer, LX, LX V6,		
ES manual trans.	500	400
ES automatic trans.	395	295
Automatic day/night rearview mirror	150	120
Includes compass.		

Prices are accurate at time of publication; subject to manufacturer's change.

MAZDA

Appearance and Miscellaneous

	Retail Price	Dealer Invoice
Rear spoiler	$395	$295
Fog lights	250	200
Alloy wheels, LX	450	383

MAZDA MIATA

Mazda Miata

Rear-wheel-drive sports car
Base price range: $21,180-$23,930. Built in Japan.
Also consider: BMW Z3 Series, Honda S2000, Toyota MR2 Spyder

FOR • Acceleration • Steering/handling • Fuel economy
AGAINST • Cargo room • Noise • Entry/exit

Miata gets an optional in-dash 6-disc CD changer but otherwise continues essentially unchanged for '02. Base and LS models are offered. Both have a manual-folding soft top with a heated glass rear window. A removable hardtop is optional. The sole engine is a 142-hp 4 cyl teamed with standard 5-speed or optional automatic transmission. A 6-speed manual is available on the LS. ABS is optional on LS, unavailable on the base model. Sixteen-inch wheels are standard on LS, optional on base Miatas in place of 15s. Optional on both are appearance packages that offer rear mud guards and more pronounced side sills. A special edition model is expected in early calendar 2002.

RATINGS

	Base, auto.	LS, man.
ACCELERATION	5	6
FUEL ECONOMY	6	6
RIDE QUALITY	3	3
STEERING/HANDLING	9	9
QUIETNESS	2	2

Specifications begin on page 551.

MAZDA

	Base, auto.	LS, man.
INSTRUMENTS/CONTROLS	8	8
ROOM/COMFORT (FRONT)	4	4
ROOM/COMFORT (REAR)	0	0
CARGO ROOM	1	1
VALUE	6	6

Miata defends front-engine sports-car tradition, while the MR2 touts mid-engine technology. Both are terrific fun, with Miata offering a measure of usable cargo room and, in base form at least, better value.

TOTAL	44	45

Average total for sports cars: 41.3

EXTENDED-USE TEST UPDATE

Shortly after it was delivered, our extended-use LS suffered marked front-end vibration at highway speeds. A dealer service department determined the cause to be unbalanced wheels, which wasn't covered under warranty. No other unscheduled maintenance has been required in its first 7812 mi.

ENGINES

	dohc I4
Size, liters/cu. in.	1.8/112
Horsepower @ rpm	142 @ 7000
Torque (lb-ft) @ rpm	125 @ 5500
Availability	S

EPA city/highway mpg
5-speed manual	23/28
6-speed manual	23/28
4-speed automatic	22/28

PRICES

Mazda Miata	Retail Price	Dealer Invoice
Base 2-door convertible	$21180	$19548
LS 2-door convertible	23930	22081
Destination charge	480	480

STANDARD EQUIPMENT

Base: 1.8-liter dohc 4-cylinder engine, 5-speed manual transmission, dual front airbags, 4-wheel disc brakes, air conditioning, power steering, leather-wrapped steering wheel, cloth upholstery, bucket seats, center console, cupholders, power mirrors, power windows, AM/FM/CD player, power antenna, digital clock, tachometer, inter-

Prices are accurate at time of publication; subject to manufacturer's change.
CONSUMER GUIDE®

MAZDA

mittent wipers, rear defogger, remote fuel-door and decklid releases, passenger-side visor mirror, floormats, theft-deterrent system, windblock panel, fog lights, 195/50VR15 tires, alloy wheels.

LS adds: limited-slip differential, cruise control, leather upholstery, power door locks, remote keyless entry, Bose sound system, 205/45WR16 tires.

OPTIONAL EQUIPMENT

	Retail Price	Dealer Invoice
Major Packages		
Convenience Pkg., Base	$795	$668
Cruise control, power door locks, remote keyless entry, upgraded sound system. NA w/Suspension Pkg.		
Suspension Pkg., Base	1025	861
LS	395	332
Sport suspension w/Bilstein shock absorbers, limited-slip differential (Base), 205/45WR16 tires (Base). NA w/detachable hardtop.		
2AP Appearance Pkg.	450	360
Small side sills, small rear mud guards.		
1AP Appearance Pkg.	800	644
Front air dam, large side sills, small rear mud guards.		
Powertrain		
6-speed manual transmission, LS	650	565
4-speed automatic transmission	900	782
LS requires antilock brakes. LS deletes limited-slip differential.		
Limited-slip differential, Base	395	332
NA w/4-speed automatic transmission.		
Safety		
Antilock brakes, LS	550	468
Comfort & Convenience Features		
AM/FM/cassette/CD player	150	120
In-dash 6-disc CD changer	500	400
Appearance and Miscellaneous		
Theft-deterrent system w/alarm	200	176
Base requires Convenience Pkg.		
Detachable hardtop	1500	1215
Rear spoiler	295	236

MAZDA MILLENIA

Front-wheel-drive near-luxury car
Base price range: $28,025-$31,025. Built in Japan.
Also consider: Acura TL, Lexus ES 300

Specifications begin on page 551.

MAZDA

Mazda Millenia

FOR • Acceleration (S model) • Steering/handling • Build quality • Exterior finish • Interior materials **AGAINST** • Transmission performance • Rear visibility

Mazda's flagship sedan line is unchanged for '02. Millenia is offered as the base "P" model with 170-hp V6, or as the uplevel S with a 210-hp supercharged V6. Standard are a 4-speed automatic transmission, antilock 4-wheel disc brakes, leather upholstery, and sunroof. Traction control is available on both models.

RATINGS	P	S
ACCELERATION	4	6
FUEL ECONOMY	5	5
RIDE QUALITY	7	6
STEERING/HANDLING	6	7
QUIETNESS	7	6
INSTRUMENTS/CONTROLS	7	7
ROOM/COMFORT (FRONT)	6	6
ROOM/COMFORT (REAR)	4	4
CARGO ROOM	3	3
VALUE	3	3

Millenia's design dates from 1995, which puts it among the oldest near-luxury cars. The newer, more-refined Mercedes-Benz C-Class, Infiniti I35, and Acura TL eclipse it overall.

TOTAL	52	53

Average total for near-luxury cars: 54.5

ENGINES	dohc V6	Supercharged dohc V6
Size, liters/cu. in.	2.5/152	2.3/138
Horsepower @ rpm	170 @ 5800	210 @ 5300
Torque (lb-ft) @ rpm	160 @ 4800	210 @ 3500

Prices are accurate at time of publication; subject to manufacturer's change.

MAZDA

	dohc V6	Supercharged dohc V6
Availability	S[1]	S[2]
EPA city/highway mpg		
4-speed automatic	20/27	20/28

1. P model. 2. S model.

PRICES

Mazda Millenia	Retail Price	Dealer Invoice
P 4-door sedan	$28025	$25891
S 4-door sedan	31025	28657
Destination charge	480	480

STANDARD EQUIPMENT

P: 2.5-liter dohc V6 engine, 4-speed automatic transmission, dual front airbags, front side airbags, antilock 4-wheel disc brakes, air conditioning w/automatic climate control, power steering, leather-wrapped power tilt steering wheel w/memory, cruise control, leather upholstery, 8-way power front bucket seats, driver seat power lumbar adjustment, center console, cupholders, rear seat trunk pass-through, power mirrors, power windows, power door locks, remote keyless entry, power sunroof, AM/FM/cassette/CD player, steering wheel radio controls, digital clock, tachometer, outside-temperature indicator, illuminated visor mirrors, variable intermittent wipers, rear defogger, automatic-off headlights, remote fuel-door and decklid releases, floormats, theft-deterrent system, fog lights, 215/55VR16 tires, alloy wheels.

S adds: 2.3-liter dohc supercharged V6 engine, traction control, Bose sound system, upgraded suspension, 215/50VR17 tires.

OPTIONAL EQUIPMENT
Major Packages

4-Seasons Pkg., P	600	504
S	300	252

Traction control (P), heated front seats, heated mirrors, heavy-duty wipers, heavy-duty battery, extra-capacity windshield-washer tank.

Comfort & Convenience Features

Bose sound system, P	800	672
In-dash 6-disc CD changer	500	420

Appearance and Miscellaneous

Two-tone paint	380	319
Chrome alloy wheels, S	600	504

Postproduction options also available.

Specifications begin on page 551.

MAZDA

MAZDA PROTEGE

Mazda Protege5 4-dr wagon

Front-wheel-drive subcompact car
Base price range: $12,955-$18,020. Built in Japan.
Also consider: Ford Focus, Honda Civic, Volkswagen Jetta

FOR • Fuel economy • Ride • Quietness **AGAINST** • Noise • Acceleration (with automatic transmission)

Mazda's '02 subcompact line offers sedans in base DX, LX, ES, and top MP3 models, along with a wagon called the Protege5. All have a 130-hp 4-cyl engine. Five-speed manual transmission is standard, automatic is optional on all but the MP3. Front side airbags and ABS are grouped together in option packages for LX, ES, and Protege5. MP3 has performance-oriented wheels and tires, special chassis tuning, unique trim, and a Kenwood audio system that plays MP3-encoded CDs. Protege5 has ES equipment and specific cosmetic touches inside and out.

RATINGS	LS w/ABS, man.	Protege5, man.	MP3
ACCELERATION	5	5	5
FUEL ECONOMY	7	7	7
RIDE QUALITY	4	4	3
STEERING/HANDLING	5	6	8
QUIETNESS	4	4	3
INSTRUMENTS/CONTROLS	7	7	6
ROOM/COMFORT (FRONT)	5	5	5
ROOM/COMFORT (REAR)	4	4	4
CARGO ROOM	3	7	2

Prices are accurate at time of publication; subject to manufacturer's change.

MAZDA

	LS w/ABS, man.	Protege5, man.	MP3
VALUE	8	7	6

Protege disappoints on ride and refinement, but matches class leaders in most other ways while offering great dollar value and an appealingly frisky personality. Recommended, but also check out the Honda Civic, Ford Focus, and Volkswagen Jetta.

TOTAL	**52**	**56**	**49**

Average total for subcompact cars: 43.7

ENGINES

	dohc I4
Size, liters/cu. in.	2.0/122
Horsepower @ rpm	130 @ 6000
Torque (lb-ft) @ rpm	135 @ 4000
Availability	S

EPA city/highway mpg

5-speed manual	25/31
4-speed automatic	25/30

PRICES

Mazda Protege	Retail Price	Dealer Invoice
DX 4-door sedan	$12955	$12517
LX 4-door sedan	14855	14043
ES 4-door sedan	15580	14567
MP3 4-door sedan	18020	NA
Protege5 4-door wagon	16335	15271
Destination charge	480	480

STANDARD EQUIPMENT

DX: 2.0-liter dohc 130-horsepower 4-cylinder engine, 5-speed manual transmission, dual front airbags, emergency inside trunk release, air conditioning, power steering, tilt steering wheel, cloth upholstery, front bucket seats, center console, cupholders, split folding rear seat, AM/FM radio, digital clock, intermittent wipers, rear defogger, visor mirrors, map lights, remote fuel door/decklid release, 195/55VR15 tires, wheel covers.

LX adds: air conditioning, cruise control, height-adjustable driver seat, power mirrors, power windows, power door locks, remote entry system, AM/FM/CD player, tachometer.

ES adds: 4-wheel disc brakes, fog lights, rear spoiler, 195/50VR16 tires, alloy wheels.

MP3 adds: 2.0-liter dohc 140-horsepower 4-cylinder engine, leather-wrapped steering wheel, Kenwood AM/FM/CD/MP3, floormats, sport suspension, 205/45ZR17 tires.

Specifications begin on page 551.

MAZDA

Protege5 adds to ES: leather-wrapped steering wheel, cargo cover, rear wiper/washer, roof rack.

OPTIONAL EQUIPMENT	Retail Price	Dealer Invoice
Major Packages		
Convenience Pkg., DX	$1095	$898
Air conditioning, AM/FM/CD player, floormats.		
Premium Pkg., LX, ES	1580	1296
Manufacturer's Discount Price, ES	*1180*	*976*
Front side airbags, antilock brakes, power sunroof, floormats.		
Powertrain		
4-speed automatic transmission	800	720
NA MP3.		
Safety		
Antilock brakes/front side airbags, LX, ES, Protege5	800	656
Comfort & Convenience Features		
Power sunroof, LX, ES, Protege5	700	560
Manufacturer's Discount Price, LX, ES	*300*	*240*
AM/FM/CD player, DX	165	132
Cassette player	150	120
In-dash 6-disc CD changer	500	400
NA MP3.		
Automatic day/night rearview mirror	230	185
Includes compass, outside temperature indicator.		
Appearance and Miscellaneous		
Theft-deterrent system w/alarm, LX, ES, MP3, Protege5	220	176
Rear spoiler, DX, LX	330	247
Fog lights, DX, LX	199	169
Alloy wheels, LX	400	320
Manufacturer's Discount Price	*NC*	*NC*
Requires power sunroof.		
Polished alloy wheels, Protege5	500	400

MAZDA TRIBUTE

Front- or all-wheel-drive compact sport-utility vehicle

Base price range: $18,155-$23,915. Built in USA.

Also consider: Honda CR-V, Subaru Forester, Toyota RAV4

FOR • Cargo room   **AGAINST** • Noise

Prices are accurate at time of publication; subject to manufacturer's change.

MAZDA

Mazda Tribute

Interior revisions keynote 2002 changes to this slightly upscale version of the Ford Escape. Tribute shares its platform and Ford engines with Escape, but has different styling and suspension settings. Like the Honda CR-V and Toyota RAV4, Tribute has unibody construction and independent suspension. Sixteen-inch wheels and a rear liftgate with separate hatch window are standard. Tribute offers front-wheel drive or all-wheel drive that lacks low-range gearing but has a dashboard switch that locks in a 50/50 front-rear torque split. The base DX model has a 4-cyl engine with manual transmission. LX and ES models have a V6/automatic combination. LX and ES can get optional ABS and front side airbags and come with a 60/40 split-fold rear seatbacks; ES also has leather upholstery. In addition to redesigned front seats, the '02 interior changes include reshaped steering-column transmission and wiper levers intended to improve access to dashboard controls. Tribute's performance and accommodations mirror those of similarly equipped Escapes. LX and ES models also gain steering-wheel audio controls.

RATINGS

	ES AWD
ACCELERATION	5
FUEL ECONOMY	5
RIDE QUALITY	6
STEERING/HANDLING	5
QUIETNESS	5
INSTRUMENTS/CONTROLS	5
ROOM/COMFORT (FRONT)	6
ROOM/COMFORT (REAR)	5
CARGO ROOM	7
VALUE	7

Substantial feeling, roomy, comfortable, even fun to drive, Tribute and Escape are compact SUV all-stars. Priced in the mid-$20,000 range full equipped, they're also sensible alternatives to any number of midsize SUVs, especially truck-based wagons less efficient in their use of space and fuel.

Specifications begin on page 551.

MAZDA

	ES AWD
TOTAL	56

Average total for compact sport-utility vehicles: 44.4

EXTENDED-USE TEST UPDATE

The dashboard low-coolant warning light on our extended-use test AWD V6 Tribute signaled a leaking coolant-overflow bottle, which was replaced under warranty. Warranty also covered a dealer service department's adjustment of the tailgate, which had become misaligned. No other unscheduled maintenance has been required in the first 22,031 mi. As of November 2001, our test vehicle had not been included among the Escapes and Tributes recalled to rectify problems with cruise-control units, steering column attachment nuts, rear wheel hubs, fuel line seals, and windshield wiper assemblies.

ENGINES

	dohc I4	dohc V6
Size, liters/cu. in.	2.0/121	3.0/182
Horsepower @ rpm	130 @ 5400	200 @ 6000
Torque (lb-ft) @ rpm	135 @ 4500	200 @ 4750
Availability	S[1]	S[2]

EPA city/highway mpg

5-speed manual	22/25[3]	
4-speed automatic		18/23[4]

1. DX. 2. LX, ES. 3. 23/27 w/2WD. 4. 19/24 w/2WD.

PRICES

Mazda Tribute	Retail Price	Dealer Invoice
DX 4-door wagon, 2WD	$18155	$16968
DX 4-door wagon, AWD	19855	18554
LX 4-door wagon, 2WD	21485	20076
LX 4-door wagon, AWD	22685	21195
ES 4-door wagon, 2WD	22715	21222
ES 4-door wagon, AWD	23915	22341
Destination charge	540	540

STANDARD EQUIPMENT

DX: 2.0-liter dohc 4-cylinder engine, 5-speed manual transmission, dual front airbags, air conditioning, power steering, tilt steering wheel, cloth upholstery, front bucket seats, center console, cupholders, folding rear seat, power mirrors, power windows, power door locks, remote keyless entry, AM/FM/CD player, digital clock, tachometer, variable intermittent wipers, visor mirrors, rear defogger,

Prices are accurate at time of publication; subject to manufacturer's change.

MAZDA • MERCEDES-BENZ

rear wiper/washer, map lights, automatic-off headlights, remote fuel door/hatch release, floormats, theft-deterrent system, rear privacy glass, roof rack, 215/70R16 tires. **AWD** adds: all-wheel drive.

LX adds: 3.0-liter V6 engine, 4-speed automatic transmission, cruise control, steering wheel radio controls, split folding rear seat, cargo cover, fog lights, 235/70R16 tires, alloy wheels. **AWD** adds: all-wheel drive.

ES adds: leather upholstery, 6-way power driver seat, leather-wrapped steering wheel, overhead console. **AWD** adds: all-wheel drive.

OPTIONAL EQUIPMENT

	Retail Price	Dealer Invoice
Major Packages		
Luxury Pkg., LX, ES	$1090	$948
Power sunroof, overhead console, AM/FM/cassette w/in-dash 6-disc CD changer, premium speakers.		
Trailer Tow Pkg., DX V6, LX, ES	355	310
Engine oil cooler, tow bar, Class II trailer hitch, trailer wiring harness.		
Safety		
Antilock brakes, LX, ES	250	218
Front side airbags, LX, ES	250	218
Requires antilock brakes.		
Comfort & Convenience Features		
6-way power driver seat, LX	250	218
Premium Audio Pkg., LX, ES	505	439
AM/FM/cassette w/in-dash 6-disc CD changer, premium speakers.		
Cassette player	200	160
Appearance and Miscellaneous		
Rear spoiler	250	220
Tubular side steps	350	269
Alarm system	115	69

MERCEDES-BENZ C-CLASS

Rear-wheel-drive near-luxury car

Base price range: $24,950-$49,900. Built in Germany.

Also consider: Acura TL, Audi A4, BMW 3-Series

FOR • Acceleration (C320, C32) • Build quality • Steering/handling • Quietness • Seat comfort **AGAINST** • Automatic transmission performance (C230, C240) • Rear visibility (C230)

A station wagon and a high-performance sedan join Mercedes'

MERCEDES-BENZ

Mercedes-Benz C230 2-door hatchback

entry-level line for 2002. Models start with the C230, a 2-dr hatchback coupe with a supercharged 4-cyl engine. The C240 sedan has a 2.6-liter V6. The C320 sedan and new C320 wagon use a 3.2 V6. The new C32 AMG sedan has a supercharged V6, 17-inch wheels vs. other models' 16s, plus sport suspension. The C230 and C240 have standard 6-speed manual transmission. A 5-speed automatic with manual shift gate is optional for those models and is mandatory on C320 and C32. (The C32's "SpeedShift" automatic is programmed for high-performance driving.) All models come with traction control, antiskid system, and antilock 4-wheel disc brakes. Also included are front and rear side airbags, curtain side airbags, and Mercedes' BabySmart child-seat recognition system. Leather upholstery is standard on C32, optional on other models. Available for sedans is a Sport Package with upgraded suspension and aero body add-ons. The coupe's optional Panorama glass sunroof opens wider than other sunroofs and includes a fixed glass panel over the rear seat, plus dual power sunshades. Mercedes' TeleAid assistance system is optional for C230 and standard elsewhere. Available for all is Mercedes' COMAND navigation system, which includes an Internet-based "InfoServices" feature that displays user-selected information.

RATINGS	C230, auto.	C240, man.	C240 w/Sport Pkg., auto.	C320 w/nav. sys.
ACCELERATION	6	5	4	7
FUEL ECONOMY	5	5	5	5
RIDE QUALITY	6	7	6	7
STEERING/HANDLING	7	7	8	7
QUIETNESS	5	7	6	7
INSTRUMENTS/CONTROLS	7	7	7	6
ROOM/COMFORT (FRONT)	6	6	6	6
ROOM/COMFORT (REAR)	3	4	4	4
CARGO ROOM	6	3	3	3

Prices are accurate at time of publication; subject to manufacturer's change.

MERCEDES-BENZ

	C230, auto.	C240, man.	C240 w/Sport Pkg., auto.	C320 w/nav. sys.
VALUE	3	4	4	4

More than a "baby Mercedes," the C-Class is a near-luxury car desirable in its own right—despite some cut-rate interior details. Sedans compete head-on with the best in class for driving enjoyment, features, and long-term value. The same should go for the new wagon. The entertaining C230 has Mercedes' lowest base price but skimps on standard luxuries, and options can bring it near an Acura CL, which has a more polished powertrain but fewer safety features.

TOTAL	54	55	53	56

Average total for near-luxury cars: 54.5

ENGINES	Supercharged dohc I4	ohc V6	ohc V6	Supercharged ohc V6
Size, liters/cu. in.	2.3/140	2.6/159	3.2/195	3.2/195
Horsepower @ rpm	192 @ 5500	168 @ 5500	215 @ 5700	349 @ 6100
Torque (lb-ft) @ rpm	200 @ 2500	177 @ 4500	221 @ 3000	332 @ 3000
Availability	S[1]	S[2]	S[3]	S[4]
EPA city/highway mpg				
6-speed manual	19/29	17/26		
5-speed automatic	21/28	19/26	19/25	17/22

1. C230. 2. C240. 3. C320. 4. C32 AMG.

PRICES

Mercedes-Benz C-Class	Retail Price	Dealer Invoice
C230 Sports Coupe 2-door hatchback	$24950	$23204
C240 4-door sedan	30550	28412
C320 4-door sedan	36950	34364
C320 4-door wagon	38450	35759
C32 4-door sedan	49900	46407
Destination charge	645	645

STANDARD EQUIPMENT

C230 Sports Coupe: 2.3-liter dohc 4-cylinder supercharged engine, 6-speed manual transmission, traction control, dual front airbags w/automatic child seat recognition system, front and rear side airbags, curtain side airbags, antilock 4-wheel disc brakes, brake assist, antiskid system, daytime running lights, emergency inside trunk release, power steering, tilt/telescoping leather-wrapped steering wheel w/radio and additional controls, cruise control, air conditioning w/dual-zone automatic climate control, interior air filter, cloth

Specifications begin on page 551.

MERCEDES-BENZ

upholstery, front bucket seats, center console, cupholders, split folding rear seat, heated power mirrors w/driver-side automatic day/night, power windows, power door locks, remote keyless entry, AM/FM/cassette w/CD changer controls, digital clock, tachometer, trip computer, map lights, rear defogger, cargo cover, heated intermittent wipers, automatic day/night rearview mirror, illuminated visor mirrors, universal garage door opener, automatic headlights, floormats, theft-deterrent system, front and rear fog lights, full-size spare tire, 205/55HR16 tires, alloy wheels.

C240 adds: 2.6-liter V6 engine, TeleAid emergency assistance system, leather/vinyl upholstery, 8-way power front seats, wood interior trim, outside temperature indicator. *Deletes:* split folding rear seat, cargo cover.

C320 adds: 3.2-liter V6 engine, 5-speed automatic transmission w/manual-shift capability, power tilt/telescoping steering wheel, 10-way power front seats, memory system (driver seat, mirrors, steering wheel, climate control), split folding rear seat (wagon), Bose sound system, cargo cover (wagon), rear heated wiper/washer (wagon), roof rack (wagon).

C32 adds: 3.2-liter V6 supercharged engine, full leather upholstery, heated front seats, split folding rear seat, power sunroof, 225/45ZR17 front tires, 245/40ZR17 rear tires.

OPTIONAL EQUIPMENT
Major Packages

	Retail Price	Dealer Invoice
Option Pkg. C1, C230, C240	$1225	$1139

10-way power front seats, power tilt/telescoping steering wheel, memory system for driver seat, steering wheel, mirrors and climate control.

Option Pkg. C2, C240, C320 sedan	1370	1274
C320 wagon	1250	1163
C230	995	925

Power sunroof, power rear sunshade (sedan), rain-sensing wipers.

Option Pkg. C3, C240, C320 sedan	435	405

Split folding rear seat, ski sack.

Option Pkg. C4, C230, C240, C320	820	763

Heated front seats and headlight washers.

Premium Option Pkg. C5, C230	2700	2511

Leather upholstery, power sunroof, Bose sound system, rain-sensing wipers.

Option Pkg. Sport C6, C240, C320	3010	2799

Full leather upholstery, sport bucket seats, aluminum interior trim, unique gauge faces, body cladding, firmer suspension, 225/50VR16 tires, unique alloy wheels.

Prices are accurate at time of publication; subject to manufacturer's change.

MERCEDES-BENZ

	Retail Price	Dealer Invoice
Wheel Option Pkg. C7, C230	$750	$698
Aluminum pedals and door sills, leather shift knob, 225/45ZR17 tires.		
Option Pkg. K2	1795	1669
Cellular telephone, 6-disc CD changer.		
Option Pkg. K2A	2190	2037
Voice-activated cellular telephone, 6-disc CD changer.		

Powertrain
5-speed automatic transmission w/manual-shift capability, C230, C240	1300	1209

Safety
TeleAid emergency assistance system, C230	750	698

Comfort & Convenience Features
Power sunroof, C240, C320 sedan	1185	1102
Navigation CD collection	140	130
Requires COMAND navigation system.		
Full leather upholstery, C230, C240, C320	1410	1311
Multicontour driver seat, C240, C320	460	428
Bose sound system, C230, C240	610	567
Power rear sunshade, C32	205	191
Rain-sensing wipers, C32	200	186

Appearance and Miscellaneous
Xenon headlights, C240, C320, C32	870	809

MERCEDES-BENZ CLK

Mercedes-Benz CLK 320 2-door coupe

Rear-wheel-drive luxury car
2001 base price range: $41,950-$67,400. Built in Germany.

Specifications begin on page 551.

MERCEDES-BENZ

Also consider: Acura CL, BMW 3-Series

FOR • Steering/handling • Acceleration **AGAINST** • Rear-seat and cargo room • Rear-seat entry/exit

Based on Mercedes' previous-generation C-Class sedan, this sporty 2-door lineup offers coupes and convertibles in three states of tune and equipment. CLK320 models have a 215-hp V6. CLK430s have a 275-hp V8. High-performance CLK55 AMG versions have a 342-hp V8, plus interior and body trim designed by Mercedes' AMG performance division. All have a 5-speed automatic transmission with manual shift feature, ABS, traction control/antiskid system, front side airbags, and Mercedes' TeleAid emergency assistance system. The convertible has a power top with heated glass rear window. For 2002, the CLK55 coupe is joined by a convertible companion. Newly optional for 320 models is a Sport package with aero bodywork and 17-inch wheels. And CLK430s gain standard aero body trim, light-gray gauges, blue-tinted windows, and new-look alloy wheels. Mercedes' COMAND system option controls audio, navigation and available cell phone from a dashboard screen. An Internet-based "InfoServices" feature displays user-selected information on the COMAND screen.

RATINGS	CLK320 cpe	CLK430 conv	CLK55 AMG cpe
ACCELERATION	7	8	9
FUEL ECONOMY	5	5	3
RIDE QUALITY	7	6	4
STEERING/HANDLING	7	7	9
QUIETNESS	6	5	5
INSTRUMENTS/CONTROLS	5	5	5
ROOM/COMFORT (FRONT)	5	5	5
ROOM/COMFORT (REAR)	2	2	2
CARGO ROOM	2	2	2
VALUE	3	2	2

As spinoffs of the previous-generation C-class sedan, CLKs are starting to feel dated in some ways, such as their lack of a tilt steering column. But they nonetheless appeal for poise, Mercedes cachet, resale value, and V8 performance.

TOTAL	49	47	46

Average total for luxury cars: 59.4

ENGINES	ohc V6	ohc V8	ohc V8
Size, liters/cu. in.	3.2/195	4.3/260	5.4/322
Horsepower @ rpm	215 @ 5700	275 @ 5750	342 @ 5500
Torque (lb-ft) @ rpm	229 @ 3000	295 @ 3000	376 @ 3000

Prices are accurate at time of publication; subject to manufacturer's change.

MERCEDES-BENZ

	ohc V6	ohc V8	ohc V8
Availability	S[1]	S[2]	S[3]
EPA city/highway mpg			
5-speed automatic	20/27	18/24	17/24

1. CLK320. 2. CLK430. 3. CLK55.

2002 prices unavailable at time of publication.

PRICES

2001 Mercedes-Benz CLK	Retail Price	Dealer Invoice
CLK320 2-door coupe	$41950	$39014
CLK320 2-door convertible	48900	45477
CLK430 2-door coupe	49650	46175
CLK430 2-door convertible	56500	52545
CLK55 2-door coupe	67400	62682
Destination charge	645	645

STANDARD EQUIPMENT

CLK320: 3.2-liter V6 engine, 5-speed automatic transmission w/manual-shift capability, traction control, dual front airbags w/automatic child seat recognition system, front side airbags, antilock 4-wheel disc brakes, anti-skid system, automatic roll bar (convertible), TeleAid emergency assistance system, air conditioning w/dual-zone automatic climate control, interior air filter, power steering, telescoping leather-wrapped steering wheel w/radio controls, cruise control, leather upholstery, 10-way power front seats w/driver seat memory, center console, cupholders, split folding rear seat, wood interior trim, heated power mirrors w/memory, driver-side mirror w/automatic day/night, passenger-side mirror w/tilt-down back-up aid, power windows, power door locks, remote keyless entry, power convertible top (convertible), wind deflector (convertible), Bose AM/FM/cassette/weatherband w/CD changer controls, digital clock, tachometer, outside temperature indicator, intermittent wipers, illuminated visor mirrors, rear defogger, automatic day/night rearview mirror, universal garage door opener, floormats, theft-deterrent system, front and rear fog lights, full-size spare tire, 205/55R16 tires, alloy wheels.

CLK430 adds: 4.3-liter V8 engine, lower-body cladding, 225/45ZR17 front tires, 245/40ZR17 rear tires.

CLK55 adds: 5.4-liter V8 engine, heated multi-contour front seats, power sunroof, rain-sensing wipers, power rear sunshade, Xenon headlights w/washers, sport suspension.

OPTIONAL EQUIPMENT
Major Packages

Option Pkg. K2	1795	1038

Integrated portable cellular telephone, 6-disc CD changer.

Specifications begin on page 551.

MERCEDES-BENZ

	Retail Price	Dealer Invoice
Option Pkg. K2A	$2190	$1355
Voice-activated cellular telephone, 6-disc CD changer.		
Option Pkg. K3, 320/430 coupe	1340	1246
Power sunroof, rain-sensing wipers, power rear window sunshade.		
Option Pkg. K4, 320/430 coupe	1545	1437
convertible	1650	1535
Heated front seats, rain-sensing wipers (convertible), Xenon headlights w/washers.		
Designo Espresso Edition	6050	5627
Light brown seat trim, light brown/charcoal steering wheel and floormats, natural maple wood console trim. Requires heated front seats or Option Pkg. K4.		
Designo Slate Blue Edition	6850	6371
Charcoal maple console trim, dark blue/charcoal seat trim, steering wheel, and floormats. Requires heated front seats or Option Pkg. K4.		

Comfort & Convenience Features

COMAND System	2035	1893
Navigation system, CD player. Deletes cassette player.		
Multi-contour front seats, 320, 430	725	674
Heated front seats, 320, 430	620	577

MERCEDES-BENZ E-CLASS

Mercedes-Benz E320 4-door wagon

Rear- or all-wheel-drive luxury car
Base price range: $48,450-$71,350. Built in Germany.
Also consider: Audi A6/allroad quattro, BMW 5-Series, Lexus GS 300/430

Prices are accurate at time of publication; subject to manufacturer's change.

MERCEDES-BENZ

FOR • Cargo room (wagon) • Acceleration • Steering/handling • Ride • Available all-wheel drive • Build quality • Exterior finish **AGAINST** • Fuel economy (E430, E55) • Navigation system controls

Mercedes' midsize line offers the V6 E320 sedan and wagon, the V8 E430 sedan, and the high-performance V8 E55 AMG sedan. Mercedes' 4Matic all-wheel drive is optional for the E430 and E320s in place of rear-wheel drive. The wagon seats seven via a rear-facing 3rd-row seat. All models have a 5-speed automatic transmission with manual shift feature, traction control/antiskid system, curtain side airbags, front/rear side airbags, and Mercedes' TeleAid assistance system. A rear obstacle warning system is optional. A Sport Package option for E320/430 sedans includes larger wheels and tires and "aero" lower-body styling. All models offer optional voice-activated cell phone and a satellite navigation system that includes an Internet-based "InfoServices" feature that displays user-selected information on the dashboard screen. New color choices and new-look alloy wheels for the E320 are the only 2002 changes.

RATINGS

	E320 sdn	E320 wgn	E430 sdn	E55 AMG
ACCELERATION	6	6	7	8
FUEL ECONOMY	5	5	4	4
RIDE QUALITY	9	9	9	7
STEERING/HANDLING	7	7	7	9
QUIETNESS	8	8	8	6
INSTRUMENTS/CONTROLS	6	6	5	6
ROOM/COMFORT (FRONT)	8	8	8	8
ROOM/COMFORT (REAR)	6	6	6	6
CARGO ROOM	4	8	4	4
VALUE	7	7	6	2

Unqualified Best Buy luxury choices, with top-notch quality, high resale value, great all-around performance, and many safety features, including available 4Matic. The E320s are the best dollar buys.

TOTAL	66	70	64	60

Average total for luxury cars: 59.4

ENGINES

	ohc V6	ohc V8	ohc V8
Size, liters/cu. in.	3.2/195	4.3/260	5.4/322
Horsepower @ rpm	221 @ 5500	275 @ 5750	349 @ 5500
Torque (lb-ft) @ rpm	232 @ 3000	295 @ 3000	391 @ 3000
Availability	S[1]	S[2]	S[3]

EPA city/highway mpg
5-speed automatic .... 20/28[4]   17/24[5]   17/24

1. E320. 2. E430. 3. E55 AMG. 4. 20/27 wagon; 20/27 4Matic sedan; 19/26 4matic wagon. 5. 17/23 w/4matic.

Specifications begin on page 551.

MERCEDES-BENZ

PRICES

Mercedes-Benz E-Class

	Retail Price	Dealer Invoice
E320 4-door sedan	$48450	$45059
E320 4-door wagon	49250	45803
E320 AWD 4-door sedan	48450	45059
E320 AWD 4-door wagon	49250	45803
E430 4-door sedan	53850	50081
E430 AWD 4-door sedan	53850	50081
E55 4-door sedan	71350	66356
Destination charge	645	645

AWD models require 4Matic all-wheel drive.

STANDARD EQUIPMENT

E320 sedan: 3.2-liter V6 engine, 5-speed automatic transmission w/manual-shift capability, traction control, dual front airbags w/automatic child seat recognition system, front and rear side airbags, curtain side airbags, antilock 4-wheel disc brakes, brake assist, antiskid system, TeleAid emergency assistance system, emergency inside trunk release, air conditioning w/dual-zone automatic climate control, interior air filter, power steering, power tilt/telescopic steering wheel w/memory feature, leather-wrapped steering wheel, cruise control, leather upholstery, 10-way power front bucket seats w/memory feature, center console, cupholders, wood interior trim, heated power mirrors w/memory feature and driver-side automatic day/night, passenger-side mirror tilt-down parking aid, power windows, power door locks, remote keyless entry, automatic day/night rearview mirror, outside-temperature indicator, AM/FM/cassette/weatherband, digital clock, tachometer, rear defogger, illuminated visor mirrors, remote fuel door and decklid releases, universal garage-door opener, variable intermittent wipers, map lights, floormats, theft-deterrent system, front and rear fog lights, full-size spare tire, 215/55HR16 tires, alloy wheels.

E320 wagon adds: cloth and leather upholstery, folding third seat, cargo cover, intermittent rear wiper and heated washer, automatic rear load leveling suspension, roof rails.

E430 adds to E320 sedan: 4.3-liter V8 engine, Bose sound system, 235/45WR17 tires.

E55 adds: 5.4-liter V8 engine, power sunroof, heated multicontour front seats, rain-sensing wipers, power rear window sunshade, Xenon headlights w/washers, sport suspension, 245/40ZR18 front tires, 275/35ZR18 rear tires.

OPTIONAL EQUIPMENT
Major Packages
E1 Option Pkg., E320, E430	1125	1046

Xenon headlamps, heated headlight washers.

Prices are accurate at time of publication; subject to manufacturer's change.

MERCEDES-BENZ

	Retail Price	Dealer Invoice
E2 Option Pkg., E320	$1645	$1530

Bose sound system, power sunroof, rain-sensing wipers.

E3 Sport Option Pkg., E320, E430	4175	3883

Front air dam, side sill skirts, rear apron, projector beam fog lights, 235/45WR17 tires, special alloy wheels. NA AWD.

ES1 Option Pkg.	1075	NA

Parktronic rear obstacle detection system, rear reading lights. Requires special order charge.

K2 Option Pkg.	1795	1669

Integrated portable cellular telephone, 6-disc CD changer.

K2A Option Pkg.	2190	2037

Voice-activated integrated portable cellular telephone, 6-disc CD changer.

designo Espresso/Silver Editions, E320	6800	NA
E430	6200	NA
E55	5400	NA

Special wood interior trim, wood/eather-wrapped steering wheel, Nappa leather upholstery, unique floormats. E320, E430 require heated front seats. Not available AWD.

COMAND System	2080	1934

Navigation system, AM/FM/CD player, steering wheel radio controls.

Powertrain

4Matic all-wheel drive, E320 AWD, E430 AWD	2850	2651

Comfort & Convenience Features

Power sunroof, E320, E430	1185	1102
Full leather upholstery, E320 wagon	1410	1311
Heated multicontour power front seats, E320, E430	740	688
Active ventilated front seats	1175	1093

Includes heated seats. Wagons require full leather upholstery.

Heated front seats, E320, E430	635	591
Power rear window sunshade, E320 sedan, E430	430	400

MERCEDES-BENZ M-CLASS

All-wheel-drive midsize sport-utility vehicle

Base price range: $36,300-$65,900. Built in USA.

Also consider: Acura MDX, Ford Explorer, Lexus RX 300

FOR • Acceleration (ML430, ML55) • Build quality
• Passenger and cargo room   **AGAINST** • Fuel economy
• Ride (ML430, ML55)

Specifications begin on page 551.

MERCEDES-BENZ

Mercedes-Benz ML500

Freshened styling, curtain side airbags, and a more powerful V8 engine lead the 2002 changes to this American-built SUV. The V6 ML320 returns, but the ML430 is replaced by the ML500 with a 288-hp 5.0-liter V8 supplanting a 268-hp 4.3 V8. Also back is the high-performance ML55 AMG. All have a 5-speed automatic transmission with manual shift gate and all-wheel drive with low-range gearing. Antilock 4-wheel disc brakes and a traction control/antiskid system are standard. A 2-person 3rd-row seat is optional except on ML55. For '02, front and rear side torso airbags are joined by standard side curtain airbags designed to cushion the head and upper-body in a side collision. New front and rear bumpers and lights add 2 inches to overall length. And the ML320 trades 16-inch wheels for the ML500's 17s (ML55 has 18s). New inside are automatic climate controls, rear-seat fan controls, and a new center console with walnut trim; leather upholstery remains optional on ML320, standard on the others. All have Mercedes' TeleAid assistance system and a dashboard screen for controlling audio and optional cell phone and navigation systems. An Internet-based "InfoServices" feature displays user-selected information on the screen.

RATINGS	ML320	ML500 w/Sport Pkg.	ML55 AMG
ACCELERATION	5	7	7
FUEL ECONOMY	4	3	2
RIDE QUALITY	4	3	2
STEERING/HANDLING	4	4	5
QUIETNESS	4	4	3
INSTRUMENTS/CONTROLS	4	4	4
ROOM/COMFORT (FRONT)	7	7	7
ROOM/COMFORT (REAR)	8	8	8
CARGO ROOM	8	8	8

Prices are accurate at time of publication; subject to manufacturer's change.

MERCEDES-BENZ

	ML320	ML500 w/Sport Pkg.	ML55 AMG
VALUE	5	2	2

Though one of the most competent and pleasant truck-type SUVs, the M-Class seems rather dated now. It's also pricey against the car-based Acura MDX and Lexus RX 300, which offer better ride comfort, driving ease and quietness. Mercedes' typical high resale values compensate, but not enough.

TOTAL	53	50	48

Average total for midsize sport-utility vehicles: 49.6

EXTENDED-USE TEST UPDATE

Extended-use ML430 required no unscheduled maintenance during its 12-month test period, but suffered poor AM radio reception in urban areas. Overall workmanship was as expected of a Mercedes, but, like other MLs we tested, this extended-use model showed occasional rough-road body shudder.

ENGINES

	ohc V6	ohc V8	ohc V8
Size, liters/cu. in.	3.2/195	5.0/303	5.4/332
Horsepower @ rpm	215 @ 5500	288 @ 5600	342 @ 5500
Torque (lb-ft) @ rpm	233 @ 3000	325 @ 2700	376 @ 2800
Availability	S[1]	S[2]	S[3]
EPA city/highway mpg			
5-speed automatic	15/19	14/17	14/17

1. ML320. 2. ML500. 3. ML55.

PRICES

Mercedes-Benz M-Class	Retail Price	Dealer Invoice
ML320 4-door wagon	$36300	$33759
ML500 4-door wagon	44950	41804
ML55 4-door wagon	65900	61287
Destination charge	645	645

STANDARD EQUIPMENT

ML320: 3.2-liter V6 engine, 5-speed automatic transmission w/manual-shift capability, all-wheel drive, 2-speed transfer case, traction control, dual front airbags w/automatic child seat recognition system, front and rear side airbags, curtain side airbags, antiskid system, antilock 4-wheel disc brakes, TeleAid assistance system, air conditioning w/automatic climate control and rear controls, interior air filter, power steering, tilt leather-wrapped steering wheel, cruise control, cloth upholstery, manual 6-way front bucket seats, center console, split folding rear seat, cupholders, wood interior trim, heated

Specifications begin on page 551.

350 CONSUMER GUIDE®

MERCEDES-BENZ

power mirrors, power front windows, power door locks, intermittent wipers, remote keyless entry, rear defogger, intermittent rear wiper/washer, AM/FM/cassette w/CD changer controls, digital clock, tachometer, universal garage door opener, illuminated visor mirrors, map lights, cargo cover, floormats, theft-deterrent system, roof rails, front and rear fog lights, front and rear tow hooks, 255/60R17 tires, alloy wheels.

ML500 adds: 5.0-liter V8 engine, leather upholstery, heated 8-way power front seats, automatic day/night driver-side and rearview mirrors, CD navigation system, trip computer, rear privacy glass, 275/55R17 tires.

ML55 adds: 5.5-liter V8 engine, power sunroof, front seat and mirror memory, Bose sound system, power rear quarter windows, rain-sensing wipers, Xenon headlights, 285/50WR18 tires.

OPTIONAL EQUIPMENT

	Retail Price	Dealer Invoice

Major Packages

	Retail Price	Dealer Invoice
M1 Luxury Pkg., ML320	$1635	$1521

Leather upholstery, 8-way power front seats, rear privacy glass. Requires M5 power sunroof.

M2 Convenience Pkg., ML320	1275	1186

Trip computer, automatic day/night driver-side and rearview mirrors, power folding outside mirrors, rain-sensing wipers, dual front seat memory, locking under-passenger-seat compartment. Requires M1 Luxury Pkg., M5 power sunroof.

M3 Convenience Pkg., ML500	800	744

Dual front seat memory, rain-sensing wipers, power folding mirrors w/memory. Requires M5 power sunroof.

M6 Sport Pkg., ML320, ML500	3350	3116

Sport bumpers, bodyside cladding, fender flares, chrome exhaust tips, 275/55R17 tires, special alloy wheels. Requires M5 power sunroof.

M7 Seat Pkg., ML320 w/M1 Pkg.,		
ML500	1180	1097
ML320	975	907
ML320/ML500 w/Designo Edition	3180	NA

Two-passenger third row seat. Deletes cargo cover. Requires M5 power sunroof.

designo Cognac Edition	4100	3813
designo Mystic Green Edition, ML320, ML500	4100	3813
designo Pearl/Sable Edition, ML320, ML500	3400	3162
designo Savanna Edition, ML320, ML500	3800	3534

All designo editions include special exterior color, specific interior color, special wood interior trim and floormats. ML320 requires heated front seats, M1 Luxury Pkg.

Prices are accurate at time of publication; subject to manufacturer's change.

MERCEDES-BENZ

Safety	Retail Price	Dealer Invoice
Parktronic rear obstacle detection system	$1015	$944

Comfort & Convenience Features
M5 power sunroof, ML320, ML500	1295	1204
Includes power rear quarter windows.		
Bose sound system, ML320, ML500	1200	1116
Includes 6-disc CD changer.		
Heated front seats, ML320	635	591
Xenon headlights, ML320, ML500	875	814

MERCEDES-BENZ S-CLASS/ CL-CLASS

Mercedes-Benz S500

Rear-wheel-drive luxury car
2001 base price range: $70,800-$117,200. Built in Germany.
Also consider: Audi A8, BMW 7-Series, Lexus LS 430

FOR • Acceleration • Build quality • Entry/exit (S-Class) • Passenger room (S-Class) • Refinement • Ride **AGAINST** • Rear-seat room (CL-Class) • Rear-seat entry/exit (CL-Class) • Fuel economy • Navigation system controls

These are Mercedes' biggest, costliest sedans and coupes. The sedans are the S430 and S500, named for their 4.3- and 5.0-liter V8 engines, respectively; the high-performance S55 AMG with its 5.4-liter V8; and the V12 S600. Coupes use corresponding engines and come as the CL500, CL55 AMG, and CL600. The V12 models' engine shuts down 6 cylinders to save fuel when full power isn't needed. AMG versions, tuned by Mercedes' high-performance AMG team, have 18-inch wheels and aero body addenda; a Sport Package option delivers their looks and upgraded tires to S430/S500/CL500 models. All have a 5-speed automatic

Specifications begin on page 551.

MERCEDES-BENZ

transmission with manual shift gate, traction/antiskid control, ABS, front and rear torso side airbags, and curtain side airbags. Mercedes' Active Body Control, designed to minimize cornering lean, is optional for S430 and S500 and standard elsewhere. New for '02 is a more-powerful air conditioning maximum-cooling setting and a 3rd memory setting for seats and related controls. Standard is Mercedes' TeleAid assistance system and COMAND video control for audio, navigation, and phone. An Internet-based "InfoServices" feature displays user-selected data on the COMAND screen. Also available is radar cruise control designed to automatically maintain a safe following distance from vehicles ahead.

RATINGS	S430	S500	S600	CL500
ACCELERATION	7	7	8	7
FUEL ECONOMY	4	4	3	4
RIDE QUALITY	10	10	10	10
STEERING/HANDLING	7	7	7	9
QUIETNESS	10	10	10	9
INSTRUMENTS/CONTROLS	4	4	4	4
ROOM/COMFORT (FRONT)	10	10	10	10
ROOM/COMFORT (REAR)	9	9	10	2
CARGO ROOM	4	4	4	2
VALUE	3	3	2	2

Some features seem needlessly high tech, and cost-cutting is evident in a detail or two. Still, these are among the world's very best luxury cars—as they should be at these prices—with Mercedes' solid-gold resale values and kid-gloves customer care part of the deal.

TOTAL	68	68	68	59

Average total for luxury cars: 59.4

ENGINES	ohc V8	ohc V8	ohc V8	ohc V12
Size, liters/cu. in.	4.3/260	5.0/303	5.4/322	5.8/353
Horsepower @ rpm	275 @ 5750	302 @ 5500	355 @ 5500	362 @ 5500
Torque (lb-ft) @ rpm	295 @ 3000	339 @ 2700	391 @ 3000	391 @ 4100
Availability	S[1]	S[2]	S[3]	S[4]
EPA city/highway mpg				
5-speed automatic	17/24	16/23	16/22	15/22

1. S430. 2. S500, CL500. 3. S55 AMG, CL55 AMG 4. S600, CL600

2002 prices unavailable at time of publication.

PRICES

2001 Mercedes-Benz S-Class/CL-Class	Retail Price	Dealer Invoice
S430 4-door sedan	$70800	$65844
S500 4-door sedan	78950	73424

Prices are accurate at time of publication; subject to manufacturer's change.

MERCEDES-BENZ

	Retail Price	Dealer Invoice
S55 4-door sedan	$98000	$91140
S600 4-door sedan	114000	106020
CL500 2-door coupe	87500	81375
CL55 2-door coupe	99500	92535
CL600 2-door coupe	117200	108996
Destination charge	645	645

S500, CL500, S55, CL55 add $1000 Gas Guzzler Tax. S600 and CL600 add $1300 Gas Guzzler Tax.

STANDARD EQUIPMENT

S430: 4.3-liter V8 engine, 5-speed automatic transmission w/manual-shift capability, traction control, dual front airbags w/automatic child seat recognition system, front and rear side airbags, curtain side airbags, anti-skid system, antilock 4-wheel disc brakes, COMAND navigation system, TeleAid emergency assistance system, daytime running lights, air conditioning w/dual-zone automatic climate control, interior air filter, variable-assist power steering, power tilt/telescoping leather-wrapped steering wheel w/memory, cruise control, leather upholstery, 14-way power front bucket seats w/adjustable lumbar support and memory, center console, cupholders, wood interior trim, heated power mirrors w/memory and driver-side automatic day/night and passenger-side tilt-down parking aid, power windows, power door locks, remote keyless entry, power sunroof, automatic day/night rearview mirror, universal garage door opener, front and rear illuminated visor mirrors, AM/FM/cassette/CD player w/Bose sound system, steering wheel radio controls, tachometer, rain-sensing intermittent wipers, automatic headlights, map lights, floormats, theft-deterrent system, outside-mirror mounted turn signal lights, front and rear fog lights, self-leveling air suspension, 225/60R16 tires, alloy wheels.

S500 adds: 5.0-liter V8 engine, upgraded leather upholstery, heated front seats, Xenon headlights, headlight washers.

CL500 adds: 6-disc CD changer, wood/leather-wrapped steering wheel, power rear sunshade, active suspension, 225/55HR17 tires. *Deletes:* rear visor mirrors, self-leveling air suspension.

S55/CL55 add to S500: 5.4-liter engine, wood/leather-wrapped steering wheel (CL55), 6-disc CD changer, power rear sunshade, multi-contour and active ventilated front seats, active suspension, 245/45YR18 front tires, 275/40YR18 rear tires. *Deletes:* self-leveling air suspension.

S600/CL600 adds: 6.0-liter V12 engine, rear obstacle detection system, rear dual-zone automatic climate controls (S600), wood/leather wrapped steering, power adjustable heated rear seats w/lumbar adjustment (S600), cellular telephone, additional leather interior trim, alcantara headliner, 225/55ZR17 tires, polished alloy wheels.

Specifications begin on page 551.

MERCEDES-BENZ

OPTIONAL EQUIPMENT	Retail Price	Dealer Invoice

Major Packages

	Retail Price	Dealer Invoice
Designo Espresso Edition, S430............................	$9500	$8835
S500, S55	8700	8091
S600	7500	6975

Special light brown leather seat trim w/two-tone door panels, elm wood interior trim, unique floormats, Designo Expresso paint. Requires climate comfort rear seats or heated rear seats.

Designo Silver Edition, S430....................................	10450	9719
S500	9750	9068
S600	8550	7952

Shell-colored leather interior trim, maple wood interior trim, unique floormats, Designo Silver paint. Requires Active ventilated seats or heated rear seats, power rear seats or Four Place Seating Pkg.

Designo Espresso Edition, CL500, CL55................	9800	9114
CL600	8300	7719

Special mocha leather interior trim, natural maple wood trim on console and doors, unique floormats. CL500 requires CL3 Comfort Pkg.

Designo Silver Edition, CL500, CL55.....................	9800	9114
S600	8300	7719

Platinum leather interior trim, natural maple wood door and console trim, unique floormats. CL500 requires CL3 Comfort Pkg.

S5/CL2 Sport Pkg., S430, S500, CL 500, S600	4900	4557

Front spoiler, side skirts, rear apron, 245/45YR18 front tires, 275/YR18 rear tires, AMG Monoblock Wheels.

K2A Option Pkg., S430, S500.................................	2190	1355

Voice-activated integrated cellular telephone, 6-disc CD changer.

Safety

Parktronic rear obstacle detection system	995	925
Tire pressure monitor, S430, S500, S600, CL500, CL600	600	558

Comfort & Convenience Features

Keyless go..	995	925

Remote keyless entry and ignition starting system.

S3 Comfort Pkg., S430	1960	1823

Multicontour front seats w/pulsating air chambers, and active lumbar support, heated and active ventilated front seats.

S3/CL3 Comfort Pkg., S500, CL500	1460	1358

Multicontour front seats w/pulsating air chambers, and active lumbar support, heated and active ventilated front seats.

Active ventilated seats, S430, S500, S55	1530	1423

Prices are accurate at time of publication; subject to manufacturer's change.

CONSUMER GUIDE®

MERCEDES-BENZ

	Retail Price	Dealer Invoice
S600	$910	$846
Includes heated rear seats. Requires power rear seat adjusters or Four Place Seating Pkg.		
Power rear adjusters, S430, S500, S55	1785	1660
Four Place Seating Pkg., S500	5655	5259
S600	3870	3599
Includes rear bucket seats, power reclining seatbacks, wood console.		
Heated front seats, S430	620	577
Heated rear seats, S430, S500, S55	620	577
Rear dual-zone climate control, S430, S500, S55	1840	1711
Distronic cruise control	2800	2604
Parktronic	995	925
Rear side sunshades	300	279
Power trunk closer	450	419

Appearance and Miscellaneous

Xenon headlights w/washers, S430	1130	1051
Active suspension, S430, S500	2900	2697
Special order charge	1000	1000
Fee for car ordered with one or more options requiring special order charge.		

2003 MERCEDES-BENZ SL-CLASS

Mercedes-Benz SL-Class 2-door convertible

Rear-wheel-drive luxury car
Base price: NA. Built in Germany.
Also consider: BMW Z8, Jaguar XK8, Porsche 911

Mercedes-Benz redesigns its flagship 2-seat convertible as an early '03 model. The new SL500 retains its predecessor's 302-hp V8, but has new styling and a retractable metal hardtop instead of a

Specifications begin on page 551.

MERCEDES-BENZ

cloth folding top. It's slightly longer, lower, and wider than the 1990-2002 version, but some 125 lb lighter. High-tech features abound, as expected now of Mercedes. Heading the list are antilock 4-wheel disc brakes with industry-first electronic "brake-by-wire" technology that modulates hydraulic pressure to each wheel by computer signal. The SL comes with a 5-speed automatic transmission with manual-shift feature, traction/antiskid control, and Mercedes' ABC active suspension designed to reduce body lean in hard cornering. Side airbags provide head and torso protection. Knee airbags are included, as is a rollover bar that automatically pops up if sensors detect an impending crash. Also standard are a navigation system; Mercedes' TeleAid communications system with emergency and concierge services; automatic climate control with temperature, humidity and pollution sensors; and a second battery, mounted in the trunk, for running power accessories.

Options include 18-inch wheels vs. standard 17s; tire-pressure monitor; Xenon high-beam headlamps; radar cruise control designed to maintain a safe following distance; voice control for audio, phone and other functions; ventilated and massaging seats; and Mercedes' "Keyless Go" system, which takes signals from a credit-card-like transmitter to allow the driver to unlock and start the vehicle by simply touching certain spots. Due at an unspecified later date is a V12 SL600 companion. Prices were not released in time for this report but are expected to mirror the $85,000 base price of the 2002 SL500. We have not yet tested the 2003 model.

ENGINES

	ohc V8
Size, liters/cu. in.	5.0/303
Horsepower @ rpm	302 @ 5600
Torque (lb-ft) @ rpm	339 @ 2700
Availability	S

EPA city/highway mpg

5-speed automatic	NA

2003 prices unavailable at time of publication.

MERCEDES-BENZ SLK-CLASS

Rear-wheel-drive sports car
2001 base price range: $38,900-$43,900. Built in Germany.
Also consider: Audi TT, BMW Z3 Series, Porsche Boxster

FOR • Acceleration • Steering/handling • Build quality • Exterior finish • Interior materials **AGAINST** • Cargo room • Entry/exit • Ride (SLK32 AMG)

A new high-performance model and a revised Sport option pack-

MERCEDES-BENZ

Mercedes-Benz SLK32 AMG

age are 2002 changes to the smaller of Mercedes' two 2-seat convertibles. These cars have a metal hardtop that lowers by powering in and out of the trunk. The SLK230 has a supercharged 4-cyl engine, the SLK320 a V6. The new SLK32 AMG has a supercharged version of the V6, plus modifications to suspension, transmission, bodywork, and interior by Mercedes' AMG performance team. Standard on the SLK230 and SLK320 is a 6-speed manual transmission. A 5-speed automatic is optional on those models and mandatory for the SLK32. Standard on all is a traction control/antiskid system, side airbags, antilock 4-wheel disc brakes, and Mercedes' BabySmart right-side airbag deactivation feature. Power seats and telescopic steering wheel are optional on the SLK230 and standard on the others. Mercedes' TeleAid assistance system is standard. The Sport package option for the SLK230 and 320 now mimics the SLK32's lower-body aero trim, wheels, and projector-beam foglamps.

RATINGS

	SLK230, auto.	SLK320, man.	SLK32 AMG
ACCELERATION	5	6	8
FUEL ECONOMY	6	6	5
RIDE QUALITY	4	4	2
STEERING/HANDLING	8	8	9
QUIETNESS	4	4	3
INSTRUMENTS/CONTROLS	7	7	7
ROOM/COMFORT (FRONT)	5	5	5
ROOM/COMFORT (REAR)	0	0	0
CARGO ROOM	2	2	2
VALUE	2	3	0

The SLK320 is the best value for refined performance. But any SLK provides soft-top fun and hard-top security in a well-built runabout with Mercedes prestige and blue-chip resale values. AMG model appeals only to the hard-core enthusiast.

| **TOTAL** | 43 | 45 | 41 |

Average total for sports cars: 41.3

Specifications begin on page 551.

MERCEDES-BENZ

ENGINES	Supercharged dohc I4	ohc V6	Supercharged ohc V6
Size, liters/cu. in.	2.3/140	3.2/195	3.2/195
Horsepower @ rpm	192 @ 5500	215 @ 5700	349 @ 6100
Torque (lb-ft) @ rpm	200 @ 2500	221 @ 3000	332 @ 300
Availability	S[1]	S[2]	S[3]
EPA city/highway mpg			
6-speed manual	20/30	17/26	
5-speed automatic	23/30	20/26	18/24

1. SLK230. 2. SLK320. 3. SLK32 AMG.

2002 prices unavailable at time of publication.

PRICES

2001 Mercedes-Benz SLK-Class	Retail Price	Dealer Invoice
230 2-door convertible	$38900	$36177
320 2-door convertible	43900	40827
Destination charge	645	645

SLK32 prices and equipment not available at time of publication.

STANDARD EQUIPMENT

230: 2.3-liter supercharged dohc 4-cylinder engine, 6-speed manual transmission, traction control, dual front airbags with automatic child recognition system, front side airbags, antilock 4-wheel disc brakes, antiskid system, navigation system, TeleAid emergency assistance system, air conditioning w/dual-zone controls, interior air filter, power steering, leather-wrapped steering wheel, cruise control, leather upholstery, bucket seats, center console, cupholders, rear defogger, universal garage door opener, heated power mirrors w/driver-side automatic day/night, power windows, power locks, remote keyless entry, automatic day/night rearview mirror, outside temperature indicator, Bose AM/FM/cassette w/CD changer controls, remote decklid release, tachometer, visor mirrors, floormats, power retractable steel hardtop, theft-deterrent system, front and rear fog lights, 205/55VR16 front tires, 225/50VR16 rear tires, alloy wheels.

320 adds: 3.2-liter V6 engine, telescoping steering wheel, 8-way power seats, wood interior trim.

OPTIONAL EQUIPMENT
Major Packages

K1 Pkg., 230	850	791
Telescoping steering wheel, 8-way power seats.		
K4 Pkg.	1545	1437
Xenon headlights, headlight washers, heated seats.		

Prices are accurate at time of publication; subject to manufacturer's change.

CONSUMER GUIDE®

MERCEDES-BENZ • MERCURY

	Retail Price	Dealer Invoice
Sport Pkg. SP1	$4135	$3846

AMG aerodynamic enhancements, 225/45ZR17 front tires, 245/40ZR17 rear tires, special alloy wheels.

Designo Copper Edition	5100	5100

Copper/charcoal-colored leather interior trim, special wood interior trim, special floormats. Requires K4 Pkg. or heated seats.

Designo Electric Green Edition	4650	4650

Charcoal-colored leather interior trim, special wood interior trim, special floormats. Requires K4 Pkg. or heated seats.

Powertrain

5-speed automatic transmission	950	884

Includes manual-shift capability.

Comfort & Convenience Features

Heated seats	620	577

MERCURY COUGAR

Mercury Cougar

Front-wheel-drive sporty coupe
Base price range: $16,520-$19,920. Built in USA.
Also consider: Acura RSX, Toyota Celica, Volkswagen New Beetle

FOR • Exterior finish **AGAINST** • Rear visibility • Rear-seat room

Cougar adds a few standard features, and treats option groups as separate models for 2002. Joining the 4-cyl price-leader are new base-trim V6 and V6 Sport, Sport Premium, and Sport Ultimate models. Automatic transmission is optional for V6s only. Cruise control, remote keyless entry, and rear wiper/washer are now standard on all Cougars. Sports come with rear disc brakes (vs. drums) and 16-inch

Specifications begin on page 551.

MERCURY

wheels (vs. 15s). Front side airbags are standard for Sport Ultimate, unavailable on other models. Sport Ultimate also includes ABS and traction control, which are available for other V6 models. Sports offer a limited-edition C2 trim option as well as a new XR package with 17-inch wheels, hood scoop, front/rear spoilers, and special interior appointments.

RATINGS	Base	V6, auto.	Sport Ultimate, man.
ACCELERATION	5	6	6
FUEL ECONOMY	6	5	5
RIDE QUALITY	3	3	3
STEERING/HANDLING	5	5	6
QUIETNESS	4	4	4
INSTRUMENTS/CONTROLS	3	3	3
ROOM/COMFORT (FRONT)	4	4	4
ROOM/COMFORT (REAR)	2	2	2
CARGO ROOM	6	6	6
VALUE	2	2	2

Cougar is average in most ways—and surprisingly dated after just three years on the market. That's why sales are slow, so don't buy without a sizable discount. Better yet, consider Acura's new RSX or the unique Volkswagen New Beetle, which can cost more but are superior products.

TOTAL	40	40	41

Average total for sporty coupes: 43.4

ENGINES	dohc I4	dohc V6
Size, liters/cu. in.	2.0/121	2.5/155
Horsepower @ rpm	125 @ 5500	170 @ 6250
Torque (lb-ft) @ rpm	130 @ 4000	165 @ 4250
Availability	S[1]	S[2]
EPA city/highway mpg		
5-speed manual	23/34	21/30
4-speed automatic		20/29

1. 4-cyl model. 2. V6, Sport, Sport Premium, Sport Ultimate.

PRICES

Mercury Cougar	Retail Price	Dealer Invoice
4 cylinder 2-door hatchback	$16520	$15333
V6 2-door hatchback	17020	15783
Sport 2-door hatchback	17520	16233
Sport Premium 2-door hatchback	18520	17133
Sport Ultimate 2-door hatchback	19920	18393
Destination charge	475	475

Prices are accurate at time of publication; subject to manufacturer's change.

MERCURY

STANDARD EQUIPMENT

4 cylinder: 2.0-liter dohc 4-cylinder engine, 5-speed manual transmission, dual front airbags, emergency inside trunk release, air conditioning, interior air filter, power steering, tilt steering wheel, cruise control, cloth upholstery, front bucket seats, power height-adjustable driver seat, center console, cupholders, split folding rear seat, heated power mirrors, power windows, power door locks, remote keyless entry, AM/FM/CD player, digital clock, tachometer, trip computer, outside temperature indicator, variable intermittent wipers, driver-side visor mirror, rear defogger, rear wiper/washer, power decklid release, front floormats, theft-deterrent system, 205/60R15 tires, alloy wheels.

V6 adds: 2.5-liter dohc V6 engine, AM/FM/cassette/CD player.

Sport adds: 4-wheel disc brakes, leather-wrapped steering wheel, illuminated visor mirrors, map lights, fog lights, rear spoiler, upgraded suspension, 215/50R16 tires.

Sport Premium adds: power sunroof.

Sport Ultimate adds: traction control, front side airbags, antilock 4-wheel disc brakes, leather upholstery, 6-way power driver seat w/power lumbar adjustment, machined alloy wheels.

OPTIONAL EQUIPMENT

	Retail Price	Dealer Invoice
Major Packages		
C2 Feature Car, Sport, Sport Premium	$515	$458
Sport Ultimate	265	236

AM/FM radio w/in-dash 6-disc CD changer, unique rear spoiler, machined alloy wheels.

XR Feature Car, Sport, Sport Premium/Ultimnate	950	846

Hood scoop, unique front and rear spoilers, special interior trim, 215/50ZR17 tires.

Powertrain

4-speed automatic transmission, V6, Sport, Sport Premium/Ultimate	995	886
Traction control, Sport Premium	235	209

Requires antilock brakes.

Safety

Antilock brakes, V6, Sport, Sport Premium	500	445

Comfort & Convenience Features

Power sunroof, 4-cylinder, V6, Sport	615	547
Leather upholstery, Sport Premium	895	797
AM/FM/cassette/CD player, 4-cylinder	80	71
AM/FM radio w/in-dash 6-disc CD changer	130	116

NA 4-cylinder.

Specifications begin on page 551.

MERCURY

Appearance and Miscellaneous	Retail Price	Dealer Invoice
Rear spoiler, 4-cylinder, V6	$235	$209
Machined alloy wheels, Sport Premium	250	223

MERCURY GRAND MARQUIS

Mercury Grand Marquis

Rear-wheel-drive full-size car
Base price range: $23,645-$28,625. Built in Canada.
Also consider: Buick LeSabre, Chrysler Concorde, Dodge Intrepid

FOR • Passenger and cargo room **AGAINST** • Fuel economy

This traditional big rear-drive sedan adds a few standard features and treats option groups as separate models for 2002. The lineup consists of GS, GS Convenience, LS Premium, LS Ultimate, and top-line LSE editions. All have a 4.6-liter V8, 4-speed automatic transmission, 16-inch wheels, 4-wheel disc brakes, and—new for '02—standard heated door mirrors, ABS, and traction control. Horsepower is 220 except on LSE, which has 235, plus performance tires and uprated suspension with rear load-leveling. The LSE also has front bucket seats with console shift vs. the other models' 3-person bench and column shift. Power-adjustable pedals are standard except on the base GS. Leather upholstery is now a no-charge option for LS models and standard for LSE. Grand Marquis shares its design with the Ford Crown Victoria and offers similar performance and accommodations.

RATINGS	LS Ultimate
ACCELERATION	6
FUEL ECONOMY	4
RIDE QUALITY	7
STEERING/HANDLING	5

Prices are accurate at time of publication; subject to manufacturer's change.
CONSUMER GUIDE®

MERCURY

	LS Ultimate
QUIETNESS	6
INSTRUMENTS/CONTROLS	4
ROOM/COMFORT (FRONT)	7
ROOM/COMFORT (REAR)	6
CARGO ROOM	6
VALUE	5

We favor more modern front-wheel-drive rivals like Buick LeSabre and Dodge Intrepid, but traditionalists won't be disappointed with the reasonably priced Crown Victoria and Grand Marquis.

TOTAL	56

Average total for full-size cars: 58.7

ENGINES

	ohc V8	ohc V8
Size, liters/cu. in.	4.6/281	4.6/281
Horsepower @ rpm	220 @ 4750	235 @ 4750
Torque (lb-ft) @ rpm	265 @ 4000	275 @ 4000
Availability	S[1]	S[2]
EPA city/highway mpg		
4-speed automatic	17/25	17/25

1. GS, GS Convenience, LS Premium, LS Ultimate. 2. LSE.

PRICES

Mercury Grand Marquis	Retail Price	Dealer Invoice
GS 4-door sedan	$23645	$22378
GS Convenience 4-door sedan	24065	22765
GS Convenience w/Discount Pkg. B3A 4-door sedan	24045	22746
LS Premium 4-door sedan	27120	25576
LS Ultimate 4-door sedan	28300	26666
LS Ultimate w/Discount Pkg. B3A 4-door sedan	26820	25300
LSE 4-door sedan	28625	26960
LSE w/Discount Pkg. B3A 4-door sedan	27140	25469
Destination charge	680	680

Discount Pkg. B3A available only in Ariz., Calif., Nev., and Hawaii.

STANDARD EQUIPMENT

GS: 4.6-liter V8 220-horsepower engine, 4-speed automatic transmission, traction control, dual front airbags, antilock 4-wheel disc brakes, emergency inside trunk release, air conditioning, power steering, tilt steering wheel, cruise control, cloth upholstery, front split bench seat, 8-way power driver seat w/power lumbar adjustment, cupholders, column shifter, heated power mirrors, power windows, power door locks, AM/FM/cassette, digital clock, variable intermittent wipers, rear defogger, passenger-side visor mirror, map

Specifications begin on page 551.

MERCURY

lights, automatic headlights, remote fuel door/decklid release, floormats, theft-deterrent system, cornering lights, 225/60SR16 whitewall tires, wheel covers.

GS Convenience adds: power adjustable pedals, remote keyless entry.

LS Premium adds: automatic climate control, 8-way power passenger seat, automatic day/night rearview mirror, compass, illuminated visor mirrors, universal garage door opener, alloy wheels.

LS Ultimate adds: wood/leather-wrapped steering wheel w/climate and radio controls, Premium sound system, electronic instruments.

LSE adds: 4.6-liter V8 235-horsepower engine, leather upholstery, front bucket seats, center console, floor shifter, upgraded suspension, rear load-leveling air suspension, 225/60TR16 tires. *Deletes:* electronic instruments.

OPTIONAL EQUIPMENT
Comfort & Convenience Features

	Retail Price	Dealer Invoice
Leather upholstery, GS Convenience	$995	$886
LS Premium/Ultimate	NC	NC
AM/FM/CD player, GS, GS Convenience	140	124
Premium sound system, LS Premium	360	321
6-disc CD changer, LS Premium/Ultimate, LSE	350	312
LS Premium requires Premium sound system.		
Trunk organizer	200	178

Appearance and Miscellaneous

Alloy wheels, LS Premium	370	329

MERCURY MOUNTAINEER

Mercury Mountaineer

Rear- or all-wheel-drive midsize sport-utility vehicle

Prices are accurate at time of publication; subject to manufacturer's change.

MERCURY

Base price range: $28,730-$30,710. Built in USA.
Also consider: Acura MDX, Dodge Durango, Lexus RX 300

FOR • Passenger and cargo room	AGAINST • Fuel economy

Mountaineer shares its design with the Ford Explorer, and both are redesigned for 2002. They have a wider stance, longer wheelbase, and gain independent rear suspension, but Mountaineer gets more expressive styling inside and out. It also has a standard 3rd-row seat for 7-passenger capacity. A V6 is standard. The optional V8 is a new overhead-cam design in place of an overhead-valve V8. Both come only with a 5-speed automatic transmission; V8 Mountaineers previously used a 4-speed automatic. Mountaineer is available with rear-wheel drive or all-wheel drive without low-range gearing (Explorer's 4WD has low range gearing). Antilock 4-wheel disc brakes and tilt/telescoping steering wheel are among the standard equipment. Options include a rear obstacle warning system, power adjustable pedals, and a driver-seat memory. Torso side airbags are not offered, but the optional curtain side airbags are designed to provide head protection in a side collision; later in the model year, they'll be programmed to deploy in a rollover. Also due later in the model year is an optional antiskid system. Mountaineer's performance and accommodations reflect those of similarly equipped Explorers.

RATINGS

	Base AWD, V6	Base AWD w/Lux. Grp., V8
ACCELERATION	4	5
FUEL ECONOMY	4	3
RIDE QUALITY	4	4
STEERING/HANDLING	4	4
QUIETNESS	4	5
INSTRUMENTS/CONTROLS	8	8
ROOM/COMFORT (FRONT)	7	8
ROOM/COMFORT (REAR)	7	7
CARGO ROOM	8	8
VALUE	6	5

Put it on your midsize-SUV shopping list. Hardly inexpensive, but better than before and available with such useful features as 7-passenger seating, adjustable pedals, curtain airbags, Reverse Sensing, and antiskid system.

TOTAL	56	57

Average total for midsize sport-utility vehicles: 49.6

ENGINES

	ohc V6	ohc V8
Size, liters/cu. in.	4.0/245	4.6/281
Horsepower @ rpm	210 @ 5250	240 @ 4750
Torque (lb-ft) @ rpm	250 @ 4000	280 @ 4000

Specifications begin on page 551.

MERCURY

	ohc V6	ohc V8
Availability	S	O
EPA city/highway mpg		
5-speed automatic	15/20[1]	14/19

1. 16/21 w/2WD.

PRICES

Mercury Mountaineer	Retail Price	Dealer Invoice
2WD Base 4-door wagon	$28730	$26345
AWD Base 4-door wagon	30710	28107
Destination charge	600	600

STANDARD EQUIPMENT

Base: 4.0-liter V6 engine, 5-speed automatic transmission, dual front airbags, antilock 4-wheel disc brakes, front air conditioning, power steering, tilt/telescoping leather-wrapped steering wheel, cruise control, cloth upholstery, front bucket seats w/manual lumbar adjustment, 6-way power driver seat, center console, cupholders, second row split bench seat, third row stowable bench seat, overhead console, power mirrors, power windows, power door locks, remote keyless entry, AM/FM/cassette/CD player, digital clock, tachometer, variable intermittent wipers, rear defogger, intermittent rear wiper/washer, visor mirrors, map lights, cargo management system, floormats, theft-deterrent system, rear privacy glass, rear liftgate, roof rack, fog lights, trailer hitch, full-size spare tire, 245/70R16 tires, alloy wheels. **AWD adds:** all-wheel drive.

OPTIONAL EQUIPMENT
Major Packages

Convenience Group	475	404

Power adjustable pedals, driver door keypad entry, universal garage door opener, illuminated visor mirrors, compass, outside temperature indicator, automatic headlights, courtesy approach lights.

Luxury Group	1685	1433

Dual-zone automatic climate control, leather upholstery, heated front seats, 6-way power passenger seat, driver seat and adjustable pedal memory, heated power mirrors, steering wheel radio controls, automatic day/night rearview mirror, message center w/trip computer, cast alloy wheels. Requires Convenience Group.

Trailer Towing Pkg.	395	336

Limited-slip differential, engine cooler, Class III/IV trailer hitch, 7-pin trailer connector.

Prices are accurate at time of publication; subject to manufacturer's change.

MERCURY

	Retail Price	Dealer Invoice
Powertrain		
4.6-liter V8 engine	$695	$591
Safety		
Front and second row curtain side airbags	495	421
Requires Convenience Group.		
Rear obstacle detection system	255	217
Requires Convenience Group.		
Comfort & Convenience Features		
Rear air conditioning	610	518
Includes rear controls, rear heater. NA w/power sunroof.		
Power sunroof	800	680
Requires Convenience Group.		
Audiophile Radio System	690	587
AM/FM radio w/in-dash 6-disc CD changer, premium sound system. Requires Convenience Group.		
Leather upholstery	655	557
Requires Convenience Group.		
Appearance and Miscellaneous		
Running boards	395	336

MERCURY SABLE

Mercury Sable 4-door wagon

Front-wheel-drive midsize car
Base price range: $19,630–$23,220. Built in USA.
Also consider: Honda Accord, Toyota Camry

FOR • Handling/roadholding • Rear-seat comfort • Cargo room **AGAINST** • Low-speed acceleration

ABS as a no-cost option heads a short list of changes for Mercury's 2002 midsize cars. Sable offers sedans and wagons in GS, new GS

Specifications begin on page 551.

MERCURY

Plus, and LS Premium trim. All GS models use a 155-hp 3.0-liter V6, LS Premiums a 200-hp V6. Both team with 4-speed automatic transmission. ABS is now a no-charge option for all Sables; wagons include rear disc brakes instead of drums. An available Secure Group bundles traction control with front side-airbags. Power adjustable foot pedals are standard except on base GS models. Front bucket seats and floorshift console are included on LS Premiums and available for all GS models in place of a split front bench, which is a no-charge LS option. Sable shares its design with the Ford Taurus and has similar performance and accommodations with comparable equipment.

RATINGS	GS Plus wgn	LS Premium sdn
ACCELERATION	4	5
FUEL ECONOMY	5	5
RIDE QUALITY	6	6
STEERING/HANDLING	6	6
QUIETNESS	5	5
INSTRUMENTS/CONTROLS	6	6
ROOM/COMFORT (FRONT)	6	6
ROOM/COMFORT (REAR)	6	6
CARGO ROOM	8	6
VALUE	7	6

Taurus and Sable boast fine road manners, terrific utility, and plenty of safety features at competitive prices. Though acceleration, ride comfort and build quality aren't tops, these are good alternatives to the midsize sales leaders, Honda Accord and Toyota Camry.

TOTAL	59	57

Average total for midsize cars: 57.0

ENGINES

	ohv V6	dohc V6
Size, liters/cu. in.	3.0/182	3.0/181
Horsepower @ rpm	155 @ 4900	200 @ 5650
Torque (lb-ft) @ rpm	185 @ 3950	200 @ 4400
Availability	S[1]	S[2]
EPA city/highway mpg		
4-speed automatic	20/27	19/26

1. GS, GS Plus. 2. LS Premium.

PRICES

Mercury Sable	Retail Price	Dealer Invoice
GS 4-door sedan	$19630	$18182
GS 4-door wagon	21040	19336
GS Plus 4-door sedan	20690	19136
GS Plus 4-door wagon	21930	20137

Prices are accurate at time of publication; subject to manufacturer's change.

MERCURY

	Retail Price	Dealer Invoice
LS Premium 4-door sedan	$22055	$20365
LS Premium 4-door wagon	23220	21298
Destination charge	625	625

STANDARD EQUIPMENT

GS: 3.0-liter V6 engine, 4-speed automatic transmission, dual front airbags, 4-wheel disc brakes (wagon), emergency inside trunk release (sedan), air conditioning, interior air filter, power steering, tilt steering wheel, cruise control, cloth upholstery, 6-passenger seating, split front bench seat, column shift, split folding rear seat (wagon), cupholders, power mirrors, power windows, power door locks, remote keyless entry, AM/FM/cassette, digital clock, power antenna (wagon), tachometer, variable intermittent wipers, rear defogger, visor mirrors, map lights, remote decklid release (sedan), cargo cover (wagon), rear wiper/washer (wagon), floormats, theft-deterrent system, roof rack (wagon), 215/60R16 tires, wheel covers.

GS Plus adds: heated power mirrors, 6-way power driver seat w/lumbar adjustment, split folding rear seat, power adjustable pedals, AM/FM/CD player, automatic day/night rearview mirror, compass, illuminated visor mirrors.

LS Premium adds: 3.0-liter dohc V6 engine, automatic climate control, leather-wrapped steering wheel, 5-passenger seating w/front bucket seats, center console, floor shifter, automatic headlights, fog lights, alloy wheels.

OPTIONAL EQUIPMENT
Major Packages

Secure Group	565	503

Traction control, front side airbags.

Safety

Antilock brakes	NC	NC

Comfort & Convenience Features

5-passenger seating, GS/GS Plus sedan	105	93

Includes center console, floor shift.

6-passenger seating, LS Premium	NC	NC
Leather upholstery, LS Premium	NC	NC
Power passenger seat, LS Premium	350	312

Requires Secure Group.

Power sunroof, LS Premium	890	792
Manufacturer's Discount Price	NC	NC

Manufacturer's discount price available only in California, Hawaii, New York City, Boston, Philadelphia, Pittsburgh, and Washington, DC.

Specifications begin on page 551.

MERCURY

	Retail Price	Dealer Invoice
Mach sound system, LS Premium	$670	$597
Includes 6-disc CD changer.		

Appearance and Miscellaneous
Alloy wheels, GS, GS Plus	395	352
Chrome alloy wheels, LS Premium	295	263

MERCURY VILLAGER

Mercury Villager

Front-wheel-drive minivan
Base price range: $19,340-$27,340. Built in USA.
Also consider: Dodge Caravan, Honda Odyssey, Toyota Sienna

FOR • Passenger and cargo room • Control layout **AGAINST** • Interior materials • Fuel economy

Unchanged for 2002, except for treating option packages as distinct models, Villager is a design twin to the Nissan Quest. Both versions end production after the 2002 model year. Mercury now offers Value, Popular, Sport, Sport Plus, Estate, and Estate Premium models. All have a 3.3-liter V6, 4-speed automatic transmission, dual sliding rear side doors, and a 3-person 3rd-row bench seat that slides on floor tracks. Sports and Estates include 2nd-row buckets, others a 2-person middle bench. Side airbags and power doors aren't available. ABS is optional for Value and Sport, standard elsewhere. Sports and Estates have 16-inch wheels instead of 15s. A rear video entertainment system is a no-charge option for Quest, an extra-cost item on the Villager Sport Plus and Estate Premium.

Prices are accurate at time of publication; subject to manufacturer's change.

MERCURY

RATINGS

	Popular	Estate Premium
ACCELERATION	2	2
FUEL ECONOMY	4	4
RIDE QUALITY	4	4
STEERING/HANDLING	4	5
QUIETNESS	5	5
INSTRUMENTS/CONTROLS	5	5
ROOM/COMFORT (FRONT)	6	6
ROOM/COMFORT (REAR)	6	6
CARGO ROOM	9	9
VALUE	4	4

Most newer-design rivals offer superior space, refinement, performance, and workmanship, not to mention side airbags. But slow Villager/Quest sales and the end of production should mean big discounts. Don't drive home without one.

TOTAL	49	50

Average total for minivans: 56.0

ENGINES

	ohc V6
Size, liters/cu. in.	3.3/200
Horsepower @ rpm	170 @ 4800
Torque (lb-ft) @ rpm	200 @ 2800
Availability	S

EPA city/highway mpg
4-speed automatic	17/23

PRICES

Mercury Villager	Retail Price	Dealer Invoice
Value 4-door van	$19340	$17667
Popular 4-door van	21340	19597
Sport 4-door van	24340	22267
Sport Plus 4-door van	25340	23007
Estate 4-door van	26340	23897
Estate Premium 4-door van	27340	24787
Destination charge: Value, Popular, Sport Plus, Estate, Estate Premium	655	655
Destination charge: Sport	665	665

STANDARD EQUIPMENT

Value: 3.3-liter V6 engine, 4-speed automatic transmission, dual front airbags, front air conditioning, power steering, tilt steering wheel, cruise control, cloth upholstery, 7-passenger seating (front bucket seats, 2-

Specifications begin on page 551.

MERCURY

passenger second row bench seat, 3-passenger third row folding bench seat), center console, cupholders, dual sliding rear doors, power mirrors, power front windows, power door locks, remote keyless entry, AM/FM/cassette, digital clock, tachometer, variable intermittent wipers, illuminated visor mirrors, rear defogger, intermittent rear wiper/washer, floormats, theft-deterrent system, roof rack, cornering lights, 215/70R15 tires, wheel covers.

Popular adds: antilock brakes, rear air conditioning w/rear controls, 6-way power driver seat w/lumbar adjustment, rear radio controls, power rear quarter windows, overhead console w/conversation mirror, map lights, flip-open liftgate, rear privacy glass.

Sport adds: second-row bucket seat, leather-wrapped steering wheel w/radio controls, universal garage door opener, adjustable rear parcel shelf, fog lights, handling suspension, 225/60R16 tires, alloy wheels. *Deletes:* antilock brakes.

Sport Plus adds: antilock brakes, 6-disc CD changer.

Estate adds: leather upholstery, memory driver seat and mirrors, 4-way power passenger seat, Premium sound system, rear headphones, heated power mirrors, automatic headlights.

Estate Premium adds: automatic climate control, electronic instruments, trip computer, outside temperature indicator, Supersound AM/FM/cassette/CD player w/6-disc CD changer.

OPTIONAL EQUIPMENT

	Retail Price	Dealer Invoice
Major Packages		
Rear Seat Entertainment System, Sport Plus, Estate Premium	$1295	$1101

Videocassette player, remote control, video game outlet, rear passenger controls, headphones. Deletes rear radio controls. Sport Plus requires Supersound AM/FM/cassette/CD player. NA w/power sunroof.

Trailer Tow Prep Group, Sport Plus, Estate Premium	250	213

Trailer tow module and jumper harness, heavy-duty battery, full-size spare tire.

Safety

Antilock brakes, Value, Sport	590	502

Comfort & Convenience Features

Rear air conditioning, Value	495	421

Includes interior air filter, rear radio controls.

Automatic climate control, Estate	245	208
Power sunroof, Sport Plus, Estate, Estate Premium	775	659
Electronic instrument cluster, Estate	295	251

Digital speedometer, digital odometer and dual trip odometers, outside temperature indicator, trip computer.

Prices are accurate at time of publication; subject to manufacturer's change.

MERCURY • MINI

	Retail Price	Dealer Invoice
586 Premium AM/FM/cassette, Sport, Sport Plus...	$310	$263
Includes rear radio controls and headphone jacks.		
58K Supersound AM/FM/cassette/CD player, Sport, Sport Plus, Estate	865	735
Includes 6-disc CD changer, upgraded sound system.		
6-disc CD changer, Sport.............................	370	314
Leather upholstery, Sport, Sport Plus	795	676

Appearance and Miscellaneous
Alloy wheels, Popular....................................	495	421

MINI COOPER

Mini Cooper

Front-wheel-drive sporty coupe
Base price: NA. Built in England.
Also consider: Ford Focus ZX3, Toyota Celica, Volkswagen Golf and New Beetle

This all-new 2-dr hatchback has the looks and spirit of Britain's iconic 1959-2000 Mini, but is chiefly a BMW design built at the German company's plant in England. The front-wheel drive Mini is positioned as a sporty coupe rather than an economy subcompact. It seats four within a boxy retro-style body and is among the smallest cars sold in the U.S., at some 18 inches shorter and 400 lb lighter (but 8 inches wider) than a Volkswagen New Beetle. Two models are offered, both with a BMW-developed 1.6-liter 4-cyl engine. Final U.S. specifications weren't available for this report, but the base Mini Cooper will have around 115 hp, the supercharged Cooper S about 163. Manual transmission is standard—a 5 speed for the Cooper, 6 speed for the S. The base Cooper

Specifications begin on page 551.

MINI • MITSUBISHI

offers an optional continuously variable automatic transmission (CVT) with a manual mode providing six separate "gears." Standard equipment includes antilock 4-wheel disc brakes, front torso and head-protecting side airbags, tire-pressure monitor, remote keyless entry, air conditioning, power windows, CD player, and 50/50 split-fold rear seat. The Cooper S gets a functional hood scoop and sport suspension with 16-inch run-flat tires vs. 15s; 17-inch wheels are an S option. The S suspension and wheels are available for the regular Cooper, as is a less-aggressive sport suspension. Options for both include antiskid control, Xenon headlamps, navigation and rear-obstacle warning systems, sunroof, wood-and-leather interior trim, and heated seats.

Minis are available at 70 major-market dealers affiliated with BMW franchises. We have not yet driven the new Mini. Prices were not available for this report, but the Mini Division of BMW expects the Cooper to start below $18,000.

ENGINES

	dohc I4	dohc I4
Size, liters/cu. in.	1.6/98	1.6/98
Horsepower @ rpm	115 @ 6000	163 @ 6000
Torque (lb-ft) @ rpm	110 @ 4500	155 @ 4000
Availability	S[1]	S[2]
EPA city/highway mpg		
5-speed manual	NA	
6-speed manual		NA
CVT automatic	NA	

1. Cooper. 2. Cooper S.

2002 prices unavailable at time of publication.

MITSUBISHI DIAMANTE

Mitsubishi Diamante
Front-wheel-drive near-luxury car
Base price range: $25,687-$28,447. Built in Australia.

Prices are accurate at time of publication; subject to manufacturer's change.

MITSUBISHI

Also consider: Acura TL, Infiniti I35, Lexus ES 300

FOR • Acceleration • Quietness • Ride **AGAINST** • Rear head room

Revised front and rear styling keynote the 2002 changes to Mitsubishi's flagship sedan. Diamante comes with a V6 engine, 4-speed automatic transmission, anitlock 4-wheel disc brakes, and 16-inch alloy wheels. Mitsubishi recommends premium fuel. Side airbags are unavailable. ES and uplevel LS models are offered. Leather upholstery and power sunroof are among standard LS features. In addition to the restyling, both models get new-design alloy wheels, with the ES's going from 15-inch diameter to 16, and the LS's 16s getting a chrome-look finish. Traction control is available in the LS All Weather Package that also includes heated front seats and mirrors.

RATINGS

	LS
ACCELERATION	6
FUEL ECONOMY	5
RIDE QUALITY	7
STEERING/HANDLING	5
QUIETNESS	6
INSTRUMENTS/CONTROLS	6
ROOM/COMFORT (FRONT)	6
ROOM/COMFORT (REAR)	5
CARGO ROOM	3
VALUE	3

Diamante's new styling can't hide such near-luxury class shortcomings as absence of side airbags and lack of a 5-speed automatic transmission. Although this is a competent car attractively priced, it's a dull one, bettered overall by a host of rivals, especially the value-packed Acura TL. It also lags in prestige and therefore resale value.

TOTAL	52

Average total for near-luxury cars: 54.5

ENGINES

	ohc V6
Size, liters/cu. in.	3.5/213
Horsepower @ rpm	205 @ 5000
Torque (lb-ft) @ rpm	231 @ 4000
Availability	S
EPA city/highway mpg	
4-speed automatic	18/25

PRICES

Mitsubishi Diamante	Retail Price	Dealer Invoice
ES 4-door sedan	$25687	$23830

Specifications begin on page 551.

MITSUBISHI

	Retail Price	Dealer Invoice
LS 4-door sedan	$28447	$26377
Destination charge	560	560

STANDARD EQUIPMENT

ES: 3.5-liter V6 engine, 4-speed automatic transmission, dual front airbags, antilock 4-wheel disc brakes, air conditioning w/automatic climate control, power steering, tilt steering wheel, cruise control, cloth upholstery, front bucket seats, height-adjustable driver seat, center console, cupholders, power mirrors, power windows, power door locks, remote keyless entry, AM/FM/CD player, power antenna, digital clock, tachometer, illuminated visor mirrors, variable intermittent wipers, rear defogger, map lights, remote fuel door and decklid release, automatic-off headlights, floormats, theft-deterrent system, full-size spare tire, 215/60VR16 tires, alloy wheels.

LS adds: leather upholstery, 10-way power driver seat w/memory and lumbar adjustment, 8-way power passenger seat, leather-wrapped steering wheel w/radio controls, power sunroof, Infinity sound system, universal garage door opener, fog lights.

OPTIONAL EQUIPMENT

All Weather Pkg., LS	720	584

Traction control, heated front seats and mirrors.

MITSUBISHI ECLIPSE

Mitsubishi Eclipse GT 2-door hatchback

Front-wheel-drive sporty coupe
Base price range: $18,087-$26,597. Built in USA.
Also consider: Acura RSX, Toyota Celica, Volkswagen New Beetle

FOR • Acceleration (V6) • Handling/roadholding **AGAINST**

Prices are accurate at time of publication; subject to manufacturer's change.

MITSUBISHI

• Road noise • Rear-seat room • Rear visibility • Rear-seat entry/exit

Eclipse offers hatchback coupe and Spyder convertible models. RS and GS versions have a 4-cyl engine, GTs a V6. Manual transmission is standard. Automatic is optional and includes a manual shift gate on GS and GT. Spyders have a power top with heated glass window. Alloy wheels, air conditioning, CD stereo, and power windows/locks are standard. Front side airbags and ABS are available only on GT models. They're in the optional Premium Package that also includes traction control for automatic-transmission versions. The only changes for 2002: two new exterior colors, a new Mitsubishi logo, and for GS and GT, glove-box and vanity-mirror lighting.

RATINGS

	RS, man.	GT, man.	GT, auto.	GT Spyder, auto.
ACCELERATION	5	7	6	6
FUEL ECONOMY	7	6	6	6
RIDE QUALITY	4	3	3	3
STEERING/HANDLING	6	8	8	7
QUIETNESS	3	3	3	2
INSTRUMENTS/CONTROLS	5	5	5	5
ROOM/COMFORT (FRONT)	4	4	4	4
ROOM/COMFORT (REAR)	1	1	1	1
CARGO ROOM	5	5	5	1
VALUE	3	3	3	3

V6 and relatively pliant suspension give Eclipse a more-conservative feel than Acura RSX and Toyota Celica, but both those rivals are newer, better built, and more fun to drive.

TOTAL	43	45	44	38

Average total for sporty coupes: 43.4

EXTENDED-USE TEST UPDATE

Extended-test Eclipse GT coupe covered 9848 mi. It required new radiator-hose clamps to stop a minor coolant leak. Intermittent engine-starting problems required replacement of a shorted-out auto-theft system relay. And service was needed when the heater failed to consistently provide warm air. All repairs were covered under warranty.

ENGINES

	ohc I4	ohc V6
Size, liters/cu. in.	2.4/143	3.0/181
Horsepower @ rpm	147 @ 5500	200 @ 5500
Torque (lb-ft) @ rpm	158 @ 4000	205 @ 4000

Specifications begin on page 551.

MITSUBISHI

	ohc I4	ohc V6
Availability	S[1]	S[2]
EPA city/highway mpg		
5-speed manual	23/30	20/28
4-speed automatic	20/27	20/28

1. RS, GS; 140 horsepower and 155 lb-ft with automatic transmission. 2. GT.

PRICES

Mitsubishi Eclipse	Retail Price	Dealer Invoice
RS 2-door hatchback, manual	$18087	$16865
RS 2-door hatchback, automatic	18887	17612
GS 2-door hatchback, manual	18957	17678
GS 2-door hatchback, automatic	19957	18610
GS Spyder 2-door convertible, manual	23617	22019
GS Spyder 2-door convertible, automatic	24607	22949
GT 2-door hatchback, manual	21147	19722
GT 2-door hatchback, automatic	22147	20654
GT Spyder 2-door convertible, manual	25597	23876
GT Spyder 2-door convertible, automatic	26597	24804
Destination charge	555	555

STANDARD EQUIPMENT

RS: 2.4-liter 4-cylinder engine, 5-speed manual or 4-speed automatic transmission, dual front airbags, power steering, tilt steering wheel, air conditioning, cloth upholstery, front bucket seat w/driver height adjustment, center console, cupholders, folding rear seat, power windows, power door locks, AM/FM/CD player, digital clock, tachometer, variable-intermittent wipers, map lights, remote hatch release, visor mirrors, rear defogger, cargo cover, automatic-off headlights, floormats, theft-deterrent system, 195/65HR15 tires, alloy wheels.

GS adds: 5-speed manual or 4-speed automatic transmission w/manual-shift capability, cruise control, leather-wrapped steering wheel, driver seat lumbar adjustment, split folding rear seat (hatchback), nonfolding rear seat (convertible), power mirrors, remote keyless entry, Infinity sound system (convertible), illuminated visor mirrors, power convertible top (convertible), fog lights (convertible), rear spoiler, 205/55HR16 tires.

GT adds: 3.0-liter V6 engine, 4-wheel disc brakes, sport suspension, fog lights, 215/50VR17 tires.

OPTIONAL EQUIPMENT
Major Packages
P3/P4 Premium Pkg., GT hatchback manual	2850	2481

Prices are accurate at time of publication; subject to manufacturer's change.

MITSUBISHI

	Retail Price	Dealer Invoice
GT hatchback automatic.....................................	$3140	$2731

Antilock brakes, traction control (automatic), front side airbags, Infinity AM/FM/cassette w/in-dash 4-disc CD changer, leather front bucket seats, 6-way power driver seat, power sunroof, rear wiper/washer, theft-deterrent system w/alarm.

P5/P6 Premium Pkg., GT convertible manual	2370	2057
GT convertible automatic......................................	2650	2308

Antilock brakes, traction control (automatic), front side airbags, leather front bucket seats, 6-way power driver seat, Infinity AM/FM/cassette w/in-dash 4-disc CD changer.

P1/P2 Sun and Sound Pkg., GS/GT hatchback......	1080	936

Infinity sound system, power sunroof.

P5 Sun, Sound and Leather Pkg., GT hatchback...	1690	1458

Sun and Sound Pkg. plus leather front bucket seats.

Comfort & Convenience Features

Leather front bucket seats, GS convertible, GT......	600	525

MITSUBISHI GALANT

Mitsubishi Galant

Front-wheel-drive compact car
Base price range: $17,707-$24,157. Built in USA.
Also consider: Subaru Outback/Legacy, Volkswagen Passat

FOR • Ride • Steering/handling **AGAINST** • Rear-seat entry/exit

Mitsubishi's top-selling car gets revised front and rear styling and a 4-cyl version with the top trim level for 2002. Galant offers 4-cyl DE, ES, and new LS models, plus ES V6, LS V6 and sporty GTZ V6 versions. All have automatic transmission. Traction control is standard on GTZ and optional for other V6 models in an All Weather Package that includes heated mirrors. ABS is optional on the 4-cyl

Specifications begin on page 551.

MITSUBISHI

ES and standard on V6s; V6 models also have 4-wheel disc brakes. Front side airbags are exclusive to and standard on LS models and the GTZ. Other '02 additions include an emergency inside trunklid release, new-look LS V6 and GTZ wheels, and altered interior trim.

RATINGS

	ES, 4 cyl auto.	GTZ
ACCELERATION	3	6
FUEL ECONOMY	6	5
RIDE QUALITY	6	5
STEERING/HANDLING	5	7
QUIETNESS	4	4
INSTRUMENTS/CONTROLS	6	6
ROOM/COMFORT (FRONT)	4	4
ROOM/COMFORT (REAR)	3	3
CARGO ROOM	3	3
VALUE	6	6

Galant matches most compact-class rivals for driving pleasure, but needs to be more solidly put together to merit a Recommended nod. Discounts should be readily available, though.

TOTAL	46	49

Average total for compact cars: 51.6

ENGINES

	ohc I4	dohc V6
Size, liters/cu. in.	2.4/143	181.0/3
Horsepower @ rpm	140 @ 5500	195 @ 5500
Torque (lb-ft) @ rpm	155 @ 4000	205 @ 4000
Availability	S[1]	S[2]
EPA city/highway mpg		
4-speed automatic	21/28	20/27

1. DE, ES, LS. 2. ES V6, LS V6, GTZ.

PRICES

Mitsubishi Galant	Retail Price	Dealer Invoice
DE 4-door sedan	$17707	$16601
ES 4-door sedan	18517	17179
ES V6 4-door sedan	20417	18938
LS 4-door sedan	21117	19588
LS V6 4-door sedan	22817	21168
GTZ 4-door sedan	24157	22410
Destination charge	555	555

STANDARD EQUIPMENT

DE: 2.4-liter 4-cylinder engine, 4-speed automatic transmission, dual front airbags, emergency inside trunk release, air conditioning,

Prices are accurate at time of publication; subject to manufacturer's change.

MITSUBISHI

power steering, tilt steering wheel, cloth upholstery, front bucket seats, height-adjustable driver seat, center console, cupholders, power windows, power door locks, AM/FM/CD player, digital clock, tachometer, rear defogger, variable intermittent wipers, driver-side visor mirror, map lights, remote fuel door and decklid release, automatic-off headlights, floormats, theft-deterrent system, 195/60HR15 tires, wheel covers.

ES adds: cruise control, power mirrors, remote keyless entry, trunk pass-through, illuminated visor mirrors, fog lights.

ES V6 adds: 3.0-liter V6 engine, antilock 4-wheel disc brakes, 205/55HR16 tires.

LS adds to ES: front side airbags, antilock brakes, leather-wrapped steering wheel, driver-seat power height-adjustment w/lumbar adjustment, power sunroof, Infinity sound system, alloy wheels.

LS V6 adds: 3.0-liter V6 engine, antilock 4-wheel disc brakes, 205/55HR16 tires.

GTZ adds: traction control, leather upholstery, 12-way power driver seat, heated power mirrors, sport suspension.

OPTIONAL EQUIPMENT
Major Packages

	Retail Price	Dealer Invoice
All Weather Pkg., ES V6, LS V6	$310	$270
Traction control, heated power mirrors.		
Premium Leather Pkg., LS, LS V6	1118	978
Leather upholstery, 8-way power driver seat. LS V6 requires All Weather Pkg.		

Safety
Antilock brakes, ES	610	500

Comfort & Convenience Features
Power sunroof, ES, ES V6	850	706

MITSUBISHI LANCER

Front-wheel-drive subcompact car
Base price range: $13,897-$16,287. Built in Japan.
Also consider: Ford Focus, Honda Civic, Volkswagen Jetta

FOR • Handling/roadholding • Fuel economy **AGAINST** • Acceleration

This new small sedan is offered in base ES, LS, and sporty O-Z Rally models. All Lancers share a 120-hp 4-cyl engine with manual or automatic transmission. Automatic is standard on the LS, along with remote keyless entry, cruise control, and 15-inch alloy wheels

Specifications begin on page 551.

MITSUBISHI

Mitsubishi Lancer LS

instead of the ES's steel 14s. ABS and front side airbags are available only on the LS, where they're grouped in an option package. Inspired by Mitsubishi's Lancer Evolution VII professional Rally racer, the O-Z comes with 15-inch O-Z brand alloy wheels, aero body trim, white-face gauges, and metal-look interior trim.

RATINGS

	ES, man.	LS, auto.	O-Z, man.
ACCELERATION	4	4	4
FUEL ECONOMY	7	6	7
RIDE QUALITY	6	6	6
STEERING/HANDLING	5	6	6
QUIETNESS	5	5	5
INSTRUMENTS/CONTROLS	6	6	6
ROOM/COMFORT (FRONT)	5	5	5
ROOM/COMFORT (REAR)	4	4	4
CARGO ROOM	3	3	3
VALUE	6	7	6

Its only significant fault is tepid acceleration, but Lancer offers little to lure buyers from higher-profile rivals such as the Honda Civic and Ford Focus. Dealers should thus be willing to discount.

TOTAL	51	52	52

Average total for subcompact cars: 43.7

ENGINES

	ohc I4
Size, liters/cu. in.	2.0/122
Horsepower @ rpm	120 @ 5500
Torque (lb-ft) @ rpm	130 @ 4250
Availability	S
EPA city/highway mpg	
5-speed manual	26/33
4-speed automatic	24/30

Prices are accurate at time of publication; subject to manufacturer's change.

MITSUBISHI
PRICES
Mitsubishi Lancer

	Retail Price	Dealer Invoice
ES 4-door sedan, manual	$13897	$13032
ES 4-door sedan, automatic	14697	13782
LS 4-door sedan, automatic	15897	14908
O-Z Rally 4-door sedan, manual	15487	14523
O-Z Rally 4-door sedan, automatic	16287	15274
Destination charge	545	545

STANDARD EQUIPMENT

ES: 2.0-liter 4-cylinder engine, 5-speed manual or 4-speed automatic transmission, dual front airbags, emergency inside trunk release, air conditioning, power steering, tilt steering wheel, cloth upholstery, front bucket seats, height-adjustable driver seat, power mirrors, power windows, power door locks, AM/FM/CD player, digital clock, tachometer, intermittent wipers, rear defogger, visor mirrors, automatic-off headlights, 185/65R14 tires, wheel covers.

LS adds: 4-speed automatic transmission, cruise control, remote keyless entry, split folding rear seat, variable intermittent wipers, floormats, 195/60HR15 tires, alloy wheels.

O-Z Rally adds: 5-speed manual or 4-speed automatic transmission, upgraded interior trim, aerodynamics pkg., unique alloy wheels.

OPTIONAL EQUIPMENT
Major Packages

ES Convenience Pkg., ES	500	440

Remote keyless entry, split folding rear seat w/armrest, additional cupholders, floormats, color-keyed door handles.

LS Preferred Equipment Pkg., LS	800	704

Antilock brakes, front side airbags.

Appearance and Miscellaneous

Rear spoiler, O-Z Rally	360	317

MITSUBISHI MIRAGE

Front-wheel-drive subcompact car
Base price range: $11,937-$15,587. Built in Japan.
Also consider: Ford Focus ZX3, Honda Civic coupe

FOR • Fuel economy • Maneuverability **AGAINST** • Acceleration (DE coupe) • Rear-seat room (2-door) • Rear-seat entry/exit (2-door)

Specifications begin on page 551.

MITSUBISHI

Mitsubishi Mirage LS 2-door coupe

Mirage is a price-leader subcompact offered only in a 2-dr coupe body style and without such features as ABS or side airbags. The DE model has a 92-hp 1.5-liter 4-cyl engine, the LS has a 111-hp 1.8-liter 4 cyl. Both offer manual transmission or an optional 4-speed automatic. Air conditioning, power windows and locks, CD stereo, and split folding rear seatback are standard on LS and optional on DE. Exclusive to the LS are an optional sunroof and a Sport Package that includes alloy wheels, rear spoiler, fog lights, and white-face gauges.

RATINGS	DE, man.	LS, auto.
ACCELERATION	3	4
FUEL ECONOMY	8	7
RIDE QUALITY	3	3
STEERING/HANDLING	4	4
QUIETNESS	3	3
INSTRUMENTS/CONTROLS	5	5
ROOM/COMFORT (FRONT)	4	4
ROOM/COMFORT (REAR)	2	3
CARGO ROOM	2	2
VALUE	2	2

Two-door versions of the Honda Civic and Ford Focus are far smarter buys than the unrefined Mirage, which lacks important features such as ABS and has as its only lure heavily discounted prices.

TOTAL	36	37

Average total for subcompact cars: 43.7

ENGINES	ohc I4	ohc I4
Size, liters/cu. in.	1.5/90	1.8/112
Horsepower @ rpm	92 @ 5500	111 @ 5500
Torque (lb-ft) @ rpm	93 @ 3000	116 @ 4500

Prices are accurate at time of publication; subject to manufacturer's change.

CONSUMER GUIDE®

MITSUBISHI

	ohc I4 S[1]	ohc I4 S[2]
Availability		
EPA city/highway mpg		
5-speed manual	32/39	29/36
4-speed automatic	28/35	26/32

1. DE. 2. LS.

PRICES

Mitsubishi Mirage	Retail Price	Dealer Invoice
DE 2-door coupe, manual	$11937	$11190
DE 2-door coupe, automatic	12737	11939
LS 2-door coupe, manual	14787	13858
LS 2-door coupe, automatic	15587	14611
Destination charge	545	545

STANDARD EQUIPMENT

DE: 1.5-liter 4-cylinder engine, 5-speed manual or 4-speed automatic transmission, dual front airbags, emergency inside trunk release, power steering, tilt steering wheel, cloth/vinyl upholstery, front bucket seats, height-adjustable driver seat, center console, cupholders, rear defogger, visor mirrors, digital clock, intermittent wipers, remote fuel-door and decklid release, floormats, 175/65R14 tires, wheel covers.

LS adds: 1.8-liter 4-cylinder engine, air conditioning, cruise control, cloth upholstery, split folding rear seat, power mirrors, power windows, power door locks, AM/FM/CD player, tachometer, variable intermittent wipers, map lights, 185/65HR14 tires.

OPTIONAL EQUIPMENT
Major Packages

Convenience Pkg., DE	1810	1591
Air conditioning, power windows and door locks, AM/FM/CD player, cloth upholstery, split folding rear seat.		
Sport Pkg., LS	1030	901
Fog lights, white-face gauges, side air dams, rear spoiler, chrome tailpipe extension, alloy wheels.		

Comfort & Convenience Features

Air conditioning, DE	880	770
Power sunroof, LS	800	700

MITSUBISHI MONTERO
4-wheel-drive full-size sport-utility vehicle
Base price range: $31,687-$35,797. Built in Japan.

Specifications begin on page 551.

MITSUBISHI

Mitsubishi Montero Limited

Also consider: Chevrolet Tahoe/GMC Yukon, Ford Expedition, Toyota Land Cruiser

FOR • Passenger and cargo room **AGAINST** • Fuel economy • Acceleration • Ride • Steering/handling

Available suedelike upholstery and revised exterior trim keynote 2002 changes to the larger of Mitsubishi's two SUVs. Montero seats seven with a 3rd-row bench seat that removes or folds flush with the cargo floor. Unlike most full-size SUVs, Montero has unibody construction instead of a body-on-frame design. And it has a right-hinged cargo door instead of a liftgate or tailgate. It also does not offer a V8 engine, using instead a 200-hp V6. The base XLS model has a 4-speed automatic transmission and 4WD that must be disengaged on dry pavement. The uplevel Limited has a 5-speed automatic with manual shift gate, plus Mitsubishi's ActiveTrac 4WD that can be left engaged on dry pavement. Both include low-range gearing. Standard are front side airbags, antilock 4-wheel disc brakes, and 16-inch wheels. The Limited comes with leather upholstery, heated power front seats, and sunroof. New XLS options include rear air conditioning, power front passenger seat, and a Touring Package with ultrasuede seat trim and a sunroof. The XLS also gains chrome grille accents, and the Limited's grille and trim are now color-keyed.

RATINGS

	XLS/Limited
ACCELERATION	3
FUEL ECONOMY	4
RIDE QUALITY	2
STEERING/HANDLING	2
QUIETNESS	4
INSTRUMENTS/CONTROLS	4
ROOM/COMFORT (FRONT)	7
ROOM/COMFORT (REAR)	7
CARGO ROOM	8

Prices are accurate at time of publication; subject to manufacturer's change.

CONSUMER GUIDE®

MITSUBISHI

	XLS/Limited
VALUE	**2**

Three rows of seats, solid construction, and reasonable fuel economy for a full-size SUV are among Montero's attractions. But they're overshadowed by mediocre acceleration; too much body lean in turns; and a harsh, trucky ride. Don't buy one without a getting sizable discount.

TOTAL	**43**

Average total for full-size sport-utility vehicles: 50.9

ENGINES

	ohc V6
Size, liters/cu. in.	3.5/213
Horsepower @ rpm	200 @ 5000
Torque (lb-ft) @ rpm	235 @ 3000
Availability	S

EPA city/highway mpg

4-speed automatic	15/19
5-speed automatic	14/19

PRICES

Mitsubishi Montero	Retail Price	Dealer Invoice
XLS 4-door wagon	$31687	$29390
Limited 4-door wagon	35797	33203
Destination charge	560	560

STANDARD EQUIPMENT

XLS: 3.5-liter V6 engine, 4-speed automatic transmission, 4-wheel drive, 2-speed transfer case, dual front airbags, front side airbags, antilock 4-wheel disc brakes, air conditioning, power steering, tilt steering wheel, cruise control, cloth upholstery, front bucket seats, height adjustable driver seat, center console, cupholders, split folding second row seat, stowable third row seat, power mirrors, power windows, power door locks, remote keyless entry, AM/FM/CD player, digital clock, tachometer, variable intermittent wipers, rear defogger, intermittent rear wiper/washer, illuminated visor mirrors, map lights, cargo cover, automatic-off headlights, remote fuel door release, floormats, theft-deterrent system, roof rack, rear privacy glass, tow hooks, skid plates, outside-mounted full-size spare tire, 265/70R16 tires, alloy wheels.

Limited adds: 5-speed automatic transmission w/manual-shift capability, limited-slip differential, power sunroof, leather upholstery, heated front seats, 10-way power driver seat w/lumbar adjustment, wood/leather-wrapped steering wheel, heated power mirrors, Infinity sound system, power antenna, compass, outside temperature display, trip computer, fog lights.

Specifications begin on page 551.

MITSUBISHI

OPTIONAL EQUIPMENT
Major Packages

	Retail Price	Dealer Invoice
P1 Touring Pkg., XLS	$1150	$1001

Limited-slip differential, Ultra Suede upholstery, power sunroof, leather-wrapped steering wheel, Infinity sound system, power antenna.

P2 Touring Pkg., XLS	2980	2594

P1 Touring Pkg. plus rear air conditioning/heater with rear controls.

Premium Pkg., Limited	1200	1044

Front automatic climate control, rear air conditioning/heater with rear controls, 8-way power passenger seat.

MITSUBISHI MONTERO SPORT

Mitsubishi Montero Sport XLS

Rear- or 4-wheel-drive midsize sport-utility vehicle
Base price range: $22,777-$32,887. Built in Japan.
Also consider: Acura MDX, Ford Explorer, Toyota Highlander

FOR • Cargo room • Instruments/controls • Build quality
AGAINST • Ride/handling • Fuel economy • Rear-seat entry/exit • Engine noise

A more-sophisticated 4WD system tops the 2002 changes for the smaller of Mitsubishi's two SUVs. Montero Sport offers ES and LS models with a 165-hp 3.0-liter V6, and XLS and Limited models with a 197-hp 3.5 V6. All have automatic transmission and offer rear-wheel drive or 4WD that can be left engaged on dry pavement. This system, which Mitsubishi calls All4-wheel drive, replaces a 4WD system that had to be disengaged on dry pavement. All4-wheel drive also includes locked-in 4WD high-range and 4WD low-range gearing. Antilock 4-wheel disc brakes are standard on 4WD models, and

MITSUBISHI

all but the ES version have 16-inch alloy wheels. Among other additions for '02: a color-keyed grille for the Limited, tube-type side steps standard on LS and XLS and optional on ES, and platinum-finish gauges on all but the ES.

RATINGS

	LS 4WD	Limited 4WD
ACCELERATION	3	5
FUEL ECONOMY	4	4
RIDE QUALITY	3	3
STEERING/HANDLING	3	3
QUIETNESS	3	3
INSTRUMENTS/CONTROLS	5	5
ROOM/COMFORT (FRONT)	5	5
ROOM/COMFORT (REAR)	4	4
CARGO ROOM	8	8
VALUE	2	3

Montero Sport sacrifices too much room and comfort for a rough-and-tumble look and attitude, and the 3.0-liter models feel underpowered. The Limited competes on price with roomier, more-refined rivals, making the XLS model the slightly better value, though discounts are readily available on all Montero Sports.

TOTAL	40	43

Average total for midsize sport-utility vehicles: 49.6

ENGINES

	ohc V6	ohc V6
Size, liters/cu. in.	3.0/181	3.5/213
Horsepower @ rpm	165 @ 5250	197 @ 5000
Torque (lb-ft) @ rpm	186 @ 4000	223 @ 3500
Availability	S[1]	S[2]
EPA city/highway mpg		
4-speed automatic	17/20[3]	16/18

1. ES, LS. 2. XLS, Limited. 3. 18/22 w/2WD. 4. 17/21 w/2WD.

PRICES

Mitsubishi Montero Sport	Retail Price	Dealer Invoice
ES 2WD 4-door wagon	$22777	$21172
ES 4WD 4-door wagon	25087	23262
LS 2WD 4-door wagon	25637	23773
LS 4WD 4-door wagon	27777	25759
XLS 2WD 4-door wagon	27607	25598
XLS 4WD 4-door wagon	29627	27475
Limited 2WD 4-door wagon	31317	29041
Limited 4WD 4-dor wagon	32887	30489
Destination charge	560	560

Specifications begin on page 551.

MITSUBISHI • NISSAN

STANDARD EQUIPMENT

ES: 3.0-liter V6 engine, 4-speed automatic transmission, dual front airbags, air conditioning, power steering, tilt steering wheel, cloth upholstery, front bucket seats w/driver-side lumbar adjustment, center console, cupholders, folding rear seat, overhead console, power mirrors, power windows, power door locks, AM/FM/CD player, digital clock, tachometer, intermittent wipers, rear defogger, rear wiper/washer, map lights, visor mirrors, floormats, theft-deterrent system, front and rear tow hooks, full-size spare, 235/75R15 tires. **4WD** adds: 4-wheel drive, 2-speed transfer case, antilock 4-wheel disc brakes, skid plates.

LS adds: cruise control, remote keyless entry, height-adjustable driver seat, split folding rear seat, variable-intermittent wipers, tubular side steps, roof rack, rear privacy glass, 255/70R16 tires, alloy wheels. **4WD** adds: 4-wheel drive, 2-speed transfer case, antilock 4-wheel disc brakes, skid plates.

XLS adds: 3.5-liter V6 engine, leather-wrapped steering wheel, automatic day/night rearview mirror, compass, outside temperature indicator, cargo cover. **4WD** adds: 4-wheel drive, 2-speed transfer case, antilock 4-wheel disc brakes, skid plates.

Limited adds: 3.5-liter V6 engine, limited-slip differential, antilock brakes, leather upholstery, heated front seats, heated power mirrors, Infinity sound system, power antenna, power sunroof, illuminated visor mirrors, fog lights. **4WD** adds: 4-wheel drive, 2-speed transfer case, antilock 4-wheel disc brakes, skid plates.

OPTIONAL EQUIPMENT
Major Packages

	Retail Price	Dealer Invoice
Appearance Pkg., ES	$1400	$1218

Remote keyless entry, black tubular side steps, fender flares, bodyside moldings, rear privacy glass, roof rack, alloy wheels.

P1 Touring Pkg., XLS	1790	1560

Limited-slip differential, power sunroof, leather-wrapped steering wheel, Infinity sound system.

P2 Luxury Pkg., XLS	2310	2010

Leather upholstery, power sunroof, Infinity sound system.

NISSAN ALTIMA

Front-wheel-drive midsize car
Base price range: $16,349-$23,149. Built in USA.
Also consider: Honda Accord, Toyota Camry, Volkswagen Passat

FOR • Acceleration (3.5 SE) • Handling/roadholding • Instruments/controls **AGAINST** • Engine noise (4 cyl)

Prices are accurate at time of publication; subject to manufacturer's change.

NISSAN

Nissan Altima 3.5 SE

Altima is slightly larger than Nissan's flagship Maxima, swelling to midsize dimensions in its 2002 redesign. It gains 7 inches in wheelbase and 5.7 in overall length against its compact-class predecessor. Altima also offers its first V6 engine, a new 240-hp 3.5 liter exclusive to the top-line 3.5 SE. Base, 2.5 S, and 2.5 SL models use a 2.5-liter 4 cyl with 175 hp, 20 more than the previous Altima's 4 cyl. All team with manual or automatic transmission; automatic 3.5 SEs qualify for optional traction control. Four-wheel disc brakes are standard. All but the base model are eligible for optional ABS, which Nissan bundles with front torso side airbags and curtain side airbags. The 3.5 SE uses 17-inch wheels, the others 16s. Leather upholstery is standard on the 2.5 SL and optional on the 3.5 SE; all have a tilt/telescoping steering wheel. Xenon headlights are a 3.5 SE option.

RATINGS	2.5 S, man.	2.5 S, auto.	3.5 SE, man.	3.5 SE, auto.
ACCELERATION	5	5	7	6
FUEL ECONOMY	6	6	5	4
RIDE QUALITY	8	8	7	7
STEERING/HANDLING	7	7	7	7
QUIETNESS	4	4	6	6
INSTRUMENTS/CONTROLS	7	7	7	7
ROOM/COMFORT (FRONT)	6	6	6	6
ROOM/COMFORT (REAR)	5	5	5	5
CARGO ROOM	4	4	4	4
VALUE	6	6	6	6

Nissan finally has a genuine Camry/Accord alternative in the moderately priced midsize class. Altima is strong on features for the money and has a spunky personality, especially in sporty 3.5 SE guise. Bundling ABS and side and curtain airbags results in a single $749 option, which isn't unreasonable for these worthwhile safety items. The gruff 4-cyl engine isn't a deal-breaker, and overall, Altima is a strong Recommended pick.

TOTAL	58	58	60	58

Average total for midsize cars: 57.0

Specifications begin on page 551.

NISSAN

ENGINES

	dohc I4	dohc V6
Size, liters/cu. in.	2.5/152	3.5/214
Horsepower @ rpm	175 @ 6000	240 @ 5800
Torque (lb-ft) @ rpm	180 @ 4000	246 @ 3600
Availability	S[1]	S[2]
EPA city/highway mpg		
5-speed manual	23/29	21/26
4-speed automatic	23/29	19/26

1. 2.5, 2.5 S, 2.5 SL. 2. 3.5 SE.

PRICES

Nissan Altima

	Retail Price	Dealer Invoice
Base 4-door sedan, manual	$16349	$15718
Base 4-door sedan, automatic	17149	16487
2.5 S 4-door sedan, manual	17999	16552
2.5 S 4-door sedan, automatic	18849	17334
2.5 SL 4-door sedan, manual	21899	19910
2.5 SL 4-door sedan, automatic	22699	20636
3.5 SE 4-door sedan, manual	22349	20319
3.5 SE 4-door sedan, automatic	23149	21046
Destination charge	540	540

STANDARD EQUIPMENT

Base: 2.5-liter dohc 4-cylinder engine, 5-speed manual or 4-speed automatic transmission, dual front airbags, 4-wheel disc brakes, emergency inside trunk release, power steering, tilt/telescoping steering wheel, cloth upholstery, front bucket seats, center console, cupholders, split folding rear seat, power windows, power door locks, tachometer, variable intermittent wipers, rear defogger, visor mirrors, map light, remote fuel door and decklid release, theft-deterrent system, 205/65R16 tires, wheel covers.

2.5 S adds: air conditioning, cruise control, height-adjustable driver seat, power mirrors, remote keyless entry, AM/FM/CD player.

2.5 SL adds: leather upholstery, 8-way power driver seat w/lumbar adjustment, leather-wrapped steering wheel w/radio controls, Bose AM/FM radio w/in-dash 6-disc CD changer, automatic day/night inside mirror, outside temperature display, trip computer, universal garage door opener, illuminated visor mirrors, alloy wheels.

3.5 SE adds: 3.5-liter dohc V6 engine, AM/FM/CD player, fog lights, upgraded suspension, 215/55R17 tires. *Deletes:* leather upholstery, Bose AM/FM radio w/in-dash 6-disc CD changer, automatic day/night rearview mirror, universal garage door opener.

Prices are accurate at time of publication; subject to manufacturer's change.

NISSAN

OPTIONAL EQUIPMENT
Major Packages

	Retail Price	Dealer Invoice
Convenience Pkg., 2.5 S	$1679	$1457

Leather-wrapped steering wheel w/radio controls, 8-way power driver seat w/lumbar adjustment, trip computer, illuminated visor mirrors, cargo net, automatic headlights, theft-deterrent system w/alarm, alloy wheels.

Cold Pkg., 2.5 SL, 3.5 SE	299	259

Heated front seats and mirror. Requires antilock brakes. 2.5 SL requires power sunroof. 3.5 SE requires Leather Pkg.

X03 Leather Pkg., 3.5 SE	1399	1272

Leather upholstery, automatic climate control, automatic day/night rearview mirror, universal garage door opener. Requires Bose AM/FM radio w/in-dash 6-disc CD changer, power sunroof.

X04 Leather Pkg., 3.5 SE	1549	1408

X03 Leather Pkg. plus woodgrain interior trim. Requires Bose AM/FM radio w/in-dash 6-disc CD changer, power sunroof.

Powertrain

Traction control, 3.5 SE automatic	299	259

Requires antilock brakes.

Safety

Antilock brakes, 2.5 S, 2.5 SL, 3.5 SE	749	650

Includes front side airbags, curtain side airbags.

Comfort & Convenience Features

Power sunroof, 2.5 S, 2.5 SL, 3.5 SE	849	737

2.5 S requires Convenience Pkg.

Bose AM/FM radio w/in-dash 6-disc CD changer, 2.5 S, 3.5 SE	899	779

Requires power sunroof. 2.5 S requires Convenience Pkg.

Automatic day/night rearview mirror, Base, 2.5 S	219	164

Includes compass, outside temperature indicator.

Appearance and Miscellaneous

Xenon headlights, 3.5 SE	499	432

Requires power sunroof.

Rear spoiler, 3.5 SE	399	346

Requires power sunroof.

Postproduction options also available.

NISSAN MAXIMA

Front-wheel-drive midsize car
Base price range: $24,699-$27,099. Built in Japan.

Specifications begin on page 551.

NISSAN

Nissan Maxima

Also consider: Honda Accord, Pontiac Grand Prix, Toyota Camry

FOR • Acceleration • Steering/handling **AGAINST** • Manual shift action • Navigation system controls

A larger engine, new 6-speed manual transmission, and moderately revised styling mark Nissan's 2002 flagship sedans. Pushed upmarket by the redesigned '02 Altima with its available 240 hp, all Maximas get a 255-hp 3.5-liter V6 with 33 hp more than the 3.0 it replaces. Clear-lens taillamps and standard Xenon headlights mark the freshened styling. Base GXE, sporty SE, and luxury GLE models return. SE substitutes a standard 6-speed manual for last year's 5-speed. A 4-speed automatic is optional on SE and standard on GXE and GLE. GXE moves from standard 15-inch wheels to 16s; the other models go from 16s to 17s. Antilock 4-wheel disc brakes are standard and add full-power brake-assist for '02. Also new is revised interior trim, standard power driver's seat, and trip computer with steering-wheel controls. A navigation system with dashboard screen is newly optional. Front side airbags are optional for SE and GLE.

RATINGS	GXE	SE, man.	SE, auto.	GLE w/nav. sys.
ACCELERATION	6	7	6	6
FUEL ECONOMY	5	5	5	5
RIDE QUALITY	7	6	6	7
STEERING/HANDLING	7	7	7	7
QUIETNESS	6	5	5	6
INSTRUMENTS/CONTROLS	8	8	8	5
ROOM/COMFORT (FRONT)	7	7	7	7
ROOM/COMFORT (REAR)	6	6	6	6
CARGO ROOM	4	4	4	4
VALUE	6	6	6	5

Maxima won its following by blending near-luxury and sport-sedan attributes at popular prices. For '02, it's being refocused to compete more directly with such cars as the Toyota Avalon and Acura TL. While still quite good, Maxima will be challenged to demonstrate the multifaceted sophistication required of its new role.

Prices are accurate at time of publication; subject to manufacturer's change.

CONSUMER GUIDE®

NISSAN

	GXE	SE, man.	SE, auto.	GLE w/nav. sys.
TOTAL	62	61	60	58

Average total for midsize cars: 57.0

ENGINES

	dohc V6
Size, liters/cu. in.	3.5/214
Horsepower @ rpm	255 @ 5800
Torque (lb-ft) @ rpm	246 @ 4400
Availability	S

EPA city/highway mpg
6-speed manual	21/28
4-speed automatic	20/26

PRICES

Nissan Maxima	Retail Price	Dealer Invoice
GXE 4-door sedan, automatic	$24699	$22326
SE 4-door sedan, manual	25449	22871
SE 4-door sedan, automatic	25449	22871
GLE 4-door sedan, automatic	27099	24354
Destination charge	540	540

STANDARD EQUIPMENT

GXE: 3.5-liter dohc V6 engine, 4-speed automatic transmission, dual front airbags, antilock 4-wheel disc brakes, emergency inside trunk release, air conditioning, interior air filter, power steering, tilt steering wheel w/radio and trip computer controls, cruise control, cloth upholstery, front bucket seats, 8-way power driver seat, center console, cupholders, split folding rear seat, power mirrors, power windows, power door locks, remote keyless entry, AM/FM/cassette/CD player, digital clock, tachometer, automatic day/night rearview mirror, universal garage door opener, trip computer, illuminated visor mirrors, variable intermittent wipers, rear defogger, remote fuel door and decklid release, map lights, automatic headlights, theft-deterrent system, Xenon headlights, 215/55HR16 tires, alloy wheels.

SE adds: 6-speed manual or 4-speed automatic transmission, leather-wrapped steering wheel, fog lights, rear spoiler, sport suspension, 225/50VR17 tires.

GLE adds: 4-speed automatic transmission, automatic climate control, leather-wrapped steering wheel, leather upholstery, driver seat memory, 4-way power passenger seat, Bose AM/FM/cassette w/indash 6-disc CD changer, 215/55HR17 tires.

Specifications begin on page 551.

NISSAN

	Retail Price	Dealer Invoice

OPTIONAL EQUIPMENT
Major Packages
Leather Trim Pkg., SE $1499 $1347
Leather upholstery, driver seat memory, 4-way power passenger seat, automatic climate control. Requires power sunroof, Bose AM/FM/cassette w/6-disc CD changer.

Meridian Edition, SE, GLE 399 346
Heated front seats, steering wheel, and mirrors. Requires power sunroof, front side airbags. SE requires Bose AM/FM/cassette w/6-disc CD changer. GLE requires traction control.

Powertrain
Traction control, SE automatic, GLE 299 259
Requires Meridian Edition.

Safety
Front side airbags, SE, GLE 249 216
Requires power sunroof. SE requires Bose AM/FM/cassette w/6-disc CD changer.

Comfort & Convenience Features
Navigation system, SE, GLE 1999 1734
Requires power sunroof. SE requires Leather Trim Pkg., Bose AM/FM/cassette w/in-trunk 6-disc CD changer.

Bose AM/FM/cassette w/in-dash 6-disc CD changer, SE. 1099 953
Requires power sunroof.

Bose AM/FM/cassette w/in-trunk 6-disc CD changer, SE 1099 953
Requires Leather Trim Pkg., power sunroof, navigation system.

Power sunroof, SE, GLE 899 779

Appearance and Miscellaneous
Rear spoiler, GXE, GLE 489 371

Postproduction options also available.

NISSAN PATHFINDER

Rear- or 4-wheel-drive midsize sport-utility vehicle
Base price range: $26,649-$31,499. Built in Japan.
Also consider: Acura MDX, Ford Explorer, Toyota Highlander

FOR • Acceleration • Cargo room • Build quality **AGAINST** • Rear-seat room • Rear-seat entry/exit

The more-expensive of Nissan's two SUVs drops last year's base model and adds features to the remaining Pathfinders for 2002.

Prices are accurate at time of publication; subject to manufacturer's change.

NISSAN

Nissan Pathfinder

Gone is the XE model, leaving SE and LE versions. This truck-based 4-dr wagon shares its design and V6 engine with the QX4 from Nissan's upscale Infiniti division. The 4WD SE Pathfinder is available with manual transmission; the other models use automatic. All offer rear-wheel drive or 4WD. The SE's 4WD must be disengaged on dry pavement. The LE uses QX4's All-Mode 4WD that can be left engaged on dry pavement. Both systems include low-range gearing. ABS is standard. Front side airbags are included with optional leather-upholstery. Also optional are navigation system and rear-seat video entertainment systems. New for '02 is a restyled grille, body-color bumpers and fender flares for the SE, and new wheels, including 17-inch alloys in place of 16s on the LE. Interior trim revisions include a new steering wheel with available audio controls.

RATINGS	SE 4WD, auto.	LE 4WD w/Leather Pkg., nav. sys.
ACCELERATION	6	6
FUEL ECONOMY	4	4
RIDE QUALITY	4	4
STEERING/HANDLING	4	4
QUIETNESS	4	4
INSTRUMENTS/CONTROLS	7	7
ROOM/COMFORT (FRONT)	5	5
ROOM/COMFORT (REAR)	3	3
CARGO ROOM	8	8
VALUE	4	3

An antiquated 4WD system weighs against the Pathfinder unless you splurge for the top-line LE with the QX4 system, in which case you might as well get the Infiniti and enjoy that brand's red-carpet customer service. Still, neither of these SUVs has what it takes to be a compelling value.

TOTAL	49	48

Average total for midsize sport-utility vehicles: 49.6

Specifications begin on page 551.

NISSAN

ENGINES

	dohc V6
Size, liters/cu. in.	3.5/214
Horsepower @ rpm	240 @ 6000
Torque (lb-ft) @ rpm	265 @ 3200
Availability	S[1]
EPA city/highway mpg	
5-speed manual	16/18[2]
4-speed automatic	15/18[3]

1. 250 hp, 240 ft-lb w/manual transmission. 2. 17/19 w/2WD. 3. 16/19 w/2WD.

PRICES

Nissan Pathfinder	Retail Price	Dealer Invoice
SE 2WD 4-door wagon, automatic	$26649	$24229
SE 4WD 4-door wagon, manual	27649	25138
SE 4WD 4-door wagon, automatic	28649	26047
LE 2WD 4-door wagon, automatic	28999	26364
LE 4WD 4-door wagon, automatic	31499	28637
Destination charge	540	540

STANDARD EQUIPMENT

SE: 3.5-liter dohc V6 engine, 4-speed automatic transmission, dual front airbags, antilock brakes, air conditioning, power steering, tilt leather-wrapped steering wheel, cruise control, cloth upholstery, front bucket seats, center console, cupholders, split folding rear seat, heated power mirrors, power windows, power door locks, remote keyless entry, AM/FM/cassette/CD player, digital clock, tachometer, variable intermittent wipers, passenger-side visor mirror, rear defogger, rear intermittent wiper/washer, map lights, automatic headlights, theft-deterrent system, rear privacy glass, roof rack, tubular step rails, tow hooks, full-size spare tire, 255/65R16 tires, alloy wheels. **4WD** adds: 4-wheel drive, 2-speed transfer case, 5-speed manual or 4-speed automatic transmission, limited-slip differential (manual).

LE adds: automatic climate control, Bose AM/FM radio w/in-dash 6-disc CD changer, steering wheel radio controls, power sunroof, universal garage door opener, outside temperature indicator, compass, illuminated visor mirrors, cargo cover, running boards, fog lights, 245/65R17 tires. **4WD** adds: 4-wheel drive, 2-speed transfer case.

OPTIONAL EQUIPMENT
Major Packages

SE Popular Pkg., SE	699	635

Bose AM/FM radio w/in-dash 6-disc CD changer, steering wheel radio controls, cargo net and cover, fog lights.

Prices are accurate at time of publication; subject to manufacturer's change.

NISSAN

	Retail Price	Dealer Invoice
Sunroof Pkg., SE	$1099	$953

Power sunroof, universal garage door opener, illuminated visor mirrors, compass, outside temperature indicator. Requires SE Popular Pkg.

Leather Pkg., SE 2WD, LE 2WD	1799	1560
SE 4WD automatic, LE 4WD	1999	1734

Leather upholstery, 8-way power driver seat w/memory, 4-way power passenger seat, heated front seats (4WD), front side airbags, dual sun visors. SE requires SE Popular Pkg. and Sunroof Pkg.

Powertrain

Limited-slip differential, SE 4WD automatic, LE 4WD	249	216

SE requires SE Popular Pkg. and Sunroof Pkg. LE requres Leather Pkg.

Comfort & Convenience Features

DVD Mobil Entertainment System	1599	1387

DVD player, LCD screen. SE requires SE Popular Pkg. and Sunroof Pkg.

VCR Mobil Entertainment System	1299	1126

VCR player, LCD screen. SE requires SE Popular Pkg. and Sunroof Pkg.

Navigation system, LE	1999	1734

Requires Leather Pkg.

Postproduction options also available.

NISSAN QUEST

Nissan Quest

Front-wheel-drive minivan
Base price range: $22,739-$27,149. Built in USA.
Also consider: Dodge Caravan, Honda Odyssey, Toyota Sienna

NISSAN

FOR • Passenger and cargo room • Control layout **AGAINST**
• Interior materials

Quest and Mercury's Villager vanish after the 2002-model-year run as Nissan and Ford end their minivan joint venture. Nissan says it will have a new minivan for 2004. New wheel designs are Quest's only major change for 2002. GXE, SE, and top-line GLE models are offered. All are 7-seaters with a Nissan V6, automatic transmission, ABS, sliding-track 3rd-row bench seat, and dual sliding rear doors. Power side doors and side airbags are not available, though a rear-seat video entertainment system is offered at no extra charge. Quest's performance and accommodations mirror those of comparably equipped Villagers.

RATINGS

	SE	GLE
ACCELERATION	2	2
FUEL ECONOMY	4	4
RIDE QUALITY	4	4
STEERING/HANDLING	5	4
QUIETNESS	5	5
INSTRUMENTS/CONTROLS	5	5
ROOM/COMFORT (FRONT)	6	6
ROOM/COMFORT (REAR)	6	6
CARGO ROOM	9	9
VALUE	4	4

Not the roomiest or most refined minivan, but a pleasant, sensibly sized family vehicle offering good value and several unique features. Sluggish sales and announced end of production means discounts should be more generous than usual.

TOTAL	50	49

Average total for minivans: 56.0

ENGINES

	ohc V6
Size, liters/cu. in.	3.3/201
Horsepower @ rpm	170 @ 4800
Torque (lb-ft) @ rpm	200 @ 2800
Availability	S

EPA city/highway mpg
4-speed automatic	17/23

PRICES

Nissan Quest	Retail Price	Dealer Invoice
GXE 4-door van	$22739	$20673
SE 4-door van	24499	22017
GLE 4-door van	27149	24398

Prices are accurate at time of publication; subject to manufacturer's change.

NISSAN

	Retail Price	Dealer Invoice
Destination charge	$540	$540

STANDARD EQUIPMENT

GXE: 3.3-liter V6 engine, 4-speed automatic transmission, dual front airbags, antilock brakes, front air conditioning, power steering, tilt steering wheel, cruise control, cloth upholstery, 7-passenger seating, front bucket seats, second-row 2-passenger bench seat, third-row sliding 3-passenger bench seat, center console, cupholders, two sliding rear doors, power mirrors, power front windows, power door locks, remote keyless entry, AM/FM/cassette, digital clock, tachometer, variable intermittent wipers, illuminated visor mirrors, rear defogger, intermittent rear wiper/washer, floormats, theft-deterrent system, rear privacy glass, cornering lights, roof rails, 215/65R16 tires, alloy wheels.

SE adds: rear air conditioning, rear climate controls, heated power mirrors, AM/FM/cassette/CD player, leather-wrapped steering wheel w/radio controls, rear audio controls, conversation mirror, map lights, second row captain chairs, under passenger-seat storage, outside temperature indicator, roof rack, fog lights, sport suspension, 225/60R16 tires.

GLE adds: leather upholstery, heated front seats, 6-way power driver seat w/manual lumbar support, 4-way power passenger seat, memory system for driver seat and mirrors, automatic climate control w/front and rear controls, in-dash 6-disc CD changer, power rear quarter windows, wood/leather-wrapped steering wheel, universal garage door opener, automatic headlights, adjustable rear parcel shelf, flip-up rear hatch glass, full-size spare tire, 215/65R16 tires. *Deletes:* fog lights, sport suspension.

OPTIONAL EQUIPMENT
Major Packages

Comfort Plus Pkg., GXE	899	779

Leather-wrapped steering wheel w/radio controls, AM/FM/cassette/CD player, rear air conditioning w/rear controls, passenger-side underseat storage, overhead console, map lights, conversation mirror, auxiliary power outlet, additional courtesy lights, cargo net, heavy-duty battery, roof rack.

Convenience Pkg., SE	899	779

6-way power driver seat w/lumbar adjustment, driver seat and mirror memory, power rear quarter windows, universal garage door opener, adjustable rear parcel shelf, flip-up rear hatch glass.

Leather Pkg., SE	1499	1300

Leather upholstery, 4-way power passenger seat, automatic headlights.

Safety

Two integrated child seats, GXE	229	199

Requires Comfort Plus Pkg. NA w/second-row captain chairs.

Specifications begin on page 551.

NISSAN

Comfort & Convenience Features

	Retail Price	Dealer Invoice
Video Entertainment System	NC	NC

Floor console w/videocassette player, monitor, remote control. GXE requires Comfort Plus Pkg.

Family Entertainment System	$249	$216

Video Entertainment System plus overhead console w/LCD screen, remote control, rear radio controls. GXE requires Comfort Plus Pkg. NA w/power sunroof.

Power sunroof, SE, GLE	899	779
Automatic day/night rearview mirror, SE, GLE	209	145
Second-row captain chairs, GXE	749	650

Requires with Comfort Plus Pkg.

Heated front seats, SE	199	172

Requires Leather Pkg.

Appearance and Miscellaneous

Fog lights, GXE	399	298
Running boards	539	373
Class II tow hitch	439	320

Postproduction options also available.

NISSAN SENTRA

Nissan Sentra GXE

Front-wheel-drive subcompact car
Base price range: $11,799-$14,899. Built in Mexico.
Also consider: Ford Focus, Honda Civic, Toyota Echo

FOR • Acceleration (SE-R) • Steering/handling (SE-R) • Fuel economy **AGAINST** • Rear-seat entry/exit • Ride (SE-R)

New sport models highlight 2002 changes to Nissan's smallest car. All Sentras are 4-dr sedans with a 4-cyl engine. Base XE and midline GXE models have 126 hp. (As does the CA model, sold only in

NISSAN

California to meet strict emissions standards.) Gone is the 145-hp SE model, replaced at the top of the line by the SE-R and SE-R Spec V. These new models have a larger engine with 165 hp in the SE-R and 175 in the Spec V. The SE-R has unique interior trim, a sport suspension, and 16-inch wheels vs. other Sentras' 14s or 15s. The SE-R Spec V gets further suspension revisions, 17-inch wheels, distinct exterior styling touches, and its own interior decor, including sport front seats. Manual transmission is standard on all models—a 6-speed on the Spec V and a 5-speed on the others. All but the Spec V are available with automatic transmission. Side airbags and ABS are optional on all but the XE and CA. SE-R and Spec V have 4-wheel disc brakes. SE-R prices were unavailable in time for this report, but Nissan expect them to range from $16,000-$18,000.

RATINGS

	XE, auto.	GXE, man.	SE-R Spec V
ACCELERATION	3	4	7
FUEL ECONOMY	6	7	5
RIDE QUALITY	5	5	3
STEERING/HANDLING	5	5	8
QUIETNESS	3	3	3
INSTRUMENTS/CONTROLS	7	7	7
ROOM/COMFORT (FRONT)	4	4	5
ROOM/COMFORT (REAR)	3	3	3
CARGO ROOM	2	2	2
VALUE	7	7	6

No Sentra is as refined as a Honda Civic or Volkswagen Jetta, or as roomy as Ford's Focus. But these are solid enough small cars, and competitive prices merit a spot on your subcompact-car shopping list.

TOTAL	45	47	49

Average total for subcompact cars: 43.7

ENGINES

	dohc I4	dohc I4
Size, liters/cu. in.	1.8/110	2.5/152
Horsepower @ rpm	126 @ 6000	165 @ 6000
Torque (lb-ft) @ rpm	129 @ 2400	175 @ 4000
Availability	S[1]	S[2]

EPA city/highway mpg

5-speed manual	27/35	24/29
6-speed manual		22/28
4-speed automatic	27/33	23/28

1. XE, GXE, CA. 2. SE-R (175 hp and 180 lb-ft w/SE-R Spec V).

PRICES

Nissan Sentra

	Retail Price	Dealer Invoice
XE 4-door sedan, manual	$11799	$11097

Specifications begin on page 551.

NISSAN

	Retail Price	Dealer Invoice
XE 4-door sedan, automatic	$12599	$11849
GXE 4-door sedan, manual	13749	12571
GXE 4-door sedan, automatic	14549	13303
CA 4-door sedan, automatic	14899	14202
Destination charge	540	540

SE-R and SE-R Spec V prices and equipment not available at time of publication. CA model available in California only.

STANDARD EQUIPMENT

XE: 1.8-liter dohc 4-cylinder engine, 5-speed manual or 4-speed automatic transmission, dual front airbags, emergency inside trunk release, power steering, tilt steering wheel, cloth upholstery, front bucket seats, center console, cupholders, rear defogger, remote fuel door and decklid release, 185/65R14 tires, wheel covers.

GXE adds: air conditioning, height-adjustable driver seat, split folding rear seat, power mirrors, power windows, power door locks, remote keyless entry, AM/FM/CD player, digital clock, tachometer, variable intermittent wipers, visor mirrors.

CA adds: 4-speed automatic transmission, theft-deterrent system, 195/60R15 tires, alloy wheels.

OPTIONAL EQUIPMENT
Major Packages

Road Trip Pkg., GXE	359	311
Cruise control, upgraded sound system, overhead console, map lights.		
Road Hugging Pkg., GXE	499	432
Fog lights, 195/60R15 tires, alloy wheels.		
Synergy Pkg., GXE manual	1049	910
GXE automatic	999	866
Road Trip Pkg. plus Road Hugging Pkg., leather-wrapped steering wheel, rear spoiler.		

Safety
Front side airbags and antilock brakes, GXE	749	650

Appearance and Miscellaneous
Rear spoiler, XE, GXE	349	269

Postproduction options also available.

NISSAN XTERRA
Rear- or 4-wheel-drive midsize sport-utility vehicle

Prices are accurate at time of publication; subject to manufacturer's change.

NISSAN

Nissan Xterra

Base price range: $17,999-$27,499. Built in USA.
Also consider: Dodge Durango, Ford Explorer Sport Trac and Sport, Toyota 4Runner

FOR • Cargo room **AGAINST** • Ride/handling • Acceleration (4 cyl) • Rear-seat entry/exit • Wind noise

The lower-priced of Nissan's two midsize SUVs gets new front styling and an available supercharged V6 for 2002. Xterra aims for younger buyers than the Pathfinder. Its base XE model comes only with a 143-hp 4-cyl engine, manual transmission, and rear-wheel drive. XE V6 and top-line SE models have a 170-hp V6. XE S/C and SE S/C models have the 210-hp supercharged V6. V6 versions come with manual or automatic transmission and 2WD or 4WD. Their 4WD must be disengaged on dry pavement but includes low-range gearing. ABS and air conditioning are standard. New for 2002 is a 4WD XE V6 off-road Enthusiast Package that eliminates the side step rails and adds a limited-slip differential, manual locking hubs, and front tow hooks. All '02 Xterras have a "power bulge" hood and a revised dashboard. SE S/Cs have 17-inch wheels; other Xterras get 16s or 15s, depending on model and engine.

RATINGS	XE 2WD, auto.	SE 4WD, man.	SE S/C 4WD, auto.
ACCELERATION	4	4	5
FUEL ECONOMY	4	4	4
RIDE QUALITY	3	3	4
STEERING/HANDLING	3	3	4
QUIETNESS	3	3	3
INSTRUMENTS/CONTROLS	5	5	5
ROOM/COMFORT (FRONT)	6	6	6
ROOM/COMFORT (REAR)	3	3	3

Specifications begin on page 551.

NISSAN

	XE 2WD, auto.	SE 4WD, man.	SE S/C 4WD, auto.
CARGO ROOM	7	7	7
VALUE	5	5	5

Xterra is priced like car-based compact SUVs, such as the Honda CR-V, Toyota RAV4, and Ford Escape/Mazda Tribute. It's less-civilized in everyday driving than those vehicles, but it charges little more for its truck toughness and superior off-road ability, plus V6 power that CR-V and RAV4 lack.

TOTAL	43	43	46

Average total for midsize sport-utility vehicles: 49.6

ENGINES

	dohc I4	ohc V6	Supercharged dohc V6
Size, liters/cu. in.	2.4/146	3.3/200	3.3/201
Horsepower @ rpm	143 @ 5200	170 @ 4800	210 @ 4800
Torque (lb-ft) @ rpm	154 @ 4000	154 @ 200	246 @ 2800
Availability	S[1]	S[2]	S[3]

EPA city/highway mpg

5-speed manual	19/24	16/18[4]	15/18[6]
4-speed automatic		15/19[5]	15/18[6]

1. XE. 2. XE V6, SE. 3. S/C models. 4. 16/19 w/2WD. 5. 16/20 w/2WD. 6. 15/19 w/2WD.

PRICES

Nissan Xterra

	Retail Price	Dealer Invoice
2WD XE 4-door wagon, manual	$17999	$16740
2WD XE V6 4-door wagon, manual	19199	17856
2WD XE V6 4-door wagon, automatic	20199	18786
4WD XE V6 4-door wagon, manual	21199	19716
4WD XE V6 4-door wagon, automatic	22199	20646
2WD XE S/C 4-door wagon, manual	22699	21111
2WD XE S/C 4-door wagon, automatic	23699	22041
4WD XE S/C 4-door wagon, manual	24699	22971
4WD XE S/C 4-door wagon, automatic	25699	23901
2WD SE 4-door wagon, manual	23199	21333
2WD SE 4-door wagon, automatic	24199	22253
4WD SE 4-door wagon, manual	25199	23173
4WD SE 4-door wagon, automatic	26199	24093
2WD SE S/C 4-door wagon, manual	24499	22529
2WD SE S/C 4-door wagon, automatic	25499	23449
4WD SE S/C 4-door wagon, manual	26499	24369
4WD SE S/C 4-door wagon, automatic	27499	25288
Destination charge	540	540

STANDARD EQUIPMENT

XE: 2.4-liter dohc 4-cylinder engine, 5-speed manual transmission, dual front airbags, antilock brakes, air conditioning, power steering,

Prices are accurate at time of publication; subject to manufacturer's change.

NISSAN

cloth upholstery, front bucket seats, center console, cupholders, split folding rear seat, AM/FM/CD player, digital clock, tachometer, tachometer, rear defogger, rear wiper/washer, roof rack, rear privacy glass, skid plates, full-sized spare tire, 265/70R15 tires.

XE V6 adds: 3.3-liter V6 engine, 5-speed manual or 4-speed automatic transmission. **4WD** adds: 4-wheel drive, 2-speed transfer case.

XE S/C adds: supercharged 3.3-liter V6 engine, limited-slip differential, tilt steering wheel, cruise control, power mirrors, power windows, power door locks, remote keyless entry, map lights, variable intermittent wipers, cargo cover, first aid kit, fog lights, side step rails, front tow hooks, 265/70R16 tires, alloy wheels. **4WD** adds: 4-wheel drive, 2-speed transfer case.

SE adds: 3.3-liter V6 engine, leather-wrapped steering wheel w/radio controls, AM/FM radio w/in-dash 6-disc CD changer, passenger-side visor mirror. *Deletes:* supercharged 3.3-liter V6 engine. **4WD** adds: 4-wheel drive, 2-speed transfer case.

SE S/C adds: supercharged 3.3-liter V6 engine, 265/65R17 tires. **4WD** adds: 4-wheel drive, 2-speed transfer case.

OPTIONAL EQUIPMENT
Major Packages

	Retail Price	Dealer Invoice
Utility Pkg., XE	$899	$779
XE V6	999	866

Tilt steering wheel, variable intermittent wipers, cargo cover, first aid kit, ceiling tie clips, additional auxiliary power outlet, side step rails, 265/70R16 tires (XE V6), alloy wheels (XE V6).

Enthusiast Pkg., XE V6 4WD	699	606

Limited-slip rear differential, front manual locking hubs, tilt steering wheel, variable intermittent wipers, first aid kit, map lights, floormats, ceiling tie clips, additional auxiliary power outlet, front tow hooks, fog lights. NA w/Power Pkg., Utility Pkg., or Sport Pkg.

Power Pkg., XE	999	866
XE V6	1199	1040

Power mirrors, power windows and door locks, remote keyless entry, cruise control, map lights, cloth door inserts. Requires Utility Pkg.

Sport Pkg., XE V6	299	259

Limited-slip rear differential, fog lights, front tow hooks. Requires Power Pkg. and Utility Pkg.

Comfort & Convenience Features

Manual sunroof, SE, SE S/C	NA	NA
Automatic day/night rearview mirror, XE, XE V6, XE S/C	219	164

Specifications begin on page 551.

NISSAN • OLDSMOBILE

Appearance and Miscellaneous	Retail Price	Dealer Invoice
Grille/taillight guards	$589	$482
Special Purpose, Wheels and Tires		
Tow hitch	349	246

NA XE.

Postproduction options also available.

OLDSMOBILE ALERO

Oldsmobile Alero GL 4-door sedan

Front-wheel-drive compact car
Base price range: $17,470-$22,315. Built in USA.
Also consider: Chrysler Sebring, Mazda 626, Volkswagen Passat

FOR • Acceleration (V6) • Control layout • Passenger and cargo room • Quietness **AGAINST** • Engine noise (4-cylinder) • Rear visibility (2-door) • Rear-seat entry/exit (2-door)

A new 4-cyl engine is the main 2002 change. Alero shares its design and powertrains with the Pontiac Grand Am, but has different styling. Coupes and sedans come in four trim levels. GX and GL1 models have a 140-hp 2.2-liter 4-cyl engine. It replaces a 150-hp 2.4, which had lower EPA fuel-economy ratings. GL2 and GLS models come with a V6 that's optional on GL1. Automatic transmission is standard, but manual is available on the 4-cyl GX and GL2. All Aleros come with antilock 4-wheel disc brakes, traction control, air conditioning, power locks, CD player, and cruise control. GX is no longer available with power windows but gains a new Sport Package option that includes manual transmission, leather-wrapped steering wheel, spoiler, and alloy wheels. This package triggers a credit off the sticker price. Alero is slated to go out of production, though GM has not said when within the phaseout of Oldsmobile it will be terminated. GM confirms 2004 as the final model year for the brand. Alero's performance and accommodations mirror those of comparably equipped Grand Ams.

Prices are accurate at time of publication; subject to manufacturer's change.
CONSUMER GUIDE®

OLDSMOBILE

RATINGS

	GL1 sdn, 4 cyl auto.	GLS cpe
ACCELERATION	4	6
FUEL ECONOMY	6	6
RIDE QUALITY	5	5
STEERING/HANDLING	5	5
QUIETNESS	4	4
INSTRUMENTS/CONTROLS	7	7
ROOM/COMFORT (FRONT)	5	5
ROOM/COMFORT (REAR)	4	3
CARGO ROOM	4	4
VALUE	5	4

Strong V6 acceleration and a long list of standard features at competitive prices are Alero's virtues. It feels more mature than cousin Grand Am, but still can't match import-brand rivals in refinement, interior design, and materials. And the phaseout of Oldsmobile means poor resale value and low lease residual values.

TOTAL	49	49

Average total for compact cars: 51.6

ENGINES

	dohc I4	ohv V6
Size, liters/cu. in.	2.2/134	3.4/207
Horsepower @ rpm	140 @ 5600	170 @ 4800
Torque (lb-ft) @ rpm	150 @ 4000	200 @ 4000
Availability	S[1]	S[2]

EPA city/highway mpg

5-speed manual	25/33	
4-speed automatic	24/32	20/29

1. GX, GL1; optional GL2. 2. GL2, GLS; optional GL1.

PRICES

Oldsmobile Alero	Retail Price	Dealer Invoice
GX 2-door coupe	$17470	$16334
GX 4-door sedan	17470	16334
GL1 2-door coupe	19680	18007
GL1 4-door sedan	19455	17801
GL2 2-door coupe	20580	18831
GL2 4-door sedan	20580	18831
GLS 2-door coupe	22315	20195
GLS 4-door sedan	22090	19991
Destination charge	585	585

STANDARD EQUIPMENT

GX: 2.2-liter dohc 4-cylinder engine, 4-speed automatic transmission,

Specifications begin on page 551.

OLDSMOBILE

traction control, dual front airbags, antilock 4-wheel disc brakes, daytime running lights, air conditioning, power steering, tilt steering wheel, cruise control, cloth upholstery, front bucket seats, center console, cupholders, split folding rear seat, power door locks, AM/FM/CD player, digital clock, tachometer, variable intermittent wipers, rear defogger, visor mirrors, power decklid release, automatic headlights, floormats, theft-deterrent system, 215/60R15 tires, wheel covers.

GL1 adds: leather-wrapped steering wheel, power mirrors, power windows, remote keyless entry, driver seat w/power height adjustment and manual lumbar support, map lights, rear spoiler (coupe), fog lights, alloy wheels.

GL2 adds: 3.4-liter V6 engine, rear spoiler, performance sport suspension, 225/50VR16 tires.

GLS adds: leather upholstery, 6-way power driver seat, AM/FM/cassette/CD player, 225/50SR16 tires, polished alloy wheels. *Deletes:* performance sport suspension, rear spoiler (sedan).

OPTIONAL EQUIPMENT	Retail Price	Dealer Invoice
Major Packages		
Sport Pkg., GX (credit)	($150)	($134)
5-speed manual transmission, leather-wrapped steering wheel, rear spoiler, alloy wheels.		
Sun and Sound Pkg., GL1, GL2	1100	979
Manufacturer's Discount Price	*845*	*752*
Power sunroof, AM/FM/cassette/CD player.		
Performance Suspension Pkg., GLS	250	223
Performance sport suspension, 225/50VR16 tires.		
Powertrain		
3.4-liter V6 engine, GL1	715	636
2.2-liter dohc 4-cylinder engine, GL2 (credit)	(1110)	(988)
Includes 5-speed manual transmission.		
5-speed manual transmission, GX (credit)	(880)	(783)
Comfort & Convenience Features		
Power sunroof, GLS	700	623
6-way power driver seat, GL1, GL2	305	271
AM/FM/cassette/CD player, GL1, GL2	400	356
Appearance and Miscellaneous		
Rear spoiler, GL1 sedan, GLS sedan	250	223

OLDSMOBILE AURORA

Front-wheel-drive near-luxury car
Base price range: $30,995-$34,990. Built in USA.

Prices are accurate at time of publication; subject to manufacturer's change.

OLDSMOBILE

Oldsmobile Aurora

Also consider: Acura TL, Buick Park Avenue, Lexus ES 300, Lincoln LS

FOR • Acceleration (V8) • Passenger room **AGAINST** • Rear visibility • Climate controls

Oldsmobile's flagship loses its V6 version partway through the 2002 model year as part of GM's phaseout of the Olds brand. Aurora shares its platform with the Pontiac Bonneville and Buick LeSabre. It offers V6 and V8 engines, both with automatic transmission. Standard are front side airbags, antilock 4-wheel disc brakes, automatic load-leveling suspension, tire-inflation monitor, and General Motors' OnStar assistance system. The V8 model includes traction control and Oldsmobile's antiskid Precision Control System; both are optional on the V6. New for '02 is a "navigational radio" system that stores maps on CDs and gives directions via a dashboard mounted screen or by audio instructions. Also new for 2002 are standard chrome exhaust tips. Olds says production of the V6 model stops in June 2002, with V8 production ceasing in May 2003.

RATINGS

	V6	V8
ACCELERATION	6	7
FUEL ECONOMY	5	3
RIDE QUALITY	8	7
STEERING/HANDLING	7	7
QUIETNESS	7	7
INSTRUMENTS/CONTROLS	5	5
ROOM/COMFORT (FRONT)	7	7
ROOM/COMFORT (REAR)	5	5
CARGO ROOM	4	4
VALUE	3	3

Few other sedans in this class offer a V8, but we doubt Aurora can tempt Lexus or BMW owners. This is, however, a pleasant, slightly sporty all-rounder that should appeal to value-minded near-luxury buyers. But you'd have to keep your Aurora 5-10 years to mitigate resale-value damage caused by the phaseout of Oldsmobile.

| **TOTAL** | 57 | 55 |

Average total for near-luxury cars: 54.5

Specifications begin on page 551.

OLDSMOBILE

ENGINES

	dohc V6	dohc V8
Size, liters/cu. in.	3.5/212	4.0/244
Horsepower @ rpm	215 @ 5600	250 @ 5600
Torque (lb-ft) @ rpm	230 @ 4400	260 @ 4400
Availability	S[1]	S[2]
EPA city/highway mpg		
4-speed automatic	18/27	18/26

1. V6. 2. V8.

PRICES

Oldsmobile Aurora

	Retail Price	Dealer Invoice
V6 4-door sedan	$30995	$28360
V8 4-door sedan	34990	32016
Destination charge	670	670

STANDARD EQUIPMENT

V6: 3.5-liter dohc V6 engine, 4-speed automatic transmission, dual front airbags, front side airbags, antilock 4-wheel disc brakes, daytime running lights, tire-pressure monitor, air conditioning w/automatic climate control, interior air filter, power steering, tilt leather-wrapped steering wheel w/radio and climate controls, cruise control, OnStar System w/one year service (roadside assistance, emergency services; other services available), leather upholstery, front bucket seats, 8-way power driver seat w/power lumbar adjustment, center console, cupholders, rear seat trunk pass-through, wood interior trim, heated power mirrors, power windows, power door locks, remote keyless entry, AM/FM/cassette/CD player, digital clock, tachometer, trip computer, illuminated visor mirrors, outside temperature indicator, overhead console, map lights, rear defogger, variable intermittent wipers, power remote decklid and fuel door release, automatic headlights, floormats, front and rear fog lights, theft-deterrent system, automatic load-leveling suspension, 225/60HR16 tires, alloy wheels.

V8 adds: 4.0-liter dohc V8 engine, traction control, antiskid system, dual-zone automatic climate control, 8-way power passenger seat, memory system including driver seat and outside mirrors, automatic day/night rearview mirror, compass, rain-sensing automatic wipers, universal garage door opener, 235/55HR17 tires.

OPTIONAL EQUIPMENT
Major Packages

All Weather Pkg., V6	575	512

Traction control, antiskid system. Requires Passenger Comfort Pkg.

Prices are accurate at time of publication; subject to manufacturer's change.

OLDSMOBILE

	Retail Price	Dealer Invoice
Passenger Comfort Pkg., V6	$440	$392

Dual-zone automatic air conditioning, rear seat ducts, 8-way power passenger seat, rear storage armrest, additional cupholders.

Convenience Pkg., V6 565   503

Memory system including driver seat and outside mirror memory, automatic day/night rearview mirror, compass, rain-sensing automatic wipers, universal garage door opener.

Comfort & Convenience Features

Power sunroof 1095   975
V6 includes universal garage door opener.
Navigational radio 935   832
Includes CD-ROM navigation system. Requires 12-disc CD changer. V6 requires Convenience Pkg. or All Weather Pkg.
Bose sound system 500   445
V6 requires Passenger Comfort Pkg. or Convenience Pkg.
12-disc CD changer 460   409
V6 requires Passenger Comfort Pkg. or Convenience Pkg.
Heated front seats 345   307
V6 requires Passenger Comfort Pkg.

Appearance and Miscellaneous

Gold Pkg. 175   156
Chrome alloy wheels 800   712

OLDSMOBILE BRAVADA

Oldsmobile Bravada

Rear- or all-wheel-drive midsize sport-utility vehicle
Base price range: $31,835–$34,367. Built in USA.
Also consider: Acura MDX, Dodge Durango, Ford Explorer,

OLDSMOBILE

Mercury Mountaineer

FOR • Passenger and cargo room • Towing ability **AGAINST** • Fuel economy

Oldsmobile's version of the redesigned General Motors midsize SUVs shares a new body-on-frame platform with the 2002 Chevrolet TrailBlazer and GMC Envoy. Each has its own styling inside and out and rides a 6-inch longer wheelbase than before, with a body that's longer, wider, and taller by five inches. All share a new inline 6-cyl engine with 80 hp more than their previous V6. A 4-speed automatic is the only transmission. Bravada for the first time is available with 2WD, which includes traction control. The 4WD version uses Oldsmobile's SmartTrac all-wheel-drive system that does not include low-range gearing. Antilock 4-wheel disc brakes and 17-inch alloy wheels are standard. GM's new SUV design does not have independent rear suspension, though Bravada uses air-spring rear suspension in place of coil springs. Standard front side airbags include head protection for the driver. Seating for five is standard. Unlike TrailBlazer and Envoy, Bravada won't offer a 7-passenger model. Bravada is slated to go out of production, though GM has not said when within the phaseout of Oldsmobile it will be terminated. GM confirms 2004 as the final model year for the brand.

RATINGS	Bravada AWD
ACCELERATION	6
FUEL ECONOMY	4
RIDE QUALITY	6
STEERING/HANDLING	4
QUIETNESS	4
INSTRUMENTS/CONTROLS	7
ROOM/COMFORT (FRONT)	7
ROOM/COMFORT (REAR)	6
CARGO ROOM	8
VALUE	3

Bravada's decent road manners make it better suited to typical street duty than the TrailBlazer, though we rate the Envoy as the best value in this GM trio. Rivals such as the Acura MDX or Lexus RX 300 offer much more refinement than Bravada for only a little more money. And Bravada's resale and lease-residual value is further harmed by the phaseout of Oldsmobile.

TOTAL	55

Average total for midsize sport-utility vehicles: 49.6

ENGINES

	dohc I6
Size, liters/cu. in.	4.2/256
Horsepower @ rpm	270 @ 6000
Torque (lb-ft) @ rpm	275 @ 3600

Prices are accurate at time of publication; subject to manufacturer's change.

OLDSMOBILE

	dohc I6
Availability...	S

EPA city/highway mpg

| 4-speed automatic.. | 15/21[1] |

1. 16/22 w/2WD.

PRICES

Oldsmobile Bravada	Retail Price	Dealer Invoice
2WD Base 4-door wagon	$31835	$28811
AWD Base 4-door wagon	34367	31102
Destination charge	600	600

STANDARD EQUIPMENT

Base: 4.2-liter 6-cylinder engine, 4-speed automatic transmission, traction control, locking rear differential, dual front airbags, front side airbags, antilock 4-wheel disc brakes, daytime running lights, air conditioning w/dual-zone automatic climate controls, rear climate controls, power steering, tilt leather-wrapped steering wheel w/radio and climate controls, cruise control, OnStar System w/one year service (roadside assistance, emergency services; other services available), leather upholstery, 8-way power front bucket seats w/lumbar adjustment, center console, split folding rear seat, heated power mirrors, power windows, power door locks, remote keyless entry, AM/FM/cassette/CD player, rear radio controls, digital clock, variable intermittent wipers, rear defogger, rear wiper/washer, automatic day/night rearview mirror, compass, outside temperature indicator, trip computer, overhead console, universal garage door opener, illuminated visor mirrors, map lights, automatic headlights, floormats, theft-deterrent system, rear liftgate, rear privacy glass, roof rack, fog lights, cornering lights, platform hitch, 7-wire trailer harness, load-leveling rear suspension, full-size spare tire, 245/65R17 tires, alloy wheels. **AWD** adds: all-wheel drive, 255/60R17 tires. *Deletes:* traction control.

OPTIONAL EQUIPMENT
Major Packages

Option Pkg. 1SB	360	310

Driver seat and mirror memory, automatic day/night outside mirrors w/reverse tilt-down and turn signal lights, digital memo recorder, cargo cover.

Option Pkg. 1SC	815	701

Option Pkg. 1SB plus rain-sensing wipers, polished alloy wheels.

Comfort & Convenience Features

Power sunroof	800	688
AM/FM radio w/in-dash 6-disc CD changer	295	254
Bose sound system	495	426

Specifications begin on page 551.

OLDSMOBILE

	Retail Price	Dealer Invoice
Heated front seats	$250	$215

Requires Option Pkg.

OLDSMOBILE INTRIGUE

Oldsmobile Intrigue GLS

Front-wheel-drive midsize car
Base price range: $22,817-$27,892. Built in USA.
Also consider: Honda Accord, Nissan Maxima, Toyota Camry

FOR • Acceleration • Passenger and cargo room • Ride • Steering/handling **AGAINST** • Climate controls

Production of the Intrigue ends in June 2002 as part of the phaseout of the Oldsmobile brand, General Motors has announced. For its final edition, a power sunroof is standard instead of optional on this midsize sedan. Intrigue shares a basic design with the Buick Century/Regal, Chevrolet Impala, and Pontiac Grand Prix. It offers GX, GL, and top-line GLS models. The only powertrain is 3.5-liter twincam V6 with automatic transmission. Standard are antilock 4-wheel disc brakes. Traction control is standard on GL and GLS and optional on GX. GLS adds General Motors' OnStar assistance system. Optional on all is Oldsmobile's Precision Control antiskid system. The sunroof remains an option on GX and GL Intrigues for 2002. Among other changes are a standard universal garage door opener for GLS and standard instead of optional CD player for GX.

RATINGS	GX/GL	GLS w/Precision Pkg.
ACCELERATION	6	6
FUEL ECONOMY	5	5
RIDE QUALITY	7	7
STEERING/HANDLING	6	7
QUIETNESS	6	6

Prices are accurate at time of publication; subject to manufacturer's change.

OLDSMOBILE

	GX/GL	GLS w/Precision Pkg.
INSTRUMENTS/CONTROLS	7	7
ROOM/COMFORT (FRONT)	6	6
ROOM/COMFORT (REAR)	5	5
CARGO ROOM	5	5
VALUE	5	5

Intrigue feels more grown up than Grand Prix, more sophisticated than Regal. It's a smart blend of features and performance at competitive prices. But with 2002 being its final model year, Intrigue does not qualify as a sound long-term investment.

TOTAL	58	59

Average total for midsize cars: 57.0

ENGINES

	dohc V6
Size, liters/cu. in.	3.5/211
Horsepower @ rpm	215 @ 5600
Torque (lb-ft) @ rpm	230 @ 4400
Availability	S

EPA city/highway mpg
4-speed automatic	20/30

PRICES

Oldsmobile Intrigue	Retail Price	Dealer Invoice
GX 4-door sedan	$22817	$20878
GL 4-door sedan	24402	22328
GLS 4-door sedan	27892	25521
Destination charge	610	610

STANDARD EQUIPMENT

GX: 3.5-liter dohc V6 engine, 4-speed automatic transmission, antilock 4-wheel disc brakes, dual front airbags, daytime running lamps, power steering, tilt steering wheel, cruise control, air conditioning, interior air filter, cloth upholstery, front bucket seats, center console, cupholders, power mirrors, power windows, power door locks, AM/FM/CD player, digital clock, tachometer, variable intermittent wipers, rear defogger, remote trunk and fuel door release, visor mirrors, map lights, automatic headlights, floormats, theft-deterrent system, cornering lights, 225/60R16 tires, alloy wheels.

GL adds: traction control, dual-zone automatic climate control, outside temperature indicator, leather-wrapped steering wheel w/radio controls, 6-way power driver seat, split-folding rear seat, remote keyless entry, AM/FM/cassette/CD player, illuminated visor mirrors, fog lights.

GLS adds: OnStar System w/one year service (roadside assistance,

Specifications begin on page 551.

OLDSMOBILE

emergency services; other services available), leather upholstery, heated front seats, 6-way power passenger seat, power sunroof, automatic day/night rearview mirror, compass, universal garage door opener.

OPTIONAL EQUIPMENT

	Retail Price	Dealer Invoice
Major Packages		
Driver Control Pkg., GX	$870	$774
Manufacturer's Discount Price	*470*	*418*
Traction control, remote keyless entry, 6-speaker sound system, 6-way power driver seat, leather-wrapped steering wheel, armrest, and shifter.		
Premium Leather Pkg., GL	1595	1420
Manufacturer's Discount Price	*995*	*886*
Leather upholstery, 6-way power passenger seat, heated front seats.		
Sun and Sound Pkg., GL	1500	1336
Manufacturer's Discount Price	*1250*	*1113*
Power sunroof, AM/FM/cassette/CD player.		
Precision Control System, GX, GL	595	530
Antiskid system, upgraded power steering, performance axle ratio, 225/60HR16 performance tires. GX requires Driver Control Pkg.		
Precision Sport Pkg., GLS	2115	1882
Manufacturer's Discount Price	*1315*	*1170*
Precision Control System plus Bose sound system, rear spoiler, chrome alloy wheels.		
Comfort & Convenience Features		
AM/FM/cassette/CD player, GX, GL	200	178
GX requires Driver Control Pkg.		
Split folding rear seat, GX	150	134
Appearance and Miscellaneous		
Rear spoiler, GX, GL	225	200
Gold Pkg.	150	134
Chrome alloy wheels, GL	695	619

OLDSMOBILE SILHOUETTE

Front-wheel-drive minivan

Base price range: $26,905-$35,450. Built in USA.

Also consider: Chrysler Town & Country and Voyager, Dodge Caravan, Honda Odyssey, Toyota Sienna

FOR • Ride • Passenger and cargo room • Available all-wheel drive **AGAINST** • Fuel economy

This upscale version of the Chevrolet Venture and Pontiac Montana gets available all-wheel drive and a DVD player for '02.

Prices are accurate at time of publication; subject to manufacturer's change.
CONSUMER GUIDE®

OLDSMOBILE

Oldsmobile Silhouette

Silhouette comes in a single body length, equivalent to the extended-length Chevy and Pontiac. GL, GLS, and top-line Premiere Edition models are offered. Premiere comes with a rear-seat video entertainment system, now with a DVD player instead of a VCR. All Silhouettes have dual sliding side doors with power operation available on one or both sides, depending on model. Front bucket seats and two 2nd-row captain's chairs are standard. The 3rd row can be fitted with two captains chairs or a 3-passenger bench. The GLS/Premiere 3rd-row bench folds flush with a floor-level storage tray. Silhouette is available with front-wheel drive or General Motors' Versatrak all-wheel drive that includes independent rear suspension and 4-wheel disc brakes. Traction control for front-drive models is optional on GL, standard on the others. All have a V6, automatic transmission, ABS, front side airbags, load-leveling suspension, and GM's OnStar assistance system. Rear obstacle detection is standard on GLS and Premiere, optional on GL. Silhouette is slated to go out of production, though GM has not said when within the phaseout of Oldsmobile it will be terminated. GM confirms 2004 as the final model year for the brand. Silhouette's performance and accommodations mirror those of similarly equipped Ventures.

RATINGS

	Premier Edition
ACCELERATION	4
FUEL ECONOMY	4
RIDE QUALITY	7
STEERING/HANDLING	5
QUIETNESS	6
INSTRUMENTS/CONTROLS	6
ROOM/COMFORT (FRONT)	6
ROOM/COMFORT (REAR)	7
CARGO ROOM	9

Specifications begin on page 551.

OLDSMOBILE

Premier Edition

VALUE — 5
Silhouette's reasonable pricing delivers impressive array of features, plus pleasant, almost sporty driving experience. Premiere makes a tempting kid-friendly vacation hauler. And only Dodge and Chrysler offer AWD among direct competitors. However, while good deals and extended warranties make Silhouette more attractive today, the phaseout of Oldsmobile does not make it a sound long-term investment.

TOTAL — 59
Average total for minivans: 56.0

ENGINES

	ohv V6
Size, liters/cu. in.	3.4/207
Horsepower @ rpm	185 @ 5200
Torque (lb-ft) @ rpm	210 @ 4000
Availability	S

EPA city/highway mpg
4-speed automatic .... 19/26[1]

1. 18/24 w/AWD.

PRICES

Oldsmobile Silhouette	Retail Price	Dealer Invoice
GL 4-door van, FWD	$26905	$24349
GLS 4-door van, FWD	30980	28037
GLS 4-door van, AWD	33550	30363
Premiere Edition 4-door van, FWD	32880	29756
Premiere Edition 4-door van, AWD	35450	32082
Destination charge	655	655

FWD denotes front-wheel drive. AWD denote all-wheel drive.

STANDARD EQUIPMENT

GL: 3.4-liter V6 engine, 4-speed automatic transmission, dual front airbags, front side airbags, antilock brakes, daytime running lights, front air conditioning, interior air filter, power steering, tilt steering wheel, cruise control, OnStar System w/one year service (roadside assistance, emergency services; other services available), cloth upholstery, front bucket seats, 6-way power driver seat, center console, cupholders, second-row captain chairs, third-row split-folding bench seat, overhead console, map lights, heated power mirrors, power windows, power door locks, remote keyless entry, AM/FM/CD player, digital clock, tachometer, variable intermittent wipers, rear defogger, rear wiper/washer, automatic headlights, illuminated visor mirrors, floormats, theft-deterrent system, rear privacy glass, fog lights, roof rack, air inflation kit, load-leveling suspension,

Prices are accurate at time of publication; subject to manufacturer's change.

OLDSMOBILE

215/70R15 tires, wheel covers.

GLS adds: traction control, rear obstacle detection system, leather upholstery, 8-way power front seats w/driver seat memory, power sliding passenger-side door, overhead console, trip computer, compass, outside temperature indicator, front dual-zone automatic climate control, rear air conditioning and heater w/rear controls, AM/FM/cassette/CD player, leather-wrapped steering wheel w/radio controls, rear-seat radio controls, headphones, universal garage door opener, 225/60R16 tires, alloy wheels. **AWD** adds: all-wheel drive, 4-wheel disc brakers. *Deletes:* traction control.

Premiere Edition adds: LCD color screen/DVD player, input jacks for video games or camcorder camera, heated front seats, third row stowable bench seat w/convenience tray, driver-side power sliding rear door. **AWD** adds: all-wheel drive, 4-wheel disc brakers. *Deletes:* traction control.

OPTIONAL EQUIPMENT

	Retail Price	Dealer Invoice
Major Packages		
Rear Comfort Pkg., GL	$575	$495
Rear air conditioning w/rear controls.		
Convenience Pkg., GL	860	740
Rear air conditioning w/rear controls, trip computer, compass, outside temperature indicator, universal garage door opener.		
Security Pkg., GL	1505	1294
Convenience Pkg. plus passenger-side power sliding rear door, rear obstacle detection system		
Towing Pkg.	195	168
Engine and transmission oil coolers, heavy-duty radiator, 6-lead wiring harness.		
Powertrain		
Traction control, GL	195	168
Comfort & Convenience Features		
Power sliding passenger-side door, GL	450	387
Power sliding driver-side door, GLS	350	301
Heated front seats, GLS	195	168
Third row split bench seat, Premiere	NC	NC
Third row captain chairs, GLS, Premiere	NC	NC
Third row stowable bench seat, GLS	NC	NC
AM/FM/cassette/CD player, GL	100	86
AM/FM w/in-dash 6-disc CD changer, GLS, Premiere	295	254
Appearance and Miscellaneous		
Alloy wheels, GL	295	254
Chrome alloy wheels, FWD GLS/ Premiere	695	598

Specifications begin on page 551.

PONTIAC AZTEK

Pontiac Aztek GT

Front- or all-wheel-drive midsize sport-utility vehicle
Base price range: $19,995-$22,995. Built in Mexico.
Also consider: Acura MDX, Ford Explorer

FOR • Passenger and cargo room • Interior storage space
AGAINST • Interior materials • Brake-pedal feel (2WD model)

Alterations to its controversial styling and more standard features mark the 2002 Aztek. This minivan/SUV crossover is based on Pontiac's Montana minivan, but aimed at young, sports-minded buyers. It has four conventional side doors and a hatchback-type glass liftgate in combination with a drop-down tailgate. The former GT trim level is dropped, leaving two base models, one with front-wheel drive, the other with General Motors' Versatrak all-wheel drive. The AWD system lacks low-range gearing. Front side airbags and ABS are standard; AWD versions add 4-wheel disc brakes. Aztek's unconventional styling contributed to slow sales in its 2001 debut year. The most notable appearance change for '02 is a revised paint scheme that substitutes body-color trim for most of last year's gray lower-body cladding. Wheel designs also change and include a 3-spoke alloys for the 2WD model. An insulated front console cooler and CD player are now standard instead of optional. Traction control is optional with 2WD. Other options include heated leather front seats, a slide-out cargo-floor section with storage bins and rollaway wheels, and GM's OnStar assistance system. Available through dealers is a camping package with clip-on tent and fitted air mattress. Maximum towing capacity is 3500 lb. The Buick Rendezvous shares Aztek's underskin design, though it's longer and has three rows of seats.

RATINGS	2WD	AWD
ACCELERATION	5	4
FUEL ECONOMY	5	5

Prices are accurate at time of publication; subject to manufacturer's change.

PONTIAC

	2WD	AWD
RIDE QUALITY	5	4
STEERING/HANDLING	4	4
QUIETNESS	5	5
INSTRUMENTS/CONTROLS	4	4
ROOM/COMFORT (FRONT)	7	7
ROOM/COMFORT (REAR)	7	7
CARGO ROOM	8	8
VALUE	3	3

Aztek is as comfortable as any SUV, and packed with features designed for active types. Its assembly quality and budget-grade cabin materials won't please the discerning, however. And if the unorthodox styling again affects sales, look for continued discounts.

TOTAL	53	51

Average total for midsize sport-utility vehicles: 49.6

ENGINES

	ohv V6
Size, liters/cu. in.	3.4/204
Horsepower @ rpm	185 @ 5200
Torque (lb-ft) @ rpm	210 @ 4000
Availability	S

EPA city/highway mpg

4-speed automatic	18/24[1]

1. 19/26 w/2WD.

PRICES

Pontiac Aztek	Retail Price	Dealer Invoice
2WD Base 4-door hatchback	$19995	$18295
AWD Base 4-door hatchback	22995	21040
Destination charge	550	550

STANDARD EQUIPMENT

Base: 3.4-liter V6 engine, 4-speed automatic transmission, dual front airbags, front side airbags, antilock brakes, daytime running lights, front air conditioning, power steering, tilt steering wheel, cloth upholstery, front bucket seats, center console w/cooler and storage, cupholders, split folding rear seat, power mirrors, power windows, power door locks, AM/FM/CD player, digital clock, tachometer, intermittent wipers, rear defogger, visor mirrors, power decklid release, automatic headlights, cargo cover, floormats, theft-deterrent system, rear quarter and liftgate privacy glass, fog lights, 215/70R16 tires, alloy wheels. **AWD** adds: all-wheel drive, 4-wheel disc brakes.

Specifications begin on page 551.

PONTIAC

OPTIONAL EQUIPMENT

	Retail Price	Dealer Invoice
Major Packages		
1SB Basic Plus Group 1	$985	$877

Remote keyless entry, cruise control, cargo nets, rear door privacy glass, roof rack.

1SC Comfort and Security Group, 2WD	3150	2804
AWD	3080	2741

Option Group 1SB plus traction control (2WD), OnStar System w/one year service (roadside assistance, emergency services; other services available), dual-zone manual climate controls, interior air filter, upgraded upholstery, 6-way power driver seat, front seat lumbar adjustment, 4-way adjustable head rests, leather-wrapped steering wheel w/radio controls, illuminated visor mirrors, front door utility packs, overhead console, driver information center, sliding rear cargo tray, theft-deterrent system w/alarm, 235/55R17 tires (AWD).

1SD Deluxe Group, 2WD	5125	4561
AWD	5055	4499

Comfort and Security Group plus leather upholstery, heated front seats, 6-way power passenger seat, Pioneer AM/FM/cassette/CD player, rear seat and cargo area radio controls, head up instrument display.

Trailer Pkg.	365	325

Heavy-duty engine oil cooler and alternator, load-leveling rear suspension, air inflation kit.

Comfort & Convenience Features

Power sunroof, w/1SB	650	579
w/1SC	240	214
w/1SD	140	125

Deletes OnStar System, rear seat radio controls.

Pioneer AM/FM/cassette/CD player, w/1SB	510	454
w/1SC	425	378

Includes leather-wrapped steering wheel w/radio controls, cargo area radio controls. Includes rear seat radio controls w/1SC Comfort and Security Group.

Pioneer AM/FM w/in-dash 6-disc CD changer, w/1SB	805	716
w/1SC	720	641
w/1SD	295	263

Includes leather-wrapped steering wheel w/radio controls, cargo area radio controls, speed compensated volume, Radio Data System. Includes rear seat radio controls w/1SC Comfort and Security Group.

6-way power driver seat	500	445

Includes sliding rear cargo tray. Requires 1SB Basic Plus Group.

Prices are accurate at time of publication; subject to manufacturer's change.

PONTIAC

Special Purpose, Wheels and Tires

	Retail Price	Dealer Invoice
17-inch alloy wheels, AWD	$200	$178
Includes 235/55R17 tires.		
215/70R16 self-sealing white-letter tires	150	134
NA AWD w/1SC or 1SD Group.		

PONTIAC BONNEVILLE

Pontiac Bonneville SE

Front-wheel-drive full-size car
Base price range: $25,530-$32,950. Built in USA.
Also consider: Dodge Intrepid, Toyota Avalon

FOR • Acceleration • Passenger and cargo room • Ride/handling **AGAINST** • Rear-seat comfort • Fuel economy

Minor styling alterations to the base SE model highlight the few 2002 Bonneville changes. SE, SLE, and SSEi models return. All come with front bucket seats, but SE is available with a front bench for 6-passenger capacity. All have automatic transmission and a 3.8-liter V6; the SSEi's engine is supercharged for more power. Standard are front side airbags, antilock 4-wheel disc brakes, tire-pressure monitor, and load-leveling rear suspension. Optional on SE and standard on the others are traction control and General Motors' OnStar assistance system. SSEi exclusives include a standard anti-skid system and head-up instrument display. Also for '02, a CD player replaces a cassette as standard on the SE, and SLE/SSEi get revised alloy wheels. Bonneville shares its basic design with the Buick LeSabre and Oldsmobile Aurora.

RATINGS

	SE	SSEI
ACCELERATION	6	7
FUEL ECONOMY	5	4
RIDE QUALITY	7	6
STEERING/HANDLING	5	6

Specifications begin on page 551.

PONTIAC

	SE	SSEi
QUIETNESS	6	5
INSTRUMENTS/CONTROLS	3	3
ROOM/COMFORT (FRONT)	7	6
ROOM/COMFORT (REAR)	4	4
CARGO ROOM	6	6
VALUE	6	5

Bonneville SE is a good big-car value, but a Grand Prix has nearly as much interior room and costs less. We like the SSEi's supercharged power, but a loaded example can top $34,000—well into the near-luxury realm, where most cars have better pedigrees and more refinement.

TOTAL	55	52

Average total for full-size cars: 58.7

ENGINES

	ohv V6	Supercharged ohv V6
Size, liters/cu. in.	3.8/231	3.8/231
Horsepower @ rpm	205 @ 5200	240 @ 5200
Torque (lb-ft) @ rpm	230 @ 4000	280 @ 3600
Availability	S[1]	S[2]

EPA city/highway mpg
4-speed automatic	20/29	18/27

1. SE, SLE. 2. SSEi.

PRICES

Pontiac Bonneville	Retail Price	Dealer Invoice
SE 4-door sedan	$25530	$23360
SLE 4-door sedan	28720	26279
SSEi 4-door sedan	32950	30149
Destination charge	655	655

STANDARD EQUIPMENT

SE: 3.8-liter V6 engine, 4-speed automatic transmission, dual front airbags, front side airbags, antilock 4-wheel disc brakes, daytime running lights, tire pressure monitor, air conditioning, power steering, tilt steering wheel, cruise control, cloth upholstery, front bucket seats, 6-way power driver seat w/lumbar adjustment, center console, cupholders, rear seat trunk pass-through, power mirrors, power windows, power door locks, remote keyless entry, AM/FM/CD player, digital clock, tachometer, overhead console, map lights, intermittent wipers, illuminated visor mirrors, rear defogger, remote decklid release, automatic headlights, floormats, theft-deterrent system, rear spoiler, fog lights, load-leveling suspension, 225/60R16 tires, alloy wheels.

SLE adds: traction control, OnStar System w/one year service (roadside assistance, emergency services; other services available),

Prices are accurate at time of publication; subject to manufacturer's change.

PONTIAC

leather-wrapped steering wheel w/radio controls, dual-zone automatic climate control, interior air filter, AM/FM/cassette/CD player, automatic day/night rearview mirror, compass, outside temperature indicator, performance suspension, 235/55R17 tires.

SSEi adds: 3.8-liter V6 supercharged engine, antiskid system, leather upholstery, articulating 12-way power front seats w/memory, head-up instrument display, Monsoon sound system, universal garage door opener, memory mirrors w/park-assist passenger-side mirror.

OPTIONAL EQUIPMENT

	Retail Price	Dealer Invoice

Major Packages

Option Group 1SC, SE	$2130	$1896

OnStar System w/one year service (roadside assistance, emergency services; other services available), traction control, performance axle ratio, leather upholstery, leather-wrapped steering wheel w/radio controls, AM/FM/cassette/CD player, dual-zone automatic climate control, automatic day/night rearview mirror.

Seat and Heat Pkg., SE, SLE	530	472
Manufacturer's Discount Price	330	294

Heated front seats, 6-way power passenger seat. NA w/front split bench seat.

Powertrain

Traction control, SE	175	156

Comfort & Convenience Features

Power sunroof	1080	961

SE and SLE include universal garage door opener.

Leather upholstery, SE, SLE	850	757
Front split bench seat, SE	150	134

NA w/Option Group 1SC or traction control.

Heated front seats, SSEi	295	263
AM/FM/cassette/CD player, SE, SLE	100	89
12-disc CD changer	595	530

SE requires Option Group.

Leather-wrapped steering wheel w/radio controls, SE	175	156

Appearance and Miscellaneous

Chrome alloy wheels, SLE, SSEi	595	530

PONTIAC FIREBIRD

Rear-wheel-drive sporty coupe
Base price range: $19,715-$31,760. Built in Canada.
Also consider: Ford Mustang, Toyota Celica

Specifications begin on page 551.

PONTIAC

Pontiac Firebird w/SLP Firehawk pkg.

FOR • Acceleration • Handling **AGAINST** • Fuel economy (V8 models) • Ride (V8 models) • Rear-seat room • Rear visibility • Wet-weather traction (without traction control) • Entry/exit

A Collector Edition trim package commemorates what is Firebird's final season in its current form. Along with the Chevrolet Camaro, which shares this design, Pontiac's sports coupe will be retired after the 2002 model year. Firebird comes in base, Formula, and Trans Am hatchback coupes, and base and Trans Am convertibles. Removable roof panels are standard on Formula and Trans Am coupes, optional on the base version. Convertibles have a power top and glass rear window. Base models have a V6 engine with 5-speed manual transmission or, as an option on coupes and standard on convertibles, an automatic. Formula/Trans Am models have a 310-hp V8 with 6-speed manual or automatic. The Trans Am WS6 Ram Air option rates 325 hp; the SLP Firehawk Package 345. Antilock 4-wheel disc brakes are standard; traction control is optional. For '02, power windows, locks, mirrors, and antenna are standard. The Collector package is based on the Trans Am and includes the WS6 equipment, yellow paint with black accents, and special wheels and trim. Firebird's performance and accommodations mirror those of like-equipped Camaros.

RATINGS	Base conv, auto.	Formula, auto.	Trans Am hatch w/WS6, man.
ACCELERATION	5	8	9
FUEL ECONOMY	5	4	4
RIDE QUALITY	3	2	2
STEERING/HANDLING	7	9	9
QUIETNESS	2	3	3
INSTRUMENTS/CONTROLS	5	5	5
ROOM/COMFORT (FRONT)	4	4	4
ROOM/COMFORT (REAR)	2	2	2
CARGO ROOM	1	3	3

Prices are accurate at time of publication; subject to manufacturer's change.

PONTIAC

	Base conv, auto.	Formula, auto.	Trans Am hatch w/WS6, man.
VALUE	3	4	3

V8 models are among the world's best high-performance values, but the Camaro/Firebird design is out of step with today's tastes and trends. In any case, this will likely be your last chance to buy a new one.

TOTAL	37	44	44

Average total for sporty coupes: 43.4

ENGINES

	ohv V6	ohv V8	ohv V8
Size, liters/cu. in.	3.8/231	5.7/346	5.7/346
Horsepower @ rpm	200 @ 5200	310 @ 5200	325 @ 5200
Torque (lb-ft) @ rpm	225 @ 4000	340 @ 4000	350 @ 4400
Availability	S[1]	S[2]	O[3]
EPA city/highway mpg			
5-speed manual	19/31		
6-speed manual		19/28	19/28
4-speed automatic	19/30	18/26	18/26

1. Base. 2. Formula, Trans Am. 3. Trans Am (345 hp w/SLP Firehawk).

PRICES

Pontiac Firebird	Retail Price	Dealer Invoice
Base 2-door hatchback	$19715	$18039
Base 2-door convertible	26630	24366
Formula 2-door hatchback	25660	23479
Trans Am 2-door hatchback	27690	25336
Trans Am 2-door convertible	31760	29060
Destination charge	575	575

STANDARD EQUIPMENT

Base hatchback: 3.8-liter V6 engine, 5-speed manual transmission, dual front airbags, antilock 4-wheel disc brakes, daytime running lights, air conditioning, power steering, tilt steering wheel, cruise control, cloth upholstery, front bucket seats, center console, cupholders, power mirrors, power windows, power door locks, AM/FM/CD player, digital clock, power antenna, tachometer, intermittent wipers, map lights, visor mirrors, remote hatch/decklid release, rear defogger, automatic headlights, floormats, theft-deterrent system, fog lights, rear spoiler, 235/55R16 tires, alloy wheels.

Base convertible adds: 4-speed automatic transmission, remote keyless entry, leather-wrapped steering wheel w/radio controls, 6-way power driver seat, Monsoon sound system, power convertible top, theft-deterrent system w/alarm.

Specifications begin on page 551.

PONTIAC

Formula/Trans Am adds: 5.7-liter V8 310-horsepower engine, limited-slip differential, leather upholstery (Trans Am), removable hatch roof (hatchback), performance suspension, 245/50ZR16 tires. *Deletes:* power convertible top (hatchback).

OPTIONAL EQUIPMENT

	Retail Price	Dealer Invoice
Major Packages		
Option Group 1SB, Base hatchback	$1755	$1562
4-speed automatic transmission, 6-way power driver seat, remote keyless entry, Monsoon sound system, theft-deterrent system w/alarm.		
3800 Performance Pkg., Base hatchback	355	316
Limited-slip differential, performance axle ratio (w/automatic transmission), upgraded steering, dual outlet exhaust.		
Sport Appearance Pkg., Base	1040	926
Aero appearance pkg., dual exhaust outlets. Requires automatic transmission. Hatchback requires Option Group 1SB.		
GT Pkg., Base hatchback	599	509
Stripe pkg., dual exhaust outlets, high-performance muffler.		
Protection Group, Base hatchback	240	214
Remote keyless entry, theft deterrent system w/alarm.		
WS6 Ram Air Performance and Handling Pkg., Trans Am	3290	2928
Ram air induction system, functional hood scoops, 325-horsepower engine, upgraded suspension, power steering fluid cooler, bright exhaust outlets, 275/40ZR17 tires, high-polished alloy wheels.		
NHRA Special Edition Pkg.,		
Formula/Tran AM w/6-speed	1095	975
Formula/Tran AM w/automatic	1070	952
Power steering fluid cooler, Hurst shifter (6-speed), rear performance axle (automatic), 245/50R16 performance tires, chrome alloy wheels.		
SLP Firehawk Pkg., Trans Am	3999	3439
Forced-air induction system, hood-mounted heat extractors, composite hood w/scoops, 345-horsepower engine, special key fobs and dash plaque, upgraded suspension, 275/40ZR17 tires, painted alloy wheels.		
10th Anniversary SLP Firehawk Pkg., Trans Am	NA	NA
10th anniversary decals, badging, dash plaque, front floormats, key fob. Car cover w/locking cable and tote bag, gold painted alloy wheels. Requires SLP Firehawk Pkg.		
Powertrain		
5-speed manual transmission, Base hatchback w/Option Group 1SB (credit)	(815)	(725)
6-speed manual transmission, Formula, Trans Am	NC	NC
4-speed automatic transmission, Base hatchback	815	725
Hurst shifter, Formula, Trans Am	325	289
Requires 6-speed manual transmission.		

Prices are accurate at time of publication; subject to manufacturer's change.

PONTIAC

	Retail Price	Dealer Invoice
Traction control, Base	$250	$223
Formula/Trans Am	450	401
Performance rear axle ratio, Formula, Trans Am	300	267

Requires automatic transmission. Includes 245/50ZR16 performance tires.

Comfort & Convenience Features

Monsoon sound system, Base hatchback	430	383
Includes leather-wrapped steering w/radio controls.		
12-disc CD changer	595	530
Base hatrchback requires Monsoon sound system.		
Leather upholstery, Base, Formula	575	512

Appearance and Miscellaneous

Removable locking hatch roof, Base hatchback	995	886
Includes sunshades, lock, stowage.		
Chrome alloy wheels	595	530
Base hatchback requires Option Group 1SB.		

Collector Edition equipment and prices not available at time of publication.

PONTIAC GRAND AM

Pontiac Grand Am 2-door coupe

Front-wheel-drive compact car
Base price range: $16,800-$22,110. Built in USA.
Also consider: Mazda 626, Mitsubishi Galant

FOR • Acceleration (V6) • Steering/handling (GT, GT1)   **AGAINST** • Rear-seat entry/exit (2-dr) • Interior materials

Pontiac's compact sedans and coupes get a new base engine for

Specifications begin on page 551.

PONTIAC

2002. SE and SE1 models trade a 150-hp 2.4-liter 4 cyl for a 140-hp 2.2 liter. GT and GT1 models retain a 3.4-liter V6. The V6 is optional on the SE1. The 4 cyl teams with manual or automatic transmission, the V6 with automatic only. Air conditioning, ABS, and traction control are standard. GTs add 4-wheel disc brakes. Grand Am shares its powertrains and underskin design with the Oldsmobile Alero.

RATINGS	SE1 cpe, 4 cyl auto.	GT sdn, V6
ACCELERATION	4	6
FUEL ECONOMY	6	5
RIDE QUALITY	5	5
STEERING/HANDLING	5	6
QUIETNESS	4	4
INSTRUMENTS/CONTROLS	3	3
ROOM/COMFORT (FRONT)	5	5
ROOM/COMFORT (REAR)	3	4
CARGO ROOM	4	4
VALUE	5	6

Strong V6 acceleration, generally enjoyable road manners, and lots of equipment at attractive prices are the main virtues of GM's compact-car duo. Neither is as refined or as well-built as the import competition, however. And while Alero has a more mature personality than Grand Am, the phaseout of the Olds brand by 2004 means it's an unsound long-term investment.

TOTAL	44	48

Average total for compact cars: 51.6

ENGINES	dohc I4	ohv V6	ohv V6
Size, liters/cu. in.	2.2/134	3.4/207	3.4/207
Horsepower @ rpm	140 @ 5600	170 @ 5200	175 @ 5200
Torque (lb-ft) @ rpm	150 @ 4000	195 @ 4000	205 @ 4000
Availability	S[1]	O[2]	S[3]
EPA city/highway mpg			
5-speed manual	25/33		
4-speed automatic	24/32	20/29	20/29

1. SE, SE1. 2. SE1. 3. GT.

PRICES

Pontiac Grand Am	Retail Price	Dealer Invoice
SE 2-door coupe	$16800	$15372
SE 4-door sedan	16950	15509
SE1 2-door coupe	18240	16690
SE1 4-door sedan	18390	16827
GT 2-door coupe	20690	18931
GT 4-door sedan	20840	19069

Prices are accurate at time of publication; subject to manufacturer's change.

CONSUMER GUIDE®

PONTIAC

	Retail Price	Dealer Invoice
GT1 2-door coupe	$21960	$20093
GT1 4-door sedan	22110	20231
Destination charge	585	585

STANDARD EQUIPMENT

SE: 2.2-liter dohc 4-cylinder engine, 5-speed manual transmission, traction control, dual front airbags, antilock brakes, daytime running lights, air conditioning, power steering, tilt steering wheel, cloth upholstery, front bucket seats, center console, cupholders, AM/FM/CD player, digital clock, tachometer, power door locks, remote fuel door and decklid release, variable intermittent wipers, rear defogger, automatic-off headlights, visor mirrors, floormats, rear spoiler, theft-deterrent system, fog lights, 215/60R15 tires, wheel covers.

SE1 adds: power mirrors, power windows, remote keyless entry, cruise control, 4-way manual driver seat w/power height adjustment, split folding rear seat, alloy wheels.

GT adds: 3.4-liter V6 engine, 4-speed automatic transmission, 4-wheel disc brakes, leather-wrapped steering wheel, Monsoon sound system, sport suspension, 225/50VR16 tires.

GT1 adds: 6-way power driver seat, AM/FM/cassette/CD player, steering wheel radio controls, power sunroof.

OPTIONAL EQUIPMENT
Major Packages

Solid Value Appearance Pkg., SE1	1630	1451
Manufacturer's Discount Price	*1005*	*895*

Power sunroof, AM/FM/cassette/CD player, Monsoon sound system, 225/50R16 tires, chrome alloy wheels. NA with 3.4-liter V6 engine.

Solid Value Appearance Pkg., GT	1535	1366
Manufacturer's Discount Price	*910*	*810*

AM/FM/cassette/CD player, power sunroof, chrome alloy wheels.

Solid Value Appearance Pkg., GT1	1220	1086
Manufacturer's Discount Price	*900*	*801*

Leather upholstery, chrome alloy wheels.

Powertrain

3.4-liter V6 engine, SE1	715	636

Includes variable-assist power steering. Requires 4-speed automatic transmission.

4-speed automatic transmission, SE, SE1	825	734

PONTIAC

Comfort & Convenience Features

	Retail Price	Dealer Invoice
Power sunroof, SE1, GT	$695	$619
Leather upholstery, GT, GT1	575	512
AM/FM/cassette/CD player, SE1	340	303
GT	195	174
SE1 includes Monsoon sound system.		
Cruise control, SE	235	209

Appearance and Miscellaneous

Chrome alloy wheels, GT, GT1	645	574
SE1	595	530

PONTIAC GRAND PRIX

CG RECOMMENDED AUTO

Pontiac Grand Prix 4-door sedan

Front-wheel-drive midsize car
Base price range: $20,965-$25,805. Built in USA.
Also consider: Ford Taurus, Honda Accord, Nissan Altima, Toyota Camry

FOR • Acceleration (3.8 V6) • Steering/handling **AGAINST** • Fuel economy (supercharged engine) • Rear-seat entry/exit (cpe)

A 40th Anniversary package and increased equipment levels mark changes to Pontiac's midsize line for 2002. Grand Prix offers a sedan in base SE trim and sedans and coupes in sportier GT form and in high-performance GTP versions. All have a V6 engine: the SE a 3.1 liter, GTs a 3.8, GTPs a supercharged 3.8. Automatic transmission, antilock 4-wheel disc brakes, traction control, and tire inflation monitor are standard. General Motors' OnStar assistance system and head-up instrument display are standard on GTP, optional on GT. Offered on GT and GTP models, the 40th Anniversary package includes a rear spoiler, hood ducts, chrome wheels, Dark Cherry paint, and unique red-and-grey interior trim. Also for 2002, the SE gains standard cruise control and dual-zone climate control, and

PONTIAC

GTs get a standard power driver's seat and CD player. Grand Prix shares its platform with the Buick Century and Regal, Chevrolet Impala and Monte Carlo, and the Oldsmobile Intrigue.

RATINGS

	SE sdn	GT cpe	GTP sdn
ACCELERATION	4	6	7
FUEL ECONOMY	6	5	5
RIDE QUALITY	7	7	6
STEERING/HANDLING	6	7	7
QUIETNESS	6	6	5
INSTRUMENTS/CONTROLS	5	5	5
ROOM/COMFORT (FRONT)	6	6	6
ROOM/COMFORT (REAR)	4	3	4
CARGO ROOM	5	5	5
VALUE	6	6	6

Assembly quality and interior materials don't match those of most import-brand rivals, but Grand Prix is a capable, sporty midsize that challenges class leaders in overall value and, in GTP form especially, beats most in performance.

TOTAL	55	56	56

Average total for midsize cars: 57.0

ENGINES

	ohv V6	ohv V6	Supercharged ohv V6
Size, liters/cu. in.	3.1/191	3.8/231	3.8/231
Horsepower @ rpm	175 @ 5200	200 @ 5200	240 @ 5200
Torque (lb-ft) @ rpm	195 @ 4000	225 @ 4000	280 @ 3600
Availability	S[1]	S[2]	S[3]
EPA city/highway mpg			
4-speed automatic	20/29	19/29	18/28

1. SE. 2. GT. 3. GTP.

PRICES

Pontiac Grand Prix	Retail Price	Dealer Invoice
SE 4-door sedan	$20965	$19183
GT 2-door coupe	22935	20586
GT 4-door sedan	23085	21123
GTP 2-door coupe	25625	23447
GTP 4-door sedan	25805	23612
Destination charge	610	610

STANDARD EQUIPMENT

SE: 3.1-liter V6 engine, 4-speed automatic transmission, enhanced traction control, antilock 4-wheel disc brakes, dual front airbags, daytime running lights, emergency inside trunk release, tire pressure monitor, air

Specifications begin on page 551.

PONTIAC

conditioning w/dual-zone manual control, power steering, tilt steering wheel, cruise control, cloth upholstery, front bucket seats, center console, cupholders, power mirrors, power windows, power door locks, AM/FM/cassette, digital clock, tachometer, visor mirrors, intermittent wipers, rear defogger, map lights, remote decklid release, automatic headlights, floormats, rear spoiler, fog lights, 205/70R15 tires, wheel covers.

GT adds: 3.8-liter V6 engine, 6-way power driver seat, rear seat trunk pass-through, remote keyless entry, AM/FM/CD player, steering wheel radio controls, overhead console, theft-deterrent system w/alarm, 225/60R16 tires, alloy wheels.

GTP adds: 3.8-liter supercharged V6 engine, full-function traction control, OnStar System w/one year service (roadside assistance, emergency services; other services available), driver seat 4-way power lumbar adjustment, head-up instrument display, leather-wrapped steering wheel, automatic day/night rearview mirror, compass, outside temperature indicator, illuminated visor mirrors, trip computer, sport suspension.

OPTIONAL EQUIPMENT

	Retail Price	Dealer Invoice
Major Packages		
Option Group 1SB, SE	$815	$725
Manufacturer's Discount Price	*390*	*347*
6-way power driver seat, rear seat trunk pass-through, cargo net, 225/60R16 tires, alloy wheels.		
Option Group 1SB, GT coupe	810	721
GT sedan	840	748
OnStar System w/one year service (roadside assistance, emergency services; other services available), leather-wrapped steering wheel, trip computer, automatic day/night rearview mirror, compass, outside temperature indicator, illuminated visor mirrors, rear reading lights (sedan), assist handles.		
Option Group 1SC, GT coupe	2680	2385
GT sedan	2710	2412
Group 1SB plus leather upholstery, driver seat 4-way power lumbar adjustment, power sunroof, head-up instrument display.		
40th Anniversary Appearance Pkg., GT, GTP	2695	2399
Manufacturer's Discount Price	*2395*	*2132*
Two-tone leather upholstery, hood ducts, unique spoiler, roof fences, exhaust tips, badging, chrome alloy wheels.		
Premium Lighting Pkg., GT coupe	610	543
GT sedan	640	570
OnStar System w/one year service (roadside assistance, emergency services; other services available), automatic day/night rearview mirror, compass, outside temperature indicator, illuminated visor mirrors, rear reading lights (sedan).		

Prices are accurate at time of publication; subject to manufacturer's change.

PONTIAC

	Retail Price	Dealer Invoice
Security Pkg., SE	$210	$187

Remote keyless entry, theft-deterrent system w/alarm.

Comfort & Convenience Features

Driver seat 4-way power lumbar support, GT	130	116
Heated driver seat, GT, GTP	100	89

Requires leather upholstery.

Leather upholstery, GT, GTP	520	463

GT requires driver seat 4-way power lumbar adjustment.

AM/FM/CD player, SE	110	98

Requires Option Group 1SB.

Bose sound system, GT	395	352
GTP	345	307

NA w/40th Anniversary Appearance Pkg.

Power sunroof, GT, GTP	795	708

Deletes overhead console.

Head-up instrument display, GT	325	289

Requires Group 1SB.

Appearance and Miscellaneous

Polished alloy wheels, GT, GTP	325	289

PONTIAC MONTANA

Pontiac Montana

Front-wheel-drive minivan

Base price range: $24,335-$33,810. Built in USA.

Also consider: Chrysler Town & Country and Voyager, Dodge Caravan, Honda Odyssey

FOR • Ride • Passenger and cargo room • Available all-wheel drive **AGAINST** • Fuel economy

Specifications begin on page 551.

PONTIAC

Pontiac's minivan gets optional all-wheel drive and a DVD player for '02. Montana is built from the same design as the Chevrolet Venture and Oldsmobile Silhouette. It offers regular- and extended-length bodies, both with dual sliding side doors. A power right-side sliding door is optional, and extended versions offer dual power doors. Seating ranges from six to eight, with two front buckets, two or three 2nd-row buckets, and two 3rd-row buckets or a 3-passenger folding bench. Extended-length models offer a 3rd-row bench that folds even with a floor-mounted parcel tray. Montana is available with front-wheel drive or General Motors' Versatrak AWD that includes independent rear suspension and 4-wheel disc brakes. Traction control for front-drive Montanas is standard on regular-length 7-passenger models, optional on extendeds. All have a V6, automatic transmission, ABS, front side airbags, puncture-sealing tires, and GM's OnStar assistance system. Options include load-leveling suspension and a tauter sport suspension. New for extended-lengths is the Thunder Sport option package with chrome 16-inch wheels instead of 15s, rear spoiler, and unique badging. Also available on extendeds is rear-obstacle detection and a rear-seat video entertainment system, now with a DVD player instead of a VCR. Montana's performance and accommodations mirror those of similarly equipped Chevrolet Ventures.

RATINGS	Base reg. length 6-pass.	Base ext. length 7-pass.
ACCELERATION	4	4
FUEL ECONOMY	4	4
RIDE QUALITY	6	7
STEERING/HANDLING	5	5
QUIETNESS	6	6
INSTRUMENTS/CONTROLS	6	6
ROOM/COMFORT (FRONT)	6	6
ROOM/COMFORT (REAR)	5	7
CARGO ROOM	9	9
VALUE	6	7

Our top-rated minivans are the Chrysler/Dodge models, Toyota Sienna, and Honda Odyssey, but Montana and its GM siblings offer lots of clever features, drive nicely, and are priced right. And only Dodge and Chrysler offer AWD among direct competitors.

TOTAL	57	61

Average total for minivans: 56.0

ENGINES

	ohv V6
Size, liters/cu. in.	3.4/207
Horsepower @ rpm	185 @ 5200
Torque (lb-ft) @ rpm	210 @ 4000
Availability	S

Prices are accurate at time of publication; subject to manufacturer's change.

PONTIAC

EPA city/highway mpg

	ohv V6
4-speed automatic	19/26[1]

1. 18/24 w/AWD.

PRICES

Pontiac Montana	Retail Price	Dealer Invoice
Regular length 4-door van 6-passenger, FWD	$24335	$22023
Regular length 4-door van w/1SA, FWD	25245	22847
Extended 4-door van w/1SA, FWD	26735	24195
Extended 4-door van w/1SE, FWD	30320	27440
Extended 4-door van w/1SX, AWD	30205	27335
Extended 4-door van w/1SY, AWD	33810	30598
Destination charge	655	655

FWD denotes front-wheel drive. AWD denotes all-wheel drive.

STANDARD EQUIPMENT

Regular 6-passenger: 3.4-liter V6 engine, 4-speed automatic transmission, driver- and passenger-side side airbags, front side airbags, antilock brakes, daytime running lights, front air conditioning, power steering, tilt steering wheel, cruise control, dual sliding rear doors, cloth upholstery, front bucket seats w/manual lumbar adjustment, second and third row bucket seats, cupholders, heated power mirrors, power windows, power door locks, remote keyless entry, AM/FM/CD player, digital clock, tachometer, visor mirrors, intermittent wipers, rear defogger, rear wiper/washer, map lights, automatic headlights, floormats, theft-deterrent system, roof rack, rear privacy glass, fog lights, 215/70R15 self-sealing white-letter tires, wheel covers.

Regular/Extended w/1SA adds: 7-passenger seating (two second row captain chairs, third row 3-passenger split folding bench seat).

Extended w/1SE adds: rear obstacle detection system, OnStar System w/one year service (roadside assistance, emergency services; other services available), front and rear air conditioning w/rear controls, 6-way power driver seat, AM/FM/cassette/CD player, leather-wrapped steering wheel w/radio controls, rear radio controls, wireless headphones, fold-down LCD screen, DVD player, power sliding passenger-side door, illuminated visor mirrors, universal garage door opener, alloy wheels.

Extended w/1SX adds to Regular/Extended w/1SA: all-wheel drive, 4-wheel disc brakes, OnStar System w/one year service (roadside assistance, emergency services; other services available), universal garage door opener, illuminated visor mirrors, trailer wiring harness, air inflation kit, load-leveling rear suspension, touring suspension, 225/60R16 self-sealing white-letter tires, alloy wheels.

Extended w/1SY adds to Extended w/1SE: all-wheel drive, 4-wheel disc

Specifications begin on page 551.

PONTIAC

brakes, trailer wiring harness, air inflation kit, load-leveling rear suspension, touring suspension, 215/60R16 self-sealing white-letter tires.

OPTIONAL EQUIPMENT

	Retail Price	Dealer Invoice
Major Packages		
PDD Convenience Pkg. 1, regular w/1SA	$610	$543
extended w/1SA, 1SX	1060	943
Front and rear air conditioning w/rear controls (extended), 6-way power driver seat, leather-wrapped steering wheel w/radio controls, rear radio controls.		
PDY Convenience Pkg. 2, regular w/1SA	540	481
Power sliding passenger-side door. Requires driver information center.		
PDY Convenience Pkg. 2, extended w/1SA, 1SX	1795	1598
Conveninece Pkg. 1 plus power siding passenger-side door, rear obstacle detection system, illuminated visor mirrors. Extended w/1SA requires driver information center.		
PCV Premium Seating Pkg., regular w/1SA	1885	1678
extended w/1SA, 1SX	2335	2078
extended w/1SA and 1SX ordered w/Convenience Pkg. 2	1275	1135
1SE, 1SY	1175	1046
Convenience Pkg. 1 plus leather upholstery, 6-way power driver seat, AM/FM/cassette/CD player. Requires alloy wheels. NA w/8-passenger seating.		
PDC Safety and Security Pkg., regular/extended w/1SA	500	445
OnStar System w/one year service (roadside assistance, emergency services; other services available), universal garage door opener, theft-deterrent system w/alarm.		
B4U Sport Performance and Handling Pkg., regular/extended w/1SA	720	641
1SE	395	352
Traction control, load-leveling rear suspension, sport tuned suspension, 215/70R15 self-sealing white-letter tires, alloy wheels.		
H4T Thunder Sport Pkg., extended	1200	1068
Rear spoiler, black interior accents, badging, 225/60R16 self-sealing white-letter tires, chrome alloy wheels. Requires Premium Seating Pkg., heated front seats, load-leveling rear suspension.		
Trailer Provisions, FWD extended	165	147
Trailer wiring harness, heavy-duty engine and transmission cooling. Requires Sport Performance and Handling Pkg. or load-leveling rear suspension. Std. AWD.		
Powertrain		
Traction control, regular/extended w/1SA, 1SE	195	174

Prices are accurate at time of publication; subject to manufacturer's change.

PONTIAC

Comfort & Convenience Features

	Retail Price	Dealer Invoice
Power sliding driver-side door, extended	$350	$312

1SA, 1SY require Convenience Pkg. 2, driver information center. 1SA also requires Safety and Security Pkg. 1SE NA w/8-passenger seating.

Driver information center, regular/extended w/1SA	185	165

Includes universal garage door opener, illuminated visor mirrors.

8-passenger seating, extended	235	209

Includes five bucket seats, rear stowable bench seat w/convenience tray. NA w/Premium Seating Pkg.

Heated front seats, regular w/1SA, extended	195	174

Requires Premium Seating Pkg.

AM/FM/cassette/CD player, extended w/1SA	440	392
extended w/1SA and Convenience Pkg. 1	100	89

Includes leather-wrapped steering wheel w/radio controls, rear seat radio controls.

AM/FM radio w/in-dash 6-disc CD changer, extended w/1SA, 1SX	735	654
1SE, 1SY	295	263

Includes leather-wrapped steering wheel w/radio controls, rear radio controls. 1SA, 1SX require Convenience Pkg. 1.

Appearance and Miscellaneous

Load-leveling rear suspension, regular/extended w/1SA, 1SE	200	178
15-inch alloy wheels, regular, extended w/1SA	325	289
16-inch alloy wheels, extended	NA	NA

Includes 225/60R16 white-letter tires.

PONTIAC SUNFIRE

Pontiac Sunfire 2-door coupe

Front-wheel-drive subcompact car
Base price range: $14,540-$16,855. Built in USA.

Specifications begin on page 551.

PONTIAC

Also consider: Ford Focus, Honda Civic, Toyota Corolla

FOR • Fuel economy **AGAINST** • Rear visibility • Rear-seat comfort • Interior materials • Rear-seat entry/exit (2-dr)

Sunfire shares its design with the Chevrolet Cavalier. It comes as a coupe or sedan in SE trim, and as a GT coupe. SEs come with a 115-hp 2.2-liter 4-cyl engine. A 140-hp twincam 2.2-liter 4 cyl replaced a 150-hp 2.4 after the start of '02 production. It's standard on the GT, optional on the SE. Manual and automatic transmissions are offered; traction control is included with the automatic. ABS and air conditioning are standard. Also for '02, the SE gets a standard tilt steering wheel (the GT already had it) and both gain a trunk release switch for the driver. Sunfire's performance and accommodations mirror those of like-equipped Cavaliers.

RATINGS	SE cpe, ohv man.	SE sdn, ohc auto.	GT, man.
ACCELERATION	3	4	5
FUEL ECONOMY	6	6	5
RIDE QUALITY	4	4	3
STEERING/HANDLING	4	4	6
QUIETNESS	3	3	3
INSTRUMENTS/CONTROLS	4	4	4
ROOM/COMFORT (FRONT)	3	3	3
ROOM/COMFORT (REAR)	2	3	2
CARGO ROOM	3	3	3
VALUE	3	4	3

They fall far short of the refinement of Japanese subcompacts, but Cavalier and Sunfire include plenty of useful standard features and should be available with discounts. Cavalier edges out Sunfire as the better overall value.

TOTAL	35	38	37

Average total for subcompact cars: 43.7

ENGINES

	ohv I4	dohc I4
Size, liters/cu. in.	2.2/133	2.2/134
Horsepower @ rpm	115 @ 5000	140 @ 5600
Torque (lb-ft) @ rpm	135 @ 3600	150 @ 4000
Availability	S[1]	S[2]
EPA city/highway mpg		
5-speed manual	23/33	25/33
4-speed automatic	24/32	24/32

1. SE. 2. GT; optional, SE.

PRICES

Pontiac Sunfire	Retail Price	Dealer Invoice
SE 2-door coupe	$14540	$13450

Prices are accurate at time of publication; subject to manufacturer's change.

PONTIAC

	Retail Price	Dealer Invoice
SE 4-door sedan	$15040	$13912
GT 2-door coupe	16855	15591
Destination charge	540	540

STANDARD EQUIPMENT

SE: 2.2-liter 4-cylinder engine, 5-speed manual transmission, dual front airbags, antilock brakes, daytime running lights, emergency inside trunk release, air conditioning, power steering, tilt steering wheel, cloth upholstery, bucket seats, center console, cupholders, folding rear seat, AM/FM/cassette, digital clock, tachometer, visor mirrors, intermittent wipers, rear defogger, power decklid release, floormats, left remote and right manual outside mirrors, theft-deterrent system, rear spoiler (coupe), 195/70R14 tires, wheel covers.

GT adds to SE coupe: 2.2-liter dohc 4-cylinder engine, leather-wrapped steering wheel, driver seat lumbar adjustment, AM/FM/CD player, fog lights, sport suspension, 205/55R16 tires, alloy wheels.

OPTIONAL EQUIPMENT
Major Packages

1SB Option Group, SE	965	859
4-speed automatic transmission, traction control, AM/FM/CD player.		
Driver's Convenience Pkg., SE	380	339
Manufacturer's Discount Price	*130*	*116*
SE coupe w/sunroof	340	303
Manufacturer's Discount Price	*90*	*80*
Cruise control, variable intermittent wipers, overhead console (without sunroof), reading lights, cargo net. Requires 1SB Option Group.		
Sun and Sound Pkg., SE coupe	1695	1508
Manufacturer's Discount Price	*1170*	*1041*
Power sunroof, 195/65R15 tires. Requires 1SB Option Group.		
Special Edition Pkg., SE sedan	1955	1740
Manufacturer's Discount Price	*1375*	*1224*
Power mirrors and windows, power door locks, remote keyless entry, theft-deterrent system w/alarm, 195/65R15 tires.		
Security Pkg., SE coupe	370	329
SE sedan	410	365
Power door locks, remote keyless entry, theft-deterrent system w/alarm. Requires 1SB Option Group.		
Power Pkg., SE coupe, GT	380	338
SE sedan	445	396
Power mirrors and windows. SE requires 1SB Option Group, Security Pkg. GT requires Option Group.		

Specifications begin on page 551.

PONTIAC • SAAB

	Retail Price	Dealer Invoice
1SB Option Group, GT	$1480	$1317

4-speed automatic transmission, traction control, cruise control, power door locks, remote keyless entry, variable intermittent wipers, theft-deterrent system w/alarm.

1SC Option Group, GT	2135	1900

1SB Option Group plus power mirrors and windows, Monsoon sound system, overhead console w/storage (without sunroof), reading lights, cargo net.

Sun and Storm Pkg. w/1SB Group, GT	2770	2020
Manufacturer's Discount Price	1770	1575

Option Group 1SB plus power sunroof, Monsoon sound system.

Sun and Storm Pkg. w/1SC Group, GT	2690	2394
Manufacturer's Discount Price	2190	1949

Option Group 1SC plus power sunroof.

Powertrain

2.2-liter dohc 4-cylinder engine, SE	NA	NA

Requires 1SB Option Group and 195/65R15 tires.

5-speed manual transmission (credit)	(810)	(721)

Requires 1SB or 1SC Option Group. SE sedan requires standard engine.

4-speed automatic transmission, GT	810	721

Includes traction control.

Comfort & Convenience Features

Cruise control, SE w/Group 1SB	235	209
AM/FM/CD player, SE	155	138
Monsoon sound system, SE coupe, GT	195	174

SE requires 1SB Option Group and Security Pkg. GT requires 1SB Option Group.

Power sunroof, SE coupe, GT w/Group 1SB	595	530
GT w/Group 1SC	555	494

Requires Option Group.

Appearance and Miscellaneous

195/65R15 tires, SE	135	120

Requires 1SB Option Group.

SAAB 9-3

Front-wheel-drive near-luxury car

2001 base price range: $26,495-$44,995. Built in Sweden, Finland.

Also consider: Acura TL, Audi A4, BMW 3-Series

Prices are accurate at time of publication; subject to manufacturer's change.

SAAB

Saab 9-3 4-door hatchback

FOR • Acceleration • Braking • Cargo room (exc. convertible)
AGAINST • Rear-seat room/comfort (convertible) • Rear visibility (convertible) • Rear-seat entry/exit (exc. sedan)

The 185-hp base-level models are gone from Saab's "junior" line for 2002. The 9-3 offers 2-dr and 4-dr hatchbacks and a 2-dr convertible, all with turbo 4-cyl engines. SE models come as the convertible and 4-dr hatchback and have 205 hp. The high-performance Viggen model is available in all three body styles and has 230 hp. SEs offer 5-speed manual transmission or optional automatic. Viggens come only with manual. The convertible has a power top with a heated glass window. Antilock 4-wheel disc brakes, traction control, and front side airbags, are standard, as are front head restraints designed to minimize whiplash injury. General Motors owns this Swedish automaker, and GM's OnStar assistance system is standard. It includes voice-activated phone, e-mail, and internet connection. Free scheduled maintenance (excluding wear items such as tires, brakes, and wiper blades) for 3-years/36,000-mi. is standard on all 9-3s except the SE hatchback, where it's part of the optional Premium Package.

RATINGS	SE 4-dr hatch, auto.	SE conv, auto.	Viggen 2-dr hatch, man.
ACCELERATION	7	7	7
FUEL ECONOMY	5	5	5
RIDE QUALITY	6	6	4
STEERING/HANDLING	7	5	8
QUIETNESS	5	4	5
INSTRUMENTS/CONTROLS	6	6	6
ROOM/COMFORT (FRONT)	7	6	7
ROOM/COMFORT (REAR)	6	3	4
CARGO ROOM	7	2	7

Specifications begin on page 551.

SAAB

	SE 4-dr hatch, auto.	SE conv, auto.	Viggen 2-dr hatch, man.
VALUE	4	2	2

Quirky describes the 9-3, and compromise is the byword for its turbo-engine performance. But 9-3s have their charms, though they're obvious mostly to Saab loyalists. For near-luxury Swedish-style, more buyers turn to Volvo's newer S60 sedans and V70 wagons.

TOTAL	60	46	55

Average total for near-luxury cars: 54.5

ENGINES	Turbocharged dohc I4	Turbocharged dohc I4
Size, liters/cu. in.	2.0/121	2.3/140
Horsepower @ rpm	205 @ 5500	230 @ 5500
Torque (lb-ft) @ rpm	207 @ 2200	258 @ 2500
Availability	S[1]	S[2]
EPA city/highway mpg		
5-speed manual	23/33	19/28
4-speed automatic	21/29	

1. SE; 184 lb-ft @ 1900 rpm with auto. trans. 2. Viggen.

2002 prices unavailable at time of publication.

PRICES

2001 Saab 9-3

	Retail Price	Dealer Invoice
Base 2-door hatchback	$26495	$25170
Base 4-door hatchback	26995	25402
SE 4-door hatchback	32595	30737
SE 2-door convertible	39995	37395
Viggen 2-door hatchback	37995	34955
Viggen 4-door hatchback	37995	34955
Viggen 2-door convertible	44995	41395
Destination charge	575	575

STANDARD EQUIPMENT

Base: 2.0-liter turbocharged dohc 4-cylinder 185-horsepower engine, 5-speed manual transmission, traction control, dual front airbags, front side airbags, front seat active head restraints, antilock 4-wheel disc brakes, daytime running lights, air conditioning, interior air filter, OnStar System w/one year service (roadside assistance, emergency services; other services available), power steering, telescoping steering wheel, cruise control, cloth upholstery, front bucket seats, driver seat manual lumbar adjustment, split folding rear seat w/trunk pass-through, cupholders, heated power mirrors, power windows, power door locks, remote keyless entry, AM/FM/cassette/weatherband w/CD changer controls, steering-wheel radio

Prices are accurate at time of publication; subject to manufacturer's change.

SAAB

controls, power antenna, digital clock, tachometer, trip computer, variable intermittent wipers, rear defogger, rear wiper/washer, illuminated visor mirrors, automatic-off headlights, floormats, theft-deterrent system, headlight wiper/washer, front and rear fog lights, cornering lights, rear spoiler, 195/60VR15 tires, alloy wheels.

SE convertible adds: 2.0-liter turbocharged dohc 4-cylinder 205-horsepower engine, leather upholstery, 8-way power driver seat, folding rear seat w/trunk pass-through, leather-wrapped steering wheel, wood interior trim, upgraded sound system, power convertible top, sport suspension, 205/50ZR16 tires. *Deletes:* rear wiper/washer, rear spoiler.

SE hatchback adds to Base: 2.0-liter turbocharged dohc 4-cylinder 205-horsepower engine, automatic climate control, leather upholstery, 8-way power front seats w/driver seat memory, leather-wrapped steering wheel, wood interior trim, power sunroof, 205/50ZR16 tires.

Viggen adds: 2.3-liter turbocharged dohc 4-cylinder 230-horsepower engine, special interior trim, front sport seats, folding rear seat w/trunk pass-through (convertible), aerodynamic body cladding, performance sport suspension, 215/45ZR17 tires. *Deletes:* power antenna.

OPTIONAL EQUIPMENT

	Retail Price	Dealer Invoice
Major Packages		
Premium Pkg., SE convertible	$1495	$1301
Automatic climate control, 8-way power passenger seat, driver seat memory, rear spoiler.		
Powertrain		
4-speed automatic transmission, Base, SE	1200	1044
Comfort & Convenience Features		
Power sunroof, Base hatchback	1150	1001
AM/FM/CD player	NC	NC
Leather upholstery, Base	1350	1175
Includes leather-wrapped steering wheel.		
Heated front seats	450	392

SAAB 9-5

Front-wheel-drive luxury car

2001 base price range: $33,995-$40,875. Built in Sweden.

Also consider: Acura RL, Lexus LS 430, Mercedes-Benz E-Class

FOR • Acceleration • Handling/roadholding • Passenger and cargo room • Build quality **AGAINST** • Road noise • Climate controls

Specifications begin on page 551.

SAAB

Saab 9-5 4-door wagon

Revised styling, an available antiskid system, and a 5-speed automatic transmission keynote 2002 additions to Saab's luxury line. All 9-5s come as sedans and wagons. Base models are called Linear for '02, and SE versions are renamed Arc. Top-line Aero models return. All have front-wheel drive, antilock 4-wheel disc brakes, traction control, and front-seat head restraints designed to counteract whiplash injuries. Front head/torso side airbags are standard; side curtain and rear side airbags are unavailable. Linear and Aero models have turbo 4-cyl engines; the Linear has 185 hp, the Aero 250 (vs. 230 last year). Arc has a 200-hp V6. All but the Arc have standard manual transmission. Standard on Arc and optional elsewhere is a 5-speed automatic transmission, which replaces a 4-speed. The new antiskid system is standard on Aero and optional on other 9-5s. It's designed to prevent skids in turns by regulating brakes and engine power. For '02, Xenon headlights are newly optional, and front airbag deployment is designed to account for occupant size and position. General Motors owns Saab and its OnStar assistance system is standard in 9-5s. Wagons do not offer 3rd-row seating.

RATINGS	Linear sdn, man.	Arc wgn	Aero sdn, auto.
ACCELERATION	6	6	7
FUEL ECONOMY	6	5	5
RIDE QUALITY	8	8	6
STEERING/HANDLING	7	7	8
QUIETNESS	6	6	5
INSTRUMENTS/CONTROLS	6	6	6
ROOM/COMFORT (FRONT)	7	7	7
ROOM/COMFORT (REAR)	7	7	7
CARGO ROOM	5	7	5

Prices are accurate at time of publication; subject to manufacturer's change.

SAAB

	Linear sdn, man.	Arc wgn	Aero sdn, auto.
VALUE	3	4	2

This year's revisions don't fully hide the fact that the 9-5 is among the oldest designs in the luxury class. Road manners and overall refinement don't match those of top European rivals, and Linears and Aeros are expensive for 4-cyl cars. The V6 Arc with the new 5-speed automatic emerges as the best all-around car in a model line that continues to appeal mostly to individualists.

TOTAL	61	63	58

Average total for luxury cars: 59.4

ENGINES	Turbocharged dohc I4	Turbocharged dohc V6	Turbocharged dohc I4
Size, liters/cu. in.	2.3/140	3.0/180	2.3/140
Horsepower @ rpm	185 @ 5500	200 @ 5000	250 @ 5300
Torque (lb-ft) @ rpm	207 @ 1800	229 @ 2500	258 @ 1900
Availability	S[1]	S[2]	S[3]
EPA city/highway mpg			
5-speed manual	22/31		21/31
5-speed automatic	20/29	18/26	20/30

1. Linear. 2. Arc. 3. Aero.

2002 prices unavailable at time of publication.

PRICES

2001 Saab 9-5

	Retail Price	Dealer Invoice
Base 4-door sedan	$33995	$31955
Base 4-door wagon	34695	32613
SE 4-door sedan	38650	36138
SE 4-door wagon	39350	36792
Aero 4-door sedan	40175	37564
Aero 4-door wagon	40875	38218
Destination charge	575	575

STANDARD EQUIPMENT

Base: 2.3-liter turbocharged dohc 4-cylinder 185-horsepower engine, 5-speed manual transmission, traction control, dual front airbags, front side airbags, front seat active head restraints, antilock 4-wheel disc brakes, daytime running lights, air conditioning w/dual-zone automatic climate control, interior air filter, OnStar System w/one year service (roadside assistance, emergency services; other services available), power steering, tilt/telescoping leather-wrapped steering wheel, cruise control, cloth upholstery, 8-way power front bucket seats, center console, cupholders, split folding rear seat w/trunk pass-through, wood interior trim, heated power mirrors, power windows, power door locks, remote keyless entry, AM/FM/cassette/CD player, steering-wheel radio controls, digital clock,

SAAB • SATURN

tachometer, trip computer, power sunroof, glove box refrigerator, illuminated visor mirrors, variable-intermittent wipers, rear defogger, remote decklid/fuel door release, automatic-off headlights, parcel shelf/cargo cover (wagon), floormats, theft-deterrent system, roof rails (wagon), front and rear fog lights, headlight wiper/washer, cornering lights, 215/55R16 tires, alloy wheels.

SE adds to Base: 3.0-liter turbocharged dohc V6 engine, 4-speed automatic transmission, leather upholstery, memory driver seat and mirrors, tilt-down passenger-side mirror, Harman/Kardon sound system, automatic day/night rearview mirror.

Aero adds: 2.3-liter turbocharged dohc 4-cylinder 230-horsepower engine, 5-speed manual transmission, bodyside cladding, sport suspension, 225/45ZR17 tires.

OPTIONAL EQUIPMENT	Retail Price	Dealer Invoice
Major Packages		
Premium Pkg., Base	$1995	$1736
Leather upholstery, driver seat memory, Harman/Kardon sound system.		
Powertrain		
4-speed automatic transmission, Base, Aero	1200	1044
Comfort & Convenience Features		
Power-ventilated front seats	995	866
Base requires Premium Pkg.		
Heated front and rear seats	595	518
Appearance and Miscellaneous		
Wheel and Tire Pkg., Base, SE	1650	1436
One-piece alloy wheels, 225/45ZR17 tires.		
Wheel upgrade, Aero	1650	1436
Two-piece alloy wheels.		

SATURN L-SERIES

Front-wheel-drive midsize car
Base price range: $16,370-$22,350. Built in USA.
Also consider: Honda Accord, Nissan Altima, Toyota Camry

FOR • Acceleration (V6 models) • Steering/handling • Dent-resistant body panels **AGAINST** • Rear-seat comfort

Curtain side airbags are among previously optional features made standard for 2002 on Saturn's midsize line. Due later is an optional rear-seat video entertainment system. The L-Series offers sedan and wagon body styles. Sedans come as L100, L200, and L300

Prices are accurate at time of publication; subject to manufacturer's change.

SATURN

Saturn L300 4-door sedan

models, the wagon as LW200 and LW300 models. All have Saturn's dent- and rust-resistant polymer panels for front fenders, doors, and bumper fascias; other body parts are steel. The 100 and 200 models have a 4-cyl engine with manual or automatic transmission, the 300s a V6 with automatic. In addition to curtain side airbags, standard features now include traction control, ABS, and, on all but the L100, 4-wheel disc brakes. Newly optional are a 6-disc in-dash CD changer. Due during the 2002 model year is a rear entertainment system with DVD video, fold-down, ceiling-mounted 7-inch screen, and wireless headphones. GM's OnStar assistance system is also slated as a midyear option. New this fall are optional 16-inch, chrome wheels for 200 and 300 models.

RATINGS

	L200 sdn, man.	LW200 wgn, auto.	L300 sdn
ACCELERATION	4	4	5
FUEL ECONOMY	7	7	5
RIDE QUALITY	6	6	6
STEERING/HANDLING	6	6	6
QUIETNESS	6	5	6
INSTRUMENTS/CONTROLS	5	5	5
ROOM/COMFORT (FRONT)	5	4	5
ROOM/COMFORT (REAR)	4	4	4
CARGO ROOM	6	8	6
VALUE	6	6	6

Not a class-leader, but a decent midsize car offering good value. Base prices are well below comparable Accords and Camrys, but Saturn's full-sticker-price policy doesn't allow negotiating. However, L-Series has been a slow seller, so lease incentives and low financing rates may be available.

TOTAL	55	55	54

Average total for midsize cars: 57.0

ENGINES

	dohc I4	dohc V6
Size, liters/cu. in.	2.2/134	3.0/183
Horsepower @ rpm	135 @ 5200	182 @ 5600

Specifications begin on page 551.

SATURN

	dohc I4	dohc V6
Torque (lb-ft) @ rpm	142 @ 4400	190 @ 3600
Availability	S[1]	S[2]
EPA city/highway mpg		
5-speed manual	25/33	
4-speed automatic	24/33	21/29

1. L100, L200, LW200. 2. L300, LW300.

PRICES

Saturn L-Series	Retail Price	Dealer Invoice
L100 4-door sedan, automatic	$16370	$14569
L200 4-door sedan, manual	17760	15806
L200 4-door sedan, automatic	18570	16527
LW200 4-door wagon, manual	19155	17048
LW200 4-door wagon, automatic	20015	17813
L300 4-door sedan, automatic	20420	18174
LW300 4-door wagon, automatic	22350	19892
Destination charge	500	500

STANDARD EQUIPMENT

L100: 2.2-liter dohc 4-cylinder engine, 4-speed automatic transmission, traction control, dual front airbags, curtain side airbags, antilock brakes, daytime running lights, emergency inside trunk release, air conditioning, interior air filter, power steering, tilt steering wheel, cloth upholstery, front bucket seats, center console, cupholders, split folding rear seat, AM/FM/CD player, digital clock, tachometer, rear defogger, remote fuel door/decklid release, variable intermittent wipers, visor mirrors, automatic headlights, theft-deterrent system, 195/65R15 tires, wheel covers.

L200/LW200 adds: 5-speed manual or 4-speed automatic transmission, antilock 4-wheel disc brakes, cruise control, height-adjustable driver seat, heated power mirrors, power windows, power door locks, remote keyless entry, illuminated visor mirrors, rear wiper/washer (wagon), cargo cover (wagon), roof rails (wagon).

L300/LW300 adds: 3.0-liter dohc V6 engine, 4-speed automatic transmission, leather-wrapped steering wheel, floormats, sport suspension, 205/65R15 tires, alloy wheels.

OPTIONAL EQUIPMENT
Major Packages

Premium Pkg., L200, L300	2860	2631
LW200, LW300	2080	1914

Leather upholstery, heated front seats, power driver seat, leather-wrapped steering wheel, (L200, LW200), AM/FM/cassette w/in-dash 6-disc CD changer, power sunroof (L200, L300), fog lights, rear spoiler (L200, L300).

Prices are accurate at time of publication; subject to manufacturer's change.

SATURN

	Retail Price	Dealer Invoice
Sport Pkg., L200, L300	$960	$883
Power sunroof, fog lights, rear spoiler.		

Comfort & Convenience Features

OnStar System, L200, LW200, L300, LW300	NA	NA
Power sunroof, L200, L300	725	667
Power driver seat, L200, LW200, L300, LW300	325	299
Leather upholstery, L200, LW200, L300, LW300	1295	1191
Includes heated front seats, leather-wrapped steering wheel (L200, LW200). Requires power driver seat.		
AM/FM/cassette/CD player, L200, LW200, L300, LW300	380	350
AM/FM/cassette w/in-dash 6-disc CD changer, L200, LW200, L300, LW300	595	547

Appearance and Miscellaneous

Fog lights, L200, LW200	225	207
Alloy wheels, L200, LW200	350	322
16-inch chrome alloy wheels, L200, LW200, L300, LW 300	NA	NA

SATURN S-SERIES

Saturn SL2

Front-wheel-drive subcompact car
Base price range: $10,570-$16,940. Built in USA.
Also consider: Ford Focus, Honda Civic, Mazda Protege

FOR • Fuel economy • Dent-resistant body panels **AGAINST** • Rear-seat room • Brake performance • Rear-seat entry/exit (SC models)

The smaller of Saturn's two cars drops its station wagon body style for 2002. Returning are sedans in SL, SL1, and SL2 models, plus 3-dr coupes in SC1 and SC2 trim. The coupes have a small, rear-hinged, left-

Specifications begin on page 551.

SATURN

side back door. All models have dent- and rust-resistant polymer front and side body panels. SL and "1" models have 100 hp, the "2" versions have 124. Manual transmission is standard; automatic is optional on all but the SL. Side curtain airbags are optional on all. The optional ABS includes traction control. A tilt steering wheel is now standard on all models.

RATINGS

	SL1, man.	SC1, auto.	SL2, man.
ACCELERATION	3	2	5
FUEL ECONOMY	7	7	6
RIDE QUALITY	4	3	3
STEERING/HANDLING	4	5	6
QUIETNESS	3	3	4
INSTRUMENTS/CONTROLS	5	5	5
ROOM/COMFORT (FRONT)	4	3	4
ROOM/COMFORT (REAR)	3	2	3
CARGO ROOM	2	2	2
VALUE	4	2	4

Saturn won its following selling reliable small cars via a one-price strategy, but has of late offered cut-rate lease deals and incentive financing to buoy sales. Design of S-Series models shows its age, but dent- and rust-resistant composite body panels help these cars look "new" longer, and resale values are relatively strong.

TOTAL	39	34	42

Average total for subcompact cars: 43.7

ENGINES

	ohc I4	dohc I4
Size, liters/cu. in.	1.9/116	1.9/116
Horsepower @ rpm	100 @ 5000	124 @ 5600
Torque (lb-ft) @ rpm	114 @ 2400	122 @ 4800
Availability	S[1]	S[2]
EPA city/highway mpg		
5-speed manual	29/40	27/38
4-speed automatic	27/37	25/36

1. SL, SL1, SC1. 2. SC2, SL2.

PRICES

Saturn S-Series	Retail Price	Dealer Invoice
SL 4-door sedan, manual	$10570	$9619
SL1 4-door sedan, manual	11850	10784
SL1 4-door sedan, automatic	12710	11566
SC1 3-door coupe, manual	12900	11223
SC1 3-door coupe, automatic	13760	11971
SL2 4-door sedan, 5-speed	13335	12135
SL2 4-door sedan, automatic	14195	12917
SC2 3-door coupe, 5-speed	16080	13990

Prices are accurate at time of publication; subject to manufacturer's change.

SATURN

	Retail Price	Dealer Invoice
SC2 3-door coupe, automatic	$16940	$14738
Destination charge	465	465

STANDARD EQUIPMENT

SL: 1.9-liter 4-cylinder engine, 5-speed manual transmission, dual front airbags, daytime running lights, emergency inside trunk release, power steering, tilt steering wheel, cloth upholstery, front bucket seats, center console, cupholders, split folding rear seat, AM/FM radio, digital clock, tachometer, rear defogger, intermittent wipers, passenger-side visor mirror, remote fuel door and decklid release, theft-deterrent system, 185/65R14 tires, wheel covers.

SL1 adds: 5-speed manual or 4-speed automatic transmission.

SC1 adds: driver-side rear door, AM/FM/CD player, rear console, rear spoiler.

SL2 adds to SL1: 1.9-liter dohc 4-cylinder engine, air conditioning, driver-seat height and lumbar adjustment, floormats, sport suspension, 185/65TR15 tires.

SC2 adds: cruise control, leather-wrapped steering wheel, driver-side rear door, power mirrors, power windows, power door locks, remote keyless entry, AM/FM/CD player, rear console, rear spoiler, fog lights, 195/60R15 tires.

OPTIONAL EQUIPMENT

Major Packages

Option Pkg. 1, SL1	1955	1796
SC1	1895	17706

Air conditioning, cruise control, power mirrors, power windows and door locks, remote keyless entry, floormats, theft-deterrent system w/alarm.

Option Pkg. 2, SL2	995	896

Cruise control, power mirrors, power windows and door locks, remote keyless entry, theft-deterrent system w/alarm.

Safety

Antilock brakes, SL	495	465
SL1, SC1, SL2, SC2	495	446

Includes traction control.

Curtain side airbags, SL	325	306
SL1, SC1, SL2, SC2	325	293

Comfort & Convenience Features

Air conditioning, SL	960	902
SL1, SC1	960	864

Specifications begin on page 551.

SATURN

	Retail Price	Dealer Invoice
Power sunroof, SL1, SC1, SL2, SC2	$725	$653
AM/FM/CD player, SL	320	301
SL1, SL2	290	261
Includes premium speakers.		
AM/FM/cassette/CD player, SL	540	508
SL1, SL2	510	459
SC1, SC2	220	198
Includes automatic tone control, premium speakers.		
Remote keyless entry, SL1, SL2	370	333
Includes power door locks, theft-deterrent system w/alarm.		
Leather upholstery, SL2, SC2	710	639
Includes leather-wrapped steering wheel. SL2 requires Option Pkg. 2.		

Appearance and Miscellaneous

Rear spoiler, SL2	225	203
Fog lights, SL2	170	153
Alloy wheels, SC1	450	405
SL2, SC2	350	315
SC1 includes 185/65R14 touring tires.		

SATURN VUE

Saturn VUE

Front- or all-wheel-drive compact sport-utility vehicle
Base price range: $16,325-$22,575. Built in USA.
Also consider: Ford Escape, Honda CR-V, Mazda Tribute

FOR • Ride • Passenger and cargo room **AGAINST** • Engine noise • Steering/handling

Saturn's first SUV is positioned against compact SUVs such as the Ford Escape and Honda CR-V, but is slightly larger and has the longest wheelbase in its class. VUE offers front- or all-wheel drive, seats five, and has Saturn's traditional dent-resistant plastic body panels.

Prices are accurate at time of publication; subject to manufacturer's change.

SATURN

Engines are from Saturn's midsize L-Series cars. The 4 cyl has front-wheel drive and uses a 5-speed manual transmission or optional continuously variable automatic. Like other CVTs, Saturn's furnishes variable drive radios instead of conventional gear changes. All V6 VUEs have AWD and a 5-speed automatic transmission. The AWD system lacks low-range gearing. Options include ABS, curtain side airbags, and General Motors' OnStar assistance system. VUE stores its spare tire under the rear load floor and has a liftgate without separate-opening glass. The split rear seat works with a fold-down front-passenger seatback to accommodate long objects.

RATINGS

	4 cyl 2WD, CVT	V6
ACCELERATION	3	5
FUEL ECONOMY	6	5
RIDE QUALITY	6	6
STEERING/HANDLING	3	3
QUIETNESS	4	4
INSTRUMENTS/CONTROLS	7	7
ROOM/COMFORT (FRONT)	7	7
ROOM/COMFORT (REAR)	7	7
CARGO ROOM	7	7
VALUE	7	7

What VUE lacks in handling it more than makes up for in versatility, ride quality, and interior comfort. Even more attractive are its competitive pricing and the high customer-satisfaction ratings for Saturn's dealership experience and no-haggle price strategy.

TOTAL	57	58

Average total for compact sport-utility vehicles: 44.4

ENGINES

	dohc I4	dohc V6
Size, liters/cu. in.	2.2/134	3.0/181
Horsepower @ rpm	143 @ 5400	181 @ 6000
Torque (lb-ft) @ rpm	152 @ 4000	195 @ 4000
Availability	S	O
EPA city/highway mpg		
5-speed manual	23/28	
5-speed automatic		19/25
CVT automatic	21/26[1]	

1. 21/28 mpg w/2WD.

PRICES

Saturn VUE	Retail Price	Dealer Invoice
2WD 4-cylinder 4-door wagon, manual	$16325	$15228
2WD 4-cylinder 4-door wagon, CVT	17265	16102
AWD 4-cylinder 4-door wagon, CVT	18860	17586

Specifications begin on page 551.

SATURN

	Retail Price	Dealer Invoice
AWD V6 4-door wagon, automatic	$22575	$21041
Destination charge	510	510

STANDARD EQUIPMENT

4 cylinder: 2.2-liter dohc 4-cylinder engine, 5-speed manual or continuously-variable automatic transmission (CVT), dual front airbags, daytime running lights, air conditioning, power steering, tilt steering wheel, cloth upholstery, front bucket seats, fold-flat passenger seat, center console, cupholders, split folding rear seat, AM/FM radio, tachometer, visor mirrors, intermittent wipers, remote liftgate release, rear defogger, intermittent rear wiper/washer, theft-deterrent system, rear privacy glass, roof rack, 215/70SR16 tires, wheel covers. **AWD** adds: all-wheel drive, fog lights, 235/65SR16 tires.

V6 adds: 3.0-liter dohc V6 engine, 5-speed automatic transmission, all-wheel drive, cruise control, power mirrors, power windows, power door locks, remote keyless entry, AM/FM/CD player, automatic day/night rearview mirror, map lights, fog lights, 235/65SR16 tires, alloy wheels.

OPTIONAL EQUIPMENT

Major Packages

Power Pkg., 4 cylinder	1360	1265

Power mirrors and windows, power door locks, remote keyless entry, cruise control, automatic day/night rearview mirror, map lights, theft-deterrent system w/alarm.

Safety

Curtain side airbags	395	367
Antilock brakes, 2WD	595	554
AWD	575	535

2WD includes traction control.

Comfort & Convenience Features

OnStar Communications System	695	646

Includes one year service (roadside assistance, emergency services; other services available). 4 cylinder requires Power Pkg., optional radio. NA w/manual transmission, AM/FM/cassette w/in-dash 6-disc CD changer.

Power sunroof	725	675
AM/FM/CD player, 4 cylinder	290	270
AM/FM/cassette/CD player, 4 cylinder	510	474
V6	220	205
AM/FM/cassette w/in-dash 6-disc CD changer,		
4 cylinder	790	735
V6	500	465

Prices are accurate at time of publication; subject to manufacturer's change.

CONSUMER GUIDE®

SATURN • SUBARU

Special Purpose, Wheels and Tires

	Retail Price	Dealer Invoice
Alloy wheels, 4 cylinder	$400	$372

SUBARU FORESTER

CG RECOMMENDED AUTO

Subaru Forester S

All-wheel-drive compact sport-utility vehicle
Base price range: $20,295-$22,895. Built in Japan.
Also consider: Ford Escape, Honda CR-V, Toyota RAV4

FOR • Visibility • Maneuverability • Cargo room **AGAINST** • Instruments/controls • Rear-seat room

Subaru's compact SUV gets a standard retractable cargo-area cover and two new option packages for '02. Forester is basically a tall wagon body on the platform used by the 1993-2001-generation Subaru Impreza subcompact car. Base L and uplevel S models are offered. Both have a horizontally opposed 4-cyl engine, manual or automatic transmission, and all-wheel-drive without low-range gearing. Standard are ABS, air conditioning, and power windows/locks/mirrors. The S model adds 4-wheel disc brakes, heated seats, heated mirrors, and intermittent wipers with de-icers. Leather upholstery is optional on both models. Replacing last year's S Premium model is the OV Premium Package option. It adds front side airbags, sunroof, and unique alloy wheels to the S. The new OK Package includes the OV equipment plus leather upholstery.

RATINGS

	S w/OK Prem. Pkg., auto.
ACCELERATION	4
FUEL ECONOMY	6
RIDE QUALITY	6
STEERING/HANDLING	5
QUIETNESS	5

Specifications begin on page 551.

SUBARU

	S w/OK Prem. Pkg., auto.
INSTRUMENTS/CONTROLS	5
ROOM/COMFORT (FRONT)	5
ROOM/COMFORT (REAR)	3
CARGO ROOM	7
VALUE	7

Forester is the most carlike of car-based quasi-SUVs, with a blend of performance, comfort, utility, and value that merits our Recommended tag. Competition is stiff, though, so check out our "Also Consider" picks.

TOTAL	53

Average total for compact sport-utility vehicles: 44.4

ENGINES

	ohc H4
Size, liters/cu. in.	2.5/150
Horsepower @ rpm	165 @ 5600
Torque (lb-ft) @ rpm	166 @ 4000
Availability	S

EPA city/highway mpg
5-speed manual	21/27
4-speed automatic	22/27

PRICES

Subaru Forester	Retail Price	Dealer Invoice
L 4-door wagon	$20295	$18506
S 4-door wagon	22895	20778
Destination charge	525	525

Prices are for vehicles distributed by Subaru of America. Prices may vary in areas served by independent distributors.

STANDARD EQUIPMENT

L: 2.5-liter 4-cylinder engine, 5-speed manual transmission, all-wheel drive, dual front airbags, antilock brakes, daytime running lights, air conditioning, power steering, tilt steering wheel, cruise control, cloth upholstery, front bucket seats, height-adjustable driver seat w/lumbar adjustment, center console, cupholders, split folding rear seat, power mirrors, power windows, power door locks, AM/FM/cassette, digital clock, tachometer, outside temperature indicator, overhead storage console, map lights, intermittent wipers, cargo cover, rear defogger, intermittent rear wiper/washer, automatic-off headlights, floormats, fog lights, roof rack, full-size spare tire, 205/70R15 white-letter tires.

S adds: limited-slip differential, antilock 4-wheel disc brakes, heated power mirrors, remote keyless entry, 6-disc CD changer, leather-wrapped steering wheel, heated front seats, variable-intermittent wipers

Prices are accurate at time of publication; subject to manufacturer's change.

SUBARU

w/deicer, visor mirrors, 215/60R16 white-letter tires, alloy wheels.

OPTIONAL EQUIPMENT

	Retail Price	Dealer Invoice
Major Packages		
OV Premium Pkg., S	$1000	$896
Front side airbags, power sunroof, monotone paint, unique alloy wheels.		
OK Premium Pkg., S	1700	1523
OV Premium Pkg. plus leather upholstery. Requires 4-speed automatic transmission.		
Feature Group 3, S	414	270
Manufacturer's Discount Price	*414*	*256*
Automatic day/night rearview mirror, compass, cargo cover, theft-deterrent system, tail pipe cover.		
Feature Group 4	195	128
Manufacturer's Discount Price	*195*	*121*
Interior air filter, cargo net, armrest extension.		
Premium Sound Group 1, L	927	640
Manufacturer's Discount Price	*695*	*525*
CD player, upgraded sound system.		
Premium Sound Pkg. 2, L	1086	759
Manufacturer's Discount Price	*795*	*600*
In-dash 6-disc CD changer, upgraded sound system.		
Premium Sound Pkg. 3, S	566	369
Manufacturer's Discount Price	*395*	*300*
Upgraded sound system.		
Interior Upgrade Group	540	353
Manufacturer's Discount Price	*540*	*335*
Automatic day/night rearview mirror, compass, woodgrain interior trim, armrest extension, cargo net.		
Protection Group	665	362
Manufacturer's Discount Price	*665*	*333*
Brush guard, hood deflector, differential protector, rear dust deflector.		
Appearance Group	493	321
Manufacturer's Discount Price	*493*	*305*
Fender flares, rear spoiler.		
Powertrain		
4-speed automatic transmission	800	719
Comfort & Convenience Features		
Leather upholstery	1295	975
Remote keyless entry, L	178	116
Special Purpose, Wheels and Tires		
Alloy wheels, L	595	447

Postproduction options also available.

Specifications begin on page 551.

SUBARU

SUBARU IMPREZA

Subaru Impreza 2.5 RS

All-wheel-drive subcompact car

Base price range: $17,495-$24,995. Built in Japan.

Also consider: Ford Focus, Honda Civic, Volkswagen Jetta/Golf

FOR • Acceleration (WRX) • All-wheel drive • Brake performance • Control layout • Steering/handling **AGAINST** • Rear-seat room • Rear-seat entry/exit • Ride

Subaru redesigns its smallest car for '02, repositioning Impreza from an entry-level to a "premium" subcompact. Coupe models are dropped. Sedans now come in 165-hp 2.5RS and 227-hp turbo WRX versions. Wagons mirror that with 2.5TS and WRX models, and add an SUV-flavored Outback with the 2.5 engine. All have new styling, 4-cyl engines with horizontally opposed cylinders, and manual or optional automatic transmissions. WRXs are patterned after Subaru's World Rally competition cars. All Imprezas come with all-wheel drive, ABS, CD player, and power windows/locks. Sedans have wider front bodywork. WRXs include a sport suspension, an aluminum hood with functional scoop, and special interior trim and seats.

RATINGS	WRX sdn, man.
ACCELERATION	7
FUEL ECONOMY	5
RIDE QUALITY	5
STEERING/HANDLING	9
QUIETNESS	4
INSTRUMENTS/CONTROLS	6
ROOM/COMFORT (FRONT)	5
ROOM/COMFORT (REAR)	3
CARGO ROOM	2

Prices are accurate at time of publication; subject to manufacturer's change.

SUBARU

	WRX sdn, man.
VALUE	5

Pricewise, Impreza has moved above Honda Civic to Volkswagen Jetta level. AWD is an asset, but the jury is out on whether shoppers will consider it a "premium" small car in terms of workmanship and refinement. WRXs are fast fun, and are expected to nab 42 percent of Impreza sales, but they may be too coltish for mature drivers.

TOTAL	51

Average total for subcompact cars: 43.7

ENGINES

	ohc H4	Turbocharged dohc H4
Size, liters/cu. in.	2.5/150	2.0/122
Horsepower @ rpm	165 @ 5600	227 @ 6000
Torque (lb-ft) @ rpm	166 @ 4000	217 @ 4000
Availability	S[1]	S[2]
EPA city/highway mpg		
5-speed manual	21/27	20/27
4-speed automatic	22/27	19/26

1. 2.5RS, 2.5TS, Outback Sport. 2. WRX.

PRICES

Subaru Impreza

	Retail Price	Dealer Invoice
2.5 TS 4-door wagon, manual	$17495	$16085
2.5 TS 4-door wagon, automatic	18295	16810
Outback Sport 4-door wagon, manual	18695	17165
Outback Sport 4-door wagon, automatic	19495	17890
2.5 RS 4-door sedan, manual	18995	17444
2.5 RS 4-door sedan, automatic	19795	18169
WRX 4-door sedan, manual	23995	21977
WRX 4-door sedan, automatic	24995	22884
WRX 4-door wagon, manual	23495	21523
WRX 4-door wagon, automatic	24495	22430
Destination charge	525	525

Prices are for vehicles distributed by Subaru of America. Prices may vary in areas served by independent distributors.

STANDARD EQUIPMENT

2.5 TS: 2.5-liter 4-cylinder engine, 5-speed manual or 4-speed automatic transmission, all-wheel drive, dual front airbags, antilock brakes, daytime running lights, air conditioning, power steering, tilt steering wheel, cloth upholstery, front bucket seats w/height-adjustable driver seat, center console, cupholders, split folding rear seat (wagon), power mirrors, power windows, power door locks, AM/FM/CD player, digital clock, tachometer, intermittent wipers, rear defogger, rear/wiper washer

Specifications begin on page 551.

SUBARU

(wagon), cargo cover (wagon), remote decklid/hatch and fuel door release, passenger-side visor mirror, automatic-off headlights, roof rails (wagon), 195/60HR15 tires, wheel covers.

Outback Sport: cruise control, outside temperature indicator, floormats, cargo tray, fog lights, rear spoiler, roof rack, raised heavy-duty suspension, 205/55SR16 tires, alloy wheels.

2.5 RS adds to 2.5 TS: antilock 4-wheel disc brakes, emergency inside trunk release (sedan), leather-wrapped steering wheel, cruise control, trunk pass-through (sedan), floormats, rear spoiler, sport suspension, 205/55VR16 tires.

WRX adds: 2.0-liter dohc turbocharged 4-cylinder engine, limited-slip differential, front side airbags, remote keyless entry, AM/FM/cassette w/in-dash 6-disc CD changer, fog lights.

OPTIONAL EQUIPMENT

	Retail Price	Dealer Invoice
Major Packages		
Popular Equipment Group 1, 2.5 TS	$420	NA
Manufacturer's Discount Price	*406*	*245*
Floormats, roof rack, mud guards, tail pipe cover.		
Premium Sound Pkg. I, WRX	462	301
Manufacturer's Discount Price	*350*	*263*
Upgraded speakers, subwoofer, amplifier.		
Premium Sound Pkg. II, 2.5TS, Outback Sport, 2.5 RS	562	366
Manufacturer's Discount Price	*425*	*319*
Upgraded speakers, tweeter kit, subwoofer, amplifier.		
Security Pkg., 2.5 TS, Outback Sport, 2.5 RS	419	NA
Manufacturer's Discount Price	*405*	*250*
Remote keyless entry, security upgrade kit.		
Comfort & Convenience Features		
Remote keyless entry, 2.5 TS, Outback Sport, 2.5 RS	175	114
Automatic day/night rearview mirror	183	119
Includes compass.		
Appearance and Miscellaneous		
Trailer hitch, 2.5 TS, Outback Sport	295	192
Fog lights, 2.5 TS, 2.5 RS	298	194
Alloy wheels, 2.5 TS	525	394

Postproduction options also available.

SUBARU OUTBACK/LEGACY

All-wheel-drive compact car
Base price range: $19,295-$31,895. Built in USA.
Also consider: Audi A4, Honda Accord, Volkswagen Passat

Prices are accurate at time of publication; subject to manufacturer's change.

SUBARU

Subaru Outback 4-door wagon

FOR • All-wheel drive • Cargo room (wagons) **AGAINST**
• Automatic transmission performance (w/4 cyl)

Outbacks are marketed as carlike alternatives to truck-based SUVs. Legacys compete compete with other compact cars. Both offer sedan and wagon body styles. They share a basic underskin design and have standard all-wheel drive, but Outbacks have a raised suspension and other SUV cues. All Legacys and the Outback base and Limited models have a 4-cyl engine. The Outback line offers a 6-cyl engine. It's standard in top-line L.L. Bean and VDC wagons and in the new-for-2002 H6 and VDC Outback sedans. Both engines are horizontally opposed designs. The 4-cyl teams with manual or automatic transmission; the six with automatic only. Front side airbags are standard for the Legacy GT Limited sedan and all Outbacks except the base wagon. All models come with antilock 4-wheel disc brakes, but an antiskid/traction control system is exclusive to Outback VDCs. Also for '02, an All-Weather Package with heated front seats and heated mirrors is standard instead of optional on Legacy GTs.

RATINGS	Legacy L wgn, auto.	Legacy GT Limited sdn, man.	Outback Limited wgn, man.	Outback VDC wgn.
ACCELERATION	4	4	4	5
FUEL ECONOMY	6	6	5	4
RIDE QUALITY	6	6	7	7
STEERING/HANDLING	5	6	5	5
QUIETNESS	4	4	4	6
INSTRUMENTS/CONTROLS	5	5	5	5
ROOM/COMFORT (FRONT)	5	5	5	5
ROOM/COMFORT (REAR)	4	4	4	4
CARGO ROOM	7	3	7	7

Specifications begin on page 551.

SUBARU

	Legacy L wgn, auto.	Legacy GT Limited sdn, man.	Outback Limited wgn, man.	Outback VDC wgn.
VALUE	4	4	6	6

Outbacks are Recommended because they offer the spirit and AWD traction of "real" SUVs without the weighty thirst and clumsy size. Though they're pricey for Subarus and not outstanding performers, the 6-cyl Outbacks are much nicer to drive than 4-cyl versions. Legacys shine mainly for standard AWD; otherwise, most rival compacts are superior values.

TOTAL	50	47	52	54

Average total for compact cars: 51.6

EXTENDED-USE TEST UPDATE

Extended-use 2000 Outback Limited wagon suffered no mechanical problems during 13-month test. However, at 5600 mi., a burning smell was traced to undercoating dripping on the exhaust pipe; it was rectified by a dealer at no charge. Subaru has recalled several thousand 2001 Outbacks to fix defects in fuel hoses and front suspension, but our extended-use 2001 VDC was not among them. It required no unscheduled maintenance during the 14,242 mi. test, though the engine was slow to turn over in subfreezing temperatures.

ENGINES

	ohc H4	dohc H6
Size, liters/cu. in.	2.5/150	3.0/183
Horsepower @ rpm	165 @ 5600	212 @ 6000
Torque (lb-ft) @ rpm	166 @ 4000	210 @ 4400
Availability	S[1]	S[2]

EPA city/highway mpg

5-speed manual	21/27	
4-speed automatic	22/27	20/26

1. Legacy; Outback Base and Limited. 2. Outback H6, L.L. Bean, and VDC.

PRICES

Subaru Outback/Legacy

	Retail Price	Dealer Invoice
Legacy L 4-door sedan	$19295	$17565
Legacy L 4-door wagon	19995	18192
Legacy GT 4-door sedan	22895	20775
Legacy GT 4-door wagon	23795	21582
Legacy GT Limited 4-door sedan	24695	22383
Outback Base 4-door wagon	22895	20772
Outback Limited 4-door sedan	25995	23555
Outback Limited 4-door wagon	26295	23820

Prices are accurate at time of publication; subject to manufacturer's change.

SUBARU

	Retail Price	Dealer Invoice
Outback H6 4-door sedan	$27995	$25349
Outback L.L. Bean Edition 4-door wagon	29495	26692
Outback VDC 4-door sedan	30395	27500
Outback VDC 4-door wagon	31895	28844
Destination charge	525	525

Prices are for vehicles distributed by Subaru of America. Prices may vary in areas served by independent distributors.

STANDARD EQUIPMENT

L: 2.5-liter 4-cylinder engine, 5-speed manual transmission, all-wheel drive, dual front airbags, antilock 4-wheel disc brakes, daytime running lights, emergency inside trunk release (sedan), air conditioning, power steering, tilt steering wheel, cruise control, cloth upholstery, front bucket seats, rear seat trunk pass-through (sedan), split folding rear seat (wagon), power mirrors, power windows, power door locks, AM/FM/cassette, digital clock, tachometer, outside temperature indicator, map lights, intermittent wipers, rear defogger, intermittent rear wiper (wagon), cargo cover (wagon), automatic-off headlights, roof rails (wagon), 205/60HR15 tires, wheel covers.

GT adds: limited-slip differential, leather-wrapped steering wheel, 6-way power driver seat w/lumbar adjustment, remote keyless entry, single power sunroof (sedan), dual power sunroofs (wagon), illuminated visor mirrors, variable intermittent wipers, floormats, fog lights, sport suspension, 205/55HR16 tires, alloy wheels.

GT Limited adds: front side airbags, leather upholstery, heated front seats, heated power mirrors, AM/FM/weatherband/cassette/CD player.

Base adds to L: limited-slip differential, 6-way power driver seat w/lumbar adjustment, remote keyless entry, AM/FM/weatherband/cassette, illuminated visor mirrors, overhead console, variable intermittent wipers, floormats, fog lights, roof rack (wagon), trailer wiring harness, raised suspension, 225/60HR16 white-letter tires, alloy wheels.

Limited adds: 4-speed automatic transmission (sedan), front side airbags, leather-wrapped steering wheel, leather upholstery, heated front seats, heated power mirrors, dual power sunroofs (wagon), single power sunroof (sedan), AM/FM/weatherband/cassette/CD player, variable intermittent wipers w/de-icer.

H6 adds: 3.0-liter dohc 6-cylinder engine, 4-speed automatic transmission, automatic climate control, interior air filter, wood/leather-wrapped steering wheel, 8-way power driver seat, McIntosh sound system.

L.L. Bean Edition adds: two-tone leather upholstery, automatic day/night rearview mirror, compass, theft-deterrent system. *Deletes:* McIntosh sound system.

VDC adds: traction control, antiskid system, single-tone leather uphol-

SUBARU

stery, McIntosh sound system. *Deletes:* interior air filter, automatic day/night rearview mirror, theft-deterrent system.

OPTIONAL EQUIPMENT	Retail Price	Dealer Invoice
Major Packages		
Popular Equipment Group 1, L wagon	$336	$211
Manufacturer's Discount Price	*336*	*193*
Roof rack, floormats, mudguards.		
Popular Equipment Group 2, L sedan	164	105
Manufacturer's Discount Price	*164*	*97*
Floormats, mudguards.		
Popular Equipment Group 4, L	305	173
Manufacturer's Discount Price	*305*	*160*
Automatic day/night rearview mirror, illuminated visor mirrors.		
Popular Equipment Group 6, GT, GT Limited, Base, Limited, H6, VDC	373	243
Manufacturer's Discount Price	*373*	*229*
Automatic day/night rearview mirror, Security System Upgrade Kit.		
Premium Sound Pkg. 1A/1B, L, GT, Base	934	644
Manufacturer's Discount Price	*695*	*525*
CD player, upgraded speakers, subwoofer, amplifier, tweeter.		
Premium Sound Pkg. 2, GT, Base	1093	763
Manufacturer's Discount Price	*795*	*600*
In-dash 6-disc CD changer, upgraded speakers, tweeter, subwoofer, amplifier.		
Premium Sound Pkg. 3, GT Limited, Limited, L.L. Bean	787	564
Manufacturer's Discount Price	*635*	*475*
In-dash 6-disc CD changer, subwoofer, amplifier.		
All-Weather Pkg., Base	500	452
Heated front seats and mirrors, front windshield wiper de-icer.		
Rough Road Group, wagons	265	164
Manufacturer's Discount Price	*265*	*147*
Acrylic hood protector, rear differential protector, rear window dust deflector.		
Powertrain		
4-speed automatic transmission, Legacy, Base, Limited wagon	800	722
Comfort & Convenience Features		
CD player, L, GT, Base	361	271
In-dash 6-disc CD changer, GT, GT Limited, Base, Limited, H6, L.L. Bean	520	390
Remote keyless entry, L	175	114
Automatic day/night rearview mirror	183	119
Includes compass. Std. L.L.Bean Edition.		

Prices are accurate at time of publication; subject to manufacturer's change.

SUBARU • SUZUKI

Appearance and Miscellaneous

	Retail Price	Dealer Invoice
Fog lights, L	$259	$168
Rear spoiler, wagons	295	192
sedans	325	212
Roof rack, L/GT wagon	172	106
Alloy wheels, L	525	394

Postproduction options also available.

SUZUKI ESTEEM

Suzuki Esteem 4-door sedan

Front-wheel-drive subcompact car
Base price range: $13,299-$16,599. Built in Japan.
Also consider: Ford Focus, Honda Civic, Nissan Sentra, Toyota Echo

FOR • Fuel economy • Cargo room (wagon) • Maneuverability
AGAINST • Rear visibility • Noise • Ride

Suzuki drops the entry-level Swift hatchback for 2002 and continues its Esteem sedan and wagon with few changes. Esteem comes in GL, GLX, and GLX-Plus models, all with a 1.8-liter 4-cyl engine. GLX-Plus includes automatic transmission and ABS; others have standard manual transmission and do not offer ABS. All get an in-trunk emergency release and revised upholstery for '02. And GLX and GLX-Plus now have 14-inch alloy wheels in place of 15s.

RATINGS	GLX sdn, man.	GLX Plus wgn, auto.
ACCELERATION	3	3
FUEL ECONOMY	7	6
RIDE QUALITY	3	3
STEERING/HANDLING	4	4
QUIETNESS	2	2
INSTRUMENTS/CONTROLS	4	4

Specifications begin on page 551.

SUZUKI

	GLX sdn, man.	GLX Plus wgn, auto.
ROOM/COMFORT (FRONT)	3	3
ROOM/COMFORT (REAR)	3	3
CARGO ROOM	2	7
VALUE	2	2

Slow, rough-riding, and noisy, Esteem is a subpar subcompact in most respects and doesn't compare well with most rivals, especially our Also Consider models. If you can't resist, though, a GLX-Plus with its standard ABS is the way to go.

TOTAL	33	37

Average total for subcompact cars: 43.7

ENGINES

	dohc I4
Size, liters/cu. in.	1.8/112
Horsepower @ rpm	122 @ 6300
Torque (lb-ft) @ rpm	117 @ 3500
Availability	S

EPA city/highway mpg

5-speed manual	27/34
4-speed automatic	26/33

PRICES

Suzuki Esteem	Retail Price	Dealer Invoice
GL 4-door sedan, manual	$13299	$12767
GL 4-door sedan, automatic	14299	13727
GL 4-door wagon, manual	13799	13247
GL 4-door wagon, automatic	14799	14207
GLX 4-door sedan, manual	14299	13727
GLX 4-door sedan, automatic	15299	14687
GLX 4-door wagon, manual	14799	14207
GLX 4-door wagon, automatic	15799	15167
GLX-Plus 4-door wagon, automatic	16599	15935
Destination charge	500	500

STANDARD EQUIPMENT

GL: 1.8-liter dohc 4-cylinder engine, 5-speed manual or 4-speed automatic transmission, dual front airbags, daytime running lights, emergency inside trunk release (sedan), air conditioning, power steering, cloth upholstery, front bucket seats, center console, folding rear seat, AM/FM/CD player, intermittent wipers, rear defogger, rear wiper/washer (wagon), remote fuel-door and decklid releases, cargo cover (wagon), roof rails (wagon), 185/60R14 tires, wheel covers.

GLX adds: cruise control, power mirrors, power windows, power

SUZUKI

door locks, remote keyless entry, tachometer, split folding rear seat, passenger-side visor mirror, rear spoiler (wagon), alloy wheels.

GLX-Plus adds: 4-speed automatic transmission, antilock brakes, AM/FM/cassette/CD player, power sunroof.

Options are available as dealer-installed accessories.

SUZUKI VITARA

Suzuki Grand Vitara 4-door wagon

Rear- or 4-wheel-drive compact sport-utility vehicle 2001 base price range: $13,899-$22,999. Built in Japan.
Also consider: Ford Escape, Honda CR-V, Mazda Tribute, Subaru Forester, Toyota RAV4

FOR • Maneuverability • Cargo room **AGAINST** • Rear-seat room • Rear visibility • Acceleration • Rear-seat entry/exit (Convertible)

Suzuki's best-selling line offers more V6 power, fewer models, and adjusted features for 2002. Price-leader 1.6-liter 4-cyl models are dropped. That leaves 2.0-liter 4-cyl JLS and JLX convertibles and wagons. Top-line V6 Grand Vitara wagons get an extra 10 hp. All offer rear-wheel drive or 4WD that must be disengaged on dry pavement but includes low-range gearing. Automatic transmission is optional. In other changes, ABS becomes standard for JLX Grand Vitaras as well as top-line Limited Grand Vitaras. Heated door mirrors are now standard on 4WD models. And all Vitaras and Grand Vitaras gain rear child-seat mountings with upper and lower anchors and tethers. Grand Limiteds gain a leather-wrapped steering wheel and shift knobs, woodgrain plastic console trim, and with 4WD, heated front seats. Chevrolet's Tracker uses the same Suzuki-sourced body-on-frame design, but differs in models and features. Vitaras

Specifications begin on page 551.

SUZUKI

match equivalent Trackers in performance and accommodations.

RATINGS	JLX wgn 4WD, auto.	Grand Limited 4WD, auto.
ACCELERATION	1	3
FUEL ECONOMY	5	4
RIDE QUALITY	2	2
STEERING/HANDLING	2	2
QUIETNESS	2	2
INSTRUMENTS/CONTROLS	3	3
ROOM/COMFORT (FRONT)	3	3
ROOM/COMFORT (REAR)	3	3
CARGO ROOM	6	6
VALUE	2	2

No standout in any way in any form. Low-range 4WD is a plus off-road, but few buyers need it. Any of our Also Consider choices offers superior refinement, room, comfort, and all-around performance.

TOTAL	29	30

Average total for compact sport-utility vehicles: 44.4

ENGINES	dohc I4	dohc V6
Size, liters/cu. in.	2.0/122	2.5/152
Horsepower @ rpm	127 @ 6000	165 @ 6500
Torque (lb-ft) @ rpm	134 @ 3000	162 @ 4000
Availability	S[1]	S[2]
EPA city/highway mpg		
5-speed manual	22/25	19/21[3]
4-speed automatic	22/25	18/20[4]

1. Vitara. 2. Grand Vitara. 3. 19/22 w/2WD. 4. 19/21 w/2WD.

2002 prices unavailable at time of publication.

PRICES

2001 Suzuki Vitara

	Retail Price	Dealer Invoice
JS 2WD 2-door convertible, manual	$13899	$13343
JS 2WD 2-door convertible, automatic	14899	14303
JLS 2WD 2-door convertible, manual	15399	14783
JLS 2WD 2-door convertible, automatic	16399	15743
JX 4WD 2-door convertible, manual	15499	14569
JX 4WD 2-door convertible, automatic	16499	15509
JLX 4WD 2-door convertible, manual	16999	15979
JLX 4WD 2-door convertible, automatic	17999	16919
JS 2WD 4-door wagon, manual	15599	14663
JS 2WD 4-door wagon, automatic	16599	15603
JLS 2WD 4-door wagon, manual	16599	15603
JLS 2WD 4-door wagon, automatic	17599	16543

Prices are accurate at time of publication; subject to manufacturer's change.

SUZUKI

	Retail Price	Dealer Invoice
JLS 2WD 4-door wagon w/alloy wheels, manual	$17099	$16083
JLS 2WD 4-door wagon w/alloy wheels, automatic	18099	17023
JX 4WD 4-door wagon, manual	17099	15731
JX 4WD 4-door wagon, automatic	18099	16651
JLX 4WD 4-door wagon, manual	18099	16651
JLX 4WD 4-door wagon, automatic	19099	17571
JLX 4WD 4-door wagon w/alloy wheels, manual	18599	17123
JLX 4WD 4-door wagon w/alloy wheels, automatic	19599	18043
Grand JLS 2WD 4-door wagon, manual	18399	16927
Grand JLS 2WD 4-door wagon, automatic	19399	17847
Grand JLS Plus 2WD 4-door wagon, manual	19599	18031
Grand JLS Plus 2WD 4-door wagon, automatic	20599	18951
Grand JLX 4WD 4-door wagon, manual	19599	18031
Grand JLX 4WD 4-door wagon, automatic	20599	18951
Grand JLX Plus 4WD 4-door wagon, manual	20799	19135
Grand JLX Plus 4WD 4-door wagon, automatic	21799	20055
Grand Limited 2WD 4-door wagon, automatic	21799	20055
Grand Limited 4WD 4-door wagon, automatic	22999	21159
Destination charge: JS/JX convertible, JLS/JLX convertible	470	470
Destination charge: JS/JX wagon, JLS/JLX wagon, Grand JLS/JLX, Grand JLS Plus/Grand JLX Plus, Grand Limited	480	480

STANDARD EQUIPMENT

JS/JX convertible: 1.6-liter 4-cylinder engine, 5-speed manual or 4-speed automatic transmission, dual front airbags, daytime running lights, power steering, tilt steering wheel, cloth/vinyl upholstery, front bucket seats, center console, cupholders, folding rear seat, AM/FM/CD player, tachometer, passenger-side visor mirror, intermittent wipers, automatic headlights, folding convertible top, dual outside mirrors, full-size spare tire, 195/75R15 tires. **4WD** models add: 4-wheel drive, 2-speed transfer case, 205/75R15 tires.

JLS/JLX convertible adds: 2.0-liter dohc 4-cylinder engine, air conditioning, interior air filter, power mirrors, power windows, power door locks, cloth upholstery, map lights, 215/65R16 tires. **4WD** models add: 4-wheel drive, 2-speed transfer case.

Specifications begin on page 551.

SUZUKI

JS/JX wagon adds to JS/JX convertible: 2.0-liter dohc 4-cylinder engine, cloth upholstery, map lights, rear defogger, cargo cover, rear wiper/washer, roof rails, 215/65R16 tires. *Deletes:* folding convertible top. **4WD** models add: 4-wheel drive, 2-speed transfer case.

JLS/JLX wagon adds: air conditioning, interior air filter, cruise control, power mirrors, power windows, power door locks, remote keyless entry, steel or alloy wheels. **4WD** models add: 4-wheel drive, 2-speed transfer case.

Grand JLS/JLX adds: 2.5-liter dohc V6 engine, split folding rear seat, driver-side visor mirror, floormats, 235/60R16 tires. *Deletes:* alloy wheels. **4WD** models add: 4-wheel drive, 2-speed transfer case.

Grand JLS Plus/Grand JLX Plus adds: antilock brakes, AM/FM/cassette/CD player, alloy wheels. **4WD** model adds: 4-wheel drive, 2-speed transfer case.

Grand Limited adds: 4-speed automatic transmission, leather upholstery, power sunroof, rear privacy glass, fog lights. **4WD** model adds: 4-wheel drive, 2-speed transfer case.

Other options are available as dealer-installed accessories.

SUZUKI XL-7

Suzuki XL-7

Rear- or 4-wheel-drive midsize sport-utility vehicle
2001 base price range: $19,799-$25,999. Built in Japan.
Also consider: Ford Explorer, GMC Envoy, Toyota Highlander

FOR • Cargo room   **AGAINST** • Acceleration • Steering/handling • Noise

More power and revised equipment make news for the 2002 ver-

SUZUKI

sion of Suzuki's midsize SUV. XL-7 is basically the compact Grand Vitara wagon with a 12.1-inch longer wheelbase and 19.1 inches of added length. It uses a larger version of Grand Vitara's V6, which gains 13 hp for '02. Manual and automatic transmission are available. XL-7 offers rear-wheel drive or 4WD that must be disengaged on dry pavement but has low-range gearing. In other changes, the Standard XL-7 goes from 7- to 5-passenger status, losing the 3rd-row seat that remains standard on other models. And all models adopt the LATCH rear child-seat system with upper and lower anchors and tethers. Also, the ABS standard on Touring and top-line Limited models is now also included on Standard and midrange Plus 4WDs. All 4WD versions gain heated door mirrors, and Limiteds add heated front seats, leather-wrapped steering wheel and shift knobs, and woodgrain plastic console trim.

RATINGS

	Touring 4WD, man.	Touring 4WD, auto.
ACCELERATION	4	3
FUEL ECONOMY	5	5
RIDE QUALITY	4	4
STEERING/HANDLING	3	3
QUIETNESS	3	3
INSTRUMENTS/CONTROLS	5	5
ROOM/COMFORT (FRONT)	4	4
ROOM/COMFORT (REAR)	3	3
CARGO ROOM	7	7
VALUE	3	3

Prices may seem attractive, but XL-7 is no bargain given its subpar refinement, labored acceleration, stiff and nervous ride, poor handling, and antiquated 4WD system. Basically, it's a mediocre compact SUV stretched to become a mediocre midsize SUV, with a cramped 3rd-row seat of questionable usefulness its one asset.

TOTAL	41	40

Average total for midsize sport-utility vehicles: 49.6

ENGINES

	dohc V6
Size, liters/cu. in.	2.7/167
Horsepower @ rpm	183 @ 6000
Torque (lb-ft) @ rpm	180 @ 4000
Availability	S
EPA city/highway mpg	
5-speed manual	17/20[1]
4-speed automatic	17/20

1. 18/20 w/2WD.

2002 prices unavailable at time of publication.

Specifications begin on page 551.

SUZUKI • TOYOTA

PRICES

2001 Suzuki XL-7

	Retail Price	Dealer Invoice
2WD Standard 4-door wagon, manual	$19799	$18611
4WD Standard 4-door wagon, manual	20999	19739
2WD Plus 4-door wagon, manual	21299	19595
2WD Plus 4-door wagon, automatic	22299	20515
4WD Plus 4-door wagon, manual	22499	20699
4WD Plus 4-door wagon, automatic	23499	21619
2WD Touring 4-door wagon, automatic	23299	21435
4WD Touring 4-door wagon, automatic	24499	22539
2WD Limited 4-door wagon, automatic	24799	22815
4WD Limited 4-door wagon, automatic	25999	23919
Destination charge	500	500

STANDARD EQUIPMENT

Standard: 2.7-liter dohc V6 engine, 5-speed manual transmission, dual front airbags, daytime running lights, air conditioning, interior air filter, power steering, tilt steering wheel, cruise control, cloth upholstery, front bucket seats, center console, cupholders, second-row split folding seat, third-row split folding seat, power mirrors, power windows, power door locks, remote keyless entry, intermittent wipers, rear defogger, rear wiper/washer, automatic headlights, floormats, rear privacy glass, roof rails, full-size spare tire, 235/60R16 tires. **4WD** adds: 4-wheel drive, 2-speed transfer case.

Plus adds: 5-speed manual or 4-speed automatic transmission, rear air conditioning w/rear controls, AM/FM/CD player, alloy wheels. **4WD** adds: 4-wheel drive, 2-speed transfer case.

Touring adds: 4-speed automatic transmission, antilock brakes, power sunroof, AM/FM/cassette/CD player, rear spoiler, fog lights. **4WD** adds: 4-wheel drive, 2-speed transfer case.

Limited adds: leather upholstery, running boards. **4WD** adds: 4-wheel drive 2-speed transfer case.

Other options are available as dealer-installed accessories.

TOYOTA 4RUNNER

Rear- or 4-wheel-drive midsize sport-utility vehicle
Base price range: $26,335-$36,105. Built in Japan.
Also consider: Acura MDX, Lexus RX 300, Mercedes-Benz M-Class

FOR • Cargo room • Build quality • Exterior finish • Interior materials **AGAINST** • Entry/exit • Fuel economy

Prices are accurate at time of publication; subject to manufacturer's change.

TOYOTA

Toyota 4Runner

Toyota's truck-based midsize SUV is offered in SR5 and top-line Limited models. Both have a V6 engine, automatic transmission, and choice of rear- or 4WD. Traction/antiskid control is standard. Four-wheel-drive 4Runners have Toyota's Multi-Mode drive system that allows 4WD to remain engaged on dry pavement and has low-range gearing. For '02, 4Runner gets a new optional Chrome Package that adds bright exterior trim. Also new are standard instead of optional air conditioning, remote keyless entry, and alloy wheels for SR5s.

RATINGS	SR5 4WD	Limited 4WD
ACCELERATION	4	4
FUEL ECONOMY	4	4
RIDE QUALITY	4	4
STEERING/HANDLING	3	3
QUIETNESS	4	4
INSTRUMENTS/CONTROLS	7	7
ROOM/COMFORT (FRONT)	6	6
ROOM/COMFORT (REAR)	6	6
CARGO ROOM	8	8
VALUE	6	5

This aged SUV design is among the pricier in its class and is less refined than car-based SUVs such as Toyota's Highlander. Those facts keep it off our Recommended list. But if you're committed to a truck-type midsize SUV, 4Runner is worth considering for its antiskid control and all-surface 4WD, plus typical Toyota quality, reliability, and strong resale value.

TOTAL	52	51

Average total for midsize sport-utility vehicles: 49.6

ENGINES

	dohc V6
Size, liters/cu. in.	3.4/207

Specifications begin on page 551.

TOYOTA

	dohc V6
Horsepower @ rpm	183 @ 4800
Torque (lb-ft) @ rpm	217 @ 3600
Availability	S

EPA city/highway mpg
4-speed automatic .... 17/19[1]
1. 16/19 w/AWD.

PRICES

Toyota 4Runner	Retail Price	Dealer Invoice
SR5 2WD 4-door wagon	$26335	$23516
SR5 4WD 4-door wagon	28875	24783
Limited 2WD 4-door wagon	33455	29874
Limited 4WD 4-door wagon	36105	32242
Destination charge	510	510

Prices are for vehicles distributed by Toyota Motor Sales, U.S.A., Inc. The dealer invoice and destination charge may be higher in areas served by independent distributors.

STANDARD EQUIPMENT

SR5: 3.4-liter dohc V6 engine, 4-speed automatic transmission, traction control, dual front airbags, antilock brakes, antiskid system, daytime running lights, air conditioning, power steering, tilt steering wheel, cruise control, cloth upholstery, front bucket seats, center console, cupholders, split folding rear seat, heated power mirrors, power windows including tailgate window, power door locks, remote keyless entry, AM/FM/cassette/CD player, power antenna, digital clock, tachometer, variable intermittent wipers, passenger-side visor mirror, map lights, rear defogger, intermittent rear wiper, cargo cover, remote fuel-door/tailgate release, automatic-off headlights, rear privacy glass, full-size spare tire, 225/75R15 tires, alloy wheels. **4WD** models add: 4-wheel drive, 2-speed transfer case, skid plates.

Limited adds: automatic climate control, leather-wrapped steering wheel, leather upholstery, heated power front seats, wood interior trim, universal garage door opener, driver-side visor mirror, illuminated passenger-side visor mirror, floormats, theft-deterrent system, fog lights, fender flares, running boards, 265/70R16 tires. **4WD** adds: 4-wheel drive, 2-speed transfer case, skid plates.

OPTIONAL EQUIPMENT
Major Packages

GH Upgrade Value Pkg. 1, SR5............................ 415 332
Sport seats w/4-way adjustable headrests, leather-wrapped steering wheel, cloth door trim, alloy wheel caps.

Prices are accurate at time of publication; subject to manufacturer's change.

TOYOTA

	Retail Price	Dealer Invoice
AG Upgrade Value Pkg. 2, SR5	$890	$712

GH Upgrade Value Pkg. 1 plus special axle ratio, 265/70R16 tires. Requires fender flares or chrome wheel lip moldings.

Sport Edition, SR5	1585	1268

AG Upgrade Pkg. 2 plus heavy-duty brakes, metallic instrument panel, special floormats, fog lights, hood scoop, color-keyed bumpers and grille, fender flares, front skid plate.

Leather Pkg., SR5	1250	1000

Leather upholstery, manual 6-way front sport seats w/4-way adjustable headrests, leather-wrapped steering wheel. NA w/Sport Edition.

CH Chrome Pkg., SR5	150	120

Chrome grille, mirrors, taillight trim, and exhaust tips. Color-keyed bumpers. NA w/Leather Pkg., Sport Edition, fender flares, chrome wheel lip moldings, or alloy wheels AL.

CW Chrome Pkg., SR5	695	556

CH Chrome Pkg. plus special axle ratio, heavy-duty brakes, chrome wheel lip moldings, 265/70R16 tires. NA w/Leather Pkg., or Sport Edition.

Convenience Pkg.	810	523

Cargo mat, roof rack, rear wind deflector, towing receiver hitch.

Comfort & Convenience Features

Rear heater	170	136
Includes rear storage console w/cupholders.		
Power sunroof	815	652
AM/FM/cassette w/in-dash 6-disc CD changer, Limited	200	150

Appearance and Miscellaneous

Fog lights, SR5	269	180
Roof rack	275	165
Black running boards, SR5	345	209
Fender flares, SR5	230	184
Requires alloy wheels AL or AG Upgrade Value Pkg. 2.		
Chrome wheel lip moldings, SR5	70	56
Requires alloy wheels AL or AG Upgrade Pkg. 2.		

Special Purpose, Wheels and Tires

Alloy wheels AL, SR5	475	380

Includes 265/70R16 tires, heavy-duty brakes, special axle ratio. Requires fender flares or chrome wheel lip moldings.

Postproduction options also available.

Specifications begin on page 551.

TOYOTA

TOYOTA AVALON

Toyota Avalon

Front-wheel-drive full-size car
Base price range: $25,845-$30,405. Built in USA.
Also consider: Buick LeSabre, Chrysler Concorde, Dodge Intrepid

FOR • Build quality • Acceleration • Automatic transmission performance • Quietness • Passenger room • Ride/handling
AGAINST • Brake-pedal feel

America's only import-brand full-size sedan is offered in XL and uplevel XLS versions. Both Avalon models have a V6 engine, automatic transmission, antilock 4-wheel disc brakes, front side airbags, and choice of bench or bucket front seats. XLS offers optional anti-skid system that includes traction control and Toyota's full-power Brake Assist emergency-stop feature.

RATINGS	XL w/bench seat	XLS w/bucket seats
ACCELERATION	5	5
FUEL ECONOMY	5	5
RIDE QUALITY	8	8
STEERING/HANDLING	6	6
QUIETNESS	7	7
INSTRUMENTS/CONTROLS	8	8
ROOM/COMFORT (FRONT)	7	8
ROOM/COMFORT (REAR)	8	8
CARGO ROOM	4	4

Prices are accurate at time of publication; subject to manufacturer's change.
CONSUMER GUIDE®

TOYOTA

	XL w/bench seat	XLS w/bucket seats
VALUE	7	7

Roomy, quiet, smooth-riding, and quite roadable for a family-oriented sedan, Avalon rivals more expensive near-luxury sedans in many respects. Toyota's strong track record for quality, reliability, and resale value adds to the appeal, making this a solid Recommended pick.

TOTAL	65	66

Average total for full-size cars: 58.7

ENGINES

	dohc V6
Size, liters/cu. in.	3.0/181
Horsepower @ rpm	210 @ 5800
Torque (lb-ft) @ rpm	220 @ 4400
Availability	S

EPA city/highway mpg
4-speed automatic 21/29

PRICES

Toyota Avalon

	Retail Price	Dealer Invoice
XL 4-door sedan, front bucket seats	$25845	$23000
XL 4-door sedan, front bench seat	26665	23730
XLS 4-door sedan, front bucket seats	30405	26756
XLS 4-door sedan, front bench seat	30305	26668
Destination charge	485	485

Prices are for vehicles distributed by Toyota Motor Sales, U.S.A., Inc. The dealer invoice and destination charge may be higher in areas served by independent distributors.

STANDARD EQUIPMENT

XL: 3.0-liter dohc V6 engine, 4-speed automatic transmission, dual front airbags, front side airbags, antilock 4-wheel disc brakes, daytime running lights, emergency inside trunk release, air conditioning w/dual-zone manual control, power steering, tilt steering wheel, cruise control, cloth upholstery, manual front bucket seats w/center console or power split bench seat, cupholders, rear seat trunk passthrough, power mirrors, power windows, power door locks, AM/FM/cassette/CD player, digital clock, tachometer, outside temperature indicator, rear defogger, illuminated visor mirrors, variable intermittent wipers, remote fuel door and decklid releases, automatic headlights, full-size spare tire, 205/65R15 tires, wheel covers.

XLS adds: dual-zone automatic climate control, interior air filter, leather-wrapped steering wheel, power front seats, heated power

Specifications begin on page 551.

TOYOTA

mirrors, JBL sound system, remote keyless entry, trip computer, compass, automatic day/night rearview mirror, universal garage door opener, theft-deterrent system, fog lights, alloy wheels.

OPTIONAL EQUIPMENT

	Retail Price	Dealer Invoice
Major Packages		
Pkg. 1, XL w/bucket seats	$1150	$920
Power front seats, remote keyless entry.		
Pkg. 2, XL w/bucket seats	1540	1232
Power front seats, remote keyless entry, alloy wheels.		
Pkg. 3, XL w/bucket seats	2755	2204
Pkg. 2 plus leather upholstery, leather-wrapped steering wheel and shift knob.		
Pkg. 3, XL w/bench seat	705	564
Remote keyless entry, alloy wheels.		
Pkg. 4,		
XL w/bench seat	1900	1520
Leather upholstery, leather-wrapped steering wheel and shift knob, remote keyless entry, alloy wheels.		
Luxury Pkg.,		
XL w/bucket seats	1915	1724
XL w/bench seat	1060	954
Leather upholstery, leather-wrapped steering wheel and shift knob, power front seats (bucket seats), remote keyless entry, JBL sound system.		
Pkg. 6, XLS	470	424
Leather upholstery, driver seat and mirror memory, AM/FM/cassette w/in-dash 6-disc CD changer, 205/60R16 tires.		
Pkg. 7, XLS	785	707
Pkg. 6 plus heated front seats.		
Pkg. 8, XLS	330	252
In-dash 6-disc CD changer, 205/60R16 tires.		
Safety		
Antiskid system,		
XLS	650	520
Includes traction control and brake assist.		
Comfort & Convenience Features		
Power sunroof	900	720
JBL sound system, XL	360	270
XL w/bucket seats requires Pkg. 1, 2, or 3.		
Appearance and Miscellaneous		
Alloy wheels, XL	592	440

Postproduction options also available.

Prices are accurate at time of publication; subject to manufacturer's change.

CONSUMER GUIDE®

TOYOTA

TOYOTA CAMRY

CG BEST BUY AUTO

Toyota Camry LE

Front-wheel-drive midsize car
Base price range: $18,970-$25,405. Built in USA.
Also consider: Ford Taurus, Honda Accord, Nissan Altima

FOR • Acceleration (V6) • Ride • Quietness • Build quality • Interior storage space **AGAINST** • Navigation system controls

Toyota redesigns one of America's best-selling cars for 2002. Camry has new styling and a 2-inch longer wheelbase than its 1997-2001 predecessor. It's slightly taller and longer overall, too, but little heavier. Base LE, uplevel XLE, and sporty new SE models are offered. Standard is a new 2.4-liter 4-cyl engine with 21 hp more than the 2.2 it replaces. A V6 is available on all models. V6s and the 4-cyl XLE have standard automatic transmission and ABS; both are optional on other Camrys. New options include front torso side airbags and curtain side airbags; V6 models can combine these features with a newly available antiskid system. Also new is an optional navigation system with dashboard touch screen. The SE includes a firmer suspension, fog lights, rear spoiler, and special trim. Optional power-adjustable foot pedals are due later in the model year for automatic-transmission Camrys. The ES 300 from Toyota's luxury Lexus division shares Camry's basic new design.

RATINGS	LE, 4 cyl man.	LE, 4 cyl auto.	SE, V6 auto.	XLE w/nav. sys., V6
ACCELERATION	5	5	6	6
FUEL ECONOMY	7	6	5	5
RIDE QUALITY	8	8	8	8
STEERING/HANDLING	6	6	7	6
QUIETNESS	7	7	8	8

Specifications begin on page 551.

TOYOTA

	LE, 4 cyl man.	LE, 4 cyl auto.	SE, V6 auto.	XLE w/nav. sys., V6
INSTRUMENTS/CONTROLS	10	10	10	8
ROOM/COMFORT (FRONT)	8	8	8	9
ROOM/COMFORT (REAR)	6	6	6	6
CARGO ROOM	5	5	5	5
VALUE	10	10	10	10

Camry's redesign brings laudable new safety features and lifts comfort, convenience, and refinement to near-Lexus levels. Although all these cars still engage the head more than the heart, Toyota reliability and resale values are always tough to beat, and slightly lower 2002 prices make Camrys an even stronger value than before. Don't buy a midsize car without shopping this one.

TOTAL	72	71	73	71

Average total for midsize cars: 57.0

ENGINES

	dohc I4	dohc V6
Size, liters/cu. in.	2.4/144	3.0/183
Horsepower @ rpm	157 @ 5600	192 @ 5300
Torque (lb-ft) @ rpm	162 @ 4000	209 @ 4400
Availability	S[1]	S[2]

EPA city/highway mpg

5-speed manual	24/33	
4-speed automatic	23/32	20/27

1. 4-cyl models. 2. V6 models.

PRICES

Toyota Camry

	Retail Price	Dealer Invoice
LE 4-cylinder 4-door sedan, manual	$18970	$16976
LE 4-cylinder 4-door sedan, automatic	19800	17721
LE V6 4-door sedan, automatic	22260	19810
SE 4-cylinder 4-door sedan, manual	20310	18076
SE 4-cylinder 4-door sedan, automatic	21140	18813
SE V6 4-door sedan, automatic	23700	21093
XLE 4-cylinder 4-door sedan, automatic	22295	19840
XLE V6 4-door sedan, automatic	25405	22610
Destination charge	485	485

Prices are for vehicles distributed by Toyota Motor Sales, U.S.A., Inc. The dealer invoice and destination charge may be higher in areas served by independent distributors.

STANDARD EQUIPMENT

LE : 2.4-liter dohc 4-cylinder engine or 3.0-liter dohc V6 engine, 5-

Prices are accurate at time of publication; subject to manufacturer's change.

TOYOTA

speed manual or 4-speed automatic transmission, dual front airbags, antilock 4-wheel disc brakes (V6), daytime running lights, emergency inside trunk release, air conditioning, interior air filter, variable-assist power steering, tilt steering wheel, cruise control, cloth upholstery, front bucket seats, height-adjustable driver seat, center console, cupholders, split folding rear seat, power mirrors, power windows, power door locks, AM/FM/cassette/CD player, digital clock, tachometer, overhead console, outside temperature indicator, visor mirrors, map lights, variable intermittent wipers, rear defogger, remote fuel door and decklid release, automatic-off headlights, full-size spare tire, 205/65R15 tires, wheel covers.

SE adds: leather-wrapped steering wheel, fog lights, rear spoiler, sport suspension, 215/60R16 tires, alloy wheels.

XLE adds to LE: 4-speed automatic transmission, antilock brakes, heated power mirrors, power front seats w/driver-side lumbar adjustment, remote keyless entry, automatic climate control, JBL sound system, automatic day/night rearview mirror, compass, trip computer, universal garage door opener, illuminated visor mirrors, rear sunshade, theft-deterrent system, 215/60R16 tires, alloy wheels (V6).

OPTIONAL EQUIPMENT
Major Packages

	Retail Price	Dealer Invoice
Pkg. 1, LE, SE 4-cylinder	$585	$468
Power driver seat, remote keyless entry.		
Pkg. 2, LE, SE	875	686
Pkg. 1 plus JBL AM/FM/CD player. NA w/navigation system.		
Pkg. 3, LE, SE	2065	1628
Pkg. 3 plus power sunroof, in-dash 6-disc CD changer, sunshade, cargo net. NA w/navigation system.		
Pkg. 4, SE V6	3115	2468
Pkg. 3 plus leather upholstery.		
Pkg. 5, SE V6	3695	3036
Pkg. 3 plus navigation system.		
Pkg. 6, SE V6	4745	3876
Pkg. 5 plus leather upholstery.		
Pkg. 7	1150	950
Antiskid system, traction control, front side airbags, curtain side airbags. Requires V6 engine.		
Pkg. 8, XLE 4-cylinder	2730	2174
XLE V6	2320	1846
Leather upholstery, power front seats, power sunroof, JBL AM/FM/cassette w/in-dash 6-disc CD changer, alloy wheels (4-cylinder).		
Pkg. 9, XLE 4-cylinder	4360	3581
XLE V6	3950	3253
Leather upholstery, power front seats, navigation system, power sunroof, alloy wheels (4-cylinder).		

Specifications begin on page 551.

TOYOTA

	Retail Price	Dealer Invoice
Safety		
Antilock brakes, LE/SE 4-cylinder	$300	$258
Front side airbags/curtain side airbags	500	430
Comfort & Convenience Features		
Navigation system, SE	2120	1776
XLE	1830	1557
SE 4-cylinder automatic requires antilock brakes.		
Power sunroof	900	720
JBL sound system, SE	490	368
JBL AM/FM/cassette w/in-dash 6-disc CD changer, XLE	200	150
Remote keyless entry, LE, SE	245	196
Heated front seats, SE V6, XLE	315	252
Camry SE requires Pkg. 4 or 6. XLE requires Pkg. 8 or 9.		
Appearance and Miscellaneous		
Alloy wheels, SE/XLE 4-cylinder	410	328

Postproduction options also available.

TOYOTA CELICA

Toyota Celica GTS

Front-wheel-drive sporty coupe
Base price range: $17,085-$22,255. Built in Japan.
Also consider: Acura RSX, Volkswagen New Beetle

FOR • Acceleration (GT-S 6-speed) • Handling/roadholding
AGAINST • Noise • Passenger room • Entry/exit

Toyota's sporty 4-cyl hatchback coupe gets a new optional appearance package for '02. Celica is offered as the 140-hp GT model and the sportier 180-hp GT-S. The GT comes with a 5-speed manual transmission, the GT-S with a 6-speed. Automatic is optional for both

Prices are accurate at time of publication; subject to manufacturer's change.

TOYOTA

and provides the GT-S with steering-wheel buttons for manual shifting. ABS and front side airbags are optional, as is a sunroof and rear spoiler. GT-S options include leather upholstery and 16-inch wheels instead of 15s. The new optional Action appearance package for GT and GT-S adds an adjustable rear spoiler along with unique sill panels/front and rear fascia.

RATINGS

	GT, auto.	GT-S, man.
ACCELERATION	6	7
FUEL ECONOMY	8	6
RIDE QUALITY	4	4
STEERING/HANDLING	7	8
QUIETNESS	3	3
INSTRUMENTS/CONTROLS	6	6
ROOM/COMFORT (FRONT)	3	3
ROOM/COMFORT (REAR)	1	1
CARGO ROOM	5	5
VALUE	4	4

This high-strung sporty coupe is more for Gen-X hotbloods than Baby Boomers, who will likely find Acura RSX or Volkswagen New Beetle more appealing. But Toyota's reputation for quality, reliability, and high resale value boost Celica's appeal enough to make it a Recommended pick.

TOTAL	47	47

Average total for sporty coupes: 43.4

ENGINES

	dohc I4	dohc I4
Size, liters/cu. in.	1.8/109	1.8/110
Horsepower @ rpm	140 @ 6400	180 @ 7600
Torque (lb-ft) @ rpm	126 @ 4200	130 @ 6800
Availability	S[1]	S[2]
EPA city/highway mpg		
5-speed manual	28/33	
6-speed manual		23/32
4-speed automatic	29/36	23/30

1. GT. 2. GT-S.

PRICES

Toyota Celica	Retail Price	Dealer Invoice
GT 2-door hatchback, manual	$17085	$15460
GT 2-door hatchback, automatic	17885	16184
GT-S 2-door hatchback, manual	21555	19398
GT-S 2-door hatchback, automatic	22255	20028
Destination charge	485	485

Specifications begin on page 551.

TOYOTA

Prices are for vehicles distributed by Toyota Motor Sales, U.S.A., Inc. The dealer invoice and destination charge may be higher in areas served by independent distributors.

STANDARD EQUIPMENT

GT: 1.8-liter dohc 4-cylinder 140-horsepower engine, 5-speed manual or 4-speed automatic transmission, dual front airbags, daytime running lights, air conditioning, power steering, tilt steering wheel, cloth upholstery, front bucket seats, center console, cupholders, split folding rear seat, power mirrors, AM/FM/cassette/CD player, digital clock, tachometer, rear defogger, intermittent wipers, visor mirrors, automatic headlights, 195/60R15 tires, wheel covers.

GT-S adds: 1.8-liter dohc 4-cylinder 180-horsepower engine, 6-speed manual or 4-speed automatic transmission w/manual-shift capability, 4-wheel disc brakes, leather-wrapped steering wheel, cruise control, power windows, power door locks, upgraded sound system, intermittent rear wiper, fog lights, 205/55R15 tires, alloy wheels.

OPTIONAL EQUIPMENT

	Retail Price	Dealer Invoice
Major Packages		
Upgrade Pkg., GT	$820	$656
Cruise control, power windows and door locks.		
All Weather Guard Pkg., GT	270	223
Intermittent rear wiper/washer, heavy-duty rear defogger, heavy-duty battery and starter. Std. GT-S.		
Action Pkg.	1590	1272
Unique bumpers, bodyside cladding, rear spoiler.		
Safety		
Antilock brakes	300	258
Front side airbags	250	215
Comfort & Convenience Features		
Power sunroof	900	720
GT requires Upgrade Pkg.		
Leather upholstery, GT-S	660	528
Requires power sunroof.		
Premium sound system, GT	330	248
6-disc CD changer	550	381
Automatic day/night rearview mirror	280	190
Security System	499	299
Remote keyless entry, theft-deterrent system. GT requires Upgrade Pkg.		
Appearance and Miscellaneous		
Rear spoiler, GT	545	436

Prices are accurate at time of publication; subject to manufacturer's change.

TOYOTA

	Retail Price	Dealer Invoice
GT-S	$435	$348
GT includes fog lights.		
Alloy wheels, GT	385	308
205/50VR16 tires, GT-S	60	48

Postproduction options also available.

2003 TOYOTA COROLLA

Toyota Corolla S

Front-wheel-drive subcompact car
Base price: NA. Built in Canada, USA.
Also consider: Ford Focus, Honda Civic, Volkswagen Jetta

FOR • Fuel economy • Build quality **AGAINST** • Acceleration (automatics) • Handling

The world's best-selling car and Toyota's oldest model is redesigned for 2003. Corolla continues its conservative tradition as a 4-dr sedan, while Toyota aims for younger buyers with the new Matrix wagon offshoot. Corolla gets new styling and, compared to the 1998-2002 version, gains 5.4 inches in wheelbase and 4.3 inches in body length. A 1.8-liter 4 cyl returns with 5 hp more and manual transmission or 4-speed automatic. Base CE, uplevel LE, and sporty S model designations continue.

Antilock brakes and front side airbags are optional; curtain side airbags are unavailable. Power mirrors and CD player are standard. Air conditioning and power locks are standard on LE and S. LE has standard woodlike interior trim, power windows, and exclusive optional leather upholstery. The S has aero body trim, fog lights, and leather wrapped steering wheel and shift lever. A sunroof is optional on S and LE. Prices were not available in time for this report.

Specifications begin on page 551.

CONSUMER GUIDE®

TOYOTA

Chevrolet's Corolla clone, the Prizm, will not carry over to the '03 design.

RATINGS	CE, man.	LE, auto	S, man.
ACCELERATION	4	3	4
FUEL ECONOMY	8	7	8
RIDE QUALITY	5	5	5
STEERING/HANDLING	4	4	4
QUIETNESS	5	5	5
INSTRUMENTS/CONTROLS	7	7	7
ROOM/COMFORT (FRONT)	4	4	4
ROOM/COMFORT (REAR)	3	3	3
CARGO ROOM	3	3	3
VALUE	6	6	6

Corolla's strong points—value, reliability, and comfort—emerge intact with this redesign. Improvements are subtle but enough to stay abreast of the best subcompacts. Honda Civic, Ford Focus, and VW Jetta sedans have more spice, but no more utility. Corolla should be on any subcompact-sedan shopping list.

TOTAL	49	47	49

Average total for subcompact cars: 43.7

ENGINES

	dohc I4
Size, liters/cu. in.	1.8/110
Horsepower @ rpm	130 @ 6000
Torque (lb-ft) @ rpm	125 @ 4200
Availability	S
EPA city/highway mpg	
4-speed manual	30/38
5-speed manual	32/40

2003 prices unavailable at time of publication.

TOYOTA ECHO

Front-wheel-drive subcompact car
Base price range: $9,995-$11,385. Built in Japan.
Also consider: Ford Focus, Honda Civic, Mazda Protege

FOR • Fuel economy • Maneuverability **AGAINST** • Acceleration (automatic transmission) • Rear-seat entry/exit (2-door)

Echo is offered in 2- and 4-dr models both with a 1.5-liter 4-cyl engine and manual or optional automatic transmission. Power steering is optional, as are ABS, front side-airbags, and a split-fold rear

Prices are accurate at time of publication; subject to manufacturer's change.

TOYOTA

Toyota Echo 2-door coupe

seatback. An in-dash CD changer, power locks, and remote keyless entry are also available.

RATINGS

	Base cpe, man.	Base sdn, auto.
ACCELERATION	4	4
FUEL ECONOMY	8	8
RIDE QUALITY	5	5
STEERING/HANDLING	4	4
QUIETNESS	4	4
INSTRUMENTS/CONTROLS	5	5
ROOM/COMFORT (FRONT)	5	5
ROOM/COMFORT (REAR)	4	5
CARGO ROOM	3	3
VALUE	7	7

Echo is slightly quirky, but it's a pleasant, efficient small car with keen pricing and Toyota's strong reputation for quality and reliability. Sales have been tepid despite low prices, so discounts should be readily available.

TOTAL	49	50

Average total for subcompact cars: 43.7

ENGINES

	dohc I4
Size, liters/cu. in.	1.5/91
Horsepower @ rpm	108 @ 6000
Torque (lb-ft) @ rpm	105 @ 4200
Availability	S
EPA city/highway mpg	
5-speed manual	34/41
4-speed automatic	32/38

Specifications begin on page 551.

TOYOTA

PRICES

Toyota Echo

	Retail Price	Dealer Invoice
Base 2-door coupe, manual	$9995	$9393
Base 2-door coupe, automatic	10855	10203
Base 4-door sedan, manual	10585	9948
Base 4-door sedan, automatic	11385	10700
Destination charge	485	485

Prices are for vehicles distributed by Toyota Motor Sales, U.S.A., Inc. The dealer invoice and destination charge may be higher in areas served by independent distributors.

STANDARD EQUIPMENT

Base: 1.5-liter dohc 4-cylinder engine, 5-speed manual or 4-speed automatic transmission, dual front airbags, tilt steering wheel, cloth upholstery, front bucket seats, center console, cupholders, AM/FM radio, driver-side visor mirror, 175/65R14 tires, wheel covers.

OPTIONAL EQUIPMENT

Major Packages

Upgrade Pkg. 1	1020	832

Power steering, intermittent wipers, split folding rear seat, digital clock, remote control outside mirrors, bodyside cladding.

Upgrade Pkg. 2, coupe	1375	1087
sedan	1470	1163

Air conditioning, power door locks, AM/FM/cassette/CD player. Requires Upgrade Pkg. 1 or bodyside cladding.

Upgrade Pkg. 3, coupe	375	300
sedan	475	380

Power windows, remote keyless entry. Requires Upgrade Pkg. 1 and 2.

All Weather Pkg.	275	220

Rear defogger, heavy-duty battery, rear seat heater ducts. Requires Upgrade Pkg. 1.

Safety

Antilock brakes	340	290

Includes daytime running lights. Requires Upgrade Pkg. 2 and All Weather Pkg.

Front side airbags	250	215

Comfort & Convenience Features

Power steering	270	231
Air conditioning	925	740
AM/FM/cassette	170	128

Prices are accurate at time of publication; subject to manufacturer's change.

TOYOTA

	Retail Price	Dealer Invoice
AM/FM/cassette/CD player	$270	$203
In-dash 6-disc CD changer	589	414
NA w/Upgrade Pkg. 2 or AM/FM/cassette/CD player.		
Power door locks, coupe	180	144
sedan	275	220
Requires Upgrade Pkg. 1.		
Remote keyless entry	175	140
Requires power door locks or Upgrade Pkg. 2.		
Rear defogger	205	164
Split folding rear seat	165	132

Appearance and Miscellaneous

Rear spoiler	100	80
Alloy wheels	499	375

Postproduction options also available.

TOYOTA HIGHLANDER

Toyota Highlander

Front- or all-wheel-drive midsize sport-utility vehicle
Base price range: $23,880-$30,795. Built in Japan.
Also consider: Acura MDX, Ford Explorer, Lexus RX 300

FOR • Passenger and cargo room • Instruments/controls
AGAINST • Fuel economy

Toyota's car-based midsize SUV is an underskin sibling to the Lexus RX 300. Both are built on the Toyota Camry sedan platform, but Highlander has a 4-inch longer wheelbase than the costlier RX 300. Highlander has 5-passenger seating only; no 3rd row seat is available. Four-cyl or V6 models are offered, both with 4-speed auto-

Specifications begin on page 551.

TOYOTA

matic transmission and choice of front-wheel drive or all-wheel drive without low-range gearing. The top-line Limited version includes automatic climate control, power driver seat, and alloy wheels. Antilock 4-wheel disc brakes and 16-inch wheels are standard. An antiskid system and front side airbags are optional. Other options include sunroof, running boards, and, on Limiteds, heated front seats and leather upholstery. For 2002, Highlander gains a standard rear seat armrest, cabin air filter, and a redesigned center console.

RATINGS

	AWD, V6
ACCELERATION	5
FUEL ECONOMY	4
RIDE QUALITY	6
STEERING/HANDLING	6
QUIETNESS	5
INSTRUMENTS/CONTROLS	7
ROOM/COMFORT (FRONT)	7
ROOM/COMFORT (REAR)	7
CARGO ROOM	8
VALUE	6

Aside from slightly elevated ground clearance, Highlander doesn't really do anything better than an AWD minivan would, sacrificing in the bargain such agreeable features as space-efficient sliding side doors and 7-passenger seating. That said, Highlander is a far smarter buy than a truck-based SUV for most people, and its all-around competence, pricing, and Toyota design make it more than a match for midsize SUVs of any stripe. It's an easy Best Buy value.

TOTAL	**61**

Average total for midsize sport-utility vehicles: 49.6

ENGINES

	dohc I4	dohc V6
Size, liters/cu. in.	2.4/144	3.0/183
Horsepower @ rpm	155 @ 5600	220 @ 5800
Torque (lb-ft) @ rpm	163 @ 4000	222 @ 4400
Availability	S[1]	S[2]
EPA city/highway mpg		
4-speed automatic	19/24[3]	18/22[4]

1. 4-cyl versions. 2. V6 versions. 3. 22/27 w/2WD. 4. 19/23 w/2WD.

PRICES

Toyota Highlander	Retail Price	Dealer Invoice
2WD 4-cylinder 4-door wagon	$23880	$21251
AWD 4-cylinder 4-door wagon	25280	22497
2WD V6 4-door wagon	25460	22658
AWD V6 4-door wagon	26860	23904

Prices are accurate at time of publication; subject to manufacturer's change.

TOYOTA

	Retail Price	Dealer Invoice
2WD Limited 4-door wagon	$29395	$26159
AWD Limited 4-door wagon	30795	27405
Destination charge	510	510

Prices are for vehicles distributed by Toyota Motor Sales, U.S.A., Inc. The dealer invoice and destination charge may be higher in areas served by independent distributors.

STANDARD EQUIPMENT

4-cylinder: 2.4-liter dohc 4-cylinder engine, 4-speed automatic transmission, dual front airbags, antilock 4-wheel disc brakes, air conditioning, interior air filter, power steering, tilt steering wheel, cruise control, cloth upholstery, front captain chairs, center console, cupholders, split folding rear seat, power mirrors, power windows, power door locks, AM/FM/cassette/CD player, digital clock, tachometer, map light, variable intermittent wipers, visor mirrors, intermittent rear wiper/washer, remote fuel door release, automatic-off headlights, 225/70R16 tires. **AWD** adds: all-wheel drive.

V6 adds: 3.0-liter dohc V6 engine. **AWD** adds: all-wheel drive.

Limited adds: daytime running lights, automatic climate control, leather-wrapped steering wheel, 8-way power driver seat, heated power mirrors, remote keyless entry, JBL sound system, illuminated visor mirrors, universal garage door opener, outside temperature indicator, cargo cover, automatic headlights, theft-deterrent system, rear privacy glass, roof rack, rear spoiler, fog lights, full-size spare tire, alloy wheels.

OPTIONAL EQUIPMENT
Major Packages

Preferred Pkg., 4-cylinder, V6	645	516

8-way power driver seat, illuminated visor mirrors, universal garage door opener, theft-deterrent system w/alarm. 4-cylinder requires Quick Order Pkg. V6 requires Convenience Pkg.

Quick Order Pkg. QO, 4-cylinder	630	504

Remote keyless entry, cargo cover, rear privacy glass.

Convenience Pkg., V6	320	256

Remote keyless entry, cargo cover.

Appearance Pkg., V6	910	728

Rear privacy glass, mud guards, alloy wheels.

Towing Prep Pkg.	160	128

Powertrain

Limited-slip differential, AWD	390	322

Specifications begin on page 551.

TOYOTA

	Retail Price	Dealer Invoice
Safety		
Front side airbags	$250	$215
Antiskid system	850	731
Includes traction control. NA w/limited-slip differential.		
Comfort & Convenience Features		
Leather Pkg., Limited	1070	856
Leather upholstery.		
8-way power driver seat, 4-cylinder, V6	390	312
Heated front seats, Limited	440	352
Requires Leather Pkg.		
Power sunroof	900	720
4-cylinder, V6 require alloy wheels.		
Heated power mirrors, 4-cylinder, V6	30	24
JBL AM/FM/cassette w/in-dash 6-disc CD changer, Limited	200	150
Appearance and Miscellaneous		
Running boards	625	405
Rear privacy glass, 4-cylinder, V6	310	248
Roof rack, 4-cylinder, V6	220	176
Special Purpose, Wheels and Tires		
Tow hitch and converter	290	232
Requires Towing Prep Pkg.		
Alloy wheels, 4-cylinder, V6	520	416

Postproduction options also available.

TOYOTA LAND CRUISER

All-wheel-drive full-size sport-utility vehicle
Base price: $52,595. Built in Japan.
Also consider: Chevrolet Tahoe and Suburban, Ford Expedition, GMC Yukon/Denali

FOR • Passenger and cargo room • Acceleration • Ride • Quietness • Build quality **AGAINST** • Fuel economy • Entry/exit • Navigation system controls

Toyota's luxury SUV gets standard instead of optional 3rd-row seating, plus rear-seat automatic climate control for 2002. Somewhat smaller but much costlier than Toyota's big-truck-based Sequoia SUV, Land Cruiser is the basis for the Lexus LX 470. They share a basic body, chassis, V8 engine, automatic transmission, all-wheel drive with low-range gearing, ABS, and standard traction control/antiskid system. An available navigation system displays maps

Prices are accurate at time of publication; subject to manufacturer's change.

TOYOTA

CG RECOMMENDED AUTO

Toyota Land Cruiser

stored on DVDs. It also has a 6-disc CD changer and can play movies on an in-dash screen with the transmission in Park. For '02, Land Cruiser gets standard 3rd-row seating, rear-seat climate control, and power swing-out rear side windows. This equipment previously comprised a $2265 option package. The 3rd-row seat can hold 3 passengers and is removable. Unlike the American-built Sequoia, Land Cruiser and LX 470 are made in Japan, do not offer a rear-wheel drive version, and lack side and curtain airbags.

RATINGS

	Base
ACCELERATION	5
FUEL ECONOMY	2
RIDE QUALITY	7
STEERING/HANDLING	3
QUIETNESS	8
INSTRUMENTS/CONTROLS	7
ROOM/COMFORT (FRONT)	8
ROOM/COMFORT (REAR)	8
CARGO ROOM	8
VALUE	5

Expensive, but these are true premium SUVs: highly capable off-road, quick and comfortable on, and built to a high standard. Land Cruiser is Recommended for better dollar value, though spending for the LX 470 brings Lexus's longer warranty and superior customer care.

TOTAL	61

Average total for full-size sport-utility vehicles: 50.9

ENGINES

	dohc V8
Size, liters/cu. in.	4.7/285

Specifications begin on page 551.

498   CONSUMER GUIDE®

TOYOTA

	dohc V8
Horsepower @ rpm	230 @ 4800
Torque (lb-ft) @ rpm	320 @ 3400
Availability	S
EPA city/highway mpg	
4-speed automatic	13/16

PRICES

Toyota Land Cruiser	Retail Price	Dealer Invoice
Base 4-door 4WD wagon	$52595	$46018
Destination charge	510	510

Prices are for vehicles distributed by Toyota Motor Sales, U.S.A., Inc. The dealer invoice and destination charge may be higher in areas served by independent distributors.

STANDARD EQUIPMENT

Base: 4.7-liter dohc V8 engine, 4-speed automatic transmission, all-wheel drive, 2-speed transfer case, locking rear differential, traction control, dual front airbags, antilock 4-wheel disc brakes, antiskid system, daytime running lights, front and rear air conditioning w/front and rear automatic climate controls, interior air filter, rear heater, power steering, tilt leather-wrapped steering wheel, cruise control, leather upholstery, heated front bucket seats w/power lumbar support, 10-way power driver seat, 8-way power passenger seat, center console, overhead console, cupholders, split folding seat second and third row seats, heated power mirrors, power windows, power door locks, remote keyless entry, JBL AM/FM/cassette w/in-dash 6-disc CD changer, power antenna, digital clock, tachometer, power sunroof, illuminated visor mirrors, variable intermittent wipers, automatic day/night rearview mirror, compass, outside temperature indicator, rear defogger, rear variable-intermittent wiper/washer, automatic headlights, theft-deterrent system, fog lights, rear privacy glass, front and rear tow hooks, skid plates, full-size spare tire, 275/70R16 tires, alloy wheels.

OPTIONAL EQUIPMENT
Major Packages

C7 Convenience Pkg. 1	1676	1057

Running boards, roof rack, rear wind deflector, cargo net, wheel locks.

Comfort & Convenience Features

Navigation system	3000	2550

Included DVD player.

Postproduction options also available.

Prices are accurate at time of publication; subject to manufacturer's change.

TOYOTA

2003 TOYOTA MATRIX

Toyota Matrix XR

Front- or all-wheel-drive subcompact car
Base price: NA. Built in Canada.
Also consider: Ford Focus wagon, Subaru Forester and Impreza, Volkswagen Jetta wagon

FOR • Fuel economy • Cargo room • Acceleration (XRS)
AGAINST • Engine noise • Ride (XRS)

Trying to lure younger buyers, Toyota creates a new crossover wagon based on its redesigned 2003 Corolla subcompact sedan. Matrix shares engines and transmissions with Corolla and the Toyota Celica, but offers both front-wheel drive and all-wheel drive. Due at midyear is the 2003 Pontiac Vibe, which uses the Matrix design, but has different styling. Matrix offers Standard, XR, and XRS models. All have a swing-up tailgate with separate opening window. AWD is optional on Standard and XR; XRS is front-drive only. All use a 4-cyl engine. Standard and XRS have 130 hp with front-drive and 123 with AWD. XRS has 180 hp. Standard and XR come with a 5-speed manual transmission, XRS with a 6-speed. Automatic transmission is optional, but is included with AWD. AWD versions retain the front-drive ride height and are not intended for serious off-road use.

Antilock 4-wheel disc brakes are standard on XRS and AWD models, optional on other versions. Front side airbags are optional on all; curtain side airbags are unavailable. Standard models feature 16-inch wheels and tires, tilt steering wheel, and an in-dash CD player. XR adds air conditioning, power locks and windows, keyless entry, power mirrors, and a 115-volt power outlet for laptops or other household appliances. XRS adds lower-profile 16-inch tires, cruise control, fog lamps, aero body package; 17-inch wheels are XRS

Specifications begin on page 551.

TOYOTA

options. A navigation system and in-dash 6-disc CD changer are optional on all models. Matrix prices were unavailable in time for this report.

RATINGS	Standard, man.	XR AWD, auto	XRS, man.
ACCELERATION	4	3	6
FUEL ECONOMY	8	7	7
RIDE QUALITY	4	4	3
STEERING/HANDLING	4	4	6
QUIETNESS	4	4	3
INSTRUMENTS/CONTROLS	5	5	5
ROOM/COMFORT (FRONT)	4	4	4
ROOM/COMFORT (REAR)	3	3	3
CARGO ROOM	7	7	7
VALUE	5	5	5

Matrix is an interesting alternative to both typical subcompact wagons and compact SUVs. Toyota reliability and utility are its strong points. Sadly, Standard and XR models have Milquetoast performance and XRS is probably too noisy, hard-riding, and high-revving for the mainstream buyer.

TOTAL	48	46	49

Average total for subcompact cars: 43.7

ENGINES

	dohc I4	dohc I4
Size, liters/cu. in.	1.8/110	1.8/110
Horsepower @ rpm	130 @ 6000	180 @ 7600
Torque (lb-ft) @ rpm	125 @ 4200	130 @ 6800
Availability	S[1]	S[2]

EPA city/highway mpg

5-speed manual	29/35	
6-speed manual		24/29
4-speed automatic	27/32[3]	24/30

1. Standard and XR; 123 hp and 125 lb-ft w/AWD. 2. XRS. 3. 25/30 mpg w/AWD.

2003 prices unavailable at time of publication.

TOYOTA MR2 SPYDER

Rear-wheel-drive sports car
2001 base price: $23,585. Built in Japan.
Also consider: BMW Z3 Series, Honda S2000, Mazda Miata

FOR • Acceleration • Brake performance • Steering/handling • Instruments/controls **AGAINST** • Cargo room • Entry/exit

Prices are accurate at time of publication; subject to manufacturer's change.

TOYOTA

Toyota MR2 Spyder

- Rear visibility (top up)

Toyota's midengine 2-seat convertible offers a unique new transmission for 2002. MR2 Spyder has a 1.8-liter 4-cyl engine and comes with a conventional 5-speed manual transmission. The new optional sequential manual transmission doesn't have a clutch pedal or a traditional "H" pattern shifter. It substitutes computer control for the clutch pedal; shifting requires only moving a floor-mounted lever forward for upshifts, back for downshifts. Gear changes can also be done via an optional pair of steering wheel mounted buttons. The sequential manual transmission has no automatic shifting capability, and no automatic transmission is offered on MR2. Standard are antilock 4-wheel disc brakes and a manual-folding top with heated glass rear window. Leather upholstery in tandem with a tan top (vs. black) is optional. Side airbags are unavailable.

RATINGS

	Base, man.
ACCELERATION	6
FUEL ECONOMY	7
RIDE QUALITY	4
STEERING/HANDLING	9
QUIETNESS	3
INSTRUMENTS/CONTROLS	7
ROOM/COMFORT (FRONT)	4
ROOM/COMFORT (REAR)	0
CARGO ROOM	1
VALUE	3

The nimble MR2 delivers genuine sports-car thrills, but compared to its natural rival, the Mazda Miata, it's more short-haul commuter or weekend toy. Miata is more practical day-to-day—and a better dollar value.

TOTAL	44

Average total for sports cars: 41.3

Specifications begin on page 551.

TOYOTA

ENGINES

	dohc I4
Size, liters/cu. in.	1.8/109
Horsepower @ rpm	138 @ 6400
Torque (lb-ft) @ rpm	125 @ 4400
Availability	S |//

EPA city/highway mpg
5-speed manual	25/30
SMT manual	25/30

2002 prices unavailable at time of publication.

PRICES

2001 Toyota MR2 Spyder	Retail Price	Dealer Invoice
Base 2-door convertible	$23585	$21344
Destination charge	455	455

Prices are for vehicles distributed by Toyota Motor Sales, U.S.A., Inc. The dealer invoice and destination charge may be higher in areas served by independent distributors.

STANDARD EQUIPMENT

Base: 1.8-liter dohc 4-cylinder engine, 5-speed manual transmission, dual front airbags, antilock 4-wheel disc brakes, daytime running lights, air conditioning, power steering, tilt leather-wrapped steering wheel, cruise control, cloth upholstery, bucket seats, center console, cupholders, power mirrors, power windows, power door locks, AM/FM/cassette/CD player, digital clock, tachometer, rear defogger, variable intermittent wipers, map lights, 185/55R15 front tires, 205/50R15 rear tires, alloy wheels.

OPTIONAL EQUIPMENT
Major Packages

Leather Pkg.	620	496
Leather upholstery, tan-colored convertible top.		

Comfort & Convenience Features

Acculaser carbon fiber dashboard	369	199

TOYOTA PRIUS

Front-wheel-drive subcompact car
Base price: $19,995. Built in Japan.
Also consider: Ford Focus, Honda Civic, Volkswagen Jetta

FOR • Fuel economy • Maneuverability **AGAINST** • Rear visibility

Prices are accurate at time of publication; subject to manufacturer's change.
CONSUMER GUIDE®

TOYOTA

Toyota Prius

Toyota's hybrid-power subcompact now offers optional front side airbags, a navigation system, and cruise control. Prius seats five and is powered by both a 4-cyl gasoline engine and an electric motor. The two automatically work in tandem or separately, depending on power needs. Standard are a continuously variable automatic transmission, ABS, and air conditioning. Prius's batteries are in effect kept charged by the gas engine and neither it nor the similar Honda Insight needs plug-in charging. However, Insight is a smaller, 2-seat hatchback with a smaller gas engine that teams with manual transmission or CVT automatic. Prius's warranty includes 8-year/100,000 mi. powertrain coverage and roadside assistance. Prius and Insight are both built in limited quantities.

RATINGS

	Base
ACCELERATION	2
FUEL ECONOMY	9
RIDE QUALITY	5
STEERING/HANDLING	4
QUIETNESS	4
INSTRUMENTS/CONTROLS	3
ROOM/COMFORT (FRONT)	5
ROOM/COMFORT (REAR)	5
CARGO ROOM	2
VALUE	4

Prius, like Insight, is basically a high-tech alternative to a traditional economy car and rather costly as such. Toyota's own Echo delivers similarly pleasant fuel mileage at lower initial cost, and Volkswagen's Jetta/Golf diesel returned over 40 mpg in our tests. Still, Prius is roomier, more-pleasant daily transport than Insight, with 4-dr convenience to boot.

TOTAL	43

Average total for subcompact cars: 43.7

Specifications begin on page 551.

TOYOTA

ENGINES

	dohc I4/electric
Size, liters/cu. in.	1.5/91
Horsepower @ rpm	70 @ 4500
Torque (lb-ft) @ rpm	82 @ 4200
Availability	S[1]

EPA city/highway mpg
CVT automatic 52/45

1. Gas engine; electric motor has 44 hp @ 1040 rpm and 258 lb-ft @ 0-400 rpm.

PRICES

Toyota Prius	Retail Price	Dealer Invoice
Base 4-door sedan	$19995	$18793
Destination charge	485	485

Prices are for vehicles distributed by Toyota Motor Sales, U.S.A., Inc. The dealer invoice and destination charge may be higher in areas served by independent distributors.

STANDARD EQUIPMENT

Base: 1.5-liter dohc 4-cylinder engine, electric drive motor, continuously-variable transmission, dual front airbags, antilock brakes, daytime running lights, emergency inside trunk release, air conditioning w/automatic climate control, power steering, tilt steering wheel, cloth upholstery, front bucket seats, center console, cupholders, heated power mirrors, power windows, power door locks, remote keyless entry, AM/FM/cassette, variable intermittent wipers, rear defogger, visor mirrors, theft-deterrent system, rear spoiler, 175/65R14 tires, alloy wheels.

OPTIONAL EQUIPMENT

Safety
Front side airbags	250	215

Comfort & Convenience Features
Cruise control	250	200
Navigation system	1900	1615
In-dash 6-disc CD changer	589	414

Postproduction options also available.

TOYOTA RAV4

Front- or all-wheel-drive compact sport-utility vehicle
Base price range: $16,525-$18,975. Built in Japan.

Prices are accurate at time of publication; subject to manufacturer's change.

TOYOTA

Toyota RAV4

Also consider: Ford Escape, Honda CR-V, Subaru Forester

FOR • Maneuverability • Instruments/controls • Visibility • Build quality **AGAINST** • Acceleration • Engine noise • Rear-seat room

Toyota's smallest SUV has a 2.0-liter 4-cyl engine with manual or optional automatic transmission. RAV4 is offered with front-wheel drive, or all-wheel drive without low range gearing. Side airbags aren't available, but ABS is, as are optional leather upholstery, alloy wheels, and sunroof. The Upgrade L Package option includes air conditioning, cruise control, and power windows/locks/mirrors. It also includes a hard cover for the outside spare tire and color keyed body trim.

RATINGS	Base AWD, man.	Base AWD, auto.
ACCELERATION	4	4
FUEL ECONOMY	6	6
RIDE QUALITY	5	5
STEERING/HANDLING	4	5
QUIETNESS	4	4
INSTRUMENTS/CONTROLS	7	7
ROOM/COMFORT (FRONT)	4	4
ROOM/COMFORT (REAR)	3	3
CARGO ROOM	7	7

Specifications begin on page 551.

TOYOTA

	Base AWD, man.	Base AWD, auto.
VALUE	5	6

RAV4 is more suited to suburban errand-running than long-distance people-hauling or off-roading. Nonetheless, it's an attractive compact SUV. Many rivals offer more space and stronger performance, but only Honda matches Toyota's reputation for quality, durability, and high resale value. So don't buy without also shopping the redesigned CR-V.

TOTAL	49	51

Average total for compact sport-utility vehicles: 44.4

ENGINES

	dohc I4
Size, liters/cu. in.	2.0/122
Horsepower @ rpm	148 @ 6000
Torque (lb-ft) @ rpm	142 @ 4000
Availability	S

EPA city/highway mpg

5-speed manual	22/27[1]
4-speed automatic	23/27[2]

1. 25/31 w/2WD. 2. 24/29 w/2WD.

PRICES

Toyota RAV4

	Retail Price	Dealer Invoice
2WD Base 4-door wagon, manual	$16525	$15285
2WD Base 4-door wagon, automatic	17575	16255
AWD Base 4-door wagon, manual	17925	16311
AWD Base 4-door wagon, automatic	18975	17265
Destination charge	510	510

Prices are for vehicles distributed by Toyota Motor Sales, U.S.A., Inc. The dealer invoice and destination charge may be higher in areas served by independent distributors.

STANDARD EQUIPMENT

Base: 2.0-liter dohc 4-cylinder engine, 5-speed manual or 4-speed automatic transmission, dual front airbags, power steering, tilt steering wheel, cloth upholstery, front bucket seats w/height adjustable driver seat, center console, cupholders, split folding rear seat, AM/FM/cassette, digital clock, tachometer, intermittent wipers, visor mirrors, map lights, rear defogger, intermittent rear wiper, dual outside mirrors, rear-mounted full-size spare tire, 215/70R16 tires. **AWD** adds: all-wheel drive, skid plates.

Prices are accurate at time of publication; subject to manufacturer's change.

TOYOTA

	Retail Price	Dealer Invoice
OPTIONAL EQUIPMENT
Major Packages
Quick Order Pkg. $2380 $1881
Air conditioning, cruise control, power mirrors, power windows and door locks, AM/FM/cassette/CD player, floormats.
Upgrade L Pkg. 3100 2457
Quick Order Pkg. plus heated power mirrors, tonneau cover, rear privacy glass, fog lights, color-keyed bumpers and bodyside moldings, hard spare tire cover. Requires alloy wheels AW or AY.
Leather Pkg. 840 672
Leather upholstery, leather-wrapped steering wheel. Requires Upgrade L Pkg.
Power Pkg. 760 608
Power windows and door locks.

Powertrain
Limited-slip differential, AWD 390 322
Requires Quick Order Pkg. or Upgrade L Pkg.

Safety
Antilock brakes 300 258

Comfort & Convenience Features
Air conditioning 985 788
Power sunroof 900 720
Requires Quick Order Pkg. or Upgrade L Pkg.
Remote keyless entry 230 184
Requires Power Pkg. or pkg. including power door locks.
CD player 275 194
In-dash 6-disc CD changer 589 414
NA w/Quick Order Pkg. or Upgrade Pkg. L.

Appearance and Miscellaneous
Roof rack 220 176
Rear spoiler 200 160
Requires Upgrade L Pkg.
Rear privacy glass 310 248
Special paint 220 187
Requires Upgrade L Pkg.

Special Purpose, Wheels and Tires
Alloy wheels AW 400 346
Alloy wheels AL/AY, AWD 895 819
Includes 235/60R16 mud/snow tires, matching spare wheel, painted overfenders. Requires Quick Order Pkg.

Postproduction options also available.

Specifications begin on page 551.

TOYOTA

TOYOTA SEQUOIA

Toyota Sequoia

Rear- or 4-wheel-drive full-size sport-utility vehicle
Base price range: $31,265-$42,725. Built in USA.
Also consider: Chevrolet Tahoe and Suburban, Ford Expedition, GMC Yukon/Denali

FOR • Automatic transmission performance • Build quality • Passenger and cargo room • Instruments/controls **AGAINST** • Fuel economy • Brake-pedal feel • Maneuverability

Toyota's biggest SUV is based on the company's full-size Tundra pickup truck; both are assembled in Indiana. With standard seating for eight, Sequoia is larger than Toyota's Japanese-built Land Cruiser and close in size to Ford's Expedition. SR5 and uplevel Limited models continue for 2002, both with Tundra's V8 and automatic transmission. Antilock 4-wheel disc brakes, 16-inch wheels, and an antiskid system are standard. Sequoia offers rear-wheel drive or 4WD that must be disengaged on dry pavement but includes low-range gearing. Front torso side airbags and curtain side airbags are optional as a package. Remote keyless entry and fog lights are new SR5 options for 2002.

RATINGS	SR5 2WD	Limited 4WD
ACCELERATION	4	4
FUEL ECONOMY	3	2
RIDE QUALITY	3	3
STEERING/HANDLING	2	2
QUIETNESS	6	6
INSTRUMENTS/CONTROLS	7	7
ROOM/COMFORT (FRONT)	7	7
ROOM/COMFORT (REAR)	9	9

Prices are accurate at time of publication; subject to manufacturer's change.

TOYOTA

	SR5 2WD	Limited 4WD
CARGO ROOM	9	9
VALUE	3	3

Sequoia exhibits all the usual big-SUV vices, but is nonetheless a strong competitor that merits serious consideration as a refined, well-equipped Toyota. Still, rivals match it in many ways while typically towing more than Sequoia's 6500-lb maximum. And they carry bigger price discounts, too.

TOTAL	53	52

Average total for full-size sport-utility vehicles: 50.9

ENGINES

	dohc V8
Size, liters/cu. in.	4.7/285
Horsepower @ rpm	240 @ 4800
Torque (lb-ft) @ rpm	315 @ 3400
Availability	S

EPA city/highway mpg

4-speed automatic	14/17[1]

1. 14/18 w/2WD.

PRICES

Toyota Sequoia	Retail Price	Dealer Invoice
2WD SR5 4-door wagon	$31265	$27824
4WD SR5 4-door wagon	34795	30965
2WD Limited 4-door wagon	39405	35070
4WD Limited 4-door wagon	42725	37811
Destination charge	510	510

Prices are for vehicles distributed by Toyota Motor Sales, U.S.A., Inc. The dealer invoice and destination charge may be higher in areas served by independent distributors.

STANDARD EQUIPMENT

SR5: 4.7-liter dohc V8 engine, 4-speed automatic transmission, traction control, dual front airbags, antilock 4-wheel disc brakes, antiskid system, front air conditioning w/automatic climate control, power steering, tilt steering wheel, cruise control, cloth upholstery, front captain chairs, center console, cupholders, second- and third-row split-folding bench seats, power mirrors, power windows, power door locks, AM/FM/cassette/CD player, digital clock, tachometer, overhead console, variable intermittent wipers, rear defogger, rear wiper/washer, map lights, visor mirrors, remote fuel door release, automatic-off headlights, theft-deterrent system, rear privacy glass, 245/70R16 tires. **4WD** adds: 4-wheel drive, 2-speed transfer case,

Specifications begin on page 551.

TOYOTA

skid plates, 265/70R16 tires.

Limited adds: leather upholstery, heated front seats, 8-way power driver seat, front and rear automatic climate controls, rear air conditioning, heated mirrors w/power fold-in, remote keyless entry, compass, outside temperature indicator, trip computer, universal garage door opener, illuminated visor mirrors, JBL sound system, automatic headlights, running boards, roof rack, fog lights, towing hitch, wiring harness, 265/70R16 tires, alloy wheels. **4WD** adds: 4-wheel drive, 2-speed transfer case, skid plates.

OPTIONAL EQUIPMENT

	Retail Price	Dealer Invoice
Major Packages		
Preferred Pkg., SR5	$3180	$2508
Leather upholstery, power front seats, JBL AM/FM/cassette w/6-disc CD changer.		
Convenience Pkg., SR5	255	204
Heated power mirrors, universal garage door opener, trip computer, compass, outside temperature indicator.		
Alloy Wheel Pkg., 2WD SR5	1535	1228
4WD SR5	1325	1060
Running boards, overfenders (2WD), additional rear privacy glass, tow hitch, 265/70R16 tires (2WD), alloy wheels.		
Safety		
Front side-impact airbags and curtain airbags	500	430
Comfort & Convenience Features		
Rear air conditioning w/front and rear automatic climate controls, SR5	570	456
Remote keyless entry, SR5	245	196
Power sunroof	1000	800
Power front seats, SR5	745	596
JBL sound system, SR5	515	386
AM/FM/cassette w/in-dash 6-disc CD changer, Limited	200	150
Appearance and Miscellaneous		
Fog lights, SR5	110	88
Roof rack, SR5	220	176
Rear spoiler, Limited	200	160
Special Purpose, Wheels and Tires		
Tow hitch, SR5	380	304

Postproduction options also available.

Prices are accurate at time of publication; subject to manufacturer's change.

TOYOTA

TOYOTA SIENNA

Toyota Sienna

Front-wheel-drive minivan
Base price range: $23,905-$28,012. Built in USA.
Also consider: Chevrolet Venture, Dodge Caravan, Honda Odyssey

FOR • Passenger and cargo room • Build quality • Exterior finish **AGAINST** • Fuel economy • Radio placement

Toyota's minivan gets a new option package for 2002 that includes an upgraded CD audio system and a host of interior amenities. Sienna is built in Kentucky and is based on Toyota's Camry sedan platform. It's available in a single body length with dual sliding side doors. Midline LE and top-line XLE models offer a power right-side sliding door, and the XLE offers dual power doors. Sienna's 3rd-row seat is split 50/50 and slides forward 6 inches for extra rear storage. The only engine is a 3.0-liter V6. Standard are automatic transmission, ABS, and a tire-pressure monitor. Front side-airbags and an antiskid system are optional, as is a rear-seat video entertainment system. The new Symphony Package adds to the LE a JBL 8-speaker AM/FM/cassette/CD audio system, plus leather-wrapped steering wheel, power driver seat, front- and 2nd-row captains chairs, and body-color exterior cladding. Also included are "Symphony" logo floor mats, cargo mat, and exterior badging.

RATINGS	CE/LE	XLE
ACCELERATION	5	5
FUEL ECONOMY	5	5
RIDE QUALITY	6	6
STEERING/HANDLING	4	4
QUIETNESS	5	5

Specifications begin on page 551.

TOYOTA

	CE/LE	XLE
INSTRUMENTS/CONTROLS	7	7
ROOM/COMFORT (FRONT)	7	7
ROOM/COMFORT (REAR)	7	8
CARGO ROOM	9	9
VALUE	8	6

Sienna is very capable and quite well-suited for family hauling duties. Delivered prices balloon fast with options, but Toyota's typically high resale values and outstanding reliability/durability record can't be ignored.

TOTAL	63	62

Average total for minivans: 56.0

EXTENDED-USE TEST UPDATE

Our extended-use Sienna LE was a 2000 model and not different in any significant way from the '02 model. It was mechanically trouble-free over its 12-month test, but suffered an instrument-panel rattle traced to an insulation panel omitted during manufacture. It was installed under warranty by a dealer service department. Another test Sienna suffered an irritating rattle from the 2nd-row seating area.

ENGINES

	dohc V6
Size, liters/cu. in.	3.0/183
Horsepower @ rpm	210 @ 5800
Torque (lb-ft) @ rpm	220 @ 4400
Availability	S

EPA city/highway mpg

4-speed automatic	19/24

PRICES

Toyota Sienna

	Retail Price	Dealer Invoice
CE 4-door van	$23905	$21514
LE 4-door van	25755	22922
XLE 4-door van	28012	24930
Destination charge	510	510

Prices are for vehicles distributed by Toyota Motor Sales, U.S.A., Inc. The dealer invoice and destination charge may be higher in areas served by independent distributors.

Prices are accurate at time of publication; subject to manufacturer's change.

CONSUMER GUIDE®

TOYOTA
STANDARD EQUIPMENT

CE: 3.0-liter dohc V6 engine, 4-speed automatic transmission, dual front airbags, antilock brakes, tire pressure monitor, daytime running lights, front and rear air conditioning w/rear controls, power steering, tilt steering wheel w/radio controls, cloth upholstery, front captain chairs, cupholders, overhead console, 2-passenger second-row seat, 3-passenger split-folding third row seat, AM/FM/cassette/CD player, digital clock, visor mirrors, variable intermittent wipers, rear defogger, rear intermittent wiper/washer, automatic-off headlights, 205/70R15 tires, wheel covers.

LE adds: power mirrors, power windows, power door locks, cruise control, tachometer, illuminated visor mirrors, map lights, rear privacy glass, full-size spare tire.

XLE adds: power driver seat, automatic climate control, heated power mirrors, JBL sound system, quad captain's chairs, leather-wrapped steering wheel, remote keyless entry, universal garage door opener, automatic headlights, floormats, roof rack, theft-deterrent system, fog lights, 215/65R15 tires, alloy wheels.

OPTIONAL EQUIPMENT
Major Packages

	Retail Price	Dealer Invoice
Extra Value Pkg., CE	$757	$681

Cruise control, heated power mirrors, power windows and door locks, remote keyless entry, floormats, rear privacy glass, roof rack, full-size spare tire.

Extra Value Pkg., LE	312	281

Heated power mirrors, remote keyless entry, quad captain chairs, floormats, cargo mat, roof rack.

Symphony Pkg., LE	1077	969

Extra Value Pkg. plus JBL sound system, leather-wrapped steering wheel, 6-way power driver seat, unique cloth upholstery, quad captain chairs, universal garage door opener, unique floormats and cargo mat, color-keyed mirrors and bumpers, bodyside cladding, 215/65R15 tires, alloy wheels.

Upgrade Pkg. 1, XLE	1690	1342

Leather upholstery, leather-wrapped steering wheel, in-dash 6-disc CD changer.

Luxury Pkg., XLE	3385	2698

Upgrade Pkg. 1 plus dual power rear doors, power sunroof.

Towing Pkg.	160	128

CE includes rear air conditioning controls. CE requires Extra Value Pkg.

Safety

Front side airbags	250	215

TOYOTA

	Retail Price	Dealer Invoice
Antiskid system	$550	$440

Comfort & Convenience Features
Video Entertainment System	1795	1495
JBL sound system, LE	435	326
Power passenger-side rear door, LE, XLE	395	316
LE requires Extra Value Pkg. or Symphony Pkg.		
Power dual sliding rear doors, XLE	795	636
Power sunroof, XLE	900	720
Heated front seats, XLE	440	352
Requires Luxury Pkg. or Upgrade Pkg. 1.		
Automatic day/night rearview mirror	280	190

Appearance and Miscellaneous
Running Boards, CE, LE	520	335
XLE	650	420
Split spoke alloy wheels, CE, LE	592	440
Alloy wheels, LE	490	392
Includes 215/65R15 tires.		

Postproduction options also available.

TOYOTA SOLARA

Toyota Solara 2-door convertible

Front-wheel-drive midsize car
Base price range: $19,365-$30,525. Built in Canada.
Also consider: Acura CL, BMW 3-Series, Chrysler Sebring

FOR • Acceleration (V6) • Ride (Coupe) • Quietness (Coupe) • Build quality (Coupe) **AGAINST** • Rear visibility • Rear-

Prices are accurate at time of publication; subject to manufacturer's change.

TOYOTA

seat entry/exit

Toyota's midsize coupe and convertible gain a new engine but retain the foundation of the 1997-2001 Camry sedan. Solara is an offshoot of the far-better-selling Camry, which for 2002 is redesigned on a new, slightly larger platform. Solara styling is freshened inside and out for '02, and 4-cyl models switch to the new Camry 2.4-liter engine, which has 21 hp more than the 2.2 it replaces. V6 Solaras retain a 200-hp 3.0. Coupes are available with manual or automatic transmission regardless of engine; all convertibles have automatic. Convertibles come with a power folding top with heated glass rear window. Front side airbags are a Solara option. Antilock 4-wheel disc brakes and leather upholstery are among features standard on the uplevel Solara SLE and optional on the base SE model.

RATINGS	Solara SE cpe, 4 cyl auto.	Solara SLE conv
ACCELERATION	5	6
FUEL ECONOMY	6	5
RIDE QUALITY	7	6
STEERING/HANDLING	6	6
QUIETNESS	7	5
INSTRUMENTS/CONTROLS	10	10
ROOM/COMFORT (FRONT)	7	7
ROOM/COMFORT (REAR)	3	3
CARGO ROOM	3	2
VALUE	8	6

Solara is polished in most every control and movement. It favors ride comfort over sporty road manners, though V6 versions have good acceleration. The 2-dr body style complicates rear-seat entry/exit, but the back seat itself is no penalty box. The convertible suffers unexpectedly pronounced top-down body flex with the roof lowered, making the solid coupe the more solid value.

TOTAL	62	56

Average total for midsize cars: 57.0

ENGINES	dohc I4	dohc V6
Size, liters/cu. in.	2.4/144	3.0/183
Horsepower @ rpm	157 @ 5600	198 @ 5300
Torque (lb-ft) @ rpm	162 @ 4000	212 @ 4400
Availability	S[1]	S[2]
EPA city/highway mpg		
5-speed manual	24/33	20/27
4-speed automatic	23/32	20/27

1. 4-cyl models. 2. V6 models.

Specifications begin on page 551.

TOYOTA

PRICES

Toyota Solara	Retail Price	Dealer Invoice
SE 4-cylinder 2-door coupe, manual	$19365	$17427
SE 4-cylinder 2-door coupe, automatic	20165	18147
SE 4-cylinder 2-door convertible, automatic	25495	22943
SE V6 2-door coupe, manual	21685	19514
SE V6 2-door coupe, automatic	22485	20236
SE V6 2-door convertible, automatic	28045	25239
SLE V6 2-door coupe, automatic	24675	22294
SLE V6 2-door convertible, automatic	30525	27472
Destination charge	485	485

Prices are for vehicles distributed by Toyota Motor Sales, U.S.A., Inc. The dealer invoice and destination charge may be higher in areas served by independent distributors.

STANDARD EQUIPMENT

SE 4-cylinder: 2.4-liter dohc 4-cylinder engine, 5-speed manual or 4-speed automatic transmission, dual front airbags, daytime running lights, emergency inside trunk release, air conditioning, interior air filter, variable-assist power steering, tilt steering wheel, cruise control, cloth upholstery, front bucket seats, height-adjustable driver seat, center console, cupholders, split folding rear seat, power mirrors, power windows, power door locks, AM/FM/cassette/CD player, digital clock, tachometer, overhead console, illuminated visor mirrors, map lights, variable intermittent wipers, rear defogger, remote fuel door and decklid release, power convertible top (convertible), automatic headlights, fog lights, rear spoiler (convertible), full-size spare tire, 205/65R15 tires, wheel covers.

SE V6 adds: 3.0-liter dohc V6 engine, antilock 4-wheel disc brakes.

SLE adds: 4-speed automatic transmission, leather upholstery, 8-way power driver seat, leather-wrapped steering wheel, automatic climate control, heated power mirrors, remote keyless entry, JBL sound system, automatic day/night rearview mirror, universal garage door opener, outside temperature indicator, theft-deterrent system, rear spoiler, 205/60R16 tires, alloy wheels.

OPTIONAL EQUIPMENT
Major Packages

Upgrade Pkg. 1, SE 4-cyl	1192	1073
Manufacturer's Discount Price	*292*	*258*
SE 4-cyl convertible	935	732
SE V6 coupe	1272	1145

Prices are accurate at time of publication; subject to manufacturer's change.

TOYOTA

	Retail Price	Dealer Invoice
Manufacturer's Discount Price	$272	$245

Remote keyless entry, upgraded sound system, floormats, mudguards, alloy wheels.

Upgrade Pkg. 2, SE V6 convertible	1187	901

Remote keyless entry, 8-way power driver seat, upgraded sound system, floormats, 205/60R16 tires, alloy wheels.

VH Sport Trim Pkg., SE 4-cyl coupe	1627	1467
Manufacturer's Discount Price	527	474
SE V6 coupe	1707	1536
Manufacturer's Discount Price	507	456

Remote keyless entry, JBL sound system, mudguards, rear spoiler, alloy wheels.

VL Sport Trim Pkg.,

SE V6 coupe manual	3277	2622
Manufacturer's Discount Price	2077	1652
SE V6 coupe automatic	3337	2670
Manufacturer's Discount Price	2137	1777

VH Sport Trim Pkg. plus leather upholstery, 8-way power driver seat, leather-wrapped steering wheel.

Appearance Pkg.,

SE coupe manual	110	88
SE coupe automatic	170	136

Leather-wrapped steering wheel, black pearl emblems.

Powertrain

Traction control, SLE	300	240

Safety

Antilock brakes, SE 4-cyl	300	258
Front side airbags	250	215

Comfort & Convenience Features

Power sunroof, coupe	900	720

SE requires power driver seat.

JBL AM/FM/cassette w/in-dash
6-disc CD changer, SLE	200	150

Heated front seats,
SE V6 coupe, SLE	315	252

SE requires VL Sport Trim.

Power driver seat, SE	390	312

Appearance and Miscellaneous

Rear spoiler,
SE coupe	435	348

Postproduction options also available.

Specifications begin on page 551.

VOLKSWAGEN

VOLKSWAGEN CABRIO

Volkswagen Cabrio GLX

Front-wheel-drive sporty coupe

2001 base price range: $19,600-$23,175. Built in Mexico.

Also consider: Chrysler Sebring, Ford Mustang, Mitsubishi Eclipse

FOR • Steering/handling **AGAINST** • Cargo room • Rear visibility • Rear-seat entry/exit

Based on VW's previous Jetta/Golf design, this 4-seat convertible gets only minor changes for 2002. Cabrio comes with a 2.0-liter 4-cyl engine, antilock 4-wheel disc brakes, front side airbags, air conditioning, and alarm. The convertible top has a glass rear window with electric defroster; the GLX-model's roof is powered. For '02, the self-dimming rearview mirror gains an on/off switch, the trunk gets an emergency escape release, and silver Cabrios are available with a gray instead of a white top. VW's bumper-to-bumper warranty is now 4 years/50,000 mi. instead of 2/24,000, and the powertrain warranty is 5/60,000 instead of 10/100,000. Cabrio will continue on the 1994-1998 Jetta/Golf platform until at least 2003.

RATINGS

	GL/GLS/GLX, auto.
ACCELERATION	3
FUEL ECONOMY	7
RIDE QUALITY	5
STEERING/HANDLING	6
QUIETNESS	4
INSTRUMENTS/CONTROLS	5
ROOM/COMFORT (FRONT)	5

Prices are accurate at time of publication; subject to manufacturer's change.

VOLKSWAGEN

	GL/GLS/GLX, auto.
ROOM/COMFORT (REAR)	3
CARGO ROOM	1
VALUE	3

Cabrio is fuel efficient, fun-to-drive, well-equipped, and well-made. It is not inexpensive, but it is one of the few moderately priced convertibles with four usable seats. And resale values are strong.

TOTAL	**42**

Average total for sporty coupes: 43.4

ENGINES

	ohc I4
Size, liters/cu. in.	2.0/121
Horsepower @ rpm	115 @ 5400
Torque (lb-ft) @ rpm	122 @ 3200
Availability	S
EPA city/highway mpg	
5-speed manual	24/31
4-speed automatic	23/29

2002 prices unavailable at time of publication.

PRICES

2001 Volkswagen Cabrio	Retail Price	Dealer Invoice
GL 2-door convertible, manual	$19600	$17974
GL 2-door convertible, automatic	20475	18811
GLS 2-door convertible, manual	20600	18856
GLS 2-door convertible, automatic	21475	19720
GLX 2-door convertible, manual	22300	20400
GLX 2-door convertible, automatic	23175	21264
Destination charge	550	550

STANDARD EQUIPMENT

GL: 2.0-liter 4-cylinder engine, 5-speed manual or 4-speed automatic transmission, dual front airbags, front side airbags, antilock 4-wheel disc brakes, integral roll bar, daytime running lights, emergency inside trunk release, air conditioning, interior air filter, power steering, tilt leather-wrapped steering wheel, cloth upholstery, front bucket seats w/height adjustment, center console, cupholders, folding rear seat, heated manual mirrors, power door locks, remote keyless entry, AM/FM/cassette w/CD changer controls, digital clock, tachometer, rear defogger, intermittent wipers, heated washer nozzles, illuminated visor mirrors, remote decklid release, floormats, manual folding top, theft-deterrent system, 195/60HR14 tires, wheel covers.

Specifications begin on page 551.

VOLKSWAGEN

GLS adds: cruise control, heated power mirrors, power windows.
GLX adds: leather upholstery, heated front seats, power folding top, fog lights, alloy wheels.

OPTIONAL EQUIPMENT

	Retail Price	Dealer Invoice
California and Northeast emissions	$100	$99

Required on cars purchased in Calif., N.H., N.Y., Mass., Conn., R.I., Pa., N.J., Del., Md., Va., Vt., and Washington, D.C.

VOLKSWAGEN EUROVAN

Volkswagen EuroVan

Front-wheel-drive minivan
2001 base price range: $26,200-$27,700. Built in Germany.
Also consider: Chrysler Town & Country, Dodge Caravan, Honda Odyssey, Toyota Sienna

FOR • Passenger and cargo room • Visibility   **AGAINST** • Control layout • Steering/handling • Noise

After gaining an antiskid system and 61 hp in mid 2001—while also cutting $5000 from its price—Volkswagen's slow-selling minivan returns virtually unchanged for 2002. EuroVan offers people-mover GLS and recreation-oriented MV (MultiVan) models, both with a 201-hp V6 and automatic transmission. A long-wheelbase Camper conversion with stove, sink, furnace, and refrigerator can be special-ordered through dealers. Antilock 4-wheel disc brakes are standard, but side airbags aren't offered. EuroVan comes only with a manual right-side sliding door; there's no left-side door or power-door option. GLS and MV seat seven with a folding 3rd-row bench and twin 2nd-row seats (rear facing on MV). Optional for MV is a "pop-top" roof incorporating a 2-person bed. For 2002, the MV joins the GLS in offering green, silver, and black exterior colors. Also, VW's bumper-to-bumper warranty is now 4 years/50,000 mi. instead of 2/24,000, and the powertrain warranty is 5/60,000 instead of 10/100,000.

Prices are accurate at time of publication; subject to manufacturer's change.

VOLKSWAGEN

RATINGS

	GLS	MV
ACCELERATION	3	3
FUEL ECONOMY	5	5
RIDE QUALITY	4	4
STEERING/HANDLING	3	3
QUIETNESS	3	3
INSTRUMENTS/CONTROLS	3	3
ROOM/COMFORT (FRONT)	4	4
ROOM/COMFORT (REAR)	8	7
CARGO ROOM	8	10
VALUE	2	2

It's quirky, noisy, and lacks such basic features as a left-side sliding door. On the upside, the stubbornly unorthodox EuroVan is roomy and is reasonably priced considering its level of standard equipment.

TOTAL	43	44

Average total for minivans: 56.0

ENGINES

	dohc V6
Size, liters/cu. in.	2.8/170
Horsepower @ rpm	201 @ 4500
Torque (lb-ft) @ rpm	181 @ 2500
Availability	S

EPA city/highway mpg
4-speed automatic 17/20

2002 prices unavailable at time of publication.

PRICES

2001 Volkswagen EuroVan	Retail Price	Dealer Invoice
GLS 3-door van	$26200	$23810
MV 3-door van	27700	25165
Destination charge	615	615

Camper prices and equipment not available at time of publication.

STANDARD EQUIPMENT

GLS: 2.8-liter V6 engine, 4-speed automatic transmission, traction control, dual front airbags, antilock 4-wheel disc brakes, antiskid system, daytime running lights, front and rear air conditioning w/dual-zone automatic climate control, power steering, cruise control, cloth upholstery, front bucket seats, two center-row bucket seats, rear 3-passenger folding bench seat, center console, cupholders, heated power mirrors, power windows, power door locks, remote keyless entry, AM/FM/cassette, digital clock, tachome-

Specifications begin on page 551.

VOLKSWAGEN

ter, illuminated visor mirrors, variable intermittent wipers, rear defogger, intermittent rear wiper/washer, cargo cover, fog lights, rear privacy glass, full-size spare tire, 225/60HR16 tires, alloy wheels.

MV adds: two center-row rear facing bucket seats, 3-passenger rear bench/bed, side fold-up table. *Deletes:* cargo cover.

OPTIONAL EQUIPMENT
Major Packages

	Retail Price	Dealer Invoice
Weekender Pkg., MV	$3235	$2856

Pop-up roof, 2-person bed, fixed driver-side rear facing seat, refrigerator, auxiliary battery, heavy-duty alternator, sliding window curtains, screen for rear hatch. Deletes dual-zone automatic climate control, rear air conditioning.

Comfort & Convenience Features

Power sunroof	1000	883
Heated front seats	400	353

VOLKSWAGEN JETTA/GOLF

Volkswagen Jetta 1.8T 4-door sedan

Front-wheel-drive subcompact car
Base price range: $15,050-$26,375. Built in Mexico.
Also consider: Ford Focus, Honda Civic, Mazda Protege

FOR • Cargo room (Golf) • Acceleration (V6) • Build quality • Fuel economy (exc. V6) • Ride (base suspension) • Visibility • Interior materials **AGAINST** • Acceleration (2.0 4-cyl automatic) • Automatic transmission performance • Rear-seat entry/exit (Golf 2dr)

More power and two new transmissions highlight changes to Volkswagen's subcompact line for 2002. Jetta comes as a 4-dr sedan and wagon. Golf shares Jetta's platform, interior, and powertrains, and comes as a 2-dr and 4-dr hatchback. Base engine for

Prices are accurate at time of publication; subject to manufacturer's change.

VOLKSWAGEN

both is a 2.0-liter 4 cyl. The 1.8T models and the Golf GTI have a turbo 4 cyl with 180 hp vs. 150 last year. The Golf GTI VR6 and Jetta GLS VR6 and GLX have a V6. They enter the '02 model year with 174 hp, but are scheduled to get 201 at midyear. TDI Golfs and Jettas use a 1.9-liter 4-cyl turbodiesel. All are available with manual or automatic transmission. The automatic in turbo 4-cyl gas models is a new 5 speed with manual shift gate vs. a 4 speed in other models. The 201-hp V6 will be available with a new 6-speed manual, replacing a 5 speed. All have standard antilock 4-wheel disc brakes, front torso side airbags, and curtain side airbags. All but GL models have traction control. For '02, the Golf GL hatchback is available with four doors as well as two. VW cuts the base price of the 4-cyl Golf GTI $515 and the GTI VR6 $2700 by making some equipment optional. An in-dash cassette/CD player is now standard on all but GL models. VW's bumper-to-bumper warranty is now 4 years/50,000 mi. vs. 2/24,000, and the powertrain warranty is 5/60,000 vs. 10/100,000.

RATINGS	Golf GLS TDI, man.	Golf GTI VR6	Jetta GL, man.	Jetta 1.8T w/Sport Lux. Pkg., auto.
ACCELERATION	3	6	3	5
FUEL ECONOMY	9	6	7	7
RIDE QUALITY	6	4	6	4
STEERING/HANDLING	6	8	6	8
QUIETNESS	5	5	6	5
INSTRUMENTS/CONTROLS	7	7	7	7
ROOM/COMFORT (FRONT)	6	6	6	6
ROOM/COMFORT (REAR)	2	2	2	2
CARGO ROOM	6	6	3	3
VALUE	6	5	7	6

These VWs are rather pricey for subcompacts, so they're not quite Best Buys. But any Jetta or Golf is strongly recommended for its suave Euro personality, safety features, build quality, and adroit design.

TOTAL	56	55	53	53

Average total for subcompact cars: 43.7

ENGINES	ohc I4	Turbocharged dohc I4	ohc V6	Turbodies el ohc I4
Size, liters/cu. in.	2.0/121	1.8/109	2.8/170	1.9/116
Horsepower @ rpm	115 @ 5200	180 @ 5500	174 @ 5800	90 @ 3750
Torque (lb-ft) @ rpm	122 @ 2600	174 @ 1950	181 @ 3200	155 @ 1900
Availability....................	S[1]	S[2]	S[3]	S[4]

Specifications begin on page 551.

VOLKSWAGEN

EPA city/highway mpg	ohc I4	Turbocharged dohc I4	ohc V6	Turbodiesel ohc I4
5-speed manual	24/31	24/31	20/28	42/49
4-speed automatic	23/29		19/26	34/45
5-speed automatic		22/29		

1. Jetta GL and GLS, Golf GL and GLS. 2. Jetta GLS 1.8T, Golf GLS 1.8T and GTI. 3. Jetta GLS VR6 and GLX, Golf GTI VR6. 4. TDI.

PRICES

Volkswagen Jetta/Golf

	Retail Price	Dealer Invoice
Golf GL 2-door hatchback, manual	$15050	$14044
Golf GL 2-door hatchback, automatic	15925	14908
Golf GL 4-door hatchback, manual	15250	14228
Golf GL 4-door hatchback, automatic	16125	15092
Golf GL TDI 2-door hatchback, manual	16345	15239
Golf GL TDI 2-door hatchback, automatic	17220	16103
Golf GL TDI 4-door hatchback, manual	16545	15424
Golf GL TDI 4-door hatchback, automatic	17420	16288
Golf GLS 4-door hatchback, manual	16600	15475
Golf GLS 4-door hatchback, automatic	17475	16339
Golf GLS TDI 4-door hatchback, manual	17650	16445
Golf GLS TDI 4-door hatchback, automatic	18525	17309
Golf GTI 2-door hatchback, manual	18910	17225
Golf GTI 2-door hatchback, automatic	19985	18298
Golf GTI VR6 2-door hatchback, manual	20295	18476
Jetta GL 4-door sedan, manual	16850	15364
Jetta GL 4-door sedan, automatic	17725	16228
Jetta GL 4-door wagon, manual	17650	16087
Jetta GL 4-door wagon, automatic	18525	16951
Jetta GL TDI 4-door sedan, manual	18145	16902
Jetta GL TDI 4-door sedan, automatic	19330	18052
Jetta GL TDI 4-door wagon, manual	NA	NA
Jetta GL TDI 4-door wagon, automatic	NA	NA
Jetta GLS 4-door sedan, manual	17900	16312
Jetta GLS 4-door sedan, automatic	18775	17176
Jetta GLS 4-door wagon, manual	18700	17035
Jetta GLS 4-door wagon, automatic	19575	17899
Jetta GLS TDI 4-door sedan, manual	18950	17646
Jetta GLS TDI 4-door sedan, automatic	20135	18796
Jetta GLS TDI 4-door wagon, manual	NA	NA
Jetta GLS TDI 4-door wagon, automatic	NA	NA
Jetta GLS 1.8T 4-door sedan, manual	19550	17803
Jetta GLS 1.8T 4-door sedan, automatic	20625	18876
Jetta GLS 1.8T 4-door wagon, manual	20350	18526
Jetta GLS 1.8T 4-door wagon, automatic	21425	19599
Jetta GLS VR6 4-door sedan, 5-speed	20200	18390

Prices are accurate at time of publication; subject to manufacturer's change.

CONSUMER GUIDE®

VOLKSWAGEN

	Retail Price	Dealer Invoice
Jetta GLS VR6 4-door sedan, automatic	$21075	$19254
Jetta GLS VR6 4-door wagon, 5-speed	21000	19112
Jetta GLS VR6 4-door wagon, automatic	21875	19976
Jetta GLX 4-door sedan, 5-speed	24700	22455
Jetta GLX 4-door sedan, automatic	25575	23319
Jetta GLX 4-door wagon, 5-speed	25500	23178
Jetta GLX 4-door wagon, automatic	26375	24042
Destination charge	550	550

STANDARD EQUIPMENT

Golf/Jetta GL: 2.0-liter 4-cylinder engine, 5-speed manual or 4-speed automatic transmission, dual front airbags, front side airbags, curtain side airbags, antilock 4-wheel disc brakes, daytime running lights, emergency inside trunk release (Jetta sedan), air conditioning, interior air filter, power steering, tilt/telescoping steering wheel, cloth upholstery, height-adjustable front bucket seats, cupholders, split folding rear seat, heated manual mirrors, power door locks, remote keyless entry, AM/FM/cassette w/CD changer controls, digital clock, tachometer, map lights, variable intermittent wipers, illuminated visor mirrors, rear defogger, intermittent rear wiper/washer (Golf, Jetta wagon), remote decklid/hatchback and fuel door releases, cargo cover (Golf, Jetta wagon), floormats, theft-deterrent system, roof rails (Jetta wagon), full-size spare tire, 195/65HR15 tires, wheel covers.

Golf/Jetta GL TDI add: 1.9-liter turbodiesel 4-cylinder engine, traction control, cruise control, alloy wheels (Jetta automatic).

Golf/Jetta GLS add to Golf/Jetta GL: cruise control, center console, heated power mirrors, power windows, AM/FM/cassette/CD player.

Golf/Jetta GLS TDI add: 1.9-liter turbodiesel 4-cylinder engine, traction control, alloy wheels (Jetta automatic).

Jetta GLS 1.8T adds to Jetta GLS: 1.8-liter dohc 4-cylinder turbocharged engine, 5-speed manual or 5-speed automatic transmission w/manual-shift capability, traction control.

Golf GTI adds: fog lights, sport suspension, 205/55HR16 tires, alloy wheels.

Golf GTI VR6 adds: 2.8-liter dohc V6 engine, 5-speed manual transmission, trip computer, outside temperature indicator, 225/45HR17 tires.

Jetta GLS VR6 adds to Jetta GLS: 2.8-liter dohc V6 engine, traction control.

Jetta GLX adds: leather upholstery, heated 8-way power front seats w/driver seat memory, leather-wrapped steering wheel w/radio con-

Specifications begin on page 551.

VOLKSWAGEN

trols, wood interior trim, automatic climate control, power sunroof, Monsoon Sound System, automatic day/night rearview mirror, trip computer, outside temperature indicator, rain-sensing wipers, heated washer nozzles, rear window sunshade, fog lights, 205/55HR16 tires, alloy wheels.

OPTIONAL EQUIPMENT

	Retail Price	Dealer Invoice
Major Packages		
Luxury Pkg., GLS, GLS TDI, GLS 1.8T	$1225	$1082
GLS VR6	1425	1258

Power sunroof, 205/55HR16 tires (GLS V6), alloy wheels. NA Jetta GLS TDI automatic. NA Jetta GLS TDI wagon.

Luxury Pkg., GTI, GTI VR6	1240	1095

Monsoon Sound System, power sunroof.

Sport Luxury Pkg., GLS 1.8T, GLS VR6	2025	1788

Power sunroof, sport suspension, 225/45R17 tires, alloy wheels.

Leather Pkg., Jetta GLS, Jetta GLS TDI, GLS 1.8T, GLS VR6	1050	929
GTI, GTI VR6	900	793

Leather upholstery, heated front seats and washer nozzles, leather-wrapped steering wheel and shifter, steering wheel mounted cruise and radio controls (Jetta). Jetta sedan requires Luxury Pkg. or Sport Luxury Pkg., except GLS TDI automatic which requires power sunroof.

Technology Pkg., GTI VR6	755	667

Automatic climate control, automatic day/night rearview mirror, rain-sensing wipers.

Cold Weather Pkg.	150	133

Heated front seats, heated washer jets. NA GL, GL TDI. Std. GLX.

Powertrain

California and Northeast emissions, GL/GLS TDI, GLS 1.8T, GLS VR6, GTI, GTI VR6, GLX	100	99

Required on cars purchased in Calif., N.H., N.Y., Mass., Conn., R.I., Pa., N.J., Del., Md., Va., Vt., and Washington, D.C.

Comfort & Convenience Features

Power sunroof, Jetta GLS TDI automatic	915	808
Monsoon Sound System, GLS, GLS TDI, GLS 1.8T, GLS VR6	325	287

Appearance and Miscellaneous

Sport suspension, GLS 1.8T, GLS VR6, GLX	200	177
Sport suspension w/17-in. alloy wheels, Jetta GLX	600	530

Includes 225/45R17 tires.

Prices are accurate at time of publication; subject to manufacturer's change.

CONSUMER GUIDE®

VOLKSWAGEN

	Retail Price	Dealer Invoice
17-inch alloy wheels, GTI	$400	$353

Includes 225/45R17 tires.

VOLKSWAGEN NEW BEETLE

Volkswagen New Beetle GLX

Front-wheel-drive sporty coupe
Base price range: $15,900-$22,375. Built in Mexico.
Also consider: Acura RSX, Ford Focus ZX3, Toyota Celica

FOR • Handling/roadholding • Fuel economy • Build quality • Exterior finish • Interior materials **AGAINST** • Rear-seat head room • Visibility • Rear-seat entry/exit

A sport model with more turbocharged power and a new transmission mark the 2002 New Beetle. This retro-styled 2-dr hatchback coupe recalls the original Beetle, but is built on the modern front-wheel-drive Jetta/Golf chassis. All models are powered by a 4-cyl engine: 2.0-liter and turbo 1.8-liter gasoline units, and a 1.9-liter turbodiesel. The 1.8 turbo in GLS Turbo and GLX models has 150 hp. The new Turbo S model due midyear has 180 hp and a new 6-speed manual transmission. Other models have a 5-speed manual or optional automatic. Front side airbags, antilock 4-wheel disc brakes, and 16-inch wheels are standard. Turbo models add traction control. Also new for 2002 are restyled wheels and wheel covers, and a Lifestyle option package for the GLS Turbo that includes Snap Orange paint and interior trim. VW's bumper-to-bumper warranty is now 4 years/50,000 mi. instead of 2/24,000, and the powertrain warranty is 5/60,000 instead of 10/100,000.

Specifications begin on page 551.

VOLKSWAGEN

RATINGS	GL, man.	GL, auto.	GLS TDI, man.	GLS Turbo w/Sport Lux. Pkg., auto.
ACCELERATION	5	4	3	6
FUEL ECONOMY	7	5	9	7
RIDE QUALITY	6	6	6	4
STEERING/HANDLING	6	6	6	7
QUIETNESS	5	6	6	6
INSTRUMENTS/CONTROLS	6	6	6	6
ROOM/COMFORT (FRONT)	7	7	7	7
ROOM/COMFORT (REAR)	3	3	3	3
CARGO ROOM	3	3	3	3
VALUE	5	5	5	5

The retro styling has its drawbacks, but the entertaining and well-built New Beetle is quite practical for a sporty coupe. Nostalgic appeal aside, it's a good value in this class.

TOTAL	53	51	52	54

Average total for sporty coupes: 43.4

ENGINES	ohc I4	Turbodiesel ohc I4	Turbocharged dohc I4
Size, liters/cu. in.	2.0/121	1.9/116	1.8/109
Horsepower @ rpm	115 @ 5200	90 @ 3750	150 @ 5700
Torque (lb-ft) @ rpm	122 @ 2600	155 @ 1900	155 @ 1750
Availability	S[1]	S[2]	S[3]
EPA city/highway mpg			
5-speed manual	24/31	42/49	24/31
4-speed automatic	23/29	34/45	23/29

1. GL, GLS. 2. GLS TDI. 3. GLS Turbo, GLX, Turbo S (Turbo S: 180 hp, 174 lb-ft).

PRICES

Volkswagen New Beetle	Retail Price	Dealer Invoice
GL 2-door hatchback, manual	$15900	$15151
GL 2-door hatchback, automatic	16775	16015
GLS 2-door hatchback, manual	16850	15706
GLS 2-door hatchback, automatic	17725	16570
GLS TDI 2-door hatchback, manual	17900	16675
GLS TDI 2-door hatchback, automatic	18775	17539
GLS Turbo 2-door hatchback, manual	19200	17876
GLS Turbo 2-door hatchback, automatic	20075	18740
GLX 2-door hatchback, manual	21500	20001
GLX 2-door hatchback, automatic	22375	20865
Turbo S 2-door hatchback, manual	NA	NA
Destination charge	550	550

Prices are accurate at time of publication; subject to manufacturer's change.

VOLKSWAGEN

STANDARD EQUIPMENT

GL: 2.0-liter 4-cylinder engine, 5-speed manual or 4-speed automatic transmission, dual front airbags, front side airbags, antilock 4-wheel disc brakes, emergency inside trunk release, daytime running lights, air conditioning, interior air filter, power steering, tilt/telescoping steering wheel, cloth upholstery, front bucket seats w/height adjustment, center console, cupholders, folding rear seat, heated power mirrors, power door locks, remote keyless entry, AM/FM/cassette w/CD changer controls, digital clock, tachometer, illuminated visor mirrors, rear defogger, map lights, remote fuel door and hatchback releases, variable intermittent wipers, cargo cover, floormats, theft-deterrent system, full-size spare tire, 205/55HR16 tires, wheel covers.

GLS adds: cruise control, power windows, fog lights.

GLS TDI adds: 1.9-liter 4-cylinder turbodiesel engine.

GLS Turbo adds to GLS: 1.8-liter dohc turbocharged 4-cylinder 150-horsepower engine, traction control, rear spoiler, alloy wheels.

GLX adds: leather upholstery, heated front seats, leather-wrapped steering wheel, power sunroof, Monsoon sound system, automatic day/night rearview mirror, rain-sensing wipers, heated windshield washer nozzles.

Turbo S adds: 1.8-liter dohc turbocharged 4-cylinder 180-horsepower engine, 6-speed manual transmission, 225/45HR17 tires. *Deletes:* automatic day/night rearview mirror.

OPTIONAL EQUIPMENT

	Retail Price	Dealer Invoice

Major Packages

Luxury Pkg., GLS, GLS TDI $1225 $1081
 Alloy wheels, power sunroof.
Sport Luxury Pkg., GLS Turbo 1625 1435
 Power sunroof, 225/45R17 tires, alloy wheels.
Leather Pkg., GLS, GLS TDI, GLS Turbo 900 795
 Leather upholstery, heated front seats, leather-wrapped steering wheel, heated windshield washer nozzles. GLS, GLS TDI require Luxury Pkg. GLS Turbo requires Sport Luxury Pkg. or power sunroof.
Lifestyle Pkg., GLS Turbo .... NA NA
 Leather upholstery w/orange inserts, power sunroof, Monsoon sound system, Snap Orange paint, 225/45R17 tires.
Cold Weather Pkg., GLS, GLS TDI, GLS Turbo 150 133
 Heated front seats, heated washer jets.

Powertrain

California and Northeast emissions 100 99
 Required on gasoline engine cars purchased in Calif., N.H., N.Y., Mass., Conn., R.I., Pa., N.J., Del., Md., Va., Vt., and Washington, D.C.

VOLKSWAGEN

Comfort & Convenience Features	Retail Price	Dealer Invoice
Power sunroof, GLS Turbo	$915	$808
Monsoon sound system, GLS, GLS TDI, GLS Turbo	325	287

Appearance and Miscellaneous

17-inch alloy wheels, GLX	400	353
Includes 225/45R17 tires.		

VOLKSWAGEN PASSAT

Volkswagen Passat GLX 4-door sedan

Front- or all-wheel-drive compact car
Base price range: $21,750-$32,375. Built in Germany.
Also consider: Chrysler PT Cruiser, Mazda 626, Mitsubishi Galant

FOR • Ride • Passenger and cargo room • Build quality • Exterior finish • Interior materials **AGAINST** • Acceleration (GLS 1.8T w/automatic) • Tire noise

After a revamp that created "2001.5" models, Volkswagen's compact sedan sees few changes for 2002 as it awaits introduction of an 8-cyl model. Base GLS Passats have a 170-hp turbo 4-cyl engine, GLS V6 and GLX a 190-hp V6. All come with manual or 5-speed automatic transmission with manual shift gate and front-wheel drive with traction control. VW's 4Motion all-wheel drive is available on V6 models with automatic transmission. Standard equipment includes front side airbags, curtain side airbags, and antilock 4-wheel disc brakes. For 2002, VW's bumper-to-bumper warranty is 4 years/50,000 mi. instead of 2/24,000, and the powertrain warranty is 5/60,000 instead of 10/100,000. Due in summer 2002 is the W8 model with a unique 275-hp 8-cyl engine consisting of four banks of

Prices are accurate at time of publication; subject to manufacturer's change.

VOLKSWAGEN

two cylinders. It will be available as an AWD sedan or wagon at a starting price of around $40,000.

RATINGS	GLS sdn, 4 cyl man.	GLS/GLX sdn, V6 auto.	GLX 4Motion wgn
ACCELERATION	5	5	5
FUEL ECONOMY	6	5	4
RIDE QUALITY	8	8	8
STEERING/HANDLING	7	7	7
QUIETNESS	6	6	6
INSTRUMENTS/CONTROLS	7	7	7
ROOM/COMFORT (FRONT)	7	7	7
ROOM/COMFORT (REAR)	6	6	6
CARGO ROOM	4	4	8
VALUE	7	7	7

Acceleration doesn't impress in 4-cyl/automatic-transmission form, and Passats are pricier than most every other compact car. But they match some near-luxury models for quality, spaciousness, and features. They also brim with European flair and offer the bonus of 4Motion AWD. It's enough to earn Best Buy status.

TOTAL	63	62	65

Average total for compact cars: 51.6

ENGINES	Turbocharged dohc I4	dohc V6
Size, liters/cu. in.	1.8/109	2.8/169
Horsepower @ rpm	170 @ 5900	190 @ 6000
Torque (lb-ft) @ rpm	166 @ 1950	206 @ 3200
Availability	S[1]	S[2]

EPA city/highway mpg

5-speed manual	22/31	20/28
5-speed automatic	21/30	20/27[3]

1. GLS 1.8T. 2. GLS V6, GLX. 3. 19/26 w/4Motion.

PRICES

Volkswagen Passat	Retail Price	Dealer Invoice
GLS 4-door sedan, manual	$21750	$19790
GLS 4-door sedan, automatic	22825	20863
GLS 4-door wagon, manual	22550	20513
GLS 4-door wagon, automatic	23625	21586
GLS V6 4-door sedan, manual	24250	22049
GLS V6 4-door sedan, automatic	25325	23122
GLS V6 4-door wagon, manual	25050	22772
GLS V6 4-door wagon, automatic	26125	23845
GLS V6 4Motion AWD 4-door sedan, automatic	27075	24951
GLS V6 4Motion AWD 4-door wagon, automatic	27875	25674
GLX 4-door sedan, manual	28750	26114

Specifications begin on page 551.

VOLKSWAGEN

	Retail Price	Dealer Invoice
GLX 4-door sedan, automatic	$29825	$27187
GLX 4-door wagon, manual	29550	26837
GLX 4-door wagon, automatic	30625	27910
GLX 4Motion AWD 4-door sedan, automatic	31575	29016
GLX 4Motion AWD 4-door wagon, automatic	32375	29739
Destination charge	550	550

STANDARD EQUIPMENT

GLS: 1.8-liter dohc 4-cylinder turbocharged engine, 5-speed manual or 5-speed automatic transmission w/manual-shift capability, traction control, dual front airbags, front side airbags, curtain side airbags, antilock 4-wheel disc brakes, daytime running lights, emergency inside trunk release, air conditioning, interior air filter, power steering, tilt/telescoping steering wheel, cruise control, cloth upholstery, height-adjustable front bucket seats w/lumbar adjustment, center console, cupholders, split folding rear seat, heated power mirrors, power windows, power door locks, remote keyless entry, map lights, trip computer, outside temperature indicator, AM/FM/cassette/CD player, digital clock, tachometer, rear defogger, remote fuel door/decklid release, variable intermittent wipers, illuminated visor mirrors, cargo cover (wagon), intermittent rear wiper/washer (wagon), floormats, theft-deterrent system, fog lights, roof rails (wagon), full-size spare tire, 195/65HR15 tires, wheel covers.

GLS V6 adds: 2.8-liter dohc V6 engine, wood interior trim. **AWD** adds: all-wheel drive, trunk pass-through. *Deletes:* traction control, split folding rear seat.

GLX adds: leather upholstery, heated 8-way power front seats w/driver seat memory, leather-wrapped steering wheel w/steering wheel radio controls, wood interior trim, automatic climate control, passenger-side mirror tilt-down parking aid, power sunroof, Monsoon sound system, automatic day/night rearview mirror, universal garage door opener, rear window sun shade (sedan), rain-sensing wipers, heated windshield washer nozzles, 205/55HR16 tires, alloy wheels. **AWD** adds: all-wheel drive, trunk pass-through. *Deletes:* traction control, split folding rear seat.

OPTIONAL EQUIPMENT
Major Packages

Leather Pkg.,		
GLS, GLS V6	1500	1325
Leather upholstery, heated front seats and windshield washer nozzles, leather-wrapped steering wheel w/radio controls.		
Luxury Pkg., GLS/GLS V6 sedan	1550	1369

Prices are accurate at time of publication; subject to manufacturer's change.

VOLKSWAGEN • VOLVO

	Retail Price	Dealer Invoice
GLS/GLS V6 wagon	$1435	$1267

Power sunroof, rear sunshade (sedan), alloy wheels.

Cold Weather Pkg., GLS, GLS V6	325	287

Heated front seats and windshield washer nozzles.

Comfort & Convenience Features

Monsoon sound system, GLS, GLS V6	325	287
Universal garage door opener, GLS, GLS V6	130	115

VOLVO 40 SERIES

Volvo S40

Front-wheel-drive near-luxury car

2001 base price range: $23,550-$28,400. Built in The Netherlands.

Also consider: Acura TL, BMW 3-Series, Lexus ES 300

FOR • Ride • Steering/handling • Cargo room (wagon)
AGAINST • Rear-seat room

Volvo's slow-selling S40 sedan and V40 wagon get an in-trunk emergency release for sedans and twin cupholders front and rear for 2002. Both share a turbo 4-cyl engine mated to a 5-speed automatic transmission. Torso front side airbags, curtain side airbags, antilock 4-wheel disc brakes, and antiwhiplash front-seat head restraints are standard. Options include an antiskid system, sunroof, and integrated dual rear child booster seats. Sport Editions feature standard leather upholstery, spoiler, fog lights, and unique interior trim, but do not alter engine, suspension, or tires.

Specifications begin on page 551.

VOLVO

RATINGS	S40	V40
ACCELERATION	6	6
FUEL ECONOMY	5	5
RIDE QUALITY	7	7
STEERING/HANDLING	6	6
QUIETNESS	5	5
INSTRUMENTS/CONTROLS	6	6
ROOM/COMFORT (FRONT)	5	5
ROOM/COMFORT (REAR)	3	3
CARGO ROOM	3	7
VALUE	3	4

The smallest Volvos have a nice array of standard safety features, but their uneven turbo power delivery and shortage of cabin space are serious shortcomings at these prices, which rise quickly with just a few options.

TOTAL	49	54

Average total for near-luxury cars: 54.5

ENGINES

	Turbocharged dohc I4
Size, liters/cu. in.	1.9/116
Horsepower @ rpm	160 @ 5200
Torque (lb-ft) @ rpm	177 @ 1800
Availability	S

EPA city/highway mpg

5-speed automatic	22/32

2002 prices unavailable at time of publication.

PRICES

2001 Volvo 40 series

	Retail Price	Dealer Invoice
S40 Base 4-door sedan	$23550	$22140
V40 Base 4-door wagon	24550	23080
S40 Sport Edition 4-door sedan	27400	25461
V40 Sport Edition 4-door wagon	28400	26401
Destination charge	625	625

STANDARD EQUIPMENT

Base: 1.9-liter dohc turbocharged 4-cylinder engine, 5-speed automatic transmission, dual front airbags, front side airbags, curtain airbags, front seat active head restraints, antilock 4-wheel disc brakes, daytime running lights, air conditioning w/automatic climate control, interior air filter, power steering, tilt steering wheel, cruise control, cloth upholstery, front bucket seats, center console, cupholders, split folding rear seat, rear seat trunk

Prices are accurate at time of publication; subject to manufacturer's change.

VOLVO

pass-through (sedan), heated power mirrors, power windows, power door locks, remote keyless entry, AM/FM/cassette w/CD changer controls, power antenna (sedan), digital clock, outside temperature display, tachometer, variable intermittent wipers, rear defogger, intermittent rear wiper/washer (wagon), map lights, illuminated visor mirrors, cargo cover (wagon), floormats, theft-deterrent system, rear fog lights, 195/60VR15 tires, alloy wheels.

Sport Edition adds: leather/cloth upholstery, power driver seat, leather-wrapped steering wheel, power sunroof, AM/FM/CD player w/CD changer controls, trip computer, front fog lights, rear spoiler.

OPTIONAL EQUIPMENT	Retail Price	Dealer Invoice
Major Packages		
Sport Pkg., Base	$750	$636
Manufacturer's Discount Price	*550*	*467*
Leather-wrapped steering wheel, front fog lights, rear spoiler.		
Leather/Audio Pkg., Base	2435	2069
Manufacturer's Discount Price	*1900*	*1615*
Leather upholstery, AM/FM/cassette/CD player, premium speakers, trip computer, 10-spoke wheels (wagon).		
Sunroof/Audio Pkg., Base	2435	2069
Manufacturer's Discount Price	*1900*	*1615*
Power sunroof, AM/FM/cassette/CD player, premium speakers, trip computer, 10-spoke wheels (wagon).		
Cold Weather Pkg.	950	807
Manufacturer's Discount Price	*850*	*722*
Traction control, heated front seats, headlight wiper/washer.		
Safety		
Dual child booster seats, Base	300	255
Comfort & Convenience Features		
Leather upholstery, Base	1300	1105
Power driver seat, Base	450	382
Audio Upgrade Pkg., Base	885	752
Manufacturer's Discount Price	*800*	*680*
AM/FM/cassette/CD player, premium speakers.		
Power sunroof, Base	1200	1020

VOLVO S60

Front- or all-wheel-drive near-luxury car
Base price range: $27,125-$34,025. Built in Sweden.
Also consider: Acura TL, BMW 3-Series, Lexus ES 300

FOR • Available AWD • Front seat comfort **AGAINST** • Rear

VOLVO

Volvo S60 AWD

visibility • Navigation system controls

Volvo's near-luxury sedan is available with all-wheel drive for 2002. The S60 is essentially the sedan version of Volvo's better-selling V70 station wagon, and both share a basic structure and some features with Volvo's S80 flagship. All S60s use an inline 5-cyl engine. The base 2.4-liter model, the more-powerful turbo 2.4T, and the sporty turbo 2.3-liter T5 all have front-wheel drive. The new 2.4T AWD apportions power to the rear wheels when the front tires begin to slip. Base and T5 models offer manual transmission or an optional 5-speed automatic. The 2.4Ts come only with automatic. Front side airbags, curtain side airbags, antilock 4-wheel disc brakes, and Volvo's anti-whiplash front seatbacks are standard. The base model has 15-inch wheels and offers optional 16s. The 2.4Ts have 16s and offer 17s. The T5 comes with 17s. Traction control is standard on all S60s and an antiskid system is standard on the T5, optional for the 2.4T models. Optional on all is a navigation system with popup dashboard screen. An emergency in-trunk release and rear cupholders round out the '02 additions.

RATINGS	2.4T	2.4T AWD w/ nav. sys.	T5, man.
ACCELERATION	5	5	6
FUEL ECONOMY	5	5	4
RIDE QUALITY	7	7	5
STEERING/HANDLING	6	7	7
QUIETNESS	5	5	5
INSTRUMENTS/CONTROLS	7	5	7
ROOM/COMFORT (FRONT)	7	7	7
ROOM/COMFORT (REAR)	3	3	3
CARGO ROOM	3	3	3

Prices are accurate at time of publication; subject to manufacturer's change.

CONSUMER GUIDE®

VOLVO

VALUE	2.4T	2.4T AWD w/ nav. sys.	T5, man.
	4	4	3

Arguably the most stylish Volvo ever, and the best-handling Volvo sedan yet. But compromises in rear seat room, ride quality, and powertrain smoothness are hard to overlook in the hotly contested near-luxury class, especially at the $36,000 sticker price of our 2.4T and T5 test cars. The 2.4T AWD is an asset to this line, but not enough to threaten the Acura TL and Lexus ES 300 for overall value.

TOTAL	52	51	50

Average total for near-luxury cars: 54.5

ENGINES

	dohc I5	Turbocharged dohc I5	Turbocharged dohc I5
Size, liters/cu. in.	2.4/149	2.4/149	2.3/141
Horsepower @ rpm	168 @ 5900	197 @ 6000	247 @ 5200
Torque (lb-ft) @ rpm	170 @ 4500	210 @ 1800	243 @ 2400

	dohc I5	Turbocharged dohc I5	Turbocharged dohc I5
Availability	S[1]	S[2]	S[3]

EPA city/highway mpg

5-speed manual	21/28		21/28
5-speed automatic	21/28	21/28	20/27

1. Base. 2. 2.4T, 2.4T AWD. 3. T5.

PRICES

Volvo S60	Retail Price	Dealer Invoice
Base 4-door sedan	$27125	$25226
2.4T FWD 4-door sedan	31625	29411
2.4T AWD 4-door sedan	33375	31038
T5 4-door sedan	34025	31643
Destination charge	625	625

AWD denotes all-wheel drive. FWD denotes front-wheel drive.

STANDARD EQUIPMENT

Base: 2.4-liter dohc 5-cylinder engine, 5-speed manual transmission, traction control, dual front airbags, front side airbags, curtain side airbags, front seat active head restraints, antilock 4-wheel disc brakes, emergency inside trunk release, air conditioning, interior air filter, power steering, tilt/telescoping steering wheel, cruise control, cloth upholstery, front bucket seats, center console, cupholders, split folding rear seat w/trunk pass-through, heated power mirrors, power windows, power door locks, remote keyless entry, AM/FM/cassette, digital clock, tachometer, rear defogger, power decklid release, illuminated visor mirrors, map lights, variable intermittent wipers, floormats, theft-deterrent system, rear fog light, 195/65HR15 tires, alloy wheels.

Specifications begin on page 551.

VOLVO

2.4T adds: 2.4-liter dohc turbocharged 197-horsepower 5-cylinder engine, 5-speed automatic transmission, 8-way power driver seat w/memory, automatic climate control, steering wheel radio controls, 205/55HR16 tires. **AWD** adds: all-wheel drive, 5-speed automatic transmission w/manual-shift capability. *Deletes:* traction control.

T5 adds: turbocharged 2.3-liter dohc 247-horsepower 5-cylinder engine, 5-speed manual transmission, antiskid system, cloth/vinyl upholstery, 8-way power passenger seat, leather-wrapped steering wheel, AM/FM/cassette/CD player, trip computer, universal garage door opener, automatic day/night rearview mirror, front fog lights, 235/45HR17 tires.

OPTIONAL EQUIPMENT

	Retail Price	Dealer Invoice
Major Packages		
Premium Pkg., Base	$3435	$2919
Manufacturer's Discount Price	*2300*	*1955*
Leather upholstery, 8-way power driver seat, power sunroof, AM/FM/cassette/CD player.		
Premium Pkg., 2.4T	2635	2239
Manufacturer's Discount Price	*1600*	*1360*
Leather upholstery, power passenger seat, leather-wrapped steering wheel, power sunroof, AM/FM/CD player, additional speakers, simulated wood interior trim.		
Touring Pkg., Base	900	764
Manufacturer's Discount Price	*600*	*510*
2.4T	1025	870
Manufacturer's Discount Price	*700*	*595*
Trip computer, automatic day/night rearview mirror, universal garage door opener, interior air quality system (2.4T), grocery bag holder, security laminated side windows.		
Touring Pkg., T5	550	467
Manufacturer's Discount Price	*440*	*374*
Interior air quality system, grocery bag holder, security laminated side windows.		
Cold Weather Pkg., Base, FWD 2.4T, T5	450	382
Heated front seats, headlight washers/wipers.		
Powertrain		
5-Speed automatic transmission, Base	1000	1000
5-speed automatic transmission w/manual-shift capability, T5	1200	1200
FWD 2.4T	200	200
Dynamic Stability Traction Control, 2.4T	1100	935
Antiskid system.		
Comfort & Convenience Features		
Power sunroof, Base	1200	1020

Prices are accurate at time of publication; subject to manufacturer's change.

CONSUMER GUIDE®

VOLVO

	Retail Price	Dealer Invoice
Navigation system	NA	NA
Leather upholstery, Base, 2.4T	$1300	$1105
T5	1350	1147
T5 includes sport seats.		
Leather/cloth upholstery, T5	1050	892
Max AM/FM/cassette w/in-dash 4-disc CD changer, T5	1020	1200

Appearance and Miscellaneous

Sport Chassis, T5	250	212
Mimas alloy wheels, Base	500	425
Includes 205/55HR16 tires.		
Sirus alloy wheels, 2.4T	250	212
Includes 215/55HR16 tires.		
Tethys/Arnalthea alloy wheels, 2.4T, T5	500	425
Includes 235/45HR17 tires.		

VOLVO S80

Volvo S80

Front-wheel-drive luxury car

2001 base price range: $38,150-$48,750. Built in Sweden.

Also consider: Acura RL, BMW 5-Series, Lexus LS 430, Mercedes-Benz E-Class

FOR • Acceleration (T6) • Passenger and cargo room • Build quality **AGAINST** • Radio and navigation system controls • Rear visibility

Volvo's flagship sedan offers three models: the base 2.9, the turbo 2.8-liter T6, and the posh T6 Executive. All have an inline 6-cyl engine and 4-speed automatic transmission; T6s have a manual-

VOLVO

shift gate. (Volvo recommends premium fuel for all models.) Antiskid and navigation systems are also available. For 2002, both engines are slightly retuned in an effort to provide more power at lower rpm. Also, the T6 now comes with 17-inch wheels, which are optional on other models in place of the standard 16s. And all models gain an in-trunk emergency release and new-design alloy wheels. Standard features include antilock brakes, traction control, front side airbags, curtain side airbags, antiwhiplash front seats, and leather upholstery. The Executive's rear seat is divided by a center console, heated, and angled to provide 2 inches more leg room. It also has wider-opening doors, a power sunshade, entertainment system with DVD video and TV tuner, refrigerated compartment, and available wireless fax/copier. Due during the model year, an Elite option gives standard S80s the expanded rear compartment but with a 3-passenger bench seat.

RATINGS	2.9	T6 w/nav. sys.	Executive
ACCELERATION	5	7	7
FUEL ECONOMY	5	5	5
RIDE QUALITY	8	7	7
STEERING/HANDLING	6	7	7
QUIETNESS	7	7	7
INSTRUMENTS/CONTROLS	6	4	6
ROOM/COMFORT (FRONT)	8	8	8
ROOM/COMFORT (REAR)	7	7	9
CARGO ROOM	4	4	4
VALUE	3	4	3

S80s are roomy, well built, and competitively priced. The navigation system is a hassle to use, and the 2.9 model lacks acceleration and handling befitting a luxury sedan. The faster T6 is pricier, but actually a better value. The Executive pampers rear-seaters like a Lexus LS 430, which, comparably equipped, costs thousands more.

TOTAL	59	60	63

Average total for luxury cars: 59.4

ENGINES	dohc I6	Turbocharged dohc I6
Size, liters/cu. in.	2.9/178	2.8/170
Horsepower @ rpm	194 @ 5000	268 @ 5400
Torque (lb-ft) @ rpm	210 @ 3900	280 @ 1800
Availability	S[1]	S[2]
EPA city/highway mpg		
4-speed automatic	19/27	18/26

1. S80 2.9. 2. S80 T6, Executive.

2002 prices unavailable at time of publication.

Prices are accurate at time of publication; subject to manufacturer's change.

VOLVO

PRICES

2001 Volvo S80	Retail Price	Dealer Invoice
2.9 4-door sedan	$38150	$35768
T6 4-door sedan	42150	39528
Executive 4-door sedan	48750	45828
Destination charge	625	625

STANDARD EQUIPMENT

2.9: 2.9-liter dohc 6-cylinder engine, 4-speed automatic transmission, traction control, dual front airbags, front side airbags, curtain side airbags, front seat active head restraints, antilock 4-wheel disc brakes, daytime running lights, air conditioning w/dual-zone automatic climate control, interior air filter, power steering, tilt/telescoping leather-wrapped steering wheel, cruise control, leather upholstery, 8-way power front bucket seats w/driver seat memory, center console, cupholders, split folding rear seat, heated power mirrors w/memory, power windows, power door locks, remote keyless entry, power sunroof, AM/FM/cassette/CD player, steering-wheel-mounted radio and climate controls, tachometer, trip computer, variable intermittent wipers, rear defogger, illuminated visor mirrors, automatic day/night rearview mirror, outside temperature indicator, universal garage door opener, floormats, theft-deterrent system, rear fog light, 215/55R16 tires, alloy wheels.

T6 adds: 2.8-liter dohc turbocharged 6-cylinder engine, 4-speed automatic transmission w/manual-shift capability, variable-assist power steering, front fog lights, 225/55R16 tires.

Executive adds: heated rear seats, DVD player w/remote control, television tuner, rear video screen, refrigerator, rear center console, power rear sunshade, 2-inch additional rear leg room. *Deletes:* power sunroof.

OPTIONAL EQUIPMENT

Major Packages

Warm Weather Pkg., 2.9, T6	700	594
Manufacturer's Discount Price	*500*	*425*
Infrared reflective windshield, rear and side sunshades.		
Cold Weather Package	450	382
Heated front seats, heated headlight wipers/washers.		
Security System	635	539
Manufacturer's Discount Price	*500*	*425*
Movement sensors, incline sensor, laminated security side glass, Air Quality System.		

Powertrain

Dynamic Stability Traction Control	1100	935
Includes antiskid system.		

Specifications begin on page 551.

VOLVO

Comfort & Convenience Features

	Retail Price	Dealer Invoice
Navigation system..	$2500	$2125
Fax/copier, Executive..	900	765
Requires cellular telephone w/fax data and capability, mobile office adapter kit.		
Power sunroof, Executive..	1200	1020
In-dash 4-disc CD changer	1000	850
Deletes cassette player.		
Air Quality System, Executive..	125	106
Requires Security Pkg.		

Appearance and Miscellaneous

Special alloy wheels, 2.9	500	425
T6, Executive...	400	340
Includes variable-assist power steering (2.9), 225/50R17 tires.		

VOLVO V70

Volvo V70 XC

Front- or all-wheel-drive near-luxury car
Base price range: $30,025-$36,500. Built in Sweden.
Also consider: Audi A4, Audi A6/allroad quattro, BMW 3-Series

FOR • Acceleration (T5) • Brake performance
• Instruments/controls • Cargo room • Interior materials
AGAINST • Fuel economy (T5) • Low-speed acceleration (T5)
• Ride comfort (T5) • Navigation system controls

Addition of a "regular" all-wheel drive model highlights the 2002 changes to Volvo's best selling line. All V70s are station wagons built on a slimmed-down version of Volvo's flagship S80 sedan platform. All have an inline 5-cyl engine. The base 2.4, the turbo 2.4T, and the sporty T5 models have front-wheel drive. The XC ("Cross Country")

Prices are accurate at time of publication; subject to manufacturer's change.

VOLVO

has the 2.4T engine, a raised suspension, SUV-influenced trim, and all-wheel drive. Joining it with AWD for '02 is the 2.4T AWD, which uses the standard suspension and trim. Base 2.4 and T5 offer manual or 5-speed automatic transmission; other models are automatic only. A manual shift-gate feature for the automatic is available on all but the front-drive 2.4 model. Traction control is standard on front-drive models. An antiskid system is standard on the T5 and optional on all other V70s except the base 2.4 model. All V70s feature antilock 4-wheel disc brakes, front side airbags, curtain side airbags, and antiwhiplash front seats. Options include a rear-facing 3rd seat, navigation system, and 17-inch wheels.

RATINGS	2.4, auto.	2.4T	T5, auto.	XC w/nav. sys.
ACCELERATION	4	5	6	5
FUEL ECONOMY	5	5	4	5
RIDE QUALITY	7	7	5	6
STEERING/HANDLING	6	6	6	6
QUIETNESS	6	6	5	5
INSTRUMENTS/CONTROLS	6	6	6	4
ROOM/COMFORT (FRONT)	7	7	7	7
ROOM/COMFORT (REAR)	6	6	6	6
CARGO ROOM	7	7	7	7
VALUE	4	5	4	4

Not as refined or well-built as Audi and BMW competitors, and less fuel-efficient than you might expect. Examples we tested also had some loose interior panels and other quality gaffes. Still, this is Volvo's best wagon yet. The XC provides some SUV flavor without SUV drawbacks, but the 2.4T and new 2.4T AWD are the best V70 values.

TOTAL	58	60	56	54

Average total for near-luxury cars: 54.5

ENGINES	dohc I5	Turbocharged dohc I5	Turbocharged dohc I5
Size, liters/cu. in.	2.4/149	2.4/149	2.3/141
Horsepower @ rpm	168 @ 5900	197 @ 6000	242 @ 5200
Torque (lb-ft) @ rpm	170 @ 4500	210 @ 1800	243 @ 2400
Availability	S[1]	S[2]	S[3]
EPA city/highway mpg			
5-speed manual	21/28		21/28
5-speed automatic	21/28	20/27[4]	20/26

1. 2.4. 2. 2.4T, 2.4T AWD, XC. 3. T5. 4. 18/22 w/XC.

PRICES

Volvo V70	Retail Price	Dealer Invoice
FWD 2.4 4-door wagon	$30025	$27923
FWD 2.4T 4-door wagon	34225	31829
AWD 2.4T 4-door wagon	35975	33456

Specifications begin on page 551.

VOLVO

	Retail Price	Dealer Invoice
FWD T5 4-door wagon	$36425	$33875
AWD XC 4-door wagon	36500	33945
Destination charge	625	625

AWD denotes all-wheel drive. FWD denotes front-wheel drive.

STANDARD EQUIPMENT

2.4: 2.4-liter dohc 5-cylinder engine, 5-speed manual transmission, traction control, dual front airbags, front side airbags, curtain side airbags, front seat active head restraints, antilock 4-wheel disc brakes, daytime running lights, air conditioning w/manual dual-zone controls, interior air filter, power steering, tilt/telescoping steering wheel, cruise control, cloth upholstery, front bucket seats, center console, cupholders, split folding rear seat, heated power mirrors, power windows, power door locks, remote keyless entry, AM/FM/cassette, digital clock, tachometer, outside temperature indicator, intermittent wipers, illuminated visor mirrors, map lights, rear defogger, rear wiper, remote fuel door/tailgate release, floormats, theft-deterrent system, rear fog lights, 195/65HR15 tires, alloy wheels.

2.4T adds: 2.4-liter dohc turbocharged 5-cylinder 197-horsepower engine, 5-speed automatic transmission, dual-zone automatic climate control, 8-way power driver seat, memory system for driver seat and mirrors, power sunroof, steering wheel radio controls, 205/55HR16 tires. **AWD** adds: all-wheel drive, 5-speed automatic transmission w/manual-shift capability. *Deletes:* traction control.

T5 adds: 2.3-liter dohc turbocharged 5-cylinder 247-horsepower engine, 5-speed manual transmission, antiskid system, 8-way power passenger seat, AM/FM/cassette/CD player, trip computer, automatic day/night rearview mirror, universal garage door opener, cargo cover, front fog lights, 215/55HR16 tires.

XC adds to 2.4T: all-wheel drive, 5-speed automatic transmission w/manual-shift capability, cargo cover, front fog lights, roof rails, raised ride height, 215/65HR16 tires. *Deletes:* traction control.

OPTIONAL EQUIPMENT
Major Packages

Premium Pkg., 2.4	3435	2919
Manufacturer's Discount Price	*2300*	*1955*

Leather upholstery, power sunroof, 8-way power driver seat, AM/FM/cassette/CD player.

Premium Pkg., 2.4T	2635	2239
Manufacturer's Discount Price	*1600*	*1360*
XC	2685	2281
Manufacturer's Discount Price	*$1600*	*$1360*

Leather upholstery, 8-way power passenger seat, leather-wrapped steering wheel, AM/FM/cassette/CD player, simulated wood interior trim.

Prices are accurate at time of publication; subject to manufacturer's change.

VOLVO

	Retail Price	Dealer Invoice
Touring Pkg., 2.4	$1250	$1061
Manufacturer's Discount Price	*925*	*786*
2.4T	1375	1167
Manufacturer's Discount Price	*1100*	*935*
XC	1350	1146
Manufacturer's Discount Price	*1100*	*935*

Trip computer, automatic day/night rearview mirror, universal garage door opener, interior air quality system (2.4T, T5, XC), additional cupholder, grocery bag holder, cargo area auxiliary power outlet, cargo net, security laminated side windows.

Touring Pkg., T5	900	764
Manufacturer's Discount Price	*800*	*680*

Interior air quality system, additional cupholder, grocery bag holder, cargo area auxiliary power outlet, cargo net, security laminated side windows.

Versatility Pkg., 2.4, 2.4T, T5	1675	1423
Manufacturer's Discount Price	*1300*	*1105*
XC	1350	1146
Manufacturer's Discount Price	*1175*	*998*

Rear-facing third row seat, integrated booster seat, folding table (2.4, 2.4T, T5), trash bin.

Cold Weather Pkg.	450	382

Heated front seats and headlight washers.

Powertrain

5-speed automatic transmission, 2.4	1000	1000
5-speed automatic transmission w/manual-shift capability, T5	1200	1200
Automatic transmission manual-shift capability, FWD 2.4T, XC	200	200

Safety

Dynamic Stability and Traction Control, 2.4T	1100	935

Antiskid system.

Dual booster seats, 2.4, 2.4T, T5	300	255
XC	175	148

Comfort & Convenience Features

Power sunroof, 2.4	1200	1020
AM/FM w/in-dash 4-disc CD changer, T5, XC	1200	1020

Includes premium sound system.

Appearance and Miscellaneous

Mimas alloy wheels, 2.4	500	425

Includes 205/55HR16 tires.

Amalthea/Thor alloy wheels, 2.4T, T5	500	425

Includes 235/45HR17 tires.

Specifications begin on page 551.

SPECIFICATIONS

Dimensions and capacities are supplied by the vehicle manufacturers. **Body types:** 2-door coupe or 4-door sedan = a standard-body car with a separate trunk; hatchback = car with a rear liftgate; wagon = car or sport-utility vehicle with an enclosed cargo bay; regular-cab pickup truck = standard-length cab with room for one row of front seats; extended-cab pickup truck = lengthened cab with seating positions behind the front seats; crew-cab pickup truck = lengthened cab with two forward-opening rear doors. **Wheelbase:** distance between the front and rear axles. **Curb weight:** weight of base models, not including optional equipment. Weight listed for 4-wheel-drive version. **Height:** overall height of base models, not including optional equipment (on sport-utility vehicles, this is the overall height of the 4-wheel drive model). **Cargo volume** *(does not apply to pickup trucks)*: coupes and sedans = maximum volume of the trunk; hatchbacks and station wagons = maximum volume with the rear seat folded; minivans and sport-utility vehicles = maximum volume with all rear seats folded or removed, when possible. **Standard payload** *(applies to pickup trucks)*: maximum weight the base model can carry, including passengers.

SUBCOMPACT CARS	Wheelbase, in.	Overall length, in.	Overall width, in.	Overall height, in.	Curb weight, lb	Cargo volume, cu ft	Fuel capacity, gal	Seating capacity	Front head room, in.	Max. front leg room, in.	Rear head room, in.	Min. rear leg room, in.
Chevrolet Cavalier 2-door coupe	104.1	180.9	68.7	53.0	2617	13.2	14.1	5	37.6	41.9	36.6	32.7
Chevrolet Cavalier 4-door sedan	104.1	180.9	67.9	54.7	2676	13.6	14.1	5	38.9	41.9	37.2	34.4
Chevrolet Prizm 4-door sedan	97.1	174.2	66.7	53.7	2403	12.1	13.2	5	39.3	42.5	36.9	33.2
Daewoo Lanos 2-door hatchback	99.2	160.4	66.1	56.4	2447	31.3	12.7	5	38.9	42.8	37.8	34.6
Daewoo Lanos 4-door sedan	99.2	166.8	66.1	56.4	2522	8.8	12.7	5	38.9	42.8	37.8	34.6
Daewoo Nubira 4-door sedan	101.2	177.0	66.9	56.3	2800	13.1	13.7	5	39.0	42.0	38.1	34.7
Daewoo Nubira 4-door wagon	101.2	179.0	67.7	57.9	2888	65.0	13.7	5	39.0	42.0	39.5	34.7
Dodge Neon 4-door sedan	105.0	173.1	67.4	56.0	2590	13.1	12.5	5	38.4	42.2	36.7	34.8
Ford Focus 2-door hatchback	103.0	168.1	66.9	56.3	2551	18.6	13.2	5	39.3	43.1	38.7	37.6
Ford Focus 4-door hatchback	103.0	168.1	66.9	56.3	2600	18.6	13.2	5	39.3	43.1	38.7	37.6
Ford Focus 4-door sedan	103.0	174.9	66.9	56.3	2564	12.9	13.2	5	39.3	43.1	38.5	37.6
Ford Focus 4-door wagon	103.0	178.2	66.9	53.9	2717	55.8	13.2	5	39.3	43.1	40.0	37.6
Honda Civic 2-door hatchback	101.2	165.6	66.7	56.5	2744	21.6	13.2	5	37.8	42.2	36.7	33.0
Honda Civic 2-door coupe	103.1	174.7	66.7	55.1	2405	12.9	13.2	5	39.0	42.5	35.4	32.8
Honda Civic 4-door sedan	103.1	174.6	67.5	56.7	2421	12.9	13.2	5	39.8	42.2	37.2	36.0
Honda Insight 2-door hatchback	94.5	155.1	66.7	53.3	1847	16.3	10.6	2	38.8	42.9	—	—

Prices are accurate at time of publication; subject to manufacturer's change.

SPECIFICATIONS

SUBCOMPACT CARS (CONTINUED)

	Wheelbase, in.	Overall length, in.	Overall width, in.	Overall height, in.	Curb weight, lb	Cargo volume, cu ft	Fuel capacity, gal	Seating capacity	Front head room, in.	Max. front leg room, in.	Rear head room, in.	Min. rear leg room, in.
Honda Insight 2-door hatchback	94.5	155.1	66.7	53.3	1847	16.3	10.6	2	38.8	42.9	—	—
Hyundai Accent 2-door hatchback	96.1	166.7	65.7	54.9	2255	16.9	11.9	5	38.9	42.6	38.0	32.8
Hyundai Accent 4-door sedan	96.1	166.7	65.7	54.9	2290	11.8	11.9	5	38.9	42.6	38.0	32.8
Hyundai Elantra 4-door sedan	102.7	177.1	67.7	56.1	2635	11.0	14.5	5	39.6	43.2	38.0	35.0
Hyundai Elantra 4-door hatchback	102.7	177.1	67.7	56.1	2635	NA	14.5	5	39.6	43.2	38.0	35.0
Kia Rio 4-door sedan	94.9	165.9	65.9	56.7	2242	9.2	11.9	5	39.4	42.8	37.6	32.7
Kia Rio 4-door wagon	94.9	165.9	65.9	56.7	2436	44.3	11.9	5	39.4	42.8	37.6	32.7
Kia Spectra 4-door sedan	100.8	177.6	67.9	56.1	2661	10.4	13.2	5	39.6	43.1	37.6	34.4
Kia Spectra 4-door hatchback	100.8	178.1	67.9	56.1	2686	11.6	13.2	5	39.6	43.1	36.6	34.4
Mazda Protege 4-door sedan	102.8	175.3	67.1	55.5	2634	12.9	14.5	5	39.3	42.2	37.4	35.4
Mazda Protege 4-door wagon	102.8	170.5	67.1	57.8	2716	NA	14.5	5	39.3	42.2	37.4	35.4
Mitsubishi Lancer 4-door sedan	102.4	177.6	66.7	54.1	2646	11.3	13.2	5	38.8	43.2	36.7	36.6
Mitsubishi Mirage 2-door coupe	95.1	168.1	66.5	53.5	2183	11.5	12.4	4	38.6	43.0	35.8	31.1
Nissan Sentra 4-door sedan	99.8	177.5	67.3	55.5	2548	11.6	13.2	5	39.9	41.6	37.0	33.7
Pontiac Sunfire 2-door coupe	104.1	182.0	68.4	53.0	2606	12.4	15.0	5	37.6	42.1	36.6	32.6
Pontiac Sunfire 4-door sedan	104.1	181.8	67.9	54.7	2644	13.1	15.0	5	38.9	42.1	37.2	34.3
Saturn S-Series 3-door coupe	102.4	180.5	68.2	53.0	2367	11.4	12.1	4	38.6	42.6	35.8	31.0
Saturn S-Series 4-door sedan	102.4	178.1	66.4	55.0	2341	12.1	12.1	5	39.3	42.5	38.0	32.8
Subaru Impreza 4-door sedan	99.4	173.4	68.1	56.7	2965	11.0	15.9	5	38.6	42.9	36.7	33.0
Subaru Impreza 4-door wagon	99.4	173.4	66.7	58.5	3045	61.6	15.9	5	39.7	42.9	37.3	33.7
Suzuki Esteem 4-door sedan	97.6	166.3	66.1	53.9	2271	12.0	12.7	5	39.1	42.3	37.3	34.1
Suzuki Esteem 4-door wagon	97.6	172.2	66.5	55.9	2403	60.2	12.7	5	38.8	42.3	38.0	34.1
Toyota Corolla 4-door sedan	102.4	178.3	66.9	57.4	2490	13.6	13.2	5	39.1	41.3	37.1	35.4
Toyota Echo 2-door coupe	93.3	163.2	65.4	59.4	2035	13.6	11.9	5	39.9	41.1	37.6	35.2
Toyota Echo 4-door sedan	93.3	163.2	65.4	59.4	2055	13.6	11.9	5	39.9	41.1	37.6	35.2

Specifications begin on page 551.

SPECIFICATIONS

SUBCOMPACT CARS (CONTINUED)

	Wheelbase, in.	Overall length, in.	Overall width, in.	Overall height, in.	Curb weight, lb	Cargo volume, cu ft	Fuel capacity, gal	Seating capacity	Front head room, in.	Max. front leg room, in.	Rear head room, in.	Min. rear leg room, in.
Toyota Matrix 4-door wagon	102.4	171.3	69.5	60.6	2670	53.2	13.2	5	40.6	41.8	39.8	36.3
Toyota Matrix AWD 4-door wagon	102.4	171.3	69.5	61.0	2930	53.2	11.9	5	40.6	41.8	39.8	36.3
Toyota Prius 4-door sedan	100.4	169.6	66.7	57.6	2765	11.8	11.9	5	38.8	41.2	37.1	35.4
Volkswagen Golf 2-door hatchback	98.9	164.9	68.3	56.9	2772	18.0	14.5	5	38.6	41.5	37.4	33.5
Volkswagen Golf 4-door hatchback	98.9	164.9	68.3	56.9	2869	18.0	14.5	5	38.6	41.5	37.4	33.5
Volkswagen Jetta 4-door sedan	98.9	172.3	68.3	56.9	2893	13.0	14.5	5	38.6	41.5	36.9	33.5
Volkswagen Jetta 4-door wagon	99.0	173.6	68.3	58.5	3079	70.6	14.5	5	38.6	41.5	38.1	33.5

COMPACT CARS

	Wheelbase, in.	Overall length, in.	Overall width, in.	Overall height, in.	Curb weight, lb	Cargo volume, cu ft	Fuel capacity, gal	Seating capacity	Front head room, in.	Max. front leg room, in.	Rear head room, in.	Min. rear leg room, in.
Chrysler PT Cruiser 4-door wagon	103.0	168.8	67.1	63.0	3108	64.2	15.0	5	40.4	40.6	39.6	40.8
Daewoo Leganza 4-door sedan	105.1	183.9	70.0	56.6	3086	14.1	15.8	5	39.3	42.3	37.8	38.2
Hyundai Sonata 4-door sedan	106.3	186.9	71.7	56.0	3181	14.1	17.2	5	39.3	43.3	37.6	36.2
Kia Optima 4-door sedan	106.3	186.2	71.7	55.5	3157	13.6	17.2	5	39.0	43.3	37.6	36.2
Mazda 626 4-door sedan	105.1	187.4	69.3	55.1	2864	14.2	16.9	5	39.2	43.6	37.0	34.6
Mitsubishi Galant 4-door sedan	103.7	187.8	68.5	55.7	3031	14.6	16.3	5	39.9	43.5	37.7	36.3
Oldsmobile Alero 2-door coupe	107.0	186.7	70.1	54.5	2946	14.6	14.1	5	38.3	42.1	37.0	36.2
Oldsmobile Alero 4-door sedan	107.0	186.7	70.1	54.5	3021	14.6	14.1	5	38.3	42.1	37.5	36.3
Pontiac Grand Am 2-door coupe	107.2	186.3	70.4	55.1	3066	14.6	14.3	5	38.3	42.1	37.3	35.5
Pontiac Grand Am 4-door sedan	107.2	186.3	70.4	55.1	3116	14.6	14.3	5	38.3	42.1	37.6	35.5
Subaru Legacy 4-door sedan	104.3	184.4	68.7	55.7	3255	12.4	16.9	5	38.9	43.3	36.6	34.2
Subaru Legacy 4-door wagon	104.3	187.4	68.7	59.6	3345	68.6	16.9	5	40.2	43.3	39.1	34.3
Subaru Outback 4-door sedan	104.3	184.4	68.7	58.3	3495	12.4	16.9	5	38.1	43.3	36.6	34.2
Subaru Outback 4-door wagon	104.3	187.4	68.7	62.2	3425	68.6	16.9	5	40.2	43.3	39.1	34.3

Prices are accurate at time of publication; subject to manufacturer's change.

SPECIFICATIONS

COMPACT CARS (CONTINUED)	Wheelbase, in.	Overall length, in.	Overall width, in.	Overall height, in.	Curb weight, lb	Cargo vol. cu ft	Fuel capacity, gal	Seating capacity	Front head room, in.	Max. front leg room, in.	Rear head room, in.	Min. rear leg room, in.
Subaru Outback 4-door wagon	104.3	187.4	68.7	62.2	3425	68.6	16.9	5	40.2	43.3	39.1	34.3
Volkswagen Passat 4-door sedan	106.4	185.2	68.7	57.6	3199	15.0	16.4	5	39.7	37.8	41.5	35.3
Volkswagen Passat 4-dr sdn 4Motion	106.4	185.2	68.7	57.6	3333	10.0	16.4	5	39.7	37.8	41.5	35.3
Volkswagen Passat 4-door wagon	106.5	184.3	68.7	59.0	3296	79.0	16.4	5	39.7	39.7	41.5	35.3

MIDSIZE CARS	Wheelbase, in.	Overall length, in.	Overall width, in.	Overall height, in.	Curb weight, lb	Cargo vol. cu ft	Fuel capacity, gal	Seating capacity	Front head room, in.	Max. front leg room, in.	Rear head room, in.	Min. rear leg room, in.
Buick Century 4-door sedan	109.0	194.6	72.7	56.6	3353	16.7	17.5	6	39.4	42.4	37.4	36.9
Buick Regal 4-door sedan	109.0	196.2	72.7	56.6	3461	16.7	17.5	5	39.4	42.4	37.4	36.9
Chevrolet Impala 4-door sedan	110.5	200.0	73.0	57.3	3308	18.6	17.0	6	39.2	42.2	36.8	38.4
Chevrolet Malibu 4-door sedan	107.0	190.4	69.4	56.2	3053	17.3	14.1	5	39.4	41.9	37.6	38.0
Chevrolet Monte Carlo 2-door coupe	110.5	197.9	72.3	55.2	3340	15.8	17.0	5	38.1	42.4	36.5	35.8
Chrysler Sebring 2-door coupe	103.7	190.2	70.3	53.7	3099	16.3	16.3	5	38.5	42.3	36.0	34.0
Chrysler Sebring 2-door convertible	106.0	193.7	69.4	55.0	3394	11.3	16.0	4	38.7	42.4	37.0	35.2
Chrysler Sebring 4-door sedan	108.0	190.7	70.6	54.9	3201	16.0	16.0	5	37.6	42.3	35.8	38.1
Dodge Stratus 2-door coupe	103.7	190.2	70.3	53.7	3012	16.3	16.3	5	38.5	42.3	36.0	34.0
Dodge Stratus 4-door sedan	108.0	191.2	70.6	54.9	3226	16.0	16.3	5	37.6	42.3	35.8	38.1
Ford Taurus 4-door sedan	108.5	197.6	73.0	56.1	3336	17.0	18.0	6	40.0	42.2	38.1	38.9
Ford Taurus 4-door wagon	108.5	197.7	73.0	57.8	3502	81.3	18.0	8	39.4	42.2	38.9	38.5
Honda Accord 2-door coupe	105.1	186.8	70.3	54.9	2967	13.6	17.1	5	39.7	42.6	36.5	32.4
Honda Accord 4-door sedan	106.9	189.4	70.3	56.9	2943	14.1	17.1	5	40.0	42.1	37.6	37.9
Hyundai XG350 4-door sedan	108.3	191.5	71.9	55.9	3651	14.5	18.5	5	39.7	43.4	38.0	37.2
Mercury Sable 4-door sedan	108.5	199.8	73.0	55.5	3338	16.0	18.0	6	39.8	42.2	36.7	38.9

Specifications begin on page 551.

SPECIFICATIONS

MIDSIZE CARS (CONTINUED)	Wheelbase, in.	Overall length, in.	Overall width, in.	Overall height, in.	Curb weight, lb	Cargo volume, cu ft	Fuel capacity, gal	Seating capacity	Front head room, in.	Max. front leg room, in.	Rear head room, in.	Min. rear leg room, in.
Subaru Outback 4-door wagon	104.3	187.4	68.7	62.2	3425	68.6	16.9	5	40.2	43.3	39.1	34.3
Volkswagen Passat 4-door sedan	106.4	185.2	68.7	57.6	3199	15.0	16.4	5	39.7	37.8	41.5	35.3
Volkswagen Passat 4-dr sdn 4Motion	106.4	185.2	68.7	57.6	3333	10.0	16.4	5	39.7	37.8	41.5	35.3
Volkswagen Passat 4-door wagon	106.5	184.3	68.7	59.0	3296	79.0	16.4	5	39.7	39.7	41.5	35.3
Mercury Sable 4-door sedan	108.5	199.8	73.0	55.5	3338	16.0	18.0	6	39.8	42.2	36.7	38.9
Mercury Sable 4-door wagon	108.5	197.8	73.0	57.8	3501	81.3	18.0	8	39.4	42.2	38.9	38.5
Nissan Altima 4-door sedan	110.2	191.5	70.4	57.9	2983	15.6	20.0	5	40.8	43.9	37.6	36.4
Nissan Maxima 4-door sedan	108.3	191.5	70.3	56.3	3248	15.1	18.5	5	40.4	44.8	37.2	35.4
Oldsmobile Intrigue 4-door sedan	109.0	195.9	73.6	56.6	3434	17.3	14.3	5	39.3	42.4	37.4	36.2
Pontiac Grand Prix 2-door coupe	110.5	197.5	72.7	54.7	3429	16.0	17.5	5	38.3	42.4	36.5	36.1
Pontiac Grand Prix 4-door sedan	110.5	197.5	72.7	54.7	3384	16.0	17.5	6	38.3	42.4	36.7	35.8
Saturn L-Series 4-door sedan	106.5	190.4	68.5	56.4	2989	17.5	15.7	5	39.3	42.3	38.0	35.4
Saturn L-Series 4-door wagon	106.5	190.4	68.5	57.3	3070	79.0	15.7	5	39.3	42.3	39.6	35.4
Toyota Camry 4-door sedan	107.1	189.2	70.7	58.3	3086	16.7	18.5	5	39.2	41.6	38.3	37.8
Toyota Solara 2-door coupe	105.1	191.5	71.1	54.3	3075	13.8	18.5	5	38.3	43.3	36.3	35.2
Toyota Solara 2-door convertible	105.1	191.5	71.1	55.5	3362	8.8	18.5	4	38.8	43.3	37.8	35.3

FULL-SIZE CARS	Wheelbase, in.	Overall length, in.	Overall width, in.	Overall height, in.	Curb weight, lb	Cargo volume, cu ft	Fuel capacity, gal	Seating capacity	Front head room, in.	Max. front leg room, in.	Rear head room, in.	Min. rear leg room, in.
Buick Le Sabre 4-door sedan	112.2	200.0	73.5	57.0	3567	18.0	18.5	6	38.8	42.4	37.8	39.9
Chrysler Concorde 4-door sedan	113.0	207.7	74.4	55.9	3479	18.7	17.0	6	38.3	42.2	37.2	41.6
Dodge Intrepid 4-door sedan	113.0	203.7	74.7	55.9	3469	18.4	17.0	6	38.3	42.2	37.4	39.1

SPECIFICATIONS

FULL-SIZE CARS (CONTINUED)

	Wheelbase, in.	Overall length, in.	Overall width, in.	Overall height, in.	Curb weight, lb	Cargo volume, cu ft	Fuel capacity, gal	Seating capacity	Front head room, in.	Max. front leg room, in.	Rear head room, in.	Min. rear leg room, in.
Mercury Grand Marquis 4-door sedan	114.7	211.9	78.2	56.8	3957	20.6	19.0	6	39.4	42.5	38.1	38.4
Pontiac Bonneville 4-door sedan	112.2	202.6	74.2	56.6	3590	18.0	18.5	6	38.7	42.6	37.3	38.0
Toyota Avalon 4-door sedan	107.1	191.9	71.7	57.7	3417	15.9	18.5	6	38.8	41.7	37.9	40.1

NEAR-LUXURY CARS

	Wheelbase, in.	Overall length, in.	Overall width, in.	Overall height, in.	Curb weight, lb	Cargo volume, cu ft	Fuel capacity, gal	Seating capacity	Front head room, in.	Max. front leg room, in.	Rear head room, in.	Min. rear leg room, in.
Acura CL 2-door coupe	106.9	192.0	69.2	53.3	3446	13.6	17.2	4	37.5	42.4	36.7	33.0
Acura TL 4-door sedan	108.1	192.5	70.7	53.7	3494	14.3	17.2	5	39.9	42.4	36.8	36.8
Audi A4 4-door sedan	104.3	179.0	69.5	56.2	3252	13.4	18.5	5	38.4	41.3	37.2	34.3
Audi S4 4-door sedan	102.6	176.7	72.7	54.9	3593	13.6	16.4	5	38.1	41.3	36.8	33.4
Audi S4 4-door wagon	102.6	176.7	72.7	54.9	3704	63.7	16.4	5	38.1	41.3	36.8	33.4
BMW 3-Series 2-door coupe	107.3	176.7	69.2	53.5	3020	9.5	16.6	4	37.5	41.7	36.5	33.2
BMW 3-Series 2-door convertible	107.3	176.7	69.2	54.0	3560	7.7	16.6	4	38.3	41.7	36.9	32.0
BMW 3-Series 4-door sedan	107.3	176.0	68.5	55.7	3153	10.7	16.6	5	38.4	41.4	37.5	34.6
BMW 3-Series 4-door wagon	107.3	176.3	68.5	55.5	3351	48.0	16.6	5	38.4	41.4	37.7	34.0
Buick Park Avenue 4-door sedan	113.8	206.8	74.7	57.4	3778	19.1	18.5	6	39.8	42.4	37.4	41.4
Cadillac CTS 4-door sedan	113.4	190.1	70.6	56.7	3509	12.8	17.5	5	38.5	42.4	36.9	37.0
Chrysler 300M 4-door sedan	113.0	197.8	74.4	56.0	3581	16.8	17.0	5	38.3	42.2	37.7	39.1
Ford Thunderbird 2-door convertible	107.2	186.3	72.0	52.1	3775	6.9	18.0	2	37.2	42.7	—	—
Infiniti G20 4-door sedan	102.4	177.5	66.7	55.1	2923	13.5	15.9	5	40.0	41.5	36.8	34.6
Infiniti I35 4-door sedan	108.3	193.7	70.2	57.0	3342	14.9	18.5	5	40.5	43.9	37.4	36.2
Jaguar X-Type 4-door sedan	106.7	183.9	70.4	54.8	3428	16.0	16.0	5	37.3	42.4	37.5	34.4

SPECIFICATIONS

NEAR-LUXURY CARS (CONTINUED)	Wheelbase, in.	Overall length, in.	Overall width, in.	Overall height, in.	Curb weight, lb	Cargo volume, cu ft	Fuel capacity, gal	Seating capacity	Front head room, in.	Max. front leg room, in.	Rear head room, in.	Min. rear leg room, in.
Jaguar X-Type 4-door sedan	106.7	183.9	70.4	54.8	3428	16.0	16.0	5	37.3	42.4	37.5	34.4
Lexus ES 300 4-door sedan	107.1	191.1	71.3	57.3	3439	14.5	18.5	5	38.5	42.2	37.4	35.6
Lexus IS 300 4-door sedan	105.1	176.6	67.9	55.5	3285	10.1	17.5	5	39.1	42.7	37.7	30.2
Lexus IS 300 4-door wagon	105.1	177.0	67.9	56.7	3410	21.8	17.5	5	39.1	42.7	37.7	30.2
Lincoln LS 4-door sedan	114.5	193.9	73.2	56.1	3603	13.5	18.0	5	40.4	42.8	37.5	37.4
Mazda Millenia 4-door sedan	108.3	191.6	69.7	54.9	3358	13.0	18.0	5	37.9	43.3	36.5	34.1
Mercedes-Benz C-Class 2-door hatchback	106.9	171.0	68.0	54.3	3306	38.1	16.4	4	38.5	42.0	36.3	33.0
Mercedes-Benz C-Class 4-door sedan	106.9	178.3	68.0	55.2	3310	12.2	16.4	5	38.9	41.7	37.3	33.0
Mercedes-Benz C-Class 4-door wagon	106.9	178.3	68.0	55.2	3495	63.6	16.4	5	38.9	41.7	37.3	33.0
Mitsubishi Diamante 4-door sedan	107.1	194.1	70.3	53.9	3439	14.2	19.0	5	39.4	43.6	37.5	36.6
Oldsmobile Aurora 4-door sedan	112.2	199.3	72.9	56.7	3627	14.9	18.5	5	38.6	42.5	37.7	38.0
Saab 9-3 2-door hatchback	102.6	182.3	67.4	56.2	3130	46.8	17.0	5	39.3	42.3	37.9	34.1
Saab 9-3 2-door convertible	102.6	182.3	67.4	56.0	3200	12.5	17.0	4	38.9	42.3	37.9	33.0
Saab 9-3 4-door hatchback	102.6	182.3	67.4	56.2	3020	46.8	17.0	5	37.9	42.3	37.5	33.6
Volvo 40 series 4-door sedan	100.9	177.8	67.6	56.0	2767	13.2	15.9	5	38.7	41.4	37.2	32.7
Volvo 40 series 4-door wagon	100.9	180.2	67.6	56.1	2822	68.1	15.9	5	38.7	41.4	38.3	32.7
Volvo S60 4-door sedan	107.0	180.2	71.0	56.2	3146	13.9	21.1	5	38.7	42.6	37.9	33.3
Volvo V70 4-door wagon	108.5	185.4	71.0	58.7	3369	71.5	21.1	5	39.3	42.6	38.9	35.2
Volvo XC 4-door wagon	108.8	186.3	73.2	61.5	3699	71.5	18.5	5	39.3	42.6	38.9	35.2

CONSUMER GUIDE®

SPECIFICATIONS

LUXURY CARS	Wheelbase, in.	Overall length, in.	Overall width, in.	Overall height, in.	Curb weight, lb	Cargo volume, cu ft	Fuel capacity, gal	Seating capacity	Front head room, in.	Max. front leg room, in.	Rear head room, in.	Min. rear leg room, in.
Acura RL 4-door sedan	114.6	196.6	71.6	56.5	3858	14.0	18.0	5	38.8	42.1	36.8	35.4
Audi A6/allroad quattro 4-door sedan	108.7	192.0	71.3	57.2	3516	17.2	18.5	5	39.3	41.3	37.9	37.3
Audi A6/allroad quattro 4-door wagon	108.6	192.0	71.3	58.2	3924	73.2	18.5	5	39.3	41.3	38.7	37.3
Audi allroad quattro	108.5	189.4	76.1	62.0	4167	73.2	18.5	5	37.5	41.7	38.4	37.3
BMW 5-Series 4-door sedan	111.4	188.0	70.9	56.5	3450	11.1	18.5	5	38.7	41.7	37.8	34.2
BMW 5-Series 4-door wagon	111.4	189.2	70.9	56.7	3726	65.2	18.5	5	38.7	41.7	38.5	34.2
BMW 745i 4-door sedan	117.7	198.0	74.9	58.7	4376	NA	23.3	5	39.2	41.3	38.5	37.2
BMW 745 Li 4-door sedan	123.2	203.5	74.9	58.4	4464	NA	23.3	5	39.2*	41.3	NA	NA
Cadillac De Ville 4-door sedan	115.3	207.0	74.4	56.7	3984	19.1	18.5	6	39.1	42.4	38.3	43.2
Cadillac Eldorado 2-door coupe	108.0	200.6	75.5	53.6	3814	15.3	19.0	5	37.8	42.6	38.3	35.5
Cadillac Seville 4-door sedan	112.2	201.0	75.0	55.7	3992	15.7	18.5	5	38.2	42.5	38.0	38.2
Infiniti Q45 4-door sedan	113.0	199.6	72.6	58.9	3880	13.7	21.4	5	38.6	44.0	38.1	37.3
Jaguar S-Type 4-door sedan	114.5	191.3	71.6	55.7	3816	11.7	18.4	5	38.6	43.1	36.4	37.7
Jaguar XJ Sedan 4-door sedan	113.0	197.8	70.8	52.7	3995	12.7	23.1	5	37.2	41.2	38.5	34.3
Jaguar XJ Sedan (V. Plas, Sup. V8) 4-door sedan	117.9	202.7	70.8	53.2	4006	12.7	23.1	5	37.2	41.2	36.9	39.2
Jaguar XK8 2-door coupe	101.9	187.4	72.0	50.5	3759	11.5	19.9	4	37.4	43.0	33.3	23.7
Jaguar XK8 2-door convertible	101.9	187.4	72.0	51.0	3990	10.8	19.9	4	37.0	43.0	33.2	23.1
Lexus GS 300/430 4-door sedan	110.2	189.2	70.9	56.7	3638	14.8	19.8	5	39.0	44.5	37.4	34.3
Lexus LS 430 4-door sedan	115.2	196.7	72.0	58.7	3955	20.2	22.2	5	39.6	44.0	38.0	37.6
Lexus SC 430 2-door convertible	103.2	177.8	72.0	53.1	3840	8.8	19.8	4	37.2	43.6	33.9	27.1
Lincoln Continental 4-door sedan	109.0	208.5	73.6	56.0	3848	18.4	20.0	6	38.9	41.9	38.0	38.0
Lincoln Town Car 4-door sedan	117.7	215.3	78.2	58.0	4047	20.6	19.0	6	39.3	42.6	37.6	41.1
Lincoln Town Car (L) 4-door sedan	123.7	221.3	78.2	58.0	4215	20.6	19.0	6	39.3	42.6	37.6	47.1

554 CONSUMER GUIDE®

SPECIFICATIONS

LUXURY CARS (CONTINUED)	Wheelbase, in.	Overall length, in.	Overall width, in.	Overall height, in.	Curb weight, lb	Cargo volume, cu ft	Fuel capacity, gal	Seating capacity	Front head room, in.	Max. front leg room, in.	Rear head room, in.	Min. rear leg room, in.
Mercedes-Benz CLK 2-door coupe	105.9	180.2	67.8	54.0	3265	11.0	16.4	4	36.9	41.9	35.8	31.2
Mercedes-Benz CLK 2-door convertible	105.9	180.2	67.8	54.3	3650	9.4	16.4	4	37.5	41.9	36.5	27.4
Mercedes-Benz E-Class 4-door sedan	111.5	189.4	70.8	56.7	3624	15.3	21.1	5	37.6	41.3	37.2	36.1
Mercedes-Benz E-Class 4-door wagon	111.5	190.4	70.8	59.3	3856	82.6	18.5	7	38.6	41.3	37.0	36.1
Mercedes-Benz CL-Class 2-door coupe	113.6	196.6	73.1	55.0	4070	12.3	23.3	4	36.9	41.7	36.8	30.8
Mercedes-Benz S-Class 4-door sedan	121.5	203.1	73.1	56.9	4133	15.4	23.2	5	37.6	41.3	38.4	40.3
Mercedes-Benz SL-Class 2-door convertible	100.8	178.5	71.5	51.1	4000	11.2	21.1	2	37.7	NA	—	—
Saab 9-5 4-door sedan	106.4	190.0	70.5	57.0	3470	15.9	18.5	5	38.7	42.4	37.6	36.6
Saab 9-5 4-door wagon	106.4	190.1	70.5	57.0	3620	73.0	18.5	5	38.7	42.4	38.2	36.6
Volvo S80 2.8, T6 4-door sedan	109.9	189.8	72.1	57.2	3583	14.4	21.1	5	38.9	42.2	37.6	35.9
Volvo S80 Executive 4-door sedan	109.9	189.8	72.1	57.2	3583	14.4	21.1	5	38.9	42.2	37.6	37.8

SPORTY COUPES	Wheelbase, in.	Overall length, in.	Overall width, in.	Overall height, in.	Curb weight, lb	Cargo volume, cu ft	Fuel capacity, gal	Seating capacity	Front head room, in.	Max. front leg room, in.	Rear head room, in.	Min. rear leg room, in.
Acura RSX 2-door hatchback	101.2	172.2	67.9	55.1	2694	17.8	13.2	4	37.8	43.1	30.1	29.2
Chevrolet Camaro 2-door hatchback	101.1	193.5	74.1	51.2	3323	32.8	16.8	4	37.2	43.0	35.2	26.8
Chevrolet Camaro 2-door convertible	101.1	193.5	74.1	51.8	3524	7.6	16.8	4	38.7	43.0	39.4	26.8
Ford Mustang 2-door coupe	101.3	183.2	73.1	53.1	3066	10.9	15.7	4	38.1	42.6	35.5	29.9
Ford Mustang 2-door convertible	101.3	183.2	73.1	53.2	3208	7.7	15.7	4	38.0	42.6	35.8	29.9
Ford ZX2 2-door coupe	98.4	175.2	67.4	52.3	2478	11.8	12.8	4	38.0	42.5	35.1	33.4
Mercury Cougar 2-door hatchback	106.4	185.0	69.6	52.2	3013	24.0	15.5	4	37.8	42.6	34.7	33.2
Mini Cooper 2-dr hatchback	97.1	142.8	75.8	55.0	2316	5.6	13.2	4	39.4	40.2	NA	17.7
Mitsubishi Eclipse 2-door hatchback	100.8	175.4	68.9	51.6	2855	16.9	16.4	4	37.9	42.3	34.9	30.2
Mitsubishi Eclipse 2-door convertible	100.8	175.4	68.9	52.8	3042	7.2	16.4	4	39.4	42.3	34.5	29.4

CONSUMER GUIDE®

SPECIFICATIONS

SPORTY COUPES (CONTINUED)

	Wheelbase, in.	Overall length, in.	Overall width, in.	Overall height, in.	Curb weight, lb	Cargo volume, cu ft	Fuel capacity, gal	Seating capacity	Front head room, in.	Max. front leg room, in.	Rear head room, in.	Min. rear leg room, in.
Pontiac Firebird 2-door hatchback	101.1	193.3	74.4	51.2	3323	33.7	16.8	4	37.2	43.0	35.2	28.8
Pontiac Firebird 2-door convertible	101.1	193.3	74.4	51.8	3402	12.9	16.8	4	38.7	43.0	39.4	28.8
Toyota Celica 2-door hatchback	102.4	170.5	68.3	51.4	2425	16.9	14.5	4	38.4	43.6	35.0	27.0
Volkswagen Cabrio 2-door convertible	97.4	160.4	66.7	56.0	2825	8.0	13.7	4	38.7	42.3	36.6	31.1
Volkswagen New Beetle 2-door hatchback	98.9	161.1	67.9	59.5	2794	12.0	14.5	4	41.3	39.4	36.7	33.5

SPORTS CARS

	Wheelbase, in.	Overall length, in.	Overall width, in.	Overall height, in.	Curb weight, lb	Cargo volume, cu ft	Fuel capacity, gal	Seating capacity	Front head room, in.	Max. front leg room, in.	Rear head room, in.	Min. rear leg room, in.
Acura NSX 2-door coupe	99.6	174.2	71.3	46.1	3153	5.0	18.5	2	36.3	44.3	—	—
Audi TT 2-door hatchback	95.4	159.1	73.1	53.0	2921	24.2	14.5	4	37.8	41.2	32.6	20.2
Audi TT 2-door convertible	95.4	159.1	73.1	53.0	3131	7.8	14.5	2	38.3	41.2	—	—
BMW Z3 Series 2-door hatchback	96.3	158.5	68.5	51.4	2943	9.0	13.5	2	36.7	41.8	—	—
BMW Z3 Series 2-door convertible	96.3	158.5	66.6	50.7	2701	5.0	13.5	2	37.6	41.8	—	—
Chevrolet Corvette 2-door coupe	104.5	179.7	73.6	47.7	3118	13.3	18.5	2	37.8	42.7	—	—
Chevrolet Corvette 2-door hatchback	104.5	179.7	73.6	47.7	3246	24.8	18.5	2	37.9	42.7	—	—
Chevrolet Corvette 2-door convertible	104.5	179.7	73.6	47.8	3248	13.9	18.5	2	37.9	42.7	—	—
Honda S2000 2-door convertible	94.5	162.2	68.9	50.6	2809	5.0	13.2	2	34.6	44.3	—	—
Mazda Miata 2-door convertible	89.2	155.7	66.0	48.4	2387	5.1	12.7	2	37.1	42.8	—	—
Mercedes-Benz SLK-Class 2-door conv.	94.5	157.9	67.5	50.4	3055	9.5	15.9	2	37.4	42.7	—	—
Toyota MR2 Spyder 2-door convertible	96.5	153.0	66.7	48.2	2195	1.9	12.7	2	37.3	42.2	—	—

MINIVANS

	Wheelbase, in.	Overall length, in.	Overall width, in.	Overall height, in.	Curb weight, lb	Cargo volume, cu ft	Fuel capacity, gal	Seating capacity	Front head room, in.	Max. front leg room, in.	Rear head room, in.	Min. rear leg room, in.
Chevrolet Astro 3-door van	111.2	189.8	77.5	74.9	4302	170.4	27.0	8	39.2	41.6	37.9	36.5

SPECIFICATIONS

MINIVANS (CONTINUED)	Wheelbase, in.	Overall length, in.	Overall width, in.	Overall height, in.	Curb weight, lb	Cargo volume, cu ft	Fuel capacity, gal	Seating capacity	Front head room, in.	Max. front leg room, in.	Rear head room, in.	Min. rear leg room, in.
Chevrolet Venture 4-door van	112.0	186.9	72.0	67.4	3699	119.8	20.0	7	39.9	39.9	39.3	36.9
Chevrolet Venture (extended) 4-door van	120.0	200.6	72.0	67.4	3838	140.7	25.0	7	39.9	39.9	39.3	39.0
Chrysler Town & Country 4-door van	119.3	200.6	78.6	68.9	4107	167.9	20.0	7	39.6	40.6	39.6	37.5
Chrysler Voyager 4-door van	113.3	189.1	78.6	68.9	3869	142.3	20.0	7	39.8	40.6	39.3	36.6
Dodge Caravan 4-door van	113.3	189.3	78.6	68.9	3869	146.7	20.0	7	39.7	40.6	39.7	36.5
Dodge Grand Caravan 4-door van	119.3	200.5	78.6	68.9	4011	167.9	20.0	7	39.6	40.6	39.1	39.0
Ford Windstar 4-door van	120.7	201.5	76.6	66.1	4017	136.4	20.0	7	39.3	40.7	41.1	36.8
Honda Odyssey 4-door van	118.1	201.2	75.6	68.5	4299	146.1	26.0	7	41.2	41.0	40.0	40.0
Kia Sedona 4-door van	114.6	194.1	74.6	69.3	4709	127.5	19.8	7	39.4	40.6	39.2	37.2
Mercury Villager 4-door van	112.2	194.9	74.9	70.1	3997	127.6	20.0	7	39.7	39.9	40.1	36.4
Nissan Quest 4-door van	112.2	194.6	74.9	64.2	3915	135.6	20.0	7	39.7	39.9	39.9	36.4
Oldsmobile Silhouette 4-door van	120.0	201.4	72.2	68.1	3948	141.9	25.1	8	39.9	39.9	39.3	39.0
Pontiac Montana 4-door van	112.0	187.3	72.0	67.4	3803	119.8	20.0	8	39.9	39.9	38.9	36.9
Pontiac Montana (extended) 4-door van	121.0	200.9	72.0	68.2	3942	140.7	25.0	8	39.9	39.9	39.3	39.0
Toyota Sienna 4-door van	114.2	194.1	73.4	66.9	3919	133.5	20.9	7	40.6	41.9	40.7	36.5
Volkswagen EuroVan 3-door van	115.0	188.5	72.4	76.4	4285	178.0	21.1	7	39.3	37.8	41.3	NA

COMPACT SPORT-UTILITY VEHICLES	Wheelbase, in.	Overall length, in.	Overall width, in.	Overall height, in.	Curb weight, lb	Cargo volume, cu ft	Fuel capacity, gal	Seating capacity	Front head room, in.	Max. front leg room, in.	Rear head room, in.	Min. rear leg room, in.
Chevrolet Tracker 2-door convertible	86.6	151.8	67.3	66.5	2811	33.7	14.8	4	40.9	41.4	39.5	35.9
Chevrolet Tracker 4-door wagon	97.6	162.8	67.3	66.3	2987	44.7	17.4	5	39.9	41.4	39.6	35.9
Ford Escape 4-door wagon	103.1	173.0	70.1	69.1	3152	63.3	15.0	5	40.4	41.6	39.2	36.4
Honda CR-V 4-door wagon	103.2	178.6	70.2	66.2	3318	72.0	15.3	5	40.9	41.3	39.1	39.4

SPECIFICATIONS

COMPACT SPORT-UTILITY VEHICLES (CONTINUED)

	Wheelbase, in.	Overall length, in.	Overall width, in.	Overall height, in.	Curb weight, lb	Cargo volume, cu ft	Fuel capacity, gal	Seating capacity	Front head room, in.	Max. front leg room, in.	Rear head room, in.	Min. rear leg room, in.
Hyundai Santa Fe 4-door wagon	103.1	177.2	72.6	65.9	3455	78.0	17.2	5	39.6	41.6	39.2	36.8
Isuzu Rodeo Sport 2-door convertible	96.9	170.3	71.4	67.1	3686	62.5	17.7	5	38.9	42.1	37.3	33.3
Isuzu Rodeo Sport 2-door wagon	96.9	170.3	71.4	67.1	3986	62.5	17.7	5	38.9	42.1	37.3	33.3
Jeep Liberty 4-door wagon	104.3	174.7	71.6	70.9	3826	69.0	18.5	5	40.7	40.8	42.1	37.2
Jeep Wrangler 2-door convertible	93.4	155.4	66.7	70.9	3110	46.6	19.0	4	41.9	41.1	40.6	35.0
Kia Sportage 2-door convertible	92.9	156.8	68.1	65.0	3230	30.4	15.8	4	39.6	41.3	38.2	31.0
Kia Sportage 4-door wagon	104.3	170.3	68.1	65.0	3352	55.4	15.8	5	39.6	44.5	37.8	31.1
Land Rover Freelander 4-door wagon	101.0	175.0	71.1	69.2	3444	46.6	15.6	5	38.4	41.8	38.9	36.8
Mazda Tribute 4-door wagon	103.1	173.0	71.9	69.9	3245	63.9	15.3	5	40.3	41.7	38.9	36.9
Saturn VUE 4-door wagon	106.6	181.3	71.5	66.5	3361	63.5	15.5	5	40.4	41.2	39.9	36.4
Subaru Forester 4-door wagon	99.4	175.6	68.3	65.0	3140	63.1	15.9	5	40.2	43.0	39.6	33.4
Suzuki Vitara 2-door convertible	86.6	152.0	67.3	65.8	2877	33.7	14.8	4	40.9	41.4	39.5	35.9
Suzuki Vitara 4-door wagon	97.6	163.0	67.3	65.8	3053	44.7	16.9	5	39.9	41.4	39.6	35.9
Toyota RAV4 4-door wagon	98.0	166.2	68.3	65.3	2877	68.3	14.7	5	41.3	42.4	38.4	32.6

MIDSIZE SPORT-UTILITY VEHICLES

	Wheelbase, in.	Overall length, in.	Overall width, in.	Overall height, in.	Curb weight, lb	Cargo volume, cu ft	Fuel capacity, gal	Seating capacity	Front head room, in.	Max. front leg room, in.	Rear head room, in.	Min. rear leg room, in.
Acura MDX 4-door wagon	106.3	188.5	76.3	68.7	4328	81.5	19.2	7	38.7	41.5	39.0	37.8
BMW X5 4-door wagon	111.0	183.7	73.7	67.2	4519	54.4	24.3	5	39.9	39.3	38.5	35.4
Buick Rendezvous 4-door wagon	112.2	186.5	73.6	68.9	4024	108.9	18.0	7	40.9	40.5	40.1	39.0
Chevrolet Blazer 2-door wagon	100.5	177.3	67.8	64.7	3848	60.6	19.0	4	39.6	42.4	38.2	35.6
Chevrolet Blazer 4-door wagon	107.0	183.3	67.8	64.6	4049	67.8	18.0	6	39.6	42.4	38.2	36.3
Chevrolet TrailBlazer 4-door wagon	113.0	191.8	72.0	69.8	4442	80.5	18.6	5	40.3	43.1	39.8	38.3

SPECIFICATIONS

MIDSIZE SPORT-UTILITY VEHICLES (CONTINUED)	Wheelbase, in.	Overall length, in.	Overall width, in.	Overall height, in.	Curb weight, lb	Cargo volume, cu ft	Fuel capacity, gal	Seating capacity	Front head room, in.	Max. front leg room, in.	Rear head room, in.	Min. rear leg room, in.
Dodge Durango 4-door wagon	116.2	193.5	71.3	72.0	4629	88.0	25.0	8	39.8	41.9	40.2	37.3
Ford Explorer 4-door wagon	113.7	189.5	72.1	71.9	4334	88.0	22.5	7	39.9	43.9	38.9	37.2
Ford Explorer Sport 2-door wagon	101.8	180.4	70.2	68.3	3963	71.4	17.5	4	39.4	42.4	39.1	36.6
Ford Explorer Sport Trac 4-door crew cab	125.9	205.9	71.8	70.1	4310	—	23.0	5	39.4	42.4	38.9	37.8
GMC Envoy 4-door wagon	113.0	191.5	72.0	69.8	4442	80.5	18.7	5	40.3	43.1	39.8	38.3
Honda Passport 4-door wagon	106.4	184.2	70.4	68.8	4013	81.1	19.5	5	38.9	42.1	38.3	35.0
Infiniti QX4 4-door wagon	106.3	183.1	72.4	70.7	4352	85.5	21.1	5	39.5	41.7	37.5	31.8
Isuzu Rodeo 4-door wagon	106.4	183.7	70.4	69.4	4124	81.1	20.0	5	38.9	42.1	38.3	35.0
Jeep Grand Cherokee 4-door wagon	105.9	181.6	72.6	70.3	3970	72.3	20.5	5	39.5	41.7	39.3	35.1
Land Rover Discovery 4-door wagon	100.0	185.2	74.4	76.4	4576	63.3	24.6	7	40.4	42.3	40.1	37.3
Lexus RX 300 4-door wagon	103.0	180.3	71.5	65.7	3924	75.0	19.8	5	39.5	40.7	39.2	36.4
Mercedes-Benz M-Class 4-door wagon	111.0	182.6	72.4	71.7	4786	81.2	22.6	7	39.8	40.3	39.7	38.0
Mercury Mountaineer 4-door wagon	113.7	190.7	72.1	71.1	4410	88.0	22.5	7	39.1	43.9	38.9	37.2
Mitsubishi Montero Sport 4-door wagon	107.3	181.1	66.7	67.7	4105	79.3	19.5	5	38.9	42.8	37.3	33.5
Nissan Pathfinder 4-door wagon	106.3	182.7	69.7	67.9	4131	85.0	21.1	5	39.5	41.7	37.5	31.8
Nissan Xterra 4-door wagon	104.3	178.0	70.4	74.0	4034	65.6	19.4	5	38.6	41.4	37.8	32.8
Oldsmobile Bravada 4-door wagon	113.0	191.6	74.7	71.9	4628	83.3	18.7	5	40.2	44.6	39.6	37.1
Pontiac Aztek 4-door wagon	108.3	182.1	73.7	66.7	4043	93.5	18.0	5	39.7	40.5	39.1	38.0
Suzuki XL-7 4-door wagon	110.2	183.6	70.1	68.0	3682	73.0	16.9	7	40.0	41.4	39.2	36.4
Toyota 4Runner 4-door wagon	105.3	183.3	66.5	66.5	4070	79.8	18.5	5	39.3	42.6	38.7	34.9
Toyota Highlander 4-door wagon	106.9	184.4	71.9	66.1	3715	81.4	19.8	5	40.0	40.7	39.8	36.4

CONSUMER GUIDE®

SPECIFICATIONS

FULL-SIZE SPORT-UTILITY VEHICLES	Wheelbase, in.	Overall length, in.	Overall width, in.	Overall height, in.	Curb weight, lb	Cargo volume, cu ft	Fuel capacity, gal	Seating capacity	Front head room, in.	Max. front leg room, in.	Rear head room, in.	Min. rear leg room, in.
Cadillac Escalade 4-door wagon	116.0	198.9	78.9	74.2	5809	138.4	26.0	7	40.7	41.3	39.0	39.1
Cadillac Escalade EXT crew cab	130.0	221.4	79.5	75.6	5752	NA	30.9	5	40.7	41.3	38.6	38.9
Chevrolet Suburban 4-door wagon	130.0	219.3	78.8	75.7	5260	131.6	33.0	9	40.7	41.3	39.4	38.6
Chevrolet Tahoe 4-door wagon	116.0	198.8	78.8	76.5	5177	104.6	26.0	9	40.7	41.3	39.4	38.6
Ford Excursion 4-door wagon	137.1	226.7	79.9	80.2	7087	146.4	44.0	9	41.0	42.3	41.1	40.5
Ford Expedition 4-door wagon	119.1	205.8	78.6	76.6	5345	106.1	26.0	9	39.3	41.2	39.8	38.6
GMC Yukon/Denali 4-door wagon	116.0	198.8	78.8	76.5	5050	104.6	26.0	9	40.7	41.3	39.4	38.6
GMC Yukon XL/Denali XL 4-door wagon	130.0	219.3	78.9	75.7	5219	131.6	28.9	9	40.7	41.3	39.8	39.1
Isuzu Trooper 4-door wagon	108.7	187.8	72.2	72.2	4455	90.2	22.5	5	39.8	40.8	38.2	36.5
Land Rover Range Rover 4-door wagon	108.1	185.5	74.4	71.6	4960	58.0	24.6	5	38.1	42.6	39.4	34.3
Lexus LX 470 4-door wagon	112.2	192.5	76.4	72.8	5401	90.4	25.4	8	40.0	42.3	39.8	39.7
Lincoln Navigator 4-door wagon	119.0	204.8	79.9	76.7	5746	109.9	30.0	8	39.8	42.8	40.6	35.2
Mitsubishi Montero 4-door wagon	109.7	189.2	74.0	71.3	4600	96.4	23.8	7	41.5	42.3	38.8	34.3
Toyota Land Cruiser 4-door wagon	112.2	192.5	76.4	73.2	5115	90.8	25.4	8	39.2	42.3	40.6	38.4
Toyota Sequoia 4-door wagon	118.1	203.9	78.0	74.0	5270	128.1	26.1	8	41.1	41.6		

Specifications begin on page 551.